PHASES OF PRACTICE

Fields of Practice	Case Name	Levels of Practice	Engagement	Data Collection	Assessment and Contract Planning	Intervention	Evaluation	Termination
Education	Jim G	micro mezzo macro	193–194	235–237	278–280	329–332, 376–377	417, 419–422	456–457
	Mrs. B	micro mezzo macro	159–171					
	Jerry	micro		217				
	Student	micro mezzo macro	143–144					
Corrections	Youth group	mezzo	194–196	238–239	280–285	332–335, 377	421, 423–424	457–459
Homelessness	Mr. R	micro	197–198	239–240	285–289	335–338, 377	425–428	459–461
Health	Mrs. Armez	micro mezzo	176–182	209–210				
	Mr. D	micro		215–216				
Mental Health	Group	mezzo		221–222				
	C Family	mezzo			254–256			
	Mr., Mrs. S	mezzo					381–384, 390–394	

FIFTH EDITION

Generalist Social Work Practice

A Strengths-Based Problem-Solving Approach

Elizabeth M. Timberlake
The Catholic University of America

Michaela L. Zajicek-Farber
The Catholic University of America

Christine Anlauf Sabatino
The Catholic University of America

PEARSON

Boston • New York • San Francisco
Mexico City • Montreal • Toronto • London • Madrid • Munich • Paris
Hong Kong • Singapore • Tokyo • Cape Town • Sydney

Senior Acquisitions Editor: *Patricia Quinlin*
Editorial Assistant: *Nakeesha Warner*
Marketing Manager: *Laura Lee Manley*
Production Supervisor: *Roberta Sherman*
Electronic Production Service: *Publishers' Design and Production Services, Inc.*
Composition Buyer: *Linda Cox*
Manufacturing Buyer: *Debbie Rossi*
Electronic Composition: *Publishers' Design and Production Services, Inc.*
Interior Design: *Denise Hoffman*
Photo Researcher: *Annie Pickert*
Cover Administrator: *Kristina Mose-Libon*

For related titles and support materials, visit our online catalog at www.ablongman.com.

Between the time website information is gathered and then published, it is not unusual for some sites to have closed. Also, the transcription of URLs can result in typographical errors. The publisher would appreciate notification where these errors occur so that they may be corrected in subsequent editions.

ISBN-10: 0-205-51682-3
ISBN-13: 978-0-205-51682-7

Cataloging-in-Publication data unavailable at press time.

Printed in the United States of America

10   9   8   7   6   5   4   3   2   1   RRD-VA   11   10   09   08   07

Photo credits appear on page 486, which constitutes an extension of the copyright page.

Contents

2

Human Diversity: Multiculturalism, Social Pluralism, and Socio-Demographic Variability   32

3

Building Empirical Evidence for Practice   77

4

Strengths-Based Problem-Solving Interviews   129

PART II
The Phases and Processes of the General Method

5

Engagement   157

6

Data Collection   200

7

Assessment and Contract Planning   242

8

Intervention in Micro and Mezzo Generalist Practice   291

9

Intervention in Macro Generalist Practice   340

10

Evaluation   379

11

Termination   430

Preface

This fifth edition of our book, *Generalist Social Work Practice*, presents the General Method as a *strengths-based problem-solving approach* for social workers serving

- individuals, families, and groups that are experiencing problems-in-living and functioning in increasingly complex environments, and
- organizations and communities that are experiencing entrenched social justice issues.

The approach takes into account the influence of multiculturalism, social pluralism, and socio-demographic diversity on the individual and collective functioning of persons in their environments, their worldview, and their patterns of seeking and using help. The integrative conceptual framework has been expanded to include *an ecological systems perspective, a problem/strengths focus, a strengths/needs orientation, a multilevel approach, an open selection of theories and interventions, a strengths-based problem-solving process*, and *practice/program evaluation*. We use Pincus and Minahan's (1973) conceptual framework of client, action, and target system in identifying goals and practice tasks to be accomplished in the General Method change effort. *Client systems* are persons asking for help and establishing contracts to work for change. *Action systems* are persons with whom the social worker collaborates in accomplishing change goals. *Target systems* are persons in need of change prior to or concurrent with accomplishing client system goals. In each system, the persons may be individuals, families, groups, organizations, or communities.

Throughout the book, emphasis is on preparation for culturally competent, ethical, effective, and accountable generalist social work practice at the entry level and provision of a platform for specialized social work practice at the advanced level. Figures and tables clarify concepts and practice examples. Learning exercises facilitate development of self-awareness and practice skills. Practice vignettes highlight the micro, mezzo, and macro levels of generalist social work practice from engagement to termination with client, action, and target systems in child welfare, gerontology, public social welfare, community services, education, corrections, and homelessness. New exercises facilitate discussion of diversity across the General Method phases in relation to each of the seven ongoing cases.

Two new chapters discuss the use of empirical evidence in monitoring and evaluating practice and interviewing from a strengths-based problem-solving stance. This material is also integrated throughout the book. In addition, two intervention chapters expand the discussion of micro, mezzo, and macro practice. Other new features include boxed definitions of concepts, additional macro case examples, information about monitoring the processes and achievements of each General Method phase, photos of selected historical figures in social work, reflection points to strengthen critical thinking and mastery of key points in each chapter, and supplemental reference resources of selected Internet sites and social work journals.

Part I provides an overview of the General Method. **Chapter 1, The Foundation for Generalist Practice in Social Work,** presents social work's valuing of persons as self-determining human beings who reveal their needs and strengths, seek services, and solve problems within the context of their environmental life space. It describes the foundation for social work practice and the core elements in the General Method's strengths-based problem-solving in micro, mezzo, and macro practice.

Chapter 2, Human Diversity: Multiculturalism, Social Pluralism, and Socio-Demographic Variability, presents a paradigm for understanding cultural, social, and socio-demographic variations in worldview and help-seeking behavior among human beings. Attention is also directed toward how oppression, prejudicial bias, and conflict affect individuals, families, groups, and communities. Discussion of similarities and differences among and within groups facilitates cultural competence in strengths-based problem-solving with an empowerment orientation.

Chapter 3, Building Empirical Evidence for Practice, explores the nature of empirical evidence in practice and ways to collect it (such as goal attainment scaling and rapid assessment instruments) in order to develop services and evaluate outcomes. The chapter addresses social workers' ethical obligation to base their practice on (1) the best information available from research, theory, and practice experience; (2) the strengths and resources the client system brings to the General Method; and (3) the information and evidence applicable to the client system's needs and the circumstances at hand. Reflecting the profession's values, what the client system brings to the helping process has been found to account for 30 percent of the empirical variance in intervention outcome (Tallman & Bohart, 1999).

Chapter 4, Strengths-Based Problem-Solving Interviews, presents empowerment, the strengths perspective, and risk and resilience as the conceptual frameworks used to craft interview questions. This new chapter is critical since the professional relationship developed through the interview process is a common factor in the helping process and has been found to account for 30 percent of the empirical variance in intervention outcome (Tallman & Bohart, 1999).

Part II presents the practice phases, guiding principles, processes, and techniques of the General Method in order to provide a conceptual understanding of both the *what* and *how to* of strengths-based problem-solving at micro, mezzo, and macro levels of practice. Each chapter also addresses monitoring social work processes at that phase of the General Method. Each contains case vignettes and seven ongoing cases.

Chapter 5, Engagement, identifies focal points of problems and needs, strengths and assets, feelings and reactions, and goals in the initial interactions between the social worker and micro, mezzo, and macro client and action systems.

Chapter 6, Data Collection, directs inquiry to gathering subjective and objective information about the nature and severity of the client system's presenting problems and needs, strengths and assets, and risk and protective factors and the environmental resources and barriers affecting their person-in-environment circumstances.

Chapter 7, Assessment and Contract Planning, appraises the data collected in order to prioritize problems and goals, identify strengths, plan and contract interventions, and set the structure for evaluating outcomes. The chapter includes drawing inferences from the data and formulating a goal-oriented action plan that addresses problems and needs, barriers to psychosocial functioning and well-being, and strategies for the enhancement of strengths, resources, and protective factors.

Chapter 8, Intervention in Micro and Mezzo Generalist Practice, presents strengths-based problem-solving principles, processes, and techniques organized as models of counseling, information and referral, crisis intervention, small group intervention, case management, and teamwork.

Chapter 9, Intervention in Macro Generalist Practice, discusses strengths-based problem-solving principles, processes, and techniques organized as models of social and political advocacy, social planning and community development, locality development, and internal organizational change.

Chapter 10, Evaluation, explores the methodology and tools for assessing practice outcomes. The chapter focuses on documenting effectiveness and analyzing goal attainment in strengths enhancement and problem reduction.

Chapter 11, Termination, addresses the core processes used in planning to cease contact and provide a transition period for client and action systems. Although primary attention is given to the celebratory and strengths elements of ending as graduation and beginning anew, the losses in ending are acknowledged and examined.

Available with MyHelpingLab

This text is available packaged with MyHelpingLab, which is an exciting new interactive online resource for social work and family therapy students. MyHelpingLab contains video clips of actual therapist–client sessions, case worker–client interactions, over 80 interactive cases, licensing/career resources, career interviews with actual practitioners, articles from the *New York Times*, Study Aids, and Research Navigator.

MyHelpingLab is available with or without course management tools. MyHelpingLab addresses individual teaching and learning needs by providing multiple modes of learning and practice. It saves in-class time for faculty and helps increase student success in many courses by providing a multimedia "shared experience" that can be accessed conveniently—24 hours a day, seven days a week.

Discover where practice comes to life! Log on to **www.myhelpinglab.com** and begin exploring the many features of MyHelpingLab today!

To offer MyHelpingLab to your students at no extra cost, you will need to obtain a special package ISBN from your local Allyn & Bacon representative: www.ablongman.com/replocator. Your representative can also assist you with your request for other instructor supplements such as Instructor's Manual/Test Bank and PowerPoint slides.

Acknowledgments

We gratefully acknowledge Dr. Maria Joan O'Neil McMahan's groundbreaking work in producing the first (1984) and subsequent (1990, 1996) editions of this book. Without her work as a base, the fourth and fifth editions would not have come into being.

We also appreciate the comments and suggestions from the following reviewers: Ronald Dolon, Ball State University; Margaret A. Twiname-Dungan, St. Cloud University; and Gary Viltereal, Western Kentucky University. Last but not least, we thank Patricia Quinlin, Senior Acquisitions Editor Social Work and Family Therapy for Allyn & Bacon, and editorial assistant Sara Holliday for their invaluable assistance in preparing the manuscript and bringing this fifth edition to fruition.

In Her Own Words:
A Commitment to Service Today
Maria Joan O'Neil McMahon

For Maria Joan O'Neil McMahon (1937–1996), social work represented a calling of service to others and provided meaning and fulfillment in her life. Throughout her social work career, she served as a model of professional excellence in practice, teaching, community service, and scholarship. Her publications focused on poverty, child welfare, the general method of practice, and social work education. Dr. McMahon received multiple honors, including Outstanding Social Worker of the Year in Connecticut and distinguished alumna of the National Catholic School of Social Service of The Catholic University of America. The following excerpts are from a 1990 talk delivered by Dr. McMahon to social workers in public social services.

It is very fitting that at least once a year social workers take a little distance from the pressures, demands, policies, and procedures to reflect and recommit ourselves to what, in fact, we are all about. We know that there was a time when our country went through a depression. We were in trouble and people were going under. At that time, our nation decided that it was not going to be a society built on survival of the fittest and instituted a means to care and help people meet their needs through the rough times so that they could once again become productive members of society. Thus, the 1935 Social Security Act reflects the highest value of our nation—that is, the value of the potential and worth of every human being. To demonstrate that value and to serve the institution of public assistance, government officials looked at many disciplines and people. They did not choose individuals from psychology or psychiatry who deal primarily with the individual. They did not choose people from the fields of sociology or social planning who deal primarily with the social environment. They sought people who understood both, because they knew that the purpose of the Social Security Act was to help individuals function effectively in society.

They chose social work as the primary discipline to carry out the job, because social workers have always had the dual person and environment perspective.

So even with your pressures, your stresses, and your often difficult jobs, what keeps you going and what keeps so many other noble, seasoned, wonderful people in public sector jobs has been the fact that there is meaning and purpose to what these jobs are about and the fact that they and you have a commitment—a commitment to human service. What does *commitment* mean? Dictionaries (*Webster's*, 1990) define it as a "declaration of adherence to an ideal or doctrine" or as a "decisive moral choice for a definite course of action." Commitment is a decisive choice. What about *service?* The definition of *service* is "to meet the needs of others" or "to repair or provide maintenance for others." Within the public social service system, there is the need for a decisive choice or declaration of adherence to the ideal and a definite course of action in serving, in meeting the needs of others, and in repairing or providing maintenance for others. So often, the larger the service system gets, the less social workers realize how important they are. And yet, the larger the service gets, the more important every single link is, because that chain has gotten so large that if one link weakens, the whole thing breaks down. Thus, no matter what your role is, if you are a member of a public social service department, you are in a public service role and you are needed.

What's going on today? Have you noticed that in the literature we now hear about homeless families? People out on the streets are no longer called bums or bag ladies. Today in America, we have children and mothers and fathers walking our streets because they are homeless. Do we as a society realize that when we decrease opportunities for people, pull back on our programs and services for those in need, there is a corresponding increase in crime, suicide, drug addiction, and family breakdown? We see that result in society today where there is obviously a pulling back of basic opportunities for food, clothing, and shelter for people in need. Who is there to be a voice? Who is there to hold on to those high values that say, yes, we care; yes, we are going to meet needs and provide opportunities? Who is there, as the Bible says, "When I was hungry, you fed me. When I was homeless, you found a place for me to live. When I was anxious, you calmed my fears. When I was naked, you clothed me"? Who is there today to feed, clothe, and find homes for others? You know who's doing it. You are.

Our poor and our needy have a real problem called poverty, and it is a multifaceted problem that involves the health system, the education system, the social service system, transportation, housing, unemployment, and more. There is no simple answer to poverty. You are not to blame and your service system is not to blame because poor people are dependent on you. The sad thing is that there are not enough resources to give you the basics of what the poor need or the opportunities to go beyond that bare subsistence. To truly serve today, we have to grow in our knowledge and skills, to become more sophisticated ourselves in doing justice to what social work is all about. Just as one of the key messages we have learned is that poverty is not a simple problem, one of the things we have also learned is that there's a need for teamwork, holistic understanding, and commitment. Everybody is called to care.

Now where do we begin? We begin with a sense of unity in our own services—teamwork—we're in it together. Shared commitment is what brings us together. As we work together toward our goal, we grow in seeing that it is not enough. Others are needed. Well, come to us, schools of social work committed to the same goals, because commitment and caring are what bring us together. If we are preparing students to get out there, to take responsible leadership roles in human services, then they had better be taught what it is really all about out there. How are we going to teach them today's reality if we practiced 20 years ago and have been in academia ever since? We need you to keep us informed about what is going on. We need your field placements; we need your data; we need your information; we need your communication. What do you need from us? You need someone with the time to take a more distant view, to research and document human needs and practice issues, to share in spreading the news of the needs of people today. For example, you have people coming to you without housing, who are hungry, who are drowning. You're meeting those immediate needs. Some of us in this audience have the time and expertise to gather information, to do research on the causes, effects, and interventions, and to publicize our findings. We are needed to teach and prepare people to work with you, to join you when you need more people coming into your agencies who know what it is all about, or to take over when you are ready to retire.

Yes, we need each other—the servers and the academics. Yes, it is a team effort and not just for social workers and agencies or educators and schools of social work but we need political support and power. How do we get it? I'll tell you how. It involves a story about a man who was awakened in the night by someone who was hungry. The man said, "I have a neighbor who has bread. Let us go and get some for you." So he knocked at the door, but the neighbor didn't answer. He kept knocking, and the neighbor came to the top window and said, "Who is it? Go away, I'm sleeping." You know that story? The man didn't swear and curse; he just said, "We have someone here who is hungry." The neighbor said, "I'm sleeping. Don't bother me," and went back to bed. What did the man do? He kept knocking. So the neighbor came again to the window and said, "I told you to leave me alone." The man said, "We have someone here who is hungry." You know that story? The neighbor went back to bed. The man kept knocking. Finally, what happened? The neighbor said, "I can't get any sleep; for God's sake here is the bread." That is a story in the Bible and that is who we are. We are the people who keep knocking, who don't go away, because if we do, what's going to happen? Who will be there? What would happen in an uncaring, survival-of-the-fittest society? What keeps us going so that we don't give up, burn out, get tired of knocking? What keeps us going is what was brought out by John Steinbeck in *The Grapes of Wrath* or by Abraham Maslow when he described how people become self-actualized. What keeps us going is the recognition that we have meaning and purpose in our lives. Yes, we have our goals and we have our dreams and we have our past experiences. But most of all, what keeps us going is the belief in human life and our commitment to human service. We know we can't do it all. But we sure can do something, and that's what keeps us going. We are doing what we can to make a difference, and that gives us purpose and meaning. That makes us more than just alive; it truly helps us live.

But most of all, we find meaning here and now in the present moment, and that's what it is all about—to live the present fully. No matter what you're doing when you work within the human service system, you have meaning and purpose within the present moment for persons currently in need. Whether these human beings know it or not, we value them and believe in the potential of human life. Think about your call to really live the gift of the present moment. To quote Buechner (1983, p. 86), "Listen to your life. See it for the fathomless mystery that it is. In the boredom and pain of it, no less than in the excitement and gladness: touch, taste, and smell your way into the holy and hidden of it because in the last analysis, all moments are key moments, and life itself is a grace."

My parting words are: Know that you are a grace to many in your own way. You might be the *only* grace to many. My hope is that through your recommitment, you will continue to do the marvelous job that those of you in public social services, and those of you who stay in public social services, are really doing today.

About the Authors

Elizabeth M. Timberlake, Ph.D., is Ordinary Professor Emerita of social work at The Catholic University of America. She has taught social work practice model development and advanced research for doctoral students, taught social work theory and practice with children and their families for master's students, and served as field instructor for undergraduates. Dr. Timberlake has specialized in direct and indirect practice with children and their parents and has worked with them and on their behalf for over 40 years in child welfare, family service agencies, mental health centers, school settings, and private practice. She has worked to empower families in housing projects and on the streets and has served on the governing boards of social agencies such as United Way, Associated Catholic Charities, Christ Child Society School Counseling Program, Good Shepherd Center, and Christ Child Institute. Dr. Timberlake has served on the editorial boards of *Social Thought, Child and Adolescent Social Work Journal,* and *Social Work in Education.* She is Director Emerita of The Catholic University of America's National Research Center for Child and Family Services. Her extensive research and over 100 publications have focused on children's coping and adaptation in the face of various life stressors, child and family coping with homelessness, physical and mental illness of children and adults, treatment process and outcome, improving social work practice and social service delivery for children and youth, the impact of federal laws on school social work practice, social work personnel issues, practice and program outcomes, and current trends and future directions in social work practice.

Michaela L. Zajicek-Farber, Ph.D., B.C.D., LCSW-Clinical, is Assistant Professor of social work at The Catholic University of America. She has earned a bachelor's degree in both social work and psychology, and master's and doctoral degrees in social work. Dr. Farber has taught foundation social work practice, human behavior and the social environment, basic research, program and practice evaluation, and context of social work practice with children and families. She has practiced social work in the context of agency and private practice settings for over 20 years with children and adults affected by chronic health conditions, developmental disabilities, mental illness, trauma, and substance abuse. Dr. Farber is currently Director of The Catholic University of America's National Research Center for Child and Family Services. She has worked through research to understand and empower families of infants and toddlers in Early Head Start, conducted needs assessments to strengthen the ability of social agencies to respond to changing client needs and resources, conducted social agency program evaluations to improve client service delivery, designed and implemented community programs to respond to the needs of high-risk teens in multicultural urban environments, and provided ongoing consultation to community agencies promoting the well-being of children and their families. She has contributed and served on a task force for the American Board of Examiners for Clinical Social Work in developing a position statement on standards for clinical social work practice with children and their families. Dr. Farber's scholarship focuses on addressing the needs and services of children and their families and practice/program evaluation.

Christine Anlauf Sabatino, Ph.D., LICSW, LCSW-Clinical, is Associate Professor of social work at The Catholic University of America. She has taught the General Method of social work practice and the concurrent integrative field internship seminars at the baccalaureate and master's levels, human behavior and the social environment, school social work, and doctoral-level critique of social work practice theories. Dr. Sabatino has earned baccalaureate, master's, and doctoral degrees in social work. She has 33 years of social work practice as a school social worker, practice and research consultant, group home social worker, and clinical social worker, and has served as program director and clinical supervisor of a private inner-city school counseling program. She has served as research associate for the National Evaluation of Early Head Start, Administration for Children, Youth and Families, U.S. Department of Health & Human Services, and currently serves as research associate for The Catholic University of America's National Research Center for Child and Family Services and the Community Development and Research Center. Dr. Sabatino serves on the editorial board for *Children & Schools* and is a certified school social worker and diplomate under the auspices of NASW. She also serves on the board of Edgewood/Brookland Family Service Collaborative in Washington, DC. She is a member of the Society of Social Work Research and the Council of Social Work Education. Her research and scholarship have focused on school social work practice, the impact of federal policies on social work and pupil personnel services, early intervention, research issues in school social work, homeless children, social work personnel issues, and current trends and future directions in social work practice.

Generalist
Social Work Practice

CHAPTER 1

The Foundation for Generalist Practice in Social Work

Given societal changes and the evolving nature of the social work profession, achieving precision in identifying and unifying social work's values, knowledge, and methods remains an ongoing challenge. In undertaking this task, this book draws on the rich written and oral traditions of twentieth-century social work as the point of departure for (1) integrating the various dimensions of the profession into a unified whole and (2) providing a comprehensive conceptual framework for understanding and practicing entry-level professional social work in the twenty-first century. Building on McMahon's (1996) generalist book, this edition depicts an entry-level professional social worker whose practice is framed within a holistic ecological-systems perspective, grounded in various theories and social work practice concepts, and guided by strengths-based problem-solving methodology and social work precepts.

Holism and Social Work

In social work, there is a philosophical valuing of persons as whole human beings who are individually unique and self-determining as they reveal needs and strengths, set goals, seek services, and solve problems within the context of their environmental life-space. Persons and populations are viewed holistically when the focus is on

▶ The total person and the interdependent dimensions of body, spirit, mind, and feelings;
▶ The person nested within and transacting with the environment; and
▶ The environment as consisting of social, physical, economic, psychological, and political forces that support and impede individual and collective social functioning and well-being.

Thus, the family, culture, physical surroundings, community, and society of the individual are seen as essential parts of a holistic view of person-in-environment.

■ **CONCEPT 1.1**

A *holistic* view of person-in-environment includes family, culture, physical surroundings, organizations, community, and society.

In considering the needs and resources of human beings holistically, the focus is on the whole hierarchy of needs, wants, and strengths and the necessary relationship of each to the others and to the resources that are available, accessible, and acceptable. Maslow (1970), for example, identifies the needs of a person as crossing over the physical (bodily needs), intellectual (cognitive needs), socio-affective (social/emotional needs), and spiritual (aesthetic needs) dimensions of persons. In this context, a *need* is something crucial for a reasonable level of living, human development, and psychosocial functioning. A *want*, by contrast, is a desire for something beyond basic survival needs and includes those desires and aspirations that motivate human beings toward goal achievement, enhance human satisfaction, and promote a sense of well-being (Wall, Timberlake, Farber, Sabatino, Liebow, Smith, & Taylor, 2000). Some common human needs (Towle, 1957) are universal across all environments; other needs and wants are influenced by the transactions between persons and their environments and by persons' goals and aspirations for their lives.

In Maslow's (1970) tradition, needs and wants are intertwined with aspirations and form a hierarchical pyramid that progresses from a wide base of physical survival needs in most environments toward a peak of creative self-actualization that reflects individual goals in particular environments. This holistic view highlights the interdependence of human needs and goals and the personal strengths and environmental resources for meeting them.

■ C O N C E P T S 1 . 2

> *Strengths* refer to the capacities, competencies, and resources of client and action systems within their environments.
>
> A *strengths perspective* focuses on enhancing the ability to cope with ordinary and extraordinary situations and potential for change.
>
> *Resources* refer to the collective supplies and social supports available in the environment to meet needs and provide assistance.

Within the broad resource network of human services, social workers and other providers become increasingly aware of the interdependence of the community service network as they strive to apply a holistic helping approach in their work with client, action, and target systems. During service delivery, the interrelationships of various professionals with one another and with their client and action systems may evolve smoothly, but more often, working together requires shared effort. Thus, case coordination and teamwork with their group building, collaboration, mediation, negotiation, management, and strengths-based problem-solving processes become essential professional tools for effective holistic service delivery. Although persons, families, groups, organizations, and communities with particular needs, strengths, and resources may come to the attention of individual practitioners or single agencies, holistically minded helpers do not lose sight of the fact that each is very much a part of other persons, families, groups, organizations, and communities; that each need and goal is strongly related to other needs and goals; and that a single service can meet neither all the needs and goals of any one entity nor one need and goal for all entities.

■ C O N C E P T S 1 . 3

> *Client system* refers to individuals, families, groups, organizations, and communities "who sanction or ask for [social work] services, who are the expected beneficiaries of services, and who have a working agreement or contract with the [social worker]" (Pincus & Minahan, 1973, p. 63).
>
> *Action systems* are formed when a social worker joins with clients and other professionals, agencies, organizations, and community members to work with and through them in order to influence a particular *target system* in need of change if the action system is to accomplish specific goals (Pincus & Minahan, 1973).

Generalist Practice in Social Work

Professional social workers engaged in *generalist practice* may be entry-level or graduate-level practitioners. The concept of *general* or *generalist* refers to a type of practice that is "not confined by specialization or careful limitation" (*Webster's*, 1990, p. 379) and includes the following major dimensions:

1. *A professionally derived knowledge, values, and skill base that is*
   - Built on liberal arts knowledge
   - Anchored in the mission and foundation of social work practice
   - Transferable between multiple fields of practice and problems in social functioning
   - Implemented across micro, mezzo, and macro levels of practice contexts
   - Applicable to different client and action systems: individual, family, group, organization, and community
2. *An ecological-systems conceptual framework that reflects*
   - The interrelatedness of human functioning and a person-in-environment focus
   - The inclusion of human competence within the intervention paradigm
   - An open selection of theories of human behavior to explain and address human functioning
3. *A holistic assessment that*
   - Identifies the target of change
   - Includes information about the client system's demographics and culturally based characteristics, behavior, and environment
   - Includes information about the client system's strengths in relation to identified needs and problems
   - Draws on the ecological-systems conceptual framework
   - Explicates client system and social worker views on the presenting situation
4. *A strengths-based problem-solving intervention that incorporates*
   - Needs in relation to presenting problems and situations
   - Competencies, resources, and assets
   - Goals, objectives, and task activities within a specified time frame and context
   - Plans for monitoring and evaluating accomplishments and outcomes
   - The minimal goal accomplishment necessary for termination of service delivery

Thus, to practice effectively, a social work generalist is expected to have acquired a basic core of knowledge of professional social work within a holistic philosophical perspective and to have integrated the core social work knowledge with the four essential dimensions of generalist practice.

The Foundation of Social Work Practice

As described in the classic working definition of the social work profession (Commission on Social Work Practice, NASW, 1956, as cited in Bartlett, 1958), the five elements of *purpose, sanction, values, knowledge,* and *methods* that are rooted in the identity of all social workers form the common base for their practice within the holistic perspective of person-in-environment. Whereas the fundamental elements of purpose and values generally remain the same today, the sanction, knowledge, and methods of contemporary social work practice have been greatly influenced by legal regulatory trends, the exponential explosion of knowledge, and changing needs, strengths, and goals of various client systems.

Purpose

The twofold purpose or mission of social work continues to be

1. Enhancing the social functioning of individuals, families, and groups in their social environments (Richmond, 1917) and
2. Modifying environmental conditions associated with population need, limited resources, and risk factors (Addams, 1910).

That is, social workers enable individuals, families, groups, organizations, and communities to function more effectively within their various environments (Meyer, 1993; Miley, O'Melia, & DuBois, 2001). They also work to improve environmental conditions for vulnerable and marginalized populations (Gutierrez & Cox, 1998). The ways in which social workers implement their purpose take different forms, approaches, roles, and methodologies. For example, social workers engage in *direct practice with persons* in such roles as counselor, enabler, broker of services, and case manager and in *indirect practice with persons* in such roles as advocate, consultant, team member, and administrator. They engage in *direct practice with environments* in such roles as consultant, organizer, advocate, group facilitator, mediator, and administrator and in *indirect practice with environments* in such roles as researcher, analyst, planner, programmer, and fund-raiser. More specifically, social workers prevent, remediate, or minimize human problems and risk factors while enhancing human strengths, resources, and protective factors. They also prevent, ameliorate, and minimize environmental conditions associated with population need, limited resources, and risk factors while enhancing population strengths and protective factors.

■ CONCEPT 1.4

Social work's *mission* is directed toward the development of the maximum potential of individuals and environments in order that client systems may improve their social functioning and achieve the highest quality of individual and collective well-being.

As stated in the *Code of Ethics* (NASW, 1999, p. 1; see also www.socialworkers.org):

The primary mission of the social work profession is to enhance human well-being and help meet the basic human needs of all people, with particular attention to the

JANE ADDAMS (1860–1935), a social reformer, worked with immigrant and poor families to improve living conditions and protect children and women from economic exploitation. Her publications include *Twenty Years at Hull House* and *Peace and Bread in Time of War*. Founder of the settlement house movement, Ms. Addams was the first American woman to receive the Nobel Peace Prize (1931).

needs and empowerment of people who are vulnerable, oppressed, and living in poverty. A historic and defining feature of social work is the profession's focus on individual well-being in a social context and the well-being of society. Fundamental to social work is attention to the environmental forces that create, contribute to, and address problems in living.

Sanction

Philosophically, the profession's tradition of social responsibility may be traced back to such early socio-political and religious writings as the 1750 B.C. Babylonian Code of Hammurabi, the sixth-century B.C. writings of Confucius, the writings of the Greco-Roman empires, and the various codifications of the Judeo-Christian traditions (Reamer, 1993). As a societal philanthropical endeavor, social work is rooted in the Elizabethan Poor Law of 1601 and seventeenth-century human welfare measures in the American colonies.

■ CONCEPT 1.5

The sources of authority and permissions that *sanction* the practice of social workers in society include (1) the clients served; (2) human service agencies under public, private, or religious auspice; (3) the organized profession; and (4) governmental agency boards with the responsibility for legal regulation.

As a societally sanctioned profession, however, social work in the United States did not come of age until the twentieth century. Being a societally sanctioned profession simply means having governmental authorization to perform designated tasks and activities in carrying out the profession's explicit mission and purpose. Specifically, federal, state, and local governments authorize social work practice through legislation that:

▶ Creates social programs and social work role positions in multidisciplinary service programs
▶ Allocates funding for social work programs, role positions, and practice activities
▶ Legally incorporates and licenses agencies, organizations, and institutions that employ social workers to establish programs and serve client systems
▶ Regulates or licenses individual social work professionals

Employing agencies provide authority and permission for social workers to engage in practice within the service boundaries specified in their legal charters of incorporation. Consumers of social work services further authorize social workers to serve them in order to enhance specified aspects of their social functioning and modify specific environmental conditions. To work for change as a collective body, social workers act through professional organizations such as the National Association of Social Workers (NASW), Council on Social Work Education (CSWE), and Federation of Clinical Social Workers to name a few.

Internet sites provide additional information about NASW (www.socialworkers .org), the social work membership organization, and CSWE (www.CSWE.org), the educational accrediting arm of the profession.

Values and Ethics

Values and ethics in social work form three interrelated dimensions, which include preferred ways of thinking about persons and society, preferred instrumentalities for dealing with people-in-environment, and preferred goals and outcomes (Levy, 1973). Social work's preferred view of persons as inherently good and possessing worth, dignity, strengths, and capacity for change and society as containing resources, opportunities, and barriers forms the ideological foundation of the profession. Specifically, social workers recognize that every human being possesses the potential for fulfill-

MARY E. RICHMOND (1861–1928), practitioner and researcher, authored *Social Diagnosis,* the first formulation of the principles and techniques of social investigation and the culmination of 17 years of social work research and practice. She served as a friendly visitor with the Baltimore Charity Organization Society and later became director of the Russell Sage Foundation through which she conducted major social work research.

ment and well-being but acknowledge that human beings are fallible, with needs and goals that may necessitate protection, support, and resources from their environments. They also recognize that a just and caring society is both a resourceful system with open doors and a social environment that, at times, requires influence and direction by responsible, compassionate professionals. This value foundation guides social workers' preference for client and action system outcomes that mobilize environmental resources and opportunities and enhance human dignity and social functioning. These outcomes are attained through the preferred instrumentalities or tools—such as the professional self, social work knowledge, ethical decision making, and intervention methods and skills—that social workers use in working with people and their environments.

Although the profession's values draw heavily from the Judeo-Christian ideological traditions, some principles such as that of compassion for vulnerable persons are also central tenets in other spiritual traditions, including Islam and Buddhism (Bullis, 1996; Canda & Furman, 1999). Thus, social workers' commitment to engage in activities that promote the potential of both persons and environments may flow not only from the profession's value base but also from their own personal beliefs and spiritual traditions that are congruent with the profession's core values.

■ C O N C E P T 1 . 6

The *value* foundation guides social workers' preference for client and action system outcomes that enhance human dignity and social functioning and mobilize environmental resources.

As a profession, social work is guided by explicit values, a moral commitment, and a written code of ethics (NASW, 1999). Social work's values are rooted in the fundamental ideals of belief in the inherent dignity and worth of every human being and recognition of the need for a democratic and caring society. This ideological base is identifiable in social welfare policies, programs, and practices that (1) seek to preserve the right of all persons to experience a sense of safety and well-being in everyday life and (2) are set into motion through democratic participatory government in which equality of rights is enforced and social justice becomes the norm (Tropman, 1999). That is, social workers strive to modify, develop, and sustain the capabilities of individuals and the resources of societies so that together they may promote improved social functioning and the highest quality of well-being for communities and persons. Not surprisingly, these ideals emphasize the centrality and interrelatedness of person and environment for carrying out social work's mission.

Social work values reflect the ultimate goal of the profession and have been formally organized into a code of ethics and practice principles. As first identified by Biestek (1957), the basic prescriptive principles of social work practice were conceptualized as individualization, purposeful expression of feelings, controlled emotional involvement, acceptance, nonjudgmental attitude, self-determination, and confidentiality. Although initially framed as principles for casework, more recent authors have noted their generic applicability for practice with systems of any size (Biestek, 1957; McMahon, 1996). Essentially, these principles guide the social worker in:

▶ Recognizing that every client system is unique and deserving of consideration and respect (individualization)
▶ Understanding the human need to express one's feelings and the value in this expression as a means of fostering growth (purposeful expression of feelings)
▶ Using one's feelings and emotions appropriately for the service of others (controlled emotional involvement)
▶ Demonstrating that human beings have a right to be accepted as they are (acceptance)
▶ Avoiding passing judgments on people (nonjudgmental attitude)
▶ Respecting the right of client systems to choose for themselves as much as possible (self-determination)
▶ Keeping information obtained from or about clients confidential (confidentiality)

The National Association of Social Workers (NASW, 1999, pp. 5–6) has promulgated a similar but somewhat different listing of core professional values together with corresponding ethical principles:

▶ *Service:* "Social workers' primary goal is to help people in need and to address social problems."
▶ *Social justice:* "Social workers challenge social injustice."
▶ *Dignity and worth of the person:* "Social workers respect the inherent dignity and worth of the person."
▶ *Importance of human relationships:* "Social workers recognize the central importance of human relationships."
▶ *Integrity:* "Social workers behave in a trustworthy manner."
▶ *Competence:* "Social workers practice within their areas of competence and develop and enhance their professional expertise."

These values and principles comprise the rules of conduct and ethical standards for professional responsibility, decision making, and conduct that are set forth in the NASW *Code of Ethics* (1999).

As further codified, these standards include social workers' ethical responsibilities to clients, colleagues, practice settings, and the profession. More specifically, the NASW *Code* identifies a range of professional responsibilities to client systems, including commitment, self-determination, informed consent, competence, cultural competence and social diversity, conflicts of interest, privacy and confidentiality, access to records, appropriate maintenance of boundaries, safeguarding interests and rights, and interruption and termination of services (section 1). In addition, the *Code* identifies the need for social workers to maintain appropriate boundaries in their professional relationships (sections 1.09–1.13) and not to allow "personal problems, psychosocial distress, legal problems, substance abuse, or mental health difficulties" to interfere with their professional performance (section 4.05). Also stressed is the need for social workers with personal difficulties that do interfere with professional performance to "immediately seek consultation and take appropriate remedial action by seeking professional help, making adjustments in workload, terminating practice, or taking any other steps necessary to protect clients and others" (section 4.05). Finally, the *Code* speaks to social workers' collegial responsibility for the profession. That is, any social worker who is aware of a colleague with personal difficulties is expected to consult with the person and assist him or her in "taking remedial action" (sections 2.09, 2.10). Thus, working within agencies, society, and the profession and with client and related systems, the social worker is able to draw on the *Code of Ethics* for direction and support.

Knowledge

Standing at the interface of person and environment with a dynamic two-sided value base, social workers simultaneously relate to both person and environment. To carry their value commitment forward into professional action, they need to possess empirical and theoretical knowledge of persons, environments, their interdependence, and their transactions. Whereas values form the ideological basis for professional action, conceptual and empirical knowledge forms the objective basis for practice principles (Linzer, 1999; Reamer, 1993). Therefore, the foundation knowledge base of professional social work has been purposely selected to provide a theoretically framed and empirically grounded understanding of:

► The thoughts, feelings, behaviors, needs, resources, and goals of human systems within the context of their strengths, risks, protective factors, multiple cultures, social pluralism, and socio-demographic variance
► The structures and processes of the environment that influence human development and biopsychosocial functioning, organizational and community functioning, and the planned change process
► The transactions occurring between persons and environments
► Hypotheses, principles, processes, and empirical evidence associated with change in client, action, and target systems
► Transactions among the various systems and hierarchical levels that constitute their work environments

■ **C O N C E P T S 1.7**

Empirically grounded knowledge refers to substantive matter or evidence that has been subjected to systematic inquiry in order to discover or check facts.

Theoretically framed knowledge refers to a coherent group of abstract propositions used in a systematic explanation of particular practice phenomena and intervention methods.

Empirical explanations of practice phenomena and intervention methods are assumed to represent known truth—that is, information derived from actual experience, experimentation, or observation. By contrast, *theoretically framed knowledge* refers to a coherent group of abstract propositions used in a systematic explanation of particular practice phenomena and intervention methods. Theoretical explanations both derive from and inform practice. They represent a way of organizing ideas, thoughts, and information in order to understand professional issues, practice phenomena, and intervention goals and plans, and they guide intervention with client, action, and target systems. Without organizing theoretical frameworks, social work knowledge simply becomes an overwhelming array of disparate facts, ideas, and assumptions about the many facets of helping found in professional practice. Without the order imposed by theory and empirical evidence, it is not possible for social workers to function professionally.

The source of this empirically grounded and theoretically framed knowledge is twofold. Much of it is drawn from the disciplines of biology, anthropology, psychology, sociology, political science, and economics as well as the profession of medicine. Increasingly, however, knowledge is being generated from within the social work profession in such areas as social welfare policies and services, social work practice methods, the social work relationship, person-in-environment, and individual, family, group, organizational, and community dynamics, to name a few. Much of today's emerging knowledge from outside and within the profession is interrelated and relevant to social work practice. Yet, when viewed as a whole, the huge amount of contemporary knowledge appears overwhelming and unmanageable. To counter this, social workers systematically organize and present established and emerging knowledge in relation to their triplex classification schema of (1) person, (2) environment, and (3) the transactions between them (see Table 1.1). Since the categories of this classification schema are not mutually exclusive, however, the items in the table are grouped according to their predominant focus.

For example, to understand the *person,* a social worker calls on the assorted information that collectively provides a comprehensive, dynamic view of the everevolving total person, complete with strengths, needs, and aspirations. This knowledge includes the psychological, biological, social, sexual, cognitive, moral, and spiritual dimensions of the human person, which are conceptualized according to subsystems, developmental stages, and life course developmental milestones. It also includes understanding the common human needs and basic goals for human development and self-actualization. Knowledge about the *person* is presented both as aggregate commonalities and individual uniqueness.

Information about the numerous systems that constitute the *environment* for each person includes resources and barriers to opportunity in relation to family, kinship networks, informal and formal social structures, professionals and institutions, and policy matters. It also includes knowledge about risk and protective factors, cultures, economics, politics, organizations, and communities as social systems.

The middle, or *In,* category of Table 1.1 lists knowledge that focuses on the *transactions* that take place as persons and environmental systems interface. These transactions are explored in terms of their functional relationship over time to the

TABLE 1.1 ■ Foundation Knowledge for Social Work

Social Work		
Person	*In*	*Environment*

Holistic Analytic Paradigm

Person	In	Environment
Well-being	Goodness-of-fit	Just and fair society
Resilience, strengths	Coping	Access to opportunity
Needs, wants, aspirations	Role fulfillment	Resource utilization
Appraisal	Exchange/stress/conflict	Resource allocation
Diversity	Variability	Diversity
Risk factors	Barriers	Risk factors
Protective factors	Support	Protective factors
Empowerment	Strengths-based problem-solving	Access to resources

Unit of Attention

Person	In	Environment
Individuals	Interaction	Groups
Children	Intrapersonal	Organizations
Adolescents	Interpersonal	Communities
Adults	Familial	Societal institutions
Older adults	Communal	National
Couples	Societal	International
Traditional	Behavioral actions	Culture as context
Nontraditional	Relationship formation	Social policies
Families	Continuing education	Legislative
Nuclear	Work, employment	Economic
Nontraditional	Role fulfillment	Health
Blended	Play, recreation	Education
Extended	Communication	Social welfare
Foster	Verbal	
Adoptive	Nonverval	
	Symbolic	

Concepts	**Theories**	**Concepts**
Human development	Psychodynamic	System development
Biology	Psychosocial	Barriers to resources
Neurology	Behavior	Access to opportunity
Genetic, heredity	Cognitive	Risk, protective factors
Physical motor	Social learning	Social justice
Cognitive	Role	Nurturing, sustaining institutions
Language, communication	Symbolic interaction	Support systems
Emotional, affective	Social exchange	Informal
Nutritional	Conflict	Formal
Sexual, intimacy	Family	Open/closed systems
Moral	Group	
Spiritual	Organization	
	Community	
	General systems	

characteristics and processes of both the environment and the developing person. Throughout life, for example, people grow and mature through the progressively more complex and reciprocal processes actively taking place between them and the individuals, objects, and symbols in their immediate and distant environments (Bronfenbrenner, 1999). Indeed, these influences on the person are at the center of theories such as psychodynamic, psychosocial, behavioral, and cognitive and interventive approaches such as crisis and empowerment. Similarly, communities grow and develop through complex transactional processes between environmental resources and protective factors, personal needs and goals, and barriers and opportunities in relation to resource availability, acceptability, and accessibility. These influences on the environment are at the center of such theories as symbolic interaction, learning, exchange, and conflict.

Although Table 1.1 does not provide an exhaustive list of all the knowledge used in social work, the categories do form an organizing framework both for social work's existing knowledge and for building its future knowledge base. When the items in the three categories are juxtaposed, the result enables social workers to gain a holistic perspective and acquire greater understanding of the person-in-environment.

Methods and Skills

■ CONCEPT 1.8

Social work *methods and skills* contain preventive, maintenance, restorative, and enhancement functions.

For social workers' actions to be more than an expression of values and mere technical application of information about person-in-environment, their professional intervention must be directed by critical thought and disciplined application of the knowledge base to specific client, action, and target systems under particular circumstances. Therefore, guided by *purpose, sanction, values,* and *knowledge,* social workers execute a series of activities within the framework of a specific *method* to achieve identified goals with client, action, and target systems. These activities constitute the methods and skills of the social worker (see Table 1.2). For example, social workers are known for using interpersonal relationships in a helping process. Sensitivity to feelings and disciplined use of self with various client systems have been consistently recognized as an essential part of the professional repertoire, as have problem-solving, goal setting, and task defining. That is, through an open, supportive professional relationship, social workers help client systems identify tasks and goals and proceed toward problem resolution and goal accomplishment. Thus, in a list of practice skills, relational and problem-solving skills obviously would be included (see the *Person* and *In* columns of Table 1.2).

Sometimes in environmental work, however, there are occasions when social workers need to interact with systems, organizations, and communities that are not

TABLE 1.2 ■ Foundation Methods/Skills for Social Work

Social Work		
Person	*In*	*Environment*

Professional interviewing skills
Ethnographic interviewing skills
Empathic responding skills
Relationship bonding skills
Skill in enhancing client strengths
Skill in empowering clients
	Strengths-based problem-solving skills
	  Problem identifying
	  Data collecting
	  Assessing/goal setting
	  Planning/task defining
	  Selecting/implementing
	    intervention
	  Evaluating
	  Terminating
	Case management
	Crisis intervention
	Family preservation
	Social worker-centered skills
	Skill in disciplined use of
	  professional self
	Skill in disciplined application
	  of foundation knowledge
	Skill in ethical decision making
	Professional skills
	  Time management
	  Teamwork
	  Documentation
	  Research
		Socio-political skills
		  Advocacy
		  Social action
		  Giving testimony
		  Bargaining
		  Organizing
		  Publicizing
		  Demonstrating
		  Mediating
		  Consciousness raising
		  Uncovering
		Locality development skills
		  Educating
		  Facilitating
		  Brokering
		  Empowering
		Social planning skills
		  Technology
		  Fact gathering
		  Analysis

client but action systems (Pincus & Minahan, 1973, p. 63). An example would be joining with a group of welfare mothers to address the quality of preschool care provided by a housing project. In exploring causes of problems or sources for meeting needs, social workers may identify target systems in either the immediate or distant environment as needing change in order to achieve goals.

When an environmental *target system* is dysfunctional and refuses to accept the change efforts of social workers and clients, the use of a supportive, enhancing relationship, together with problem-solving skills, is inappropriate and ineffective. An example would be a housing or social service program that rejects applicants on the basis of marital status. In such instances, the social worker stands at the interface of person and environment and uses research, political, and advocacy skills in goal-directed work to change the environmental target system. In addition to the basic relational and problem-solving skills of micro- and mezzo-level practice with individuals, families, and small groups, social workers need a range of macro-level practice skills and strategies with large groups, organizations, and communities. These include the ability to conduct needs assessments, document evidence, build coalitions, advocate for particular points of view, publicize issues, bring legal action, organize demonstrations, and seek legislative action (see the *Environment* column in Table 1.2).

Besides working with client systems, action systems, and environmental target systems, social workers are expected to perform certain activities as employees within their agencies and as members of their profession. Thus, professional responsibility requires such skills as keeping records; maintaining confidentiality; using supervision, collaborating with multiple disciplines, and building teams; and managing time effectively and efficiently. Research skills—particularly for monitoring client system progress, evaluating outcomes, and identifying trends in their own agency practice—are equally important.

In summary, the person-in-environment perspective provides a comprehensive framework for conceptually organizing the many complex foundation methods and skills of social workers today. In turn, this framework clearly conveys that a whole array of methods and skills is available for responsible choice and flexible individualized selection, depending on the circumstances of a given situation.

The Generalist Perspective

■ CONCEPT 1.9

Generalist practice elements include:

1. An ecological-systems perspective
2. A problem/strengths focus
3. A strengths/needs orientation
4. A multilevel approach
5. An open selection of theories and interventions
6. A strengths-based problem-solving process
7. Practice and program evaluation

In generalist practice, the social work foundation—which consists of *purpose, sanction, values, knowledge, skills,* and the *person-in-environment perspective*—is developed and expanded through an overlay and integration of seven practice elements. These practice elements interrelate and overlap as the generalist social worker provides services to individuals, families, groups, organizations, and communities in a manner that provides an integrated picture that may be called the *generalist perspective.* By definition, a *perspective* means a "broad view of events or ideas in their true nature and relationships" (*Webster's,* 1990, p. 677).

In other words, generalist practice assumes that the foundation is rudimentary to all social work practice and that the conceptual frameworks, focus, and methodology identified in the practice elements are essential means for using foundation knowledge, values, and skills. Whereas the generalist perspective refers to a view of what a social worker *brings* to a problem(s)-person(s)-situation(s), generalist practice refers to what a social worker *does* in a problem(s)-person(s)-situation(s) in micro-, mezzo-, and macro-system practice. Thus, entry-level generalist social workers are prepared to work directly with a variety of people, populations, and problems as well as the families, groups, organizations, and communities that comprise their environments. Over and above this common foundation for all social work practice, the intervention of graduate-level social workers is described according to the theoretical frameworks, focus, and methodology used in various specialized intervention models, such as clinical social work, developmental play therapy, family therapy, community organization, program administration, and social planning and policy.

An Ecological-Systems Perspective

To address the interactions and transactions of person and environment, generalist practice combines general systems, social systems, and ecological concepts and processes. The resulting ecological-systems approach portrays human and environmental systems at the micro (individual), mezzo (family, small group), and macro (large group, organization, community) levels as open, self-organizing, self-regulating, and adaptive functional units of action, interaction, and transaction and as comprised of intricate, interdependent subsystems (Robbins, Chatterjee, & Canda, 1998). In support of this combination, Kirst-Ashman and Hull (1999, p. 16) note that "both systems theory and the ecological perspective provide major tools for social work."

To understand the ecological-systems perspective as a central element in generalist practice, however, definitions of *systems* and *ecology* are essential.

■ C O N C E P T S 1 . 1 0

"A *system* is a dynamic order of parts and processes standing in mutual interaction" (von Bertalanffy, 1968, p. 208).

"*Ecology* is the science concerned with the adaptive fit of organisms and their environments and with the means by which they achieve a dynamic equilibrium and mutuality" (Germain, 1973, p. 326).

Social systems attempt to protect their survival through adaptation *and* self-preservation *and are interrelated and* interdependent; *human systems and their environments are intimately connected to one another. Thus,* people *and their* environments *are involved in a process of continued adaptation to one another and must be viewed holistically.* (Robbins, Chatterjee, & Canda, 1998, pp. 27–28)

Thus, in an ecological-systems perspective, *systems* and *ecology* are integrated by viewing the *person(s)* as a *system(s),* the *environment(s)* of the person as a *system(s),* and the *fit* and *transactions* between person(s) and environment(s) *ecologically.* As depicted in Figure 1.1, the person is seen as a system with various interdependent parts that include biological, psychological, political, economic (occupational), educational, spiritual, social, and sexual, to name a few (see Table 1.1). The environment is viewed as a system consisting of two major parts that nurture (family, friends, groups, community) and sustain (institutions, organizations, programs in society at large) (Bronfenbrenner, 1999). In sum, the ecological-systems perspective enhances understanding of person-in-environment by highlighting the actions, interactions, and transactions that may take place among the various parts and at the boundary where the person (organism) and environment interface.

A precursor for the application of the ecological-systems perspective to social work practice is found in William Gordon's (1962) writings on boundary work. Just as ecology concerns itself with the adaptive fit of organisms and their environments, Gordon's seven basic ideas constitute extensive consideration of what occurs at the

FIGURE 1.1 ■ An Ecological-Systems Perspective of Person in Environment

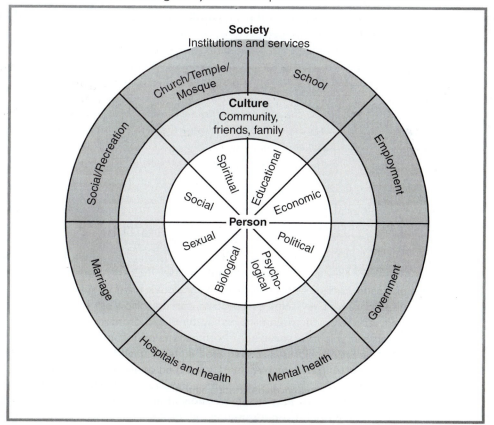

boundary between a client system and its environment. As summarized by Hearn (1979, pp. 350–351):

1. Social work has a simultaneous dual focus . . . upon the person and . . . situation, upon the system and its environment.
2. It occurs at the interface between the human system and its environment. . . .
3. The phenomenon which occurs at the interface is a transaction between system and environment. . . .
4. Transaction is a matching effort, whose focus is the coping behavior of the organism on the system side, and the qualities of the impinging environment on the environmental side. . . .
5. An encounter between the organism and the environment leaves both changed. . . .
6. The best transactions are those which promote the growth and development of the organism while at the same time being ameliorative to the environment. . . .
7. Unattended systems proceed . . . toward disorder, . . . disorganization, . . . or . . . a positive increase in entropy. . . . Thus, for growth . . . , there has to be a continuous redistribution of entropy between organism and environment.

Rooted in general systems theory, Gordon's boundary work provides the branch for the ecological-systems perspective to bear fruit in social work. Although they evolved over a 30-year period, the similarities between the early ideas of Gordon (1962) and the more recent ideas of Germain and Gitterman (1995) and Mattaini, Lowery, and Meyer (1998) as they define *ecology* are readily seen:

> *Ecology is a science concerned with the relations between living organisms—in this case, human beings and all the elements of their environments. It is concerned with how organisms and environments achieve a goodness-of-fit or adaptive balance and equally important, how and why they sometimes fail to do so. (Germain & Gitterman, 1979, p. 362)*

An ecological perspective also notes transactional processes and serves as a "metaphor for human relatedness through mutual adaptation" (Mattaini, Lowery, & Meyer, 1998, p. 6). As a way of integrating or synthesizing elements into a whole, the ecological-systems perspective "directs the vision of the client [system] and social worker toward the complex transactions in cases, helping connect them, and recognizing their interactions" (Mattaini, Lowery, & Meyer, 1998, p. 6).

In the ecological-systems perspective, the interactions, transactions, and interdependence between the organism (subsystem) and the environment (macrosystem) are seen as crucial for the survival of both. Any change in one may have a positive or negative effect on the other (Germain & Gitterman, 1995). The complexity and diversity among people and the various systems that constitute their immediate and distant environments as they act, exchange, interact, and transact continuously for survival are highlighted. In a recent revision of his original 1943 conceptualization of the ecological model, Bronfenbrenner (1999) added the prefix *bio,* with the result that his revised dynamic model incorporated the role of the environment into the processes of human development and change throughout the life cycle. His revised bio-ecological model defines environmental process in terms of its functional relationship to and reciprocal transaction with various characteristics of the environment and the developing person. In other words, both person and environment are constantly, mutually, and actively exchanging with and influencing each other for better or worse at the boundaries of their existence.

For social workers, the ecological-systems perspective and its newer bio-ecological variant help reinforce the holistic perspective of person-in-environment. This perspective is clear that it is not enough to look at or work with either people or environments alone or in isolation from each other. Rather, the emphasis needs to be on the critical nature of the lifeline between person and environment, because it is at the boundary where the two meet that many stresses and problems occur and resources are found.

A Problem/Strengths Focus

■ C O N C E P T   1 . 1 1

A *problem/strengths focus* is a broad concept referring to the issue, need, question, or difficulty and the concomitant strengths and resources brought to the generalist practitioner's attention for study and action at any given time.

In social work, the word *problem* is often used in describing the purpose, definition, focus, and process of the profession. Multiple authors over the past 50 years, for example, have asserted that social work is a problem-solving process (Hepworth, Rooney, & Larsen, 1997; Levy, 1973; Perlman, 1957; Siporin, 1975, 1993). Indeed, the classic 1956 "Working Definition of Social Work Practice" states the purpose of the profession: "To assist individuals and groups to identify and resolve or minimize problems arising out of disequilibrium between themselves and their environment" (Commission on Social Work Practice, NASW, 1956, as cited in Bartlett, 1958, p. 6).

Some years later, Siporin (1975, p. 3) refers to *social problems* in his definition of *practice:* "Social work is defined as a social institutional method of helping people to prevent and resolve their social problems, to restore and enhance their social functioning." More recently, Bisman (1994, p. 27) adds the social agency as a dimension of problem focus, noting that

> *what has been called the dual perspective of person and environment actually has three components. Person and environment mean the consideration of individuals within the context of the community and its resources, social policies and regulations, and the service delivery of the organization.*

On the one hand, the meaning and use of the concept *problem* in social work have been debated and criticized as too limiting and tied to pathological or negative situations and conditions. The concept has also been criticized as too general a term for distinguishing the essence of social work from other professions that describe their work as problem-solving. On the other hand, *problem* has been defined as any "question proposed for solution or discussion" (*Webster's*, 1990, p. 721). In social work, the question is: *What does this client system need for problem resolution?* When defined in this manner, the concept has room not only for needs, pathological conditions, risk factors, and negative situations but also for the strengths, assets, resilience, protective factors, and micro, mezzo, and macro resources essential to the prevention, maintenance, restoration, and enhancement functions of social work.

■ CONCEPT 1.12

Problems in social functioning arise out of disequilibrium between persons and their environments and take the form of questions proposed for discussion or resolution. This disequilibrium includes both negative and positive forces:

▶ Needs, pathological conditions, issues, risk factors, and situations
▶ Strengths, assets, resilience, protective factors, and resources

Perlman (1957, p. 133) normalized the term *problem* for social workers when she wrote that "living is a problem-solving process" and noted that the goal for social workers was to enhance problem-solving capacities. In clarifying problems as a source of difficulty in everyday person-to-person or person-to-task relationships, Perlman (1957, pp. 146–148) pointed out that the problem identified by a client system is not necessarily *the problem* (meaning the basic causative agent in the person's difficulty, the problem of major importance). "It is simply a problem in the helpseeker's current life situation which disturbs or hurts him in some way, and of which he would like to be rid." She saw the social worker's task with the client system as collaborative and focused on identifying what the client system needs in order to cope with or be rid of the focal problem. She also noted that for the majority of people seeking help from social workers, the problem is based on forces outside of themselves and within their social role transactions.

Following Merton's (Merton & Nisbet, 1971) theoretical tradition, Germain and Gitterman (1979, p. 371) conceptualized *problems* in terms of *dysjunction* and *stress* between the person and environment:

> *In the Life Model, therefore, human problems and needs are conceptualized as outcomes of transactions between the parts of that whole. Thus they are defined as problems in living which have created stress and taxed coping abilities. Within the interface where person and environment touch, the problem or need reflects a dysjunction between coping needs and environmental nutriments.*

For a social situation to be defined as a problem implies that it has been evaluated by someone as undesirable. That is, there must be an evaluator or definer for a problem to exist as such (Pincus & Minahan, 1973).

In generalist practice, *the problem* is the initial focus and pervasive issue attended to throughout a strengths-based problem-solving procedure with individuals, families, groups, organizations, and communities. As an essential element of generalist practice, problem focus is a broad concept referring to the issue, need, question, or difficulty brought to the generalist's attention for study and action at any given time.

In the past, the focus of attention for study and intervention by social workers was often determined according to their method of practice. The traditional methods were casework, group work, and community organization. Today, in generalist practice, however, the focal problem presented to generalists directs the conceptual explanations of both the problem and the interventions used in strengths-based problem-solving methodology. That is, depending on the problem, needs, strengths, and related goals, the social worker selects the most appropriate explanations for problem assessment and strengths identification and the most appropriate interventions for problem resolution. The problem thus becomes the pivotal point of the spiraling strengths-based problem-solving process to be explained further throughout this book.

A Strengths/Needs Orientation

■ CONCEPT 1.13

> A *strengths/needs orientation* involves joining with the client or action system in discovering and mobilizing the strengths, assets, and resources of both persons and environments in order to effect change in problems and life trajectories.

From a strengths/needs orientation, the problem focus in generalist practice enables individuals, families, groups, organizations, and communities to "build something of lasting value from the materials and capital within and around them" (Saleebey, 1997, p. 233). As used in the General Method of social work practice, the strengths/needs orientation contains five assumptions:

1. Client systems at the micro, mezzo, and macro levels of practice have the inherent capacity for growth and change (Saleebey, 1997).
2. Each client system brings not only problems, adverse experiences, and needs but also a wide range of knowledge, beliefs, ordinary experiences, survival skills, capacity for resourcefulness, capabilities, resources, preferences, and aspirations to the problem-solving process (Fraser & Galinsky, 1997; Weick, Rapp, Sullivan, & Kisthardt, 1989).
3. Resources may be personal or communal; micro, mezzo, or macro level; and naturally occurring or formally constituted. They may include monetary and social capital. They may involve concrete realities—such as the physical environment, shelter, food, and instrumental supports—or more abstract realities—such as intrapersonal strengths, interpersonal relationships and support networks, environmental climate, and emotional supports.
4. Adversity may be experienced as both injurious and as a source of challenge and opportunity (McMillen, 1999).
5. The environment contains an ever-evolving mixture of demands and supportive resources, stresses and challenges, barriers and opportunities. The opportunities

involve alternative options and choices, ways of being and doing, and routes to change (Friedman & Wachs, 1999).

Based on these strengths-oriented assumptions, the generalist practitioner joins with client and action systems in seeking solutions to problems, questions, and needs by

▶ Focusing on strengths, assets, and competencies while exploring problems and needs as catalysts for change, and creating opportunities for competencies to be displayed (Dunst, Trivette, & Deal, 1994)
▶ Strengthening the internal and external forces that serve to meet need and ameliorate or prevent risks (Fraser & Galinsky, 1997)
▶ Expanding resources, options, and choices that are available, acceptable, and accessible, and mobilizing strengths and competencies in the service of problem-solving and goal achievement

■ CONCEPT 1.14

Practice tasks in *strengths-based problem-solving* involve solving problems and meeting needs while reducing risk factors, increasing protective factors, and stimulating generative factors in the service of the client and action system's strengths, needs, goals, and aspirations.

Integrating these strengths-oriented assumptions into the generalist perspective adds another dimension to the entry-level practitioner's way of thinking about and working with client, action, and target systems at the micro, mezzo, and macro levels. According to Saleebey (1997, p. 235), a strengths/needs orientation also changes the "nature of the contractual relationship . . . in the direction of power equalization, mutual assessment, and evolving agreements." Thus, the strengths/needs orientation of the General Method is closely linked to the concept of empowerment, which

includes combining a sense of personal control with the ability to affect the behavior of others, a focus on enhancing existing strengths in individuals or communities, a goal of establishing equity in the distribution of resources, an ecological (rather than an individual) form of analysis for understanding individual and community phenomena, and a belief that power is not a scarce commodity but one that can be generated. (Gutierrez, 1990, p. 150)

■ CONCEPT 1.15

Empowerment is a generative process through which the powerless and vulnerable are enabled to (1) mobilize personal, familial, organizational, and communal resources; (2) exercise greater control over their environment; and (3) meet their needs and attain their aspirations (Cowger, 1997; Pinderhughes, 1995).

A Multilevel Approach

■ CONCEPTS 1.16

> *Micro-level practice* refers to one-on-one intervention or work with individuals.
>
> *Mezzo-level practice* refers to work with families and small groups.
>
> *Macro-level practice* refers to large-scale practice with large groups, organizations, communities, and society at large.

As noted earlier, generalist practitioners work with multiple client, action, and target systems. That is, their focus, conceptual framework, and methodology do not constrict their practice or expertise to working only, or mainly, with individuals, families, groups, organizations, or communities as *client systems* seeking help. Any one of these systems may also be seen as an action or target system. As a *target,* a system is viewed by the generalist as requiring change in order to meet the needs and goals of the client system. As a member of an *action* system, a social worker mobilizes that action system to work to bring about change in a target system and thereby accomplish the established goals (Pincus & Minahan, 1973).

Another way to categorize systems is according to the level of practice. As noted earlier, the *micro* practice level means one-on-one or individual work, *mezzo* refers to family and small group work, and *macro* refers to large-scale practice, such as with large groups, organizations, communities, institutions, or society (Brueggeman, 1996). In generalist practice, social workers practice at whatever level is needed with whatever type system, depending on the problem and strengths in focus as assessed from an ecological-systems perspective. Thus, the generalist may be working at a particular practice level at a given time or with more than one level concurrently or sequentially. This *multilevel systems approach* connotes a readiness for variability in practice based on the problem and strengths in focus and the generalist's knowledge and skills for strengths-based problem-solving.

An Open Selection of Theories and Interventions

■ CONCEPT 1.17

> *Open selection of theories and interventions* means that use of theories and interventions to direct the social worker's actions varies according to the problems and strengths in focus and the goals set.

Use of an *open selection of theories and interventions* means that generalists theoretically frame their practice but do not specialize in any one theoretical approach. Their only constriction may be due to limited ability and experience in using particular theoretical frameworks and specialized models of interventions. When the situation, problem, needs, and strengths call for a more specialized approach, generalists make referrals.

The scope of attention for intervention by the generalist practitioner may extend from a person, to a family, to a group, to an organization, to a community, to society at large. In focusing on a problem, a whole range of possible causes, needs, strengths, and alternative solutions must be considered. Although generalists do not have depth of knowledge or specialized competence, entry-level social workers are expected to think with conceptual clarity and complexity, identify the particular client system and point of interface in need of attention, and use theory and other foundation knowledge to inform their practice. In summary, generalist practitioners are open to select the most appropriate conceptual explanation for an accurate assessment and planned intervention in the particular person-problem-situation.

■ CASE EXAMPLE

Peter, 18 years old, was referred to the community service center because of his withdrawn behavior and failing grades during his senior year in high school. Intake assessment revealed that he had cognitive abilities below age level and lacked physical stamina. He had always been a student with marginal grades. His withdrawal from school and neighborhood social activities was precipitated by increasing family demands to help with his father's business. According to his family's culture, the eldest son is expected to work in and eventually take over the family business. At the point of seeking help, Peter was feeling rejected by his father and relatives and experiencing difficulty coping with the multiple pressures in his life.

The social worker in this case needs to be able to translate the *person-in-environment* framework into assessment via several knowledge pathways. For example, developmental theory would be used to assess Peter's potential for fulfilling developmentally appropriate life tasks and for securing a health evaluation of his physical capabilities. Cognitive theory would be used to assess Peter's attributed meanings to his problems as well as his cognitive potential for grappling with possible solutions. Role theory would be used to assess Peter's role (skills, expectations, and enactment) within the context of his family and community. The ecological-systems perspective would be used to identify the multiple systems impinging on Peter: his developmental self, family, school, and culture. A strengths/needs orientation would be used to assess his role performance competencies and social skills.

Figure 1.2 shows how the social worker applies knowledge. The lines of the circle in Figure 1.2 are the places where knowledge under the *in* category (Table 1.1) falls. Role theory is indicated as RT at the interfaces between person and family and between family and employment/society. The knowledge categorized under *person* or *environment* in Table 1.1 falls in the sections within the circles. For example, cognitive theory (CT) is in the *education* section; biological development (BD) is in the *biological* section; and knowledge about culture (C) is in the second circle with *community, friends,* and *family.* The application of this knowledge involves boundary work at the interfaces between Peter and his family and between his family and employment/society.

FIGURE 1.2 ■ Use of Knowledge in Case Example

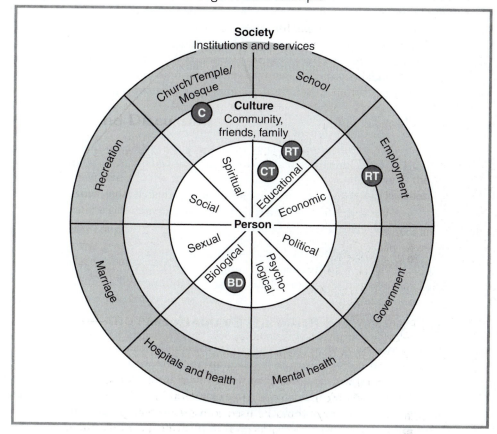

Thus, generalist practitioners selectively and collectively apply foundation knowledge to practice. They understand the meaning of this knowledge; grasp the concepts, statements, and sources for each theory; and selectively apply knowledge and theory to the person-environment situation. In addition, with the help of the ecological-systems framework, the generalist social worker is able to view the relationships and complementarity among basic practice concepts and principles of foundation knowledge for collective application and more effective practice.

A Strengths-Based Problem-Solving Process

Multiple authors have noted that the purpose of social work intervention is to help client systems cope more effectively with problems in living and thereby improve their quality of life. They agree that each phase of the multiphase intervention process has distinct objectives and operations and note that these operations usually, but not always, proceed successively through sequential phases. Experts also agree that the helping relationship, activities, and skills used in each phase of the process differ more in prevalence, intensity, and purpose than in type (Perlman, 1957; Shulman, 1999).

Other authors (Lippitt, Watson, & Westley, 1958; Sheafor, Horejsi, & Horejsi, 1997), however, focus more on problem-solving as a *planned change process*. From a more macro perspective, Lippitt, Watson, and Westley (1958, p. 130) were among the first to identify the problem-solving process as applicable to work with individuals, groups, organizations, and communities. Their seven phases include:

1. The development of a need for change
2. The establishment of a change relationship
3. The clarification or diagnosis of the client system's problem
4. The examination of alternative routes and goals, and establishment of goals and intentions
5. The transformation of intentions into actual change efforts
6. The generalization and stabilization of change
7. Achieving a terminal relationship

These and other authors concur that the progression of these sequential intervention phases is spiral, with frequent recycling or reworking of tasks and activities. That is, the cycle begins anew as problems are solved and new ones encountered.

A Practice and Program Evaluation

Social workers have an obligation to their client systems, public and private agency settings, and communities to be accountable for their practice and program outcomes. They are responsible for using or creating programs and interventions that have been or can be evaluated for their success. They are expected to systematically monitor the progress of their client systems throughout the helping process and evaluate the effectiveness of their intervention. Effectiveness in the General Method is usually thought of as goal achievements that fall within one or more of the following broad outcomes:

- ▶ Needs met
- ▶ Reduction of problems or risks
- ▶ Increased competencies
- ▶ Management of stress
- ▶ Reduction of environmental barriers to change
- ▶ Enhancement of strengths and skills
- ▶ Enhancement of resources

The General Method

In the "Working Definition of Social Work Practice," *method* is defined as "an orderly systematic mode of procedure" (Commission on Social Work Practice, NASW, 1956, as cited in Bartlett, 1958). According to Siporin (1975, p. 43), *method* refers to "the 'how' of helping, to purposeful, planned, instrumental activity through which tasks are accomplished and goals are achieved." Basically, *method* means an orderly process of action that connotes thought, purpose, and activity. In addition to reflection and action skills, the General Method incorporates the purpose, values, and knowledge of the profession into the *how* of intervention.

■ **CONCEPT 1.18**

General method refers to an orderly action process that incorporates reflection, purpose, values, and knowledge into the *how* of intervention.

Using the definition of *general* to mean what belongs to the "common nature" of a group and "not confined by specialization or careful limitation" (*Webster's,* 1990, p. 377) and the definition of *method* to mean "an orderly systematic mode of procedure" (*Webster's,* 1990, p. 570), it is possible to identify a general method of social work practice that is common to all the traditional methods, not bound by careful limitation, and consisting of a purposeful procedure ordered by six major phases—*engagement, data collection, assessment and contract planning, intervention, evaluation,* and *termination.*

Within each of these sequential phases there are varying clusters of practice skills, such as communicating, using self purposively in professional relationships with client systems, collecting relevant information, contracting, evaluating, and saying a planned goodbye. In reality, these phases are not mutually exclusive and may even occur simultaneously or out of order. Yet this framework serves as a systematic guideline for organizing knowledge, thoughts, and actions of social workers as they interact with diverse systems.

The General Method may be utilized when working with individuals, families, groups, organizations, and communities. It is inclusive of work with environmental target and action systems as well as with client systems (Pincus & Minahan, 1973) and is built on the holistic base of the mission, purpose, knowledge, values, and skills presented earlier.

The General Method, however, is more than the selection and sequencing of skills identified in the foundation of social work practice and more than a multiphase action chain. It is a professional strengths-based problem-solving process carried out within the context of the generalist perspective. This means that throughout the process, the social worker focuses on identifiable problems and strengths, employs an ecological-systems perspective, problem solves from a strengths/needs orientation, selects openly from a range of theories and interventions, and readily practices at multiple levels of person-in-environment (that is, at micro, mezzo, and macro levels of practice).

Entry-Level and Graduate-Level Practice

As noted earlier, entry-level generalists are guided by social work foundation knowledge, values, and skills when using the General Method as a basic strengths-based problem-solving procedure with a variety of client systems. Within the ecological-systems perspective, generalist practitioners acknowledge human individuality, environmental variance, and client system diversity. Depending on the current reality of each unique problem situation, they move back and forth across practice levels and phases of the General Method.

The more advanced methods of graduate-level practitioners include much that is found in the General Method but also reflect the usage of specialized knowledge, skills, and procedures for work with particular client systems, problems, or populations. For example, the social worker with a graduate-level concentration in the area of children may employ a specialized method for working with children through developmental play therapy (Timberlake & Cutler, 2001). The family specialist may employ a distinctive method of family preservation (Fraser, Nelson, & Rivard, 1997; Schwartz & AuClaire, 1995) or family therapy (Bardill, 1997; Nichols & Schwartz, 1995).

How do social workers decide the method of practice needed in a particular situation? To answer this question, they must consider several factors. Primarily, it is necessary to collect data on the severity of the problem or need being addressed and on the strengths and coping capacities of the client system in need. As depicted in Figure 1.3, there is a strong indication that a graduate-level social worker is needed when the severity of the problem or need is great and when the client system has few strengths and limited ability and motivation for dealing with the problem (see point 1 in Figure 1.3). To bring about the greatest possible improvement in these client situations, it is desirable that the social work practitioner have both general and specialized expertise. When the problem or need is of little severity and the client system

FIGURE 1.3 ■ Entry-Level and Advanced Methodology

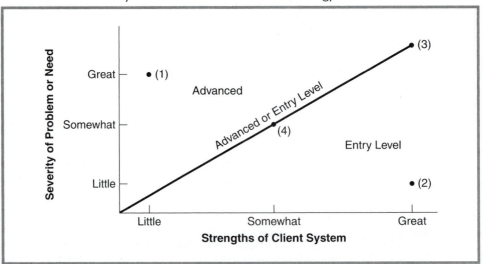

has obvious strengths and coping capacities, the entry-level generalist will be able to intervene with a high expectancy for goal accomplishment (see point 2 in Figure 1.3).

As shown in Figure 1.3, some problem situations of client systems may be addressed by either a graduate-level or entry-level generalist practitioner. That is, either the General Method or an advanced method could be used successfully. Where there is similarity in the assessed severity of the problem with the assessed strengths of the client system a balance may result. In these cases, there is greater question as to whether advanced or entry-level generalist methods should be used for effective goal accomplishment. In other cases, there may be major life and death issues but the graduate-level practitioner is not needed because there are great strengths and few needs in the client system (see point 3 in Figure 1.3).

Some client-problem-need-strengths situations fall within a middle range of problem severity, entrenchment, and dysfunction. These client systems may be served successfully by either an entry-level social worker using the General Method or a graduate-level generalist practitioner using either the General Method or a specialized method. That is, in cases where the problem or need falls in the middle of the scale of severity and the client system's strengths are assessed as moderate, the selection of method may be arbitrary (see point 4 in Figure 1.3). For example, a community concerned with an increase in neighborhood crime may have some strengths for mobilizing itself to work on this emerging problem with the help of either an entry-level generalist or a graduate-level practitioner. The strengths-based problem-solving General Method or the specialized community-organization method could be effective. Or a team approach of both graduate-level and entry-level social workers could prove efficacious.

Figure 1.3 may be a helpful tool for case assignment or planning. To use the tool, however, it is important to understand the meaning of the indicators of problem/need severity and of the client system's strengths and resources. A problem or need is assessed at little severity when it has recently emerged (time consideration) with limited scope (how many, how deeply involved) and when it has little life-or-death magnitude. When the client system is assessed as having little strength, it means that the persons or communities involved have very limited coping capacities, motivation, and resources. As the assessment moves higher on either scale, it means that there is evidence of a greater degree of client system strength or problem severity.

SUMMARY

As shown in Figure 1.4, the social work profession grows out of a liberal arts base. Its foundation is built on the five elements of *purpose, sanction, values, knowledge, and method (skills)*. From this foundation, entry-level social workers assume a holistic generalist perspective about practice that includes:

▶ An ecological systems perspective of person-in-environment
▶ A problem/strengths focus

FIGURE I.4 ■ The Generalist Perspective of the General Method

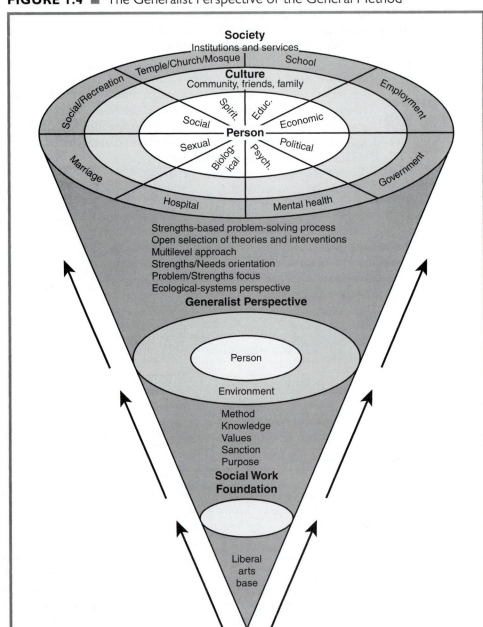

▶ A strengths/needs orientation
▶ A multilevel approach (micro, mezzo, macro systems)
▶ An open selection of theories and interventions
▶ A strengths-based problem-solving process
▶ Practice and program evaluation

From this perspective, the General Method of social work practice employs a systematically organized body of knowledge and skills that guides the generalist practitioner and the client system receiving service or the action system in their collaborative effort toward goal attainment. This collaborative effort consists of the process phases of *engagement, data collection, assessment and contract planning, intervention, evaluation,* and *termination,* which comprise the second part of this book.

REFLECTION POINTS

Becoming a skilled social work practitioner requires knowledge and skills, including the ability to reflect on practice endeavors. The following reflection points are designed to strengthen critical thinking and mastery of knowledge of key points in this chapter.

1. Define the following key elements in generalist social work practice:
   • An ecological-systems perspective
   • A problem/strengths focus
   • A strengths/needs orientation
   • A multilevel approach
   • An open selection of theories and interventions
   • A strengths-based problem-solving process
   • Practice and program evaluation
2. How might each of these elements influence your professional behavior with client, action, and target systems at micro, mezzo, and macro levels of practice?
3. Review the *NASW Code of Ethics* (www.socialworkers.org). Select one section and consider the fit between these professional values and your personal values.
4. For further reading and research, use the key words in Question 1 to locate social work references related to this chapter's content. (See Appendix A, Selected Internet Resources, and Appendix B, Selected Social Work Journals.) What concerns and issues are evident in the articles? How might these concerns and issues affect your professional behavior with client, action, and target systems?

CHAPTER 2

Human Diversity: Multiculturalism, Social Pluralism, and Socio-Demographic Variability

As noted earlier, the social work profession has a simultaneous dual commitment to social change in the interest of social justice and to social intervention in the enhancement of human life. The value base undergirding this commitment is a caring concern for the dignity, worth, and uniqueness of each and every human being. While certain common human needs are essential for all persons, individuals' frames of reference, or worldview, for thinking and feeling about these needs and seeking ways to fulfill them differ. These variations are based on the interactions of several factors:

► A person's membership in a particular cultural group (race, national origin, religion, ethnic group)
► Pluralizing social stratification influences (socioeconomic class, education, occupation, political power) and community environmental characteristics (urban, suburban, rural)
► Personal and socio-demographic variability in endowment, personality, age, gender, sexual orientation, health, and physical and mental ability

The resulting idiosyncratic worldview provides a platform for personality development and becomes the source of many individual and familial strengths and assets as well as the source of environmental resources and barriers to client system well-being that are attended to in generalist social work practice.

When social workers first enter the profession, they bring their own personal cultural values and vantage points for viewing client systems, problems and needs, strengths and vulnerabilities, and problem-solving approaches. Yet personal idiosyncratic frames of reference of person-in-environment are not sufficient tools for professional interaction with complex heterogeneous client systems. Therefore, this chapter seeks to promote awareness of, sensitivity to, and competence in working with multiculturalism, social pluralism, and socio-demographic variability.

Each section includes an exercise for self-assessment.

Multiculturalism

Concepts and Discussion

In preparing to communicate with an individual, family, group, organization, or community, a social worker takes time to study the cultural influences of the client system to be contacted. Cultural influences include goals and aspirations, patterns of resource utilization or help-seeking behaviors, self-concepts or identity, patterns of communication and emotional control, and ways of perceiving life events and social situations. To understand the full implications of cultural influences on practice, however, first requires an overview and definition of concepts central to ethnic-group membership and culturally competent service delivery.

■ CONCEPT 2.1

Culture is the set of values, beliefs, and norms for socially acceptable language patterns, behaviors, and standards for ideal role types that represent the social structure of a given society.

CULTURE   Culture is historically bound yet dynamic over time. It constructs a social reality that reduces the uncertainties in life by providing a means for understanding the world and for knowing the social location and expected behaviors for persons in this world. Cultural reality is apparent in (1) the societal structures of technology, laws and governance structures, religion and rituals, and social roles and rules (McGoldrick, Giordano, & Pearce, 1996) and (2) the cognitive, affective, and action realms associated with individual and collective values, beliefs, attitudes, ideas, and expectations in everyday life. It comprises a system of shared symbolic meanings rooted in the real and mental worlds of client, action, and target systems and is circumscribed by social factors in their environments, such as power and authority structures, access to opportunities, and institutional constraints. Through implicit and explicit group standards of behavior, culture influences personal thoughts, feelings, actions, and interactional patterns in community life. Cultural values affect the way people construe and evaluate problems, situations, and the actions taken in pursuit of important goals. Each culture has ideal role types, normative expectations, and shared symbolic interpretations that (1) give meaning to life experiences, (2) ground and identify a person's sense of self, and (3) generate a sense of individual well-being of persons-in-environment. Thus, in an individual sense, *culture* may be defined as a framework of assumptions for understanding self, making sense of the world, and communicating that understanding to others. In their practice, social workers encounter culture through

▶ Client characteristics, behaviors, and life choices
▶ Work-environment agency practices
▶ Intervention standards of care practices
▶ Society's beliefs and ethnic-group memberships
▶ Their own characteristics, behaviors, and life choices

■ CONCEPT 2.2

National origin refers to persons who share a place or country of origin and, often, a common ancestry. They also share a sense of historical circumstances, continuity, and psychosocial referents that create a sense of social group identity.

NATIONAL ORIGIN   Individuals who identify with broader cultural traditions, such as the European American culture, also tend to identify strongly with a particular subculture(s) reflecting the specific country of family origin, family immigration patterns to the United States, and migration patterns and settlement location within the United States (specific cities, rural/urban, North/South/East/West). Recent war experiences of survivor groups may intensify the cumulative effect of the historic national past with frozen grief experiences, such as those associated with terrorism, torture, and genocide, that have been passed along over the generations.

Intergenerational differences in identification with national origin wax and wane across generations as the focus shifts from who group members are by virtue of their life experiences in their nation of origin to what they have been taught about their national origin and the relationship between family teaching and life experiences in the United States. Over time, social identity defined by nation of origin as rooted in family traditions is likely to be perceived as a personal strength and maintained by leisure-time activities and festive traditions that reflect the voluntary enjoyable aspects of being an ethnic national, or, as classically termed, a symbolic national ethnic (Gans, 1979).

■ C O N C E P T S **2 . 3**

Race refers to persons who share a more or less distinctive combination of physical characteristics transmitted by their ancestors.

Racism refers to the ideologies of superiority and negative attitudes involved in judging others solely on the basis of common physical characteristics.

RACE Racial group members may or may not share the same sense of common group identity and family traditions that tie an ethnic group together and serve as a source of strength. In many instances, the common physical characteristics of race (such as skin color, hair, body size, facial features, or language patterns) are judged negatively and, thus, imbued with negative meaning. Racist attitudes lead to differential and detrimental treatment of racial group members by individuals and by social institutions. Internalization of the racist beliefs of a larger society by members of a racial group can be associated with negative self-evaluation, increased stress, and barriers to individual and communal well-being.

■ C O N C E P T **2 . 4**

An *ethnic group* is a subculture within a society that has retained distinctive characteristics and traditions associated with categories of race, national origin, and/or religion.

ETHNICITY Ethnic group members share commonalities such as values, religious beliefs and practices, language, historical continuity, and place of origin or common ancestry. These commonalities, in turn, represent shared historical circumstances and psychosocial referents that, over time, create a sense of peoplehood, togetherness, and belongingness—that is, a common ethnic group identity. Ethnic group value systems function as those learned principles and rules that have evolved to help an individual choose between alternative courses of action, resolve conflicts, and make decisions in daily life. These value systems are useful in that they guide conduct in a variety of ways. They serve as standards for

▶ Taking positions on social issues
▶ Preferring one cultural, religious, or political ideology over another

- ▶ Guiding presentation of self to others
- ▶ Evaluating and judging self and others
- ▶ Comparing self and others
- ▶ Influencing or changing others
- ▶ Rationalizing beliefs, attitudes, and actions in order to maintain and enhance self-concept
- ▶ Seeking help from others

■ CONCEPTS 2.5

Ethnic identity refers to the existence of a stable inner sense of who a person is. This identity is formed by the successful integration of the various experiences of the self into a coherent self-image and refers to that part of personal identity that contributes to a person's image of self as an ethnic group member.

Assimilation refers to members of an ethnic group who abandon traditional ways and customs and adopt the new culture fully by completely changing their personal cultural identification, attitudes and beliefs, behaviors, language, marital expectations, parenting style and expectations, and sense of social responsibility so that they are congruent with the dominant culture.

Acculturation refers to members of an ethnic group who have retained their original cultural heritage while learning about and adapting to new ways, beliefs, and behavioral expectations.

Ethnic Identity   Ethnic group socialization is intended to inculcate children with the cultural norms of behaviors, beliefs, and expectations of their subculture and thereby help them attach to their membership group and develop an ethnic identity. Ethnic assimilation and acculturation are the processes by which ethnic groups absorb characteristics of the dominant culture. The two processes, however, differ in that *assimilation* involves abandoning the old and adopting the new. In so doing, a person may, for some time, lose a sense of belonging and place. *Acculturation,* by contrast, calls for retaining one's heritage while incorporating new value standards and behaviors. During acculturation (but not in assimilation), *ethnic conflict,* or ethnic group identity struggle over opportunities and resources, is expected as part of the group members' competition within themselves and with other groups regarding cultural maintenance, empowerment, and socioeconomic parity.

Experiencing *ethnocentrism,* or viewing another way of life as inferior to that of one's own culture, and *racism,* or devaluing others on the basis of their skin color, have always been a part of the ethnic adaptation process and experience of ethnic groups. The current beliefs about acculturation promote *multiculturalism,* or the ways, customs, and practices that respect and maintain ethnic cultural distinctiveness among different ethnic groups (Gutierrez, Alvarez, Nemon, & Lewis, 1997).

At the micro, mezzo, and macro levels of social work practice, the culturally competent generalist social worker is expected to do the following:

▶ Start where the particular client system is—that is, understand the client system's problems, needs, strengths, and goals in respect to the client system's cultural beliefs, values, and perceptions.

▶ Know that the client system's beliefs, assumptions, and behaviors are rooted in the client system's cultural and acculturating experiences and that these may vary for different individuals (even within the same ethnic group).

▶ Avoid assuming that the client system will see the world the same way the social worker does (even when both share the same ethnic background).

▶ Assume that the client system will have different perceptions and find out the specific differences.

▶ Value the uniqueness and individuality of each client system.

▶ Use multicultural sensitivity in promoting individual, family, group, organizational, and community strengths-based problem-solving, collaborative facilitation, data collection, assessment, planning, intervention, action, research, and analysis of needs, strengths, and goals.

▶ Keep up with the professional literature about the effectiveness of policies and practices with different ethnic client systems.

■ CONCEPT 2.6

Minority refers to the extent of a cultural group's power and access to the resources and opportunities available in a society.

MINORITY   Minority group members are likely to have less control over the circumstances of their lives than majority group members. That is, they are likely to experience economic, social, and political inequality, whereas the majority group tends to dominate society in the economic, social, and political realms. Although for some persons ethnic identity provides access and privilege, the social meaning of race/ethnicity for many members of minority groups often results in stigma, discrimination, and prejudice. Thus, minority status captures differential exposure to social, economic, and political stressors, variation in the social and personal resources available for coping with stress, and different value styles in coping and adaptation.

In 2003, the U.S. Census (www.census.gov) listed about 96 million persons who were classified as minority (of about 293 million total U.S. residents). They belonged to the following six distinct racial-ethnic-cultural groupings which are ordered by size: Hispanic or Latino (39.9 million), Black or African American (37.1 million), Asian (11.9 million), biracial or multiracial (4.3 million), American Indian and Alaskan Native (2.8 million), and Native Hawaiian and Other Pacific Islander (495,000). From 2000 to 2003, the Hispanic or Latino group showed the largest growth by far (an increase of 4.6 million) compared to the Black or African American group (an increase of 1.4 million) and the Asian group (an increase of 1.3 million).

For a social worker to be culturally sensitive and competent, knowing about the general characteristics of these major U.S. cultures is not sufficient. For example, careful research has revealed great intragroup cultural variation and diversity apart from pluralizing social influences (socioeconomic class, education, occupation, political power, community environment) and personal and socio-demographic distinctions (endowment and personality, age and developmental stage, gender, sexual orientation, physical and mental ability). Specifically, 14 distinguishable subcultures have been identified among African Americans (Valentine, 1971; Williams, 1983); 98 subcultures are distributed across over 200 Native American tribes (Coggins, 1991); at least five Latino and Hispanic subgroups exist (Marin & Marin, 1991); and there are 23 Asian/Pacific Islander subgroupings (Morales, 1976). Each of these subcultures has distinctive historical traditions, values, customs, attitudes, lifestyles, and languages or dialects. Although some common biological and social characteristics may exist among the members of a racial/ethnic minority group—such as the Samoan, Guamanian, Chinese, Japanese, Vietnamese, and Koreans of the Asian/Pacific cluster—a social worker needs to comprehend what it means for subgroup members to have a history and dynamic culture of their own and yet find themselves repeatedly linked to other subgroups that are similar but different.

In assessing the functioning of ethnic minority client systems, it is important for the social work generalist to consider the degree to which the client system has been socialized into the mainstream culture. Ethnic minority clients are members of two cultures. Thus, their functioning must be considered in relation to both their culture of origin and the majority culture. For example, first-generation minority clients adhere closely to their traditional beliefs, values, and patterns of behavior. By the third generation, clients have usually internalized many patterns of the dominant culture, although they typically maintain many traditional patterns of family relationships. Caution must be exercised, however, in considering the degree of acculturation of any client system, as errors can be easily made when the practitioner fails to recognize and attend to the uniqueness of each. The following factors have been identified as affecting the degree of bicultural socialization and interaction of ethnic minority client systems with mainstream society (Devore & Schlessinger, 1999; Pedersen, 1997; Sue & Sue, 1999) and have been recommended in carrying out ethnically sensitive and culturally competent social work services:

► Assess the degree of commonality between the two cultures with regard to norms, values, beliefs, perceptions, and problem(s) being presented by the client system.
► Consider the client system's command of language or bilingualism within each culture as related to educational and/or occupational achievement and fulfillment of daily tasks.
► Assess the client system's degree of biculturalism or the degree to which the client system identifies with features of each culture in the pursuit of daily functioning.
► Consider the degree of dissimilarity of the client system's physical appearance from the majority culture (facial features, skin color, body appearance), the degree to which this dissimilarity is valued or devalued by each culture, and the client system's response to such valuation.

▶ Assess the client system's past and present experience with cultural role models (cultural translators and mediators) by identifying the importance and competence of significant persons who shaped their learning about the norms and expectations for each culture as related to the presenting problem.

▶ Consider the client system's degree of ethnic identification through their affective perception and interpretation of the immigration experience, family narrative, and present generational standing.

▶ Assess the degree to which the client system's conceptual and affective problem-solving style meshes and blends with the prevalent or valued style of the dominant culture as it pertains to the presenting problem.

Multicultural competence is a necessary prerequisite to effective, affirming, and ethical professional social work. As such it is defined through the generalist social worker's awareness, knowledge, and skills necessary to counsel, educate, and link client, action, and target systems effectively and ethically across cultural difference. Toward this end, the *Journal of Multicultural Social Work,* the *Journal of Ethnic and Cultural Diversity in Social Work,* and the following websites can be accessed for further learning:

International Association for Cross-Cultural Psychology (www.iacco.org)
Center for Cross-Cultural Behavioral Pediatric Health (www.unt.edu/pediatric)
National Center for Cultural Competence (www.gucdc.georgetown.edu/ncc)
Transcultural Mental Health Care (www.tmhc.nsw.gov.au)

■ C O N C E P T 2 . 7

Ethnic-group membership refers to the ways in which historical experiences, cultural values, and worldview influence the way individual and collective members cognitively construe and affectively experience persons, situations, needs, problems, resources, and solutions.

ETHNIC-GROUP MEMBERSHIP The social worker's cultural sensitivity can, in part, be fostered through a conceptual understanding of the role personal values play in everyday life experiences, knowledge of an ethnic group's particular history, and knowledge of its members' fundamental value orientations to various aspects of daily living.

At times, however, value clashes among ethnic groups and between particular ethnic groups and mainstream U.S. cultures become apparent. In these instances, the social worker has an obligation to go beyond cultural sensitivity and understanding and to become the interpreter of the value conflict. That is, the social worker helps the client system become aware that the two focal value systems are not congruent and syntonic with selected life dimensions. Specifically, the social worker needs to

▶ Clarify how the two values of concern differ socially and culturally within the two cultural systems.

▶ Identify positive and negative social consequences for adhering to either value position.

▶ Identify legal consequences for either value position.

▶ Identify any value position and any legal obligations of the agency service delivery system.

■ CONCEPT **2.8**

Well-being is determined by the interaction of physical and mental health with values reflecting general beliefs and sense of desirable ways of being and behaving.

WELL-BEING   As values reflect people's beliefs and ways of being and behaving, they provide members with a sense of societal and family norms, expectations, and stability. They also provide standards for evaluating actions and outcomes, justifying opinions and conduct, planning and guiding behavior, deciding between alternative options, comparing self with others, influencing others, and presenting self to others. Only when exclusive identification labels, such as Jewish or AME (African Methodist Episcopal) values, are placed on particular cultural value systems do value orientations seem to stand on their own and be applicable by themselves with minimal reference to individuals, families, and peer groups (Tropman, 1999).

In each life area, cultural value systems provide living guides and usable frameworks for daily life choices and decision making. When an ethnic group value system is insufficient for an individual in a particular situation or life domain, the individual is likely to draw on his or her internal values that reflect (role) identification and sense of well-being as well as the family and significant peers. When these identifications are congruent, people experience a sense of support and well-being.

The value orientations of different ethnic groups may be assessed and understood through exploring the group's philosophical orientation toward nature and humanity, social orientation toward time and space, personal orientation toward self and others, life goals, and social responsibilities (Reid & Popple, 1992; Rothenberg, 2001; Wakefield, 1993):

1. *Philosophical orientation toward nature in general and humanity in particular*
   • Do the values reflect harmony with or mastery over nature?
   • Do the values reflect submissive sharing with or assertive achieving over nature?
   • Does the value orientation portray human nature as basically good and worthy or basically evil and unworthy?
2. *Social orientation in time and space*
   • Are the values congruent with a sense of societal clock time or a sense of personal time?
   • To what degree is the time orientation focused toward the past, the present, or the future?
   • To what degree is the spatial orientation focused toward personal space or communal space?

3. *Personal orientation toward self and others*
   - To what degree does the self-concept reflect the meaning of personal self-reliance versus reliance on family, neighborhood, and community?
   - To what degree is interaction with others reflected by values promoting assertive competition for scarce resources versus values reflecting cooperative interdependency?
   - Does social status reflect sharp boundaries between "us" and "them"?
   - To what degree is social mobility viewed as a permanent or a shifting status?
4. *Personal orientation toward life goals*
   - To what degree do the social rules of engagement reflect the concept of individualism and fair play versus communalism and fair share?
   - Does goal achievement reflect an attitude valuing personal optimizing and being first or an attitude valuing group affiliation and team achievement?
5. *Personal orientation toward social responsibilities*
   - Does the sense of social responsibility primarily attend to the causation of problems and sources of situational risks or to the conditions to be addressed and the issues to be resolved?
   - Are work, wealth, and material goods valued as part of self or as resources for self and others?

Cultures often interlock as individuals from varied backgrounds come together. An Anglo social worker, for example, with a future time perspective may become very annoyed with a Mexican American, present-oriented client who does not conserve her money to last throughout the month. This client, in turn, may become irritated with the social worker, who is seen as taking too much time to collect data before providing a direct service. A Pakistani American family oriented to the notion of extended family and collective family space may ignore the social worker's point that simultaneous and lengthy visits by grandparents, siblings, spouse, children, nieces, and nephews to a 35-year-old relative in a semi-private hospital room are intruding on the personal space, health care expectations, and comfort level of the room's other occupant.

The well-being of ethnic group members, however, is contingent on

- ▶ Group values and stability
- ▶ Economic and familial survival
- ▶ The interactions of members' personal characteristics with
  - cultural norms and expectations
  - the status of the ethnic subgroup
  - the fit of the ethnic subgroup with the dominant culture
- ▶ Cultural resources such as family supports and religious affiliation

Personal and cultural resources, thus, offer shields from adverse consequences of stress related to tensions in ethnic group membership. The common tension polarities that confront all minority group members have been identified as (1) oppression versus liberation, (2) powerlessness versus empowerment, (3) exploitation versus parity, (4) assimilation versus acculturation, and (5) stereotyping versus individuality (Lieberman & Lester, 2004; Lum, 1999; Pedersen, 1997). To work with minorities, social workers need to understand these existing tensions and provide the support necessary to empower minorities to speak, act, and assume responsibility for themselves as they organize to overcome particular tensions. Rather than expecting assimilation or conformity to exploitation, social workers demonstrate an understanding of each minority group and multicultural appreciation by supporting a client system's efforts to achieve cultural maintenance, empowerment, and parity.

■ **C O N C E P T S 2 . 9**

Religion refers to an "institutionalized pattern of beliefs, behaviors, and experiences, oriented toward spiritual concerns, shared by a community and transmitted over time in traditions" (Canda & Furman, 1999, p. 37).

Religious affiliation refers to group membership in a formal institutional system of religious beliefs and practices.

Spirituality is related "to a universal and fundamental aspect of what it is to be human—to search for a sense of meaning, purpose, and moral frameworks for relating with self, others, and the ultimate reality" (Canda & Furman, 1999, p. 40) and is expressed through religious and nonreligious forms.

Faith refers to personal beliefs and relationship with a greater being.

Mystical experiences transcend the human capacity for thinking and expression and involve "direct, personal encounters with aspects of reality that are beyond the limits of language and reason to express" (Canda & Furman, 1999, p. 40).

RELIGION AND SPIRITUALITY   Religion, spirituality, and faith play important roles in different cultures. They each reflect multiple levels of religious identification and value commitments (see Figure 2.1). At the core are the essential cultural beliefs and attitudes that comprise the central ideas and feelings to which value commitments are attached. At the next level, the outward form of this belief system is the ethic, or body of moral principles and spiritual beliefs, that reflects both core religious values and religiously influenced values on matters of daily living involving self and others, social roles and human interaction, achievement and work, and material goods and money. At the third or middle level, religious value orientations are embodied in the organizational structures of church, temple, synagogue, or sect. The codified policies of the fourth level reflect the formal institutionalized values of organized religion. The fifth and last level of religious identification and value commitments involves institutionally sanctioned religious practices (Tropman, 1999). At each of these five levels, members of a religious group may adhere to the essence of the cultural values and belief systems or to very specific and concrete ritualistic representations and procedures.

Increasingly, attention is being addressed to the impact of group membership in mainstream religions (Judaism, Christianity, Islam, Buddhism), alternative religions,

FIGURE 2.1 ■ Levels of Identification and Commitment to Religious Values

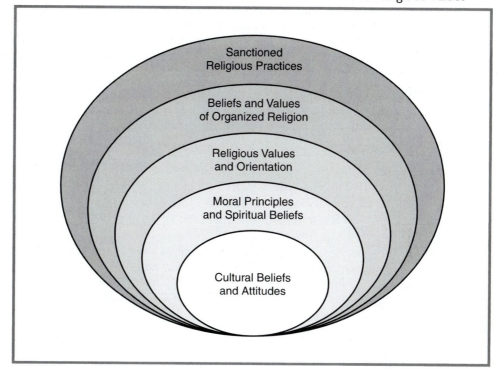

Sanctioned
Religious Practices

Beliefs and Values
of Organized Religion

Religious Values
and Orientation

Moral Principles
and Spiritual Beliefs

Cultural Beliefs
and Attitudes

and newer religious movements on the personal faith beliefs and the ordinary and extraordinary life experiences and choices of client, action, and target systems. This impact is apparent in the members' perceptions of their problems and needs, in their use of formal and informal support and advocacy systems, and in their actions to solve problems, achieve empowerment, overcome adversity, mobilize resources, meet needs, and achieve aspirations. Values, spiritual beliefs, and religious memberships are often key determinants in client, action, and target systems' thinking, feeling, and acting in relation to environmental circumstances and major life events such as the following:

▶ Getting married, using reproductive technology, having children, rearing children, staying married
▶ Selecting an occupation, accepting certain kinds of employment, losing employment, changing jobs
▶ Coping with personal losses of family and friends, illness and trauma, community disasters
▶ Living in poverty, obtaining education and job training, finding housing, using day care

In addition, many of the larger social justice issues addressed in macro practice have religious dimensions. For example, societal provision of basic food, clothing, and shelter for the poor is tied up in centuries-old, value-laden issues of who is worthy to receive community aid. Similarly, today's capitation practices of managed care affect health care rationing and service provision to poor families as well as child welfare services to children most in need.

As noted in Chapter 1, social work and religion are connected historically and philosophically. At the operational level of practice method, however, the social work profession has not yet fully clarified the role of spirituality and faith in engagement, data collection, assessment and contract planning, intervention, evaluation, and termination. Nor has the profession systematically addressed which spiritual or faith-based practices (such as religious literature, prayer, meditation, religious ritual, to name a few) are effective with which client, action, or target systems. A small cadre of social work scholars began to address these issues in the 1950s (Biestek, 1957; Spencer, 1956). A few more joined them in the 1970s and 1980s (Berl, 1979; Canda, 1983; Cornett, 1982; Joseph, 1975, 1987; Keith-Lucas, 1972, 1985; Loewenberg, 1988). More recently, this early cadre of scholars has expanded in number, productivity, and nuance of issues associated with policy and practice (Bullis, 1996; Canda, 1998; Canda & Furman, 1999; Cnaan, 1999; Cnaan & Boddie, 2002; Derezotes, 1995; Doe, 2004; Garland & Conrad, 1990; Graham, Kaiser, & Garrett, 1998; Joseph, 1997; Siporin, 1993; Smith, 1995; Sullivan, 1994; Tangenberg, 2004, 2005; Van Hook, Hugen, & Aguilar, 2001).

In problem-solving situations in which it is appropriate to address the underlying spiritual nature of the dilemma and inherent religiously based value conflicts, the social worker first gains an understanding of the client system's religious and spiritual beliefs, traditions, and ritual practices and then learns about any related federal laws or court rulings. For example, the natural hallucinogen of the peyote plant may be used in Native American ceremonials, animal sacrifices are part of Santeria faith practices, and religious cults may act to isolate members from the outside world (Bullis, 1996). These and other somewhat unusual religious practices and rituals are afforded First Amendment protection when they are central to the spiritual belief system of a particular organized religion. In all circumstances, however, the client system's spiritual beliefs are the major determinants in social work service provision in relation to a wide variety of life decisions. Each decision reflects client system choices that advance certain values at the expense of others. The rights guaranteed by the First Amendment and the social work ethic of the right of client systems to self-determination guarantee their right and responsibility in making their own value-based choices and being accountable for the consequences. It is clear that the social worker should not engage in professional practices that have the potential to harm client systems or their environments, convey the appearance of trying to convert a client system to the social worker's own religious beliefs, or employ professional practices that do not have demonstrated efficacy.

Social workers in secular and sectarian settings have an obligation to work within and carry out agency policy concerning the role of spirituality in social service delivery in that agency and, in the case of public agencies, to follow the laws and judicial system rulings that govern the separation of church and state. Agency governing boards have a fiduciary right and responsibility to assure that agency funds are being spent as directed by explicit agency mission. These and other governing board policies have been upheld by the judicial system. The right of client systems to rely on the fit between explicit agency mission, social work services, and practice methods has also been supported by the social work profession. When a social worker ethically disagrees with an agency service delivery position based in a particular religious value orientation, she or he has a professional obligation to make an explicit decision and take one of the following courses of action:

- ▶ Seek to understand the reasons for and adhere responsibly and professionally to agency policy in day-to-day social work practice.
- ▶ Request and work for a policy change (which may not be possible if the issue in a sectarian agency is central to the mission or if the issue in a public agency is legally regulated).
- ▶ Register a complaint to administration, explain the professional/personal dilemma, and ask to be reassigned to a different service unit within the agency.
- ▶ Register a complaint to administration, explain the professional/personal dilemma, and seek employment elsewhere.

■ CONCEPT 2.10

Social justice incorporates social work's commitment to individual well-being and the welfare of society and represents the profession's moral commitment to advocacy on behalf of the poor, dispossessed, oppressed, and disadvantaged.

SOCIAL JUSTICE Although racism, prejudice, and oppression may be expressed in interpersonal transactions, they are also embedded in the policies and programs of governments and private institutions and sustained by political, economic, and social factors. These factors create populations-at-risk by limiting access to services, depriving people of basic needs, discriminating against certain populations, and promoting social injustice. In promoting social change and social justice for these at-risk populations, social workers raise the question: *To what extent and how should society redress these inequities?*

In macro-level practice, social workers, individually and in action systems, engage in political and community activism and advocacy for improved social conditions with and on behalf of vulnerable and stigmatized populations (Belanger, 2001; Ferguson, 2004; Larkin, 2004; Polack, 2004). Improving social conditions may include, for example, decreasing social stressors, opening up access to services, meeting basic needs, and eliminating discrimination. In micro- and mezzo-level practice, social workers engage with their client systems to (1) increase social functioning; (2) change the deprivations, obstacles, barriers, and stressors in the environment; and (3) develop environmental supports and resources (Finn & Jacobson, 2003; Parker, 2003; Wrenn, 2002).

LESTER B. GRANGER (1896–1976), a social advocate, worked nationally and internationally for equal opportunity and justice for all persons. He directed the National Urban League for 20 years and served as president of the National Conference of Social Welfare and the first American president of the International Conference on Social Welfare (1961).

■ **CONCEPT 2.11**

Help-seeking attitudes and behavior are reflected in the client system's cultural values about self-sufficiency, type of help sought, and preferred patterns of problem-solving and communicating.

HELP-SEEKING ATTITUDES AND BEHAVIOR   Distress is both a personal and a communal experience. It is shared when client systems want relief and help. Receiving and giving help are part of day-to-day caring experiences and involve preferences, choices, and decision making by client systems as to how they manage their lives. Help-seeking attitudes and behavior involve (1) selecting specific others to provide assistance, confirm decisions, and offer advice; (2) communicating about needs, wants, and preferences; and (3) setting goals and problem solving.

For example, Asian Americans of Japanese and Korean ancestry may view persons with psychological problems as weaklings and the need to seek help for mental health problems as shameful (LeResche, 1992). They may attribute mental illness to supernatural forces (displeasure of ancestral spirits, spirit intrusion, somatic-natural condition) and may deal with such problems by internalizing them to avoid a loss of face. They may be distrustful of professional helpers (Duryea & Gundison, 1993). Such beliefs share much in common with those of Native Americans but the approach to treatment differs markedly. Whereas Native Americans may turn to indigenous folk healers (medicine men), Asians more often consider family care to be the most logical and effective treatment, as the cause is believed to be primarily interpersonal disharmony within the family. Jewish Americans, by contrast, freely seek help, including psychotherapy, as they tend to view mental health problems as the result of individual unresolved intrapsychic forces (McGoldrick, Garcia-Preto, Hines, & Lee, 1989). African Americans (Taylor, Ellison, Chatters, Levin, & Lincoln, 2000), Asian and Pacific Americans (Yamashiro & Matsuoka, 1997), Caribbean Africans (Brice-Baker, 1996), and Latinos (McMiller & Weisz, 1996), on the other hand, prefer to seek help from family, friends, and churches. They may perceive questions as prying and intrusive, become belligerent and inarticulate, and require more time than Caucasian Americans to trust and become comfortable with a professional helper. European Americans usually prefer to seek help first from extended family members, religious organizations, and neighborhood clinic associations (McMiller & Weisz, 1996).

Different cultural communication styles may result in miscommunication and misunderstanding. In many Native American cultures, for example, direct eye contact is considered insulting and is avoided, whereas avoiding eye contact seems evasive and dishonest to European Americans. Many Asian cultures expect a period of polite conversation at the beginning of a visit to a professional. Rushing to the reason for the visit without some exchange of pleasantries is considered rude. Some cultures place importance on silence as a form of respect; others tend to be very expressive. Symbolic behaviors (such as time orientation, social distance, spacing, touching, facial expression, and gesturing) vary dramatically from culture to culture (Pedersen, 1997).

Effective communication with client systems involves good attending skills, high level of awareness of nonverbal behaviors, and an understanding of the cultural context of the language. Individuals learn their first or native language (or regional dialect) at an early age and at home. Thus, the first language is associated with intimacy, spontaneity, and informality. When speaking in their native language or dialect, client systems tend to be more emotionally open and expressive than in their second language or standard English (Kochman, 1981). A social worker's use of native language in conjunction with standard English directly affects a client system's perception of the social worker's credibility and the degree to which they demonstrate a change in attitudes and behaviors (Lum & Lu, 1999).

Patterns of communication are bound in culture and personal and social experience. Client systems differ in the way they assign meanings to words, say things, and express themselves with gestures. Sensitivity to these differences is necessary in engaging people from different cultural backgrounds. Social workers, therefore, need to assess presenting problems, needs, and strengths based on the client system's

▶ Own language used to label a problem, express a need, and describe a strength
▶ Symbolic meaning assigned to the problem and need
▶ Typical patterns of communication in presenting self and seeking help
▶ Prior experience with help seeking and successful problem-solving
▶ Expectation for self-sufficiency
▶ Orientation toward professional or indigeneous care and use of resources
▶ Own criteria for deciding whether satisfactory solution has been achieved

Self-Assessment of Cultural Sensitivity

In the General Method of social work practice, sensitivity to cultural diversity may be demonstrated within each phase of the process. A social worker's sensitivity to the culture of a client, action, or target system is reflected in the way in which that social worker (1) engages the system of contact in identifying problems, needs, and strengths, (2) collects data and makes an assessment and contract, (3) intervenes, (4) evaluates, and (5) terminates. Timing, communications, and actions show the extent to which a generalist social worker realizes the value orientations of a culture. The social worker's attitude and approach also indicate an awareness of the pressures, problems, strengths, and supports that persist in the lives of persons from diverse ethnic cultures.

EXERCISE 2.1
Cultural-Sensitivity Exercise

1. What is your cultural background?

2. Do you identify with a particular ethnic group?

3. Select an ethnic group you come the closest to identifying with, and describe the group's customary behaviors regarding each of the following:
   a. Role of father, mother, children, and extended family members
   b. Dating patterns
   c. Eating patterns
   d. Education and work patterns
   e. Illness, death, and dying

4. How do you feel about your ethnic identity? What are the strengths and weaknesses you perceive in your ethnic group?

5. What ethnic groups lived in your home environment when you were growing up? How did your family relate to families of other ethnic groups (consider attitudes, experiences, power relationships; i.e., was one dependent on, or subordinate to, another)?

6. What are your earliest memories of meeting people of minority groups (i.e., African American, Alaskan Native, American Indian, Asian Pacific American, Native Hawaiian, Hispanic or Latino)? Of biracial or multiracial groups? How did your family relate to people of minority groups? (Consider attitudes, power relationships, experiences.)

7. Are your feelings about your own ethnic group related to any power relationship you experienced with other ethnic groups?

8. Are your feelings about *other* ethnic groups related to any power relationships you experienced with other ethnic groups?

9. With someone from a different ethnic background, compare your ethnic groups according to the factors given in item 3.

10. How do your feelings for your ethnic group compare with this person's feelings for his or her ethnic group?

For effective multicultural practice, a social worker needs to be consciously aware of his or her own culture as well as that of the client, action, or target system receiving service. Continued growth in self-awareness enables a social worker to recognize and appreciate the nuances within and among diverse cultures and begin to identify his or her own ethnocentric attitudes. As noted earlier, *ethnocentrism* is basically the belief that one's own ethnic group has the only appropriate and acceptable practices, values, and customary behaviors.

In Exercise 2.1, questions are proposed for reflection and discussion. The purpose of the exercise is to enhance cultural sensitivity and self-awareness. Through identifying, sharing, and comparing the facts, feelings, and experiences addressed in the exercise, social workers may gain a more empathic understanding of diverse groups.

Social Pluralism

■ CONCEPT 2.12

Social pluralism refers to expressions of values and behavior that vary along social structures comprising systems of socialization, social control, social gratification, and social change.

Knowledge of multiculturalism alone, however, does not provide sufficient understanding of the worldview and the value frame of reference of a client, action, or target system to be contacted. Within cultural groups, value, attitudinal, and behavioral variance may be accounted for by social pluralism. The social structural dimensions of social pluralism include socioeconomic class, poverty, political power, and community environment characteristics. Together, these social structures convey the social status or social worth of a person or group in the view of others.

Concepts and Discussion

■ CONCEPTS 2.13

Socioeconomic class is a socially constructed perspective that reflects an understanding of the world, where a person fits within it, and a distinctive lifestyle. The social patterns attributed to groups on the basis of status or class may also be explained as a reaction to environmental conditions, including income. Socioeconomic class affects what persons have as available choices and what they perceive the choices to be (Farley, 1994; Wright, 1985).

Ethnic reality is the socioeconomic cultural environment that influences the behaviors and dispositions of individuals, families, groups, organizations, and communities.

SOCIOECONOMIC CLASS AND PARITY   The U.S. economy involves the production, distribution, and consumption of goods and services. The institutions that operationalize the U.S. economy are founded on principles of economic capitalism that include the pursuit of profit and private ownership. These principles evoke specific societal conditions and a dual labor market that includes (1) a primary labor market characterized by high wages, opportunities for advancement, benefits, and rules of due process that protect employment rights and (2) a secondary labor market characterized by low wages, little opportunity for advancement, few benefits, and minimal job protection. Although beginning to change, the primary labor market is dominated by white males; the secondary market consists primarily of women, minorities, legal and illegal immigrants, and the working poor of all backgrounds. Apparent changes in the economic structure in the twenty-first century include new information technologies based on increasingly sophisticated computer hardware and software, increasing global economic interdependence, and the growing dominance of the information and service sectors over basic industrial manufacturing. These changes are associated with a high demand for increasingly specialized knowledge and skills and dramatic fluctuations in wages. At the same time, however, there is structural unemployment, many low–income-generating employment options, and changes in the distribution pattern of jobs. Furthermore, the federal government does not have a policy for a *living wage.*

Although salaries, investments, and the real estate market together with a rising stock market have increased the wealth of those at the top, the wages of the middle class have stagnated in comparison, and medical and pension benefits have declined. In addition, many U.S. workers have experienced a sharp slowdown in income with the advent of corporate downsizing, increased use of temporary and illegal workers, declining union membership and clout, fewer well-paid industry jobs, lack of affordable housing, and increased difficulties in making an adequate living through farming. Together, these economic data trends suggest a shrinkage of the middle class and a narrowing of avenues for social mobility. Thus, these changes appear to be reinforcing the *status quo,* to be placing the middle class at risk, and not likely to enable the poor and working poor to achieve economic and social parity (Danziger & Haveman, 2001).

Socioeconomic class involves more than the amount of money and economic security available to a person, family, group, or community. It is identified through such variables as income, occupation, education, residence, and group identification. It is all encompassing and reflected in how a person thinks, acts, talks, looks, dresses, moves, and walks; in the shops, businesses, and restaurants patronized; in the friendships made; and in the schools attended, jobs attained, and neighborhoods lived in.

In the myth of a classless U.S. society, intelligence and ambition are highlighted as responsible for life success. Such a myth creates a false sense of hope or expectation that an individual and family can experience different life opportunities and get ahead. This hope and the occasional well-publicized success story tend to keep the hierarchical class structure in place and to place the blame for not moving up on the individual. Yet the reality is that class-based societal structures keep the poor and the working class locked into social positions of servitude. If class-oppressed people believe in equality of opportunity, they are likely to internalize the blame for their socioeconomic position and less likely to develop conscious awareness of socially imposed class limitations (Erikson & Goldthorpe, 1993).

Conversely, the myth of a classless society also keeps middle- and upper-class individuals and families entrenched in the socioeconomic privileges available. That is, the myth reinforces their beliefs that their privileges must be deserved due to their own personal merits and superiority and therefore are to be enjoyed and defended. In those instances in which their economic status may decline, they still have the language, thought, and behavior patterns to fall back on. Thus, they maintain the privilege of choice.

Personal well-being is contingent on economic survival and family and social stability. The accumulation of material goods and wealth provides a person with more options, opportunities, freedom, and leisure time. Accumulation of wealth is also associated with greater influence and power over others. Inequality of social resources brings with it a wide range of associated differences that may impact the social functioning of individuals, families, groups, organizations, and communities. When people experience *classism,* it is both because they lack money, choices, and power and because of the way they think, talk, act, move, and make decisions.

As the point where socioeconomic class and ethnicity intersect, ethnic reality influences the dispositions that arise out of a group's (1) cultural values, as embodied in its history, rituals, and religion; (2) migration experiences; (3) encounters with mainstream culture; (4) approach to family organization; and (5) language adaptation (Erikson & Goldthorpe, 1993; Rothenberg, 2001). As ethnicity and socioeconomic class interlock, the client system experiences pressures and forces that arise from the incongruence between the two. For example, although a family may have moved into a higher social class (blue-collar to white-collar occupation, public to private school, smaller to bigger house, less well-off to wealthier neighborhood), family members may not be given full participation in the politics and activities of their new social environment because of their ethnicity and recently achieved socioeconomic strata. To the degree that the family's ethnicity is perceived as a devalued one by the majority of the community culture, the family may not be accorded political power and access to environmental resources.

Although people of color are often class-bound due to racial discrimination as well as socioeconomic differences, not all within a group are equally oppressed in respect to education, position in the occupational structure, and income. For example, although the adult Vietnamese community has fared poorly in California, their children's legendary success has become part of the common folklore (Caplan, Choy, & Whitmore, 1992).

Ethnicity and culture provide motivation and a source of strength for individuals who draw on their ethnic identity and cultural beliefs. Yet, their minority status and social class struggles continually reinforce negative determinism in their move toward social equality and social justice. The culturally competent social worker must be aware of the dynamics of the prejudice and discrimination that accompany the ethnic acculturation process and the struggle for parity.

■ CONCEPTS 2.14

Rural refers to the country or means country-like. Rural localities are often defined in terms of low population density (2,500 to 50,000 inhabitants) and relative isolation.

Urban pertains to cities or jurisdictions. Urban areas are highly populated (over 50,000).

A *suburb* is defined as an incorporated municipality within a standard metropolitan statistical area other than a central city (Lineberry, 1975).

ENVIRONMENT AND COMMUNITY DIFFERENCES   A knowledge of distinguishing characteristics of community environments helps social workers better understand the people of particular localities and the interactions and interrelationships that take place between different people and different environments. As brought out in the ecological-systems perspective, an environment is affected by the persons contained within it and, conversely, persons are affected by their environments. More specifically, an environment's growth is directly influenced by the endowment, personalities, values, and functioning of its residents. Interdependently, the growth and development of people are directly influenced by the nature, resources, values, and functioning of their environments. Thus, an understanding of rural, urban, and suburban localities can help a social worker become aware of diverse ways in which environments and persons may affect each other. If an individual, family, group, organization, or community is located in a rural environment, for example, their needs, strengths, experiences, values, resources, and development may be very different from those in urban or suburban areas. These differences may include income sources and occupations (agriculture and agri-business versus business and industry), lifestyle (simple versus complex), and structure and number of available human resources (highly structured and numerous versus informal and sparse) (Ginsberg, 1998).

General characteristics make urban, suburban, and rural localities distinguishable from one another. Urban locations, for example, generally offer various organized human services that are highly structured, with clearly stated policies and procedures. Rural areas may be devoid of formal, professional services but usually contain informal, natural helping networks that provide assistance. Whereas the power structure of an urban area may be described as pluralistic, with several complex interacting systems, the power structure of a rural area may be seen as elitist, with community decision makers often not holding formal positions of authority. There is often a blurring of boundaries between political and sociocultural life in homogeneous rural communities (Ginsberg, 1998). The laws and procedures of an urban legal control system are more explicitly articulated and executed than those of a rural area; in the latter, informal means of regulation are frequently preferred for solving local problems (Johnson, 1993; Martinez-Brawley, 1990).

The central and distinguishing problems of rural areas often include generational poverty, conservative mores and thinking, an increasing loss of youth from the area, and 60 percent of the nation's substandard housing (Conger & Elder, 1994). By contrast, core problems for those who live in the city have been described in terms of depersonalization, loss of individuality, and inadequate housing options. From the Model Cities Programs of the 1960s War on Poverty to the present, federal programs to improve inner-city ghettoes have had only short-term success at best. By contrast, grass-roots community groups working to improve their surroundings have achieved some success. One exemplar is a public housing project in Macon, Georgia, in which the Housing Authority used community organization principles of self-help, empowerment, responsibility, and dignity to enable families to move toward self-sufficiency and to integrate public housing residents and their agendas into the mainstream political and social service policy-making circles of the community (Center for Visionary Leadership, 1998).

In recent years, urban development has led to the renovation of many old buildings in cities. These structures have been changed into upper- or upper-middle-class condominiums or apartments. As a result of such gentrification, poor and lower-middle-class city residents are often unable to find local housing. The absence of low-income housing in urban and suburban areas and the resistance by suburban residents to building such housing, along with the presence of restrictive zoning laws, have contributed to the contemporary housing crisis for the urban poor. Social workers have found that when low-income persons are relocated to surrounding areas, they often have problems locating transportation to and from their place of employment, child care, and other needed human services.

People from rural areas discuss their problems and seek out professional help less readily than those from urban and suburban localities (Conger & Elder, 1994; Coward & Dwyer, 1993). Spillover and conflicts from events of the past often run deep, affect the present-day behavior of rural residents, and create barriers to community problem solving and collaborative work. When informal networks are not providing the assistance needed, and social workers are not accepted by certain individuals in rural communities, a social worker may try to work cooperatively and collaboratively with the local power structure of community leaders and neighbors in order to connect the client system-in-need with a particular resource. For example, if a family is suffering because of problems such as mental illness or alcoholism and refuses to discuss its problems with a social worker, then the natural support systems of local clergy, doctor, or a friend may be willing to speak with the family to sanction the services of the social worker and to mobilize the network of nontraditional service providers such as informal caregivers, mutual self-help groups, church sisterhoods, or voluntary service groups.

In urban or suburban areas, a somewhat similar but more formal approach is used when community leaders or paraprofessionals are hired to serve as outreach workers to link services with persons-in-need. The generalist in the metropolis is usually better able to locate specialized services to help with problems such as those described in the earlier example (i.e., mental illness or alcoholism). In a rural area, however, the social worker may be the only professional resource available. It may be possible to work directly with the family, or it may be necessary to develop a program or write a grant to bring the needed service into the area. During the 1980s, severe economic losses in rural areas, particularly in farm communities, led to a decrease in informal social interactions and an increase in family breakdown. Major withdrawals of federal financial supports, soaring interest rates, declining land values, declining prices, and rising surpluses have led to an increasing number of farm foreclosures and bankruptcies. The economic crisis of farmers has been little understood; it has resulted in a high incidence of depression, family violence, and suicide. As stated by one farmer, "The loss of the land is not just the loss of one's job, it's the loss of one's life" (O'Neil & Ball, 1987, p. 2). This feeling exists especially when the land has belonged to a family for several generations. The farmer who experiences property foreclosure by a bank usually sees this as both a personal loss and a family disgrace.

Existing services in rural areas, such as Agricultural Extension Programs or Farm Bureaus, are often unable to cope effectively with the financial, social, and emotional crises facing poverty-stricken rural communities. Human service professionals and social service programs have made some efforts to join with such services in reaching out to farmers in crisis. They have helped farmers organize groups to advocate fairer policies and prices and locate other sources of income (Martinez-Brawley & Blundell, 1989; Messenger, 2004).

Whereas specialists are utilized in urban localities, generalists have been recognized for years as the most appropriate practitioners for rural communities (Ginsberg, 1998). In applying the General Method when working in a rural area, a social worker would find it helpful to have knowledge of rural economics (agriculture, mining, industry), regional planning and development, labor organizations, employment patterns, and relationships between public administration and services and also local rural governments and services (Conger & Elder, 1994; Ungar, Manuel, Mealey, & Campbell, 2004). In addition, a social worker in a rural area needs to be sensitive to local etiquette, folkways, values, the probable strong suspicion of outsiders, and the presence of natural helping networks. As Jenkins and Cook (1961, p. 415) point out:

> Agents of formal services often try to impose a program designed for an urban setting on rural people, ignoring rural values and attitudes. The professional worker frequently fails to respect the local residents who serve as natural helpers. Conversely, those in the natural helping network tend to reject the detached, professional behavior of the formal helper, preferring to "take care of their own."

A social worker in an urban or suburban area should have some understanding of the political struggles that take place in their localities over the metropolitan turf (Lineberry, 1975). As the subsystems in an urban or suburban area (whether they are organizations, cultural groups, churches, or geographic communities) compete for space and power in order to live out their values and aspirations, they frequently become involved with the complex political system. Political power, coalitions, public policy, and legal regulation are among the tools used in suburban and urban areas to secure and maintain land and resources.

Cities have been economically drained as people and many businesses have moved to suburbia. As suburbs have been incorporated with strict zoning, land-use restrictions, and population growth controls, the boundary lines between the suburbs and the central city have been tightened and the number and types of people allowed to enter suburban borders have been increasingly proscribed by suburban localities.

While a decrease in suburban growth may result from existing discrimination, increasing growth controls, and competition between growth and no-growth groups, such a decrease may also reflect a depressed national economy or local energy shortage. Social workers need to be aware of attempts that have been made to consolidate or coordinate city and suburban governments. In some instances, consolidation has resulted in a loss of space and resources for particular groups. Through an understanding of urban politics, social workers are better able to assist and support local groups and individuals in organizing to advocate for fair distribution of finite resources within a locality.

Knowledge, skills, and experience beyond those of an entry-level generalist may be needed both by the social worker who becomes involved with urban or suburban politics or who works in a rural area with extensive problems, no formal service delivery system, and limited natural helping networks. The rural social worker would very likely be expected to assume service roles in administration, teaching, program development, and policy formation in addition to direct practice. The urban social worker would need to have expertise in the use of the various political tools cited earlier.

The social worker with a sensitivity to diversity in environments comes to a geographic area with more realistic expectations and preparation. Social workers who are realistically prepared are then better able to help client systems, as well as to help themselves cope, develop professionally, and bring about change in the environment (Jones & Zlotnick, 1998).

Self-Assessment of Sensitivity to Social Pluralism

Social workers and social welfare systems, as well as client systems and other work-related systems, may have contrasting values. On this point, Keith-Lucas (1972) identifies three major types of value systems found in U.S. society: (1) capitalist-puritan (CP), (2) humanist-positivist-utopian (HPU), and (3) Judeo-Christian (JC). Capitalist-puritan value systems incorporate basic assumptions of individualism, materialism, and the perspective that life success or failure is associated with internal personal traits, constraints, and strengths. Humanist-positivist-utopian value systems incorporate basic assumptions of communal well-being, public interest and the common good, and the perspective that life success or failure is associated with external environmental constraints, barriers, and resources. Judeo-Christian and other religious value systems incorporate basic assumptions of concern for vulnerable persons, the collective moral body, and the perspective of distributive justice in allocating essential resources to deserving persons. Basic assumptions for each of these three value systems are given in Exercise 2.2. Capitalist-puritan value assumptions are described in items 1, 2, 7, 8, and 13 of the exercise. Humanist-positivist-utopian assumptions are given in items 3, 4, 9, 10, and 14. Assumptions of the Judeo-Christian system are indicated in items 5, 6, 11, 12, and 15. Completion of the instrument and summation of the item scores for each of the three major value assumptions provide a self-assessment of a social worker's underlying value orientations. Usually, a social worker is dominant in one but not totally identified with any value system. This exercise helps social workers grow in awareness of their own values and in sensitivity to the diversity of value systems that often conflict in human service delivery.

EXERCISE 2.2
Value System Index

Assumptions	Totally Disagree 0	1	2	3	4	Totally Agree 5
1. Human beings are responsible for their own success or failure.						
2. Human nature is basically evil, but it can be overcome by an act of will.						
3. The primary purpose of society is to fulfill human needs, both material and emotional.						
4. If human needs were fulfilled, then we would attain goodness, maturity, adjustment, and productivity, and most of society's problems would be solved.						
5. Human beings are fallible but at the same time are capable of acts of great courage or unselfishness.						
6. People are capable of choice, in the "active and willing" sense, but may need help in making their choices.						
7. The primary purpose of life is the acquisition of material prosperity, which people achieve through hard work.						
8. The primary purpose of society is the maintenance of law and order, which make this acquisition possible.						
9. What hampers people from attaining fulfillment is external circumstance, not in general under their control.						
10. These circumstances are subject to manipulation by those possessed of sufficient technical and scientific knowledge, using the scientific method.						
11. Love is always the ultimate victor over force.						
12. The greatest good lies in terms of people's relationships with their fellows and with their creator.						
13. Unsuccessful or deviant individuals are not deserving of help, although efforts should be made up to a point to rehabilitate them or to spur them to greater efforts on their own behalf.						
14. Humanity and society are ultimately perfectible.						
15. Human beings are created beings; one of their major problems is that they act as if they were not and try to be autonomous.						
CP 1, 2, 7, 8, 13						
HPU 3, 4, 9, 10, 14						
JC 5, 6, 11, 12, 15						

Socio-Demographic Variability

In addition to multiculturalism and social pluralism, human variability is influenced by endowment and personality as well as socio-demographic variance in age and developmental stage, gender, sexual orientation, and challenges in mental and physical ability.

Concepts and Discussion

■ CONCEPTS 2.15

> *Endowment* refers to the genetic traits and characteristics that serve as the basis for persons' innate mental, physical, and cognitive abilities. It also includes persons' natural gifts, talents, and subsequent developmental abilities.
>
> *Personality* consists of the combination and integration of characteristics and experiences that give a person his or her unique personhood. Personality development takes place in human beings as they use endowment and interact with others in their environment.

ENDOWMENT AND PERSONALITY   *Endowment and personality* are additional diversity variables of *person*. The endowment of a person is a major contributor to his or her bio-psychosocial development and personality. Basically, personality is influenced by (1) the endowment of a person, (2) the inherent qualities and opportunities found within a person's environment, and (3) the transactions that take place between person and environment. The personality of a human being consists of the combination and integration of characteristics and experiences that give a person his or her unique personhood. Social workers realize that a person's behavior and problems may relate to individual endowment and personality as well as to culture, class, sexual orientation, age, and developmental stage.

■ CONCEPT 2.16

> *Developmental stage* (see Table 2.1) refers to the evolving levels or phases of a person's psychosocial development and includes physical, mental, social, sexual, cognitive, spiritual, and moral growth.

AGE AND DEVELOPMENTAL STAGE   Human systems are dynamic and naturally go through various stages in their evolution. They also form complex wholes with diverse functions that may progress independently of each other. The knowledge base of the social worker includes theories about the developmental processes that take place physically, socially, sexually, cognitively, spiritually, and morally in a person. Although an individual may be at one age chronologically, he or she may not be at a corresponding psychosocial or cognitive stage developmentally. For example, a 12-

Get Photo copied!

TABLE 2.1 ■ A Multidimensional Perspective of Human Development

Age	Physical	Psychosexual	Psychosocial	Cognitive	Moral	Spiritual
0–3	Marked growth; teething (6–8 months); crawling (9–12 months); self-feeding; walking (1–); bowel and bladder control (1–2)	Oral stage (0–1) Anal stage (1–3)	Trust versus mistrust (0–1) Autonomy versus shame and doubt (1–3)	Sensorimotor stage (0–18 months) Object permanence (18 months)	Preconventional level Stage 1: Punishment and obedience	Sensing oneness, being cared for
3–6	First permanent teeth; stronger voice; receptive alert brain; manual and motor power	Phallic (Oedipal stage)	Initiative versus guilt	Preconceptual stage (2–4)	Stage II: Naive instrumental hedonism—conformity for reward	Beginning sense separateness, self-will
6–12	Increased muscular ability and coordination; girls' growth rate exceeds boys'	Latency stage	Industry versus inferiority	Intuitive stage (4–7) Concrete-operational stage (7–11)	Conventional level Stage III: "Good boy/good girl" conformity to avoid disapproval Stage IV: Authority, maintaining law and order	Experiencing God's attributes through parents and environment; beginning to hear and use religious words Social responses: formal religious education ritual; loyalty to faith of parents; anthropomorphic religious concepts

Age	Physical	Psychosexual	Psychosocial	Cognitive	Moral	Spiritual
13–18	Girls: Development of breasts, pubic hair, complexion changes, onset of menstruation Boys: Development of pubic hair, sperm, voice changes, complexion changes	Adolescence (genital stage)	Identity versus identity diffusion	Formal-operational (11–15)	Postconventional level Stage V: Morality of contract; standards of society; individual rights	Religious questioning; religious awakening; varying sense of faith; rebelliousness
18–35	Leveling off of growth	Maturity—to love and to work	Intimacy versus isolation		Stage VI: Morality of individual principles of conscience; universal ethical principles	Crisis/conversion experience Affiliation with (or withdrawal from) organized religious sect
35–65	Change in weight distribution; metabolism and sensory abilities slow down; menopause—women		Generativity versus stagnation or self-absorption			Search for and deepening of personal religious experience, active church participation
65–	Marked decrease in motor coordination; taste buds decline; organs begin to dysfunction		Ego integrity versus despair			Deepening of personal religion; finding religion to give meaning and support for death

Note: The primary theorists who have conceptualized the processes and stages identified above are: physical—Theodore Litz; psychosexual—Sigmund Freud; psychosocial—Erik Erikson; cognitive—Jean Piaget; moral—Lawrence Kohlberg; spiritual—Gordon Allport and Maria Joan O'Neil. Specific references for each would be too numerous to print here.

year-old youngster may be operating at a 3-year-old level cognitively, or a 30-year-old may be functioning psychosocially at a developmental level similar to that of an adolescent.

Using knowledge of human development in the social environment, the social worker considers the psychosocial, cognitive, and spiritual developmental level at which a person is functioning from the multidimensional perspective of *person*. In Table 2.1, conceptualizations for considering stages of development according to complementary theories are outlined and juxtaposed. When a lag is observed in any dimension of development, the social worker may have a beginning idea of the needs, problems, strengths, and tasks confronting the person at that time. A social worker should keep in mind that each person's development is unique and that a number of interrelated and interacting factors contribute to and direct development. These factors include endowment, culture, and gender.

Sensitivity to age and developmental stage helps the social worker find the most appropriate way to communicate with a client, action, or target system and to understand the problems and challenges each may be facing. There are distinct communication approaches that are more effective than others when working with particular age groups. For example, small children (approximately up to age 3) have been helped through directly involving the child's parents or significant others in providing the service. The social worker supports the parent figure, who works directly with the child. Children from approximately ages 4 through 11 often find it difficult to carry on a verbal conversation with a new adult. They are used to having adults teach, direct, or parent them. Social workers are usually more effective with children at this age when they communicate through the use of play. For adolescents (ages 12 to 17), a challenging type of play—such as sports, chess, or other game activities— may help reduce their apprehensions. Using peer groups is also an effective way to reach adolescents, as hearing from peers rather than adults is generally more acceptable. The adult, on the other hand, functions in a verbal world. Here, too, however, the social worker needs to be sure that the language and vocabulary used are appropriate for the particular adult client system receiving service. Those who may be considered elderly (over age 70) often feel more secure when the social worker comes to them in their own homes. Yet here, too, depending on need, strengths, and attitude toward social workers who may be much younger, those who are older may be helped through meeting with elderly colleagues with whom they share common concerns and experiences.

Just as individuals pass through developmental stages, so do human systems containing more than one person (couple, family, group, organization, community). In general, there are six basic stages to this group developmental process: (1) testing/tunneling in, (2) role clarifying, (3) working, (4) reformulating, (5) accomplishing, and (6) terminating (Toseland & Rivas, 2005). In the beginning stage of testing, system members usually observe and conform. As there is movement for role clarification, power struggles may become apparent. With the acceptance of positioning, purpose, rules, and guidelines, these human systems move into the work stage. As tasks and goals begin to be accomplished, members of the system grow in confidence and may venture out into new behaviors and goals. Reformulating roles and responsibilities may cause tensions and conflicts among members. If communication is open and members are able to change, a more mature, equal, or democratic type of functioning may be reached with a high level of system accomplishment. Eventually, individual members of the group may terminate as a whole. Members often join with outside individuals or human systems to form new functioning units.

Just as social workers recognize diversity in the human developmental process, they also recognize the different growth levels of families, groups, organizations, and communities. Such knowledge and sensitivity help a social worker in engagement, problem assessment, progress evaluation, and ongoing facilitation of growth and development within various size systems.

■ CONCEPTS 2.17

> *Gender roles* refer to the expected behavior patterns of masculinity and femininity dictated by society (Davis & Proctor, 1989; Nussbaum, 2000).
>
> *Gender identity* is part of the unchanging core of personality formation.
>
> *Sexism* means the subjugation of one gender to another and refers to the existing attitudes, policies, and practices that demonstrate this discrimination.

GENDER

Women The patriarchal ideology found in United States society and in other societies fosters institutional sexism through which women have long experienced inequality and victimization. This treatment and the acceptance of male dominance are due to differences in gender roles rather than to physiological differences between the sexes. Thus, if social workers are to be helpful to women, it is important that they understand:

▶ The nature and scope of the female gender role as it has evolved within a sexist society

▶ The more recent perspective of feminine identity development as involving interconnectedness, or self-in-relation

The feminist gender role in vogue today highlights the importance of relational development and interconnectedness. According to Gilligan (1982, pp. 7–8),

> *Female identity formation takes place in a context of ongoing relationship since mothers tend to experience their daughters as more like and continuous with themselves. . . . [Girls], in identifying themselves as female, experience themselves as like their mothers, thus, fusing the experience of attachment with the process of identity formation.*

In other words, females experience themselves as more continuous with and related to the external world and know themselves through their relationships with others (Chodorow, 1978; Gilligan, 1982; Jordan, Kaplan, Miller, Stiver, & Surrey, 1991; Miller, 1976).

Socialization, gender-based life experiences, and role expectations of women differ from those of men. The traditional gender role imposed on a woman as a dependent, conforming, and emotionally nurturing female has not been a satisfying and health-promoting role for many. Women have often felt constricted and ineffective in this role. They have experienced tensions and conflict that are due to lack of privilege and power. Some have internalized society's image of themselves and have accepted a self-concept in which they are helpless, inadequate, and submissive. These women often need help to reject such negative self-attributes and to become resocialized as competent and whole persons (Jordan, Kaplan, Miller, Stiver, & Surrey, 1991; Nussbaum, 2000).

In the past, service providers worked to help women adjust to their feminine role. Today, however, there is an increasing recognition of the need for social workers to help women become consciously aware of how they have been socialized and to find ways for them to grow in self-actualization. Social workers need to realize that difficulties that in the past may have been identified as individual, personal problems of women are actually a social problem, with a social cause and possible political solution. As a woman discusses her problems with a social worker, she may be surprised and supported in learning that other women have had similar experiences and that, collectively, they are victims of sexism in society (Gutierrez & Lewis, 1999). Through joining together, women have begun to develop a sense of empowerment and to expose the destructive forces they experience. Organized movements—such as the Suffrage Movement, the Women's Trade Union, the National Consumer's League, and the National Organization for Women—have greatly contributed to improving the status of women in U.S. society.

Social workers can help women develop additional coping skills in assertiveness, self-confidence, self-reliance, expression of anger, confrontation, organization, and leadership. A sense of independence can be enhanced if the social worker assumes the role of a facilitator more than that of expert. In the General Method, a collaborative approach is used in which the social worker and the client system engage in a shared strengths-based problem-solving process. Thus, this method aptly lends itself to working with women in a sensitive responsive manner.

Men   Whether men are responsible for the development and maintenance of sexism in society can be debated endlessly. However, it is more important for women and for men to become involved in searching out the positives and the potential for both as they go through the process of redefining gender roles. These issues are currently affecting the basic foundation and institutions of U.S. society. Men may struggle with accepting changes in the feminine gender role because such acceptance necessitates their letting go of power and privilege. Nevertheless, there are possible advantages for men if the results of women's liberation include a change in the demands and expectations for men in a sexist society (Davis & Proctor, 1989).

Men also may be seen as victims of sexism. Having to assume the strong, dominant, breadwinning, protector role has had negative and sometimes fatal effects on men. They have been expected to perform with total success at work and at home. A man's occupation has been seen as his primary status determinant and basic identity. As a result, failure in work is perceived as failure in personhood for many men.

The drive to succeed has also influenced men's suicidal actions. The instruments used by men to commit suicide are more certain to complete the task successfully than those used by women. Over 70 percent of all completed suicides are committed by men (Horwitz & Scheid, 1999).

Being cast in the role of a strong male has restricted men's freedom to acknowledge and express emotions. Supportive relationships have been generally limited to a man's wife, with few sustained peer friendships. Even emotional displays with children have been considered out of character for a man. The stress and tensions felt by men and left unexpressed have resulted in stress-related illnesses and an earlier death rate for men than for women. Such problems, directly related to the masculine gender role, can now begin to be identified and possibly resolved if men join in the movement to overcome existing sexism in society. As pointed out by Goldberg (1978, p. 1), "The social revolutions of recent years can lessen the male's time-honored burdens, help him reclaim denied emotion, expand his sensual responsiveness, bring new dimensions of honesty and depth to his heterosexual relationships, as well as alert him to the self-destructive compulsions within him."

Rather than respond openly and hopefully to women's expanded roles, some men are feeling extremely threatened by the changes they witness in their wives, daughters, friends, and associates. They experience shock, hurt, and fear as women change, compete, and achieve in the workplace, the political field, and the family. Some fight the changes; others react by withdrawal from encounters with women. Although it may be difficult for a man to seek help with his feelings, a sensitive social worker can help him understand and express what he is experiencing. With support, men may begin to see some value in letting go of social norms and moving into more collaborative sharing with women.

Contemporary social changes have resulted in a variety of significant problems for men. These may include problems in areas such as custody battles, male single parenting, and fathering after divorce when children remain with their mothers or when parents have joint custody. Social workers are able to help men with these problems through such efforts as counseling and establishing support groups for single fathers.

Although sexism has a direct effect on men and women in U.S. society, the problems of racism and poverty overshadow and compound the situation for minority men and women. Nonwhite males have a shorter life expectancy than all females and all other males (Horwitz & Scheid, 1999). Black males, in particular, have the highest rate of being victimized by crime and robbery, of experiencing job injuries, of being in low-status service jobs, and of being unmarried. The lack of opportunities in society has frequently led them to try to improve their economic status by participating in illegal activities. Social workers can demonstrate sensitivity to the high-risk status of black men through such efforts as promoting community groups to serve as support networks for black males and through advocating social policies that are responsive to their employment and economic needs. Unless efforts to overcome racism and poverty are sustained and achieved, success in gender egalitarianism will be of little significance for poor minority men and women (Gutierrez & Lewis, 1999).

It is possible that the changes taking place in gender roles may result in new, ongoing problems for men and women in general. Women may go to such an extreme in their efforts to prove their equality with men that they may become engrossed in competition and power struggles. They, too, may develop stress-related illnesses and a lower life expectancy pattern as they suppress feelings and stress achievement. With men changing their masculine role, one development may be a shift toward their demonstrating strength through interpersonal and intellectual skills. This change, however, may prove to be equally stressful for men as they strive for success and mastery in these skill areas.

Instead of evolving into new problems, the movement for change in gender roles can be a reciprocal process that produces growth and gains for both sexes. Social workers may contribute to making this a reality by helping men and women clarify who they are, why they are the way they are, and where they are in the process of becoming. As men and women strive for wholeness, a beneficial goal to work for is the separation of role and status from gender. Emphasis needs to be placed on individuality with an acceptance of flexible roles as appropriate to each situation. Social workers can help men and women develop a definition of self and role that is individualized and sensitive to the person's as well as others' needs and growth. The General Method of social work practice is based on the practice principle of *individuality*. In applying the method to gender issues, a social worker keeps in mind the unique needs and circumstances of each client system.

Self-Assessment of Gender Sensitivity   As with other types of human diversity, social workers need to be aware of their own personal attitudes and possible stereotypical ideas regarding gender roles. A simple exercise that may assist a student or social worker to grow in self-awareness in this area is found in Exercise 2.3.

SEXUAL ORIENTATION.   A *homosexual* person has been defined as "one who is motivated in adult life by a definite preferential erotic attraction to members of the same sex and who usually (but not necessarily) engages in overt sexual relations with them" (Marmor, 1980, p. 85). McNaught (1981) describes two primary types of homosexuals: (1) *transitional*—an individual who is basically heterosexual but engages in homosexual behavior when no one of the opposite sex is available (as in prisons or military service) and (2) *constitutional*—an individual whose sexual orientation toward the same sex is set at around the ages of 3 to 5 years.

Basically, *homosexuality* is a general term used to describe men or women. Many homosexual men prefer to be referred to as *gay* and many homosexual women prefer the term *lesbian*. To be gay or lesbian involves psychological and sociological experiences as well as sexual attractions or behaviors. The individual can be better understood if seen in relation to his or her environment and in relation to those who live within that environment. A term frequently used to describe the negative emotional reactions of heterosexual people toward gay men, lesbians, bisexuals, and transgendered persons is *homophobia*. This reaction is associated with a deep-rooted fear and accompanying hatred of homosexual lifestyles and individuals. Historically, homosexuality was described in the helping professions as a disturbance or illness. Today, it is referred to as a sexual orientation.

EXERCISE 2.3
Gender-Sensitivity Questions

1. What would be your immediate reaction when hearing about a 40-year-old woman marrying a 20-year-old man?

2. How do you feel about having a woman in charge of
   a. Your bank (president)
   b. Your place of employment
   c. The military
   d. Your church
   e. The executive branch of the government (president of the United States)

3. Who did the cooking, cleaning, and shopping in your house when you were growing up?

4. Who does the cooking, cleaning, and shopping in your present home?

5. Who do you think should be responsible for household tasks?

6. What do you think of a man who walks out of a door before a woman who is also trying to leave?

7. Do you ever use the expressions

   a. Woman driver
   b. Henpecked husband
   c. Female gossip
   d. Man-sized job
   e. Catty women
   f. The girls

The problems or needs brought to the attention of social workers by lesbian, gay, bisexual, and transgendered (LGBT) client systems are not necessarily related to sexual variations in lifestyle. There are, however, a number of tensions, needs, and problems an individual may experience as a result of being LGBT. A knowledgeable and sensitive social worker may assist the individual in these problematic areas. For example, as a person (at any age) begins to recognize an attraction to members of the same sex or to explore the possibility that he or she may be homosexual, he or she may experience strong feelings of fear, confusion, or guilt. For many, there is no one to turn to for an open, honest discussion about their questions and concerns. Some, particularly adolescents, find the internal conflict so overwhelming that they turn to drugs or suicide (McNaught, 1981). Social workers can be very helpful as individuals struggle over questions about their sexual identity or decision to choose or not choose a gay or lesbian lifestyle, or to "come out" (make their sexual orientation known). Help may be needed in planning when and how they will share their decisions with significant persons in their lives. Coming out can be extremely traumatic for a person unless there has been careful planning with supports available. What is at stake may include the loss of a job, marriage, children, or self-esteem (Appleby & Anastas, 1998).

Lesbian, gay, bisexual, and transgendered persons also may seek help from social workers because of problems with interpersonal relationships (Saulnier, 2002). Individuals or couples may seek help to decide about improving, maintaining, or terminating a relationship or lifestyle. If two LGBT people decide to make a lifelong commitment to each other, they may ask a social worker to help them find a way to legitimate their relationship. They may not know about relationship contracts or joint wills. Problems and needs may develop after one of the two dies. The remaining partner may need someone else to help him or her grieve over the loss of the other. Biological family members may have legal access to the remaining assets of the deceased. Even if there has been a joint will, the family may contest it (Laird & Green, 1996; Mallon, 2004).

As LGBT individuals get older, a number of institutional, legal, emotional, and medical problems may emerge. Institutional problems may include housing or nursing home practices that do not permit two nonrelated members to dwell together. If one partner is in a nursing home or hospital, the other may not be allowed to visit or make medical decisions for the institutionalized person without legal documents, such as durable and medical powers of attorney, because there is no legal or blood relationship. Legal problems may include restrictive laws regarding property or wills as well as the absence of laws to prevent discriminatory practices by judges, police, or insurance companies. The emotional problems of elderly LGBT persons may include feelings of rejection by the LGBT community and feelings of abandonment or loss after the death of a partner. The medical problems of homosexuals at any age may include sexually transmitted diseases (pharyngeal or anal gonorrhea or AIDS, for example) (Laird, 1999).

In addition to the help offered directly by the social worker, LGBT persons may need support and services from a variety of professionals and other systems. As they interact with people in diverse settings, they need to be understood and accepted as unique individuals. Social workers can assist by locating available, appropriate resources. The resources needed may include knowledgeable and accepting physicians, lawyers, clergy, and insurance companies. LGBT persons also may be enabled to deal with their tensions and problems through active participation in self-help groups, supportive networks, and related political action movements. Sometimes social workers provide services for members of families of LGBT individuals. For example, counseling sessions or groups led by social workers for wives of gay and bisexual men may help them deal with such feelings and issues as anger, betrayal, homophobia, sexuality, care of children, and support.

Self-Assessment of Homophobia   There is clearly a need for social workers to understand their attitudes and assumptions about gay and lesbian persons. The questions in Exercise 2.4 constitute a brief exercise for self-reflection and discussion about sexual orientation and homophobia.

EXERCISE 2.4
Sensitivity to Sexual Orientation

1. If you learned that a person is LGBT, would it influence your decision about sitting next to him or her?

2. Have you worked with LGBT client systems?

3. Do you think LGBT individuals could benefit from being placed in a mixed group (heterosexuals and homosexuals)?

4. Would you protest if an antihomosexual joke were told?

5. Do you think LGBT individuals have had disturbed relationships with one or both parents?

6. Do you have social contacts with LGBT persons?

7. Would you ever discourage LGBT clients from disclosing their sexual orientation to their family, friends, or co-workers? Why?

8. Do you think of homosexuality as a sickness or as a natural variant in human sexuality?

9. What would be your response if you learned that your sibling or child was LGBT?

10. Do LGBT persons have a right to be ministers, schoolteachers, social workers, or legislators?

◄ **PERCEPTIONS OF ILLNESS BEHAVIOR AND HEALTH**   Culture exerts a fundamental and far-reaching influence on the interpretation of health and illness. Culturally derived perceptions of thoughts, feelings, and acts pertaining to symptoms, the meaning of illness and disabilities, and the consequences have always been associated with illness behavior. For example, in some cultural groups, people are expected to be stoic in bearing pain. In others, they are expected to express pain vociferously and publicly. Illness reflects an adaptive social process in which participants are often actively striving to meet their social roles and responsibilities, to control their environment, and to make their everyday circumstances less uncertain and therefore more tolerable and predictable (Mechanic, 1978). Determining a client system's view of illness, physical aberrations, disabling conditions, and mental symptoms becomes an important part of social work assessment in the General Method. In modern Western society, most people continue to attribute illness to physical causes (i.e., associated with biological factors such as chemical or hormonal imbalances, genetic predispositions, degenerative processes, and hereditary malformations; environmental factors such as infections and toxins; and individual factors such as improper nutrition, lack of physical exercise, and difficulty coping with stress). Their beliefs are predominantly secular, rational, and future oriented. Because people tend to be receptive to diagnoses and treatments that match their expectations, mainstream Americans seek to eradicate the cause of illness with antibiotics, vitamins, hormones, medications, surgical procedures, radiation and chemotherapy, exercise, proper rest, and psychotherapy as preferred ways of treatment. They remain skeptical of alternative treatment approaches that do not immediately or easily fit into their cultural perceptions of illness. Thus, the U.S. health care system is, in large measure, an outgrowth of reverence for science and technology as well as a conviction that nature can be mastered.

By contrast, many ethnic minority clients espouse markedly different beliefs (frequently related to spirituality, magic, and family rules of behavior) about the causes of illness and other health afflictions. For example, Native Americans view good health as a balance of living in harmony with nature, a view that depends on adhering to a strict set of cosmic laws (Applewhite, 1995). Thus, healing means that the individual must be recreated, reconnected, and live in balance with nature. Many Hispanic groups believe that health is subject to God's judgment and that suffering is a consequence of having sinned and is a punishment *(castigo)* for disobeying God's laws. Thus, only a *curandero* (folk healer who has been chosen by God) can provide an appropriate cure (Applewhite, 1995). Puerto Ricans have *espiritistas,* who are believed to have supernatural inspiration for dealing with health and illness through exorcising harmful spiritual influences and strengthening benign spiritual influences (Guarnaccia, 1993). Asian/Pacific Islanders tie their views about health and illness to beliefs about magic, spirituality, and family ancestral rules of behavior. Many use a combination of healers ranging from traditional folk healers to homeopathic herbalists and acupuncturists (Pearl, Leo, & Tsang, 1995).

Most non-Western societies represented by ethnic minorities in the United States, especially those who are poorly educated and from low socio-economic levels, hold onto beliefs about health and sickness that are primarily rooted in traditional cultural folkways. These typically involve beliefs in supernatural forces, the use of home remedies, and the assistance of folk healers as ways to eliminate illness and restore good health. When major discrepancies exist between a client system's expectations and medical recommendations for treatment, client systems often reject both medical diagnosis and treatment. To the extent these types of belief systems intertwine with Western health care systems, experienced practitioners recommend that health care professionals, including social workers, learn to convey any discussion about health and treatment in ways that the individual may understand, using language, expressions, and services that are culturally salient. For example, the client system's primary language may be used in conveying treatment recommendations. Cultural community brokers may be used to find appropriate alternative medicine treatments and community supports (Land & Hudson, 1997).

CHALLENGES IN PHYSICAL AND MENTAL ABILITY   Deviations in human physical and mental abilities carry different meanings for different societies throughout the world. Values attached to disability vary both geographically and historically as well as based on various cultural beliefs associated with the meaning of individual responsibility. In ancient Greece, for example, malformed babies were thrown over a precipice. In other societies, persons with disabilities have been imbued with supernatural divine powers (on the primitive Truk Islands) and accorded positive societal attitudes (in modern-day Denmark) (Mackelprang & Salsgiver, 1996).

Today, more than two million people in the United States have serious and persistent mental illnesses such as schizophrenia, bipolar disorder, and major depression (Horwitz & Scheid, 1999). Nine to ten million are afflicted with alcoholism and other drug addictions; the highest percentage are those of ethnic minority descent who have low incomes (Native American Indians, African Americans, Hispanics, and Pacific Islanders) (Substance Abuse and Mental Health Services Administration, 1995). These neurobiological illnesses, addictions, and other disabilities have a devastating effect on individual functioning and ability to work and live independently. They also carry social stigma and result in much discrimination.

Congress's passage of the Americans with Disabilities Act of 1990 (P.L. 101-336) represents acknowledgment that the 43,000,000 Americans with disabilities have been subject to serious discrimination without legal recourse (Mackelprang & Salsgiver, 1996). Historically, these patterns of discrimination were based on (1) beliefs from the Middle Ages that people with physical and mental disabilities had experienced God's wrath, (2) stereotypes that people with disabilities and health problems were nonproductive, and (3) the sick role that Western culture expected persons with disabilities to fulfill. Such attitudes and resulting policies were shaped primarily by philosophies of utilitarianism, humanitarianism, and human rights (Newman, 1991). Fears about social disorder, for example, created a shift from home care to institutionalization in early to mid–nineteenth-century U.S. society. The creation of institutions paralleled the influx of large numbers of immigrants. As families became more transient and society encountered varying ethnic attitudes about sickness, health, and disability, institutional care began to be seen as a socially unifying force and began replacing certain welfare functions (Berkowitz, 1987). Concurrently, describing deviance from social norms, including disability, came to be defined as a social problem, and institutional services were deemed better than those available in individual communities. The subsequent shift from institutional care toward deinstitutionalization, which took place in the latter part of the twentieth century, has been credited with the following:

▶ Revealing the inhumanity and financial drain of large residential settings that abrogated individual and family needs and did not produce the promised rehabilitation of persons who deviated from societal norms

▶ Producing improvements in general knowledge about health, illness, and disability disorders as well as new medical treatments involving advanced technology, drugs, surgery, and various therapies to alter human behavior

▶ Recognizing the role of holistic protective factors, such as personal strength and resiliency, and the use of personal and community social supports in facilitating the goodness-of-fit between individuals and their environmental systems

▶ Stimulating the special education, mental health, independent living, and grassroots self-help treatment movements that emphasized principles of normalization, least restrictive settings, and recovery in service delivery and human rehabilitation

The Individuals with Disabilities Education Act (IDEA) of 1997 supported the notion that persons with disabilities should be active and in control of their own lives by assuring six rights for children (Timberlake & Sabatino, 2006; Turnbull & Turnbull, 1998):

1. The right to attend school
2. The right to a fair appraisal of strengths and needs
3. The right to a beneficial experience in school
4. The right to be included in the general education curriculum and other activities
5. The right to be treated fairly
6. The right to be included in the decision-making process

These principles and rights created a perspective of people with disabilities as active and responsible consumers of services and as persons entitled to control their own lives.

■ C O N C E P T S **2.18**

> The *normalization principle* suggests that all people, whether different or not, should be integrated to the maximum extent possible into the mainstream service delivery system and that services should promote those personal behaviors and characteristics that are culturally as normative as possible (DeJong, Batavia, & McKnew, 1992).

> The *least restrictive environment principle* supports normalization beliefs by shifting the focus from large impersonal institutional settings to community and family care as the primary environmental settings for service delivery to people with exceptional physical and mental needs (Seligman & Darling, 1997).

> The *recovery principle* further underscores the deeply personal process that takes place in coping with health limitations (caused by mental illness, drug addiction, and deteriorating physical or emotional functioning) by documenting that people who are afflicted with such health problems are able to carry on a rich, satisfying, and productive life (Anthony, 1993).

Currently in the health care service delivery system, *rehabilitation* focuses on restoring human capacities that have been lost due to poor health, illness, or injury. *Habilitation* extends this focus into maximizing and promoting normal human potential in all health functioning and across all life situations. Social work helping strategies with client systems experiencing challenging conditions typically involve the following:

1. *Micro approaches* that focus on
   • Individual and family education about the conditions and options for (re)habilitation (Seligman & Darling, 1997), the process of recovery (Taylor, 1997), and the availability of community resources (Laborde & Seligman, 1991)

- Change strategies for reframing the personal meaning of the affliction (Marshak & Seligman, 1993) and for coping with and adapting to the chronicity (Deselle & Proctor, 2004)
- Skills training and parent management (Marsh, 1992)

2. *Mezzo approaches* that use
   - Collective group education and mutual self-help to improve and empower specific groups of people (Van Soest & Garcia, 2003)
   - Community outreach to mobilize specific group community services (Rivera & Erlich, 1998)

3. *Macro strategies* that focus on
   - Education and training to improve the quality of services and service delivery to specific groups of clients (Mackelprang & Santos, 1992)
   - Education and training to increase community awareness and understanding of various social problems and challenging conditions (Gill, 1998)
   - Social planning for the development and coordination of human services (Hardcastle, Wenocur, & Powers, 2004)
   - Community development (Rubin & Rubin, 1992), coalition building (Mizrahi & Rosenthal, 1993), and class advocacy to promote specific group and community empowerment while engaging political, economic, and legislative systems to facilitate equitable redistribution of resources and justice for disadvantaged or oppressed populations (Lewis, 1991)

A Holistic Framework for Sensitivity to Human Variability

All people have basic needs of food, clothing, and shelter and share similar desires and goals to improve the quality of their lives (Maslow, 1968). The way people seek to achieve these desires and goals, however, usually depends on their experience with multiculturalism, stratification influences of social pluralism, and personal sociodemographic variability in endowment, personality, age, gender, sexual orientation, health, and physical and mental abilities. Thus, although all persons have the same problems, concerns, and aspirations, the "isms" (such as racism, classism, sexism, and ageism, to name a few) block opportunities, compound the problems experienced by certain groups of people, and lead to oppression and social injustice.

For example, besides poverty, racism continues to be one of the pervasive problems facing people of color and their communities. It is viewed as a root cause of generational poverty, diminished self-esteem that promotes community violence and self-medicating through drugs and alcohol, and disproportionate involvement in the criminal justice system. But despite the fact that wages and income, promotion rates, middle and top management, contractors, and manufacturing firms all document the same historical story of continued discrimination, there is a growing perception that white Americans, especially white males, are now experiencing reverse discrimination as an outcome of affirmative action policies and practices (Axinn & Levin, 1997). A survey by the National Opinion Research Center, however, found that, although 70 percent of the U.S. public believed that whites were being hurt by affirmative action policies, only 7 percent reported experience with reverse discrimination (Patterson, 1995). This backlash against people of color is further evident in several recent pieces of legislation that underpin the present climate of delivering services. For example, Propositions 187 and 209 in California respectively prohibited social services to all persons who could not document their legal status and prohibited preferences based on race and gender in public education, employment, and state contracting (Karger & Stoesz, 1990).

Although discrimination based on race is illegal, it is still prevalent and continues to be the basis for many macro issues that affect societal participation, relationships, and resource distribution for all people in general but people of color in particular. Social workers must guard against institutionalized practices that perpetuate unequal treatment of communities of color as well as unequal practices with individuals of color. They must use practice approaches that are suited to work with particular multicultural groups. Such approaches acknowledge the existence of multicultural, socio-pluralistic, and socio-demographic differences while celebrating the resourcefulness and creativeness of human potential. They focus on social justice and human empowerment within the context of the client system's environment.

In summary, the values of social justice, life choice, and individuality are key tenets of the social work profession. Therefore, social workers are expected to:

- Help oppressed client systems obtain freedom and growth.
- Respect the need of individuals to choose for themselves.
- Avoid judging the choice and morality of others' behavior as long as the behavior and choice do not threaten or deprive another of life, choice, or expression.
- Promote the tenet that to be human is to have choice in values, lifestyles, and behaviors.
- Avoid stereotyping a member of any group.

These expectations highlight the necessity for knowledge of client system diversity as an essential guide for social workers' thoughts and actions.

Such strengths-based social work practice helps client systems uncover and promote strengths from within (Saleebey, 1997). Cultural values and traditions, resources, coping strategies, family, friends, and community support networks represent potential individual strengths. Collective history and traditions, mutual support, and group resources represent collective community strengths. The client system is viewed as an expert in identifying past successes and in developing solutions based on past experiences. These past experiences are particularly emphasized in the strengths-based problem-solving of the General Method. Empowerment seeks to promote a power-shared relationship, competency-based assessment, collectivity for mutual aid, education for critical thinking, and knowledge and skills for finding resources and taking action within the context of the client system's environment (Parsons, Jorgensen, & Hernandez, 1994). It requires a holistic view (as found in Figure 2.2) about the interactive effect of people's concerns, strengths, perceptions, values and beliefs, unique persona, and cultural risks and resiliencies.

Photocopy

FIGURE 2.2 ■ Holistic View of Human Diversity

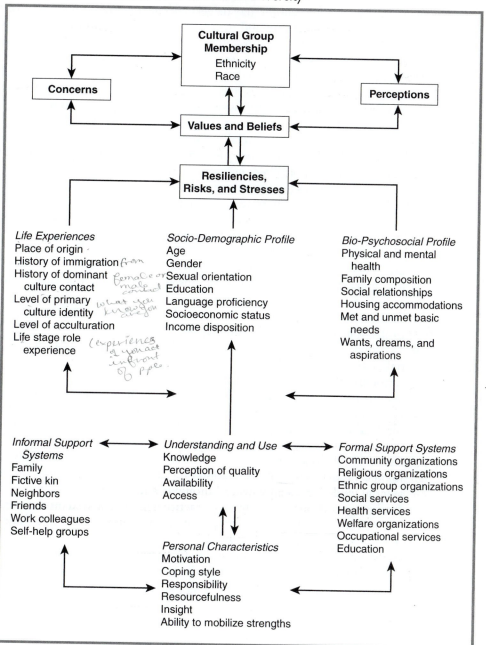

To help client systems identify the micro-, mezzo-, or macro-level problem(s) for which social work intervention may be needed, client systems must be allowed to tell their stories in their own way and to construct their own versions of reality (Salee-bey, 1997). In many cultures, storytelling or narration has long been used to record history. Since it allows for the incorporation of cultural references and perceptions, it is a natural way to develop the helping relationship across diverse client systems. However, the social worker needs to become an active listener and participant in this two-way interaction process by using professional skills to guide client systems through their narration and to uncover and construct the meaning of their personal or collective social reality. The social worker may also need to learn to use metaphor as a way of linking past history to present interpretation of perceived needs and problems and thereby facilitate client systems' recognition of strengths. In this narrative approach, client systems tell their story from the beginning to the present or from the end back to its origin. In the process, clients' conceptions of self, relationships, life, and communal experiences take shape and provide meaning and purpose (Goldstein, 1990). This ethnically sensitive approach requires one to:

- ▶ Listen actively and nonjudgmentally to each client system.
- ▶ Recognize that client system perceptions are shaped by individual, personal, and collective experiences.
- ▶ Understand that cultural values affect all human individual, family, group, organization, and community interaction.
- ▶ Acknowledge that all people translate nonverbal communication (such as spatial observances, handshaking, and eye contact) in different ways.
- ▶ Recognize that within each culture there exists much human variability in how people think, feel, act, and express their physical and emotional characteristics.
- ▶ Recognize that the route for seeking services (or help seeking) is affected by cultural values underpinning the delivery of human services, personal resiliencies, social stratification of access to resources, historical client systems, life experiences, and the placement of societal values on personal and collective responsibilities for self-care, financial independence, social relationships, and the client system's past experiences with discrimination.
- ▶ Recognize that verbal communication patterns differ based on personal and collective community cultural interpretations and experiences, life-stage development, and language competency.
- ▶ Acknowledge that cultural values affect personal perceptions and behavior in all facets of human interaction across all levels of service delivery.

SUMMARY

The knowledge areas of multiculturalism, social pluralism, and socio-demographic variability and their accompanying self-awareness exercises serve two purposes. They help social workers organize their own personal and group membership value orientations, attitudes, assumptions, biases, and prejudices that may become barriers in understanding and communicating with others. Second, these knowledge areas set the stage for social workers' lifelong learning about their client, action, and target systems and themselves in their professional roles. The purpose of this approach to human diversity is to increase sensitivity and empathy and also build an inclusionary professional worldview. Specifically, the professional worldview created here:

▶ Extends the professional self beyond the ethnocentrism and bias inherent in the boundaries and blinders of personal experience and own worldview
▶ Respects and understands the protective role that multiculturalism, social pluralism, and socio-demographic variability play in adaptive social functioning and social enhancement
▶ Understands the impact of societal "isms" and human service delivery biases on individual and collective stress, resilience, and well-being at the micro, mezzo, and macro levels of practice
▶ Uses the knowledge of multiculturalism, social pluralism, and socio-demographic variability to communicate clearly, interact respectfully, and act facilitatively with client, action, and target systems as well as human service providers in order to mobilize strengths and resources, solve problems, meet needs, empower the vulnerable, and provide sensitive and competent services across diverse groupings of persons

A sensitivity to human diversity from a holistic multivariant perspective is essential for effective generalist social work practice. This sensitivity becomes competency in diversity when the social worker's experiential awareness and knowledge of multiculturalism, social pluralism, and socio-demographic variability join with the social worker's skill in providing effective and sensitive services to meet the needs of diverse client systems. This is a process in which the social worker needs to integrate knowledge about multicultural, social stratification, and socio-demographic influences on human perceptions, beliefs, values, and actions with a reflection about self-awareness and insight as well as honed skills.

In micro-level service competency with diverse client systems, a primary social work task is to assist the client system at the point of interface between the client system and environment in empowering the client system to sort out needs, wants, and goals and in providing assistance with the client system's coping, strengths and competence, and resource utilization in achieving those goals. In mezzo-level service competency, a social worker's primary task is to facilitate family or group development, encourage mutual support, and empower toward mastery. In guiding the family or group through its normal developmental process, the social worker pays particular attention to how the "isms" and their issues of oppression, prejudice, bias, and perceptions of conflict affect family or group cohesion, developmental progress, and goal accomplishment.

In macro-level service competency, the social worker involves community and large client and action systems in addressing diversity issues in the delivery of services to all persons, promoting social equality and justice, and reducing social violence. The tasks of communities self-identified by commonalities of race, ethnicity, social stratification, sexual orientation, physical or mental challenges, or other diversity involve bringing together various community support networks (churches, indigenous service providers, and public and private human service organizations) and mobilizing their resources to provide a safe and just path for community development or community acculturation in the case of immigrant ethnic groups. Through social organization and planning for social action, the social worker helps community systems uncover common bonds around values and goals while creating community coalitions, mobilizing resources, advocating, negotiating, and brokering services.

Following through each phase of the General Method, the social worker embarks on a journey of knowledge and skill development and sensitivity to diversity. The integration of content on multiculturalism, social pluralism, and socio-demographic variability within each chapter is a deliberate attempt to highlight the importance of cultural sensitivity and competence throughout the use of the General Method. Besides gaining knowledge and skill development in the application of the method, each chapter focuses on human diversity issues with different client systems in a variety of fields of practice.

REFLECTION POINTS

Becoming a skilled social work practitioner requires knowledge and skills, including the ability to reflect on practice endeavors. The following reflection points are designed to strengthen critical thinking and mastery of knowledge of key points in this chapter.

1. Define the following key concepts in generalist social work:
   - Multiculturalism
   - Social pluralism
   - Socio-demographic diversity
2. Choose one aspect from each of these three concepts (as described in this chapter) and explore how a personal experience or issue related to each aspect might influence your personal viewpoint. Then, examine the fit between your personal and professional viewpoints.
3. How might each of these concepts influence your professional behavior in practice with client, action, and target systems at micro, mezzo, and macro levels of practice?
4. Review Section 1.05, Cultural Competence and Social Diversity, in the *NASW Code of Ethics* (www.socialworkers.org). How will these standards influence your professional behavior?
5. For further reading and research, use the key concepts in Question 1 to locate social work references related to this chapter's content. (See Appendix A, Selected Internet Resources, and Appendix B, Selected Social Work Journals.) What issues or concerns are evident in the articles? How might these influence your professional behavior with client, action, and target systems?

CHAPTER 3

Building Empirical Evidence for Practice

Generalist social work practice in today's environmental context demands knowledge about *best practices*, or the optimal ways of delivering services to meet an ideal *standard of care* for a given client population under given circumstances. *Best practices, standard of care,* and *cost effectiveness* have been combined by public and private funding sources into a *managed care* approach to service delivery. In *managed care,* funding sources have become external arbiters of practice decisions about who gets what services for how long. In this context, generalist social work practice efforts are heavily scrutinized, monitored, and evaluated not only for the relevance and soundness of intervention but also for service accountability, brevity, impact, efficiency, and cost effectiveness. Best practices, which rely primarily on expert opinion and client testimonials, are now being supplemented by best practices that increasingly use empirically derived and driven evidence in making practice decisons.

Buffeted by the external pressures of managed care trends, federal and state laws, trends in the applied social and behavioral sciences, and a growing stakeholder demand for accountability, the social work profession's use of empirical practice evidence in the General Method is guided by its mission, values and ethics, and holistic person-in-environment practice approaches (O'Hare, 2005). In this context, generalist practice endeavors are expected to use theoretically and empirically derived intervention models of practice, be transparent, and adhere to ethical practice standards.

Thus, the purpose of this chapter is to help generalist practitioners become informed about building empirical evidence for the foundation knowledge and values of the social work profession and the conceptual framework of the General Method. To accomplish this purpose, Chapter 3 addresses:

▶ The reasons for evaluation
▶ A brief history and scope of practice research in social work
▶ The steps in building empirical evidence for social work
▶ The role of theory in building empirical evidence for practice
▶ The essential components of building evidence for practice
▶ The development of a scientific approach to practice
▶ The common strategies for engaging in practice evaluation

Reasons for Evaluation

Ongoing Process of Service Delivery

Evaluation is part of the continuous process of service delivery throughout the six phases of the General Method. Although evaluation is typically carried out during and after the intervention phase, planning for evaluation begins prior to intervention. Indeed, thinking about evaluation begins during the engagement phase when the social worker and client system first meet and begin exploring client system issues, problems, needs, strengths, resources, and goals. In defining problems and needs, they collectively make decisions about which information facilitates understanding the identified needs, strengths, and goals. This preliminary information sets the stage for making further decisions about data collection, assessment, and evaluation to monitor intervention quality and quantity and to evaluate the client system outcomes and benefits.

During the assessment and contract planning phase, the evaluation process is formalized in the planning contract. This contract is a formal written agreement to

(1) employ specific General Method intervention strategies in order to achieve identified client system goals within a specified time frame and (2) participate in an explicit monitoring process throughout the intervention. Thus, throughout the General Method, the client system and the social worker are collaboratively involved in ongoing monitoring and evaluation of their joint work to achieve positive changes for the client system. Sometimes, the monitoring and evaluation process may yield evidence that the client system's goals and objectives have been met. At other times, it may identify a need to redefine the problem, reassess goals and objectives, reexamine the effectiveness of goal-directed activities and tasks, or alter the intervention plan. Although practice evaluation proceeds from a beginning to an end point, it is a cyclical process that informs and is a key part of the strengths-based problem-solving approach of the General Method:

▶ *Engagement phase* (Chapter 5): The client system (individuals, families, groups, organizations, and communities) and the social worker begin developing a working relationship to understand the client system's problems, issues, strengths, and resources and to develop a preliminary agreement about information necessary to understand the needs and resources and document client system change.

▶ *Data-collection phase* (Chapter 6): With the client system's consent, the generalist social worker and the client system begin gathering information. They explore, evaluate, and decide whether the information being collected is sufficient for understanding the problem and identifying available resources and whether additional information is needed to facilitate prioritizing which issue or need will be targeted for further assessment so that positive change can occur.

▶ *Assessment and contract planning phase* (Chapter 7): The client system and the social worker conduct an assessment of problems, needs, strengths, and resources; establish priorities and goals; and reach agreement about the preintervention data-collection activities necessary to provide a baseline for evaluating change. They formalize their working agreement into an explicit written contractual agreement.

▶ *Intervention phase* (Chapters 8 and 9): The client system and the social worker participate in the contracted intervention process and activities. They monitor goal accomplishment, track changes, and discuss whether the desired changes are occurring or whether the contract needs to be renegotiated and the intervention modified for goal achievement.

▶ *Evaluation phase* (Chapter 10): The client system and the social worker analyze the accomplishment of goals and objectives and identify positive, negative, and unanticipated changes. They discuss whether the client system is satisfied with services and is ready to move toward termination or desires a different service.

▶ *Termination phase* (Chapter 11): The client system and the social worker revisit the change process and goal accomplishments, discuss maintenance of positive gains, and discuss ending the collaboration and the possibility of future contact should the need arise.

Quality Assurance

In addition to professional values and ethics, knowing how to help requires social workers to possess both relevant knowledge and practice skills. For example, in the child welfare field, obtaining permanent homes for children removed from their parents requires knowledge and practice skills specific enough to address the needs of the individual children (micro focus), the needs of their parents and extended families (micro and mezzo focus), and the needs of the organizations and communities serving and supporting them (mezzo and macro focus). Thus, central reasons for gathering empirical evidence and engaging in evaluation include:

▶ Maintaining quality service delivery for the client system
▶ Documenting service quality for different stakeholders such as program directors, funding sources, policymakers, and future client systems
▶ Establishing empirical evidence about the effectiveness of different practice models and intervention strategies for meeting different client system's needs

Specifically, client systems want to know whether they have benefited by General Method intervention and if the services were worth the time, effort, and money spent. Generalist practitioners want to know which interventions are likely to help with what problems for which client systems under what conditions and with what evaluation protocols to show the results. Program directors want to know how well specific interventions serve particular client systems and how effective and cost efficient they are. Policymakers, governmental bodies, administrators, and funding sources want to know comparative information about the efficacy, efficiency, and costs of the services and the operation of the entire program or agency. The general public and prospective client systems want to know whether particular interventions actually help individuals, families, groups, organizations, and communities accomplish goals.

Accountability

Another reason for engaging in empirical evaluation is to demonstrate professional accountability in delivering services and assuring that client systems actually benefit. In addition, empirical documentation is used to assure that service delivery is in compliance with applicable laws and policies about client entitlements, confidentiality, privacy of records, occupational and health safety, affirmative action, and any specific conditions for service delivery. Empirical documentation provides evidence that service delivery funds are appropriately spent.

Goal Attainment

Finally, empirically based practice allows social workers to document attainment of client system goals. Client systems and other stakeholders such as program directors and funding sources want to know:

▶ Is the client system better off now than before the intervention?

▶ Were all of the targeted goals and objectives reached? If yes, how well? If no, what were the barriers to goal accomplishment?

▶ What environmental conditions were essential in reaching goal accomplishment?

Brief History and Scope of Practice Research in Social Work

The emergence of empirically based practice in social work is not new. In the early twentieth century, Mary Richmond's (1917) *Social Diagnosis* represented the culmination of seventeen years of practice and research. At mid-century, Ann Shyne's 1948 research question *Can planned short-term intervention be effective?* and her later research questions about placement prevention and family reunification yielded positive results supporting brief intervention services to children in their own homes (Shyne, 1959, 1973). Florence Hollis's (1964) *Social Casework: A Psychosocial Therapy* summarized content analyses of written and taped case records that identified techniques used in direct work with clients and demonstrated the relationship among psychosocial study, diagnosis, and intervention.

These and other early practitioners/researchers set the stage for the 1970s emergence of a more scientific approach to practice research in keeping with new developments in the evaluation field. The classic *Evaluation of Social Intervention* (Mullen & Dumpson, 1972) included the known field experiments of social work interventions conducted through 1971. This book, in turn, led to a national conference that resulted in the first major call for the profession to move toward empirically based practice. Other authors in the 1970s (Fisher, 1973; Jayaratne & Levy, 1979) underscored the importance of carefully documented research to determine the effective-

GRACE ABBOTT (1878–1939), chief of the U.S. Children's Bureau, was instrumental in establishing laws providing the first federal grants-in-aid for social welfare purposes and promoting maternal and child health. She also incorporated research into legislative policymaking and developed systems for collecting data from states about child labor, delinquency, and dependency. While a faculty member at the University of Chicago School of Social Service Administration, Abbott served as editor of *Social Service Review*.

ness of social work practice and advocated that social workers seek empirical evidence, measure client progress, and document intervention outcomes in order to provide objective rather than subjective evidence and guides to practice. Gambrill (1999) brought home the importance of evidence-based practice when she noted that social workers would not want to be treated by practitioners whose intervention methods were solely derived from their idiosyncratic expertise, opinions from colleagues, findings from one or two outcome studies, or findings from studies documenting only consumer satisfaction with services.

By the turn of the twenty-first century, the premise that social work practice should be based on empirically tested and verified knowledge has become widely accepted and endorsed by many leaders in the profession (Rosen & Proctor, 2003). Concerns, however, still persist that research-derived evidence may not be easily accessed by practitioners or easily translated into practice efforts (Gambrill, 2001). Recently, Gilgun (2005, p. 52) identified the four cornerstones of evidence-based practice in social work as consisting of research and theory, practice wisdom and values, person of the practitioner, and what client systems bring to practice situations. She noted that how to use research evidence and what types of research are available remain important issues, along with encouraging social workers to conduct research. Today, a wide range of practice research activities is contributing to building empirical evidence for social work practice and much effort is being directed into delineating practice guidelines in multiple fields of social work practice (Rosen & Proctor, 2003). Many of these activities include the process of developing and documenting:

▶ Socio-demographic and cultural profiles of social work client systems
▶ Theoretical frameworks that conceptualize the link between intervention and the meaning of the client system problems, needs, strengths, and resources
▶ The practice model and the operational procedures in a selected intervention
▶ The propositions about the client system problem(s) and needs in relation to the client system goals and objectives
▶ The process for determining and selecting appropriate research design for monitoring and evaluating the selected client system outcomes
▶ The degree of experimental rigor present in the selected evaluation design
▶ The process of monitoring the implementation of the intervention
▶ The criteria and process of participant intervention selection and how individual participants are assigned to different intervention conditions or options
▶ The process and methods of data collection and whether these methods were self-reported or examiner assessed and reported with population norms
▶ The process of selecting variables for monitoring interventions (length of sessions, number of sessions attended, etc.) and assessing intervention impact on client system outcomes
▶ The validity and reliability of instruments measuring client system outcomes
▶ The role of funding sources in the evaluation process and the relationship of the lead investigator to the funding sources
▶ The data analysis and the process of drawing conclusions from findings
▶ The impact of interventions on client system outcomes and their relevance and importance for practitioners, evaluators and researchers, and policymakers

It is important to note that the connection between social work practice and practice evaluation research is a two-way street (Mullen & Streiner, 2006). Evaluation evidence about the type and process of intervention provided to and absorbed by client systems informs practice. However, in order to be relevant and meaningful for client systems, social work practitioners, and the generation of knowledge for future practice, the evaluation must be well executed, informed by actual practice methods, conceptually or theoretically framed, and subjected to public and professional peer scrutiny. Thus, practice in social work includes the following expectations:

1. Practice decisions about intervention will be based on empirically derived interventions that have documented their level of effectiveness and have had their level of effectiveness subjected to professional scrutiny.
2. If untested interventions are being used, they will be evaluated and subjected to some level of professional peer scrutiny.
3. All practice interventions will be automatically subjected to some degree of empirically based evaluation that documents progress and outcomes (Roberts, Yeager, & Regehr, 2006).

Steps in Building Empirical Evidence for Social Work

Cournoyer and Powers (2006, p. 799) suggest that

> whenever possible, practice should be grounded on prior findings that demonstrate empirically that certain actions performed with a particular type of client or client system are likely to produce predictable, beneficial, and effective results . . . and that every client system should be individually evaluated to determine the extent to which the predicted results have been attained as a direct consequence of the practitioner's actions.

Within this context, conducting empirically driven practice and *doing* evidence-based work translates into the following steps (Gibbs & Gambrill, 2002; Sackett, Straus, Richardson, Rosenberg, & Haynes, 2000):

1. Identify the client system's problems, needs, strengths, and resources, and the method of intervention being sought.
2. Formulate answerable questions such as *What is the best way to help client systems with these kinds of problems and needs, and with these kinds of characteristics and value preferences, under these kinds of environmental conditions?*
3. Search, gather, and critically examine the available evidence in light of available scientific information using nationally and internationally recognized websites (see Appendix A).

4. Critically appraise the evidence for its research validity, experimental rigor, impact or the size of effect on client system, meaningfulness to the client system, and practice applicability or usefulness for generalist practice.

It is understood and assumed that all evaluative empirical evidence about interventions can be organized according to their scientific strength. This scientific strength rests on the belief that only rigorous experimental designs applied with randomly selected participants, or participants subjected to random assignment in experimental intervention conditions, have the capability to provide the best evidentiary information about whether it can be claimed that the *intervention is responsible for the client system outcome*. Needless to say, not all practice evaluative efforts have the capability or suitability of being subjected to this degree of experimental rigor. The range of the scientific evaluative rigor in investigations can be seen in Figure 3.1.

These steps do not necessarily create a guide about whether the obtained evidentiary information addressing intervention effectiveness can be applied to the individual client system. The decision about whether to accept or reject evidence and how best to apply the obtained evidence about the intervention's effectiveness rests on the formal working relationship between the generalist practitioner and the client system. Together, the generalist practitioner and the client system consider whether:

▶ The evidenced results about the intervention meet the needs of the client system
▶ There is real access to the interventive services described
▶ The evidence meets the client system's values, characteristics, and preferences
▶ The evidence found can be actually applied to the individual client system

As shown in Figure 3.1, levels of evidence have been organized on the basis of scientific principles for judging evaluation research designs in different studies. These principles do not exclude the importance of multidimensional knowledge in judging the soundness, importance, and efficacy of interventions with different client systems within various environmental conditions. Thus, in intervening, generalist social workers:

▶ Collaboratively work with client systems to identify and prioritize problems and needs while using a strengths-based problem-solving approach to practice
▶ Collaboratively work with client systems to reframe their problems and needs into goals and objectives that can be translated into client system outcomes
▶ Collaboratively work with client systems to translate their unique needs into propositions and questions that can be tested and investigated so that practice evaluation efforts can determine whether client goals have been reached
▶ Use professional expertise to locate the best available evidence that answers questions about client system needs
▶ Collaboratively work with client systems to appraise the collected evidence and weigh the pros and cons of the relevance of the findings to the client system
▶ Use professionally honed practice judgment to assist client systems in critically examining the potential consequences of selecting different interventions used to address identified needs and priorities in light of strengths and resources

FIGURE 3.1 ■ Levels of Empirical Evidence for Judging Intervention Studies

Level 1 (Best Scientific Evidence)

Interventions derived by research studies with most experimental scientific rigor.

Studies that have been subjected to research meta-analysis or quantitative experimental replications using randomized controlled trials (RCTs) that included comparison/control intervention conditions or that have been derived from quantitative analytical studies applied to different environmental conditions and clients with various characteristics or that have been supported by recommendations by a national consensus panel of systematically reviewed randomized or controlled research studies.

Level 2

Interventions derived by research studies that use experimental conditions but need further replication and substantiation of effectiveness under multiple conditions with multiple samples of client systems.

Studies that have been subjected to at least one RCT with a comparative or placebo intervention condition, or multiple studies using multiple time series design, or national consensus panel recommendations based on uncontrolled design findings in which positive client system outcomes show dramatic positive effects of interventions.

Level 3

Interventions derived by research studies that use quasi-experimental conditions and need further experimental testing and replication.

Studies that have been subjected to uncontrolled trials or experimental qualitative and quantitative studies with small samples of least 10 or more subjects, or studies with quasi-experimental group-design conditions or studies with basic pre-post comparisons of client system outcomes, or quasi-experimental studies that have been based on reports of some systematic review or expert consensus, or studies that have used explanatory rigorous single-subject qualitative designs with at least 10 or more subjects.

Level 4 (Least Scientific Evidence)

Interventions derived by research studies or efforts that are usually non experimentally based.

Studies that have been based on practitioners' individual anecdotal case reports; or unsystematic clinical qualitative observations using monitoring and descriptive single-subject qualitative designs, or studies based on program descriptive reports of implementation efforts of the intervention without any or minimal analytic testing of intervention effectiveness.

▶ Use professional skills in educating client systems about options in evaluation strategies for monitoring and documenting change in outcomes

In sum, generalist social workers are expected to:

1. Think critically during the strengths-based problem-solving process found in the General Method phases of engagement, data collection, assessment and contract planning, intervention, evaluation, and termination.

2. Use a multidimensional approach for assessment that is empirically driven and provides some degree of baseline (preintervention) information documenting the extent of the client system's problems, needs, strengths, and resources.
3. Use the selected monitoring and assessment process to track changes in client system outcomes for appraising the impact of the intervention.
4. Become knowledgeable about the different ways, means, and research evaluation methodology for deriving evidence-based interventions.

The Role of Theory in Building Evidence for Practice

All practice interventions and their evaluation processes are enhanced when their underpinning conceptual or theoretical frameworks are made explicit (Marsh, 2004). Such conceptualizations and practice-oriented theories organize ideas and beliefs about how people develop and function, how problems occur, and how problems and people change. They represent conceptual frameworks that practitioners bring to bear in their practice decision making (Berlin & Marsh, 1993). Payne (2005) suggests that practice-oriented theories or conceptual frameworks that underpin practice efforts are used to provide propositions about practice values and beliefs as well as to describe ordered patterns of practice activities, not just simply to deduce propositions about client system problems or to produce evaluation hypotheses about client system outcomes. Some practice-oriented theories are well articulated, especially when the original design of the intervention or delivery of program services is based on explicit social science theory.

For example, Fraser, Nash, Galinsky, and Darwin (2000) developed a practice intervention approach (subsequently translated into a package of program services) that taught social problem solving to young children and their parents. The services were based on human behavior theories about child development, theories of risk and resilience in human functioning, and theories about parenting and childrearing. These theoretical foundations about the nature of problems and intervention approaches necessary to change them were translated into a model of practice intervention. In turn, this practice model was carefully outlined in an intervention (treatment) manual subsequently used for implementing the program services and for replication.

More often, however, programs and interventions are developed in practice settings in such a way that theory or conceptual frameworks driving the practice efforts or services tend to remain implicit (Rossi, Freeman, & Lipsky, 1999), or known only to the practitioners who uniquely use them. To become knowledgeable about creating and using evidence in practice, generalist social workers must assume responsibility for making the implicit explicit by synthesizing literature reviews, conducting joint interviews with experienced practitioners, observing program operation, reviewing program documents, learning to use logic models (conceptual graphic road maps showing how the intervention affects client system outcomes), and documenting their own practice (Alter & Egan, 1997). This process of creating empirical evidence requires that social work practitioners, researchers, and evaluators work together to produce program and practice theory or a detailed description of the relationship between program resources, program activities, and program outcomes in order to show how the program intervention is supposed to bring about the intended change in the client system outcomes (Rossi, Freeman, & Lipsky, 1999, p. 160).

All programs (and thus their interventions and services) are based on some idea about which mechanisms contribute to client system change and why. Therefore, articulating the underpinning conceptual framework or theoretical beliefs about how and in what way the practice efforts are meant to help client system problems is a necessary process for gathering and creating evidentiary knowledge for best practices. Toward this purpose, Marsh (2004) suggests that social workers may find it useful to think about and distinguish among three types of practice theories:

1. *Problem-based theories* focus on explaining the etiology of personal and social problems; the characteristics and conditions that shape or constrain them; and the ways problems change at micro, mezzo, and macro levels. For example, Finney and Moos (1992) discuss that these theories explain how and why problems occur (e.g., substance abuse in adolescents), but do not address how and why selected interventions affect specific client system outcomes.

2. *Theories of intervention or service delivery* specify the processes, resources, and activities used by social work practitioners and client systems to achieve desired outcomes at micro, mezzo, and macro levels of practice. These intervention-oriented theories explain the steps through which the client system change is expected and they lead to specific client system outcomes. For example, Marlatt and Gordon (1985) use cognitive behavior therapy (CBT) for relapse prevention of substance abuse.

3. *Theories of problem-service matching* focus on the interactional fit between client systems needs and interventions at micro, mezzo, and macro levels. These theories address interactional issues that occur when practice guidelines and standards of care mandates come into contact with specific client system needs. To test their effectiveness, these theories and their concepts are translated into specific intervention practice models that are applied to targeted client system problems or needs within standards of care. For example, Smith and Marsh (2002) demonstrate how the process of matching client system needs with intervention can result in a significant reduction in substance use.

Overall, understanding and appreciating the role of theory in the development and application of practice interventions or the conceptualization of client systems' problems and needs allows generalist social workers to:

▶ Consider the underlying beliefs about the cause and effect of different client system problems and needs and their interaction with strengths and resources.
▶ Identify which theories and concepts serve what purpose in assessment, intervention, service delivery processes, and evaluation.
▶ Empirically test intervention models developed from theoretical propositions.

▶ Ultimately influence knowledge and understanding of the nature and evolution of different client system problems in the context of risk and protective factors.

Essential Components of Building Evidence for Practice

Conceptual and Operational Definitions

In addition to identifying the theoretical propositions that underpin social work interventions in service delivery programs, it is essential to ascertain the appropriateness of the intervention based on scientific evidence and practice relevance. In order to accomplish this, all practice concepts, including interventions and outcomes, must be clearly defined using both theoretical concepts and operational actions in behavioral practice terms (Rosen & Proctor, 1978). For example, consider a case in which a social work generalist is working with a client system to increase social support. The client system and the social work generalist conceptually define what is meant by *social support*. Although both may be thinking about increasing personal social support from a spouse or partner, they have to identify the type of personal social support being sought. Are they concerned about more personal time together, less verbal conflict, help with household chores, or child care? Or is the concern about increasing extended family support? Then again, the client system's concerns may be to gain not only personal support but also formal social support involving services from community agencies.

Conceptual definitions usually reflect the mutually agreed-on meaning of the word concept being addressed. Once the social worker and the client system reach agreement about meaning, they can begin addressing the *operational action definition:*

▶ How will this social support be obtained (in goals and intervention plans)?
▶ What measures or observations will be used to collect evidence that the social support is increased?

In other words, after the conceptual definition is collaboratively achieved, the social worker and the client system have to agree on an operational definition of what social support means to the client system, how it will be obtained, and how the client system will convey changes and goal achievement to the social worker. Will the client system be asked to report verbally on a weekly basis about changes in the amount of social support? Will the client system be asked to complete a data-collection instrument (e.g., questionnaire or survey) that asks about the range of social support received *before the intervention* was applied (baseline period) and *during and after the intervention?* Or will the client system be asked to provide written consent for obtaining collateral information about changes in social support from someone else (spouse or partner, or professional)?

Operational definitions focus on types, how, and by what means the socia port can be provided, measured, and changes evaluated. For these definition match those in expected standards of care, the generalist social worker may need to consult the current professional literature to identify how client systems with similar problems may be served so that benefits are obtained. In drawing on this body of evidence, generalist practitioners must go beyond labels to ensure correspondence between the concepts in the professional literature and those in practice with a particular client system (Rosen, Proctor, & Staudt, 1999). In order to do so, generalist social workers need to have a sound understanding of client system outcomes and their relationship to interventions.

■ C O N C E P T 3 . 1

Outcomes refer to any condition that an intervention is intended to affect or change. They are targets toward which intervention is directed.

Outcomes

Client system outcomes are changes or benefits for client systems that are achieved during or after participating in intervention activities. Outcomes may relate to behavior, skills, knowledge, attitudes, values, conditions, or other attributes. They are what participants know, think, or can do; how they behave; or what their condition is following the program. *Ultimate outcomes* refer to those conditions that best address change in client system needs given the presenting problems and resources. Their attainment constitutes justification for rendering intervention a success. However, some client system circumstances call for identifying *intermediate or short-term outcomes* that are prerequisite conditions for achieving ultimate outcomes. Hence, it is critical that accurate conceptual and operational formulations of intermediate and ultimate outcomes take place during intervention planning.

Client system outcomes are also influenced by program service-delivery *inputs, activities, and outputs.* Program inputs include resources dedicated to or consumed by the intervention program and client system. Examples include money, staff and staff time, volunteers and volunteer time, facilities, equipment, and supplies. Inputs for a parent education class might include the hours of staff time spent designing and teaching the class, client system contributions of ideas and time, and social resources such as money and available supports from other sources. Inputs also include constraints on the program such as laws, policy regulations, and funding source requirements.

Program service-delivery *activities* are what the program intervention does with the inputs to fulfill its mission and achieve client system goals and objectives. Activities include intervention types, strategies, and techniques that comprise the program's service methodology. Examples of program activities include sheltering and feeding homeless families and training homeless adults in preparation for seeking jobs.

Program *outputs* are the direct products of service activities and are measured in terms of the volume of work accomplished such as numbers of parenting classes taught and attended, counseling sessions conducted and participated in, educational materials developed and distributed, and the number of client systems served at the micro, mezzo, and macro levels of practice. Program outputs are important because they lead to a desired benefit for client systems. For example, an adult client system has a problem with age-appropriate parenting of children. The desired ultimate outcome for this client system is improved parenting skills. The intermediate outcome is to increase the client system's knowledge of age-appropriate parenting and disciplinary practices. The program output of providing parent education classes could be measured as the numbers of classes held, parents served, and classes actually attended.

Figure 3.2 provides a graphic depiction of the process of getting from input to services to output and client system outcome. As seen in this figure, getting to client system outcomes involves not only problem specification and assessment but also the process of identifying and assessing strengths that can be used in meeting goals and objectives and facilitating ultimate client system outcomes. This strengths-based problem-solving process of the General Method takes into account client system values, personal preferences and expectations, and cultural context. The careful specification of client system outcomes further facilitates assessment and contract planning, program service delivery, and evaluation by optimizing the generalist practitioner's ability to distinguish between desired consequence or outcomes of the intervention and unanticipated consequences or outcomes. In the earlier example, an adult woman reaches the desired parenting outcome of appropriately parenting and disciplining her child. An unintended and unanticipated consequence, however, may be increased marital tension between the parenting couple. This example highlights the need to be vigilant in identifying early indicators of both desired and unintended outcomes in generalist social work practice.

FIGURE 3.2 ■ Practice Approach to Client System Outcomes

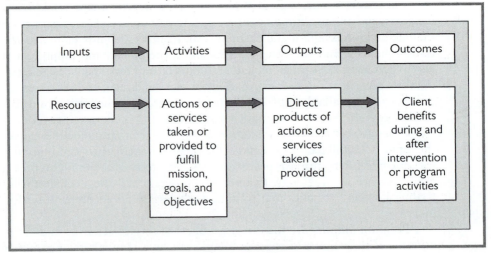

■ CONCEPT 3.2

Interventions are defined as activities and processes that are facilitated by the generalist social worker for the purpose of achieving desired client system outcomes.

Interventions

Without delivering ethical, responsible, and effective intervention (Chapters 8 and 9), there is little basis for expecting that the client system's desired outcomes will be realized. The effectiveness of interventions is determined according to the scientific standards of evidence that form the basis of practice (Rosen & Proctor, 2006). For interventions to be considered part of the evidentiary standards of care in professional practice, they must be scientifically testable and evaluated in a way that clearly shows what works (and what needs improvement), for whom, and under what conditions. As noted earlier, for interventions to be assessed and evaluated scientifically, they must be defined conceptually and operationally. This degree of specification enables the intervention to be applied in the manner intended. Practically speaking, this approach benefits from the development of an intervention protocol or a procedural manual that outlines the conceptual aspects of the intervention and the sequence of action steps to be taken by the generalist social worker and the client system. When practice interventions are well described and converted into specific operational protocols, they are likely to be applied in the manner intended with a certain amount of fidelity and integrity (Yeaton & Sechrest, 1981). This approach facilitates intervention replication and testing under different conditions and with different client systems to assess their impact. That is, the less clearly an intervention is described and the concepts defined, the greater the room for variability and error in interpreting the meaning of the intervention and identifying the actions required for appropriate implementation.

It is critical in evidence-based practice that there be a close correspondence between the way interventions are conceptualized, operationalized, and implemented. To achieve this correspondence, the development of intervention manuals is considered helpful (Fraser, Nash, Galinsky, & Darwin, 2000). In using practice intervention manuals, however, generalist practitioners face the challenge not only of mastering the intervention but also of relying on their knowledge and experience to:

▶ Adapt the content of intervention manuals to specific practice situations.
▶ Evaluate the client system outcomes achieved.
▶ Document the practice process, adaptations, and final outcomes.

Practice Guidelines

Ideally, in an evidence-based approach to social work practice, all interventions become synthesized into scientifically tested practice guidelines. These guidelines will provide social workers with organized and synthesized knowledge about interventions having an established degree of scientific effectiveness in achieving targeted outcomes (Rosen & Proctor, 2006). In the absence of practice evidence that meets the minimum scientific criteria (or Level 1 in Figure 3.1), preliminary guidelines for the strengths-based problem-solving approach of the General Method of social work practice reflect expert-derived information about how and why this particular intervention approach is viewed as helpful with specific client systems.

To move the General Method forward in documenting its effectiveness, generalist social workers are called on to:

▶ Join forces with research-oriented social workers specializing in program and practice evaluation to evaluate General Method interventions.
▶ Engage in critical thinking about research findings and evidence-based decision-making in practice.
▶ Become more knowledgeable and research literate about what constitutes scientific evidence in social work practice (Roberts & Greene, 2002).

Development of a Scientific Approach to Practice

The body of knowledge that informs social work practice is both descriptive and prescriptive in nature. Descriptive knowledge is typically used when a social worker is trying to understand or explain the different phenomena encountered in the practice process. Prescriptive knowledge, on the other hand, is used when the purpose or the goal is to effect a meaningful change in the phenomena observed or outcomes planned. In both cases, the knowledge must withstand the scientific scrutiny of testing and evaluation to be considered evidence according to the rules of science. Thus, in evidence-based practice, the social worker's professional judgment and behavior are guided by distinct but interdependent principles (Gambrill, 1999). First, social workers are expected to seek effectiveness information about interventions so that they can assist their clients in making *an informed decision* about the likelihood that a recommended intervention will actually be helpful. Second, social work practice efforts need to be grounded on prior findings that demonstrate empirically that intervention actions performed with specific client systems are likely to produce beneficial and predictable results. Third, practice efforts with client systems need to be evaluated individually to determine the extent to which the predicted results have been attained as a consequence of practitioner and client system efforts. Fourth, at some later point, interventions need to be subjected to rigorous, experimental evaluations to determine if the scientific claim can be made that the intervention and not something else produced the targeted client system outcomes.

Implicit in these expectations is the assumption that evidence-based practice is a rational systematic process of inquiry and problem solving that involves a series of informed decisions. These decisions are inherently contingent on the retrieval and application of readily available information, the degree of scientific validation of collected information, and professional judgment about the relevance and applicability of the evidence for specific client systems. This process requires using rational systematic decision making about what constitutes evidence and an interactive search strategy employing controlled language designed to increase the probability of locating and evaluating relevant empirical information (Cournoyer & Powers, 2006).

Ethical and Evidentiary Decision-Making Process

Ethical and evidentiary issues are linked through professional codes of ethics and accreditation standards (Gambrill, 2006). For example, the NASW *Code of Ethics* (1999) states that *social workers should critically examine and keep current with emerging knowledge relevant to social work.* Obviously, if social workers are not familiar with the evidence status of various practices and policies, they cannot pass this information on to their clients and honor their obligation for facilitating informed consent with their client systems prior to participating in social work intervention. In turn, if client systems are not sufficiently informed or are actually misinformed, they are deprived of just and fair opportunities for achieving their self-determined outcomes. The ethical obligations and accountability expectations for social work practice are examined in Figure 3.3.

Social work engagement in ethical decision making for delivering evidence-based practice also requires paying close attention to client system preferences, values, and expectations, and how these factors may mesh or conflict with the generalist social worker's own personal and professional value system. Factors such as culture, poverty, socio-economic status, literacy, English language competency, and other environmental factors account in part for differences among client systems in help-seeking behavior and decision making. Also, generalist practitioners need to be aware of prejudice, discrimination, oppression, and racism at micro, mezzo, and macro societal levels and their potential impact on client systems (Chapter 2). In addition, factors of age, gender, ethnicity/race, education, living situation, coping skills, and relationships with others become equally important for client system decision making. Thus, in the process of planning and selecting the intervention, generalist social workers need to bear in mind that best practice evidence may not necessarily work in the same way with all client systems or with similar clients in different environmental contexts.

Who the client system is (in respect to possessing micro, mezzo, and macro risks and protective factors) and what critical information this system brings about the presenting problems, strengths, and resources, and collateral issues are critical in (1) assessing the client system's scope of problem(s), (2) making decisions, and (3) searching for alternative intervention options. In brief, generalist practitioners are expected to use the following steps in working with empirically derived practice evidence within the strengths-based problem-solving approach of the General Method (see Chapters 5 through 11):

1. Engage the client system in identifying, defining, and assessing the problems, needs, strengths, and resources that are present in seeking problem resolution.

FIGURE 3.3 ■ Evidence-Based Social Work Practice Obligations

Social Work Ethical Obligations	Social Work Expected Actions
1. Assist clients while avoiding harm.	Access and become informed about research evidence that shows that selected treatment or intervention is likely to benefit the client.
2. Maximize client self-determination and autonomy.	Provide clients with information about risks and benefits of recommended approach to intervention. Accurately describe available status of evidence, consider the consequences of this evidence for clients' anticipated desired outcomes, and assist clients with considering consequences of alternative methods of intervention.
3. Respect and support the integrity of client decision making.	Avoid coercion in trying to co-opt client decision making and involve clients in weighing the pros and cons, or risks and benefits, of recommended interventions. Assist clients in envisioning the possible anticipated and unanticipated consequences of their choices. Model the use of reflective rather than directive practice approach unless a client's life is in danger or in crisis.
4. Provide competent practice methods.	Become knowledgeable and learn skills that reflect an evidence-based approach to practice and evaluation of practice. Keep up to date with reading and learning practice and evaluation-related knowledge.
5. Provide accountable services and practice.	From the beginning to the end of delivering services, engage clients in ongoing feedback about progress and discussion about whether targeted outcomes are being pursued and met. Assist clients in regular critical examination of strengths and barriers in selected actions. Provide clients with any new information about intervention as it becomes available.
6. Promote social justice.	With client permission, advocate on behalf of individual clients for changes in their environmental systems that contribute to individual problems. For all clients, become an active advocate for changing societal conditions that contribute to personal problems.
7. Engage in lifelong learning to maintain professional competence.	Become proactive in own assessment of professional needs, knowledge, and skills. Engage in appropriate professional peer consultation and supervision. Become knowledgeable about other allied disciplinary knowledge that is relevant for own practice skill development and client outcome application. Participate in continuing education.

Source: Adapted from Gambrill (2006), p. 226.

2. Provide the client system with an informed consent statement about planned intervention recommendations.
   • Include evidentiary information about the proposed intervention.
   • Assist the client system in weighing the presented evidence.
   • Assist the client system in exploring available alternatives and consequences.
3. Utilize empirical literature and research to facilitate collaborative decisions.
4. Use a systematic approach in developing practice hypotheses that can be tested by an intervention matched to the client system's problems and needs.
   • Start with careful assessment of the *person-in-environment* situation.
   • Assist the client system in setting short-term and long-term goals with measurable, observable objectives aligned with intervention task activities.
   • Develop and agree on an individualized evaluation process.
   • Engage in monitoring progress toward goals with frequent review and modification of services as needed to accomplish goals and objectives.

These decision-making steps also involve decisions about how and what kind of questions the social worker asks to *understand the client system problem* and to *judge what available evidence exists to solve the problem.* Both questions play a role in the social worker's recommended intervention options. The knowledge-related aspects of client system problems contained in the General Method of practice and what can be done about them are explored in detail in Chapters 5 through 11. Therefore, the following section primarily focuses on how social work practitioners can *formulate questions for searching and learning about available evidence* for different intervention approaches.

Identifying Sources for Building Evidence in Practice Information

As noted in Chapter 1, generalist social workers serve individuals, families, groups, organizations, and communities. They assist with psychosocial, behavioral, and social problems; advocate for social justice; and plan and administer social policies and community programs. In view of the profession's mission and broad scope, values and ethics, and the multiplicity of practice roles and functions, generalist social workers often find it challenging to reach consensus about best evidence to resolve client systems' problems. In searching for evidence to support decisions and actions, they may need to draw on the knowledge and practice-related information generated not only by social workers but also by other professionals in other disciplines.

To support the development of social work knowledge during the last two decades, the National Institute of Mental Health (NIMH) has provided funding to create and sustain several research-oriented organizations and Social Work Research Development Centers (SWRDC). These organizations are listed in Appendix A.

To start searching websites and journals blindly is rarely useful, considering that it takes time to synthesize the information and decide whether it is actually relevant

FIGURE 3.4 ■ Steps in Searching for Evidence-Based Practice Information

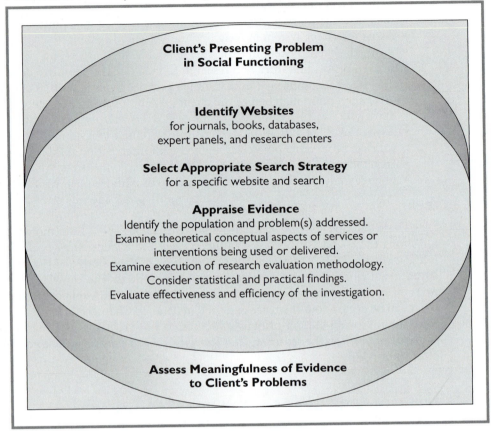

Client's Presenting Problem
in Social Functioning

Identify Websites
for journals, books, databases,
expert panels, and research centers

Select Appropriate Search Strategy
for a specific website and search

Appraise Evidence
Identify the population and problem(s) addressed.
Examine theoretical conceptual aspects of services or
interventions being used or delivered.
Examine execution of research evaluation methodology.
Consider statistical and practical findings.
Evaluate effectiveness and efficiency of the investigation.

Assess Meaningfulness of Evidence
to Client's Problems

to practice decision making. As exemplified in Figure 3.4, constructing well-formulated, answerable questions that are searchable is both a technical skill and an art.

The purpose of a search is to obtain a reasonably accurate answer to the practice question of concern. Thus, it is important to know what one is searching for and to prioritize search sources. Often, it is useful to start with reference sources and research reviews to identify model programs, model intervention guidelines, professional journals for specific topic areas, and government and other agency websites for informational reports.

Questioning

Evidence-based practice requires a willingness to say *I do not know* and acknowledge that there is often a gap between what is known and what is needed in the General Method to assist client systems in attaining their preferred outcomes while avoiding harm (Gambrill, 2006). Thus, a key step in beginning to search for evidence is translating the information needed about intervention practices and policy decisions into answerable search questions that facilitate a productive search in various databases. Well-formulated search questions need to be about problems important to client systems.

Gibbs (2003) refers to such questions as COPES questions in that they are client-oriented questions that are of practical importance to guide evidence searches. As part of developing a searchable query about intervention effectiveness, questions can be organized in four parts for conducting searches (originally developed by Sackett, Straus, Richardson, Rosenberg, & Haynes, 2000; adapted by Yeager & Roberts, 2006, pp. 51–52). These four parts are:

1. *Who is the client system and what problem is being addressed?*
   First, the generalist practitioner needs to consider who the client system is and what unique characteristics this client system possesses. Second, the practitioner needs to identify the main problem area for which goals, objectives, and outcomes are going to be developed and intervention sought. This process may require in-depth meetings with the client system as well as proceeding further along from the engagement phase, to the data-collection phase, to the assessment and contract planning phase of the General Method in order to narrow down and prioritize what intervention will actually be researched for its effectiveness in goal achievement.

2. *What intervention?*
   As noted earlier, once the generalist practitioner and the client system have settled on goals and objectives, work can proceed in determining which intervention is likely to be most effective in resolving the client system's identified problem(s). The searchable question seeks information about intervention effectiveness and alternative ways of intervening. It is important to remember that there is seldom one single intervention that is best for all client systems. In this search process, the generalist practitioner needs to remember: *Who is the client? What is the scope of the problem? Does the scope of the problem and need reach across micro, mezzo, and macro environmental contexts?*

3. *Which alternative interventions?*
   Once the generalist social worker begins considering the intervention in relation to the scope of the client system's problems, needs, strengths, and resources across various contexts, more questions arise: *What is considered the standard of care? How does usual care differ from an alternate intervention, doing nothing, a control group, or being on a waiting list?* This comparative approach is then built into the search process.

4. *What client system outcome(s)?*
   Last, it is important to have a client system outcome in mind. The outcome is agreed on by the generalist practitioner and the client system and needs to be observable or measurable by some means to determine success. For example, consider a micro client system—adults with schizophrenia experiencing problems with substance abuse. What are the goals of intervention or outcomes for these individuals: to reduce addictive behavior or to prevent relapse or both? For a mezzo client system—a group of high-risk adolescents struggling with juvenile delinquency—is the

group's outcome to increase the youths' conflict management skills or school participation or both? For a macro client system—an advisory community group of representatives from different human service agencies—is the goal to inform the community about their collective needs or to take social action to reduce social injustice or something else?

These search-related questions contain several common elements that can be used to guide the generalist practitioner in searching for relevant practice evidence:

► The type of client system
► The type and scope of the client system problem
► The targeted intervention deemed helpful
► The type of alternate intervention actions available
► The client system goals being sought

In order to learn how to formulate search questions, Gambrill (2006) and Gibbs (2003) recommend that such questions be formulated in very specific ways. Examples of these different kinds of search questions that serve various purposes are provided here:

1. *Effectiveness question:* For parenting adults with substance-abuse problems who receive parent education services compared to wait-listed participants, which results in better parenting skills, parenting knowledge, and nurturing of children?

2. *Prevention question:* For high school teens at risk for pregnancy who are exposed to a Think It Over curriculum program compared to other high school health class participants, which teens have more knowledge of birth-control methods and/or report more pregnancies?

3. *Assessment question:* For elderly adults with depression and memory problems who complete a screening test for depression compared to those completing the *DSM-IV* short mental health status examination, which assessment or measurement approach best discriminates between depression and dementia?

4. *Description question:* For task groups of employment managers with structured leadership compared to such task groups with unstructured leadership, which task groups are more likely to accomplish their selected task goals efficiently?

5. *Prediction question:* For training programs designed for health professionals with interdisciplinary training in developmental disabilities compared to programs with multidisciplinary training, which programs are likely to result in a more effective service delivery for individuals with developmental disabilities?

6. *Risk question:* For mothers evidencing abusive behavior toward their children who complete the Child Endangerment Risk Assessment Protocol (CERAP) measure of risk assessment compared to those completing a clinical interview assessment, which measure better predicts risk of future abuse of children?

7. *Harm question:* In high-risk communities with a high proportion of liquor stores per capita in one census track compared to communities with a low proportion of liquor stores per census track, which communities show a greater proportion of violent crimes per census track?

8. *Cost-benefit question:* For homeless shelters that provide individual clients with case management services compared to those shelters without case management, which shelters are more cost effective in reducing homelessness?

■ **CONCEPT 3.3**

Search questions are formulated by separating them into four components:

1. Describe the client system type with what kind of problem.
2. Indicate who gets what intervention or action.
3. Specify an alternative or what kind of alternative intervention or action.
4. Specify what kind of outcome this intervention produces.

Searching

Searching effectively and efficiently for empirically based information related to practice is key to evidence-based practice. Preparing well-formed search questions facilitates the search process. Every search involves identifying important search terms for locating the requested information. Different databases, however, require different ways of inputting information and use different quality filters for conducting searches. *Quality filters* are specific terms that a particular database recognizes in retrieving the information being researched. Gibbs (2003) calls these MOLES (*m*ethodology-*o*riented *l*ocators for *e*vidence *s*earch). For example, a social work practitioner may be interested in *child maltreatment* for which other filters may be *child abuse* or *child neglect*. Using *and* retrieves articles with both terms (child abuse and child neglect), whereas using *or* retrieves all articles with either term (child abuse or child neglect). The term *not* excludes materials containing certain words. Parentheses can be used to group words such as (abuse and neglect). Brackets or quotation marks may need to be used with certain databases. For those just starting out in learning to search on the Internet, investing time in learning from a librarian is time well spent.

Analyzing

Analyzing information requires critical thinking: "*There are always many different opinions and conventions concerning any one problem or subject matter*" (Popper, 1994, p. 39). Critical thinking involves purposeful thought in which one uses standards such as clarity and fairness and carefully examines implicit conceptual beliefs and explicit operational actions in order to arrive at well-reasoned observations (Gambrill, 2006). Critical thinkers are aware that there may be many legitimate points of view, each of which may yield some level of insight. Critical thinking examines information by considering the following questions:

► Is this information, claim, or evidence accurate?
► What critical tests have been performed?
► What biases are evident in results or to what extent are the results free of any bias?

▶ What values are supported by the interventive strategy?

▶ Have the results been replicated? If so, how and with what results?

▶ How representative were the samples of participants selected?

▶ Who is presenting the results and for what purpose?

▶ What measuring instruments were used? Are these reliable and valid?

▶ Are there vested interests apparent in presenting the conclusions being drawn?

▶ Have any facts been omitted?

▶ Are there any alternative explanations for the findings?

Critical thinking for analyzing evidence also requires a certain amount of skepticism. This skepticism values critique, public transparency, and scrutiny. It tolerates ambiguity, looks for alternative possibilities and goals, values rationality and systematic process, is deliberate in uncovering goals and the process of obtaining goals, and considers evidence against initial views (Glathorn & Baron, 1991). Analyzing evidence thus requires critical thought, flexibility, and keen interest in discovering mistakes in thinking. Consider the statement: *"In our infinite ignorance we are all equal"* (Popper, 1992, p. 50). This statement reflects an attitude for, belief in, and respect for the intrinsic worth of all human beings, the value of learning and truth without self-interest, and opinions that differ from one's own (Nickerson, 1988–1989, p. 507).

Besides critical thinking, generalist social workers need to be able to communicate effectively in analyzing evidence. Clear language is important whether speaking or writing (Perkins, 1992). Client systems, for example, will not understand jargon or garbled sentences. Clear communication requires use of a language (English, Spanish, Chinese, etc.) in accord with agreed-on meanings. If terms are not clear, confused discussion may result from assuming "one word, one meaning." For example, although social work practitioners may know what they mean by using a term such as *abuse* or *empowerment,* consider the different definitions or perceptions these words may elicit from client systems depending on their age, gender, and other characteristics that provide their frames of reference. That is not to say, however, that in analyzing evidence, one should spend enormous amounts of time defining terms. Rather, what is needed is *starting where the client system is* in the identification and definition of the meaning of the nature of problem(s); engaging the client system in a critical discussion while paying attention to the client system's diverse needs (personal, developmental, cultural, situational); and then testing the conceptual propositions through empirical means to uncover language and perception confusions or fallacies. Examples of misleading influences in language include (Gambrill, 2006, p. 113):

▶ *Conviction through repetition:* One believes something because one often hears it reported. For example, *There are jobs that no one but immigrants will take.*

▶ *Jargoning:* Vague or very specialized terms are used to conceal ignorance or impress others. For example, *The client's ego-defenses are the cause.*

▶ *Misleading metaphors:* The phrase *War on Drugs* is used as a way to describe intervention efforts to decrease substance abuse.

▶ *Emotional buzzwords:* The phrase *Just Say No* is used as a way to guide intervention efforts with teens. Such words may arouse affect rather than guide.

▶ *Uninformative labels:* Think about the various controversies and the consequences of using the following labeling statements. The client system is a group of *illegal aliens,* or a community of *left-wing organizations.*

▶ *Assuming one word, one meaning:* Consider, for example, the word *empowerment.* Give examples of at least three different meanings and how these meanings could differ based on different client system characteristics.

▶ *Vague terms:* Consider the words *uncommunicative, unstable,* and *difficult* and the different meanings that can be attributed to these words.

▶ *Reifying:* One mistakenly assumes that a word concept corresponds to something real. For example, consider the natural statement of fact, *John's height is 6 feet tall.* Now consider the reified statement, *Mary says John's height is 6 feet tall.*

Knowledge of these communicative or language-related fallacies can help social workers understand how evidence is perceived. Gibbs and Gambrill (1999) have identified seven fallacies that practitioners have a tendency to fall into when considering evidence about intervention effectiveness:

1. *Relying on case example:* Drawing conclusions about many client systems from one or a few unrepresentative individuals
2. *Relying on testimonials:* Accepting claims that a method is effective based on one's own experience
3. *Being vague:* Using nonspecific descriptions of problems and outcomes in a way that makes it impossible to determine whether progress has occurred or to replicate findings
4. *Assuming soft-hearted means soft-headed:* Mistakenly believing that being empathic and caring is not compatible with rational scientific practice
5. *Relying on newness or tradition:* Accepting an assertion that what helps client systems is based on it being new, cutting edge, or traditional
6. *Appealing to authority:* Assuming that evidence about the intervention's helpfulness is true because it is based on the expertise and authority of the person making the argument instead of critical examination of empirical evidence
7. *Overanchoring or not making sufficient adjustment:* Tending to base estimates of client system behavior on initial pieces of information and not adjusting these estimates in light of new evidence

Types of Research Studies

Being informed about different kinds of research and their advantages and disadvantages, including their biases, assists social workers in drawing on findings in an informed and ethical manner. Research studies differ in purpose, the questions they raise and investigate, and the likelihood that the method used may provide accurate information about the questions and hypotheses being studied. Examples include the following:

▶ *Analytic studies* are studies designed to make *cause-and-effect* inferences about specified hypotheses or variable relationships—for example, about the relationship between poverty and child abuse. Some analytic studies are *experimental* with intervention manipulated in such a way that specific groups of participants receive the intervention while other groups receive traditional services, are wait-listed, or receive a comparative intervention. Some are randomized trials, whereas others are nonrandomized trials. For example, see a randomized clinical trial of cognitive group intervention with adolescents of depressed parents (Clarke et al., 2001).

▶ *Descriptive studies* provide information about prevalence and incidence of client system problems. They describe the state of affairs of a problem, such as child abuse or domestic violence, in a given environmental context. For example, see a study about prevalence of AIDS in young men (Valleroy et al., 2000).

▶ *Prospective studies* are longitudinal studies in which participants are selected by particular means and followed over a period of time. Some are also partially analytical and descriptive. For example, see studies that examine the effectiveness of public support for child care using Head Start or Early Head Start services: www.acf.hhs.gov.

▶ *Retrospective studies* investigate events that have already occurred in relation to a present problem. Information in these studies is collected through recall or memory of participants or examination of case records. For example, see a study on the relationship between child abuse and teen pregnancy (Boyer & Fine, 1992).

▶ *Contemporary comparison studies* investigate groups of participants based on their experience with risk factors at the same time they are being compared. For example, see a study on child abuse potential of parents with a history of substance abuse disorder (Ammerman, Kolko, Kirisci, Blackson, & Dawes, 1999).

These and the following study types produce different degrees of research methodology control of study biases and varying *levels of evidence* (see Figure 3.1). Understanding this idea is integral to the analysis and interpretation of findings and their application in generalist practice. This idea includes understanding that different kinds of research evidence or findings related to certain kinds of questions offer different degrees of methodological control over research study biases and limit the conclusions that can be inferred. This degree of control over all aspects of evaluation is reflected in the most rigorous experimental studies and randomized trials to the least controlled studies using single-case designs, expert-based opinions, or focus groups (see Figure 3.5).

In *experimental* studies, such as randomized clinical trials, it is expected that participants will be grouped into different intervention conditions on the basis of a mathematical random assignment procedure. Typically, these studies use an experimental group-based design in which some participants (e.g., youths) receive the specified intervention (e.g., social skills training) while others receive controlled conditions. The controlled conditions can involve giving a placebo (instead of target intervention); placing *control* participants on a waiting list while they are being evaluated on the same designated outcome (e.g., social skills) and then receive the intervention at a later point; providing them with a different intervention such as the typical standard of current care (case management and referral for similar training); or providing

FIGURE 3.5 ■ Degree of Control over Methodological Application in Studies

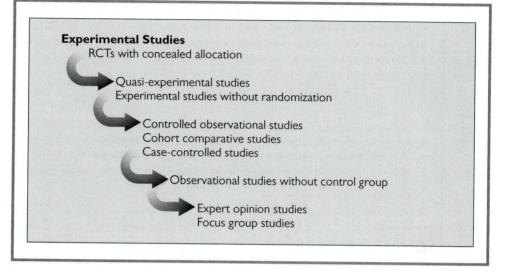

them with a comparative package of interventions (e.g., social skills training and talk therapy). The participants in the controlled conditions serve as the comparison or control group in the study. Randomization of participants into the different intervention conditions assures a fair and mathematically known selection process for each group condition. Further, concealing the allocation of participants into different intervention conditions from participants, data collectors, or facilitators of the intervention conditions protects against bias that can affect the scientific interpretation of experimental findings. Without having a comparison or control group condition, it is not possible to conclude logically or rationally that the intervention rather than something else was responsible for the client system outcome, and concealed allocation of different conditions further assures that process.

To become skilled in assessing and understanding the evidence derived from experimental studies, the generalist practitioner needs to be able to answer the questions in Figure 3.6. Although it is very difficult to carry out experiments in the natural environments in which people live, it is important that such studies be pursued.

In *quasi-experimental studies,* the allocation of participants to intervention or controlled conditions in the research design is arranged by the researcher but without randomization or concealed allocation of the conditions. Thus, selection bias and other biases pertaining to the internal validity of designs affect how findings can be interpreted (see research methodology texts such as Rubin & Babbie, 2001).

It is important to note that the more the evaluation design departs from a true experimental approach (which has randomly selected participants who are randomly allocated to experimental intervention and controlled conditions while measuring client system outcomes before and after the intervention conditions are applied), the more biases enter into the investigative process and limit the scientific value of inference. For example, in such studies that are *natural experiments,* there is typically a

FIGURE 3.6 ■ Assessing Quality Criteria in Experimental Studies

Questions for Assessing the Scientific Rigor in Experimental Studies

▶ How were the participants assigned to intervention or treatment conditions?
▶ Was the assignment by a random method or by something else?
▶ Was the intervention allocation concealed, and from whom?
▶ Were all the participants in the evaluation reasonably similar in their characteristics and prognostic criteria or reasons for seeking the intervention?
▶ Were the eligibility criteria for participation in the intervention specified?
▶ Were the care providers blinded to intervention conditions?
▶ Were the research evaluation questions or hypotheses clearly outlined?
▶ Was the intervention conceptually or theoretically and operationally defined?
▶ Was the purpose of the evaluation relevant to participants' needs or problems?
▶ Were the instruments or tools used to assess and measure client outcomes valid and reliable?
▶ Were the procedures for data collection from participants noninvasive and nonreactive?
▶ Did the results describe the procedural steps for intervention and controlled conditions?
▶ Did the analytical statistical results describe the characteristics of the participants and their needs?
▶ Were the findings statistically significant, practically meaningful, and theoretically important?
▶ Did the analyses explore attrition of participants and its impact on findings?
▶ Did the authors address alternate or rival explanations of their findings?
▶ Can the study make a reasonable scientific claim that the intervention influenced the client system's outcomes based on its overall experimental rigor?

lack of control over assignment of participants into the intervention and controlled conditions. In these studies, different groups of participants are recruited because they *naturally* exist in their different conditions. For instance, consider studies about children's exposure to lead and the consequences of that condition to children's development. Some children happen to live in a lead environment (the experimental condition), whereas other children live in a nonlead environment (the control condition). By careful selection of study participants (usually performed by matching various characteristics) these two groups of children can be compared on the impact of lead on their development. This example and other natural experiments have analytic and descriptive components.

Cohort studies are similar to natural experiments because they also assess cohort groups of participants exposed to certain situations (domestic violence, hurricanes, disasters). These cohort groups are followed and compared on various selected outcomes over time. Although cohort groups cannot be assigned to experimental conditions by random means, they can be randomly selected from an identifiable group of people who have some important condition that is valuable to examine (e.g., population groups who seek social support services following a disaster and the effect that different interventions may have on their physical and mental health over a period of time). Due to lack of random assignment, cohort studies are prone to methodological biases. They are, however, important in identifying risks and resiliencies of cohort group participants.

Case-controlled studies have a small degree of experimental control of what happens to participants. They are retrospective observational studies that examine the relationship between certain characteristics of participants and some past occurring event. For example, one case-controlled study reported on a relationship between the drug diethylstilbestrol (DES) given in the past to pregnant women and their subsequent likelihood of developing vaginal cancer (Herbst, Ulfelder, & Poskanzer, 1971). This important study used eight women with cervical cancer, of whom seven took the drug DES during their pregnancy as the case group (experimental condition) and 32 women who did not use DES during pregnancy as the control group to draw conclusions about the likelihood of developing cancer.

Cross-sectional studies take a snapshot at one point of time in the cross-section of participants' behavior or attitudes and draw inferences about their behaviors or attitudes on the basis of the observed relationships among different variables. For example, such studies may be used to describe various relationships between client system problems and certain characteristics. Since such studies tend to be correlational studies, they lack the ability to determine which variable occurred first (or could have been the cause) and which came second (or could have been the outcome). For example, examine the national alcohol survey studies conducted by the National Institute of Alcohol Abuse and Alcoholism (NIAAA) of the National Institutes of Health (www.arg.org/studies.html#NAS).

Pre-post studies, called before-and-after studies, have a minimal ability to provide information about the cause-and-effect relationship between an intervention and client system outcomes unless the evaluation included some form of control group condition. Pre-post studies are considered essential precursors for conducting more costly quasi-experimental or experimental studies as they show whether participants changed in the expected (hypothesized) direction and how much they changed. For example, see a study that tested a violence prevention curriculum with middle school students (Durant, Treiber, Getts, McCloud, Linder, & Woods, 1996).

Case-series studies describe selected characteristics of a series of case examples. Due to lack of comparison, no assumptions can be made about causes. A case report is essentially a descriptive anecdotal report or a description of a single-case client system. At a minimum, the practitioner examining a case report needs to ask many of the following questions in order to judge their utility (Center for Reviews and Dissemination, University of York, U.K. www.york.ac.uk/inst/crd/pdf/crd4_ph5.pdf):

▶ Is the case study based on a representative sample selected from a relevant population? Or is the individual representative of others with similar problems?
▶ How was the single case selected and on what criteria?
▶ Are the subjects in this case report similar in the progression of their problem?
▶ Was the intervention systematically applied?
▶ Were client system outcomes assessed using objective tools or measures?

▶ If comparisons are being made, is there a sufficient and clear description of the process on which comparisons are being made?

Just as there are many questions to consider about what it takes to provide sound intervention, there are many important questions to ask about issues that can result in harm to participants. For example, Petrosino, Turpin-Petrosino, and Finkenauer (2000) presented a *meta-analysis* (a study using a statistical procedure for combining data from multiple studies; see more information on the procedure at www .edres.org/meta/) of seven randomized experiments that investigated the effect of the intervention program called *Scared Straight*. All seven studies found that this program was statistically and practically harmful in that the experimental group of offending teens exposed to prison life and interaction with incarcerated offenders had statistically significant higher recidivism rates than the control groups of offending teens not exposed to the program conditions. As this example illustrates, practitioners are expected to use questions (Guyatt & Rennie, 2002) found in Figure 3.7 to assess studies' risks for causing harm.

Applying and Evaluating

Each client system is unique, undoubtedly differing in many ways from the descriptions in various studies. Some client systems may not actually reflect the characteristics commonly observed among members of targeted populations that participate in evaluations. Others may not respond favorably to service approaches usually deemed effective under certain conditions or in a laboratory setting. Therefore, as generalist social workers search for evidence and locate information about intervention effectiveness, in addition to reviewing research empirical findings and considering individual client system needs, they also need to consider authority-based recommendations from experts and professional organizations to identify information relevant to the client system under consideration. Further caution is indicated as interventions may have been tested only with small samples of client systems or under different environmental conditions. Thus, the generalist practitioner needs to remember that the client system under consideration may not necessarily share the same characteristics.

Given the possibility of client systems differing from study participants, having a solid foundation of empirical evidence does not necessarily guarantee that a given intervention will meet the needs of a particular client system. Therefore, after identifying the evidence and locating an array of alternative interventions with some level of empirical support, the generalist practitioner must select the intervention that appears to be most relevant for meeting the client system's unique needs and goals. In this process, the practitioner and the client system appraise the evidence together. They discuss the risks and benefits of using the identified intervention against alternatives. They also examine the anticipated consequences of using alternatives, and eventually agree on the best available intervention given the client system's needs, strengths, goals, and objectives. Specifically, in this appraisal process, using critical thinking skills for decision making and assessment in the General Method of social

FIGURE 3.7 ■ Questions for Assessment of Harm in Studies

Are the results valid?

▶ Did the experimental and control groups begin the investigation with similar prognosis for selected outcomes?

▶ Did the study analyses adjust or analyze differences in the baseline measures of outcomes between experimental and control groups?

▶ Were the participants in the experimental and control groups similar in descriptive characteristics and baseline outcome measures?

▶ Were the experimental and control group participants in different treatment conditions?

▶ Were the outcomes measured in the same way in groups being compared?

▶ Was the follow-up sufficiently complete?

What are the results?

▶ How strong is the association between treatment condition exposure and the outcome?

▶ How precise is the estimate of risk?

How can results be applied to client system care?

▶ Were study clients similar to the clients under consideration?

▶ Was the duration of treatment and/or follow-up adequate based on what is known about "standard of care"?

▶ What was the magnitude of risk for participants in the study compared to clients under consideration?

▶ What is likely to happen if the exposure of current clients stopped?

work practice, the generalist practitioner examines the fit between the empirical evidence and the client system's:

▶ Unique problem(s)—severity, duration, and co-occurring conditions

▶ Strengths—motivation, capacity, preferences, and knowledge and use of resources and supports

▶ Environmental, cultural, and other diversity effects

▶ Knowledge and awareness that a problem exists

Obviously, it is not realistic to expect a perfect fit between an empirically supported intervention and the needs of a particular client system. If there are sound, logically derived reasons for *not applying* the evidence-based intervention (e.g., a reason based on knowledge of culture, local community needs or setting, prior experience, or ethical reasons), the practitioner is expected to supplement, modify, or adapt the most appropriate and best supported intervention approach with knowledge drawn from practice and experience. It is important to realize, however, that adaptations and modifications of interventions carry risks about which client systems need to be informed and an evaluation needs to be performed. A number of sources provide more information about methodological aspects of practice evaluation with different client systems (Bloom, Fischer, & Orme, 2003; Roberts & Greene, 2002).

Common Strategies for Engaging in Practice Evaluation

Social workers use a variety of evaluative strategies and approaches to identify the client system's beginning or baseline needs, goals, and objectives and to evaluate the extent of changes taking place during and after service provision. The strategies most commonly used by generalist practitioners include using rapid assessment instruments (RAIs), developing client system focused measures that provide self-observation data, and applying single-subject research designs (that meet the standards of generating Level 1 and Level 2 empirical evidence for judging practice effectiveness) (see Figure 3.1). These measuring strategies are used to

▶ Assess the client system's initial presentation of the extent and severity of problems and needs and the extent and amount of the strengths, assets, and resources available for strengths-based problem solving.
▶ Prioritize client system needs in respect to agreed-on goals and objectives.
▶ Identify the client system's preferred outcomes.
▶ Monitor and evaluate change in client system outcomes.
▶ Assist in making decisions about termination and maintenance of changes.

Rapid Assessment Instruments (RAIs)

Rapid assessment instruments are standardized pencil-and-paper or computerized rating scales and questionnaires to be completed by client systems and scored by practitioners. They document the level of a specific problem experienced by a client system at any given point in time and over a period of time. Problems for which RAIs have been developed are myriad. A few examples include social support, family functioning, coping and adaptation, marital adjustment, organizational climate, group cohesion, hardiness, social skills, self-esteem, self-control, and depression. Many of these standard measures are copyrighted and usable only by permission and purchase. Examples may be found in instrument reference texts such as those of Nugent, Sieppert, and Hudson (2001), Fisher and Corcoran (1994), and Magura and Moses (1986) and in social work research journals.

■ **C O N C E P T   3 . 4**

Standardized measures or instruments are designed to measure particular knowledge, aptitudes, feelings, or behaviors as diagnostic measures. They are administered, scored, and interpreted in a systematic standard objective manner on the basis of norms established for a large number of persons with similar problems. Since these measures have established scientific instrument validity and reliability, their application during testing must be executed in a uniform way to assure continued validity.

Client System Focused Measures for Self-Observed Data

Client system focused measures are scales constructed to document and provide clients with direct observable feedback about their self-observed states (feelings, emotions, behaviors, or reactions), perception of self-in-environment, and the state of their problems, strengths, and goals. Typically, these individualized measures include client logs, individualized rating scales, and goal attainment scaling systems. Since they are based on presenting problems and client system needs, they are developed and constructed with the client system's direct input, and thus they may more accurately reflect a client system's situation than standardized measures or instruments.

■ **C O N C E P T   3 . 5**

> *Client system focused measures* are evaluative tools or instruments developed to individually assess, monitor, and evaluate quantitative and qualitative changes in client system outcomes and the overall situation. They may include client logs, self-rating scales, self-monitored observations, and goal attainment scaling.

Client system logs are structured journals or other such individually developed recording devices (e.g., computer blogs, audiotapes, or videotapes) that document client system changes in relation to identified problems, needs, goals, and objectives. As individually developed recording devices, logs serve as practice-based tools to measure qualitative and quantitative changes in the client system's situation. These change outcomes may be represented as events, actions, feelings, reflections, behaviors, and goal accomplishments to name a few possibilities.

The purpose of logs is twofold. First, individualized recordings and documentation are intended to jog the client system's memory so that full and accurate data are conveyed to the generalist social worker at different points of time during service. Second, such documentation can reveal unsuspected connections between events so that the practitioner and the client system can formulate new propositions (hypotheses) about what is happening in the client system's life context. For example, a mother who is having trouble obtaining her teenager's cooperation may record that she feels anxiety about her youth's school participation every time she asks about homework. The generalist practitioner may hypothesize that this parent may be conveying her anxiety to the child and thereby increasing the child's own anxiety. In turn, the interactive effect of their anxiety may increase the likelihood of conflict between the two. After the generalist practitioner and the mother review and discuss her notes and observations, an intervention strategy that addresses parental feelings and behavior can be formulated.

All client system logs are structured to include a description of the event under scrutiny; the time, day, and date the event took place; and the client system's reaction to the event. In addition, the client system may be asked to note who else is present and what takes place before and after the event in question. The intent of log-journaling is to help facilitate a dialogue about *what took place, when, where, why,* and *how* and to maintain documentation that can be tracked over a period of time and be reviewed to help the client see and reflect on the recorded observations. Figure 3.8 provides an example of a log partially completed by a client system experiencing difficulties managing anger. Because logs consist of information provided by the client system, they are confidential and should be handled and stored according to the rules of confidentiality governing ethical social work practice and federal privacy regulations.

Rating scales are individually developed, empirically rank-ordered judgments or evaluative rating scales that track a specified client system outcome. Typically, these scales are used for client systems to self-rate their feelings, behaviors, traits, problems, changes in objectives, and accomplishments, among other things. Such scales are used not only for self-observation by client systems but also for observation and monitoring by collateral persons associated with the client system, such as parents, spouse/partner, supervisors, teachers, and other helping practitioners. The idea in using such scales with collateral others is to triangulate their observations with the

FIGURE 3.8 ■ Example of Client Exploratory Log

Client Name					
Time	Place	Who was there?	What did you want?	What happened?	What was your reaction?
8:00 A.M.	My home at breakfast time	I and my wife	Time to read the morning paper and have quiet conversation	My wife and I argued about our kids	I was upset, yelled, slammed the door, and left without eating
8:45 A.M.	Driving to work in my own car	Just myself	Wanted to get to work and just have peace	Traffic became congested, a driver cut in front of me	I slammed on the breaks, then honked at the driver, opened my window and yelled at the driver, and followed the driver out of my way until the driver got off the road
10:00 A.M.	My office (I am a supervisor at a building company)	I and my secretary	Get the work done: correspondence and organization of plans	She was trying to explain why things were not finished	I got tired of listening to her explanations and yelled and berated her

client system's self-observation to obtain a better sense or picture of the objective reality. In other words, *triangulation* is a way for increasing the objectivity of the client system's self-observation by using multiple sources of evidence that either support or contrast with the client system reality. Triangulation increases the objective reality of observations. Graphic rating scales, self-anchored scales, and summated rating scales are three types of rating systems used for this purpose.

Graphic rating scales are developed and structured according to the client system's goals and objectives or the generalist social worker's plan for meeting client system needs. These scales are organized according to a numbered continuum, from a possible low score to a possible high score, to measure the client system behavior, attitudes, problems, or goals. For example, Figure 3.9 shows a feeling thermometer designed to rate the client system's feelings of stress. This kind of thermometer rating scale can be used to measure fluctuations in feelings of individuals as well as cohesiveness of groups or organizational climate of institutions.

Another example of a general graphic rating scale involves asking client systems to provide feedback about an intervention process that is taking place during counseling sessions, collaborative team meetings, or local community development meetings. The objective is to increase the generalist's understanding of how the client system views the effectiveness of the working process that is taking place (see Figure 3.10).

The major advantage of rating scales is that they are easy to construct and use. Their validity rests on their salience or meaningfulness in accurately measuring or describing the client system's state of being. For example, when constructing such scales, using descriptive statements that are extremes, such as *extremely* stressed, *hugely* distressed, or *unbelievably* upset, is not useful, and can actually be confusing as people vary in their general perceptions and reactions to such extreme labels. Such rating

FIGURE 3.9 ■ Rating Scale Thermometer

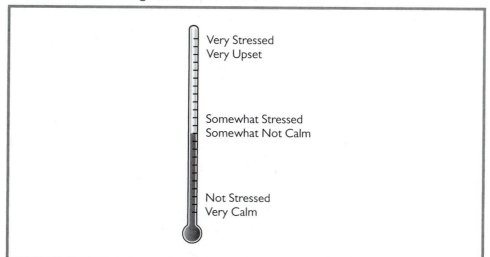

FIGURE 3.10 ■ General Rating Scale

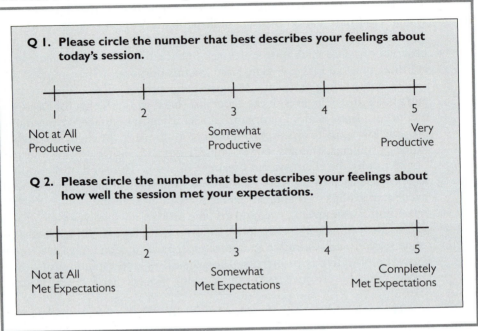

scales can also have more than one question. Their usefulness increases when they are constructed in a way that exhaustively measures the client system's perception about some concern (e.g., anger, social support, family need, community violence).

Some client system focused rating scales, particularly those that are used in counseling sessions or community meetings, are constructed in such a way that clients are asked to define specific referents, or anchors, on a three-point continuum when describing their feeling or attitudinal reactions to some state of being. An anchor point is the point on a scale where a concrete descriptor is given to define the condition represented by that point as it is understood or defined by the client system. *Anchored rating scales* are particularly useful when measuring the client's response to intensity of feeling, or some other reaction involving an emotional or behavioral response. For example, as seen in Figure 3.11, client systems can be asked to describe their feelings about their level of comfort in coming to a group session or testifying at a congressional hearing. These questions can be repeated over time and serve as a monitoring system for tracking changes in the client system's state of being. When rating scales contain several questions to capture some overall state of the client system's response or state of being, they can be summed to create a total score for the overall client system response. Thus, *summative rating scales* combine responses to all the questions into a single summated composite score that represents the client system's overall state of being. Such scales are widely used for assessing individual, family, group, and organizational problems; conducting needs assessments; and conducting case and program level evaluations.

FIGURE 3.11 ■ Anchored Rating Scale

Q 1. Please circle the number that best describes your level of comfort about joining the group treatment.

| 1 | 2 | 3 | 4 | 5 | 6 | 7 | 8 | 9 | 10 |

Not at All   Somewhat   Very
Comfortable   Comfortable   Comfortable

Q 2. Please circle the number that best describes your level of concern about joining the group treatment.

| 1 | 2 | 3 | 4 | 5 | 6 | 7 | 8 | 9 | 10 |

Not at All   Somewhat   A Lot
Concerned   Concerned   Concerned

In addition to the advantages presented, there are disadvantages to instruments constructed with direct input from client systems. One drawback is reactivity. That is, client systems may intentionally or unintentionally distort their responses in order to appear more worthy or deserving of services, or to please the social worker. Another disadvantage is that these rating scales are based on the assumption that client systems have the knowledge, experience, and confidence that enables them to rate their emotional or attitudinal state. Yet another drawback may be the social worker's unintentional coercion in seeking evidence-based empirical documentation. Client systems from non-Western worlds or children do not necessarily know how to rate themselves, or they may have a different way of thinking and capturing the degree of their emotional response. Thus, when using or constructing such rating scales, the generalist practitioner should ascertain that a client system has the required cognitive developmental capacity, has the literary and overall comprehension of the rating scale process, and is willing and comfortable with this approach to learning about self. Also, the entire process must meet the social worker's ethical practice obligations of obtaining informed consent and must promote a client system's self-determination and competence.

Goal attainment scaling system (GAS) is another form of rating scales used to measure the accomplishment of client system goals or objectives (see Figure 3.12). This approach to scaling or ranking progress in achieving client system outcomes is intended as a way of helping client systems and generalist practitioners collaborate in defining and measuring goals and objectives. Since its inception, GAS has been applied to individual, family, group, organizational, and community activities and in a broad range of service settings. The basic procedures for developing GAS involve (see Figure 3.12):

▶ Identifying client system goals and objectives based on needs and preferences
▶ Assigning weights to selected goals or objectives

FIGURE 3.12 ■ Client System Goal Attainment Scaling System

For each selected goal, use the GAS scale to operationalize objectives:

Rating Level Options	Assign* Weight Priority (1–10)	Define or Specify Outcome Level for the Identified Objective	Description or Meaning
−2 or 1		Very Unsatisfactory Goal Level of Attainment Most Unfavorable Outcome	Lowest probability of occurring—the objective does not get addressed
−1 or 2		Unsatisfactory Goal Level of Attainment Unfavorable Outcome	Lower probability of occurring—the objective gets addressed in minimal terms showing initial efforts
0 or 3		Minimum Desirable Goal Level of Attainment Expected Level of Outcome Basic Realistic Outcome	Highest probability of occurring—the objective standard has been realistically set and occurs as expected
+1 or 4		More Favorable Goal Level of Attainment More than Expected Level of Outcome	Lower probability of occurring—the objective has been met somewhat beyond the expected minimum performance standard
+2 or 5		Most Favorable Goal Level of Attainment Best or Ideal Outcome	Lowest probability of occurring—the objective has been met well beyond the basic expectations

*Note: If your objectives for a given goal are about equally important, you may choose NOT to weight the objectives, and the total objective GAS score at a given time for each objective then reflects just the scaled ranking you choose; the total GAS score is the sum of all the total objective GAS scores.

▶ Defining, translating, or estimating each objective by expected outcome on a scale (−2, −1, 0, +1, +2) in which the client system and the social worker define the minimum level of progress expected for a successful outcome to be achieved

▶ Obtaining a weighted score for each goal (based on the number of weighted objectives) during a designated time period (e.g., at baseline and then at a later point, or monthly, quarterly, and/or annually)

It is useful, at this point, to remember that goals are broad statements about the direction and intent of the intervention services to be provided. Objectives, on the other hand, are more precise, specified statements that are intended to highlight how the goal is to be achieved—by whom, when, and by what means. Outcomes are targeted goal referents for expected behaviors, attitudes, and skills, or for organizational activity achievement. The expected outcome levels for each goal or objective must be made operational by specified statements that indicate the referents for the degree of goal attainment. The weighting of each goal or objective along a range from 1 to 10 is meant to indicate its importance to the intervention plan. Two goals or objectives may have the same weight. However, the intent of assigning weights is to communicate priorities. Thus, assigning weights of 10 to all three objectives defeats the purpose of this process. If all goal-objectives are equally important to a client system, it is not necessary to assign weights. The choice of whether to weight client system goals and objectives is usually based on knowledge about the client system's needs or the goals of the service program (see Figure 3.13).

The scoring process begins by determining the baseline score or the beginning point for the GAS score for any specified objective or outcome (see Figure 3.13):

1. *If weights are used to prioritize objectives for each goal,* multiply the initial scaled score for each goal or objective by its respective weight. Then sum the goal-objective scores to obtain the total GAS score for a given goal.
2. *If weights are not used* and all goal-objectives have about equal weight, sum or add the goal or objective rankings for each goal to obtain the total GAS score.
3. Scoring is based on weighing of objectives. For example, in Figure 3.13:

Objective 1:
   Weight = 10
   Rating = -1
   Score = $10 \times -1 = -10$

Objective 2:
   Weight = 6
   Rating = -2
   Score = $6 \times -2 = -12$

Objective 3:
   Weight = 8
   Rating = -1
   Score = $8 \times -1 = -8$

The total goal attainment score at baseline, then, is the total summated score for all three objectives $[(-10) + (-12) + (-8)]$ or -30.

The advantage of the goal attainment system for tracking evidence is based on its flexibility and adaptability. It can track processes as well as outcomes and it can be used to aggregate information across many client systems or programs. Its validity, however, rests on the process of how well each measured scale level is conceptualized or defined. The scale levels are anchored in the reality of what the client system believes or how well each level can be documented by some objective assessment of what is happening to the client system.

FIGURE 3.13 ■ Example of GAS System in Delivering Program Services

Umbrella Goal:

To prevent premature institutionalization of at-risk elderly, aged 60+ years, through providing case-management services at the St. J. Senior Center.

Subgoal

To serve 300 unduplicated individual clients with nutritional center meals within one operational time period.

Objective 1

Assigned Priority Weight = 10

Provide nutritional meals to all enrolled senior participants who are not on specialized diets according to state nutritional standards within one week of program enrollment (See: Program Performance Standards)

GAS Scale System:

1 or −2	= Only 25% of enrolled participants received meal services [this level reflects that things are not working and need major adjustment]
2 or −1	= 50% of enrolled participants received meal services
3 or 0	= 75% of enrolled participants received meal services = Expected Level
4 or +1	= 85% of enrolled participants received meal services
5 or +2	= 100% of enrolled participants received meal services = Ideal Level

Objective 2

Assigned Priority Weight = 6

Assess participating seniors' satisfaction with meal services at the center within six months of their enrollment.

GAS Scale System:

1 or −2	= Only 30% of participants express satisfaction
2 or −1	= 50% of participants express satisfaction
3 or 0	= 80% of participants express satisfaction: Documented by using Client Attendance Logs
4 or +1	= 95% of participants express satisfaction
5 or +2	= All enrolled participants express satisfaction

Objective 3

Assigned Priority Weight = 8

Provide nutritional education through periodic group-based workshop for newly enrolled participating seniors.

GAS Scale System:

1 or −2	= Only 10% of enrolled new seniors attend planned workshop
2 or −1	= 35% of enrolled new seniors attend planned workshop
3 or 0	= 60% of enrolled new seniors attend planned workshop as documented in Attendance Log
4 or +1	= 80% of enrolled new seniors attend planned workshop
5 or +2	= All enrolled seniors have participated in a nutritional workshop within a specified target period

Instrument Validity, Reliability, and Other Issues

All constructed instruments used for documenting or collecting evidence about some client system state are expected to be valid and reliable. *Valid instruments* are those that measure *what* they are supposed to measure and not something else. For example, if the instrument is supposed to measure client system satisfaction with delivery of nutritional services (see Figure 3.13), then it should contain questions pertaining to client satisfaction with the nutritional domain and not other concerns. *Reliable instruments,* on the other hand, are instruments that consistently give the same result with the same unchanged client system every time they are used. Of course, no instrument remains completely unchanged from one time to the next, but the idea is that when the client system remains generally unchanged, a reliable instrument will show similar client system response from one time to the next. It is useful to remember that valid instruments are reliable instruments, but reliable instruments may not be necessarily valid. Consider the following example: *A person approaches you and asks for directions to a train station. You provide those directions in the same way every time you are asked but unintentionally give the wrong directions. The person does not end up at the train station.* Your directions are consistent and reliable but not valid.

Instruments can also have different degrees of sensitivity, reactivity, and utility. Considering that client system changes are likely to be small, instruments must be able to detect small changes in order to accurately track a given level of a real problem. The key to sensitivity in measurement is to select not only the appropriately valid instrument but also an appropriate measuring method. For example, consider that a client system objective is to reduce group conflict of agency employees. Let's say you choose to administer a group conflict questionnaire at the beginning of each staff meeting during which time not many group conflicts occur and employees have very little privacy. In this instance, although you may have a valid instrument, your method of administration is insensitive to the client system's needs for privacy and confidentiality.

Similarly, measurement sensitivity can be an issue when a problem is indicated by more than one client system behavior. For example, members of a team may show problems with accomplishing tasks by not coming on time and responding rudely to each other during meetings. If behaving rudely occurs more frequently than not attending meetings, then it is sensible to count incidents of rudeness behavior rather than focus on nonattendance. High-frequency behaviors are more likely to reveal small changes in process (understanding, beliefs, attitudes, skills) than low-frequency behaviors or events.

Sometimes the very act of measurement affects how client systems respond during measurement. Knowledge, experience, cultural beliefs, literacy, gender, and other diversity-related issues may affect how client systems react to being assessed or evaluated and thus create evaluation bias. The more obtrusive the measure or measuring process, the more likely some reactive bias may affect the results. Further, if a measuring instrument is to be useful, it has to be practical in a particular situation with a particular client system. Its utility is affected by the complexity and length of items included. Consider the previous example of having an instrument measuring group conflict. If this instrument has many complex questions, such as *If you answered yes to the question above, then state. . .* , contains over 100 questions, and has a complicated scoring system, then the instrument would have a very low utility in practice. Instruments that have sound practice utility are those measuring devices that are acceptable to client systems, easy to administer and score, and accurately reflect the client systems' state of being.

Single-Subject Design Measuring Process

Although many practice situations warrant informal case-level evaluations, such as case consultations and case conferences, these informal ways of evaluation do not have the capacity in and of themselves to adequately track client system outcomes. They are, however, considered useful and practical in service delivery and in the application of the General Method with different client systems. They serve a practical purpose in providing the generalist with informal ways of obtaining evidence. For example, case consultation with other professional provider systems can assist the generalist social worker in gaining a better understanding of the client system problem, or in the client system gaining a better knowledge of another system's perspective on a given problem. Case conferences are equally important ways of making sure that different members of a particular service system gain similar awareness or understanding about process and outcomes being addressed. Focus groups offer a particular way of gaining information from a collection of individuals about a specific topic. The major advantage of these informal approaches for collecting evidence is their practical utility. The major disadvantage, however, is their lack of empiricism or systematic application in collecting evidence. A more formal way of systematically tracking and collecting client system outcomes is the use of *single-subject designs*. These research designs (in comparison to group-based designs) are primarily focused on client systems, singly or a few at a time.

■ **C O N C E P T   3 . 6**

> *Single-subject designs* are case-level empirical methods of evaluation. They assess change in practice objectives or client system outcomes by repeated frequent measurement. The evaluated subject can include a single individual, couple, group, family, organization, or community. These case-level replications can be aggregated to determine program effectiveness.

Single-subject designs share the following features (Tripodi, 2002):

1. They establish measurable client system objectives that are relevant to client system needs, strengths, and goals.
2. They establish the state of the client system before intervention by measuring the client system outcomes during the baseline phase of measurement.
3. They use repeated measurement or tracking of client system outcomes.

4. They graphically display the monitored change process to visually document changes in the client system outcomes.
5. They use simple analytical procedures for determining client system changes.

Today, most programs have developed ways to track and quantify the characteristics of the client systems being served (e.g., see Figure 3.14).

Single-subject designs vary along a continuum that can be described as exploratory, descriptive, and explanatory. All three can be used for purposes of quality improvement, knowledge building, and client outcome documentation.

Exploratory single-subject or single-case designs are most commonly used for quality improvement because they involve continuous monitoring of client system progress. These designs are meant to explore, assess how things are going, and build a foundation of general ideas and tentative propositions that can be confirmed or abandoned later by using more rigorous design process. They do not produce conclusive or statistically definitive results and they cannot prove, for example, that the intervention *caused* or is responsible for change with some statistical certainty for the client system outcome. These designs, however, provide ongoing feedback about the progress of the client system, allowing practitioners to make intervention decisions based on documentation of empirical evidence about some important aspect of the client system behavior, attitude, and skills targeted for intervention. This monitoring process makes it likely that ineffective service delivery will be fairly quickly discontinued. Figure 3.15 provides an example of an exploratory single-subject design used for monitoring community group members' reported average number of collaborative activities.

Descriptive single-subject designs evaluate client system change over a period of time and can include quasi-experimental design method of evaluation. That is, these designs can make comparisons but typically do not have a way to control the influence of other factors on client system change (apart from the interventive process). They do, however, compare client system outcomes across baseline (graphically designated as Phase A) and intervention (graphically designated as Phase B) periods (see Figure 3.16).

Another variation of this design includes the process of comparing what happens to the client system outcome not only during baseline and intervention time periods but also when using different types of interventive strategies (see Figure 3.17). Sometimes the social work generalist uses different kinds of supportive services that can be applied individually in a sequential order or as a combined package of services. For example, a micro-level client system (an individual) may need individually applied intervention (during Phase B) followed by group-applied intervention (during Phase C), or the individual client system may need to start using group-based services followed by a successive intensification of individual services (Phases $B_1 B_2 B_3 \ldots$) (see Figure 3.18).

The advantage of differentiating interventions or the intensive application of a particular intervention provides a way of seeing what may be happening to the client system outcome when changes in the intervention occur. The disadvantage in this design is that what happens in different intervention (Phases B, C, D or $B_1 B_2 B_3 \ldots$) can-

FIGURE 3.14 ■ Common Graphic Display of Data or Information

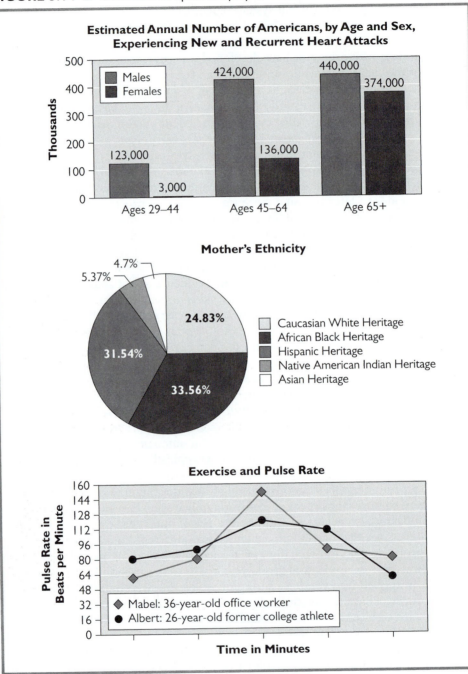

FIGURE 3.15 ■ Exploratory Nonexperimental Monitoring Single Subject Design

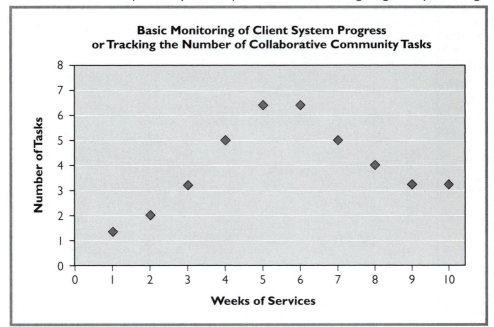

FIGURE 3.16 ■ Descriptive Quasi-Experimental Single-Subject Design

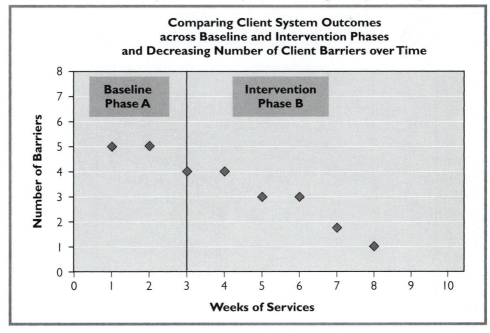

FIGURE 3.17 ■ Variation of Descriptive Intervention Single-Subject Design

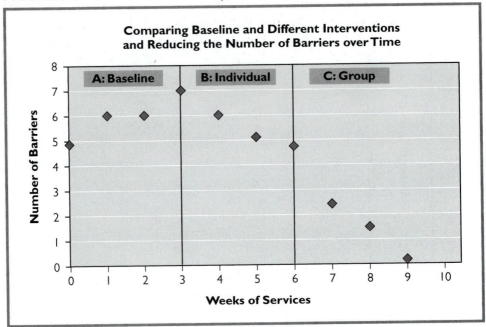

FIGURE 3.18 ■ Variation of Intervention Intensity Single-Subject Design

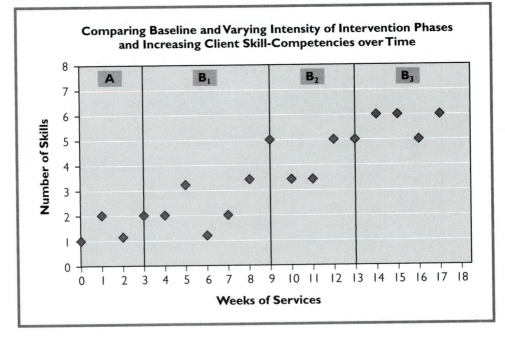

not be compared with the baseline phase because either Phase B or B_1 has already occurred. In addition, the effect of Phase C alone cannot be distinguished from the combined effects of Phases B and C. Therefore, the practitioner will not really know whether the intervention might have worked without the introduction of Phase B. In turn, this difficulty also means that the more interventions there are, the more difficult it becomes to interpret what is happening and the harder it is to ascribe the observed client system outcome to any particular interventive strategy.

Explanatory single-subject designs are experimental case-level designs interested in demonstrating the *cause-and-effect* relationship between client system outcome and the applied intervention across time. These designs are the most rigorous (see Figure 3.19) and their explanation rests on how well the design can show what happens to the client system outcome when the baseline condition (or nonintervention Phase A) is reapplied throughout the tracking process. That is, under controlled and agreed circumstances, the intervention is withdrawn (now called Phase A_2) while the client system continues to monitor the selected targeted outcome(s). Obviously, withdrawing or stopping the intervention requires much forethought, ethical practice planning, and client knowledge about how to get immediate support if the *unanticipated were to happen.* It is useful at this point to note that the principles of demonstrating *causal relationship* between any two variables (e.g., between intervention and client system outcome) rests on scientific principles of causality between variables.

FIGURE 3.19 ■ Explanatory Single-Subject Design

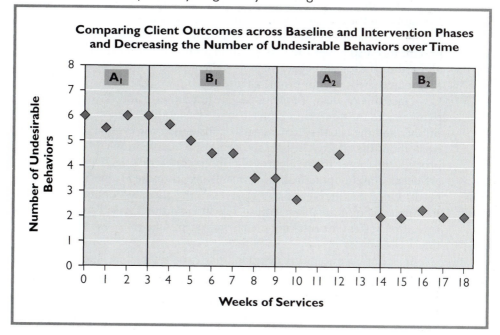

The *principles of causality* between variables rest on the fulfillment of three conditions:

1. The two variables (e.g., intervention and outcome variables) being examined must have an observable and statistically documentable relationship.
2. The causative variable must occur first in the time order of the observed variables, and the *effect or outcome variable* must occur second.
3. The relationship between the cause-and-effect variables cannot be spurious or cannot be explained by the relationship with any other variable.

Thus, using single-subject designs consists of asking questions, defining the elements of the question that will be investigated or tracked over time, testing the question through the application of selected design and chosen instruments for measuring the investigated elements, and accepting or rejecting the assumptions on which the question is based. For example, a client system seeks assistance and, during the engagement phase in the Generalist Method, agrees to collect baseline information (in Phase A_1) about a targeted outcome that has been linked with the client system's presented problems, needs, and strengths. To be able to analyze whether the client system outcome changes statistically, the baseline period and other tracking periods require that the targeted client system outcome is observed or measured at least three times within each monitored phase. The three observations can take place within one week, one day, or any specified time period that makes sense or is relevant to the client system's needs and that has been negotiated and agreed on by the generalist social worker and the client system. Prior to, during, or at the conclusion of the baseline phase, the practitioner and the client system assess the client system's needs, strengths, and selected outcome(s) and make decisions about intervention, monitoring, and evaluation of the client system's outcomes. During this beginning phase, the practitioner also poses a *search question* and searches for the best available evidence about the efficacy and effectiveness of the potential intervention that could be used to mitigate client system problems and needs.

Once this process is concluded, the practitioner and the client system are ready to move into the intervention phase in the Generalist Method. In this phase the practitioner and the client system start by considering the evidence that may or may not exist about the effectiveness of the proposed intervention. At the conclusion of this process, they agree to use a particular intervention or a package of interventions that are deemed useful, practical, and ethically appropriate for meeting the client system's needs. Once the intervention is agreed on, the client system enters into Phase B, or the application of the intervention. The intervention Phase B_1 is monitored using an agreed-on system for tracking the client system outcome over a designated period of time.

In the application of the explanatory experimental design, at some point, when the client system's state would not be endangered, the practitioner and the client system discuss and agree to *withdraw the intervention* for a specified period to investigate the effect of intervention removal on the client system outcome. For example, sometimes this process can take place quite naturally when the practitioner is away because of planned vacation, attending a conference, or other reasons. Whatever the reason, however, this reapplication of baseline (Phase A_2) has to be ethically planned, discussed fully with the client system, and ethically implemented with appropriate supports in place. The generalist social worker should prepare the client system for what to do for support and what to do in case of an unexpected emergency situation. The idea is that the client system is *more or less ready to consider or envision* the upcoming process of termination of services. This envisioning process helps to prepare the client system since it provides an immediate feedback about what may need to be in place for termination to actually occur, while it tests the client system's response by withdrawing the intervention temporarily. Subsequently, at the conclusion of Phase A_2, the client system resumes receiving the intervention as previously (B_2) (see Figure 3.19). There are many variations in how this design can be implemented and statistically analyzed. To appreciate the complexity of these designs, see texts such as Bloom, Fischer, and Orme (2003).

The formal process in which single-subject designs are applied has many advantages for the client system and the generalist social work practitioner:

- ▶ The practitioner is responsible for data planning and gathering.
- ▶ The focus is on the client system.
- ▶ Decisions about intervention can be made as data are being collected.
- ▶ Analysis and review of problems in relation to outcomes is facilitated.
- ▶ The process incurs small costs in time and disruptiveness.
- ▶ The client system's situation can be taken into account directly.
- ▶ The data collected can be useful for practice and program level evaluations.

Although the outcome data may be collected by the client system or others in the client system's environment, the practitioner is expected to assume ethical responsibility and to control how this process takes place. That is, although the practitioner decides what data should be collected where, when, under what conditions, by whom, and for what purpose, the decision for implementing the data-collection process rests on the collaborative agreement forged by the practitioner–client system working relationship. Given these parameters, it is possible to organize data collection in a way that confirmational data from collateral sources (e.g., a teacher or a community member) can be obtained efficiently in time to assist with decision making. In addition, social work practitioners are free to follow their own theoretical approaches to practice. The collected data do not determine the practice approach used but are likely to be determined by it. For example, see a study by Briggs, Leary, Cox, and Shibago (2005) that examines the effects of group treatment on separated parents and their interaction with their children.

All single-subject designs are adaptable to meet the client system's needs. For example, it may be necessary to intervene with a particular client system once without establishing a baseline. On the other hand, if a client system can provide data about the duration, frequency, or intensity of the problem prior to the actual initial interview with the generalist social worker, a *retroactive baseline* may be established based on the strength of the client system's recollected report. In addition, the systematic measurement of client system outcome provides immediate feedback about whether any intervention or phase of intervention is effective. For example, the generalist social worker may start with a basic descriptive design AB and quickly realize that the B-level intervention is not really having the desired effect and immediately intensify the same intervention or switch the client to a C-type intervention, depending on the professional judgment and the client system's response. Decisions about client system progress are ongoing and useful for making decisions not only for continuing, augmenting, or changing services but also for envisioning and planning for termination of services.

Case-level designs also require that the practitioner develop measurable and observable client system goal-oriented practice objectives—for example: *What precisely is the individual client system's anxiety or meaning of behavior that needs to be measured? Is the individual client system anxious because something recently happened, or does the anxiety signify a recurring problem in the environment?* If the client system is anxious because of recent specific events, then resolving this situation may be approached differently as opposed to when the client system's discomfort is related to past events. This level of detailed knowledge in posed questions is necessary for developing a good understanding of the client system's problems and needs, knowing how to find out about client system's resource capacities, and planning an appropriate intervention.

There is no doubt that using and applying single-subject designs and any other measurement process takes time and practice. It is useful to remember that all case-level designs are flexible in order to meet a client system's individualized needs. For example, a rating scale designed to meet a community's need for assessing crime can be designed to meet that individual community's various members' needs and capacities (related to literacy, English language, culture, experience, etc.) in order to facilitate accurate data information. Instruments can be completed at home, in the office, or somewhere else at times convenient to the client system.

In addition, data collected on individual client systems can be aggregated to provide program evaluation information. For example, a charitable organization that funds different agencies might require each agency to document a minimum level of successful case outcomes in order to continue the funding. The individual agencies and their individual practitioners would provide evidence related to successful client system outcomes, complete with data clearly displayed in some graphic presentation. Agencies that are staffed with practitioners who are familiar with using case-level empirical designs have less difficulty demonstrating documentable success than agencies with staff who do not use an empirical approach to practice.

Furthermore, client system data collected over time can also be useful in creating eligibility criteria for delivering program services as a whole. For example, it may be determined that client systems that achieve a certain score or observed state on an outcome tend to do better in the program, or complete the services, than client systems that achieve a lower score at a given point of time in service delivery. A minimum score might then be considered as a criterion for admittance.

Disadvantages of single-subject designs are primarily twofold: They have limited generalizability and the explanatory designs are difficult to implement. The findings on client system outcomes are limited in their inference or generalizability to the targeted client system. However, a number of similar results obtained in similar situations with similar client systems make it more likely that the findings can be generally applicable. The generalist social worker may not initially have such comparative data available, except with time and replication. Generalist social workers are cautioned to resist the temptation to assume that because a selected intervention worked once with one client system, it must necessarily work again with another client system.

Implementation of explanatory case-level designs requires great care to assure ethical implementation of the experimental approach. For ethical reasons, such designs may be applied by the happenstance of natural absences but their rigor suffers. In this instance, the measurement of the problem often does not continue between the first intervention Phase B (or B_1) and the withdrawal of the intervention phase (or Phase A_2), as the client system that believes a problem has been solved is unlikely to keep records between an apparent solution and the reappearance of problems. Therefore, there can be a gap in data that prevents inference that the reappearance of the problem had anything to do with the removal of the intervention. Perhaps the problem would have reappeared even if the intervention continued. Consequently, the application of a second baseline period (A_2) in the explanatory design (such as $A_1B_1A_2B_2$) eliminates one argument for causality—that the problem reappears when the intervention is removed. Descriptive case-level designs, then, are easier to implement than explanatory designs, as they require only a baseline phase followed by as many intervention phases as are necessary to meet the client system needs. Although descriptive designs are practical and easy to arrange, they are limited in their ability to infer that the intervention can be held responsible for the client system outcomes.

SUMMARY

An empirically based approach to General Method practice encourages the integration of ethical, evidentiary, and application concerns. It involves a systematic approach to improving and maintaining quality of client system services. Such an approach includes steps that convert information needs related to practice decisions into answerable questions; searches for the best evidence with which to answer them; critically appraises that evidence for its validity, impact, and applicability to the practice with a given client system; applies the results of this appraisal to practice and policy decisions; and evaluates the effectiveness and efficiency in carrying out the previous steps and seeks ways to improve them in the future.

REFLECTION POINTS

Becoming a skilled social work practitioner requires knowledge and skills, including the ability to reflect on practice endeavors. The following reflection points are designed to strengthen critical thinking and mastery of knowledge of key points in this chapter.

1. Define the following key concepts:
   - Evidence-based practice
   - Client system outcome(s)
   - Client system intervention(s)
   - Search questions
   - Fallacies in critical thinking
   - Client system focused measures
   - Single-subject evaluation designs
2. How might human diversity influence the formulation of search questions in searching for evidence about intervention effectiveness?
3. Provide examples of evidence-based search questions using the four identifiable parts as presented in Concept 3.3.
4. Review Social Workers' Ethical Responsibility to Clients in the *NASW Code of Ethics* (www.socialworkers.org) in relation to your professional behavior for conducting evidence-based practice while considering different phases of the General Method.
5. For further building of knowledge about empirical evidence in practice, find the referenced studies in this chapter (e.g., analytic studies, retrospective studies, experimental studies, cohort studies, cross-sectional survey studies, or single-subject studies) and discuss what sort of evidence was being studied, for what purpose, what the study found, and how this evidence could be used in practice.

Strengths-Based Problem-Solving Interviews

The professional interview is the cornerstone of strengths-based problem-solving in generalist social work practice. Professional interviews differ from conversations because they have a specific purpose, focused direction, and clear communication. The purpose of a professional interview is to exchange information in order that the generalist social worker and the client system may track the client system's needs and wants, identify the preferred goals and objectives, and implement a plan to solve problems and address issues and needs. The direction of a professional interview is guided by the mission, purpose, goals, and programs of the service agency and by the needs, wants, and resources of the client system.

Whether the generalist practitioner is engaged with a client, action, or target system on a micro, mezzo, or macro level, the key to effective generalist social work intervention is purposeful, adept communication throughout the strengths-based problem-solving interviews. These interviews also use specific methods, skills, and techniques, and are accomplished by means of the professional relationship, methods, skills, and techniques involving exploration, reflection, and validation. They use a wide variety of technical interviewing skills to sustain the dialogue between the client system and the generalist social worker and thereby further the development of the professional relationship and the strengths-based problem-solving process.

In this chapter, interviewing is explored in depth to prepare the generalist practitioner for work in all phases of the strengths-based problem-solving approach of the General Method. As shown in Figure 4.1, the empowerment perspective, the strengths perspective, and the risk and resilience perspective establish the attitudinal and belief framework that will guide the generalist practitioner in working with individuals, families, groups, organizations, and communities as client, action, and target systems in micro, mezzo, and macro practice. These three perspectives set the stage for exploring specific techniques of interviewing that will facilitate excellence in the helping relationship and avoidance of common interviewing mistakes. Their overarching purpose is to help the generalist social worker achieve best practices in strengths-based problem-solving interviews.

The General Method

Overview

As noted in Figure 4.1, the General Method strengths-based problem-solving interview is guided by three distinct and overarching paradigms: the empowerment perspective, the strengths perspective, and the risk and resilience perspective. Each paradigm framework must be kept in mind as the generalist practitioner prepares for every interview, if the General Method interview is to rise to the level of professional social work discourse. Together these frameworks provide a structure to guide the professional social work interview so that no matter what problem, person, or situation one encounters, the generalist practitioner can be assured that he or she is using a holistic perspective in each phase of the General Method.

The *empowerment* perspective calls on the generalist social worker to presume that the client system has the capacity to effect change and transform itself individually and collectively in order to achieve a fuller life. In other words, the generalist practitioner approaches the client system as an expert who has much knowledge to help explain the situation and many skills to draw on in meeting identified needs. Approaching the client system as an expert helps establish a co-equal relationship that underscores the authority and influence the client system brings to the General Method interview.

FIGURE 4.1 ■ Elements of Strengths-Based Problem-Solving Interview with Micro, Mezzo, and Macro Client Systems

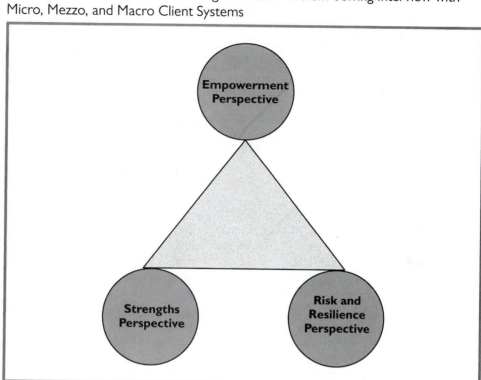

The *strengths* perspective means that the generalist practitioner moves beyond a problem-saturated discussion of the current situation and explores the client system's aspirations, competencies, and confidence as well as environmental resources, social networks, and opportunities. The generalist practitioner looks on the client system as a "whole" and draws out its talents for self-direction and self-actualization. Doing this requires the social worker to view the client system situation from alternative points of view and multiple perspectives.

Finally, the General Method interview examines the concurrent client system's *risks and resiliencies* at the macro, mezzo, and micro levels that impact the present situation. By examining these risks and resiliencies, the generalist practitioner learns which protective factors are missing that must be set in place to aid in bringing about a problem resolution or meeting a special need. Only by conducting interviews through these three paradigm frameworks of empowerment, strengths, and risks and resiliencies does the generalist practitioner conform to the knowledge base of the strengths-based problem-solving approach of the General Method. In addition, these paradigm frameworks assure that the strengths-based problem-solving interview incorporates questions about human diversity that further enhance professional understanding of the problem-person-situation.

The Interview Process

> *The social work interview is a set of communications with four special characteristics: (1) has a context or setting; (2) is purposeful and directed; (3) is limited and contractual; and (4) involves specialized role relationships. (Compton & Galaway, 1994, p. 310)*

The strengths-based problem-solving interviews of the General Method usually take place within the auspice of an agency whose mission, purpose, and setting revolve around a specific field of practice with defined service programs and practice methods developed to meet the needs of a particular target population. Within this context, the *professional interview* may be defined as a formal set of communications that centers on defining the client system's needs, wants, personal strengths, and environmental resources. Interview content focuses on issues, problems, and needs that the agency or program has the sanction and authority to address.

General Method interview questions are aimed at collecting information in all relevant domains of the bio-psycho-social-spiritual development of the person and all pertinent subsystems related to the client system. In this instance, the reference point for question relevance is whether it elicits information that facilitates understanding the problems, issues, needs, strengths, and resources of the client system. The professional interview is limited to examining only those topics that further the generalist practitioner's understanding and the client system's point of view about the issue at hand. It is essential to remember that all persons choosing to be included in a professional social work interview at the micro, mezzo, or macro level have a contribution to make in illuminating the situation and a responsibility to advance the joint problem-solving endeavors.

■ CONCEPT 4.1

> *Empowerment* is a "process of increasing personal, interpersonal, or political power so that individuals, families and communities can take action to improve their situations" (Gutierrez, 1994, p. 202). Empowerment consists of recognizing and identifying the processes of oppression, facilitating client system learning, and promoting client system actions to obtain needed assets.

The Empowerment Perspective

Overview

Social work helps people help themselves. This overly broad statement is often very difficult for the beginning generalist social worker to grasp and put into practice. When this idea is studied in depth, however, the generalist begins to learn about the historical, political, psychological, sociological, and economic roots that give meaning to this abstraction. Specifically, the empowerment perspective is guided by a particular set of knowledge, skill, and language that has been implicitly included in the problem-solving process since the inception of social work and has helped give birth to the notion that social work is a unique profession. On further examination, empowerment comes into focus in social work's early years in the United States as the professional attitude that formed the foundation for the General Method.

Historical Roots

At the end of the nineteenth century and the beginning of the twentieth century, there was a growing debate about the role of what was then known as the *charity worker,* the proper moral underpinnings and authority of this *friendly visitor,* and whether this role and authority constituted a profession of social work (Flexner, 1915). Another debate arose between those who saw the primary purpose of social work as one that addresses the *cause* (the reform movement) of problems (*content*) versus one that addresses the *function* (the direct practice movement) of problems (*process*).

Historical giants of the profession, from each group, were able to show through practice, scholarship, and teaching that this is a false dichotomy. In fact, the uniqueness of the social work profession and its contribution to society rests on the simultaneous and dual focus on persons in transaction with their environments. In the following discussion, it becomes clear that the founders of the social work profession set the course for the profession's commitment to social change in the interest of social justice and the enhancement of human well-being.

Jane Addams (1860–1935) developed Chicago's Hull House in 1889. In the tradition of the reform movement, this settlement house program sought to improve social conditions for underserved peoples and their communities. In working with immigrant families, Jane Addams came to understand that much of their distress was rooted in causes that lay in social and economic conditions related to urbanization, industrialization, and immigration. Some of these conditions included the need for employment, child care, education, and health care. Consequently, over the years, through its centers, programs, and advocacy work, Hull House established an employment bureau, English lessons, citizenship classes, child-care facilities, kindergarten classes, libraries, and theatre, music, and art programs.

Addams's neighborhood development work eventually extended beyond local concerns to the national suffrage movement, the progressive education movement, and the pacifist movement in World War I, which she saw as directly linked to issues of power, knowledge, and politics (Addams, 1910). Thus, her settlement house work serves as an archetypal and classical brand of what has become known today as social planning and community development, locality development, social action, social policy, and social and political advocacy methods of social work practice. These methods all recognize the power of personal and communal social capital and the politics of institutional barriers to social justice and well-being.

Mary E. Richmond (1861–1928) joined the Charity Organization Society in 1888. She became trained as a "friendly visitor" who went to the homes of people in need and tried to help them improve the quality of their life situation. Consistent with her preparation, she believed that social problems were to be explained by weaknesses within the individual. However, she expanded her investigations to include an examination of the close social ties of the individual—connections such as the family, schools, employment, and religious institutions—in an effort to help clients make social adjustments and improve their life situations. She began to develop ideas about specific methods to help those in need. These methods became known as *scientific philanthropy*. They included social diagnosis, social casework, group work, and what we know today as the therapeutic relationship. She advocated for the establishment of schools for the study of social casework and began to stress the need for formal education. In an effort to establish a professional environment for what was previously considered mere charity work in the homes of the poor, Richmond authored several books, including *Social Diagnosis* (1917) and *What Is Social Case Work?* (1922).

Bertha C. Reynolds (1885–1978) was a renowned direct social work practitioner. She received professional training and earned a certificate in social work from Smith College. In addition, she underwent intensive personal psychoanalysis, which was the formal training curriculum for becoming an analyst at that time. Reynolds combined psychological, sociological, and social work concepts with social justice and civil rights issues to create a truly psychosocial practice model that gave full recognition to the impact of intrapsychic dynamics along with the role of macro activities of advocacy and social action. Reynolds believed that the social work profession should "make an imprint upon the society of our time" (Reynolds, 1951, p. 163).

In time, Reynolds moved away from the diagnostic school of thought that had been championed by Mary Richmond and away from its emphasis on problem causation in which she had been trained. Instead, Reynolds advocated the notion that psychological growth was the central feature of social work practice. Consistent with analytic theory, she stressed the importance of the relationship between the social worker and the client and emphasized that the value of the relationship was in its growth-enabling processes and not its curative effect. Reynolds envisaged change as

BERTHA C. REYNOLDS (1885–1978) was a community organizer, clinician, and educator in social work. She sought to change poverty and racism through a Marxist philosophy of social justice. Her practice and writings employed a perspective of human behavior as occurring within and in response to systemic, structural, and institutional frameworks, not just psychopathology. Her publications include *Learning and Teaching in the Practice of Social Work* and *An Uncharted Journey*.

the responsibility of the client, not the practitioner. The social worker was expected to take into account social and cultural factors and help client systems make their own choices and release their own growth potential—that is, to *help* the client rather than *cure* the client. In other words, the social worker entered the helping relationship at the point of initial contact without first interviewing to take an extensive history, classifying the client problem, prescribing a particular treatment plan, or assuming responsibility for an anticipated outcome (Dunlap, 1996).

Over the last quarter century, the person-in-environment context has become a central construct in professional social work (Rapp, 1998). These early leaders, all women, seeded the ideas that we know today as empowerment. *Empowerment* is defined as the "process of increasing personal, interpersonal, or political power so that individuals, families and communities can take action to improve their situations" (Gutierrez, 1994, p. 202). In colloquial terms, empowerment means *the personal is political.*

The Empowerment Paradigm and Processes

Empowerment is the synthesis of a wide range of knowledge that connects issues of social and economic justice with personal anguish and difficulty (Mancoske & Hunzeker, 1990). It uses strategies that are directed toward achieving actions that are liberating and transforming for the client system. Through empowerment, client systems are helped to take control of their needs and issues and to shape their own destinies. Empowerment is intended to free the client system from fear and immobilization.

Empowerment begins with the development of a partnership and collaborative relationship that acknowledges client system reality and uniqueness and gives special attention to issues of diversity and oppression. The generalist social worker brings power to the strengths-based problem-solving process through professional expertise, interpersonal skills, and legitimized agency authority. In addition, each client system has its own innate power in the form of self-knowledge, competencies, and capabilities. Empowerment is not something that is given by the generalist practitioner. It is found through the joint search for understanding the significance of the problem in social functioning or the unmet need according to the client system's point of view and through reviewing and learning from previous efforts to conquer powerlessness.

The empowerment process consists of helping the client system to:

▶ Develop critical thinking skills.
▶ Reduce self-blame.
▶ Assume responsibility.
▶ Enhance self-efficacy.

Critical thinking skills require the client system to move beyond description of a life space issue to an analysis of the forces that have placed or kept in place barriers to the client system securing rights and benefits. In bringing empowerment processes into play, the generalist practitioner becomes a teacher and provides information and resources for the client system to reach a higher level in its understanding of its situation. Such knowledge is power.

After years of mistrust and injustice, many client systems mistakenly blame themselves for their current life space issues. They see themselves as helpless in the face of historical, economic, and political forces. To counter this perspective, the social worker must help the client system review the institutional pressures that have maintained its powerlessness. In addition, the social worker must provide encouragement and convey a sense of hope and expectation for the client system in order that the system may begin to believe that the future has many possibilities.

If this process is not undertaken, the client system will not be able to take responsibility for defining the problem, selecting solutions, and seeking resources that are consistent with its own perceptions of the current situation. The notion of taking responsibility in examining the forces of oppression may create a new future, may elicit anger, and may lead to frustration in the client system. The social worker must respond empathically and build self-esteem and self-confidence in the face of what might appear to be insurmountable odds.

Through this consciousness raising, the client system comes to believe that it has the ability to accomplish tasks that will achieve larger goals. Self-efficacy is seen in greater self-confidence in the strengths-based problem-solving process, individual and collective mutual supports, and successful coping with oppressive situations. Informal social networks are a significant source of support to aid the client system in maintaining a sense of competency and mastery. The generalist assists the client system in gaining access to these personal assets and environmental resources (DuBois & Miley, 2005).

In the empowerment paradigm, there is *no one* solution to any situation, problem, need, or issue. Indeed, the complex situations presented by client systems require multiple actions to bring about solutions. The generalist practitioner's main stance is to listen carefully and avoid telling the client system what should be done to address the current needs or issues.

Thus, the empowerment tasks of the generalist social worker are to bolster motivation, offer psychological comfort, enhance problem-solving, and promote self-direction. These tasks are undertaken while the generalist social worker supports a client system in increasing its knowledge and understanding of the situation, facilitating the application of critical thinking to the problem-solving process, and reflecting with the client, action, or target system on the decision choices available prior to action (Lee, 1996). Empowerment tasks require the generalist social worker to enter a co-equal relationship that identifies options for the client system and ascribes authority to the client system to make its own choices.

For the generalist social worker, the nature of the empowerment relationship means that the practitioner brings to the professional social work interview a set of attitudes and beliefs about help-giving processes that:

▶ Validates the client system's reality
▶ Focuses on the present and future rather than the past
▶ Concentrates on solutions rather than on problems

Empowerment is a *can do* way of thinking brought to the strengths-based problem-solving partnership. Through knowledge building, reflection, and action, the generalist practitioner aids the client system in identifying goals, selecting objectives, and implementing tasks that reflect the idiosyncratic nature of the consumer's reality.

■ CONCEPT 4.2

The *strengths perspective* is a distinctive lens wherein "everything you do as a social worker will be predicated, in some way, on helping to discover and relish, explore and exploit clients' strengths and resources in the service of assisting them to achieve their goals, realize their dreams, and shed the irons of their own inhibitions and misgivings" (Saleebey, 1997, p. 3).

The Strengths Perspective

Overview

Many beginning generalist practitioners wonder how to begin with their client systems. They look for a specific formula or instructions to use as a guide for their interview. Often the rationale for seeking a prescription is to allay anxiety for both the social worker and the client system. The reality is that there is never one set of directions to follow when conducting an interview. Rather than having a formula or prescription, it is far more important to recognize that all professional social work interviews actually begin in the mind of the generalist practitioner long before the social worker–client system dialogue even begins.

The strengths perspective offers a noteworthy set of principles to consider when preparing to undertake an interview. It is a paradigm that requires generalists to move beyond only a problem-focused view of the client, action, or target system in order to include an examination of manifest and latent personal and environmental strengths and resources that may be applied to the issue at hand. The strengths perspective helps the generalist practitioner to identify and examine categories of asset-based information for successful strengths-based problem-solving that can motivate the client system and inspire hope for the future.

Historical Roots

In the twentieth century, the early theories and methods of the helping professions were redeveloped in concert with the scientific approach, which favored empiricism, objectivity, and linear relationships between variables. Known as *logical positivism*, this scientific model of knowledge building required the practitioner to develop interviewing skills for the study, diagnosis, and treatment of deficits or problems. This model set up a hierarchical power structure in the helping relationship wherein the social worker, taking a neutral stance, was assumed to have the expertise that was required for any type of solution. Pathology dominated the dialogue with less focus on the uniqueness of each client system, its view of the situation, or its potential strengths and resources. Further, the role of the environmental context was no longer part of the interview lexicon.

In today's postmodern approaches, known as *social constructivism*, problem-saturated stories are deconstructed by the social worker and the client system so that client systems can begin to expand their view of reality and see important facets of the personal situation and social environment that previously had been unrecognized. Consequently, the strengths model does not subscribe to the classical assessment and treatment approach in which the social worker draws on professional authority in a way that minimizes client system contributions.

In the social constructivist approach to interviewing and strengths-based problem-solving, the client system is considered to be the expert who is most knowledgeable about the current difficulty and possible remedies. Client system values, subjective perceptions, and socio-cultural experiences are all seen to carry meanings that are central to resolving the issues at hand. The generalist practitioner is viewed as a co-constructionist who aids in separating the person from the problem and in helping the client system keep in mind that the problem is not intrinsic to the client. Through questions, comments, and summarizing, the generalist practitioner aids the client system in reconstructing a new personal story that facilitates development of revised ways to view, manage, and control issues of concern, and thereby meet needs using previously unrecognized strengths and assets (Kelley, 1996).

Using the social constructivism paradigm, Saleebey and various colleagues (1992, 1997, 2006) began to introduce the idea that social work practice needed to move beyond the pathology, pessimism, and inequality prevalent in the helping relationship. In addition, they helped bring back and move forward the inclusion of social context, personhood, and community as central features critical to the helping process. These researchers and practitioners also began to articulate underlying assumptions and techniques of interviewing, which have become known today as the *strengths perspective.*

Wellness (Weil, 1995), solution-focused (DeJong & Berg, 2002), asset-based community development (Kretzmann & McKnight, 1993), and narrative stories (Kelley, 1996) are other strengths-based approaches with similar social constructionist characteristics. The term *strengths-based* sounds simpleminded, yet taking into account the assets and resources rather than the deficits or problems of a client, action, and target system and employing these assets and resources in the strengths-based problem-solving approach of the General Method requires a great deal of professional sophistication.

Principles

The central strengths-based principles offered by Saleebey (2006) clarify the social worker's thoughts in preparation for an interview and sharpen the use of critical thinking skills when preparing interview questions and comments. First, the social worker notes that every client, action, and target system has strengths and assets. Individuals, couples, families, groups, agencies, organizations, neighborhoods, and communities have personal and communal social capital, assets, and resources as well as specialized knowledge in relation to their situation. The task of the generalist practitioner is to uncover the wealth of underutilized and unrecognized assets available to the client system. Second, the generalist practitioner must recognize that difficulties, no matter how acute or chronic, bring with them innate opportunities for growth and change. Thus, the task for the generalist social worker is to help the client system recognize all the previous work done to overcome or cope with seemingly insurmountable difficulties. This recognition ties directly into the third principle of working with the client system to envision aspirations and set high expectations for resolving the situation and meeting needs. The intent of this task is to bring hope to the current endeavors and create a working environment wherein the client system senses the possibilities of growth, change, and tangible outcomes for a better future.

Consistent with the empowerment perspective, the strengths perspective engages the client, action, and target systems whenever possible, as a partner or collaborator in the strengths-based problem-solving process. Taking this position requires that the generalist practitioner view the client system as the expert in understanding, coping with, and responding to the client system's issues of concern. The social worker offers specialized knowledge to expand and deepen the client system's view of the situation. The task, however, is to work *with* the client system rather than *for* the system. In other words, the client system is the expert and knows more than the generalist practitioner about what will work and what will not work to bring about problem resolution.

The final principle of the strengths-based perspective is to recognize that no matter how impoverished a client, action, or target system situation or setting appears to be, there are, in fact, an abundance of resources, assets, and strengths that may be brought to bear on the difficulty. The task of the generalist social worker, then, is to identify the social wealth available in the environmental context and intermediate services and to position this social capital for use by the client system.

In summary, the five principles of the strengths-based perspective are:

1. Every client, action, and target system has strengths and assets.
2. Difficulties bring opportunities for growth and change.
3. Every client, action, and target system has aspirations for change.
4. The client, action, and target systems are the experts in understanding, coping with, and responding to their problems, needs, and issues of concern.
5. Every client, action, and target system has strengths, resources, and assets to bring to bear on the difficulty.

Thus, the strengths perspective is in direct contrast to a deficit-based model of practice that depicts the person as the problem, creates skepticism, engenders a disconnectedness, and overlooks the ecological context of the difficulty. Rather, the strengths perspective is characterized by practice that centers on competencies, capacities, and courage; promise, possibilities, and positive expectations; and resilience, reserves, and resources (Saleebey, 2006).

Interview Questions

These principles and assumptions may appear to be very simplistic but the application of the interview questions will demonstrate how complex and difficult it is to move the client, action, and target system from a perspective focusing on the present and past to a strengths-based problem-solving framework with a future perspective in which the client system must embrace the possibilities inherent in a situation rather than being hemmed in by seemingly intractable limitations. Several authors (De Shazer, 1988; Saleebey, 2006) discuss different types of specific interview questions that shift the frame of reference from a deficit model to a strengths perspective framework. The most well-known interview questions are the Miracle Question, the Exception Question, and the Difference Question.

MIRACLE QUESTION   The Miracle Question (DeJong & Miller, 1995) helps the client system envision solutions to its issues or needs. It takes this form: Ask the client system to imagine that the problem has been miraculously solved overnight while the client slept. Next, ask the client system to describe all the signs one would see during the next day that would indicate the miracle had occurred. The effectiveness of this question depends on helping the client system articulate as many features as possible that focus on the solution. The purpose of the Miracle Question is to bring the mindset of the client system to the point of seeing where the system wishes to go. This vision of the future engenders hope and often leads the client system to fill in the picture of how to get there. When the vision and the plan are created by the client system, there is a great deal more interest and motivation to undertake the work involved in achieving problem resolution.

EXCEPTION QUESTION   A second type of interview question used in strengths-based problem-solving work is the Exception Question (DeJong & Miller, 1995). It takes the form of asking the client system if there are times when the problem is not present or is less severe. Saleebey (1997) assumes that there are exceptions to all problems, issues, and needs. By describing these instances of exception, the client system is actually describing strengths, resources, and abilities. Rather than having the generalist explore specific domains of social functioning regarding the system's aspirations, competencies, and confidences as well as the environmental resources, social networks, and opportunities, the Exception Question allows the client system to guide the discussion to the relevant areas where satisfaction and success are envisioned.

DIFFERENCE QUESTION   The Difference Question is another type of strengths-based interview question. The purpose of this question is to help client systems realize they have the ability to do something different than what has been tried in the past. In that way, the question reinforces the intention of changing, reaching a goal, and taking purposeful action. *"What difference did doing that differently make for you?" "What difference would you say that made for you?"* (Saleebey, 2006, p. 123).

OTHER QUESTIONS   Other strengths-based interview questions (DeJong and Miller, 1995; Saleebey, 1997) center on:

► How the client system has managed to survive the challenges
► On whom the client system depends for support
► When there was a time that things were going well
► What the client system wishes to get out of life
► What gives the client system a sense of pride and accomplishment

These are described as survival questions, support questions, exception questions, possibility questions, and esteem questions. All are meant to help the generalist social worker and the client system find the strengths that will be instrumental in the strengths-based problem-solving general method.

Risk and Resilience Perspective

Overview of Component Parts

Another important paradigm to use when preparing for an interview and thinking about talking points with the client system was introduced into the social work literature by Fraser (1997). Similar to the empowerment and strengths perspectives in viewing the client, action, and target systems within a positivistic viewpoint, this paradigm further sorts information according to risk, resilience, and protective factors for micro, mezzo, and macro levels of systems.

■ **C O N C E P T   4 . 3**

> *Resilience* is a general framework of experiences and beliefs that allows client systems to define problematical situations "as an opportunity and to act with understanding, confidence, and persistence in overcoming or rebounding from the consequences of associated adversities through environmental mastery and individual adaptation." (Richman & Bowen, 1997, p. 101)

Risk factors are defined as "any influence that increases the probability of onset, digression to a more serious state, or maintenance of a problem condition" (Kirby & Fraser, 1997, p. 10). This definition encompasses conditions that impact the individual's biological, constitutional, developmental, psychological, social, and spiritual nature as well as intermediate familial and distal environmental conditions that increase the probability of negative future outcomes.

The term *resilience* describes client systems who have achieved positive outcomes in the face of risk (Kirby & Fraser, 1997). This process is characterized by three different types of resilience. The first is characterized by the attainment of a positive outcome despite a high-risk situation. This is sometimes referred to as *overcoming the odds.* The second type of resilience is the ability to retain or restore equilibrium in the face of interpersonal or environmental stress, or *competence under stress.* Finally, resilience incorporates the notion that one successfully adapts in the face of great adversity, or *recovery from trauma.* For both risk and resilience factors, the generalist social worker must keep in mind that different cultures will have variant definitions of what constitutes risk and resilience.

Risk and resilience must be examined within the detailed context of the specific social stressors that bring about the need for client system intervention. To apply this paradigm, the generalist practitioner's work centers on identifying *protective factors* that reduce risk and, by inference, augment resilience. Protective factors may be internal or external forces that ameliorate risk, but, by definition, they also include efforts associated with the three domains of micro, mezzo, and macro systems. By identifying factors that produce risk and promote resilience on all three levels of systems, the social worker has moved far beyond the individual pathology-focused assessment and intervention model prevalent at the end of the last century.

Environmental protective factors are broadly related to opportunities that bring about individual and societal well-being. At the community or macro-system level, protective factors include access to employment, housing, education, health and mental health care, transportation, communication, and child care, to name a few. Risk factors consist of circumstances that act as barriers to accessing these opportunities and include the additional obstacles inherent in social injustice such as discrimination, poverty, and inadequate education.

Mezzo systems are medium-size systems—for example, the family, the neighborhood, and the local school district. Protective factors on this system level include positive family relationships such as effective parenting, the presence of supportive neighbors, a safe community, and strong home-school-community relationships. Risk factors include rejection of nontraditional family structures, negative responses to immigrant or other targeted families in a neighborhood, intrafamily communication problems, child maltreatment, isolation from the community, and family failure to partner with their child's school.

The micro system refers to individual characteristics related to biological, cognitive, constitutional, developmental, psychological, social, and spiritual growth. Physical health, normal intelligence, a balanced temperament, self-esteem, and freedom to be a believer or nonbeliever are all characteristics correlated with protective factors for individuals. Risk factors are deficits in any of these biomedical or psychosocial domains or barriers to personal expression. Furthermore, age, gender, race, ethnicity, and sexual orientation may pose a risk factor for certain individuals given the prevalence of "isms" and the state of current American laws and public policies.

Population Specificity

Each field of practice, agency setting, and population has a set of problem-specific risk factors that it specializes in addressing. It is the professional obligation of the generalist social worker to study the current empirical evidence about the etiology of the various client system conditions that are addressed by his or her agency and to understand the key dimensions and processes of those personal and environmental circumstances that must be addressed in planned change if the risk factors are not to worsen. In other words, it is assumed that there are multiple determinants for all problems in psychosocial functioning. The values and ethics of the social work profession call on the generalist to be well versed in and keep current with the complex issues associated with the mission and nature of the agency and its service population. Keeping the individual, family, and community risk and protective factors in mind is a sure way to integrate a set of knowledge, skills, and assurance into the strengths-based problem-solving interview.

■ CASE EXAMPLE

You are the school social worker in a public elementary school. A student has been referred to you because of teacher concerns about poor social and behavioral performance. In addition, the student has limited academic success. In meeting with the family, you collect the following information that is sorted and outlined in Table 4.1 according to a risk and resilience perspective.

In this case, it became quickly apparent that the current problems in social functioning for this student were transitional in nature. Despite the initial concerns about the student's cognitive abilities due to a premature birth, testing indicated that this child has basic skills and normal intelligence. The family is under stress due to the recent move to a new community and their limited English skills. However, they, too, have basic skills in spoken and written English and continue to improve on them in county adult education courses. The greatest risk to this family is its immigration status. This concern is being sorted out with the help of the Catholic Spanish Center and its office of legal services.

In summary, the generalist social worker first prepares to engage the client, action, or target system in a professional interview by creating a "mental Rubik's Cube" consisting of a variety of mental rows and columns that are changed to create different patterns of questions and that empower a system to take action in the face of difficulties, to discover strengths and resources that may be brought to bear on the planned change effort, and to bring forward protective factors for successful strengths-based problem-solving at the micro, mezzo, and macro system levels. In order to take on these specific attitudes and beliefs, the generalist practitioner must first reflect on the ways the current difficulty is affected by social, psychological, political, and economic issues that have brought about some incapacity that negatively affects the client system. Second, the generalist practitioner prepares to engage the client system from its base of strengths and resources rather than its deficits. Finally, the generalist practitioner reviews the capacities and barriers at the micro, mezzo, and macro systems that add to the current predicament.

These three paradigms help distinguish professional social work interviews from any other type of interview. These ideas and beliefs guide the generalist practitioner to ask questions, think about issues, and take actions in a manner that is fundamentally different from all other medical, psychological, social science, and educational counseling experts.

TABLE 4.1 ■ Risk and Resilience Factors: A School Case Example

	Risks	Resiliencies	Protective Factors
Micro System	Premature birth	Normal developmental milestones	Intensive care
	Lacking early childhood education or kindergarten experience in country of origin (Central America)	Likes to draw, color, play, and be with other children	Educational screening shows normal intelligence
	English is a second language	Student has basic skills in reading, writing, and speaking English	Student qualifies for ESL classes
	School failure	Attend school daily	Access to student study team, evaluation services, referrals for special school programs for children at risk
Mezzo System	International family new to the community	Involved family	Extended family lives in the same community
	Limited knowledge of formal and informal support services for children	Responds to school social work request for a home visit	Sees education as the key to future success for children
	English is a second language	Able to speak English and have working knowledge of written English	Enrolled in adult education English language classes
Macro System	Immigration status	Family for whom mother babysits will sponsor Green Card Application	Spanish legal services

Professional Relationship

A professional relationship is formed by the generalist social worker and client system out of their mutual concern about and intent to resolve the problems, needs, and issues experienced by the client system. The purpose of the General Method is to create a secure working environment, provide a means for carrying out the strengths-based problem-solving process, and facilitate client system goal accomplishment. Professional relational processes take place within interviews. The relationship tone of respectful collaboration is established through principles drawn from the General Method's empowerment perspective, strengths perspective, and risk and resilience perspective and integrated into the interview process. Relationship boundaries are established by the values and ethics of the social work profession and by federal laws and regulations. The professional relationship has no utility apart from the practice situation and has no value apart from its contribution to goal achievement (Biestek, 1957; Applegate & Bonovitz, 1995; Gutierrez, Parsons, & Cox, 1998; Perlman, 1957).

Within this context, the professional relationship involves a purposeful, collaborative exchange process that is respectful of the needs, strengths, assets, and resources that the client system brings to the strengths-based problem-solving process. The relationship is the catalyst for change and the medium through which the generalist social worker employs interview strategies and techniques in strengths-based problem-solving to:

▶ Enable client systems to establish their preferred goals and objectives.
▶ Facilitate development of the strengths-based problem-solving ability of micro, mezzo, and macro client systems.
▶ Enable client systems to mobilize their dormant capacities and resources in the interest of meeting their needs and achieving their goals.

As both catalyst and medium, the professional relationship carries the generalist social worker's and the client system's joint collaborative work forward to the contracted goals and objectives established by the client system during the assessment and contract planning phase (Chapter 7).

The professional relationship begins:

▶ When the generalist social worker and client system meet
▶ When the client system starts sharing problems, needs, and issues of concern
▶ When the generalist social worker demonstrates affective engagement coupled with professional competence that conveys respect, acceptance, support, and expectation designed to facilitate considering these difficulties in a new way (Gutierrez, Parsons, & Cox, 1998; Perlman, 1957)

The professional relationship ends when the client system's goals are achieved (termination phase; Chapter 11).

The General Method Interview

Interviewing Techniques

The interview, as depicted in Figure 4.2, is the primary tool through which the generalist social work practitioner engages the client system. It is also the main data-

FIGURE 4.2 ■ Strengths-Based Problem-Solving Interviews Guided by the Empowerment Perspective, the Strengths Perspective, and the Client System's Risk and Resilience Perspective

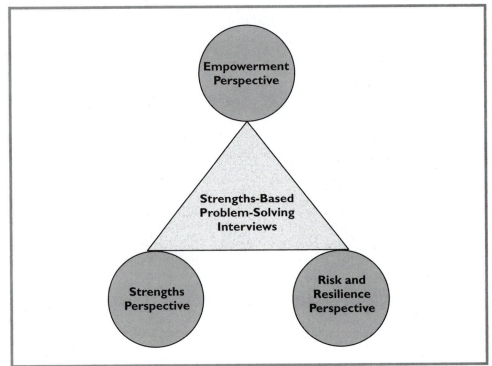

collection instrument for the social work profession. For years, scholars have written about and researched this skill and the essential elements that bring about a successful interview (Garrett, 1972; Kadushin & Kadushin, 1996; Truax & Carkhuff, 1967). Further, the interview serves as the platform for all the phases of the General Method.

What do I say tomorrow when Mrs. Martinez comes to see me? This is a common question among beginning generalist practitioners and is often accompanied by worry and anxiety as they prepare to take the first steps in establishing a collaborative relationship with the client, action, or target system. The current professional literature consistently identifies the following dozen elements as central to the strengths-based problem-solving interview process (Bisman, 1994; Compton, Galaway, & Cournoyer, 2005; Cummins, Sevel, & Pedrick, 2006; DeJong & Berg, 2002; Hepworth, Rooney, Rooney, Strom-Gottfried, & Larsen, 2006; Ivey & Ivey, 2007; Sevel, Cummins, & Madrigal, 1999).

I. LISTENING As paradoxical as it might seem, the first, best, and most important technique of interviewing is to *listen* to the client. Often client systems have not experienced the luxury of a professional social worker or anyone giving his or her full attention to the content and affect of their concerns. DeJong and Berg (2002) recommend that the social worker listen for who and what are important to client systems as they describe their issues of concern.

Good quality listening skills involve:

▶ Tuning in to the client system's frame of reference and understanding the client system's perception of the situation.
▶ Guarding against evaluating what the client system is saying. Listening requires generalist practitioners to suspend their personal beliefs about the situation and not filter the client system's beliefs through their own frame of reference.
▶ Providing aid in using the client system's perspective in the General Method's strengths-based problem-solving approach rather than leaping forward with the social worker's own ideas and plans about how to address the issue.

It is also important to remember that the generalist practitioner's presence and commitment to the strengths-based problem-solving relationship is, in itself, a form of communication. Indeed, all behavior is a form of communication, so the generalist social worker must pay attention not only to how a person listens but also to how a person presents himself or herself in dress, voice, body and verbal language, and manners when the interview begins.

For some client systems, it is important to dress in the role of a professional. This does not mean buying expensive clothing or wearing the most recent fashions. It does mean that the generalist social worker dresses and presents himself or herself as being in the business of helping. It is a sign of respect for the client system and an indication of one's competence as a social worker.

Vocal qualities also help further one's presentation of self. For example, tone of voice is very important even when the client system is highly distressed and talking loudly or using inappropriate language. One conveys a sense of balance in the relationship and confidence in the process by maintaining measured, soft, even vocal tone rather than mirroring the client's distress as revealed through tone of voice.

Another technique is to use the same rate or pace of speech as the client system. It is important to ask colleagues how one comes across to others in verbal communication—loud or quiet, assertive or receptive, rapid fire or tortoise slow. Marked regional differences in speech and language patterns, including pace and style, can be very real impediments to open and full communication. By mirroring the rate and pace of speech and language patterns and not appearing as a distant professional stranger, the social work practitioner is more easily heard by the client system. The ability to conduct such mirroring takes awareness and practice.

Eye contact, visual tracking, head nodding, facial expressions, hand gestures, smiles, and physical proximity are all forms of communication. Ideally, they indicate attentiveness, respect, and openness to the interview without invading the client system's space. In the end, the time taken to prepare oneself mentally and physically before the interview will result in more focus during the interview (Sevel, Cummins, & Madrigal, 1999).

Further, client systems have more information about their problems, issues, needs, and potential solutions than they know. They are the actual experts in identifying their concerns and understanding which actions will be most effective in bringing about a solution to their concerns. Thus, the interview is a partnership and is most successful when client systems are allowed to tell their story and express their concerns uninterrupted by frequent questions. DeJong and Berg (2002) describe this as the *not knowing* stance that is critical to building interviews that will lead to solutions. In the interview, the generalist social worker's expertise lies in exploring the client system's frame of reference and bringing out those resources the client system perceives will shift the situation to elicit balance and well-being. Only client systems can convey how they want their lives changed, what will be different once the change has occurred, and what resources exist for bringing about this change.

2. OPEN-ENDED QUESTIONS   After beginning the interview by greeting the client, the generalist practitioner usually begins by making a general comment such as *Welcome* and following up by asking, *How may I help you?* or *Tell me what brought you to our agency.* These are *open-ended questions and comments.* Open-ended questions cannot be answered by a simple yes or no answer (Bisman, 1994). They are broad questions that call for an unstructured response. Open-ended questions and comments give client systems the choice of where they wish to start their story and what information they wish to share. Such questions solicit information that reflects the client system's frame of reference and are a way to show respect and promote client self-determination (DeJong & Berg, 2002). By contrast, closed-ended questions and comments center on the generalist practitioner's frame of reference.

The purpose of the open-ended question is to draw out detailed information and encourage client systems to elaborate their ideas. Open-ended questions are frequently used during the first part of the interview when the generalist practitioner is inviting the client system to open up and share its problematic concern and how it has tried to handle the situation. In order to bring depth of thought to the interview, open-ended questions must be relevant to the issues at hand and help achieve the overall purpose of the interview.

3. CLOSED-ENDED QUESTIONS   *Closed-ended questions* are in direct contrast to open-ended questions. Closed-ended questions ask for specific facts. They reflect the generalist social worker's frame of reference and what the social worker wants to know, thereby restricting the client system's responses (Hepworth, Rooney, Rooney, Strom-Gottfried, & Larsen, 2006). Beginning generalists may overuse this type of question or comment in an effort to obtain information they believe will demonstrate a successful interview. Paradoxically, however, a string of closed-ended questions usually results in a very superficial interview and closes down client system communication. The practitioner will know that this type of question is ineffective if communication becomes blocked or the answers do not further the interview process. At times, it is necessary to employ closed-ended questions, but the skillful generalist practitioner will use them judiciously and in conjunction with open-ended questions.

4. CLARIFICATION QUESTIONS   Open-ended questions are often paired with *clarification questions*. When the client system speaks in vague or overly general terms, it is necessary for the generalist to determine if he or she has correctly understood the thought, feeling, or experience conveyed by the client, action, or target system. It is a way to elicit feedback while at the same time help the client system sharpen its narrative story. Sometimes, the verbal language used by the client system is unfamiliar to the social worker or the nonverbal language is unclear. Other times, the client system draws conclusions that leave the generalist practitioner without any understanding of how this judgment was made. In either case, clarification questions are designed to help the generalist social worker fully understand the client system's perception of and reaction to the situation. More than any other type of interview question, the nature of the clarification question draws the social worker and client system together into a reciprocal dialogue not matched by other types of questions or comments.

5. PARAPHRASING   *Paraphrasing* is another form of clarification. The generalist practitioner synthesizes the content, thoughts, feelings, and actions expressed by the client system and restates them to confirm the meaning of the original message. The technique of paraphrasing uses statements, not questions, in response to the client system. The generalist practitioner simplifies the client system's message using his or her own words and communicates the paraphrase back to the client system for approval, amendment, or rejection. The goal of paraphrasing is to capture the essence of the presentation and mirror it back to convey that the client system has been heard and may continue to expand on the difficulties (Cummins, Sevel, & Pedrick, 2006; Compton, Galaway, & Cournoyer, 2005).

6. FURTHERING   *Furthering* is another interviewing technique which consists of minimal prompts to encourage the client system to continue presentation of the narrative. These prompts may be verbal or nonverbal. Both types of prompts convey attentiveness and interest, in effect asking the client system to continue. Client systems may make vague statements or overgeneralizations that make it difficult to understand the true meaning of what is being said. Furthering is a way of eliciting more details, clarifying what has been said and not said, and amplifying the content, affect, and meaning of the presentation for both the generalist social worker and the client system what is being described.

7. REFLECTION OF FEELINGS   *Reflection of feelings* or empathic communication plays a pivotal role in strengths-based interviews. It is the ability to accurately perceive and sensitively communicate back to the client system the inner feelings being expressed. Often client systems experience a cluster of feelings and reactions that are difficult for them to separate, explain, or even comprehend how each is related to the other. Reflecting feelings is the skill not only to be empathically attuned to the feelings being expressed but also to distinguish between the clearly apparent feelings and the unidentified or latent feelings behind the obvious feelings. In other words, the generalist practitioner brings depth to the interview by sensitively acknowledging the expressed feelings and articulating for the client system the unacknowledged or unexpressed feelings. However, a note of caution is in order to ensure that the generalist social worker is reflecting the client system's feelings and not projecting his or her own upon the client system's narrative. This interview technique helps the generalist practitioner explore not only the breadth and depth of the issues being discussed but also the extent to which the client system is aware of the intensity of the feelings. When the client system recognizes the hidden feelings, insight is gained about the issue and this movement begins to alleviate the overall distress (Hepworth, Rooney, Rooney, Strom-Gottfried, & Larsen, 2006; Sevel, Cummins, & Madrigal, 1999).

8. SUMMARIZATION *Summarization* pulls together the thoughts, feelings, experience, and content expressed by the client system. It may be used to begin an interview in order to tie together the previous interview with the current interview. Summarization may also be used throughout the interview to focus the discussion, clarify complex issues, or provide a transition to the next interview topic. In addition, it may be used to complete the interview, identify the highlights of the session, and set an agenda for the next interview (Hepworth, Rooney, Rooney, Strom-Gottfried, & Larsen, 2006; Ivey & Ivey, 2007). Caution is indicated, however, in that summarization is not simply a list of items discussed but rather the weaving together of subject matter, patterns, and reactions.

9. INFORMATION GIVING Strengths-based problem-solving in generalist practice often requires the social work practitioner to provide concrete information, topical literature, or community resource materials to the client, action, or target system. This *information giving* is meant to assist the client system in making decisions based on consideration of multiple alternatives that will further the client system's plans to address its need or issue or to act in new ways. It differs from the pitfall of *advice giving* in which the generalist practitioner indicates what he or she believes is the best approach to a situation (Ivey & Ivey, 2007; Sevel, Cummins, & Madrigal, 1999).

10. CONFRONTATION *Confrontation* is a technique of interviewing that is often misunderstood by beginning generalist practitioners. It simply consists of identifying discrepancies in the client system's messages within the narrative. These discrepancies may be in verbal communication, nonverbal communication, or behaviors. The discrepancies also may occur between verbal and nonverbal communication or between verbal communication and behavior. Before using this technique of interviewing, it is crucial that the generalist social worker develop a strong relationship with the client system—one that is characterized by acceptance, trust, support, mutuality, and respect.

11. INTERPRETATION *Interpretation* consists of statements made by the generalist practitioner that tie together seemingly disparate thoughts, feelings, reactions, and experiences for the purpose of facilitating client system insight into the source, pattern, or continuation of difficulties. It is a way of surfacing an underlying issue or eliciting deeper meaning about the situation. The goal is to assist the client system in examining the current circumstances and seeing them in a new light. Interpretation is a technique of interviewing that requires a high degree of skill and is to be used judiciously. If a client system disagrees or discounts the interpretation, the generalist social worker needs to accept this stance gracefully and move the interview forward with other techniques (Sevel, Cummins, & Madrigal, 1999).

12. SILENCE   Interviews are about talking, but sometimes *silence* is a useful form of interpersonal communication (Ivey & Ivey, 2007). Silence can be frightening, but it really does not hurt anyone. It allows the generalist social worker and the client system to reflect on what is being discussed. The practitioner takes the cue from the client system. If there are nonverbal or verbal indications of discomfort with the silence, the social work practitioner takes the lead in asking another question or allows the client system to take the lead in continuing the narrative. In the end, it is important to keep in mind that silence has more interview power than filling up the silence with chatter.

Pitfalls to Avoid in Interviews

Everyone makes mistakes during an interview. Whether a beginning generalist social work practitioner or a senior clinical social worker, the individual learns that for every interview there is more than one opportunity to spoil the ongoing communication through a variety of missteps. When the strengths-based problem-solving relationship is built on mutual respect and openness, the practitioner finds that client systems are very forgiving of mistakes, invested in returning to a collaborative partnership, and committed to moving forward in the strengths-based problem-solving process.

The following are some communication style patterns and reasons why they are best avoided (Sevel, Cummins, & Madrigal, 1999):

- ▶ *Advice giving* is not consistent with a co-equal collaborative relationship.
- ▶ *Inappropriate use of humor* minimizes the problem.
- ▶ *Interrupting the client system* does not allow the system to express the complete idea or finish the train of thought.
- ▶ *Abrupt transitions* do not allow for closure on a topic that the client system has chosen to discuss.
- ▶ *Inappropriate and irrelevant questions* move the professional interview away from a collaborative approach toward an intrusive and investigative style of communication.
- ▶ *Judgmental responses* impede the development of trust by placing the generalist social worker in a role of authority.
- ▶ *Offering false assurance* minimizes the problem and prevents the client system from coming to terms with the difficulty and consequences of the situation.
- ▶ *Inappropriate social worker self-disclosure* takes the focus off the client system and distracts from client system concerns.
- ▶ *Premature confrontation* may hinder the development of trust and interfere with the development of the professional relationship.

▶ *Overwhelming the client with too much information* confuses critical issues and inhibits decision making and action.

▶ *Premature problem-solving* is a barrier to achieving complete understanding of the complex psychosocial issues brought by the client system and bars the client system from fully exploring the issue and participating in the strengths-based problem-solving efforts.

▶ *Insincerity* is a form of dishonesty and creates an artificial helping relationship.

▶ *Minimizing the problem* is an effort to downplay the depth, breadth, and complexity of the situation and is antithetical to the helping process. It does not give the message that the client system is understood.

Summary (see Figure 4.3)

The professional social work interview is a specialized form of communication in which the generalist social work practitioner seeks to elicit a variety of client system

FIGURE 4.3 ■ The Professional Relationship Supports the Strengths-Based Problem-Solving Interview

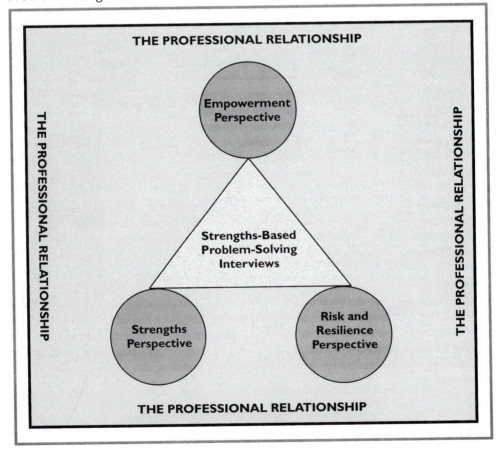

expressions of thoughts, feelings, and experiences related to the presenting problems, issues, or needs (Compton, Galaway, & Cournoyer, 2005). Although generalist social workers may use evidence-based practice manuals as guides in exploring certain practice questions and taking specific actions during the process of service delivery, procedural steps in a manual are not meant to limit or control the strengths-based problem-solving discourse between the generalist practitioner and the client system.

The strengths-based problem-solving interview process is guided by principles of empowerment and the strengths perspective. Professional social work interviews also include information on universal and problem-specific risk factors at the micro, mezzo, and macro levels for the purpose of identifying protective factors that can strengthen multisystem resilience. All of these factors are considered and incorporated into the interview process in the service of developing a professional relationship between the generalist practitioner and the client, action, or target system.

To this end, generalist practitioners can monitor and reflect on their interviewing skills by examining the degree to which their communication has supported client system expertise, focused on strengths and assets rather than problems, and integrated protective factors by asking themselves:

1. How well do I listen to the client system? Am I aware of both explicit and implicit statements?
2. Do I acknowledge the client system's expertise?
3. Am I sensitive to the client system's diverse characteristics and needs?
4. Do I silently discount the opinion of the client system because of sociodemographic and cultural diversity or prejudice? If so, what can I do to exchange silences for dialogue with the particular client system? What can I do to address my own biases and discomforts with certain diversity?
5. Have I taken enough time to help the client system explore the pros and cons of the proposed actions while exploring and examining alternative courses of action?
6. Have I asked the client system for feedback in a way that the client system would be comfortable in offering such feedback?
7. Have I acknowledged what I have learned from the client system and how that knowledge has been helpful in assisting the client system with finding possible solutions?
8. Have I used language that the client system understands?
9. When there have been barriers to communication, have I invited the client system to teach me a better system of collecting information?
10. When professional obligations require me to carry out actions that the client system opposes, have I subsequently taken time to explore this decision in an open, direct, and respectful way?
11. When I am feeling anxious about the client system's behavior or circumstance, do my feelings negatively impact the interview?
12. Are my professional actions a benefit to the client system rather than to myself or are they geared to alleviating my own anxiety?
13. Have I made a conscious effort to explore the client system's strengths and environmental assets as much as I have spent exploring the problems, needs, or barriers?

SUMMARY AND TRANSITION

When students choose social work as their professional career path, they soon discover that society in general, other professionals, immediate family, and close friends are unclear about what social work is and what it does. This uncertainty is sometimes captured in the expression, *The good news is that social work is a big tent. The bad news is that social work is a big tent.* But the very same features that make this axiom true are the distinguishing characteristics that cause professional social work to be fundamentally different from psychiatry, psychology, education, political science, and sociology.

Each of these lines of work has a view of client systems and of the processes for attending to a client system's problems and needs. The psychiatrist addresses the question of whether physical and/or mental health is interfering with the patient's well-being. The primary tool used to answer this question is the clinical interview. The psychologist is interested primarily in mental disorders and uses tests and measurements to ascertain what cognitive features are involved in the patient's complaint. Educators disseminate general knowledge, information, and skills that assist the student in acquiring literacy and in acculturating individuals to societal norms and expectations. They use lectures, seminars, workshops, media and materials, laboratory experiences, small group discussions, modeling, and performance measures to impart their expertise. Political scientists study the decision-making processes of governments and social institutions. By examining economic, political, and social issues, a political scientist and a public policymaker attempt to influence the course of action taken by various societal institutions in an effort to reinforce certain values and beliefs about the best policies, funding sources, and program services for specific populations with specific needs. Sociologists investigate critical questions encountered in social institutions and the social processes that influence societal groups. This work is accomplished through the research and study of social problems and their anthropological, economic, geographical, historical, political, and social psychological origins.

By contrast, social work values the knowledge base and methods of each and every one of these various disciplines and occupations. In fact, social work integrates components from each in such a unique way that this singular profession has developed its own unique purpose, sanctions, values, knowledge, and methods.

Social work is the first profession to approach the helping process from a holistic perspective that always views the person within the context of his or her family, culture, physical surroundings, community, civil institutions, and society. It is not enough to study the individual or society discretely without efforts to enhance the social functioning of individuals, families, and groups and to modify organizations, communities, and larger environments so that those efforts prevent, ameliorate, or minimize conditions associated with risk factors, population needs, and resource limitations. In other words, social work is the only profession historically committed by its knowledge and methods to developing the maximum potential of micro, mezzo, and macro client systems. A further defining feature of the social work profession is the central tenet that achieving the highest level of social functioning and general welfare is accomplished only by working at the interface of the person-in-environment and micro, mezzo, and macro systems. It is only through exploration of the transactions between these three different system levels that one can truly bring about enduring change for the benefit of all.

Furthermore, society sanctions these precepts and assigns authority to the profession for implementing the aims and goals that are regulated by a written professional Code of Ethics and implemented according to core professional values that exemplify professional standards and basic principles of practice. These standards and practices are guided by classical and modern theoretical and conceptual knowledge and by knowledge of human diversity. Anyone is able to collect facts and information, but it is only when these are examined in relation to existing social work literature, research, and scholarship that the information rises to the level of professional knowledge that allows the social worker to understand and explain a client system problem situation and collaboratively select a method of planned change.

As shown in Figure 4.4, strengths-based problem-solving interviews with diverse micro, mezzo, and macro client systems do not stand alone in the General Method. This interview approach combines with social work foundation knowledge, the ecological systems perspective, the knowledge of human diversity, and the empirical ap-

FIGURE 4.4 ■ Generalist Social Work Practice: Knowledge and Tools for the General Method

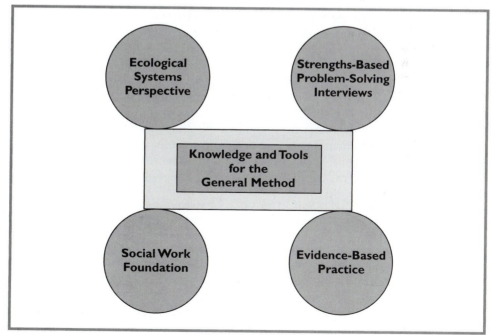

proach to practice to form the knowledge base and tools for the General Method. Thus, the four chapters in Part I of this book have provided an overview of the General Method and a basis for moving forward to Part II, which focuses on the practice principles, processes, and techniques used during the six phases of the General Method: engagement, data collection, assessment and contract planning, intervention, evaluation, and termination.

REFLECTION POINTS

Becoming a skilled social work practitioner requires knowledge and skills, including the ability to reflect on practice endeavors. The following reflection points are designed to strengthen critical thinking and mastery of knowledge of key points in this chapter.

1. Define and discuss the following key elements that frame the generalist social work interview:
   • Empowerment
   • Strengths perspective
   • Risk and resilience
   • Professional relationship
2. Discuss how human diversity influences the interview process.
3. Discuss with a classmate an interview in which you were "not heard." Identify the specific elements that served as a barrier to communication.
4. Engage in a role-play with a colleague in which you try out the different interview techniques discussed in this chapter. Be explicit about the techniques you are using.
5. Review the *NASW Code of Ethics* (www.socialworkers.org). How do these standards support strengths-based problem-solving interviews?
6. For further reading and research, use the key concepts in Question 1 to locate social work references related to this chapter's content. (See Appendix A, Selected Internet Resources, and Appendix B, Selected Social Work Journals.) What issues or concerns are evident in the articles? How might these influence your strengths-based problem-solving interviews with client, action, and target systems?

CHAPTER 5

Engagement

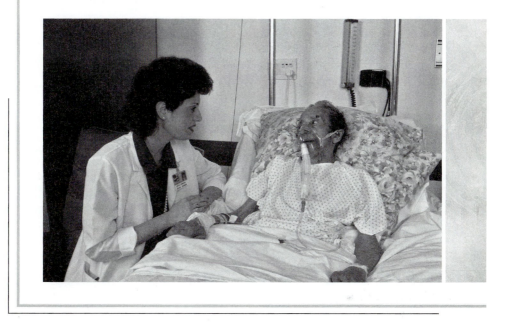

Whether the generalist social work practitioner begins to work with an individual, family, group, organization, or community as a client, action, or target system, the social worker's first task is to engage the system in strengths-based problem-solving directed toward goal accomplishment. Thus, the first phase of the General Method is termed *engagement*. Engaging a client or action system in an interactive professional exchange focused on the possibility of change, however, may trigger inhibiting barriers to service delivery in the form of negative help-seeking behavioral responses and the possibility of resistance by the system to what is perceived as outside intrusion. Therefore, from the first contact, the generalist practitioner needs to draw on foundation social work knowledge, values and ethics, and practice principles and skills for effective engagement in the strengths-based problem-solving approach of the General Method.

■ **C O N C E P T   5 . 1**

The *engagement phase* consists of the time and processes used in establishing a professional relationship with a client or action system that is directed toward goal-oriented change.

During the engagement phase, the social worker attends to seven guiding processes:

1. Establishing professional relational boundaries
2. Identifying problems, needs, and strengths
3. Recognizing feelings and reactions
4. Increasing client system investment
5. Determining goals
6. Making initial plans
7. Monitoring the engagement phase

That all of these guiding processes are addressed at least to some degree before proceeding to the second phase of the General Method highlights the fact that these processes may be used to document progress and monitor the engagement phase.

Establishing Professional Relational Boundaries

The engagement phase of the General Method involves a purposive, interactive exchange process characterized by the interpersonal and affective connectedness that forms a professional working relationship. This professional alliance exists between the social worker and the client or action system, sets the tone for their collaborative work toward a specified goal and outcome, and serves as a catalyst for change (Applegate & Bonovitz, 1995). This professional relationship exists only within a specific practice situation and has no value apart from its contribution to the work at hand. It reflects the professional strengths, limits, and relational boundaries established by the value base and ethical imperatives of the social work profession. Using the term *reflection-in-action,* Schon (1983) notes that the purpose of the professional relationship is to establish conditions that facilitate reflective, purposive conversations with client systems about their needs, resources, and life experiences.

Since the purpose of engagement with client, action, and target systems differs, the nature of the professional working relationship will also differ. Client systems, for example, are seeking services and are the expected beneficiaries of services. Thus, the professional working alliance with a client system includes the more facilitative relational conditions of respect, empathy, warmth, genuineness, and unconditional positive regard (Carkhuff & Anthony, 1979; Rogers, 1957) and conveys energy and hope for goal accomplishment. The importance of balancing these relational qualities of acceptance, expectation, support, and stimulation (Perlman, 1957) according to particular client system strengths and needs cannot be overstated. Indeed, at the midpoint of the last century, Biestek (1957), Perlman (1957), and Simon (1960), respectively, wrote of the professional relationship with the client system as the soul and essence, the heart, and the keystone of social work intervention. By the end of the century, a positive working relationship had been identified as necessary for (Gaston, 1990) and as the best predictor of (Horvath & Symonds, 1991; Safran, Crocker, McMain, & Murray, 1990) positive direct practice outcomes. Today, the quality of the professional working relationship is considered to be the common factor in the helping process that accounts for 30 percent of the variance in client system outcome (Tallman & Bohart, 1999).

In action systems, the social worker joins with others to work with and through them in influencing a target system and accomplishing identified goals. Thus, the professional working relationship with an action system reflects the more active relational conditions of mutual respect, positive interaction, collaboration, advocacy, and political skill and conveys energy and belief in the goal-directed work of changing the target system.

Identifying Problems, Needs, and Strengths

Before actually discussing the problem with a client or action system in any depth, it is necessary for the social worker to prepare for the contact. He or she tries to learn as much as possible about the culture, needs, strengths, and resources of the system. The social worker tries not only to understand the system that he or she will interact with but also to understand his or her own culture, needs, and resources and how the two, social worker and system of contact, may form a "fit" for positive interactions. If it appears that there will be stress or difficulty in the match between social worker and client or action system, the generalist practitioner seeks help from a supervisor.

At the point of initial contact, after brief introductions, the purpose for coming together needs to be expressed. Within the description of purpose, a problem, need, or strength may be mentioned. The social worker keeps these in mind for reference when the time is appropriate.

If the service setting is concerned about a problem and initiates the contact with the client or action system, the social worker states the purpose. If the client system or a referral system initiates the contact with the service system, the social worker encourages the initiating system to say why the contact was made. For example:

■ **CASE SCENARIO 1:**

Concern Originates in Service Setting

SW: Good morning, Mrs. B. I am Mary Costello, the school social worker. I would like to talk with you about your son Johnnie and how he's doing at school.

■ **CASE SCENARIO 2:**

Concern Originates in Client System

SW: Good morning. I am Mary Costello, the school social worker. I understand you wanted to talk with me.

CLIENT: Yes, I'm Mrs. B, Johnnie's mother. His teacher said that maybe I could talk to you about the problems I've been having at home with my son lately.

The generalist asks himself or herself: *What is the issue, problem, need, or question that appears to be the major concern for this client system? Is there really a problem (or problems) that the client system will identify and invest energy in for resolution? What are the corresponding strengths and resources that will facilitate strengths-based problem-solving?* In asking these questions, the social worker begins to clarify the problems or needs he or she and the client system are going to work on together.

The General Method is permeated with the ecological-systems perspective. Thus, the generalist practitioner knows that when an environment provides a client or action system with the inputs needed for thriving, the environment expects certain system inputs in return. In other words, the environment and the client or action system have role expectations for each other that involve behaving and producing in a manner conducive to the well-being of the other. Therefore, in the General Method, the problem or need is defined initially in terms of what is taking place at the point of interface and interactions between the client or action system and the expectations and resources of the environment. From the input/output ecological-systems perspective, the problems, needs, strengths, and resources can be seen at the boundary point where a system interlocks with some aspect of its surrounding environment or with some other system in that environment. It must also be remembered, however, that strengths and resources permeate both client and action systems and their environments and are not limited to boundary points. Thus, the intervention plan to be developed is not limited to the boundary where a system and the environment come together.

As brought out by Hearn (1969, p. 69): "In short, social work activity is focused inside, outside, and at the boundary between the system and its environment." The initial problem description, however, focuses on the boundary point where there is a need or desire to direct attention to the functioning of the client or action system and the environment in relation to each other.

For example, in Case Scenario 1, the problem as presented by the social worker is between Johnnie and the school. He is not behaving or performing academically at the level expected for him to "fit" into the school system. The problem, as introduced by Mrs. B in Case Scenario 2, is between Johnnie and his mother at home. He is not acting in the manner his mother expects. Every effort should be made to relate the problem, needs, and strengths as directly as possible to the client or action system in contact with the social worker. The more distant and less explicit the problem, the more difficult it is to involve the client system in a timely change effort. Usually it is not necessary to identify clearly the causes of the problem in the engagement phase. During data collection, phase 2, there is opportunity to obtain information on causes. Sometimes, however, facts relating to cause may need to be presented to promote greater incentive for cooperation. The social worker may need to present data in order to determine the validity of the apparent causes of a problem or need presented by Mrs. B.

For example, in Case Scenario 1, if Mrs. B identifies the main problem as Johnnie's not getting along with his teacher, she may think there is little she has to work on to improve the situation. If, on the other hand in Case Scenario 2, Mrs. B is helped to see that Johnnie's problems started around the time her husband was laid off from work and she began working, Mrs. B may begin to get more involved in looking at the problem and needed resources.

The timing and techniques used in presenting facts to stimulate engagement are dependent on the sensitivity and skills of the social worker. Presenting facts too soon or too abruptly may cause the client system to become distressed or inhibited. In Case Scenario 1, Mrs. B may be overwhelmed to hear that Johnnie is late for school, skipping classes, talking back to the teacher, and not turning in homework assignments. She may not understand what her role is in resolving these problems. In Case Scenario 2, Mrs. B may find it difficult to talk about her husband or the financial constraints that necessitated her going to work. She may become distressed as she begins to see a correlation between her son's school problems and what is happening with herself and her husband. She may lose sight of family strengths and resources.

In beginning to identify the problem with a client system, the skilled generalist is sensitive to delicate, feeling-filled areas. The social worker knows that feelings relevant to the problems must be recognized, understood, and expressed if there is to be real movement toward problem resolution and strengths enhancement. As feelings are disclosed, new problems or a clearer understanding of the problem, needs, and strengths, may emerge. As stated, problems are not fixed, but clarification is evolving, and feelings and cognitions are forces that help move the problems and potential into clearer focus.

Recognizing Feelings and Reactions

Micro and Mezzo Client Systems

A basic practice principle, as described in Chapter 1, is *purposeful expression of feelings* (Biestek, 1957; National Association of Social Workers, 1999). The social worker does not encourage indiscriminate ventilation of feelings about any or every issue. The General Method is a purposeful process that calls for the social worker to have expertise in the realm of feelings. The generalist practioner strives to become aware of the feelings of the client system as they relate to the problem situation. The social worker recognizes when the client system is expressing unrelated feelings and uses skill in deciding whether these feelings indicate other problem areas in need of attention or whether their expression is an attempt to avoid facing the problem at hand. If the former, the social worker and the client system may need to reconstruct or add to the identified problem; if the latter, the social worker may need to discuss the avoidance with the client system and redirect the conversation back to the identified problem-needs-strengths configuration.

There is also the basic principle called *controlled emotional involvement* (Biestek, 1957; National Association of Social Workers, 1999). It points to the need for the social worker to have self-awareness in terms of his or her own feelings surrounding the problem-client system-environment situation. Prior to and throughout the process of working with others, the generalist social worker realizes the fact that he or she has feelings also. At times, these feelings may be very strong and in need of control while he or she works with particular client, action, or target systems or problem areas. If this is difficult for the social worker, he or she should seek help from a supervisor.

In the General Method, the identification of feelings, as well as problems and strengths, is done basically on a rational level. The knowledge foundation of social work practice looks at the whole of human nature and enables the social worker to be aware of unconscious as well as conscious factors that influence human behavior. In generalist practice, however, the feelings encouraged and expressed are mainly conscious and identifiable. The approach of the social worker may be described primarily as rational or cognitive. In the cognitive approach, conscious thought is considered the principal determinant of emotions, motives, and actions. Thus, the feelings, incentives, and action behaviors brought to the social worker's attention are problems in the client system's conscious awareness (Granvold, 1994; Robbins, Chatterjee, & Canda, 1998). The generalist practitioner does not discard the notion of the unconscious in human behavior, but recognizes that his or her competence is for working on the rational, conscious level. The feelings addressed in generalist practice are conscious or able to be brought into consciousness with a little effort.

Carkhuff and Anthony (1979, p. 243) point out that each feeling has a rational reason that can be identified:

> The thing the helper must remember is this: *Regardless of the apparent nature of the cause of a particular helpee's feelings, each of those feelings will always turn out to have a sufficient and rational reason! One of the most important goals of all helpee exploration is to identify—to the helper as well as to the helpee—the real reason for each of his or her real feelings.*

Even though feelings may be conscious, the social worker knows that often they are difficult to share. It may be awkward for a person to engage in a discussion about private feelings with a social worker in the early phases of a working relationship. As stated earlier, in some cultures, words are seldom used to express feelings, particularly with someone outside of the family (Chao, 1992; Marsella, 1993). In many cultures, feelings of inadequacy are particularly difficult to express. Among others, these may include feelings of being no good, unable to do things, unable to do something about a situation, or unable to handle affection from others. They may also include feelings about being hurt or rejected, guilt, shame, passivity, helplessness, and dependency, or they may include feelings that come from a need to be punished or a need to punish someone else (Egan, 1998).

Poor families have often been described as unable to express concerns well enough to talk about them with a social agency and so inarticulate that they literally do not have the words for their emotion. Hollis (1965) disagrees with this judgment and reports that most social workers do not have difficulty getting clients to express their feelings if the social workers themselves use appropriate language. She points out that social workers should not let simplicity of language be understood as incapacity. Often, simple words or expressions are the most valid and meaningful. "Exploration may sometimes proceed at a slower pace than with the more verbal, better educated client. But once the low-income client's confidence has been established, he is likely to speak freely, particularly of feelings of anger and frustrations, sometimes directed against the worker himself" (Hollis, 1965, p. 469).

To be able to help a client system discuss relevant feelings, the generalist social worker needs to have a broad vocabulary to describe feelings. As brought out by Hallowitz (1979, p. 111):

> The worker also helps the client with feelings that impair his ability to deal with the problems at hand—e.g., anxiety, conflict, resistance. He encourages the client to do the problem-solving work to the fullest possible extent. When the limits of this are reached, he contributes his own thinking and suggestions.

The suggestions offered to help a client system with describing feelings have to be carefully and appropriately selected. The word list in Figure 5.1 may be helpful to social workers as they search for ways to describe particular feelings most aptly. Each word may be modified for more accurate indications of degrees of intensity by using such descriptive words as *a little, somewhat, moderately,* and *very.*

Feelings are not described in one or two words. They may be expressed through phrases, behavioral descriptions, and stated desires (Egan, 1998). For example, to feel "happy" may be described as "I feel great," "I feel as free as a bird," "I feel I could jump for joy," or "I feel I would like to reach out and hug everyone here." The important point in the engagement phase is not so much *how* the feelings are expressed but that they *are* expressed in whatever manner has the most meaning to the client system. Central to the art of social work practice is the awareness of feelings in human systems and of the value in their purposeful expression.

As stated earlier, when feelings are expressed, the social worker needs to explore with the system of contact the rational reason for the feelings. A technique frequently used as the practitioner clarifies the feelings is to say, *I understand that you are feeling _____ because _____* or *Is it that you feel _____ because _____?* or *You seem to be feeling _____ because _____.*

It is always necessary to solicit feedback from the client system after a reason for feelings is suggested. This may be accomplished by adding a statement such as, *Is that correct? What do you think? Am I right?* or *Is that it?* In this way, the client system is encouraged by the social worker to participate in the process of finding reasons for feelings, and to accept, modify, or reject the suggested description of feelings offered by the social worker.

FIGURE 5.1 ■ Words to Describe Feelings

Positive Feelings	Negative Feelings
Relaxed	Uptight, nervous
All together	Spacey, mixed up
Whole	Falling apart
Confident, adequate, potent	Confused, unsure, inept
Graceful	Awkward, clumsy
Well organized	Disorganized
Accepted	Rejected, abandoned
Appreciated	Unappreciated
A part of things	Out of step, left out
Loved	Unloved
Full of life	Burned out, exhausted
Strengthened, firm	Weakened, weak
Witty	Dull
Able to cope	Overwhelmed
Good	Bad
Warm	Cold
Delighted	Unhappy, frustrated
Great	Small
Glad	Sad
Pleased	Displeased, angry, outraged
Loving	Hateful, hostile, furious
Daring	Afraid
In control	Out of control, helpless
Hopeful	Hopeless
Full	Empty
Built up	Put down, crushed
Serene	Disturbed
Energetic	Exhausted
Healthy	Sick
Powerful	Powerless
Free	Trapped

As the social worker moves with the client system from the identification of feelings to the reasons for the feelings, the social worker tries to utilize the ecological perspective. An effort is made to incorporate a view of the system in relation to the environment within the definition of the reason for feelings. The more the members of a client system see the part they play in the reason for the feelings, the more chance there is that they will begin to use their feelings in dealing with the problem. For example, the social worker in the first case scenario may say:

Mrs. B, I can see that you are troubled because you can't understand why your son is not getting along in school lately. Is that right?

or

> Mrs. B, you seem to be very upset right now. Is it because you don't want to hear that Johnnie is having school problems at a time when you and the family are having so many other difficulties?

In the second case scenario, the social worker might say:

> You are feeling very frustrated because you can't seem to get along with your son lately. Is that it, Mrs. B?

or

> You are very angry with your son lately because he is not behaving the way you expect of him. Is this correct?

The reason for the feelings may be closely related to the problem as presented, or after further exploration, the social worker may find that the reason for the feelings as clarified becomes a means for uncovering issues that need more immediate attention. In the first case scenario, for example, the social worker may begin to see that Mrs. B is currently feeling overwhelmed because of extensive family problems, and Johnnie's behavior at school is but an indicator of a very troubled family situation. In the second case scenario, Mrs. B expressed feelings that relate directly to the presenting problem. The feelings she expressed were caused by a problem in parent-child interaction.

As the feelings are refined and the problem reformulated, it may become apparent through the exploration of feelings and their reasons that there is a problem needing to be addressed, but that it is outside the scope of competence of the generalist practitioner or the agency's services. A referral to another service may be necessary. When several problems have emerged and at least one problem continues within the social worker's domain, a resource may need to be contacted for a collaborative effort. It is important for the social worker to keep in mind that every step in the process of the General Method may change the nature of the problem.

When needs or expectations are unmet, client system members begin to feel unfulfilled. Negative feelings, including anger and rage, may develop. Negative feelings drain energy from a client system. When the reason for these feelings is identified and if through some process or intervention the reason may be reversed, there is then new energy available for more effective social functioning. Positive feelings generate vitality and energy for growth-promoting transactions. The reasons for positive feelings are seen as something to be maintained or enhanced. As long as the reasons persist, the energy level continues to expand for effective social functioning.

The reasons for feelings may relate closely to the problems and also to the goals. The stating of reasons for negative or positive feelings helps to move the social worker and the client system into recognizing and discussing goals. The introduction of suggestions for preliminary goals should come only after the client system has confirmed the stated reasons for feelings. If the suggested goals are unrelated to the feelings of the client system, they may be a reflection of the social worker's hopes and expectations rather than the client system's actual goals.

Macro Client Systems

As noted earlier, the engagement phase initiates the General Method with client systems of any size or type. Even when working with an action or target system, the generalist tries to discern how the problem is perceived, what feelings or reactions exist about the situation, and what goals would be acceptable and feasible for involvement by the particular system.

Client systems request or agree to work with the social worker to receive benefits from the service. Action systems cooperate with the social worker to achieve goals or influence target systems. Target systems need to change for goal accomplishment. They may or may not wish to work with the social worker.

A target, action, or client system may be an individual, family, group, organization, community, social institution, or society. These are the systems of contact in social work practice. As the generalist works with diverse systems, an important consideration is the distinguishing characteristics that are generally recognized among the different systems. As depicted in Figure 5.2, human systems have a basic set of characteristics that vary according to the type of system. The social worker prepares for contact with a client, action, or target system by recalling or trying to find out as much as possible about the system. Working from foundation knowledge, the social work practitioner makes every effort to become aware of the system's characteristics and the degree of intensity of feelings and reactions.

For the range of major systems of contact in social work, there are characteristic polarities with intervening degree scales that may be considered (Figure 5.2). The polarities include facts versus feelings, goal orientation versus process orientation, formality versus informality, explicit nature versus implicit nature, organization versus little organization, structure versus little structure, objectivity versus subjectivity, social control versus human concern, law versus circumstance, and work versus love.

In Figure 5.2, feelings and goals are associated with certain types of client, action, and target systems. As indicated in the diagram, there are basically greater expectation and awareness of feelings and process with smaller systems and greater expectation and awareness of facts and goals with larger systems. In beginning to work with a larger system, the generalist practitioner sees the need to come prepared to present facts and to work with structure and formality.

To work with any client, action, or target system, the social worker deals with human beings who naturally have feelings. The social worker tries to identify feelings as they relate to the problem and to the social worker's efforts. Skill is used to distinguish between those feelings that are the personal feelings of individual representatives and the reactions of the larger system. Whereas the social worker may be able to discuss feelings and relationships with individuals, it often takes longer to recognize and discuss them with individuals who represent a large system. There is a possibility that the expression of feelings and reactions will not be able to influence

FIGURE 5.2 ■ Polarities in Systems

Individual . . . Family . . . Group . . . Organization . . . Community . . . Institution . . . Society

Feelings _____ Facts

Process orientation_____ Goal orientation

Informality _____ Formality

Implicit nature _____ Explicit nature

Little organization _____ Much organization

Little structure _____ Much structure

Subjectivity _____ Objectivity

Human concern _____ Social control

Circumstance _____ Law

Love _____ Work

or change a situation in a larger system because of policy and structure. Carefully presented facts, however, could be most effective.

In terms of goals, larger systems enter very readily into a dialogue about their goals and expectations. They usually have explicitly stated goals that can be utilized as the social worker tries to engage the client, action, or target system in mutual goal setting. The smaller system, however, may take more time and need more help in understanding and expressing its goals.

As implied in Figure 5.2, while working with the three major components of the engagement phase (i.e., problems and needs, feelings and reactions, and goals), the social worker usually finds a natural tendency to get into feelings and relationships with the smaller systems (i.e., individuals, families, groups, and some communities) and to get into facts and goals with larger systems (i.e., some communities, as well as organizations, institutions, and society). As stated, however, all three components—problems and needs, feelings and reactions, and goals—must be considered by the social worker for successful movement in the engagement phase.

Increasing Client System Investment

During the engagement phase, the social worker builds the basis for collaborative work with a client system by

▶ Acknowledging that the problems and concerns are real and changeable
▶ Conveying that potential for change lies in untapped capabilities and resources
▶ Using engagement techniques that increase client and action system investment in the strengths-based problem-solving process of the General Method

This approach involves active and reflective listening behavior that is attentive to the client system's verbal and nonverbal expression of thoughts, feelings, and experiences with the presenting problem, current circumstances, ways of coping, and changes that may have occurred. Key techniques include paraphrasing, clarifying, questioning, and summarizing themes and points in the client system's narrative to reflect the content and process of their messages and feelings and to inquire *Have I heard this right?* This iterative process helps the client system feel understood, reinforces ownership statements about the person-problem-situation and strengths-based problem-solving, and credits the client system with constructive problem-solving efforts and change.

The central assumption in the strengths perspective of social work practice is that the potential for change resides in untapped strengths and abilities (Saleebey, 1992; Weick, 1992). Three related assumptions in the strengths-based problem-solving of the General Method are:

1. The potential for change lies in the client system's life force and hope that push for expression and investment in a better quality of life (Smalley, 1967).
2. Every person-problem-situation configuration is multifaceted.
3. Each facet of this configuration contains inherent opportunities and challenges that tap into diverse capabilities and potential strengths and resources.

From this point of view, each facet has the potential of becoming a unique lens through which to view and clarify the person-problem-situation and create a problem-solving option that stimulates capabilities, strengths, and resources. In other words, the social worker's collaborative task with the client system involves creating a new frame of reference with innovative ways of seeing and being in the person-problem-situation configuration and then generating new strengths-based problem-solving thoughts and actions.

To further increase client and action system investment, the social worker helps the system explore its cognitive and behavioral efforts to handle the internal and external demands and adversity of the person-problem-situation by asking questions about coping that elicit strengths, capabilities, and resourcefulness.

▶ *This must be difficult for you. What are you doing to manage?*
▶ *In the face of all this, what is it that keeps you going?*
▶ *How do you handle things?*
▶ *When things have gotten really difficult, what have you said to yourself?*

Client system answers to these questions provide clues about coping resources that may be further developed and coping skills that need to be taught. In addition, the social worker asks questions that are oriented to changing the status quo.

▶ *How will you know when you don't need to come here any more?*
▶ *What will you need to see? To feel?*

The answers to these questions move the engagement process forward to a consideration of goals.

Determining Goals

The social worker begins by reflecting on several questions:

▶ *What does the client system need?*
▶ *What does the client system want?*
▶ *Are there unexpressed needs, wants, and aspirations?*
▶ *What are the client system's strengths that may facilitate meeting these needs, wants, and aspirations?*

In the first case scenario cited, the social worker hears that Mrs. B wants Johnnie to remain in school and get promoted, but she also wants and hopes for some relief from other family burdens. In the second case scenario, Mrs. B is focusing on the goal of improving her relationship with her son. Such clarification of goals is imperative for the social worker to determine how to proceed with the client system.

These two scenarios illustrate two different approaches in identifying goals for engagement. To figure out what to do, the generalist practitioner begins by uncovering the needs, wants, and aspirations behind the initial statement of problems. Client system needs may be physical, psychological, social, economic, cultural, or spiritual and represent personal and social requirements that are essential for the client system's survival, well-being, and fulfillment (Barker, 1999). Needs have to be made explicit in relation to client system wants and aspirations in order to be translated into goals. Typically, client systems focus first on problems, as these involve the sources of distress and perplexity for which they are seeking help.

For example, in the first case scenario, the mother's problems with Johnnie at school may turn out to be a reflection of different needs related to issues in the school, home, or community. In the second case scenario, the problems reflect needs related to issues in child development, parent–child interaction, and family system dynamics. In turn, these needs orient the social work practitioner toward questions about what resources are required in order to resolve the identified needs. Answers to the questions identify aims that can be directed toward resolution of needs. These aims then become focal goals. Thus, it becomes clear that problems, needs, and goals are interrelated. It is also clear that goals have to be expressed, understood, and agreed on by both client system and social worker before moving on to the second phase of the method.

What is a goal? Epstein (1985, p. 125) gives a very direct answer: "The idea of a goal is straightforward. It is the end toward which effort is directed. A goal is a point beyond which something does not or cannot go. . . . Therefore a goal is an attainable wish."

In the General Method, a goal is conceptualized as including objectives, tasks, motives, and attainable desires. Goals are the desired outcomes toward which intervention activity is directed. Although goals naturally flow out of the data collection and assessment phases, the establishment of the beginning goals needs to take place during engagement. It is during this time that the social worker and the client system not only explore the extent of the problems, needs, and strengths but also begin considering the potential consequences of their possible resolution. Typically, client system goals may take many forms (Kirst-Ashman & Hull, 1999; Sheafor, Horejsi, & Horejsi, 1997):

▶ *Learning a skill or acquiring particular knowledge* for decision making or fulfilling a particular role
▶ *Making an important decision* about a course of action, such as deciding to change a lifestyle or marital status, relinquish custody of a child, or obtain medical and mental health services
▶ *Obtaining information* in order to make a decision
▶ *Assessing problems or concerns* to decide whether attention or help may be needed
▶ *Making plans* to address a particular concern
▶ *Changing behavior* to increase a desired outcome
▶ *Altering feelings or attitudes* toward self or others
▶ *Gathering information about availability of services or programs*
▶ *Becoming connected or enrolled in a program*
▶ *Resolving a conflicted relationship*
▶ *Changing appraisal of life events or circumstances* to develop a new perspective
▶ *Drawing on underused strengths*

Goals are the end toward which the social worker and the client system direct their efforts. Goals are explicated in the General Method when there is mutual agreement by social worker and client system. It is possible that the General Method may be arrested because no goals can be established by mutual agreement. To proceed without this mutuality would be futile.

Although initial goals may be expressed in broad, general terms, the practitioner and the client system work toward formulation of concrete goals. General and specific goals of the General Method are of a social functioning nature, and they are conceptualized from an ecological-systems perspective. General goals relate to social situations in which the exchange at the interface between client system and environment is central. As the goals are stated, clarified, and refined, the social worker keeps in mind the necessity of having goals be measurable and attainable. They should be practical, limited in number, and obviously related to the identified problems and needs.

As the General Method proceeds into data collection, assessment, and planning, goals may be reformulated and refined for greater specificity. Goal setting leads to the strengths to be mobilized and the identification of specific tasks to be performed for goal accomplishment. The actions necessary to obtain the stated goals will be clarified within an identifiable and realistic time span. When the General Method is completed, the identified strengths should have been enhanced and the identified problems and needs should have been addressed, alleviated, or resolved.

Moving from identifying preliminary general goals that are stated ecologically and that are related directly to the presenting problems or needs, the generalist helps the client systems develop more specific measurable and practical objectives and tasks. For example, a general goal stated by Mrs. B may be to improve interactions between herself and her son. As the social worker gets more involved with Mrs. B and her son later on in the course of the General Method, they would be expected to agree on the general goal and to identify their specific objectives and tasks in terms of behaviors and conditions. These might include the following:

General Goal: To improve relations between Mrs. B and her son

Specific Objective 1: Mrs. B and her son will spend more time together.
- ▶ *Task 1:* Mrs. B will spend half an hour after her son gets out of school listening and talking about his day.
- ▶ *Task 2:* Mrs. B will discuss with her husband the need for him to help their son with at least two homework assignments each week.
- ▶ *Task 3:* Mrs. B will take her son to a movie or other fun activity once a month.

Specific Objective 2: Mrs. B will gain a better understanding of parenting teens.
- ▶ *Task 1:* Mrs. B will attend a parenting class once a week for eight weeks at the agency.
- ▶ *Task 2:* Mrs. B will go to the library and read at least one book on parenting boys.
- ▶ *Task 3:* Mrs. B will arrange a time for herself and her husband to discuss her concerns about parenting their son.
- ▶ *Task 4:* Mrs. B will leave the room when her feelings escalate in managing her son's discipline.

Specific Objective 3: Johnnie will gain more self-control in managing conflict.
- ▶ *Task 1:* Mrs. B, her husband, and Johnnie will attend a follow-up session with the social worker to assess the extent of their conflicts.

Goals in the engagement phase of the General Method are beginning goals and tasks in an ongoing process of goal setting. The main purpose for goal identification in the initial phase is to let the client system know that the social worker is listening and that he or she hears what the client system is saying about wants, needs, values, and strengths. The social worker skillfully begins to engage the client system in thinking about goals, with the hope that this engagement will motivate the system for deeper involvement in a collaborative strengths-based problem-solving effort. As the General Method proceeds, the social worker and the client system gain a clearer understanding of problems, feelings, and goals.

Making Initial Plans

Client Systems

Engagement creates a working climate in which the client system's fears, problems, needs, strengths, and goals are explored. First, the phase of engagement is an interpersonal exchange process during which the client system and the social worker must reach an understanding about why the client system is seeking help, what the client system hopes to accomplish from the initial encounters, and what the client system brings to the strengths-based problem-solving process. Second, the social worker and the client system engage in a mutual exchange around problem appraisal to get a sense of the number of problems and their severity, duration, and impact as well as any previous remedies sought and any success or lack thereof. Third, the social worker presents information about the agency's purpose, any eligibility requirements, policy about confidentiality, and available agency resources. Fourth, the client system and the social worker consider three possible outcomes of their actual engagement in the General Method of social work practice:

▶ *Role induction:* The client system agrees to proceed with the outlined intervention process.
▶ *Referral:* Because the client system cannot be adequately served by the present agency, and the social worker has an obligation to help the system gain access to needed services, a linking/brokering service is offered.
▶ *Discontinuation of services:* The client system and social worker agree not to continue because (1) the problems, needs, and issues presented cannot be addressed by the agency services, (2) the client system and social worker agree that the initial contacts were sufficient to mobilize strengths-based problem-solving processes and resources, or (3) the client system chooses not to invest further time, energy, or resources in pursuing help.

As the generalist social worker engages the client system in the helping process, the social worker and the client system also begin to make decisions about problem clarification and prioritization so that client system goals can be pursued. For example, the numerous problems that occur on multiple levels of many client systems may be overwhelming and immobilizing: interpersonal conflicts, dissatisfaction with social relationships, difficulties in role performance, faulty cognitive appraisals, problems in role transitions, inadequate resources, problems in decision making, problems with organizations and communities, and cultural conflicts. In sorting out and prioritizing problems with client systems, social workers have long been guided by six practice principles:

1. *Start with the problem the client system identifies as important.* Although the social worker may not agree with the client system about where the problem stands in a prioritized list of all problems involved, the social worker begins where the client system is in identifying the problem of primary concern and related needs and strengths. In the course of their discussion, the problem list may be reframed and reprioritized for purposes of their work together. It is important to note that role induction and forward progression through the next phases of the General Method cannot take place unless there is an agreement during the engagement phase about which problem and need merits mutual attention and work at this point in time.

Court-ordered and other nonvoluntary client systems, who have been brought to the social worker's attention by external authority sources, often pose particular challenges to the engagement process. Typically, these clients may resent being ordered to speak with a social worker and may deny the existence of a problem. With client systems that are reluctant to engage, social workers usually follow one of two approaches. They may recommend that a specific amount of time be spent searching for the existence of a problem or issue with which the agency can help. The client system is asked to withhold judgment about the need for service or the social worker's usefulness until the problem-needs-strengths situation has been examined in greater depth. In the event this approach is unsuccessful and when the client system understands the social worker's explanation of the possible consequences of discontinuing service, the social worker may terminate contact with the client system. In both approaches, the social worker may provide the client system with alternative resources.

2. *Redefine the problem in behavioral terms and cast the behaviors within a strengths/needs orientation.* Each problem or situation is clarified as to what exactly the need is, why it is a problem, whom the problem affects, how severe it is, how long it has been going on, what has been tried before to ameliorate it, what success was evident in the previous helping attempts, and what may resolve it.

3. *Prioritize the problems listed in order of their importance to the client.* The focus is on "what the client system wants" and not on what the social worker thinks the client system may need. The target problem is not necessarily limited to what the client system wants initially but rather to what is wanted after a mutual process of deliberation and thought—after data collection, after assessment and contract planning, or even after beginning intervention. That is, the client system's initial expression of concerns and problems to which the social worker contributes his or her own knowledge and clarifying technique often evolves into a different facet of the problem or even a different, seemingly unrelated problem focus. It is also not uncommon for client systems to renegotiate their initial agreement about problems, needs, strengths, and goals at a later phase of the helping process.

4. *Assist the client in selecting two or at most three problems and needs to which the client system attributes most priority.* The social worker helps the client system explore the identified problems in view of (a) the client system's feelings and thoughts about the problem's consequences if left unaddressed; (b) which problems and needs are of most interest to the client system; (c) which problems and needs might be corrected with only a moderate investment of time, energy, cost, or other resources; and (d) which problems and needs would require extraordinary investment, energy, and resources.

5. *Help the client system consider beliefs, strengths, and goals relevant to the problems presented.* As they explore the nature of the problems and the surrounding feelings and behaviors, the social worker also helps the client system identify beliefs, strengths, and goals related to the problems presented and how these may influence possible outcomes.

6. *Establish initial agreement with the client system to engage in the helping process while continuing to identify problems and needs that will be further addressed through data collection.* Written documentation of this initial agreement with the client system is important not only for the client system but also for assessment of goal accomplishment and for agency record keeping.

Action Systems

Making initial plans with action systems also involves an interpersonal exchange process during which the system and social worker must reach an understanding about (1) what each wants and hopes to accomplish from the initial encounters and (2) what barriers and resources each brings to the strengths-based problem-solving process. Through mutual appraisal, they begin to make decisions about problem clarification and prioritization so that action system goals can be agreed on and pursued. In this mutual decision-making process, generalist practitioners are guided by the same six practice principles used with client systems.

1. Start with the problem or need that the action system identifies as important.
2. Redefine the problem or need in behavioral terms and cast the behaviors within a strengths/needs orientation.
3. Prioritize the problems and needs listed in order of their importance to the action system.
4. Assist the action system in selecting two or at most three problems and needs to which the action system attributes most priority.
5. Help the action system consider beliefs, strengths, and goals relevant to the problems and needs presented.
6. Establish initial agreement with the action system to engage in the helping process while continuing to identify problems and needs that will be further addressed through data collection.

Monitoring the Engagement Phase

Each phase of the General Method has an evolving, dynamic, and relative nature. Thus, the expected timing of the engagement phase is not estimated because the actual timing of any phase of the General Method is not clearly predictable. Sometimes, a social worker and a client or action system may move through engagement or any other phase in one interview. Other times, it may take months or never be completed.

In this era of managed health care, however, social workers, as well as other human service professionals, are expected to be more efficient and timely in their service delivery while maintaining effectiveness. Along with the particular case record documentation required by the agency, thoughtful monitoring of each phase of the General Method enables the social worker to assess progress, or the lack thereof. Table 5.1 provides a means of assessing social worker and client system progression along the guiding principles and processes of the engagement phase. Since each process reflects social worker and client system exchange, each individual rating score monitors the mutuality of this exchange. Thus, when each engagement process is rated and a total score is obtained, then a total summated scale score can document progress. A low score necessitates clarifying with a supervisor whether the reason for the lack of progress is related to time, related to the nature of the social worker–client system exchange, or related to other factors the client system has brought to the en-

JESSIE TAFT (1882–1960), founder of the functional school of social work, was known for her work with children in foster care through the Children's Bureau and state Charities Aid Associations. Her connections with psychoanalyst Otto Rank led to her conceptualizations about the helping processes in social work, the use of a controlled professional relationship, and the use of the time element in treatment. Taft authored 87 publications, including *The Dynamics of Therapy in a Controlled Relationship.*

gagement process. For example in Table 5.1, a total summated scale score approaching or slightly greater than 14 reflects satisfactory progress in engagement. A total summated scale score of 17 or greater suggests that this phase is being appropriately accomplished and progression into the next phase of data collection is expected. Social work engagement with an action system could be rated and monitored in similar fashion.

In addition to rating the accomplishment of the engagement principles and processes, the social worker and supervisor together reflect on and review the material, which provides a means for identifying accomplishment of the phase-specific

TABLE 5.1 ■ Rating Scale for Engagement Principles and Processes

Engagement Principles and Processes	Not Initiated (0)	Initiated (1)	Making Satisfactory Progress (2)	Being Completed (3)
Establishing relational boundaries				
Identifying problems and needs				
Identifying strengths and resources				
Recognizing feelings and reactions				
Determining goals				
Making initial plans				
Monitoring engagement phase				

outcomes related to client and action system engagement. As noted earlier, these possible outcomes of the engagement phase include being inducted into the client or action system role, referral to a more appropriate resource, and discontinuing services. Outcomes with an action system in the engagement phase are reviewed in similar fashion.

Working with Different Systems

The following complex case situation is offered to provide a better understanding of the application of the engagement phase of the General Method to different systems. The social worker for the family will begin to use the General Method to work with client, action, and target systems. The systems of contact in the following case example range from an individual to a large business.

■ CASE OVERVIEW

Mrs. Armez was sent to the Unity Social Service Department by her pastor. Her husband had to go into the hospital for an operation, and, after a few weeks, was told by the doctor he could return to work. When Mr. Armez tried to return, he was told they didn't need him any longer, and he was laid off. While he had been in the hospital, Mr. Armez's place of employment had been bought by another company, and Mr. Armez thinks the new management does not like Hispanic people. Mr. Armez continues to feel weak and doesn't know if he could work the way he used to. Mrs. Armez said that since Mr. Armez's unemployment benefits ran out and the family went on welfare, he hasn't been acting right. He drinks more, and he fought with her when she began to do some part-time work. The children are not doing well in school lately, and the school social worker is afraid that they are being overly disciplined by Mrs. Armez and her husband.

Micro Practice Example 1: Generalist with Mrs. Armez (Client System)

SW: Good afternoon, Mrs. Armez. My name is Katherine Brown. I understand Rev. Sanchez suggested that you get in touch with us.

CLIENT: Yes, he thought you might be able to help me.

SW: I'd be glad to work with you, Mrs. Armez. Where would you like to begin?

CLIENT: I'm not sure. It's just that nothing seems to be working out right now, and I don't know how to explain it.

SW: I can imagine that it isn't easy for you to begin to talk with me. Was it difficult for you to come in today?

CLIENT: I came right after work. I know my husband would be mad if he knew I stopped off here. I just can't let things go on the way they've been going these last few months.

SW: It sounds like you are under a lot of pressure right now. Am I right?

CLIENT: I'm so upset with all that's happening at home. It's too much for me to take.

SW: You're feeling very upset because you just don't know how to handle the many problems at home right now.

CLIENT: Yes, please understand, I love my children and my husband. It's just that every-thing is going wrong. He's changed since he lost his job. He can't get work, and he's mad that I'm working. I can't let my children starve. I iron for some people in the morning, and that helps a little. The welfare money isn't enough. He just doesn't care—I don't know how to reach him. He's drinking so much lately.

SW: I can see that you love your children and your husband. You're feeling confused because you can't understand your husband any more, and he doesn't seem to un-derstand what you are trying to do. Is that it?

CLIENT: Yes, but—he's just a man, and in his country, women don't work. He's feel-ing bad he can't get work. I don't blame him.

SW: You are trying very hard to understand him. I can see that.

CLIENT: Yes, and it's not just him. The kids are sick a lot lately, and the school is say-ing they are not behaving themselves. I try to get after them, but they're getting so fresh. And that place where we live—it's getting worse. The landlord doesn't care. I try to clean it, but with my husband home all day—I'm tired of fighting with them.

SW: Mrs. Armez, I hear you mentioning many problems that you are facing right now— your husband can't find a job and you're worried about his drinking, your children are often sick and having troubles in school lately, you are not pleased with where you are living, and you and your husband and children are not getting along. I can un-derstand that you are feeling overwhelmed because you can't handle all of these problems by yourself.

CLIENT: (Shakes head and begins to sob.) I can't deal with it. It's just too much. I need some help.

SW: I can see that you are feeling very helpless because you can't change the situation, and you want some help with trying to deal with it all. What is it that you are hop-ing for, Mrs. Armez?

CLIENT: If only things could be different. I wish Hector could go back to work. He liked where he was, and we were getting along fine. And I wish the kids weren't so sickly and that they would mind in school. I guess I just want things the way they were. Maybe we should move away but how? It's just so bad right now. If only something could be done.

SW: I'll be glad to begin to work on it with you, Mrs. Armez. We can't tackle all of these problems at once, but we can take one at a time to see what can be done. But first, would you please talk a little more about the situation with me so that I can un-derstand it better?

In this case vignette, the generalist practitioner began with an introduction and reviewed the referral sources and purpose for Mrs. Armez's coming. She gave the client system time and encouragement to express her feelings about coming and moved on to clarify problems and needs, feelings, and goals. With the identification of so many problems, the feelings and goals remain at a very broad level until further information can be obtained and until problems are prioritized and strengths identified.

The social worker will need to offer Mrs. Armez much support as the procedure moves into data collection. The social worker will need to know information to answer such questions as: *Why was the husband laid off? How does he perceive the family problems at this time? What are the children's health problems and behavioral problems? How involved is the school or any other agency with the family? When did each problem begin? How motivated are family members to work for change? What are the family strengths in problem-solving?* These questions all fall within an ecological-systems perspective for data collection, which will be presented in the next chapter.

The generalist practitioner working with the family would use the General Method for working with several interlocking systems. The target and action systems to be contacted could include employment agencies, hospital and health services, the school, the city's Income Maintenance Department, the landlord, housing authorities, programs for alcoholics, shelters for battered wives, protective services, and other agencies or social institutions.

Mezzo Practice Example 2: Generalist with the Manager (Bill Jones), the Personnel Director (Tom Wilson), and the Foreman (Joe Casey) of the Factory Where Mr. Armez Had Been Employed (<u>Target System</u>)

(This interview takes place after the social worker had met with Mr. Armez in his home and received from him written permission to talk with his employer.)

SW: Good morning. I'm Katherine Brown, a social worker from Unity Social Service Department. I've asked to meet with you to discuss Mr. Armez, one of your past employees. I understand Mr. Armez was not accepted back to work after he recovered from his hospitalization. Is that correct?

PERSONNEL DIRECTOR: Yes, Mr. Armez was only with us about a year before he took off, and we had to hire someone else.

SW: I see. Mr. Armez wasn't with you very long before he took a sick leave. Let's see. I believe Mr. Armez said he began to work here in October of last year, making it 14 months of employment before he requested a sick leave. Is that correct?

MANAGER: I'll tell you, Miss Brown, quite honestly, the company had some concerns about taking him back. We didn't think he was able to work at the level we expect of our employees.

SW: I appreciate your honesty, Mr. Jones. You're saying that Mr. Armez wasn't accepted back because the company feared he wouldn't be able to do the work expected. May I ask why you thought that?

MANAGER: Well, let's see—do you remember, Tom?

PERSONNEL DIRECTOR: Yes, I believe we even had questions about his performance before he took off. Let's check with Joe about that. Joe Casey was the foreman over Mr. Armez. Could we get him up here, Bill?

MANAGER: (calls on phone)

SW: Thank you for trying to trace this back for me.

MANAGER: What's the matter, Miss Brown? Hasn't he found work anywhere else?

SW: No, he hasn't. I understand he liked his work here and thought he was doing a good job.

MANAGER: Here's Joe. Let's find out how he was doing. Joe, this is a local social worker asking about Hector Armez. Do you remember who he is?

FOREMAN: Oh yeah, the Spanish guy. He had to leave for some kind of operation, I think.

SW: He had trouble with his arm and needed to be hospitalized for an operation.

PERSONNEL DIRECTOR: Joe, his performance on the job wasn't that great, was it? We thought it wouldn't be wise to take him back at the time. Do you remember?

FOREMAN: I don't know. He was with us about a year or so and was coming along OK. He was still learning. After he left, we needed someone on the machine. We couldn't wait forever. He had been out a lot, and I had given him a warning.

SW: I believe I hear three reasons for not taking Mr. Armez back: (1) He was out a lot, (2) you needed a replacement, and (3) there were questions about his performance level. Is that right?

FOREMAN: Well, he was doing OK, but we just couldn't wait that long.

MANAGER: And, you know, after being in the hospital and all, maybe he wouldn't be able to man that machine. It's heavy work we do here.

SW: There was some risk involved in taking him back?

MANAGER: Well, we take risks, but not if we can avoid it. We needed to keep the machines going, and we couldn't count on him.

SW: I see. You needed to keep the machines going. May I ask how your personnel policy addresses the need for sick leave?

PERSONNEL DIRECTOR: Our employees can take a sick leave when they need it, but we get concerned when it's a new man and he's out a lot.

MANAGER: We often get new people, like Armez, who just want to take off a few weeks—or even a summer—and we can't be bothered with them.

SW: It sounds as if you really doubted that Mr. Armez had to leave for medical reasons because he's a member of a certain group of people.

MANAGER: Listen, Miss Brown, I don't have anything against Spanish people or any other group of people. We just didn't want to take him back. You heard the foreman say we gave him a warning for his absenteeism, and he continued to take off.

SW: I understand that you didn't want to take him back at the time, and I can see that it's not easy to talk about this. I really don't want to cause any difficulty, but I would like to try to see if there is any way that Mr. Armez could come back to work here. I can understand your limitations in keeping someone who misses a lot of work. Could you tell me how many days did he miss while he was working here?

PERSONNEL DIRECTOR: I'll have to review his file to find out the exact number of days he wasn't here.

MANAGER: Why are you so concerned about him, anyway? Is he asking for welfare? What do you want from us?

SW: I am working with the family while Mr. Armez is trying to find employment. Mr. Casey, the foreman, says that Mr. Armez was doing OK on the job, but he was out a lot. I know Mr. Armez had a health problem that needed medical attention. Apparently, Mr. Armez did not have the opportunity to show that he was better after his hospitalization. I hear that your personnel policy does have sick leave written in it, yet Mr. Armez was not given the chance to come back. What I'm hoping is that there will be some way that we can work together toward giving Mr. Armez the opportunity to return to work here.

MANAGER: What is he able to do now? Can he take on a heavy job?

SW: The doctor said he could return to work two weeks after the operation.

MANAGER: We never saw any doctor's statement. I don't know. We'll have to talk more about it here at our next administrative meeting. I'll meet with you again early next week. No promises.

SW: All right. I hope we will be able to work together on this.

MANAGER: We'll see what we can do. I'll need that doctor's statement. Why don't you set up another appointment with my secretary for early next week.

In this target system vignette, it is obvious that the social worker needed to have some basic facts (e.g., date employment began, reason for hospitalization, doctor's statement) to break through efforts at avoidance. She was sensitive to feelings and skillfully recognized them. Confrontation, with mention of legal action, was not needed at this time. Initial identification of problems, feelings, and goals took place. The social worker would want to move on to clarify why Mr. Armez was absent, what the company expects of its employees, and what the stated benefits are that Mr. Armez could have expected from the company.

It is possible that a social worker will not be able to get beyond the engagement phase with a target system. A social worker, either alone or with other systems (client or action), may work toward bringing about change in a target system, even if the system refuses to engage in the process. Strategies may be implemented outside of the target to create the change necessary for goal accomplishment. The social worker may use the General Method to join with other resources and services to form an action system that may address the micro, mezzo, and macro issues involved.

Mezzo Practice Example 3: Generalist with Doctor at Hospital Clinic (<u>Action System</u>)

(This interview takes place after the social worker has received and delivered release-of-information forms signed by Mr. Armez.)

SW: Good afternoon, Dr. Jackson, I'm Kathy Brown from Unity Social Services. Thank you for agreeing to meet with me to discuss Mr. Armez, one of your patients.

DOCTOR: Yes, Miss Brown, I hope I may be of some help to you.

SW: Dr. Jackson, I am working with Mr. Armez and his family. Mr. Armez has not gone back to work yet. I am wondering about Mr. Armez's condition and his ability to take on a physically taxing job at J. B. Barnes Tractor Factory. I spoke with his employer, and there is hesitancy to take Mr. Armez back. One of the reasons given is their fear he will not be able to do the job because of his operation. Mr. Armez himself says he still feels some weakness in his arm, even though you said he could resume work a few weeks after the operation. I understand that the work Mr. Armez would do calls for heavy lifting and pulling on an assembly line that make tractors. I am wondering if Mr. Armez is able to take on this kind of work, and I would appreciate your professional assistance.

DOCTOR: Yes, I'm sorry to hear that Mr. Armez hasn't gone back to work yet. There was a growth on the arm that had to be removed. It was not malignant, and when the wound healed, he was discharged from the clinic. I was not aware that Mr. Armez was continuing to feel weakness in the arm. It could be simply because it hasn't been used for a while and it needs exercise.

SW: I see. The employer has requested a written medical statement about Mr. Armez's ability to work.

DOCTOR: I am concerned that Mr. Armez continues to feel weakness in his arm. I would be glad to take another look at it, Miss Brown, and let you know what I find.

SW: I can see that you are concerned about the situation, Dr. Jackson, and I am glad you are interested in working with me to help Mr. Armez get back to work.

DOCTOR: Yes. If I find that he should be able to do the work, I'll be happy to write up a statement to that effect.

SW: I'll suggest to Mr. Armez that he contact you for an appointment and I'll call you after you have seen him. Is that all right with you?

Here too, the social worker tries to engage a mezzo action system in collaborative work on the identification of problems, strengths, feelings, and goals. The social worker senses the concern and willingness of the doctor to get involved in the situation. Without becoming defensive, the doctor agrees to reconsider his assessment. The social worker recognizes this openness and moves quickly to initial goal setting. The doctor agrees to become engaged in the process and will proceed with Miss Brown in collecting data. This phase of the General Method would not have proceeded so smoothly if the doctor had to bring up policy constraints or rules and regulations of the clinic about taking back discharged patients. In this case example, the doctor as a staff member of the clinic apparently did not find any conflict in being able to cooperate with the social worker for goal accomplishment.

As the social worker continues to work with the Armez family and their multiple problems, additional client, action, and target systems might emerge. It is possible she would begin macro practice and engage with a community or a group that would include members of the Armez family. For example, it could become apparent that poor housing conditions are felt by many people in the apartment complex of the Armez family. A community effort by all of the tenants might be the most effective means to improve the macro social situation.

It could be that the company would not take Mr. Armez back, and that Mr. Armez would tell the social worker he knew of six other Hispanic men who were laid off since the company went under new management. The social worker could meet with all six to develop an advocacy group, who might collectively agree to involve the Human Rights Commission.

With all of these examples, the generalist practitioner begins by engaging the client system in the identification and expression of presenting problems and needs, purposeful feelings, and desirable goals. As this case example illustrates, the General Method is applicable to client, action, or target systems of any size.

Using Social Work Foundation Knowledge in Engagement

As the generalist social worker begins to have contact with a client, action, or target system, and throughout the process of the General Method, the foundation knowledge, values, and skills are called into play. The perspective of the social worker is pervasively ecological as he or she observes the matching and interacting of systems and carefully applies theories and skills to practice.

As pointed out in this chapter, the generalist social worker demonstrates in words and actions an unfolding of the principles of acceptance, individualization, nonjudgmental attitude, purposeful expression of feelings, controlled emotional involvement, self-determination, and confidentiality (Biestek, 1957; National Association of Social Workers, 1999). In the engagement phase, relationship and problem-solving skills are readily applied. The social worker uses skills in listening, responding, guiding, paraphrasing, and clarifying, along with skills for identifying problems, needs, strengths, feelings, and goals. It is also possible, as in the target system example, that some political advocacy and groups skills may be needed. In trying to engage a target system in the initial phase of the General Method, the generalist may need to provide evidence, enter into bargaining, or propose legal action.

Knowledge about people, families, organizations, and communities as well as concepts from role theory and stress theory are very helpful to a social worker in exploring problems, needs, strengths, feelings, and goals during engagement. In the case vignettes just presented, the problems included the stresses associated with the major life events of Mr. Armez's illness, surgery, and job loss and how these stressors altered performance of his role within the community and spousal roles within the family. No longer able to fulfill his valued roles of worker and family breadwinner, Mr. Armez experienced family role strain, personal distress, and decreased self-esteem. In formulating descriptions of the problems, feelings, actions, and goals of the situation, the social worker used knowledge of people, their environments, and the interdependence of both. Problems were seen as taking place at the interface between a client system and other systems in the environment. Mrs. Armez's strengths were identified as the support provided by family members, her husband's work history prior to illness, and her husband's search for work. Feelings and their reasons were related to a need or failure in matching expectations between client systems and environmental systems. Goals were generally described in terms of developing or enhancing the fit and transactions among Mr. and Mrs. Armez's employment, health, and family systems.

The use of foundation knowledge, values, and skills from an ecological systems perspective and with an open selection of theories and concepts continues as a generalist moves into the second phase of the General Method. As data are collected, the social worker knows that in the evolving procedure of the method, a refinement takes place in identifying and expressing problems, needs, strengths, feelings, and goals. Although each of the six phases of the General Method has its own particular processes and landmarks to guide the social worker and client or action system, the elements of earlier phases remain present and are called on throughout the engagement.

Human Diversity in Engagement

As stated earlier, sensitivity to human variability is needed within each phase of the General Method of social work practice. During engagement, for example, as a social worker and a client or action system begin to identify purpose, problems, needs, strengths, feelings, and goals, an awareness of the culture of the system can help the social worker create an atmosphere of understanding and responsiveness. Care can be demonstrated even in the selection of place for the initial contact. To foster a sense of security and trust, it may be more appropriate to meet with members of a particular cultural client, action, or target system outside of the office or agency. Home visits or visits in community meeting spaces clearly convey a sense of acceptance of the client or action system, a mutual partnership in strengths-based problem-solving, and a pattern of collaborative interaction apart from the professional comfort zone of the social worker's office. For example, outreach in the neighborhood and home visits have proven to be effective especially within the Hispanic community (Castex, 1994; Ordaz & DeAnda, 1996). When transportation is an issue, such as with low-income families or rural families, home visits convey the social worker's comprehension of the difficulties inherent in mobilizing resources to meet basic needs and willingness to engage *where the client system is.*

Members of ethnic groups incorporate knowledge of their ethnic history and personal experiences with people of diverse cultures as they relate cross-culturally. Consumers of services may view service providers and agencies from different perspectives, particularly if there are no apparent members of the consumer's culture in the service-providing system. Guardedness, hostility, fear, and defensiveness are often present when a client or action system begins to have contact with a social worker from a different culture. Reactions vary according to ethnic backgrounds. Chinese culturally derived reactions, for example, include politeness, quietness, and friendliness when the individual is confronted with potential threatening situations (Lie, 1999).

In approaching a client, action, or target system and beginning to identify the purpose of contact, a social worker needs to be sensitive to basic communication patterns, according to the culture of the system. To give and to expect eye-to-eye contact with Native Americans or Asians, for example, would be insensitive, because eye contact is generally considered to mean lack of respect in these cultures (Devore & Schlessinger, 1999; Williams & Ellison, 1996). Although a social worker may feel more comfortable with informality toward client systems (i.e., using first names, casual dress, attitude of friendliness), members of certain cultures, such as Asian American and African American, may need and expect a formal approach from a professional social worker, at least initially. During first contacts, Asian Americans need to have the purpose and function of a service clearly stated (Browne & Broderick, 1994; Chung, 1992).

In proceeding, the social worker also keeps in mind the time orientation of a culture. Urban African Americans and Japanese Americans may need time to build up a sense of trust and openness; by contrast, Mexican Americans move quickly into relationships and decision making, relying heavily on inferential abilities. Repetition and calculations are often unwelcomed by Mexican Americans as they proceed with problem-solving (Lum, 1999; Pedersen, 1997).

Diversity is also found among cultures when it comes to identifying and expressing feelings. People from Eastern European ethnic groups, such as Poles, Hungarians, Czechs, and Slovaks, may have strong feelings of shame over having to seek professional help (McGoldrick, Giordano, & Pearce, 1996). Members of some ethnic groups are very reluctant to talk about personal feelings and problems with outsiders. This is particularly true of Asians and Native Americans. On the other hand, members of Jewish and Italian cultures are often openly expressive of their feelings, needs, and problems (Huang, 1991; McGoldrick, Giordano, & Pearce, 1996).

Problems, needs, or strengths may be perceived and described from various perspectives, according to culture. For example, Chinese Americans and Mexican Americans may tend to view problems collectively rather than individually. The troubling behavior of one may be seen as a direct assault on the pride of the community (Green, 1999). By contrast, the accomplishments and resources of one may be viewed as bolstering the community. Also, problems, needs, and resources may need to be described in material rather than emotional terms. Huang (1991) found, for example, that many Chinese clients would work on emotional problems and needs only if they were receiving concrete assistance at the time.

Although a problem may come to the attention of a social worker as a personal problem of an individual or group, a culturally sensitive social worker is cognizant of the fact that environments themselves, with their institutional pressures and prejudices, may really be the problem to be addressed. In the engagement phase, a social worker fosters a sense of openness when the person or people that make up a client system can begin to see that the social worker understands both the real problem, the needs, and the strengths and how the system perceives and experiences the problem/situation configuration.

Goals may be more clearly understood and articulated if a social worker is aware of a culture's value orientation. The aspirations and goals of individuals, families, groups, and communities usually reflect the values that have been transmitted through their culture.

The values of *person, family, tribe,* and *community* are commonly upheld by several cultures. There may be, however, discrete meaning as well as variance for such values within particular groups. For example, although individualism is valued by Puerto Rican Americans, there is a distinction that should be noted by social workers as they begin to work with Puerto Rican Americans. The Puerto Rican culture centers attention on those personal inner qualities that constitute individual uniqueness and personal worth in and of themselves, in contrast to the prevalent individualism in the United States that values individual aspiration and ability to compete for higher social and economic status (Garcia-Preto, 1996).

An astute understanding of values helps a social worker locate what motivates members of the client or action system and give direction on expressing relevant goals. Members of the Puerto Rican American culture, for example, would be motivated to work on goals that appeal to personal responsibility and leadership, rather than those that appeal to platforms or programs.

Throughout each phase of the General Method, a social worker should demonstrate sensitivity not only to multiculturalism but also to social pluralism and sociodemographic differences. During engagement—for example, as purpose, problems, needs, and strengths are identified—the social worker shows respect and acceptance by beginning where the client system is. He or she should focus on only those problems and needs that the client system wishes to address. When a social worker knows that an individual is of a lower socio-economic class, of a lesbian, gay, bisexual, or transgendered (LGBT) orientation, physically challenged, or mentally challenged, there must not be a hidden agenda on the social worker's part, in which he or she expects to discuss (or to change) the lifestyle of the individual. If the client system is having difficulties that relate to human diversity, a social worker may begin to be helpful by making known that he or she is aware of the pressures and problems persons often have to face in U.S. society. As generally found in helping relationships, a client system is usually more comfortable by beginning with external problems (related to societal institutions, policies, and practices). Eventually, as the relationship develops and the client system becomes more engaged, problems and needs that are more interpersonal (primary relationships, for example) and then more intrapersonal (dual identities, self-esteem, fears) may be shared.

During engagement, a social worker encourages and accepts a client or action system's expression of feelings and reactions. For persons who experience themselves as being apart from the mainstream, these may include loneliness, alienation, isolation, hurt, anger, and outrage toward a rejecting, condemning family or society. A social worker who becomes defensive or judgmental will be indicating a lack of self-awareness and sensitivity to the needs of the client or action system.

As initial goals are stated during engagement, the social worker carefully listens and articulates the aspirations and expectations of a client system. If the social worker cannot support the goals of a client system in any way, this circumstance should be recognized and resolved before proceeding into the second phase of the General Method. Problems associated with multiculturalism, social pluralism, and socio-demographic diversity may be caused by discriminatory practices of large institutions. The social worker takes time throughout the General Method to engage the client system in the process of realistically stating, understanding, and refining long- and short-range goals, which may be personal, interpersonal, institutional, or societal in nature.

ONGOING CASES
Engagement Phase

Each chapter of this text that describes one of the phases of the General Method contains a section that has case examples of micro, mezzo, and macro practice from diverse fields of social work practice. The examples demonstrate the applicability of the General Method with its multiple phases and major focal points, principles, and processes for each phase in all areas of practice with diverse human populations. In the following section, the application of knowledge and skills during the *engagement phase* of the General Method is demonstrated by entry-level generalist social workers in seven diverse fields of practice: child welfare, gerontology, public social welfare, community services, education, corrections, and homelessness. In Exercise 5.1, questions are proposed for reflection and discussion about how practice in each of the case examples during the engagement phase might change if the client system represented a different

▶ *Culture:* Racial/ethnic group membership, national origin and social group identity, religion and spirituality)

▶ *Social Status:* Socio-economic status, environmental, and rural/urban differences)

▶ *Socio-demographic strata:* Age and developmental stage, gender roles, sexual orientation, challenges in mental and physical ability).

EXERCISE 5.1
Impact of Human Diversity on Engagement Process

Consider the following questions with each of the seven client systems. When engaging the client system, how might change in culture, social status, or socio-demographic strata:

1. Influence the client system's help-seeking attitudes and behavior?
2. Influence professional view of the pressures, problems, needs, strengths, resources, and goals brought by this system?
3. Influence the norms, roles, and authority issues in work with each system?
4. Reveal values that influence timing, communications, and actions?
5. Affect the dynamics of the professional relationship?
6. Affect monitoring of the progress, timeliness, and effectiveness of service delivery?

In the following section, the application of knowledge and skills during the *engagement phase* of the General Method will be demonstrated by entry-level generalists in each of the seven fields of practice.

I. Child Welfare Case

A. Agency: State Department of Children's Services

B. Client System

K is a 15-year-old female of French American ethnicity. The police referred her to Children's Services two and a half years ago because she was physically abused by her mother. K had also been sexually abused by her stepfather on two occasions. She was committed to the state and placed in a group home, where she lived for over two years. She then requested and was placed in foster care. After two months in a foster home, K ran away. The police picked her up and placed her in an emergency shelter. She was at the shelter when the case was assigned to a new social worker from the State Department of Children's Services.

C. Engagement

PROBLEM: During engagement, K said she knew she had two problems: (1) she had no place to go to live and (2) she was missing school. She said she did not want to return to her foster home, but would not say why she ran away. She shared that she had run away with a boyfriend, who left her after a few days. K spoke about hating herself and knowing that no place or school would want her. She described herself as "dumb" and "ugly." During engagement, the generalist social worker identified additional problems. These included the personal problems of (1) poor self-esteem, (2) identity confusion, (3) problems concerning her sexuality and how to relate to males, and (4) depression.

FEELINGS: K expressed feelings of nervousness and loneliness. She said she knew she was "jittery" and just couldn't settle down to anything. She also said that she "hated" her mother and stepfather and never wanted to see them again. She wished she could live with her "real father."

At one point, K began to cry and left the room. When she returned, the social worker identified feelings of pain and depression. K admitted that she was "really down" and believed that no one really cared if she lived or died. She said that her "rotten boyfriend" got tired of her, even though she "gave him everything," and she knew her parents couldn't stand her either.

STRENGTHS/RESOURCES: (micro level) K's strengths include her capacity to self-preserve in dangerous situations and to express her feelings about the situation. She acknowledges her need for help and has been able to accept the help extended. She wishes to return to school.

GOALS: K's stated goals were (1) to obtain and maintain a permanent placement (permanent placement means a place to live until adulthood) and (2) to get back into school as soon as possible. K said she wanted to leave the shelter but didn't know where to go. She thought she would like to go back to the group home where she had lived before she had been placed in the foster home. The social worker hoped that K would eventually see the need for help with her more personal problems, although K was not ready to discuss this need at the time of engagement.

D. Charted Progress

By the end of the engagement period, the social worker recorded the items in Table 5.2 to begin to chart a formal plan of action (explained in detail in this chapter). The date of contract, the problems identified at the time by the social worker or the client, and the goals mutually agreed on by both K and the social worker were listed as in Table 5.2.

TABLE 5.2 ■ Initial Recording: Child Welfare Case

Date Identified	Problem/Need	Client System Feelings	Goal
1/12	No permanent home	Loneliness Restlessness Hatred of self and others	a. To obtain a permanent placement b. To maintain a permanent placement
1/12	Out of school	Depression	c. To reenter school
1/12	Personal problems a. Poor self-esteem b. Identity confusion c. Sexuality (relationships, behavior) d. Depression		

II. Gerontology Case

A. Agency: Seaside Nursing Home

B. Client System

Mrs. J is an 80-year-old Portuguese American woman who was admitted to the skilled-nursing facility at Seaside Nursing Home two weeks ago. She was released from the hospital with a diagnosis of "organic brain syndrome." The summary from the hospital social worker indicated that Mrs. J was a housewife with no formal education. Her family refused to be involved with her and left no name or address for contact. Mrs. J cannot remember where members of her family live. At the nursing home, she remained reclusive and appeared to be afraid to leave her room. An entry-level generalist was assigned to work with Mrs. J to help her adjust to the nursing home.

C. Engagement

PROBLEM: During the first interview, Mrs. J expressed displeasure with her placement in the institution. She said she did not like it at the nursing home and wished she could go somewhere else. She did not respond when asked where she would like to go. Mrs. J could not speak English fluently, and wished there was someone who could speak Portuguese with her. She said she was afraid that if she left her room, her things would be stolen. She would only leave her room if someone came to take her to the dining room for meals.

FEELINGS: Mrs. J began to express feelings of distrust, anger, and abandonment. She did not feel comfortable in a cross-cultural environment. Whenever the social worker began to talk about where Mrs. J came from or where she would like to go, Mrs. J became quiet and looked very sad and hurt. She would shake her head and look out the window. During the second interview, she said she had three children but they all had gone away and left her. She would not talk about her husband.

STRENGTHS/RESOURCES: (macro, micro levels) Mrs. J's strengths include her interest in the Portuguese community, her verbal ability, and her ability to share her past history despite memory problems. The Portuguese community may be a resource through church and civic organizations.

GOALS: Mrs. J said that she wished she were able to go out on her own. She realized that she first had to be able to leave her room before she could go anywhere else. She did not think she liked the people at the nursing home, but was willing to meet twice a week with the social worker to talk about how she was getting along. She said she hoped that someone who spoke Portuguese would come to see her.

The goals for Mrs. J that were agreed on by herself and the social worker during engagement were (1) to be able to leave her room on her own, (2) to have someone who speaks Portuguese visit with her, and (3) to get to know the staff and resources of the nursing home.

D. Charted Progress

The social worker charted progress at the end of the engagement phase, identifying dates, problems, and goals, as shown in Table 5.3. At this time, it was also possible to record the initial contract for biweekly meetings of the social worker and Mrs. J.

TABLE 5.3 ■ Initial Recording: Gerontology Case

Date Identified	Problem/Need	Client System Feelings	Goal	Task	Contract	Date Anticipated
9/25	Poor adjustment: reclusiveness— not leaving room alone	Distrust Fear Anger Abandonment	To be able to leave room alone			
9/25	Cultural isolation: need to communicate in native language		To be visited by someone who speaks Portuguese			
9/27	Unfamiliar with staff and resources of the nursing home		To get to know the staff and resources of the nursing home	Meet twice a week with social worker	Social worker and Mrs. J	10/4 and every Tuesday and Thursday thereafter

III. Public Social Welfare Case

A. Agency: State Social Services

B. Client System

Mr. and Mrs. P and their two children, ages 2 and 4, arrived at the agency with their suitcase. Mrs. P's father had called the agency a week earlier, saying that his daughter and her two children had come to live with him, but he didn't have any room. He wanted "the state" to find housing for his daughter and grandchildren. He also said that his daughter and her husband were separated, but**Client** that her husband was waiting at their old apartment to take their TANF (Temporary Assistance to Needy Families) check. Mrs. P's father wanted the check held for his daughter, who would come in to pick it up. When the P family arrived at the Social Services unit, the case was assigned to an entry-level generalist.

C. Engagement

During the initial interview, because of the urgent nature of the situation, the problem, feelings, and goals of engagement were explored and specific data were collected. Preliminary assessment, planning, and intervention also took place during the first day of contact with the family.

PROBLEM: In this situation, housing was the obvious immediate problem. Because of repeated tardiness in paying their rent, the P family had been evicted from their apartment. Mrs. P thought that she and her children could find temporary shelter with her father. After two weeks, however, he said they would have to leave. Mr. P expected to take the money from their welfare check and return to Maine, where his mother lived. He said he had planned to send for his family once he got settled. At this time, however, Mr. and Mrs. P said that they decided they would prefer to find another apartment locally.

FEELINGS: Mrs. P was feeling rejected by her father and blamed him for their current problem. Mr. P was angry at the state for not sending their check and food stamps. (After the initial call from Mrs. P's father, the check and food stamps had been held by the post office and were later returned to the central welfare office.) Both felt that no one really wanted them or cared. They appeared to be confused and said that they were feeling helpless and did not know what to do.

STRENGTHS/RESOURCES: (mezzo level) Mr. and Mrs. P's strengths include their desire to maintain the family unit despite many life stresses and their concern for their children. They are invested in obtaining housing so that the family can remain together in their local community. They are able to draw on their extended families for limited help.

GOALS: When asked what they hoped the social worker could do for them, the Ps said that they wanted him to find them a place to stay. The social worker clarified his own role and said that he could assist them by locating temporary shelter, but that they would have to become active in searching for and in documenting their search for more permanent housing. The immediate goals agreed on by the social worker and Mr. and Mrs. P were (1) to find emergency shelter for the family (short-range goal) and (2) to locate an apartment in the local or neighboring geographic area for extended residence by the family (long-range goal).

D. Charted Progress

As the social worker began recording for a formal plan of action, the basic information obtained through engagement was charted as in Table 5.4.

IV. Community Services Case

A. Agency: Clayton Neighborhood House

B. Client System

Mrs. T lives with her husband and three children in a one-room apartment at 33 L Street. She came to Clayton House to request clothing for her children and to complain about the lack of heating in their room. She informed the social worker that there were three other Hispanic families in their building who also were without heat. None of the adults in the four families spoke English. A Spanish-speaking entry-level generalist visited all four families. They met to organize and work together to obtain heating in their homes.

C. Engagement

Mrs. T was encouraged to express her problems, feelings, and goals when she met with the social worker. Her initial request for clothing was granted on the same day at the first interview. She was directed to the clothing room at Clayton House and told to take whatever she needed.

After the social worker and Mrs. T talked together about the heating problem, the client system in this case expanded to include members from the other three families who shared the problem. Before trying to resolve the issue with Mrs. T, the social worker wanted

TABLE 5.4 ■ Initial Recording: Public Social Welfare Case

Date Identified	Problem/Need	Client System Feelings	Goal
9/28	Housing for P family	Helplessness Anger Rejection Confusion	a. To find emergency shelter for the P family b. To locate an apartment for long-term residence by the family

to meet with the others who were experiencing the problem and to find out more about the situation. After visiting each family individually in their apartments, the social worker met with members of all four families in Mr. and Mrs. T's room. Together, they began to identify problems, feelings, and goals.

PROBLEM: The basic problem identified during the engagement period was the lack of heat on the second floor of the L Street apartment building. All of the residents who met with the social worker lived on the second floor. They said that they had had very little, if any, heat over the past month. There were some nights when the temperature dropped below freezing, and the only means of keeping warm was to turn on all of the burners and the ovens of their stoves.

When the social worker inquired about the residents on the first floor, she was told that they do not have a heating problem. They were described as "English speaking," and it was felt that they received better treatment from the landlord.

FEELINGS: The community of residents who met with the social worker shared feelings of frustration and victimization. They felt helpless and angry. They did not think that their landlord listened to them or cared about what happened to them. They were afraid that if they put pressure on the landlord, he would evict them and they would not be able to find another place to live.

STRENGTHS/RESOURCES: (micro, mezzo, macro levels) Mrs. T's strengths include her concerns for her family and her connectedness with other families in her apartment community. She shows personal strength and leadership in being able to articulate the needs of the community and request help for all. The families are all invested in improving their living circumstances.

GOAL: All present agreed that something had to be done. They asked the social worker to help them. A mutually agreed-on goal was to get their apartments heated. They wanted assurance that heating would be provided consistently throughout the winter.

D. Charted Progress

The social worker recorded the basic information obtained during engagement as outlined in Table 5.5. She saw a possible problem of discrimination by the landlord, but decided to wait until further data were collected before recording the problem in the record.

TABLE 5.5 ■ Initial Recording: Community Services Case

Date Identified	Problem/Need	Client System Feelings	Goal
12/3	Lack of heat on second floor	Frustration Helplessness Fear Anger	To obtain consistent, adequate heating for second-floor residents of L Street apartment house

V. Education Case

A. Agency: Keeney Elementary School

B. Client System

Jim G is an 8-year-old African American child in third grade. His teacher referred him to school social services because he began to miss school or to come late each morning. His behavior was becoming increasingly inappropriate. He often kept his head down on his desk and remained silent when his teacher called on him. He no longer raised his hand in class or showed any interest in learning. His grades were beginning to drop, and his teacher feared he would get so far behind in his work that he might have to be moved to a different classroom. The teacher also noted that Jim was not eating his lunch. These behaviors were not apparent until the second month of the school year. An entry-level generalist was assigned to talk with Jim and to make a home visit.

C. Engagement

PROBLEM: When Jim entered the social worker's office, he sat at the table and kept his head down. The social worker asked if he knew why she wanted to see him, and he shook his head negatively. She reviewed his teacher's concerns and assured Jim that the people at school wanted to try to help him so that he would not get behind in his schoolwork. The social worker wondered if Jim could talk about what was bothering him lately. Jim didn't answer, but got up and walked over to the bookcase containing toys and games. He asked who the toys were for, and the social worker explained that any of the children who came to the office could use them. Jim took out the game "Chutes and Ladders" and asked if the social worker wanted to play it with him. As they were setting up the game, the social worker said that she could see that it wasn't easy for Jim to talk about what was troubling him, but she hoped that he would eventually. With his mother's permission, the social worker began to see Jim twice a week in her office.

After the first meeting with Jim, the social worker visited his mother at home. Jim lived with his mother and father in a middle-class neighborhood. Mrs. G expressed concern over her son's regressive school behavior and said that she noticed that lately he was acting somewhat strange at home also. He wouldn't go to sleep at night unless his mother stayed in his room and kept a light on. She could not identify anything different or painful that Jim might have experienced since school began. She said that her son had done excellent schoolwork when he was in first and second grades, and she could not understand what was happening to him to bring about the changes he was going through. She offered to work with the school in whatever way possible. She stated that she would see that Jim got to school on time each day even if she or her husband had to drive him. Mrs. G agreed to come to school to talk with the social worker again in two weeks.

The problems identified during the initial interviews with Jim and his mother were (1) school tardiness and absenteeism, (2) declining academic functioning (interest, participation, grades) and (3) refusal to sleep without his mother and a light in his room.

FEELINGS: In early sessions with Jim and with his mother, very little feeling was expressed by either of them. Jim avoided talking about anything personal. Mrs. G only expressed concern over her son's school performance.

STRENGTHS/RESOURCES: (micro, mezzo, macro levels) Jim's strengths include good health, good academic progress until recently, ability to engage with others, and ability to behave appropriately when assisted by adults. His parents are invested in seeking help to increase his wellbeing. The school is invested in helping students beyond academic success and recognizes the importance of students' home life in relation to academic functioning.

GOAL: Mrs. G and the social worker agreed to work together to help Jim improve his attendance at school and his academic performance. Both agreed to talk with Jim to try to motivate him to want the same goals.

D. Charted Progress

As the social worker extended the engagement period with Jim and his mother, she recorded the initially identified problems as found in Table 5.6. She also recorded the goals and tasks that she and Mrs. G developed.

VI. Corrections Case

A. Agency: Juvenile Court

B. Client System

A group was formed for seven male adolescents, all age 14, who were on probation for burglary, theft of automobiles, or minor larceny (shoplifting). The usual probationary period was six months. If a youth attended and participated regularly in group meetings and met all of the other requirements of probation, the time of probation could be reduced to four months. All of the group participants knew that they were expected to attend weekly group meetings from four to six months, depending on when their probationary period would be over. A new B.S.W. female social worker was assigned to co-lead the group with an M.S.W. male social worker who had worked in corrections for six years and who had specialized in social group work while in graduate school.

C. Engagement

PROBLEM: The presenting problem shared by all of the youths was being on probation for illegal actions. Discussion centered on clarifying the problem. Was it being on probation

TABLE 5.6 ■ Initial Recording: Education Case

Date Identified	Problem/ Need	Client System Feelings	Goal	Task	Contract	Date Anticipated
11/1	Jim's school tardiness and absenteeism	Depressed Sad	To improve Jim's regular school atten-dance (on time each day)	1. See that Jim gets to school on time each day.	1. Mrs. G	11/5 and each school day thereafter
11/1	Jim's declining academic performance		To improve academic functioning (interest, participation, grades)	1. Talk with Jim about school problems.	1a. Social worker and Jim b. Mrs. G and Jim	11/6 and twice a week thereafter
11/2	Jim's getting to sleep at night					

or was it committing illegal acts? At this time, most of the group members saw the problem more in terms of having gotten caught rather than having broken the law. One member said that their basic problem was "law-breaking leading to probation." All agreed that this was a good way to describe it.

As group participants began to talk more about themselves, several other common problems began to surface. The youths were surprised to learn that all of them were in special classes in school because of learning disabilities. They all said that they had "bad tempers" and made some reference to problems at home. Two of the youths mentioned their drug habits.

FEELINGS: In early group sessions, members expressed strong feelings of mistrust, particularly toward the group leaders. Some members complained about having to come to the group but eventually admitted that they were angry really because they had gotten caught by the police and put on probation. They said that it was "dumb" of them to get caught. Members repeatedly indicated a sense of little self-worth.

STRENGTHS/RESOURCES: (micro, mezzo levels) The youths easily bonded in the group and worked to get off their probation. They show some problem-solving capacities or "street-smarts" that have allowed them individually to survive their academic and home life problems. These capacities can be harnessed for increasing their motivation to engage in socially appropriate behaviors in the group.

GOALS: The goal most clearly expressed by all of the participants was to get off probation as soon as possible. They also admitted that they wished they could stay out of trouble, but that it was not easy. They said, too, that they would like to be able to handle their tempers better. They expressed interest also in being able to understand more about "the changes" they were going through.

Although reference had been made to problems they were having with parents, there was not a general agreement that group members wanted to work on getting along better with their parents. They also did not like to talk about the fact that they did not think they were worth very much.

D. Charted Progress

The social worker recorded the problems and goals that were identified by the group during the engagement period, as found in Table 5.7. She did not list the problems of learning disabilities and drug habits, because the youths were receiving help with these problems from other services. The preliminary agreement of group attendance and participation in order to get off probation was recorded in the columns called "task," "contract," and "date anticipated."

TABLE 5.7 ■ Initial Recording: Corrections Case

Date Identified	Problem/ Need	Client System Feelings	Goal	Task	Contract	Date Anticipated
10/1	Law breaking leading to probation	Anger	To get off probation in four months	Attend weekly group meetings.	Seven members, two social workers	10/1 and each Monday at 4:00 P.M. for at least four months
10/1	Bad tempers		To learn to control temper in school, home, neighborhood			
10/1	Need to understand "changes" of teenagers		To learn about "changes" youths go through			
10/1	Parent-son conflicts					
10/1	Low self-worth					

VII. Homeless Ness Case

A. Agency: West End Community Shelter

B. Client System

José Romano, a 37-year-old Hispanic male, came to the emergency shelter on May 7. He had gone to the County Department of Social Services for assistance and they referred him to the shelter. During his intake interview with the shelter social worker, an experienced B.S.W., Mr. R said that he had been recently evicted from his apartment and that he was HIV positive. He had come to the mainland United States from Puerto Rico 20 years ago. He was divorced with no children.

C. Engagement

PROBLEM: Mr. R told the social worker that he had completed a drug detox program six years ago and thought he had put his life in order. He was working as a chef in a nursing home when he found out that he was HIV positive. He quit his job because he did not think he would be allowed to work in a kitchen. He did not realize that he could not be fired because he was HIV positive. He could not find another job. After his money ran out, he lost his apartment, and his friends seemed no longer to be interested in him. His immediate needs were identified by Mr. R and the social worker as shelter, food, and health care.

FEELINGS: Mr. R was feeling abandoned and depressed. He said that he had no place to turn and did not know what was going to happen to him. He knew he was not feeling well physically and was afraid that he was getting worse.

STRENGTHS/RESOURCES: (micro level) Mr. R shows personal resilience in that, despite a history of addiction and family difficulties, he has stayed sober and held a stable job for a number of years until very recently. He is invested in staying and working in the local community. Past history demonstrates that he follows through on recommendations.

TABLE 5.8 ■ Initial Recording: Homelessness Case

Date Identified	Problem/Need	Client System Feelings	Goal
5/8	HIV positive, lack of knowledge	Fear Abandonment	To obtain ongoing medical care and information
5/8	Homeless/hungry		To obtain immediate housing/food
			To obtain long-term housing
5/8	Unemployed (no financial support)		To obtain employment—part/full time
			To obtain public assistance/social security (long range)

GOALS: Mr. R said that he would like to get medical help for his condition. He also said he needed a place to stay. He understood that the shelter had a 60-day limit and he would need some place to go after that. He wondered whether the shelter would keep him even for 60 days if his sickness got worse. He said he wished he could be working. He wanted to be able to pay for his food and lodging. Goals were identified as (1) to get medical care, (2) to locate housing (short- and long-term), and (3) to locate employment (part or full time).

D. Charted Progress

The identified needs and goals agreed upon by Mr. R and the social worker were recorded (see Table 5.8). The social worker knew that Mr. R eventually would not be able to work and would need some other source of financial support. At the present time, however, Mr. R was highly motivated and appeared able to engage in some type of employment.

SUMMARY

In this chapter, focus was on the engagement phase of the General Method. Skills for working with practice processes were identified. The use of the ecological-systems perspective throughout the phase was emphasized. The traditional purpose of social work, to enhance social functioning, was evident as the engagement process was described within a strengths-based problem-solving process.

Case vignettes offered a demonstration of the use of skills, the ecological-systems perspective, and the practice processes of the engagement phase. Examples described the work of a generalist as she began to engage a family, a business employer, and a health care service in the General Method. The use of foundation knowledge, values, and skills during engagement was discussed. Additional examples included cases from diverse field areas. Several ways in which a social worker demonstrates sensitivity to human diversity during engagement were also described.

The expected timing of the engagement phase was not stated in this chapter because actual timing of any phase in the General Method is not clearly predictable. Sometimes a social worker and client system may move through engagement or any other phase in one interview. The method and each of its phases have an evolving, dynamic, and relative nature.

In the next chapter, the generalist practitioner will be seen in movement to the second phase of the method: data collection. The overlap and natural flow from the first to the second phase will be shown. In the second phase of the systematic procedure, the social worker and system of contact take a deeper and sharper look at the issue, need, question, or difficulty brought forth for study and action.

REFLECTION POINTS

Becoming a skilled social work practitioner requires knowledge and skills, including the ability to reflect on practice endeavors. The following reflection points are designed to strengthen critical thinking and mastery of knowledge of key points in this chapter.

1. Define the following key concepts in generalist social work:
   - Engagement phase
   - Professional relationship
   - Professional relationship boundaries
   - Client and action system feelings and reactions
   - Client, action, and target system goals
2. How might each of these concepts influence your professional behavior in social work practice with client, action, and target systems at micro, mezzo, and macro levels of practice?
3. How might human diversity influence the process of engagement at micro, mezzo, and macro levels of practice?
4. Review the section on Ethical Principles in the *NASW Code of Ethics* (www .socialworkers.org). How will these standards influence your professional behavior?
5. For further reading and research, use the key concepts in Question 1 to locate social work references related to this chapter's content. (See Appendix A, Selected Internet Resources, and Appendix B, Selected Social Work Journals.) What underlying theoretical concepts are evident in the articles? How are they applied in the articles? How might they be applied in one of the seven ongoing cases in this chapter or in a case in your field internship?

CHAPTER 6

Data Collection

As the social worker engages the client system in problem and goal prioritization by gathering more information, the generalist practitioner and the client system move into the second phase of the General Method. Usually, the social worker collects information first from the client system (unless referring information has been forwarded before the initial meeting) and second from sources deemed necessary for verification and comprehensiveness. Demonstrating the scientific aspect of professional social work, the generalist practitioner uses research skills to distinguish fact from impression, assumption, or conclusion. Inasmuch as possible in the data-collection phase of the General Method, the social worker strives to acquire information that is factual.

Using an ecological-systems perspective, the generalist directs inquiry to find out about the problems and needs presented, the persons involved in the problems, the strengths and assets of the persons, and the potential or actual resources and barriers in the environment that may affect the person-problem-environment situation.

Specifically, the social worker collects information about the problem, the person, and the environment.

Gathering Data

Although the social worker's unit of attention typically centers on the individual client, it can also encompass the family, small groups of unrelated persons, organizations, or communities. Usually, most of the data are gathered through the identified client about the client system. However, it may be equally important to gather information through a client's relative(s) (spouse, child, or other related member), a significant friend(s) who has an immediate impact on the client's day-to-day living, and/or sources of collateral information in the client's immediate environment. The collateral sources may include human service personnel, health personnel, treatment professionals, teachers, and employers, to name a few. To gain an understanding of the *micro system* or the client's internal frame of reference about a particular problem or situation, it is helpful to collect information in the following four major content areas:

1. *Scope of presenting problem*
   - Who has the problem: the client system, the significant other in the client's life domain, or a person outside of the client system?
   - How is the problem manifested? Can specific behaviors, actions, or events be observed?
   - Is it a new problem or an ongoing one? Why is the client system seeking help now?
   - Where does the problem occur in the client system's environment?
   - How often does the problem happen? Can a beginning frequency of problem manifestation (i.e., a baseline) be obtained?
   - What is the severity, intensity, and duration of the problem manifestation?
2. *Client system psychosocial functioning*
   - What is the client's age and developmental life stage? Are they congruent?
   - What role does the client system need to fulfill?
   - What dimensions of the whole person (cognitive, behavioral, biological, emotional, spiritual) does the problem affect?
   - Is the problem creating a crisis for the client system's social functioning and/or role fulfillment?
   - How successful is the client system in role fulfillment with and without the problem?
   - What other significant persons in the client system's life domain are affected by the presenting problem? How are they affected? What has been their response?
3. *Client system coping and strengths in problem-solving*
   - What meaning does the client system attribute to the problem presented?

- What cultural, ethnic, and spiritual beliefs and values are important to the client system and relevant to the current problem situation? Which values and beliefs may pose barriers to problem-solving? Which serve as strengths and assets?
- How difficult does the client system view the problem?
- How satisfied is the client system with his or her own role functioning in view of the problem?
- How interested or motivated is the client system in seeking resolution for the problem?
- What outside aversive or discomfort factors impinge on the client system's present degree of action or inaction?
- How resilient is the client system in coping with stress in general and with the presenting problem in particular?

4. *Availability of client system resources*
   - What personal strengths does the client possess (educational level, problem-solving approach, resilience, mood disposition, relationship with others, and health disposition)?
   - What economic and environmental resources does the client system possess for meeting the basic needs of income, child rearing and child care, housing, food, clothing, household items, personal care and recreation, health care, and access to phone and transportation?
   - What familial or informal resources does the client system possess? Which people are significant in the client's life? Does the client system have significant persons who might be enlisted for support?
   - What external or formal resources are available in the client system's life domain?

To understand the problems, needs, strengths, and goals of the *mezzo systems*, such as a family or small group, the challenge is to collect enough information about each individual member while collecting information about the whole group:

1. *Purpose of group*
   - What is the written purpose of the group system or the purpose as articulated by the leader of the group? By the members?
   - What is the purpose of members' participation? What do members hope to gain by being in the group?
   - What are the explicit and implicit tasks of the group?

2. *Function of group*
   - Is this a family group? What is its composition: nuclear or blended; traditional or nontraditional? Who are its members?
   - Is it a therapeutic group? What therapeutic mode of treatment does it use?
   - Is it a civic or advocacy group? What civic action or advocacy purpose does the group seek?
   - Is it an educational group? What knowledge does it seek to impart?
   - Is it a skills training group? What particular skills are being sought?

3. *Group operations*
   - Do individual members' beliefs and values pose a barrier to the group's cohesion?

- Do the overall beliefs and values of the group pose an asset or a barrier to some other system?
- What are the strengths of the group's beliefs and value system?

4. *Group relationships*
   - How often does the group meet? Where?
   - Is there a fee for joining or participating in the group?
   - Are there any specific responsibilities required of the participants? Are these responsibilities or tasks clearly stated or written out for participants at the time of joining?

5. *Value diversity in group functioning*
   - Does the problem reflect intragroup relationships and communication?
   - Does the problem reflect intergroup relations and operation?
   - What other external systems are involved in the problem presented?

To understand the problems of large **macro systems**, the data collection focus expands to include gathering information about the cultural, political, and economic contexts of the social structures and people involved. Societal attitudes and expectations about social problems and social institutions vary. By sanctioning or developing means of problem control, amelioration, or prevention, these attitudes and expectations influence the tasks of large macro systems. Three areas form the central organizing principles underlying data collection with macro systems: understanding the social problem, the social task or goal, and the means of social service system delivery. For example, it is often useful to collect information about the following:

1. *Locality of the social problem*
   - Is the problem found in a local community? Does it show lack of relationships? Lack of problem-solving capacities? Lack of something else?
   - Is the problem found in the community at large? Does it affect larger social systems of education, health, employment, and the general welfare of citizens?
   - Is the problem apparent in the community at large or in predominantly disadvantaged populations? Does the problem involve social injustice, deprivation, or resource inequity?

2. *Social goals*
   - Are the social goals related to the self-help capacity and integration processes of the local community?
   - Are the social goals related to community social planning or problem solving in relation to substantial community problems and specific task goals?
   - Are the social goals related to social action or a shifting of power relationships and resources? Do they seek basic institutional change? Do they require both process and task goals?

3. *Change strategies*
   - Is the typical approach to involve a broad cross-section of people in determining and solving their own problems through consensus?
   - Is the strategy to gather facts about problems and decide on the most rational course of action through seeking consensus or through conflict?

- Is the strategy to shift the power structure and/or crystallize issues and concerns in order to take a stand through seeking conflict, competition, confrontation, direct action, or negotiation?

4. *Medium of change*
   - Does the change process involve creating a new or an existing small process and task goal-oriented community group (or several groups)?
   - Does the change process involve manipulation of formal organizations and data analysis?
   - Does the change process involve manipulation of mass organizations and political process?

5. *Change boundaries*
   - Is it a local community? What are the geographic referents or endpoints? Is it one community or several?
   - Is it a subsystem or a local or large community? Is it a functional subpart of a community social system?
   - Is it a subpart or a segment of society?

6. *Social work role*
   - Does the generalist need to be primarily an enabler/catalyst, coordinator, teacher of problem-solving skills and ethical values, and/or a supporter in emphasizing common group objectives?
   - Does the generalist need to be an expert diagnostician, fact gatherer, and/or analyst in building a social plan, implementing a program, or interpreting research for practice application?
   - Does the generalist need to be an advocate, community organizer, or a social activist in organizing client or action groups to act in their own behalf in redressing injustice and promoting fairness?

Information may be gained directly through personal interviews, questioning, listening, and observing or indirectly through secondary sources such as records, documents, written materials, and verbal or written communication with outside systems. Collecting information through a personal interview may be characterized as having a conversation with a purpose. In a sense, the interview is a natural measuring instrument in which the respondent's answers to structured and unstructured questions may be translated into measures and used as data for monitoring client progress or evaluating outcomes (Kerlinger & Lee, 2000; Rubin & Babbie, 2001). Having begun to identify what information is needed for accurate assessment, the social worker begins to plan how to formulate questions for gathering the needed data. The focus is on collecting detailed information about the concrete interaction patterns, behaviors, and issues in the problem. Thus, the social worker may ask the client system:

- ▶ *Can you describe what the problem is like when it is happening?*
- ▶ *What is the timing during the day? The week?*
- ▶ *Where does it usually happen?*
- ▶ *What do you say and do when it is happening? What do others say and do?*

> *How do you feel and react when you experience the problem?*
> *What do you think about?*
> *Is the problem different from when it first started? How?*

In asking these questions, the social worker collects data about the different dimensions of the problem and of client system capabilities and resources inherent in the cognitive, affective, and behavioral responses to the problem.

Besides using the direct approach in questioning, social workers also find answers through listening and observation. Whereas direct structured questioning may sometimes elicit fear or defensiveness, skilled listening with minimal prompts or unstructured questioning and observing may disclose the needed information without provoking discomfort. If a social worker has any doubt about interpreting what is being seen or observed, the social worker has the responsibility to seek validation through multiple sources. Sometimes, this situation leads to a request for formal testing using standardized psychometric instruments. For example, the social worker may observe that the client's mood appears depressed and seems to interfere with problem solving. At the same time, the client system overtly expresses anger and denies any feelings of sadness. To get a better handle on the client's affective state and to help the client system recognize the effect of feelings on actions, the social worker may request that the client system fill out a rapid assessment instrument such as a preliminary mood screening inventory. Subsequently, the social worker and the client system discuss the results and plan for appropriate intervention. Pending the severity of the client's mood scores, observed affective expression, and psychosocial functioning and the purpose of the agency, the social worker's initial process of listening, observing, and data collecting may lead to a formal request for a full mental health evaluation by a clinical social worker, psychologist, or psychiatrist. When rapid assessment instruments are used as part of data collection, the social worker bears the responsibility of appraising the client system if further testing or professional evaluation is needed.

Data may also be collected through secondary sources, such as evaluations from other agencies and professionals, public records, and other written or verbal communication with outside systems. If data are obtained through a study of public documents (state records of births, marriages, deaths, etc.), no written permission is needed, but the client system is entitled to know why the information is being sought.

Informed Consent and Assent

Throughout the process of collecting data, the social worker demonstrates belief in the dignity of persons by respecting a client system's right to privacy. The social worker understands and upholds the principle of confidentiality when information about a client system is requested, released, and utilized. Only information that is relevant and necessary for accurate assessment should be sought by the social worker after the written informed consent of the client system has been obtained. This release of information must contain the client system's written permission to the source to release information to the agency and must explain why it is needed and how it is to be used.

According to Wilson (1978, p. 57), 10 conditions must be met if a client system is to give his or her informed consent:

1. The consumer must be told that there is a desire or a request to release certain data.
2. The consumer must understand exactly what information is to be disclosed. He cannot intelligently decide if he wants it revealed unless he knows exactly what material is in question.
3. In order for the consumer to know what is to be released, he should actually see the material and/or have it read to him and explained in terms he can understand.
4. The consumer must be told exactly to whom the information is being released—name, position, and affiliation.
5. The client must be told why the information is being requested and exactly how it will be used by the receiving party.
6. There must be a way for the consumer to correct or amend the information to ensure its accuracy and completeness before it is released.
7. The consumer must understand whether or not the receiving party has the right to pass the information on to a third party. The consumer must have the right to specify that this not be done without his knowledge and consent.
8. The consumer should be fully informed of any repercussions that might occur should he (a) grant permission for the disclosure or (b) not give permission.
9. The consumer should be advised that his consent for release of information is time-limited and revocable. He should be advised how he can withdraw his consent and be given periodic opportunities for doing so.
10. The consumer's consent for release of information must be in writing on a "Release-of-Information Consent Form."

Before any information is requested or released, a release-of-information form must be signed by the client system with a copy placed in the agency records, a copy provided to the client system, and the original sent to the source from which the information is being sought. If the client system is a child, it is of particular importance that both *Parent Informed Consent* and *Child Informed Assent* requesting collateral information be sought and documented. This document includes information about assenting to collection of the collateral information in language that the child can understand and within the scope of his or her cognitive competence. Older children are typically expected to participate more actively in the assent process and to co-sign their agreement along with their parents. An example of a release of information form may be found in Figure 6.1.

It is possible that the system of contact will not allow the social worker to collect information on some problems. In this situation, the social worker will have to limit the focus of attention to those problem areas accepted by the client system for

FIGURE 6.1 ■ Release-of-Information Consent Form

I _____ give permission

(person giving consent)

for _____ to release to

(system with information)

_____ the following

(system to receive information)

information:

_____

_____

_____

_____

_____

_____

I understand that _____

(system receiving information)

will use this information for the following purpose:

_____

_____

_____

_____

_____

This consent is to expire on   _____

                                                              (date)

Signed _____   _____

                                                              (date)

Witness _____   _____

                                                              (date)

Agency representative _____   _____

                                                              (date)

study and intervention. If a client system will not give permission to release information that must be obtained in order to proceed with a case, the social worker may have to point out that services will have to be terminated unless the information is made available.

Maintaining Confidentiality

Throughout the process of collecting data, the social worker demonstrates belief in the dignity of persons by respecting a client system's right to privacy. The social worker understands and upholds the principle of confidentiality when information about a client system is requested, released, and utilized. Prior to seeking any information about a client system, the social worker must have the written informed consent of the client system. When requesting information, the social worker has the responsibility to clarify why the information is needed, how it will be used, and who will have access to the data collected.

In interacting with client systems, the social worker helps the client understand the implications of sharing information. A client who comes to an agency for help is asking for service from the agency. Occasionally, a client may ask a social worker not to tell "anyone," including other agency employees, what is being disclosed. In this case, the social worker will need to point out that information is shared with those in the agency whose roles relate directly to service delivery, such as supervisors, secretaries, program evaluators, or other service providers who are working on the case. This type of sharing is not a breach of confidentiality. It is in accordance with the Health Information Privacy Protection Act (HIPPA) of 2000, which recognizes the need for information exchange among those employees of an agency who have a need for the record in the performance of their duties.

The client system should be assured that information shared with a social worker will not go outside of the agency without the client's permission. Exceptions to this (e.g., if the person threatens to harm another person or the social worker, or if the record is subpoenaed by the court) should be stated also. Unless a state has privileged-communication statutes for social workers, a social worker will be expected to comply if issued a subpoena requesting disclosure of information about a client to the court. A social worker who receives a subpoena should consult with the agency and an attorney to discuss how information is to be disclosed or retained.

Generally, social workers are cautious in disseminating confidential information to outside agencies. There are times, however, when social workers are somewhat careless in discussing the lives and problems of their client systems. Occasionally, social workers feel a need to let go of the heavy input received during interviews, and to find outlets during informal situations with family, friends, or colleagues. This is not only a serious failure in confidentiality, but also a failure to use supervision or other appropriate channels for ventilation and support.

As data are received, skill is needed in selecting and documenting information for the record. Client systems have the right to verify personally the accuracy of information recorded in the permanent files of the agency. When a social worker explains what will be done with the information collected, the client system should be told about the kind of record kept by the agency and the policy regarding access to records. Discussion about records and confidentiality does not have to be prolonged enough to cause alarm or suspicion. A social worker uses skill in determining when and how to talk about different aspects of confidentiality with a client system.

■ CASE EXAMPLES

Example 1: Agency Boundary

CLIENT: Miss Brown, there's a problem I'm having right now at home that I'd like to talk with you about, but I don't want Mr. Johnson, my husband's social worker, to know about it. He would tell my husband, and there would be trouble.

SW: I'd be happy to talk with you about any problem you may be having, Mrs. Armez, but I'm afraid I can't agree to withholding information from Mr. Johnson. Mr. Johnson and I are working as a team with your family, and we do share information. Is it that you are afraid that Mr. Johnson will discuss the problem with your husband?

CLIENT: Yes, I don't trust Mr. Johnson. He sees my husband every week, and I know they talk about me. He would end up telling my husband what I said.

SW: You are afraid of what would happen if your husband found out about the problem, is that it?

CLIENT: Yes, I couldn't deal with it if he found out. It would be awful. Do you think Mr. Johnson would tell my husband?

SW: Mr. Johnson and I talk together to help each other gain a more total understanding of the family situation. We respect what each of you shares with us, and we do not report back on what was said by one to the other.

CLIENT: I don't think I could risk it.

SW: I can see that you are troubled, Mrs. Armez, and I hope that you will grow in trusting us here at the clinic. I would like to see you get help with whatever is bothering you.

Example 2: Release of Information

SW: Mr. Armez, when I spoke with your employer, he said he needed a doctor's statement indicating that you are ready to go back to work. I understand that you had a doctor's examination last week. Is that right?

CLIENT: Yes, I saw the doctor last Tuesday. He said I could go back to work by Thursday.

SW: Fine. In order for me to get a statement from the doctor for your employer, I need to have your consent in writing. I will indicate on this release-of-information form that the doctor's statement will be sent to your employer with a copy to be kept in our file. Is this agreeable with you, Mr. Armez?

CLIENT: Yes, sure. That's OK.

SW: All right. Let's go over what is stated here on this consent form before you sign it.

In the first example, the social worker encourages the client system to speak about her problems but makes it clear that what she says will be shared with the co-worker for the case. It is better to have the client system hold back from sharing at this time than to have co-workers holding back information from each other. The honesty and concern expressed by the social worker in this case help strengthen the client system's trust in the social workers and in the agency. In the second case scenario, the social worker points out what information is needed, from whom, and for what purpose. The content of the consent form is carefully described and reviewed before the form is signed.

Sometimes primary and secondary data are gathered from an action system about a social service delivery system in order to obtain funding from a public or private source. In this instance, the challenge is to maintain confidentiality by collecting anonymous facts about the problems and needs, diversity, resources, and service barriers encountered by micro and mezzo client consumer systems and to collate these facts into a representative aggregate report documenting service need and cost of service delivery. For example, a state-level Juvenile Justice Division flat-lined the funding of local agencies providing formal counseling services for predelinquent children, youths, and families for 15 years despite increased requests for service. To address this social problem, the social work director of one local agency mobilized the other directors to form a statewide association of youth service agencies in order to develop an aggregate anonymous database, including:

▶ Scope, duration, and severity of problems/needs, scope of available personal and environmental resources, and diverse characteristics of client systems served and not served
▶ Number and composition of the client systems served and the modality, length, and effectiveness of the services provided
▶ Barriers encountered by client systems in seeking and receiving services
▶ Barriers encountered in delivering services to diverse client systems
▶ Delinquency-like behavior and adjudicated delinquency of youths in community environments with and without youth service agencies

Since the database would be built by agency staff and consultants and would not include identifying client system information, the standard informed consent and assent for receipt of agency services was considered sufficient protection of confidentiality.

Fact versus Assumption

As a social worker collects data, skill is needed to distinguish between fact and assumption. Interpretation of what is heard or seen may be influenced by the social worker's frame of reference, past experiences, values, needs, and impressions. Through personal experience, a social worker may quickly assume that one word, description, or event is similar to another, and a label may be given that is actually incorrect. When a social worker believes data have been found, he or she should ask: *How is this documented? Did I really see this—hear this—find this?*

Facts answer the question: *Is this true or false?* Assumptions, because they are not based on facts, may be either true or false. With assumptions, missing information is taken for granted. An activity to help refine one's skill for data collection is given in Exercise 6.1.

EXERCISE 6.1
Information

A woman was leaving the office when a man appeared at the door and demanded money. The secretary opened a drawer. The contents of the drawer were scooped up, and the man sped away.

If the following statement is true, circle *T*. If it is false, circle *F*. If the statement is an assumption, circle *?*

1. A man appeared as a client was leaving the office.	T	F	?
2. The intruder was a man.	T	F	?
3. No one demanded money.	T	F	?
4. The secretary was the woman who opened the drawer.	T	F	?
5. The man took the contents of the drawer.	T	F	?
6. Someone opened a drawer.	T	F	?
7. Money was in the drawer.	T	F	?
8. The man ran away.	T	F	?
9. The man demanded money from the woman.	T	F	?
10. There are three people in this story.	T	F	?

In this exercise, all statements contain assumptions except for number 3, which is false, and number 6, which is true. The assumptions that cannot be substantiated by the words of the story are the following:

1. It is assumed that the woman is a client.
2. It is assumed that the man is an intruder.
3. False
4. It is assumed that the secretary is a woman.
5. It is assumed that the contents were taken (not just "scooped up") and that this was done by the man.
6. (True)
7. It is assumed that the contents were money.
8. It is assumed that "sped away" means "ran away."
9. It is assumed that the money was demanded from the woman and not from the secretary.
10. It is assumed that the woman was not the secretary.

These assumptions could be correct, but they could be incorrect also. In this exercise, the question mark should have been circled for 8 out of 10 answers.

A social worker tries to tap all possible resources for reliable data before beginning to make an assessment. The validity of each piece of information is considered before an effort is made to categorize and to integrate information. If the social worker recognizes that he or she is drawn toward making an assumption, the question should be asked: *Why am I assuming this?* It is possible that the assumption comes from one's "sixth sense," which may be a useful guide to tracking down the facts for a valid assessment.

Basic Categories for Data Collection

The Problems/Needs

As stated earlier, when data are gathered, they are clustered under the three headings of "problem," "person," and "environment." The *problem* is the need, concern, issue, or difficulty that has been identified for study and action by both the social worker and the system of contact. Before deciding what needs to be done, or even which problem or need should be considered first, the social worker and the client system require a clear understanding of the scope, duration, and severity of each problem or need.

What is the scope of the problem or need? How many people are involved in the cause or the effect of the problem? What other systems are feeling this problem? Where can the boundary be drawn between those who have the problem or need and those who are outside of it?

The social worker also studies the duration of the problem or need. *When did it begin? How long has it been going on? Has it been continuous or intermittent?* The longer a problem exists, very likely, the longer it will take to break the pattern and bring about whatever change is needed. The shorter the duration, the greater the chance of quick and effective intervention.

And finally, the social worker asks: *How serious is this problem or need?* A guide for understanding the severity of a problem is to consider it in terms of a life-or-death scale. If, for example, the problem is physical, the social worker asks: *Is the illness terminal? What is the potential for cure?* If the problem is more interpersonal or social, the social worker considers the possibility of its leading to the breakdown or destruction of the family, the person, the group, the community, or the relationship.

The Persons

Another major category for data collection is the *person or persons* who are experiencing the problem or needs. A central concern is the coping capacity, strengths, and assets of the persons who have the problem. *To what extent are the persons experiencing this problem capable of maintaining or improving their level of psychosocial functioning? How have the persons been able to cope with this or similar problems before? Do the persons have physical, psychological, intellectual, social, economic, and spiritual strengths and assets for dealing with the problem or need?*

In addition to coping capacity, the social worker seeks indicators of the extent of motivation the persons have to work on the problem. *Do they express a desire to change the situation or to overcome the problem? Do they have hope that things can change? Is any person feeling distress, enthusiasm, fear, or pressure that is directly related to the problem, and can this serve as impetus for change? Where do the persons want to begin? Why there?* If any person does not seem to have hope that a particular situation can change, why not? What could be a source for motivating this person? What does this person value or want?

The Environment

The third basic category for data collection is that of the *environment* that surrounds the persons and problems/needs under study. *What is there in the environment that could be relating to this person-problem-environment situation?* An ecological-systems perspective emphasizes the necessity and potential for transactions between persons and their environments. Environmental factors, qualities, or systems may be present that could serve as resources and supports. Currently, the persons may not be utilizing these resources, owing to barriers such as to a lack of awareness, misunderstanding, or fear of rejection. To identify formal and informal resources and barriers to their use, the social worker gathers information from systems in the environment as well as from client systems. The person is asked: *What have you tried before? Did you go anywhere or to anyone to receive help with this problem before?* Explorations move from a consideration of the person's immediate environment—with informal resources of family, friends, and local community services—to a study of more formal resources, public or private, in the extended societal environment. The social worker asks: *What resources are available and appropriate to meet this need with these persons at this time? What are the barriers to resource availability?*

In addition to gathering data on environmental resources, the social worker looks for information about systems or circumstances in the environment that may have a negative influence on the persons or that may be a contributing factor to the problem. These, too, may be informal sources—family, friends, community—or formal systems, such as schools, hospitals, religious institutions, and organizations. *Is the problem caused or compounded by the person's interaction or interdependence with the environment? More specifically, what systems of the environment relate to the person-problem-environment situation, and how do they promote or prevent the growth or functioning of the persons involved?*

In summary, the social worker asks: *What is the scope, duration, and severity of the problem or need? Do the persons have the capacity and motivation to work on the problem? What resources or influences are there in the environment that could or do have an impact on the problem?* After data are gathered in all three categories for each identified problem or need, the social worker proceeds in the General Method to a collective, comprehensive study for preliminary assessments and problem prioritization.

Throughout all the phases of the General Method, the skilled social worker is recognizing and processing data. As with the identified problem and goals of other phases, the information collected is dynamic and changing. Newly acquired data may lead to a reformulation of the problem, goals, assessment, or planned intervention. It is in the second phase of the General Method that particular emphasis is given to procuring and documenting any information that is missing and believed essential for effective assessment and planning.

Recording Data

Because of the possibility of a client system's misunderstanding or misusing information found in his or her record, one might ask: *Why bother to keep records?* A social worker needs to record data for several reasons, including:

1. To enhance service delivery through monitoring progress or regression
2. To account for services and to document need
3. To allow for easy transferability if a social worker leaves an agency
4. To contribute to evaluation research leading to improved services

Each service agency has its own identified methods for keeping records. Three commonly known ways of recording in social work are (1) process recordings, (2) summary recordings, and (3) problem-oriented recordings.

Process Recordings

Most agencies do not use process recordings for their permanent records. This type of recording is a lengthy narrative that describes in detail the interactions and communications that took place during a single interview. This recording may be subdivided into four basic parts: (1) presenting situation, (2) narrative (interview), (3) social worker's impressions, and (4) future plans. An example of a process recording may be found in Figure 6.2. After stating the basic information of who, when, where, and why in the section called "presenting situation," the social worker narrates what actually took place in the interview. This narrative should include not only what the client system said but also what exactly was said by the social worker in the sequence as it happened.

The third section of a process recording is for the social worker's initial impressions of the person-problem-strengths-environment situation and of the social worker and client system relationship, based on what was said and felt during the interview. This is not a formal assessment of the case, but rather a current indication of the social worker's thoughts about the case and the interview. The social worker tries to clarify what he or she thinks now about the persons, problems, strengths, and environment and the social worker–client system interaction that just took place. Impressions may include a consideration of how the social worker thinks he or she conducted the interview.

In the fourth section of a process recording, the social worker describes future plans for the case. He or she asks the question: *What next?* This section includes what

FIGURE 6.2 ■ Process Recording

Case of Mr. D

I. Presenting Situation

Mr. D is a 40-year-old African American male who was seen by Social Services on 10/7 at his own request. He was presently hospitalized for surgery on his ankle, which did not heal properly. The initial injury occurred about a year ago, at which time, according to the patient, he fell off a ladder.

II. Narrative (Interview)

Mr. D was dozing when I entered the room but stirred and said he was willing to talk for a few minutes. I asked him how he was feeling following his surgery two days ago. He stated that his ankle was better but his hip was sore from being in bed so much. It is still painful if he moves too much.

He then asked me what I had been able to find out about financial help, since he no longer had any health insurance and the money he received for Social Security Disability could not possibly take care of the hospital bills. I said that I had been in contact with our business office, which informed me that the necessary forms had been sent to the Department of Social Services informing them of Mr. D's need for assistance. I explained that DSS would contact him following his release to try to reach an agreement regarding his bills.

At this, Mr. D expressed his impatience over his hospitalization. He said he was anxious to be released from the hospital, feeling that he can sit in bed at home as well as he could here. When I suggested that perhaps he was still in need of special services that could best be delivered in the hospital, he replied that he was not receiving any special services that would keep him from going home. Mr. D stated further that he "doesn't trust" the staff. I asked him why he felt this way. He said the doctors did not tell him the truth when he was seen in the clinic prior to his hospital admission. He said he was left with the impression that they were going to break and reset his ankle. He felt that they knew at the time that more extensive surgery was possible, and that he should have been told about this. He was not informed of their decision to do a bone graft until the day he was admitted to the hospital before his surgery. I suggested that perhaps they had not made a definite decision until they had made a more careful examination of his X-rays following his visit to the outpatient clinic. I agreed that they could have informed him that this type of surgery was a possibility. Mr. D seemed to accept what I said and made no further comments on the subject.

I then asked Mr. D how things were going at home. He said that his mother, who lived in the apartment below, continued to take care of his two boys and that the boys came to see him almost every afternoon. Mr. D. seemed a bit reluctant at this point to discuss his home situation in much depth. When asked about his divorce, he said that this did not become final until last April. Neither he nor the boys ever see his ex-wife. He stated that he had to fight to get custody of the boys but felt his wife didn't want them very much, since she makes no attempt to see them. Mr. D mentioned that during his past hospitalization, his sister, rather than his ex-wife, had taken care of his daughter. I asked where his daughter was now, and he said that she had fallen through the ice at Carney Park and drowned last winter while he was recuperating at Rocky Neck Veterans' Home. I asked him how he felt about this incident. He said, while looking out the window toward the park, that his feelings did not matter. His concern was for his sons at present, particularly the older boy, age 11, who was with his sister at the time. When asked how

(Continued)

FIGURE 6.2 ■ Continued

he felt the boys were doing, he said he thought they had recovered all right, and things were pretty much back to normal. Mr. D seemed particularly uneasy during this part of our conversation, during which time he began fidgeting with his covers and gazing out the window. Since I did not feel that he trusted me enough at this point to explore his feelings any further, I closed this part of the discussion by saying that perhaps in time it would be easier for him to talk about it. He agreed by saying "yes."

I asked Mr. D if he would like me to come back again tomorrow, if I could stop in for a few minutes to see how he was doing. I mentioned that perhaps by then he would be allowed to get up and around a bit. He added that he had hoped he would be home but if he was still here, he wouldn't mind if I came to see him.

III. Social Worker's Impressions

My impressions of this client, and this interview in particular, were that there was a great deal to be discussed here, but that at the present time, Mr. D was reluctant to discuss many of his feelings with me. He was satisfied insofar as Social Services had met his financial needs. He did not seem to want the help that could be provided in a social work relationship, helping him to work on his feelings in many areas, including his hospitalization, his divorce, and his daughter's death.

IV. Future Plans

While the patient refuses to discuss his feelings and concerns regarding areas such as his daughter's death and his divorce at this time, he may open up after a few interviews. I plan to see him again next week.

the social worker and the client system have agreed on as the next step in the process, and any other actions the social worker expects to take concerning the case.

Process recording is primarily a tool for supervision. It is submitted to a supervisor for review prior to a supervisory session. The supervisor reviews the record with the social worker and indicates strengths and weaknesses in interviewing skills. The social worker is helped to consider possible options or directions for proceeding with the case. Usually, process recordings are kept in a separate folder for the social worker and do not become a part of the permanent record.

Summary Recordings

Many agencies use a type of summary recording for their permanent records. Here, contacts for a period of time, generally not longer than three months, are summarized. In a summary recording, a social worker follows a four-part outline similar to that of process recording. The topical headings used are (1) basic information, (2) content summary, (3) social worker's impressions, and (4) future plans. The basic information given in a summary recording states the dates and places of contact, the persons interviewed, and the purpose for coming together. The content section highlights the topics and themes addressed during sessions, along with any major decisions reached during the period of time covered in the summary. The last two sections give the social worker's impressions of what has happened over the period of time covered and the future plans for continued work by social worker and client system.

Problem-Oriented Recordings

A problem-oriented recording (POR) is a clearly identified system of recording that originated with Dr. Lawrence Weed (1971) in health care systems. Several modified versions of this method are presently in use by many human service agencies (Martens & Holmstrum, 1974). Using a problem focus, recording usually begins with a list of all the problems identified to date, with an indication of when the problem was first recognized. For each problem listed, a brief assessment is given according to a "SOAP" format, which has been modified here to include strengths (SOSAP). The Subjective data (according to client's perception of the problem), the Objective data (as documented by testing, observation, and written and oral verification), the Strengths data (including strengths and resources), the Assessment (social worker's judgment), and the Plan (immediate) for each problem on the list are stated in a concise manner. In strengths-oriented problem-solving, a data list of strengths and resources precedes the assessment and changes the acronym to *SOSAP*.

For example, a problem listed for Jerry (15 years old, oldest of five children, both parents at home) was "below-average school performance—potential school dropout." The SOSAP assessment for this problem was recorded as follows:

S   7/10: Jerry says he finds school boring, and he plans to quit when he is 16. 7/12 and 7/14: His teachers say he doesn't seem to be able to grasp the material, although he tries very hard.

O   Jerry's full-scale IQ is 80 (Performance 90, Verbal 70, WISC-R, 5/21/99). He repeated eighth grade. With current grades, he may have to repeat ninth grade. There is only one ninth grade at Brown Junior High, and it is geared toward students of average or above-average intelligence.

S   Jerry's strengths and resources include a supportive family and a talent for the sports in which he participates and enjoys.

A   Jerry is finding school work difficult, owing to his limited intellectual abilities and his being placed in a class for students with average or above-average intelligence. He has a growing sense of inferiority and will probably drop out if he does not receive help.

P   1. Discuss Jerry's learning needs with Jerry, his parents, the school principal, and Jerry's teachers.

   2. Explore resources for tutoring and supportive services for Jerry.

   3. Explore other schools for Jerry.

   4. Work with all people in item 1 to provide Jerry with the learning opportunities he needs.

CHARLOTTE TOWLE (1896–1966), practitioner, administrator, and educator, linked the necessity of understanding human needs and behavior with the administration of public assistance programs in her book *Common Human Needs*. As a faculty member of the University of Chicago's School of Social Service Administration, she developed a client-centered casework curriculum that focused on the relationship between the inner life and the social environment.

Prior to closing a case with POR, a "closing summary" for each problem is stated that includes (1) status of the problem, (2) prognosis, and (3) recommendations.

The problem-oriented recording method emphasizes the importance of organization and preciseness in recording. Information is recorded in a manner that is very available for research, documentation, and evaluation. The method offers a framework for immediate recall and immediate information provision. The social worker is challenged to clarify problems and to progress in a skillful, accountable way. This recording method is particularly appropriate for general practice in which a strengths-based problem-solving approach is used throughout the process of service.

Other Record Forms

In addition to the three types of recording cited, information collected on a case may also be recorded on fact sheets and in social histories or referral summaries. In most agency files, a basic fact sheet is found inside the cover of each record (see the example in Figure 6.3). Names of the family members and related resources, dates, addresses, and other factual information are often listed on fact sheets.

In social histories, a brief narrative is given for a variety of general headings. These include family composition, family background, developmental history, education, work, health, religion, economic history, other agencies involved, problem assessment, goals, and future plans. In a referral summary, the social worker may add or delete any of these headings, depending on the nature and needs of the setting receiving the referral.

In any recording for permanent records or referrals, the information presented should be as factual as possible. Social workers need to be able to document their statements and to substantiate their conclusions. If a social worker is making a statement that is an assumption or an opinion, it should begin with such phrases as "It appears to me at this time that . . . because . . ." or "Based on . . . , my impressions

FIGURE 6.3 ■ Identification and Summary Fact Sheet

Admission no. _____ Date of admission _____ Room no. _____

Patient's name _____ Sex _____ Phone _____

Home address _____
                     street   town   state   zip

Admission date _____ Discharge date _____

Prior admission _____ Admission date _____ Discharge date _____

Admitting diagnosis _____

_____

Financially responsible party _____ Relationship _____

Address _____ Phone _____
                                                home   work

Power of attorney   Yes _____ No _____

Notify in case of emergency _____ Relationship _____

Address _____ Phone _____
                                                home   work

Date of birth _____ Age _____ Place of birth _____

U.S. citizen _____ Religion _____ Church _____

Marital status: S M W D _____ Medicare no. _____

Social security no. _____ Insurance no. _____

Welfare: Title XIX no. _____ Others _____

Attending physician: Name _____ Phone _____

Address _____

Previous physician: Name _____ Phone _____

Address _____

Pharmacist: Name _____ Phone _____

Dentist: Name _____ Phone _____

Podiatrist: Name _____ Phone _____

Funeral director: Name _____ Phone _____

Hospital preference _____ Phone _____

Discharged diagnosis _____

_____

Discharge date _____ to _____

at this time are. . . ." Accurate, effective recording calls for skill and sensitivity. As a social worker collects data in the second phase of the General Method, it is essential that he or she have skill in recognizing and recording relevant, accurate data in a systematic and professional manner.

Monitoring the Data-Collection Process

Careful monitoring of the data-collection phase focuses on the relevant facts collected about the person/problem/environment of the client system. For strengths-based problem-solving, it is important that the collected data balance problems and needs with strengths and assets and with environmental resources as well as barriers. Checklists often serve as a practical reminder in ensuring this balance as well as a way of monitoring the completeness and relevance of the dataset for the purpose intended. The *micro, mezzo,* and *macro system* data lists earlier in this chapter are easily converted into three-point checklists (data not needed, not yet collected, collected).

Working with Different Client Systems

Is there a difference in data collection when it is done with client systems of different sizes? Are there variations in the techniques or processes used when a social worker is gathering information about a group or community rather than an individual? How is information about a group or community kept confidential when it is frequently disclosed in the presence of several people who are not agency personnel? Is there a different method for recording information when working with a family, group, organization, or community?

The size of a client system does not alter the framework for organizing data under the three basic headings of "problem," "person," and "environment." The process and techniques used in collecting data, however, may differ when one is working with a larger system, such as a group or a community. Keeping in mind that the system of contact is made up of distinctive parts, the social worker is sensitive to the needs and perceptions of individual members. Focus, however, is directed toward identifying the felt needs of the client system as a whole. The social worker's focus is the client system in its entirety, while helping its members to grow in an awareness of their common identity and concerns.

Techniques are needed to locate information of a common nature and to sift out uncommon information of a personal nature. To determine the problems, motivation, and capacity of a larger system, and not just of a few outspoken members of the larger system, is a major challenge for a social worker. In the data-collection phase of the General Method, the social worker tries to become aware of the problems, persons, and environmental resources and influences of the entire client system. An effort is made to collaborate with the members of the client system in collecting information. They are encouraged to distinguish fact from assumption, to be open to diverse perceptions and feelings, and to focus on balancing common problems and needs with common strengths and resources.

Even prior to bringing the members of a client system together to engage in a working relationship, social workers frequently begin the process with a preliminary period of data collection by individual contact. Before convening the entire client system, the social worker needs to find out what constitutes the boundary of the client system and to develop an initial awareness of its members and their felt needs and available strengths and resources. A social worker will often speak with individual members of a family, group, organization, or community to give them the opportunity to share freely and in confidence their perceptions of the client system and its problems. This enables the social worker to locate motivating issues and potential leaders for the system. Once the client system and the social worker start to work together for identified goals, they jointly collect data on particular problems, related influences, strengths, and resources.

Although the categories for data collection within the ecological-systems perspective of problems, persons, and environment are basically the same for all client systems, the nature of the content addressed may differ. When working with a larger client system—such as a community, for example—the resources for and influences on the environment are generally of a formal nature. These may include foundations, federal and local policy makers, and organizations or their representatives. Information collected has to be clearly factual with documentation. Although skill for recognizing feelings is strongly needed when collecting information with smaller client systems, skill in acquiring and presenting facts is paramount in working with larger systems. Social workers need to be aware of the general feeling tones and reactions of larger client systems and their individual members, but change in larger client systems is strongly dependent on documented facts. Members of an organization may be very sympathetic toward a cause, but they may not be able to change their larger structure unless there is documented evidence of the need for and value in changing the policies or procedures of the organization. With larger complex systems, the information collected is mainly of a formal, factual nature.

As mentioned, a person may be hesitant to speak out about issues or concerns in a large client system. This hesitance may be due to a fear of reprisal later by other members of the system or by outsiders who have been informed of what the person said. Before they can develop confidence in sharing openly, members of a large system need clarification of what will happen when information is disclosed within the system. Although a social worker may state how he or she and the agency will handle information obtained, the social worker is not able to guarantee that other members of the client system will keep in confidence what will be shared. Prior to encouraging the disclosure of information within a client system, a social worker makes an effort to get the members of the client system to mutually agree on a code for themselves regarding how they will treat what is said at their meetings. This code should be restated or reconsidered whenever new members are added or there is some question whether it will continue being enacted.

■ **CASE EXAMPLE:**

Group

SW: Before we go on, I would like to talk with all of you about the confidential nature of what goes on in this group. As far as the agency is concerned, anything shared within the group is kept within the agency unless we all give our consent to have certain information shared outside. A summary of each meeting is recorded in the agency record, and any group member may request to review these recordings. The only exception for allowing information to go outside the agency would be if you revealed that you planned to injure someone or if I or our records were subpoenaed to court. Any questions about this?

MARY (GROUP MEMBER): Yeah, but what about everyone else here? How do I know that what I say won't be talked about out on the street by someone here?

SW: Well, let's talk about that. What do we think about a group member sharing what is said here with someone outside of the group? How do you want to handle what is said during our meetings?

MICHAEL (GROUP MEMBER): I don't think it's right to go and tell other people. We came here because we wanted help, but I don't want everyone in the world to know my business.

SW: I hear you saying that you don't think members should talk about what we share here with others. I wonder what the rest of the members think about this.

OTHERS: (Five others speak in support of Michael's position.)

SW: Are we saying as a group that we will keep in confidence whatever is said within this group? Are there any exceptions to this?

In terms of record keeping, the methods described earlier for recording data collected during an interview (process, summary, problem oriented) may be used to record contacts with client, action, and target systems of any size. Whether working with an individual, family, group, organization, or community, the social worker records fundamental facts about the presenting situation (who, when, where, why), the essential content addressed during the contact (problems, needs, strengths and assets, feelings, decisions), and the goals and plans that were established. In recording each contact or contacts over a period of time, a social worker may also include his or her impressions of the person-problem-environment situation.

When recording about a large system, a social worker needs to distinguish between what is recognized as a problem or need of one or some members of the system and what is seen as a common problem or need of the entire system. For example, when compiling the problem list for a problem-oriented recording for a family system, the social worker indicates when a problem belongs to one or some members rather than to the whole family.

■ **CASE EXAMPLE:**

Problem List

Active	Date
Father's unemployment	10/2
Inadequate housing	10/2
Father's drinking	11/3
Mother-father communication	11/3
Ryan's sore throat	11/3

In this example, whereas the housing need is common to all, it is apparent that there are individuals within the family who have particular problems that influence the functioning of the entire family: the unemployment and drinking problems are the father's; mother and father have a problem with communication; and Ryan has the sore throat.

In using summary recording to record an activity group session, a format may be followed such as that illustrated in Figure 6.4. Here again, the social worker

FIGURE 6.4 ■ Weekly Group Record

Date _____

Group _____ Leader _____

Attendance: Total members present: Male _____ Female _____

Visitors _____

Brief description of meeting: Please record briefly important discussions, decisions, and problems. *Give your own evaluation of the meeting.*

What was the main activity of the group at this meeting? Who initiated the main activity, and how did the group as a whole respond to the suggested activities? What program suggestions did you mention or bring up in the meeting?

Situations requiring individual attention: Please record problems, group or individual conflicts, and other incidents that you may want some help with from your supervisor.

Leader's interpretation regarding behavior of individuals: If there was any unusual behavior, why do you think the individuals and the group as a whole behaved as they did?

Plans for the next meeting:

basically indicates the presenting situation, central content (activity, process, problem), the leader's impressions, and future plans. The recording format provides opportunity for the social worker not only to describe the problems and behaviors of the group, but also to identify the problems and behaviors of individuals that influence the functioning of the group.

Making a process record of an action system, such as a community meeting, may be extremely lengthy and time consuming. The framework found in Figure 6.5 provides guidance for highlighting important aspects of a meeting. Basically, the content addressed includes facts about the presenting situation, content discussed, and future plans and goals. The topics that are covered include how the social worker perceived his or her role, before, during, and after the meeting, as well as the social worker's impressions. This recording, as with all recordings, may be used in supervision as a teaching tool. It lends itself to pointing out a social worker's skill and sensitivity for working with communities.

FIGURE 6.5 ■ Process Recording for a Community Meeting

I. *Presenting Situation*
Social worker's name
Name of community
Place of meeting
Date of meeting
Who called the meeting?
For what purpose?
Number of people attending
Who were the people at the meeting? (Whom did they represent?)

II. *Meeting*
What took place? Topics, decisions, actions (including worker's), in sequence.

III. *Social Worker's Impressions*
How do the community members see themselves? See you?
Do they see themselves as a community?
What are your impressions of the roles, behaviors, and strengths of participants?
What do they want to accomplish individually? As a community?
What do they want from you?
Did they and you come away with something as a result of the meeting?
How did you use yourself during the meeting?
How did you feel about the meeting—before, during, and after?

IV. *Future Plans*
What do they do now?
What do you do now?

Using Social Work Foundation Knowledge in Data Collection

In the second phase of the General Method, the social worker uses values, knowledge, and skills from the social work foundation identified in Chapter 1. The practice principles of confidentiality, self-determination, and nonjudgmental attitude are strongly apparent in the actions and transactions of the social worker during data collection. As pointed out, the client system has the right to choose what personal information will be disclosed, as well as to choose how this information will be used. The social worker strives to gather factual information for a documented assessment that is free from assumption or personal value judgments.

In proceeding in the helping process with collecting data about persons and environments, the social worker uses assorted theoretical and conceptual knowledge learned in human behavior, social environment, and psychopathology course work to comprehend the nature and functioning of client, target, and resource systems. Through observing and inquiring directly or indirectly, he or she obtains information in a manner that reflects the use of theories from the holistic foundation. Seeing the data collected in the light of basic theory, the social worker is able to identify such characteristics as coping capacities, strengths, developmental levels, communication patterns, and role expectations. Theory also helps the social worker recognize whether certain factors are the cause or the effect of problem situations. For example, in inquiring about the time when 8-year-old Alex started to insist that the light be kept on in his room at night, the social worker learned that it was around this same time that Alex started to have learning problems at school, to become increasingly possessive of his mother, and to act fearful toward his father. Knowledge of such theories as life cycle and psychosocial development, as well as role and stress theory, helped the social worker pursue inquiry for understanding the regressive behavior.

The skills of the social work foundation that are used in the data-collection phase of the General Method include professional skills of relationship building, communication, investigation, and strengths-based problem-solving; gathering information; and recording the collected data. In sifting out facts of importance for understanding and planning, the social worker listens, questions, and clarifies. He or she may work with various systems to identify problems, needs, and strengths or to collaborate in exchanging information for effective teamwork. Recording and research skills are used to test out and to register the findings collected.

Human Diversity in Data Collection

From an identification of problems, feelings, and goals in the engagement phase, the social worker and client system move on to gathering information for problem assessment. As a social worker begins to collect information about problem, person, and environment, some cultural systems may be hesitant to give information about personal or family problems, needs, and strengths, particularly to someone from a different ethnic group. The social worker must therefore be explicit in making known what information is needed and how it will be used. Whereas some client systems may wish to move quickly through this phase, with reliance on intuition, others may need to move cautiously, with reliance on fact and reason.

To collect data on the actual participants in a problem-person-environment situation, it is important for a social worker to understand the roles and structures in the culture of the system. For example, a fourfold structural typology often may be found among Puerto Rican American families: (1) extended family systems—a wide range of natural or ritual kin; (2) the nuclear family—father, mother, and children; (3) father, mother, their children, and children of other unions of the husband or wife; and (4) the mother-based family with children of one or more men, but no permanent male figure in the home (Garcia-Preto, 1996).

In locating resources or influences in the environment, a social worker needs to know who or what resource would be appropriate to contact for certain problems. In the Puerto Rican culture, for example, there may be ready acceptance to have *compadres* and *comadres* (godparents) become foster parents if a child needs to be placed. To mediate in matters such as property disputes, however, it may be more appropriate in this culture to use distant relatives, in order to avoid the risk of losing friendships with closer relatives if they became involved (Garcia-Preto, 1996).

During data collection in the General Method, as the three focal points of problem, person, and environment are explored, a social worker looks to see if an individual has a nurturing system as well as a sustaining system in his or her environment. The social worker also considers the values and expectations of all three (individual, nurturing system, and sustaining system), realizing that the more they share in common, the greater their congruence, goodness of fit (Germain & Gitterman, 1996), and mutual health and growth. Even if an individual is found to be different or nonacceptable by a sustaining system, he or she can grow and thrive, provided there is a strong, supportive nurturing system. Unfortunately, many individuals who are perceived as having different lifestyles or as being physically or mentally challenged have no nurturing system where they are understood and supported, and they live in a very rejecting, condemning sustaining system.

In collecting data, a social worker inquires about a client system's current and potential environment. When working on problems related to human diversity, a social worker gathers information not only about existing resources in the client system's life space but also about possible formal and informal resources that could offer support for persons in their environments.

A social worker also needs to be sensitive to cultural and social role expectations when information about problem, person, and environment is gathered. For example, men who believe they should be strong and successful might resist exposure of their personal, family, or social problems. Their environments might be limited in nurturing networks. They might withdraw from talking about themselves at any length, perhaps feeling comfortable only when talking objectively about their work or society at large with its organizations and institutions. Women might express feelings of helplessness and even fear of succeeding in resolving their problems. Perhaps they will struggle over a sense of being disloyal or ungrateful if they criticize or talk about their husbands or family problems.

In collecting data, a social worker is also sensitive to the socio-demographic variables of age and stages, endowment and personality, value systems, social class, and geographic location. The social worker's skill in inquiry, use of informative resources, and ability to recognize facts, custom, and feelings will reflect the extent of sensitivity the social worker has to various dimensions of human diversity.

ONGOING CASES
Data-Collection Phase

In this section, the application of knowledge and skills during the *data collection phase* of the General Method is demonstrated by entry-level generalist social workers in seven diverse fields of practice: child welfare, gerontology, public social welfare, community services, education, corrections, and homelessness. The case examples demonstrate the applicability of the General Method with its multiple phases and major focal points, principles, and processes for data collection in all areas of practice with diverse human populations. In Exercise 6.2, questions are proposed for reflection and discussion about how practice in each of the case examples during the data-collection phase might change if the client system represented a different

▶ *Culture:* Racial/ethnic group membership, national origin and social group identity, religion and spirituality
▶ *Social status:* Socio-economic status, environmental, and rural/urban differences
▶ *Socio-demographic strata:* Age and developmental stage, gender roles, sexual orientation, challenges in mental and physical ability.

EXERCISE 6.2
Impact of Human Diversity on Data-Collection Process

Consider the following questions with each of the seven client systems. In collecting data, how might change in culture, social status, or socio-demographic strata:

1. Influence the client system's willingness to provide information?
2. Influence the social worker's view of the information needed?
3. Reveal values that influence timing, communications, content, and actions in collecting information?
4. Affect the dynamics of the professional relationship in data collection?
5. Affect monitoring of the progress, timeliness, and completeness of data collection?

I. Child Welfare Case

A. Agency: State Department of Children's Services

B. Client System

K, a 15-year-old female is in an emergency shelter. (For more background information, see Chapter 5, Ongoing Cases: Engagement Phase, I. Child Welfare Case.)

C. Engagement Summary

The feelings expressed during engagement included loneliness, restlessness, hatred of self and others, and depression. The problems and goals identified during this phase are listed in Chapter 5.

D. Data Collection

PROBLEM: During data collection, the social worker learned that K was well liked by those who lived in the group home where she was first placed. The group parents described K as quiet and fearful. She seemed to get lost in the group; therefore, they thought a foster home was a good plan for her at the time. The foster-home parents described K as stubborn and pouty. She never seemed to get enough attention and didn't want to do her share of the work. They said they tried to tell K to stay away from the boy she ran away with, but she would not listen to them.

In school, K had been performing at an average level while she lived in the group home. During her stay in the foster home, she remained in the same school she had attended while in the group home. Her grades started to drop before she ran away. Her teachers said that K daydreamed a lot, but they thought she did have the potential for at least average achievement. As her marks started to drop, the school personnel had a pupil-appraisal team meeting. The Children's Services social worker who had the case prior to the current social worker attended the meeting. It was agreed at this meeting that K would be referred to the local mental health center for counseling. K refused to go to the center, saying she was not "crazy."

PERSON: During data collection, the social worker discovered that K was extremely motivated to work on her two stated goals. She said she missed school and even missed her teachers. She wished she could go back to the group home, where they were "nice" to her. K began to say that she knew that she was "messed up" and that she probably needed to go for counseling. She hoped someone could help her so she wouldn't feel "so awful inside." She thought that a boy at the shelter was starting to like her, but she was "afraid of getting too close." The social worker at the shelter described K as "shy" and "noninvolved with the activities or residents of the shelter."

ENVIRONMENT: The emergency shelter had a residence time limit of four weeks. In exploring possible resources for K, the social worker learned that K's biological father had moved out of state and left no forwarding address. K's stepfather had been taken to court for child sexual assault, and her mother blamed K for reporting it. K's mother did not want K to be returned home, "ever." There were no relatives interested in caring for K. K's foster parents did not want her to return either. Although there was no opening in K's previous group-home placement, the social worker located another group home with an opening in a neighboring city. Services available for residents in this home included ongoing casework

TABLE 6.1 ■ Ongoing Recording: Child Welfare Case

Date Identified	Problem/Need	Goal
1/12	No permanent home	a. To obtain a permanent placement
		b. To maintain a permanent placement
1/12	Out of school	c. To reenter school
1/12	Personal problems	Personal goals (1/19)
	a. Poor self-esteem	a. To feel better about self
	b. Identity confusion	b. To clarify identity
	c. Sexuality (relationships, behavior)	c. To be able to have good friendships with males
	d. Depression	d. To stop "feeling down"

by an M.S.W. and weekly peer-group meetings, where discussions focused on such topics as "sex," "parents," and "growing up confused."

E. Charted Progress

During the process of data collection, goals were expanded to include K's expressed desire to get help with her personal feelings and problems. These new, mutually agreed-upon goals were added to the two goals identified during engagement and were recorded as shown in Table 6.1. Since the date when these goals were agreed on was different from the date of problem identification, the later date was recorded in the "goal" column.

Note: The paperwork required throughout the process of working with K included the following:

Summary recordings of all contacts with K and related resources
Referral summary for the group home
Case summary for the court in preparation for a petition to seek continuance of commitment
Transfer summary at termination

II. Gerontology Case

A. Agency: Seaside Nursing Home

B. Client System

Mrs. J is an 80-year-old Portuguese woman in a skilled nursing facility. (For additional background information, see Chapter 5, Ongoing Cases: Engagement Phase, II. Gerontology Case.)

C. Engagement Summary

The feelings expressed during engagement included distrust, fear, anger, and abandonment. The problems and goals identified during this phase are listed in Chapter 5.

D. Data Collection

PROBLEM: The social worker attended a patient-care conference on Mrs. J with the staff of the nursing home. She learned at this time that Mrs. J was causing a disruption on her floor. She was fighting with the nurses when they came to give her a bath. She sometimes stood at the door of her room and called the other residents names. On occasion, she would refuse to go to meals or to leave her room. She was often found talking to herself in Portuguese. Also reported were minor incidents of confusion and irrational mood swings.

PERSON: As data were being collected, Mrs. J began to talk more freely with the social worker about herself and her background. She said she came to America when she was 20 years old. She married shortly after arriving and had three children by the time she was 25. Her husband left the family when the youngest child was 13 years old. Mrs. J used to clean houses and take in washing to earn money. All of her children had to leave school and get jobs. She said she was "hard" on her children and wished she had been nicer to them. Mrs. J said she wished she could go back to Portugal, where she believes her husband is living. She could not recall the marriage names of her children or the name of her husband's village.

Mrs. J began to express an interest in knowing more about the other residents. She said she yelled at them because they would not look at her. She was angry at the nurses because they tried to undress her for a bath late in the morning after she was up and dressed. She wished the nurses and the people would like her and agreed that she was willing to try to get along better with them.

ENVIRONMENT: During data collection, the social worker learned from the hospital social worker who made the referral to the nursing home that one of Mrs. J's daughters had admitted her to the hospital. During admission, the daughter stated that her father left the family several years ago and could not be located, and that Mrs. J had been living alone until she no longer could go out by herself. The daughter said that she was moving out of state and would send a forwarding address (which never arrived). She said that her sister and brother also lived out of state.

The social worker also learned that there was no one in the nursing facility who spoke Portuguese. The director of volunteers offered to try to locate someone who spoke the language and who would be willing to visit with Mrs. J. The social worker learned from Mrs. J that she used to attend a church where the pastor and several members of the congregation were Portuguese. The social worker located the church, and the pastor said he would go see Mrs. J. Other resources available to Mrs. J in the nursing home included program planning, recreational therapy, choir, and church services. There were also weekly resident meetings that Mrs. J could attend.

E. Charted Progress

During the data-collection phase, the problem list was extended to include Mrs. J's disruptive behavior on her floor. The additional problems were recorded as indicated in Table 6.2. Mrs. J's organic brain syndrome was not listed as a problem in the social service record because she was receiving treatment for this from the medical staff.

Note: The recording required throughout the process of working with Mrs. J included the following:

TABLE 6.2 ■ Ongoing Recording: Gerontology Case

Date Identified	Problem/ Need	Goal	Task	Contract	Date Anticipated	Date Accomplished
9/25	Poor adjustment; reclusiveness— not leaving room alone	To be able to leave room alone				
9/25	Cultural isolation; need to communicate in native language	To be visited by someone who speaks Portuguese				
9/27	Unfamiliar with staff and resources of the nursing home	To get to know the staff and resources of the nursing home	Meet twice a week with social worker.	Social worker and Mrs. J	10/4 and every Tuesday and Thursday thereafter	10/4, 10/9, 10/11, 10/16
10/2	Fighting with nurses over bath	To work out bath schedule with nurses				
10/2	Calling residents names	To stop calling residents names				

Intake summary

Weekly summaries of contacts with Mrs. J

Patient-care conference reports

Social service tasks, entered in the problem-oriented recordings of the nursing home

Record of outside contacts made and information obtained as data were collected

Ongoing contracted plan

Termination summary

III. Public Social Welfare Case

A. Agency: State Social Services

B. Client System

Mr. and Mrs. P and their two children, ages 2 and 4, are in need of emergency shelter and more permanent housing. (For more background information, see Chapter 5, Ongoing Cases: Engagement Phase, III. Public Social Welfare Case.)

C. Engagement Summary

The feelings expressed during engagement included helplessness, anger, rejection, and confusion. The problems and goals identified during engagement are listed in Chapter 5.

D. Data Collection

PROBLEM: Shelter is a basic human need. There is a lack of available housing for low-income families in the local city and surrounding areas. Housing is a crucial need for the P family at this time. The Ps have had several moves since their marriage five years ago. They have been evicted from apartments at least three times in the past because they failed to keep up with rent payments. The Ps said that they had to use the money they received from TANF to buy food. The social worker also learned that they currently had no money left for food. The family receives TANF because Mr. P's psychological problems prevent him from maintaining employment (confirmed by Income Maintenance Department's eligibility technician, who has letters from psychiatrists on file). The TANF check and food stamps for the month are being held at central office until the status and address of the family are clarified.

PERSONS: Although Mr. P said he bought a newspaper to see if there are any available apartments in the area, he and his wife do not appear to be motivated to get involved in apartment hunting. They are anxious to be relocated, but they expect that others (the state or Mrs. P's father) will find a place for them. They are blaming others (the state, Mrs. P's father, landlords, friends) for their problem of being homeless. They express a strong dependency on others to meet their needs. They do not seem to have the ability or the desire to become actively involved in problem solving or in changing their perspective or behavior. With Mr. P's written permission, the social worker contacted his psychiatrist at the mental health center, Saint John's Hospital (where he had been treated), and also got in touch with the Vocational Rehabilitation Department (where he had been tested). Mr. P's mental illness and continued inability to work were verified. The psychiatrist said that Mr. P is faithful in keeping his weekly appointments at the center. The children appear to be in good health. Mrs. P said that it was about time for the children to go for a checkup at the health clinic, but that she had lost their medical card. She said the income-maintenance worker was sending her another one.

ENVIRONMENT: Mr. and Mrs. P said that they have no family or friends who are willing to take them in, even for the night. Mrs. P said she knew that her father was trying to find a place where she and the children could live.

Three possible temporary shelters were located: (1) Salvation Army, (2) City Hotel, and (3) Center City Motor Inn. For more permanent housing, the social worker contacted five social service agencies in the surrounding area. None was able to provide any information on possible housing. The process of making a Section-8 (rent subsidy) application to the Housing Department was reviewed.

During the initial period of data collection, the social worker also explored possible resources for emergency food donations. The following sources were identified: (1) Community Renewal Center, (2) Salvation Army, (3) Saint Michael's Church, (4) Center City Churches Food Bank, and (5) Good News Soup Kitchen.

Throughout the entire process of working with the P family, information continued to be collected as additional needs and possible resources emerged. Data collection extended to information about the following (including referral procedures):

Protective services (possible placement of children)
Social security
Appeal process when placement extension was refused (fair hearing)
Housing resources
Emergency fuel banks
Moving coverage
Medical transportation service
Appliance repair
Resources for Thanksgiving basket and children's Christmas presents
Community health services

E. Charted Progress

Adding to the recorded problem and goals, the social worker listed the immediate need for food and the identified problem of poor money management (Table 6.3). The family agreed with the goal of securing food, but they were resistant to admitting that help was needed with managing their money (no goal recorded). Although the social worker became aware of the additional problems of Mr. P's unemployment and mental incapacity, these problems were not added to the problem list for service from the social worker, because they were already being addressed by the Income Maintenance Department and the mental health center.

Note: Information about Mr. P's unemployment and mental illness was recorded as part of data collection in the record. Additional paperwork during the total time the generalist worked with the P family included the completion of the following:

Authorization forms for placement of family
Section-8 housing application
Emergency food applications
Documentation that the Ps were searching for housing
Letter to authorize medical care
Request for medical transportation

TABLE 6.3 ■ Ongoing Recording: Public Social Welfare Case

Date Identified	Problem/Need	Goal
9/28	Housing for P family	a. To find emergency shelter for the P family
		b. To locate an apartment for long-term residence by the family
9/28	Emergency food	a. To obtain emergency food supply
		b. To find resource to supply food until TANF check is received
9/28	Poor money management	

Release-of-information forms
Request for extension of emergency placement
Request for fair hearing
Application for social security benefits
Application for energy assistance

IV. Community Services Case

A. Agency: Clayton Neighborhood House

B. Client System

Four Hispanic families are without heating in their apartments on the second floor of 33 L Street. (For more background information, see Chapter 5, Ongoing Cases: Engagement Phase, IV. Community Services Case.)

C. Engagement Summary

As the social worker engaged the families in the problem-solving process, they expressed feelings of frustration and helplessness. There were also feelings of fear and anger expressed toward the landlord. The problem of inadequate heating was identified, and all agreed on the recorded goal, "To obtain consistent and adequate heating for second-floor residences of the L Street apartment house."

D. Data Collection

PROBLEM: As the social worker explored the problem further, she learned that residents were paying a monthly rent of $250 for one-room apartments. The families were told that heating was included in the rent. Although one person in each of the families was employed, they said that they could not afford any increase in rent or to pay for heating themselves.

The social worker had brought a thermometer with her on the visit. She checked the temperature in each of the apartments, and all of them registered about 50°F.

Since none of the residents at the meeting had lived in the building the previous winter, they did not know if a similar problem had existed last year. They shared how difficult it was for them to find a place to live. No one was requesting help with relocation at this time.

PERSONS: The social worker learned that there were 15 children (ages 6 months to 16 years) and seven adults (no one over age 50) living in the four apartments. Although the residents were motivated to come together to discuss their heating problem, everyone was afraid to have a direct confrontation with the landlord. Mrs. T said that she and her husband had tried to call the landlord, but he was not available and never returned their call. Some members said he is hard to talk with, because he doesn't understand Spanish and they don't speak English. The residents were motivated to work on the heating problem with the social worker, but they asked her to contact the landlord in their behalf.

ENVIRONMENT: The social worker learned from those attending the meeting that an individual who lived downstairs worked as a janitor in the building. They said that they had complained to him about a lack of heat upstairs, but he told them they would have to tell the landlord. The social worker stopped at the janitor's apartment on the way out, but he was not home. The name and phone number of the landlord were obtained from the residents.

With further inquiry, the social worker learned that the landlord lived in a neighboring town, and that he had owned two other buildings in the same area where the L Street apartment was located. The two buildings were recently sold to the city.

When the social worker called Mr. X, the landlord, he said that he was not aware of a problem with heating for the second floor. The social worker informed him that each of the apartments on the floor was registering a temperature of 50°F or below. Mr. X said that he had asked the janitor of the building to help keep heating costs to a minimum, but he didn't realize this was being done through an uneven distribution of heat in the building. He said he would contact the janitor and have the problem taken care of right away.

The social worker inquired if Mr. X knew that his residents had tried to reach him to tell him about the heating problem. Mr. X said he was very busy and often found it hard to return all of his calls. He said also that his secretary finds it difficult to understand what the Spanish-speaking tenants are trying to say over the phone.

E. Charted Progress

The social worker entered a summary report of her visit to L Street in the record. She recorded pertinent information collected from speaking with the landlord and the residents. Paperwork completed while working with the community of residents included a planned contract that was developed with the residents (see Chapter 7).

V. Education Case

A. Agency: Keeney Elementary School

B. Client System

Jim G is an 8-year-old African American third-grader with regressive behavior in school and at home. (For more background information, see Chapter 5, Ongoing Cases: Engagement Phase, V. Education Case.)

C. Engagement Summary

Although presenting problems and goals were discussed with Jim and his mother (as outlined in Chapter 5), feelings were not expressed, and there was not a clear understanding of the cause of Jim's problems throughout the first three weeks of contact. The social worker proceeded with data collection, realizing that the engagement period needed to be extended.

D. Data Collection

PROBLEM: The social worker reviewed Jim's school record and the nurse's report. Jim was in good health and he had performed at an above-average academic level during his first two years of school. His teacher said that in September, when school first started, Jim seemed happy and interested in school. She wondered if he should be placed in a special needs classroom because he was getting so far behind in his work. Jim's previous testing and academic performance showed that he did not have a learning disability.

PERSONS: Although Jim seemed to like meeting with the social worker, he did not care if he did not do well in school. He hoped he wouldn't have to repeat a grade. He said his father had told him that school wasn't really that important and that Jim could come to work with him in the car lot when he got older. Whenever Jim or the social worker began to talk about home or his parents, Jim became restless and looked a little frightened.

In one session, after meeting for three weeks, Jim began to play with the black man and woman puppets. He had them begin to dance together and then they started to hit each other. He took the frog puppet and had him yell out, "Hey, stop that!" The social worker commented, "It sounds like froggie wants them to stop." Jim continued with the frog shouting, "Stop that fighting, do you hear?" The social worker said it looked like froggie was getting upset, and she wondered what froggie was feeling. Jim said, "He's scared. He hates it." The social worker said, "I wonder what froggie's afraid of." Jim took the woman doll and put her back on the shelf. He then became quiet and sat down. The social worker asked if that was it. "Was froggie afraid that she would go away?" Jim didn't answer. The social worker softly said that she knew that sometimes children are afraid that their parents will go away if they fight with each other. Jim looked away. The social worker asked if Jim was ever afraid that his mother might go away. Jim whispered, "Sometimes." The social worker then asked if Jim ever told his mother what he was afraid of, and Jim shook his head. The social worker wondered if Jim would mind if she told his mother what he was afraid of, and as he got up to leave the room he said, "I don't care."

ENVIRONMENT: The social worker learned from the school record that Jim's mother was a nurse and that his father managed a car lot. During the second interview with Mrs. G, the social worker asked if she could meet with Jim's father, but Mrs. G said that he was always very busy and worked long hours running the car lot. At the third meeting with Mrs. G, the social worker shared with her what had happened in play with Jim. Mrs. G's eyes filled with tears. She then told the social worker that in October, she learned that her husband had gone out with another woman. She said that she didn't think Jim noticed that she and her husband were quarreling. She recalled that at one point she did tell her husband that she might take off and leave him and the children. She said she wouldn't really do it but just wanted to scare him. She said her husband assures her that he will never see the woman again, but she finds it hard to trust him and to forgive him.

The social worker encouraged Mrs. G to talk with Jim about his fear and to assure him that she doesn't plan to leave home. The social worker also asked if Mrs. G could talk with her husband about what was happening with Jim. Mrs. G said that she would try to get her husband to take time off to come in to see the social worker with her next week.

E. Charted Progress

During the process of data collection and the extended engagement period, the social worker added the newly identified problem of Mr. and Mrs. G's strained relationship to the problem list, as shown in Table 6.4. The plan to have Mrs. G talk with Jim and to have Mr. G come in to meet the social worker with Mrs. G was also recorded.

Note: The recording of the social worker included an ongoing contracted plan developed by the social worker, Mr. and Mrs. G, and Jim (presented throughout Chapters 5 through 11), which was kept in the social service file. The social worker also recorded basic factual information in Jim's school record. In addition, a summary of each contact was included in the social service file, and a closing summary was added at the time of termination.

TABLE 6.4 ■ Ongoing Recording: Education Case

Date Identified	Problem/ Need	Goal	Task	Contract	Date Anticipated	Date Accomplished
11/1	Jim's school tardiness and absenteeism	To improve Jim's regular school attendance (on time each day)	1. See that Jim gets to school on time each day.	1. Mrs. G	11/5 and each school day thereafter	11/5—ongoing
11/1	Jim's declining academic performance	To improve academic functioning (interest, participation, grades)	1a. Talk with Jim about school problems.	1a. Social worker and Jim	11/6 and twice a week thereafter	11/6, 11/8, 11/13, 11/15, 11/20, 11/27
				b. Mrs. G and Jim	11/2	11/2
			2. Follow up.	2. Social worker and Jim	11/5	11/5, 11/21
			3. Talk with Jim about home tensions and assure him she will not leave.	3. Mrs. G and Jim	11/21	
			4. Meet to discuss Jim's problems in relation to parents' problems.	4. Social worker, Mr. and Mrs. G	11/27	
11/2	Jim's getting to sleep at night					
11/21	Strain in Mr. and Mrs. G's marital relationship					

VI. Corrections Case

A. Agency: Juvenile Court

B. Client System

A group of seven male adolescents (all 14 years old) are on probation. (For additional background information, see Chapter 5, Ongoing Cases: Engagement Phase, VI. Corrections Case.)

C. Engagement Summary

During engagement, the primary goal of getting off probation as soon as possible was clearly stated by all members of the group. The youths also wanted help both with controlling their tempers and with understanding better the "changes" they were all going through (as outlined in Chapter 5). Although they recognized problems they were having in communicating with their parents, they did not want to work on trying to improve their relationships with them. They did not want to talk about their low self-esteem. They expressed anger at having been picked up by the police and put on probation.

D. Data Collection

After an initial period of testing and attempted manipulation of the leaders, group members began to talk more openly about their family backgrounds and life experiences. In addition to collecting data from the youths themselves, the two social workers visited the homes of each group member and talked with parents. The social workers also talked with the youths' teachers and social workers at the schools they attended. The files of the court for each of the youths were also reviewed carefully (permissions obtained).

PROBLEM: The social workers learned that each member of the group had committed more than once the offense that led to his being put on probation. All seven of the youths were seen in their schools as "problem students" who had difficulties in learning and in getting along with teachers and classmates. They were described by teachers as "troublemakers" or "attention seekers." Two of the youths were believed to be junior members of the Savage Nomads or the Ghetto Brothers street gangs.

The group members said that they got into trouble usually when they were mad about something or dared to do it by friends. In one case, breaking and entering was required for initiation into a gang.

PERSONS: Three of the group members were highly motivated to get the most out of the group and to get off probation (MK, ML, and B). Two others laughed a lot and seemed to take the group "as a joke" (J and T). The remaining two were quiet and less easy to understand (A and C). C appeared very upset over being on probation.

The school reported that test scores indicated that two of the boys had borderline intelligence (A and MK). The others had average or above-average intelligence, even though they had problems with learning.

The racial/ethnic backgrounds of the group participants were as follows: one Italian American, one Irish American, two white with mixed ethnic backgrounds, two African American, and one Hispanic.

ENVIRONMENT: All of the youths came from single-parent families. Five lived with their mothers, one lived with his father, and one lived with his grandmother. All came from lower-class or lower-middle-class neighborhoods. The youths had not been active in local recreational centers or programs. Three said they used to attend some church activities for teenagers, but they only went to church when their parents made them go.

The parents and grandmother of the youths expressed interest and concern for their children. Three mothers and T's grandmother said they were afraid that they had no control over their sons (grandson). They all hoped the youths had learned their lesson and would now stay out of trouble. C's father spoke only Spanish. He appeared to be totally overwhelmed, and said he might have to send C back home to Puerto Rico. J's mother had an apparent drinking problem. She said she was thinking seriously of "putting J away" because he was getting too hard to manage. She did not say where she thought she might put him. She had heard that J's father was in jail. Three other group members had older brothers who were in jail or correctional centers (A, T, and ML).

E. Charted Progress

Summary recordings were written that briefly described contacts with the group members' parents, teachers, and school social workers. Brief entries were made each week in the records to indicate attendance and participation in the group. Later, detailed studies of each youth were written when he became eligible to be removed from probation.

VII. Homelessness Case

A. Agency: West End Community Shelter

B. Client System

José Romano, a 37-year-old Hispanic male, is homeless and HIV positive. (For additional background information, see Chapter 5, Ongoing Cases: Engagement Phase, VII. Homelessness Case.)

C. Engagement Summary

Mr. R had worked hard to lead an independent lifestyle. After testing HIV positive, he left his job and lost his apartment. During engagement, he shared with the social worker strong feelings of fear and abandonment. The goals they identified focused on locating health care, housing, and employment.

D. Data Collection

PROBLEM: Mr. R believed his illness was caused by his use of unsanitary needles during his drug addiction more than six years ago. He experienced frequent colds and fatigue. He had not been to a doctor in four months because he couldn't afford it and no longer had health insurance.

PERSON: Mr. R was hesitant to take drugs for his illness because he had previously been a drug addict. He knew he needed to talk with a doctor about this and to find out more about his illness. Mr. R said that he was willing to take any kind of job at this point because he needed money. His work history over the last five years was strong in terms of dependability and performance. Mr. R's work experience and skills were limited to cooking and farming.

ENVIRONMENT: Mr. R was not aware of any relatives in the state. His ex-wife had moved back to Puerto Rico. He said that he regretted that he had fallen away from his church and wished that he could "get back in God's graces."

In the building next to the shelter, there was a free health clinic for people in the neighborhood. The staffing of the clinic was provided through voluntary service from the doctors and interns of the city hospital. A grant provided funding for supplies and equipment. Mr. R would be able to receive medical care and information from the clinic.

With Mr. R's permission, the social worker contacted the Social Security Administration and the Department of Social Services. She learned that after Mr. R became "significantly impaired" and became active with AIDS, he would qualify for (1) Social Security and Supplemental Security Income and (2) general emergency assistance until he received his first check.

An organization called "Harmony" offered a variety of services for people with AIDS or HIV. Services included legal advocacy, a buddy system, a support group, transportation, and limited assistance with paying bills. Also, in the surrounding area, the social worker located two residences (Hope Home and Christian House) for persons with AIDS. Currently, all of their beds were full (nine beds total).

Following up on Mr. R's interest in returning to his church, the social worker was informed of the names and locations of the two Catholic churches in the area. She learned also that there was one church with a weekly service for a large Hispanic population.

Mr. R approved of the social worker's contacting his past employer. His employer said that Mr. R was never a problem and that they missed him at the nursing home. He had heard about Mr. R's illness from another employee. He did not have any job openings for Mr. R at the Hope Home. The state employment office was contacted for a listing of possible job openings, and Mr. R was encouraged to look in the employment section of the shelter's newspaper each day.

E. Charted Progress

During data collection, the social worker became aware of Mr. R's desire to return to God and the Catholic church. The need for religious enrichment was added to Mr. R's progress chart. Also added was Mr. R's desire for more information about his illness (see Table 6.5). Basic information was recorded on the fact sheet of his record. In summary recordings, additional information obtained during data collection was included.

TABLE 6.5 ■ Ongoing Recording: Homelessness Case

Date Identified	Problem/Need	Goal
5/8	HIV positive, lack of knowledge	To obtain ongoing medical care and information
5/8	Homeless/hungry	To obtain immediate housing/food To obtain long-term housing
5/8	Unemployed (no financial support)	To obtain employment—part/full To obtain public assistance/social security (long term)
5/10	Spiritual void	To return to church

SUMMARY

Although the process of data collection, which includes recording and documenting facts, may be seen as somewhat arduous and unsatisfying, it is an essential component of professional practice. In this chapter, central focus was given to identifying and organizing relevant data, distinguishing fact from assumption, understanding the meaning of informed consent, and using appropriate recording formats to document information in writing. These dimensions of data collection are basic to the process, and they prepare the social worker to move on to the next phase, assessment and contract planning. As with all of the phases of helping, circumstances change in human situations, and the art of identifying facts about current realities goes on throughout the dynamic process. A social worker must remain open to reformulating or supplementing the information collected, even after it has been organized and used in developing an assessment and planned intervention.

REFLECTION POINTS

Becoming a skilled social work practitioner requires knowledge and skills, including the ability to reflect on practice endeavors. The following reflection points are designed to strengthen critical thinking and mastery of knowledge of key points in this chapter.

1. Define the following key concepts in generalist social work:
   - Data
   - Data collection
   - Informed consent
   - Confidentiality
   - Problems and needs
   - Recording data
2. How might these concepts influence your professional behavior in social work practice with client, action, and target systems at micro, mezzo, and macro levels of practice?
3. How might human diversity influence the process of collecting data at micro, mezzo, and macro practice levels?
4. Review Sections 1.03, Informed Consent; 1.07, Privacy and Confidentiality; and 1.08, Access to Records, in the *NASW Code of Ethics* (www.socialworkers.org). How will these standards influence your professional behavior?
5. For further reading and research, use the concepts in Question 1 to locate social work references related to this chapter's content. (See Appendix A, Selected Internet Resources, and Appendix B, Selected Social Work Journals.) What underlying theoretical concepts are evident in the articles? How are they applied in one of the seven ongoing cases in this chapter or in a case in your field internship?

Assessment and Contract Planning

Throughout the helping process of the General Method, the social worker listens, reflects, analyzes, plans, and acts to facilitate client system ownership of the strengths-based problem-solving process. There is, however, a phase early in the helping process primarily designated for assessment and contract planning. Central characteristics of this phase of the General Method include client system empowerment, collaborative judgment, and mutual decision making. Inherently linked to the data-collection phase of purposive gathering of objective and subjective information from client systems and collateral sources, the *assessment and contract planning phase* emphasizes the intellectual activities of assessment, reflection, analysis, reframing, and interpretation of the collected data in order to formulate an action plan for strengths-based problem-solving. After gathering information relevant to understanding the problems and needs of the client system, the social worker conducts assessment and contract planning by

- ▶ Appraising the demands of the person-problem-environment transactional fit with the client system
- ▶ Mobilizing the process of client system discovery and activation of capabilities and resources
- ▶ Negotiating and prioritizing goals
- ▶ Exploring and planning interventions
- ▶ Outlining the steps of the intervention process, including *who, what, when, where,* and *why*
- ▶ Creating a contract
- ▶ Establishing the structure for monitoring and evaluating interventions

Assessment Process

Assessment begins with the client system's expectations about service outcome and incorporates the strengths/needs orientation. This orientation supports the cardinal values of social work—namely, belief in the value and worth of every individual and belief in client self-determination. During assessment and planning, these values direct the social worker and the client system toward identifying client system strengths, capabilities, and environmental resources and respecting the importance of client system contributions in bringing about change in itself and/or its surrounding environment.

During assessment, the client system and the social worker first actively invest in making sense of available facts, observations, and other information. In so doing, they identify the capacities, assets, resource potential, challenges, and barriers of the agency, community, or situation involving the identified problem and need; both the client system and the system's environment; and any factors in client system diversity that might come into play. Second, the client system and the social worker use their joint understanding as a basis for deciding what can be done about the client system's problems or concerns. A primary consideration is the concept of building on client system strengths and resources while addressing the obstacles or barriers to be circumvented or overcome.

Thus, assessment includes both the process of understanding and the product of the understanding that serves as the basis for action. Client systems bring significant information to the assessment process and have the ultimate power over the direction of the assessment statement. They usually know what they want, can describe what they are willing to do, and can demonstrate their own capabilities. Social workers take on the role of contributing technical knowledge and skills for analyzing the information available, constructing plans, and understanding the personal capabilities and environmental resources available to the client system for implementing the plan. In this working partnership, client systems have the right and responsibility to say what they can and will do, whereas social workers offer recommendations and provide feedback about possible consequences of chosen actions or inactions. Their use of collaborative decision-making processes during assessment serves as one means of empowering client systems through demonstrating that what they think and believe is important.

It is possible that in certain situations a social worker will have to act before a full assessment has been completed. A client system may have immediate, urgent needs that must be met before the necessary data can be collected for a formal assessment. There may not be time to plan and contract with a client system before intervening in a crisis situation. Action may have to be taken immediately in order to stabilize a life-at-risk situation. Once this is accomplished, however, every effort is made by the social worker to involve the client system in a mutual process of assessment.

Assessment Statement

After much listening and gathering of information, the social worker is expected to write an *assessment statement* for each problem identified by the client system. In the past, an assessment statement was referred to as a *diagnosis* in social work. In 1917, Mary Richmond modified the concept for greater relevance to the profession by calling it a *social diagnosis*. Problems frequently brought to the attention of generalist social workers are of a material, interpersonal, institutional, or interdependent nature. Using the term *assessment* rather than *diagnosis* helps avoid the possible inference that an identified problem is seen as a client's illness or as always residing with the client system.

In the assessment statement, the social worker begins by clearly indicating the nature of the client system's presenting problem and then identifying with the client system:

> ▶ *How does the problem relate to the client system's needs?*
> ▶ *Is the presenting problem the main problem or are there other related problems that contribute to the presenting problem?*
> ▶ *Who else in the client system's environment may be part of the presenting problem?*
> ▶ *Why does the presenting problem exist at this point in time?*
> ▶ *What has the client system (or others) tried in dealing with the presenting problem? With what success?*

By the third phase of the General Method, the social worker should have sufficient data to describe the actual scope and cause of each problem and need. A simple formula to keep in mind for initiating an assessment statement is:

_____ has _____ _____ because _____
      (who)   (what problem)   (with what level of need)   (why)

The "why," or cause of the problem, may be seen in many layers. Often, an immediate causal or contributing factor has touched off the problematic situation. In addition, several sequential factors may have led to the immediate cause. For example, Mr. L may be unemployed because he does not have marketable skills in this state, but he lacks such skills because he came from a country where he was socialized into a work world of a very different nature. Or, a client may be unemployed because he was laid off from his job, and maybe this was the result of fiscal cutbacks by the national administration or local industry.

In looking for the cause of a problem, the social worker realizes that there is a wide range of possible causes, from personal to interpersonal to structural or societal. The cause cited in an assessment statement should be the one most directly related to the presenting problem and need. If, in the social worker's judgment, it is necessary to go back further to preceding causes in order to understand the problem for contract planning and intervention, these causes should also be cited, with a clear explanation of how they are connected to the current problem and need.

In addition to the opening causal statement, an appraisal of the change potential of the problem should be presented in a full assessment statement. A problem's change potential is dependent on problem, person, and environment. All three factors are interdependent, with direct impact on the maintenance or resolution of the presenting problem.

First, the social worker and the system of contact consider the nature of the problem itself, asking how serious the problem and need are and what the change potential is. *Is this a problem, issue, or need that can be resolved? Is the problem of such a nature that it is irreversible (e.g., suicide, terminal illness, bankruptcy)? More specifically, how broad or deep is the problem or need? Are many people involved, and to what extent? How long has it been going on?*

Second, what has been tried in solving this problem before and with what success? In other words, the social worker and the client system explore the details of the problem, its triggers, and its effects on the life of the client system. They then explore the successful and unsuccessful ways in which the client system has handled this and other problems in the past and how these efforts have worked. To elicit specific details about problem-solving efforts, the social worker may ask:

▶ *What have you done about this problem so far? What happened? How successful was it?*
▶ *What have others done or suggested? What was helpful? What not?*

Third, the strengths and needs of the client system with the problem are assessed. *What is his or her or their motivation and capacity to make whatever changes may be necessary? Are they able to cope with it alone or to accept help from others? What is their change potential?* In order to document a clinical assessment of the strengths, needs, and limitations of a person or a relationship, rapid assessment instruments are available for use during interviews. A social worker's appraisal of client systems in such areas as anxiety level, social interaction, marital adjustment, assertiveness, and alcohol or drug use may be supported by scores obtained on the assessment instruments (see Chapter 3). Of course, there are limitations in the use of these instruments. A social worker would want to cite additional evidence, such as documentation from other professionals and direct observation, to support the assessment.

The fourth area to be considered before an integrated assessment of the problem's change potential can be made involves the environment in which the problem is located. *What is available in the environment in terms of formal or informal resources to promote the necessary changes? Are there restraining forces in the environment that are stronger than supportive resources? With optimum use of available resources, what is the expected outcome? What is the change potential of the environment for dealing with the problem?*

After the three variables of problem, person, and environment are assessed individually, a cumulative assessment of the potential for change may be made for the particular problem within its person-environment context. Basically, the social worker's statement may be framed as follows:

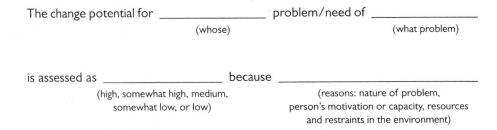

The change potential for _____ problem/need of _____
                              (whose)   (what problem)

is assessed as _____ because _____
              (high, somewhat high, medium,   (reasons: nature of problem,
                 somewhat low, or low)   person's motivation or capacity, resources
                                                   and restraints in the environment)

In addition to a causal statement and a change-potential statement, the assessment statement should include a judgment about the seriousness or urgency of the problem. The question to be asked here is: *To what extent is this a life-or-death matter for these people (or this person) at this time?* Even if the change potential for a problem is judged to be very low, immediate attention and priority has to be given to a life-endangering situation. Action must be taken in whatever way possible to protect the lives of those involved. In critical situations, the social worker may have to make an immediate referral or serve as an advocate, even though there is little support from the persons or environment involved with the problem. Further considerations of intervention will be presented in the next chapter. The point being highlighted here is that an assessment statement should include a professional judgment on the urgency and seriousness of the problem, with supportive data.

■ **CASE EXAMPLES**

Micro Example 1: Mr. L, 37 Years Old, French-Canadian, Unmarried, No Family

PROBLEM: UNEMPLOYMENT

ASSESSMENT STATEMENT: Mr. L has the problem of unemployment because he is unskilled and unmotivated to seek employment. The nature of the problem is such that the potential for change is very low. Mr. L has been out of work since he moved to this state three years ago. His capacity for work is limited because he does not have the skills sought by employers in this area. He has low motivation to seek work because he experienced a series of rejections in his early efforts to find employment. He is feeling hopeless and depressed. Resources for training or hiring unskilled laborers are extremely difficult to locate in this state. For these reasons, the overall change potential for Mr. L's problem of unemployment is assessed as very low. This is a very serious problem for Mr. L, because he does not qualify for public assistance in this state, and the savings he brought with him from Canada are depleted.

Macro Example 2: North Central City Community (Approximately 600 Families, Six-Block Area, Low-Income Housing)

PROBLEM: NO PUBLIC TRANSPORTATION

ASSESSMENT STATEMENT: The North Central City Community is a neighborhood with a need for public transportation because the local bus company recently cut off its route into the neighborhood. The problem is somewhat serious, as most people in the neighborhood do not have cars and they now have to walk eight blocks to get a bus. A strong asset is that the people of the community are highly motivated for active involvement in resolving the problem, and they have an organized leadership. The bus company has expressed an openness to reconsider its action and to meet with community representatives. In this situation, the change potential is assessed as high, since resources are available inside and outside of the community.

In assessing data according to the triplex of problem, person, and environment, a social worker needs to maintain a holistic perspective of the dynamic interrelationships of social, cultural, and psychological factors. Tools and instruments have been developed to help the professional see the relationship of a client's psychological and social needs with institutional and environmental resources. In juxtaposing one's professional assessment of the problem, person, and environment triplex, a social worker may see more clearly how to partialize and prioritize multiple problems in complex situations.

Problem Prioritization

Before entering into the goal setting and contracting of this phase of the General Method, the social worker and the client or action system need to prioritize the problems identified and assessed. The questions asked are: *What problem do we work on first? Where do we begin? On what basis should a problem or need be selected as the primary focus for intervention?*

As the social worker compiles, categorizes, and reviews data, it often becomes apparent that several problems and needs are pressing. In response to the question of where to begin, the social worker and the client or action system enter into a process for prioritizing the problems and needs identified. To select the most appropriate starting point, the social worker must reconsider the initial assessment of the information that was gathered according to the problem-person-environment triplex for each identified problem, issue, and need.

In studying each problem or triplex, the social worker keeps in mind the fact that a client system needs to build up a sense of trust in the social worker's and agency's ability to be helpful. To foster client involvement in a growing, working relationship with the social worker, there has to be an experience of success or satisfaction of need as soon as possible. The social worker therefore tries to select *first* a problem that has a high change potential for resolution or need satisfaction.

As stated earlier, in writing an assessment statement for a problem, the social worker asks: *What is the change potential of the problem itself, of the persons involved, and of the related environment? What strengths, assets, and resources are available to facilitate and support the change?* Only after assessing all three dimensions for a problem will the social worker be able to arrive at a comprehensive and accurate prognosis that can be used for problem prioritization. For some problems, the persons may have high motivation and capabilities, but the environment may contain many barriers and provide little opportunity to actualize the persons' potential. An unemployed person, for example, may have skills and high motivation to find a job, but there may be no job openings in the environment. A person may have a problem or need that does not appear to be serious in nature, such as an absence of a support system. If, however, the person has little motivation, or if there are no available support groups or resources in the environment, the prognosis for change in this problem area is low. After considering the total change potential for problems such as those just cited, the social worker would continue to try to find an initial problem or need with high potential for change in all three areas of problem-person-environment before beginning to intervene with the system.

At times, it may be impossible to find an initial problem or need with high change potential in all three areas. From a list of problems, it may be very difficult to distinguish and select the one that should be given priority. A tool has been developed to assist a social worker in conceptualizing and analyzing a number of problems. It serves as a framework to compare change expectations for different problems and, through juxtaposition, to visualize which problems have the greatest change potential.

According to the tool depicted in Table 7.1, each problem is studied and scaled according to an assessment of the change potential of the problem-person-environment triplex. On the basis of data collected previously, the social worker estimates the potential for change, using a scale of 0 to 10. Scoring criteria are as follows: 0 = no potential, 1 = very low, 2 = low, 3 = somewhat low, 4 = somewhat high, 8 = high, 9 = very high, and 10 = maximum potential for change. For example, in looking at the problem identified as "child's illness" in Table 7.1, the social worker first asks about the nature and duration of the illness. If information has been gathered that indicates the child has just developed a strep throat, and the social worker knows that there is a high incidence of cure for this illness, the change potential for "problem"

TABLE 7.1 ■ Problem Prioritization

| Problem List | Change-Potential Scores (0–10) | | | Total Change Potential | Problem Prioritization | Severity |
	Problem	Personal Strengths	Environmental Resources			
Child's illness	8	8	9	25	1	
Father's drinking	2	1	4	7	8	*
Father's unemployment	5	8	5	18	3	
Mother's depression	6	4	6	16	5	
Wife abuse	3	2	4	9	7	*
Housing conditions	6	5	3	14	6	
School truancy	8	7	8	23	2	
Husband-wife communication	6	5	6	17	4	

*Life-at-risk situation.

may be scored as high (8). If there are accessible health care resources and the parents and child will take or administer the prescribed medication, the change potential in "personal strengths" and "environmental resources" is also high (scored 8 and 9). Because the total change-potential score for the problem of "child's illness" is very high (25), this problem may be seen as the highest priority on the list of problems for initial intervention.

The change potential scores for the problem identified as "father's drinking" are not as hopeful. On the basis of data observed and obtained, the social worker has assessed all three categories with extremely low scores. In looking at the nature and duration of the problem itself, the social worker knows that the problem has gone on for years and that alcoholism is a serious physical and socially pathological illness (scored 2). In terms of the father's motivation and capacity to change at this time, the social worker assesses the "personal strengths" category also as very low (1), because the father denies he has a drinking problem and refuses to go for help. The social worker studied the formal and informal resources of the father's environment and averaged out a score of 4. Although formal resources are available in the environment to help the father with his drinking problem (Alcoholics Anonymous and local hospital and clinic), his wife and family deny that the father has a drinking problem, saying that he and most of his buddies are just heavy drinkers. Apparently, the total change potential for the "father's drinking" is very low (7). The social worker recognizes that it is a very serious problem, but one that will not be resolved in the near future.

In selecting the problem with the highest change potential for beginning intervention, the social worker is aware of the fact that there are problems of greater severity in need of ongoing attention. It is expected that these problems will probably take a long time before any marked change will occur. Because of the serious nature of these problems, the social worker continues to direct efforts toward overcoming them while at the same time working on those problems or needs for which progress and success may be expected.

For example, in Table 7.1, there are two problems with low change-potential scores (father's drinking; wife abuse). These problems are asterisked in the "severity" column because they are assessed as life-at-risk situations. The social worker will continue ongoing efforts to study and intervene in these areas while working with the family on problems that have higher potential for change.

Goal Setting

Goals emphasize client system growth and gains in specific terms. They reflect the overt and covert changes desired by the client system in the system's problems and life situation that correspond to its wants and needs. Goals have multiple functions:

▶ Provide direction and continuity for the work
▶ Provide a means for the client system and the social worker to come to agreement about the outcomes to be achieved
▶ Facilitate selection of intervention strategies
▶ Facilitate monitoring progress
▶ Serve as outcome criteria

In view of the goals' functions, goal setting is explored in the context of the client system's values as well as the goals' feasibility in light of agency functions, environmental constraints, and the reality of the situation, behaviors, and attitudes targeted for change.

Explaining the purpose of goals increases client system acceptance, participation, and sense of direction. Initially, for example, the social worker might ask:

As we've explored your problems, you've indicated several things you'd like to be different. What about identifying specific goals that you think are important?

Using the client system's language as much as possible, the social worker then explicitly reframes the goal statement, partializes the problem components as needed, and adds questions about standards, feasibility, and benefits:

You want to   • *improve _____?*
             • *increase _____?*
             • *decrease _____?*

How much of this do you want to achieve? (standards)
What risks and challenges do you foresee? (feasibility)
What benefits will you gain by achieving this goal? (benefits)

Finally, the social worker and the client system explore priorities and rank the goals from most to least important to the client system and most difficult to achieve now to least difficult to achieve now:

As a result of the services you will receive and our work together, what do you expect to achieve? To be doing?

Contract Planning

The contract planning process follows assessment and translates prioritized goals into purposively designed and sequenced action tasks with specific time frames for completion. It shifts the focus from *What's wrong?* to a concern with *How can what's wrong be fixed?* When applied to the problems in social functioning experienced by client systems, planning tasks focus on:

▶ Enhancing the adaptive capacity of client systems
▶ Stimulating client system growth potential
▶ Decreasing environmental barriers to client system growth and adaptation
▶ Increasing environmental resource availability, acceptability, and accessibility
▶ Increasing environmental resource capacity for responding to identified needs

Contract planning becomes the bridge between assessment and intervention and is the activity focused on change. After a problem, issue, or need has been selected for action, the social worker and the client or action system begin to plan what needs to be done, by whom, and when. It is possible that they will choose to work on more than one problem at a time. It is important, however, that they clearly understand which problems are being addressed and which ones are not, and the reasons for the selection.

Contract planning is a skill. As pointed out earlier, in the strengths-based problem-solving approach of the General Method, every effort is made to conceptualize and to verbalize the identified problems, strengths, and corresponding goals. During the third phase of the method, social worker, and client or action system also conceptualize and verbalize the specific tasks that need to be performed in order to accomplish the goals. Not only are the tasks identified but they are also placed in sequence. Dialogue between social worker and system includes a consideration of which tasks need to precede others. The discussion about each task extends to a consideration of possible consequences that may result from its enactment.

A contract plan specifies the reason for each component and action in the plan. Accountability is an important aspect of any contractual relationship. A well-developed plan that specifies what is to be done and why it is to be done demonstrates a means of fulfilling the responsibility for accountability to client systems, agencies, and the supporting public.

In developing a contract, a client-centered perspective and process need to be maintained. Full participation of client systems in the contract planning process increases chances of success by providing the client system with the opportunity to take ownership of the strengths-based problem-solving of the General Method, become more empowered, and improve problem-solving skills. Generally, plans are made with the client system, written down in the client system's presence, and reviewed together when finalized. This is a phase during which it is easy to leave client systems out of the process. As the social worker collects information or data, he or she might be tempted to take over and write the contract without any client or action system input. Sometimes this may happen because social workers feel pressured to complete the paperwork. Sometimes they are eager to start the change process. Other times, inexperienced social workers may feel uncomfortable with client systems being in control of the helping process. However, when client or action systems do not fully participate or at the least have their input considered, the chances of contract failure increase because client systems are deprived of an opportunity to become empowered and to improve their problem-solving skills.

Therefore, careful planning is needed in determining who should be expected to perform what task. A basic guiding principle is: *Inasmuch as possible, a client or action system should do for himself or herself.* A social worker would agree to carry out a task for a system only when it is apparent that the individual, family, group, organization, or community is unable to perform the needed task and that no other resources are available to call on. Social workers do not foster dependency. Nevertheless, they do recognize that there are certain actions that some individuals are unable to perform, owing to internal or external circumstances. When such actions are necessary for goal accomplishment, a social worker using the General Method would try first to mobilize other resources of the client or action system, such as family, friends, church, or community support systems. If no internal or informal resources are available, the social worker may initiate or execute a needed task. As quickly as possible, however, the social worker would try to enable the system to perform such tasks for himself or herself.

■ CASE EXAMPLES

Micro Example 1

A client has been trying to contact his landlord for days to register a complaint. Although the landlord has been avoiding contact with the client, he may be more readily available when an agency social worker contacts him. The social worker would try to arrange for the landlord to meet with the client to discuss the complaint. If necessary, the social worker may have to go with the client. If neither of these two options is feasible, the social worker may have to go on behalf of the client.

Macro Example 2

Thirty agency directors convened to discuss the longstanding refusal by the state legislature to increase statewide funding for gerontology services. They noted that task force reports over the last 20 years have recommended increased funding to no avail.

The group asked the social worker to locate and collate these reports and then lobby the legislature on the agencies' behalf. The social worker encouraged the group to collect the reports and then work with her in analyzing the material and preparing an advocacy plan for the directors to implement.

During the contracting period, when the social worker and the system of contact clarify who will do what, it is important for both to identify the date when each task is expected to be implemented and the date completed. Little progress can be made and time may be wasted unless timing is discussed and there is a sense of expectation for task and goal accomplishment.

As each goal is considered and contracted through mutual agreement on task assignments, an anticipated date is stated for the implementation of each task, even though the date may have to be altered due to unexpected circumstances. The projection of dates for task execution serves as a guide for general planning and review. If a task is not completed on the expected date, the social worker and the client or action system can grow in understanding the dynamics of problem, person, and environment by asking why it was not accomplished as anticipated. More realistic comprehension and planning could result from this inquiry.

A tool for use in generalist practice has been developed that integrates the essential components of a contracted plan (see Table 7.2). As a social worker proceeds in the process of strengths-based problem-solving with a client or action system, this tool may be used to state in writing what is agreed on as (1) the problems, issues, or needs to be addressed, (2) the goals to be accomplished, (3) the tasks to be performed, (4) the persons to implement each task, (5) the dates anticipated to enact each task, and (6) the actual dates of task accomplishment. Once the tool is filled out by the social worker and the client or action system, they may refer to it each time they need to assess progress or impediments to progress. Skill is needed for precise identification of the problems and needs and the goals and tasks. Ideally, the goals and tasks should focus on behaviors that can be measured or observed.

As each problem, issue, or need is selected for action, the name of the problem is entered on the instrument, along with the date when the social worker and the

TABLE 7.2 ■ Contracted Plan

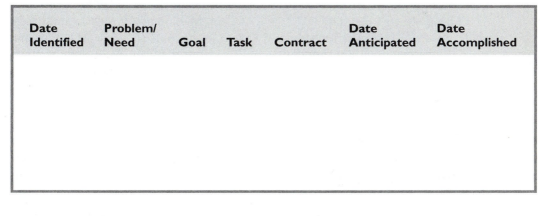

Date Identified	Problem/ Need	Goal	Task	Contract	Date Anticipated	Date Accomplished

system of contact agree that it is a problem for intervention. The list of problems and needs should be prioritized according to the criteria and process stated earlier.

Goals are conceptualized as the expected outcomes of the endeavor. Because overall client goals may be too broad, they are often partialized into long-range and short-term goals or specific objectives. Goals are written to satisfy the principle of

Who . . .
Will do what . . .
To what extent . . .
Under what conditions . . .
By when?

Therefore, the tasks to be accomplished for each goal or objective need to be written in sequence. The person or system indicated as contracting to perform each task should be identified in accordance with the principle of "doing for self as much as possible." The dates anticipated are written down after realistic consideration of what is feasible. As each task is accomplished, the final column should be filled in with the accurate date of completion.

The instrument, as shown in Table 7.2, can be placed in the front of any record for immediate identification of plan and progress. It becomes obvious, on first glance at the "date accomplished" column, whether there are tasks that were contracted but not completed. Rather than having to review all of the recordings of various contacts contained within a record to find out what has been happening with a case, the social worker (or supervisor), by reviewing the instrument, can receive a synthesis of the essence of the work being done to date.

The instrument in Table 7.2 fits well with problem-oriented recording (POR) described in Chapter 6. The contracted plan (Table 7.2) may be seen as a direct follow-up and complement to the steps taken for the POR. The problems and dates identified on the problem list of the POR are readily available for problem prioritization and listing in the first and second column of the contracted plan. Also, the "assessment" and "plan" stated in the "SOSAP" for each problem with the POR will help in the identification of goals, tasks, contracts, and dates anticipated to be listed on the contracted plan. As each task of the contract is performed, its date of accomplishment is indicated on the contracted plan. This information will facilitate the writing of summary statements, as expected for each problem in a POR.

The contracted plan (Table 7.2) is a tool for ongoing use. Problems and needs, goals, tasks, and contracted enactor may change in the course of service. Once begun, there is a need for continued updating and review of the plan. As brought out in a later chapter, this tool may also serve as a major instrument for evaluation through goal analysis.

■ CASE EXAMPLE

Mezzo Example 3

An example of a contracted plan for the problems prioritized in Table 7.1 may be found in Table 7.3. For the first problem, child's illness, it is clear in the "contract" column that

TABLE 7.3 ■ Contracted Plan: The C Family

Date Identified	Problem/Need	Goal	Task	Contract	Date Anticipated	Date Accomplished
2/8	1. Child's illness	1. To improve child's health— treat step throat	1. Call health clinic for appointment.	1. Mrs. C	2/9	2/9
			2. Take child to clinic.	2. Mrs. C and social worker	2/12	2/15
2/8	2. School truancy	2. To attend school daily	1. Speak with mother.	1. Social worker	2/9	2/9
			2. Speak with child.	2. Mrs. C and social worker	2/9	2/12
			3. Speak with teacher.	3. Mrs. C and social worker	2/12	2/12
			4. Wake child on time.	4. Mrs. C	3/1	3/1
			5. Put child on bus.	5. Mrs. C	3/1	3/1
2/8	3. Father's unemployment	3. To obtain steady employment (father)	1. Discuss with Mr. C.	1. Social worker	2/15	2/18
			2. Contact employment agencies.	2. Mr. C	2/16	2/19
			3. Check training programs.	3. Social worker	2/16	2/17
			4. Locate job or training (J/T) for Mr. C.	4. Mr. C, employment agencies, or social worker	2/25	3/15
			5. Apply for J/T.	5. Mr. C	3/16	3/16
2/8	4. Lack of communication between husband and wife	4. To improve husband-wife communication (talking out instead of fighting out)	1. Speak with Mr. C.	1. Social worker	3/22	3/22
			2. Speak with Mr. and Mrs. C.	2. Social worker	3/25	3/25
			3. Refer Mr. and Mrs. C to marital counseling center.	3. Social worker	3/25	3/25
			4. Contact marital counseling center.	4. Mrs. C	3/26	3/29
			5. Attend sessions at marital counseling center.	5. Mr. and Mrs. C	4/5	4/5
			6. Support their attendance.	6. Social worker	4/5	4/5
2/8	5. Overcrowded housing	5. To obtain larger living quarters	1. Discuss with Mr. and Mrs. C.	1. Social worker	4/7	4/7
			2. Explore housing options and contact possible resources.	2. Mr. and Mrs. C and social worker	4/8	4/8
			3. Apply for housing.	3. Mr. and Mrs. C	4/8	
			4. Move family.	4. The C family and movers	5/10	

the social worker planned to take Mrs. C and her child to the clinic. She (social worker) did this because Mrs. C had a history of missing clinic appointments. Also, Mrs. C had no way of getting to the clinic except by bus. The social worker was unable to locate any available informal resources to provide transportation.

As the social worker proceeded in strengths-based problem-solving with the family, she found that some of the problems identified during the first interview had decreased, owing to relief in other problem areas. For example, once Mr. C returned to work, Mrs. C was not so depressed and there was less physical abuse by her husband. Both Mr. and Mrs. C recognized their need to better understand and communicate with each other, and they agreed to go for marital counseling. They were also ready to begin working to find better housing. Mr. C was not ready, however, to talk about his heavy drinking. He and his wife denied that this was a problem, especially now that Mr. C was back at work. The social worker planned to continue to be involved with the family as they worked on finding better housing, but she was not able to go any further with Mr. C's drinking problem at this time.

Monitoring the Assessment and Contract Planning Process

To keep track of progress during the assessment and contract planning phase, the social worker rates the degree to which four phase-specific processes have been completed. Table 7.4 provides a rating scale for the processes of writing an assessment statement for identified problems, needs, and barriers with corresponding strengths, assets, and resources; assessing the change potential in relation to each problem and

FLORENCE HOLLIS (1907–1987), a practitioner, researcher, and educator, was instrumental in strengthening social workers' understanding of long-term clinical practice. She conducted an NIMH-funded content analysis of written and taped case records to identify techniques used in direct work with clients and published *Casework: A Psychosocial Therapy.* She served as district administrator of the Family Society of Philadelphia, the Institute of Family Service in Cleveland, and the Community Service Society of New York. Hollis was a social work faculty member at Case Western Reserve University and Columbia University.

TABLE 7.4 ■ Rating Scale for Assessment and Contract Planning Process

	Not Addressed (0)	Begun Addressing (1)	Adequately Addressing (2)	Addressed (3)
Assessment statement for problems, needs, issues, barriers, strengths, assets, and resources				
Assessment of change potential for each				
Prioritization of problems, needs, barriers for urgency, and change potential				
Contracting with time frames				

need; prioritizing each for urgency and change potential; and contracting with anticipated time frames.

Low item scores (0, 1) and low summated total scale scores (less than 8) suggest a minimal present level of assessment and contract planning. Such scores raise concerns and suggest the necessity of continuing the assessment and contract planning phase. Item scores of 3 and total summated scale scores of 12 suggest adequate completion of the assessment and contract planning phase.

Working with Different Client Systems

As stated earlier, the General Method of social work practice is applicable to working with a variety of client, action, and target systems. A social worker may be working with a family, an individual, a group, an organization, or a community, but in any case, the social worker and the client system go through an assessment and contract planning phase. A question to be considered is: *Are there any differences in writing an assessment statement, prioritizing problems and issues, or drawing up a contracted plan when working with different-size client or action systems?* Various writers in the field of social work have focused on the art of assessment with particular systems, such as group, family, organization, and community. The approach and tools presented in this chapter, however, are used in working with any type of client or action system.

In applying and adopting assessment tools to particular systems, a social worker is sensitive to the knowledge that exists about each. In working with a community, for example, the social worker knows that a community consists of a complex body of persons with a common characteristic of place, problem, heritage, values, or commitment. There are often very distinctive subsystems within a community that may contract, contest, and conflict with one another. The social worker calls on the knowledge and skills identified in the profession by those who have expertise in community work and supplements their work with the newly developed tools for generalist practice.

Ross (1995) identified the process of organizing a community according to the following six phases:

1. Identify the community's needs and objectives.
2. Order or rank the needs or objectives.
3. Develop the confidence and will to work on the needs and objectives.
4. Find resources (internal and/or external) to deal with the needs or objectives.
5. Take action in respect to the needs or objectives.
6. Extend and develop cooperative and collaborative attitudes and practices in the community.

The phases for community organization as described half a century ago and more recently (Hardcastle, Powers, & Wenocur, 2004; Kretzmann & McKnight, 1993; Tropman, Ehrlich, & Rothman, 1995) are basically consistent with the phases of the General Method. In both processes, social worker and community go through phases where problems and objectives are identified, data are collected, and action is taken. It is implicit that prior to taking action, needs assessments are conducted, problems are prioritized with an appraisal of resources, and then actions are planned. Before moving into the action phase, the social worker and community use available tools to help prioritize problems and plan interventions.

For example, in the South End Community, the stated problems and needs were listed as follows:

High prices at local grocery stores
Rat- and roach-infested housing
No local control or input in neighborhood schools
Gang wars among community youths
No traffic light at the corner of Fifth Street and Silver Street

After drawing on assessment statements for each of these problems, the tool for prioritization of problems was completed, as found in Table 7.5.

Apparently, the community was motivated to begin to work on the need for a traffic light and the problem of high prices in local stores. In addition to motivation, the social worker assessed the nature and scope of each problem, as well as the extent of related resources. After all factors were considered, it became clear that the problem with the highest change potential was the need for a traffic light. This was a serious (life-at-risk) problem with a good chance of resolution. The problem of gang wars was seen as serious (a youth having been stabbed last month), but community members did not indicate high motivation to work on this. They said gang wars had been going on for years because people from certain blocks just didn't get along. Also, few resources were available for youth in the area. The social worker, while not los-

TABLE 7.5 ■ Problem Prioritization: The South End Community

Problem List	Change-Potential Scores (0–10)			Total Change Potential	Problem Prioritization	Severity
	Problem	Personal Strengths	Environmental Resources			
High prices	3	8	3	14	2	
Infested housing	3	5	3	11	3	
No school control	2	3	2	7	5	
Youth fights	3	4	2	9	4	*
Traffic light	8	7	8	23	1	*

*Life-at-risk situation.

ing sight of this problem, would begin with an issue with high success potential in order to build up a sense of trust and accomplishment within the community.

After prioritizing problems, issues, and needs, the social worker and community would move to planning specific tasks and responsibilities for goal accomplishment. The tool for contracted planning could aptly be used at this point. An example of how a contract could be developed with this community is found in Table 7.6. In this case, as community members begin to witness success from their efforts, a sense of pride and power develops. They begin to hope for greater accomplishments and to demonstrate motivation to work on complex tasks, such as finding funding sources and writing grant proposals. In time, the community begins to focus on what could be as well as what is, on prevention as well as problem resolution. Residents begin to talk about the need for them to overcome their interpersonal conflicts because they could gain so much more by working together. Some people identify past feelings of helplessness or isolation. According to Table 7.6, once the community finds out that there is funding for building a youth recreational center, they begin to think about other projects for enriching the community. The social worker's role as leader and activator decreases as members feel more confident and assume more leadership themselves.

Although the complexity of community work may be somewhat frightening to entry-level social workers, the general tools for assessment, as demonstrated, enable a social worker to partialize and to coordinate the complex dimensions of needs and actions within community practice. As stated earlier, these assessment tools may be applied similarly when working with groups, families, or individuals.

There may be a major shift in the size of the system of contact during the helping process, as tasks become identified and implemented. Client systems may expand or decrease in number. Although a social worker may begin contact with an individual, in the course of planning it may become apparent that the social worker will need to intervene with the family or a larger system to achieve goals. Fortunately, a social worker using the General Method employs knowledge and skills that are applicable to systems of any size.

TABLE 7.6 ■ Contracted Plan: South End Community

Date Identified	Problem/Need	Goal	Task	Contract	Date Anticipated	Date Accomplished
3/15	1. Need for traffic light	1. To have a traffic light installed at Fifth and Silver Streets	1. Inquire about meeting with traffic commissioner (in three weeks).	1. Mr. G and social worker	3/19	3/24
			2. Draw up a petition.	2. Petition committee (Mr. and Mrs. K, Mr. F, Ms. Q, Mrs. R) and social worker	3/20	3/26
			3. Get 500 signatures.	3. Petition committee and six others (Rev. J, Mrs. B, Capt. P, Mr. S, Mr. and Mrs. B)	4/3	4/5
			4. Collect information on accidents at Fifth and Silver Streets.	4. Mrs. A	3/20	3/22
			5. Draw up a traffic-flow chart.	5. Traffic committee (Mr. and Mrs. M, Mr. McN, Ms. W, Mr. T) and social worker	4/3	3/31
			6. Meeting of community.	6. Whole community	4/4	4/4
			7. See commissioner with petition and information.	7. Petition committee, Mr. G, and social worker	4/9	
			8. Discuss cancellation by commissioner at committee meeting.	8. Community and social worker	4/13	4/13
			9. Arrange to meet with mayor.	9. Mr. G	4/15	

Problem	Goal (Date)	Task	Responsible	Target Date	Date Completed
		10. Meet with mayor.	Same as for contract 7	4/30	
		11. If task 9 is not possible, meet to plan a demonstration.	Community and social worker	4/20	4/20
		12. Make signs.	Traffic committee	4/22	4/22
		13. Notify communications media.	Mr. G and Mrs. P	4/26	4/26
		14. Demonstration at Fifth and Silver Streets.	Community and social worker	4/27	4/27
		15. Get traffic light.	Town officials	5/3	5/4
		16. Community meeting.	Community and social worker	5/7	5/7
2. High prices	2. To lower prices in local grocery stores (3/15)	1. Compare prices and prepare report.	Comparative price committee (Mrs. B, Mr. G, Mr. and Mrs. N, Ms. W, Mr. T)	5/12	5/12
		2. Meet with store owners and present data.	Teams a. Mr. B, Mrs. Q, Mrs. J b. Mr. and Mrs. K, Mr. F	5/20	5/27
		3. Community meeting.	Community and social worker	5/27	5/27
		4. Meet with consumer-protection worker.	Mr. G, Mr. F, Mrs. J	6/3	6/3
		5. Meet with store owners and consumer-protection worker.	Comparative price committee, Mr. F, Mrs. J, social worker, store owners, and consumer-protection worker	6/20	6/22
		6. Monitor prices.	Teams as in contract 2	6/30 and ongoing	

Table 7.6 ■ Continued

Date Identified	Problem/Need	Goal	Task	Contract	Date Anticipated	Date Accomplished
3/15	3. Infested housing	3. To exterminate rats and roaches in community housing	1. Community meeting.	1. Community and social worker	6/24	6/24
			2. Identify locations and extent of infestation—bring in housing inspector.	2. Data collection committee (Mr. and Mrs. M, Mrs. B, Mr. F, Ms. R, Mr. McW)	7/9	7/8
			3. Draw up petition and get signatures.	3. Petition committee	7/17	7/17
			4. See landlords with data and petition.	4. Teams a. Mr. F, Mrs. Q, Mr. and Mrs. M b. Mr. B, Ms. J, Mrs. R	7/30	7/31
			5. Speak with Housing Authority and Housing Court.	5. Mr. G, Mr. F, Mrs. J	8/6	8/10
			6. Community meeting.	6. Community and social worker	8/10	8/12
			7. Withhold rents.	7. Tenants of infested housing	8/31	8/31
			8. Get publicity.	8. Mrs. P and Mrs. Q	8/30	8/29
			9. Hire sanitation specialist.	9. Landlords	9/2	9/10
3/15	4. Gang wars	4. To end gang wars	1. Community meeting.	1. Community and social worker	9/7	9/7
			2. Identify scope and cause—talk with youth and with police.	2. Data collection committee (Mr. F, Mrs. Q, Ms. R, Rev. J, Mr. McN)	9/20	9/22
			3. Locate funding to build recreation hall for	3. Mr. G, Mrs. R, and social worker	9/20	9/24

		community youth—talk with local officials.			
		4. Draw up funding proposal.	Funding committee (Mr. and Mrs. S, Ms. W, Mr. T)	9/30	10/8
		5. Build recreational center (on church grounds).	Contractors and community	8/30	11/30
		6. Hire recreation director.	Recreation center committee (Rev. J, Mrs. R, Mr. and Mrs. M, Ms. Q, Mr. G)	10/30	11/20
		7. Monitor center.	Recreation center committee	11/1	
6/15	5. No school input or control	5. To have direct input into local school	1. Community meeting.	Community and social worker	8/24	8/24
			2. Study structure of school and compare with other schools.	School committee (Mr. and Mrs. K, Mr. F, Mrs. W)	8/30	9/4
			3. Meet with principal.	Mr. G, Mr. and Mrs. M	8/26	8/29
			4. Meet with Board of Education.	Mr. G, Mrs. Q, Rev. J, Mr. W	9/14	9/15
			5. Locate funding sources.	Mrs. R, Mrs. P, Mr. F	9/11	9/20
			6. Get other community people involved—elderly, singles, etc.	Rev. J, Capt. P, Mrs. R, social worker		
			7. Draw up proposal for community programs of school.	Mrs. R, Mr. W	9/30	

Using Social Work Foundation Knowledge in Assessment and Contract Planning

The skills and approach a social worker uses in the assessment and contract planning phase should reflect the foundation value of *belief in the dignity and worth of every person* (see Chapter 1). As the social worker and system of contact collaborate in assessing and contract planning, the basic practice principles—particularly individualization, self-determination, and acceptance—are demonstrated.

A client or action system needs to have an individualized assessment. No two people or systems are exactly alike. Each one has a unique combination of problems, needs, resources, and circumstances. Thus, the principle of *individualization* is highlighted in the assessment and contract planning phase of the General Method.

In prioritizing problems and needs, the social worker knows that an essential factor to consider prior to problem selection is the extent of motivation in a client or action system to work on a particular problem or need. Unless there is client *self-determination* in problem prioritization, a social worker will undoubtedly meet with resistance and failure. The social worker who forges ahead for problem resolution will be unsuccessful without the agreement and support of the client or action system.

Although it is easy to wish that a client or action system have greater strengths or motivation, the social worker must convey an attitude of acceptance toward the system as it is. If several problems are assessed as having low potential for change, the social worker may feel a sense of frustration or helplessness. He or she must begin with accepting the client or action system "as a given." Through discussion, support, and assessment, within an atmosphere of acceptance, the social worker enables the system to view itself more realistically and to consider possible and desirable goals.

In addition to foundation values and principles, a social worker in the assessment and contract planning phase uses knowledge and skills from the holistic foundation for general social work practice (see Chapter 1). When writing a statement of cause for a problem, the social worker may be using concepts from theories to explain how a client or action system has been influenced by others. Knowledge of cultures, policies, and formal and informal resources is used in developing priorities for planning and intervention. The social worker utilizes various theories to understand persons, problems, and environments and their interactions as an appraisal of their change potential is being made.

The foundation skills that are used during assessment include goal setting, planning, contracting, and recording. As the social worker involves the client or action system in contracting, interviewing skills such as clarifying, bargaining, and confronting may be needed. The supportive skills of listening, guiding, feeling, and sensing are prevalent throughout the assessment and contract planning process. With the individualization of each person-problem-environment triplex during assessment, the social worker applies foundation skills and theories as deemed appropriate to the situation.

Human Diversity in Assessment and Contract Planning

During the assessment and contract planning phase, as problems and needs are prioritized and contracts are formulated, the social worker and the client or action system may find it difficult to determine where to begin, particularly when the work is with minorities. Often, the problems identified are both personal and societal in nature. Although it may be necessary to invest major energy first in providing for immediate material needs, the social worker should also plan to deal with the larger social change issues that need to be addressed. A social worker's involvement in the larger issues helps demonstrate his or her understanding and acceptance to the client or action system. As interventions are contracted, the social worker strives to promote empowerment by strongly encouraging and supporting minority members to speak and act for themselves to meet immediate needs and to bring about institutional change.

In working out a contract with a client or action system, the social worker may find different degrees of participation and active involvement by systems, depending on cultural orientations. When a social worker is seen as an authority person in a hierarchical relationship, members of the system may show passivity and dependence. The speed with which a contract is drawn up may also be influenced by the culture of a particular client or action system.

The planning and selection of tasks on a contract should reflect a sensitivity to cultural values and beliefs. For example, to suggest institutional care of the elderly as a plan for many African Americans, Puerto Ricans, or Asians would be inappropriate. Similarly, placing a child with a relative in the tribe would be a much more acceptable plan for a Native American family than a foster-home placement would be.

As noted in Chapter 2, the core issues related to institutional racism, cultural diversity, gender-role expectations, sexual orientation, and socio-economic status need to be incorporated into the assessment and contract planning phase. This applies to assessing unmet needs and resource availability of client or action systems at the personal micro level, the family or group mezzo level, and the broader macro level.

Many personal problems may be assessed as stemming from tensions and rejections the individual has experienced when trying to participate in societal systems. The social worker and the client system study all of the identified problems and issues, but priority is given to those with high potential for change. The broad, general goals that were stated during engagement are refined during assessment into more specific, attainable, measurable goals for contract formulation. In every possible way, the social worker tries to empower the client or action system to implement independently the tasks identified in the contract or to implement them with a community of others who face similar pressures or injustices.

Information gathered about potential supportive resources is discussed during assessment, and the plan drawn up by the social worker and the client or action system may include initial contact with outside resources. If no local resources are available, the plan may be developed to organize a support group in or outside of the social worker's agency.

Using an ecological-systems perspective in planning, a social worker realizes that an individual with a goal of changing his or her behavior and image may experience pressure and negative reactions from the environment. For example, in any work on redefining gender roles—whether with men or women, individually or in groups—attention needs to be given to the possible consequences that may result from any change. The reality is that change is usually a painful process for both the individual and the environment. Although a person may become self-sufficient and independent, it is true that no person can be an island, totally independent from others, for very long. Human beings by nature are interdependent. To move into a truly collaborative, balanced interdependence, however, may be impossible for some individuals in their existing environments. Women who have been greatly dependent, for example, may have to go to the other polarity of total independence before they and others can see them as equal, complementary counterparts. The implications of these and other possible actions and reactions need to be given serious consideration before choices and changes are made. Various support systems and reinforcements need to be located and ensured if such change is to be positive and stabilized. Thus, in writing assessment statements, prioritizing problems and issues, and contracting with different systems, social workers use their knowledge of and sensitivity to multiculturalism, social pluralism, and socio-demographic diversity.

ONGOING CASES
Assessment and Contract Planning Phase

In this section, the application of knowledge and skills during the *assessment and contract planning phase* of the General Method is demonstrated by entry-level generalist social workers. In Exercise 7.1, questions are proposed for reflection and discussion about how practice in each of the case examples during the assessment and contract planning phase might change if the client system represented a different

- ▶ *Culture:* Racial/ethnic group membership, national origin and social group identity, religion and spirituality
- ▶ *Social status:* Socio-economic status, environmental and rural/urban differences
- ▶ *Socio-demographic strata:* Age and developmental stage, gender roles, sexual orientation, challenges in mental and physical ability.

I. Child Welfare Case
A. Agency: State Department of Children's Services
B. Client System

K, a 15-year-old female, is in an emergency shelter. (For more background information see Chapter 5, Ongoing Cases: Engagement Phase, I. Child Welfare Case.)

EXERCISE 7.1
Impact of Human Diversity on Assessment and Contract Planning Process

Consider the following questions in each of the seven client systems. In assessment and contract planning, how might change in culture, social status, or socio-demographic strata:

1. Influence the client system's willingness to participate in assessment and contract planning?

2. Influence the social worker's view of assessment and contract planning?

3. Reveal values that influence timing, communications, content, and actions in assessment and contract planning?

4. Affect the dynamics of the professional relationship in assessment and contract planning?

5. Affect monitoring of the progress, timeliness, and completeness of assessment and contract planning?

C. Summary of Preceding Phases

The problem, needs, and goals identified during engagement and data collection are listed in Chapter 6. During engagement, K expressed feelings of loneliness, hatred, nervousness, and depression. In collecting data, the social worker learned that K had experienced some difficulty adjusting in both the group home and the foster-home placements that she had before she ran away, particularly in the foster home. Her schoolwork had also deteriorated prior to her running away and being placed in the emergency shelter. After exploring informal and formal resources in the environment, the social worker located a group home for young women (ages 14 to 19) in Jenett City that had an opening. K expressed a strong desire to move into a group home, to return to school, and to get help with her personal problems.

D. Assessment

ASSESSMENT STATEMENT: K has no permanent residence because she cannot live at home with her abusive parents (mother and stepfather), and she ran away from her foster home. She has personal needs (problem 3 in Chapter 6) that interfere with her functioning. The etiology of K's personal problems go back to her traumatic home environment, where she was physically and sexually abused. K is out of school because she is living in a temporary shelter awaiting placement. Her school performance had dropped to below average while she was living in the foster home because she became involved with a boyfriend and was having an increasing number of arguments with her foster parents.

The change potential for K's problem of homelessness is assessed as somewhat high because K is motivated to accept a group-home placement and a resource is available. The change potential for K's need to reenter school is assessed as somewhat high because there is a school near the group home. The change potential for K's problems with adjustment to placement and school is assessed as somewhat high because K is now motivated to accept ongoing help with her personal problems and because there will be opportunity for K to receive help individually and in group while living in the group home.

PROBLEM PRIORITIZATION: The problem-prioritization tool was used by the social worker, as recorded in Table 7.7.

The need for a placement is given top priority because it has the highest change potential (24) and also because of the urgency (severity) of the situation (living in temporary shelter). Finding a school placement is not a difficult problem to resolve. It received the second-highest score and became second in priority.

The personal problems have lower change scores because it is expected that these problems will take more time for resolution. K is particularly motivated to try to get over "feeling down." She is ready to talk about how hurt and angry she is. She also wants to feel better about herself and to understand what has happened to her. She hesitates to talk about her sexuality, even though problems related to her sexual identity, behavior, and relationships are assessed as serious (severity). K ran away from home when she became involved with a boyfriend, and she fears new heterosexual friendships. Since the social worker has been able to locate environmental resources for all the problems listed, the change potential scores in the "environment" column are high (9s). Even though the problem relating to K's sexuality is prioritized last, the social worker sees the seriousness of this problem and will bring it to the attention of the person who will be working with K individually in the group home.

CONTRACTING: Building on the list of problems and goals identified during engagement and data collection, the social worker and K then began to plan the tasks that needed to be performed to achieve the stated goals. They also identified who would be responsible for carrying out each task, and they set the dates when task completion could be anticipated. Their contracted plan is given in Table 7.8.

TABLE 7.7 ■ Problem Prioritization: Child Welfare Case

| Problem List | Change-Potential Scores (0–10) | | | Total Change Potential | Problem Prioritization | Severity |
	Problem	Personal Strengths	Environmental Resources			
No permanent home	7	8	9	24	1	*
Out of school	7	7	9	23	2	
Personal problems						
Poor self-esteem	5	6	9	20	4	
Identity confusion	5	6	9	20	4	
Sexuality	5	5	9	19	6	*
Depression	5	7	9	21	3	

*Life-at-risk situation.

TABLE 7.8 ■ Contracted Plan: Child Welfare Case

Date Identified	Problem/Need	Goal	Task	Contract	Date Anticipated	Date Accomplished
1/12	1. No permanent home	1a. To obtain a permanent placement b. To maintain a permanent placement	1. Make referral. 2. Visit group home. 3. Move to group home. 4. Follow up.	1. Social worker 2. K and social worker 3. K, with social worker's help 4. Social worker, K, and group-home staff	1/19 1/22 1/24 1/30 and every second week	
1/12	2. Out of school	2. To reenter school	1. Enroll in local school. 2. Follow up.	1. K and group-home staff worker 2. Social worker, school personnel, group-home staff	1/28 1/30 and other school conferences	
1/12	3. Personal problems a. Depression b. Poor self-esteem c. Identity confusion d. Sexuality	3. Personal goals (1/19) a. To stop "feeling down" so much b. To feel better about self c. To clarify identity d. To be able to have good friendships with males	1. Have weekly individual sessions with social worker at the group home. 2. Participate in weekly peer-group meetings. 3. Follow up.	1. K and group-home social worker 2. K 3. Social worker, K, and social worker at group home	1/25 and once a week thereafter 1/25 and once a week thereafter 1/30 and every second week	

269

II. Gerontology Case

A. Agency: Seaside Nursing Home

B. Client System

Mrs. J is an 80-year-old Portuguese woman in a skilled-nursing facility. (For more background information, see Chapter 5, Ongoing Cases: Engagement Phase, II. Gerontology Case.)

C. Summary of Preceding Phases

The problems, needs, and goals identified during engagement and data collection may be found in Chapter 6. During engagement, Mrs. J expressed feelings of distrust, fear, anger, and abandonment. In collecting data, the social worker learned that Mrs. J's failure to adjust included disruptive behavior in the unit. She was agitating the nurses and the residents. More information was obtained about Mrs. J's history and her family, who could not be located. Portuguese-speaking resource people in the nursing home (a new volunteer) and in the community (the church pastor) were being located to visit with Mrs. J. The client herself was becoming more open and motivated to adjust to the nursing home.

D. Assessment

ASSESSMENT STATEMENT: Mrs. J is reclusive, uncooperative, and agitated because she is culturally isolated in the nursing home and because she has been abandoned by her family. She will not leave her room alone because she is afraid that the little she has left will be stolen. She finds it difficult to go out and meet with others because she can't speak English fluently, and she feels uncomfortable with people of a different culture. Mrs. J fights with the nurses when they come to give her a bath because it distresses her to have to get undressed at 10 o'clock in the morning. Mrs. J has been yelling at the residents and calling them names because she wants to get their attention and to make them communicate with her. She displays anger and confusion at times, as a result of her organic brain syndrome.

The change potential for Mrs. J to overcome her reclusiveness is assessed as medium high because Mrs. J is somewhat motivated to be able to leave her room on her own and because she is physically able to do so at this time. The potential to overcome her cultural isolation is assessed as medium because she can speak some English, a volunteer has been located who is Portuguese, and the pastor of Mrs. J's former church will also come to see her. The change potential for Mrs. J to get to know the staff and the resources of the nursing home is assessed as high, because Mrs. J has agreed to meet twice a week with the social worker, and she has expressed interest in meeting other staff members and hearing about available resources. Her involvement in activities at the nursing home will depend on how comfortable she feels with the activities and with those who participate in them.

The change potential for overcoming the bath-schedule problem is assessed as high because the nurses are open to reconsidering the time Mrs. J is scheduled for her bath. Mrs. J and the head nurse are willing to meet to discuss the problem. The change potential for overcoming Mrs. J's yelling at the residents is also assessed as high, because Mrs. J is motivated to work for better communication with others. She says she will stop the name-calling.

Mrs. J's overall functioning and adjustment are dependent also on the rate of deterioration due to organic brain syndrome.

TABLE 7.9 ■ Problem Prioritization: Gerontology Case

Problem List	Change-Potential Scores (0–10)			Total Change Potential	Problem Prioritization	Severity
	Problem	Personal Strengths	Environmental Resources			
Reclusiveness: not leaving room	9	7	7	23	3	*
Cultural isolation	6	8	7	21	5	
Unfamiliarity with staff and resources	9	8	9	26	1	
Fighting with nurses over bath	7	8	9	24	2	
Calling residents names	7	9	6	22	4	

*Life-at-risk situation.

PROBLEM PRIORITIZATION: The social worker prioritized the identified problems, using the prioritization tool as shown in Table 7.9.

The problem of reclusiveness has a high change-potential score (9), because in considering the nature of the problem itself, residents who are physically able to leave their rooms may do so. The change potential for "person" is assessed as somewhat high (7). Although Mrs. J has the physical capacity to leave her room and expresses a desire to get out more, she still feels afraid and strange in the nursing home. "Environment" is also assessed at a 7 for this problem. Resources (persons and programs) in the nursing-home environment are available to help Mrs. J leave her room. They do not, however, reflect her culture, except for one possible volunteer. Mrs. J's problem of reclusiveness is asterisked in the "severity" column, because it can be seen as potentially a life-or-death issue. If Mrs. J regresses to the point of refusing to leave her room even for meals, she could become seriously ill and have to be moved into the chronic-care unit.

In assessing the problem of cultural isolation, the change potential is seen as medium, and scored as a 6. People of different cultures do not have to feel or be isolated. Even though Mrs. J does not speak English fluently, she can carry on a conversation in English ("person" score of 8). She could help others in the environment to understand and respond to her cultural needs. Although there are no Portuguese residents or staff members in the nursing home at the time, this may change, because the number of Portuguese moving into the local geographic area is increasing. Mrs. J has also expressed some desire to get to understand others at the nursing home, and the staff of the home, particularly those who speak Spanish, have indicated an interest in helping Mrs. J feel welcome. They talked about serving Portuguese food and playing music from Portugal at the next resident-and-staff party. The "environment" assessment at this time is scored a 7. If a Portuguese volunteer or Mrs. J's pastor becomes actively involved with her, the environment score may be raised.

The lack of familiarity with the staff and resources of the home was seen as a problem easily remedied (9). Mrs. J is capable of understanding the staff and resources, and she is somewhat motivated to learn about them (8). The program planner, recreational director, head nurse, chaplain, and others on the staff of the nursing home are very willing to talk with Mrs. J and to develop an individualized program for her. The planned program for Mrs. J could include recreational, social, and spiritual activities. "Environment," therefore, is given a high change-potential score (9) for the problem of "unfamiliarity with staff and resources of the nursing home."

The potential for changing the problem of fighting with the nurses over the bath is assessed at 7. Even though the problem is not a life-or-death issue, changing the schedule for Mrs. J's bath time would affect the schedule for many others. It is possible, however, for the schedule to be changed and thus prevent further fighting by Mrs. J over the bath. The change potential for "person" is 8 because Mrs. J is capable of being cooperative and has said she would like to get along better with the nurses. The nurses are open to rescheduling Mrs. J's bath time, and the head nurse has agreed to meet with Mrs. J about it ("environment" score of 9).

In considering the problem of calling other residents names, the social worker assessed the change potential for the problem itself as 7. The act of holding back from name-calling is possible for Mrs. J. She realizes that it isn't right and wants to stop this behavior (9). The residents ("environment") are not interested in going near Mrs. J at this time (change potential of 6), but some will probably respond if they are encouraged by the staff to try to reach out to her.

In totaling the change potential scores, the problems become prioritized as follows: (1) unfamiliarity with staff and resources, (2) fighting with nurses over bath, (3) reclusiveness: not leaving room, (4) calling residents names, and (5) cultural isolation.

CONTRACTING: Building on the prioritized problem list, the social worker and Mrs. J began to plan and to contract for what needed to be accomplished in order to achieve their mutually agreed on goals. The contracted plan they developed is shown in Table 7.10.

III. Public Social Welfare Case

A. Agency: State Social Services

B. Client System

Mr. and Mrs. P and their two children, ages 2 and 4, are in need of emergency and permanent housing. (For additional background information, see Chapter 5, Ongoing Cases: Engagement Phase, III. Public Social Welfare Case.)

C. Summary of Preceding Phases

The problems, needs, and goals identified during engagement and data collection are listed in Chapter 6. During engagement, Mr. and Mrs. P expressed feelings of helplessness, anger, confusion, and rejection. As data were collected, the social worker learned that the P family had a history of frequent moves, often caused by evictions due to their failure to pay the rent. The Ps were receiving TANF but had difficulty in planning and budgeting their money. Mr. P was unable to maintain employment because of his psychological incapacity. He was

TABLE 7.10 ■ Contracted Plan: Gerontology Case

Date Identified	Problem/Need	Goal	Task	Contract	Date Anticipated	Date Accomplished
9/27	1. Unfamiliarity with staff and resources of the nursing home	1. To get to know the staff and resources of the nursing home	1. Meet twice a week with social worker.	1. Social worker and Mrs. J	10/4 and every Tuesday and Thursday thereafter	10/4, 10/9, 10/11
			2. Meet with program planner.	2. Social worker, Mrs. J, and program planner	10/16	
			3. Meet with a person from recreation staff.	3. Social worker, Mrs. J, and recreation staff person	10/23	
10/2	2. Fighting with nurses over bath	2. To work out bath schedule with nurses	1. Meet with head nurse to discuss bath schedule.	1. Mrs. J and head nurse	10/16	
9/25	3. Reclusiveness: not leaving room alone	3a. To leave room alone (at least once a day)	1. Walk down to nursing station alone at least once a day.	1. Mrs. J	10/25 and each day thereafter	
		3b. To attend a house activity, program, or meeting (at least once a week)	2. Go to a house activity, program, or meeting (at least once a week).	2. Social worker or staff member and Mrs. J first two times	Starting week of 10/22	
				3. Mrs. J with residents each week thereafter	Starting week of 11/5	
10/2	4. Calling residents names	4. To stop calling residents names	1. Stop name calling.	1. Mrs. J	10/16 and thereafter	
			2. Say "hello" to residents.	2. Mrs. J	10/16 and thereafter	
9/25	5. Cultural isolation	5. To share culture with others	1. Meet director of volunteers.	1. Mrs. J, social worker, and director of volunteers	10/25	
			2. Visit with Portuguese volunteer.	2. Mrs. J and volunteer	?	
			3. Visit with pastor of church.	3. Mrs. J and pastor	?	

receiving weekly outpatient treatment at the local mental health center. At the time of initial assessment, the Ps were asking for help only in locating housing and food.

D. Assessment

ASSESSMENT STATEMENT: The P family does not have a place to stay because they were evicted from their apartment two weeks ago for not paying their rent on time. They do not plan and budget the money they receive from TANF to last throughout the month. The Ps are in need of emergency food because they do not have any money left from last month, and the check and food stamps for this month are being held at central office until the family is relocated.

The change potential for the P family's housing problem is assessed as low because of the Ps limited motivation to become actively involved in searching for an apartment. Although there are possible resources for emergency shelter, the authorized payment for temporary placement is only for a maximum of 14 days.

The potential for meeting the need for food is assessed as high because several resources are available. Finding a way to transport a food supply to the Ps should not be a problem unless the social worker is unable to get an agency car.

PROBLEM PRIORITIZATION: During initial assessment, the social worker used the problem-prioritization tool for conceptualization. It was clear and urgent that the first two areas in need of immediate attention were food and temporary shelter for the family. In prioritizing, the housing problem was divided into the two parts of (1) emergency shelter and (2) long-term residence. The food need was also subdivided. Considering these two housing needs along with the two food-supply needs, the social worker drew up the prioritization shown in Table 7.11.

TABLE 7.11 ■ Problem Prioritization: Public Social Welfare Case

Problem List	Change-Potential Scores (0–10)			Total Change Potential	Problem Prioritization	Severity
	Problem	Personal Strengths	Environmental Resources			
1. Housing						
a. Emergency shelter	8	8	8	24	2	*
b. Long-term	2	1	2	5	4	*
2. Food						
a. Emergency food	9	9	8	26	1	*
b. Until check and food stamps	8	8	7	23	3	*

*Life-at-risk situation.

The problem/need with the highest change potential is obviously finding immediate food for the family. The second-prioritized area is emergency shelter. The social worker and the family will then need to plan for receiving a food supply to last until Mr. and Mrs. P receive TANF income and food stamps. The fourth problem area, the last prioritized because of its low change potential, is the need for a long-term residence for the family. There is a pressing need to work on this fourth problem, because the temporary shelter can only be for two weeks. The social worker knows also that the only way the temporary placement will be supported financially by the agency is if the Ps make ongoing efforts to secure more permanent housing. An extension in temporary placement is granted only if there is evidence that every effort is being made by the family to locate a residence. Through problem assessment and prioritization, it became clear to the social worker that pressure needed to be exerted on Mr. and Mrs. P to have them become more actively involved in the search for housing.

CONTRACTING: The social worker and Mr. and Mrs. P developed the contract identified in Table 7.12. Permission was given by Mr. and Mrs. P to have the social worker discuss their plan and progress with Mr. P's doctor and the income-maintenance technician. The social worker asked Mr. P's doctor and the family's income-maintenance technician to help with motivating the Ps to become more involved.

IV. Community Services Case

A. Agency: Clayton Neighborhood House

B. Client System

Four Hispanic families are without heat in their apartments on the second floor of the 33 L Street apartment building. (For more background information, see Chapter 5, Ongoing Cases: Engagement Phase, IV. Community Services Case.)

C. Summary of Preceding Phases

The problem, needs, and goal identified during engagement and data collection are stated in Chapter 5. During engagement, residents from four apartments met with the social worker and expressed feelings of anger, frustration, fear, helplessness, and victimization. In gathering information, the social worker learned that residents were paying $250 for one-room apartments, heat included. The name and address of the landlord was obtained and he was contacted. Because of the urgent nature of the problem, the social worker and the residents moved quickly through engagement, data collection, and assessment.

D. Assessment

ASSESSMENT STATEMENT: The four families who live on the second floor of the 33 L Street apartment building do not have adequate heating because the heating for the building has not been regulated for adequate, even distribution. There also is a problem with direct communication between residents and the landlord. The residents and the landlord do not speak the same language, and the landlord does not return calls made to him by tenants. (The social worker added the communication problem to the problem list in the record; see Table 7.13.)

TABLE 7.12 ■ Contracted Plan: Public Social Welfare Case

Date Identified	Problem/Need	Goal	Task	Contract	Date Anticipated	Date Accomplished
9/28	1. Food—emergency food	1. To obtain emergency food supply	1. Discuss resources.	1. Social worker and Ps	9/28	
			2. Contact resource.	2. Social worker and Ps	9/28	
			3. Obtain food.	3. The Ps	9/28	
9/28	2. Housing—emergency shelter	2. To move into emergency shelter	1. Locate resource.	1. Social worker	9/28	
			2. Discuss resources.	2. Social worker and Ps	9/28	
			3. Contact resource.	3. Social worker and Ps	9/28	
			4. Move to resource.	4. Ps with social worker's help	9/28	
9/28	3. Food until TANF check and food stamps arrive	3. To receive a food supply until TANF check and food stamps arrive	1. Locate resource.	1. Social worker	9/29	
			2. Discuss resource.	2. Social worker and Ps	9/29	
			3. Contact resource.	3. Social worker and Ps	9/29	
			4. Receive food.	4. Ps and resource	9/29 until check and food stamps arrive	
9/28	4. Housing—long-term	4. To move into an apartment for long-term residence	1. Explore resources.	1. Mr. and Mrs. P and social worker	9/29	
			2. Contact resources.	2. Mr. and Mrs. P	9/29	
			3. Move.	3. The Ps	10/12	
			4. Update.	4. Social worker, Mr. P's doctor, income-maintenance technician	9/29 and weekly	

TABLE 7.13 ■ Contracted Plan: Community Services Case

Date Identified	Problem/Need	Goal	Task	Contract	Date Anticipated	Date Accomplished
12/3	1. Lack of heat on second floor	1. To obtain consistent, adequate heating for second-floor residents of L street apartment house	1. Contact janitor.	1. Social worker	12/3	
			2. Contact landlord.	2. Social worker	12/4	12/4
			3. Meet for follow-up.	3. Residents and social worker	12/5	12/5
12/5	2. Communication problem with landlord					

The change potential for the problem of inadequate heating is assessed as somewhat high at this time because Mr. X, the landlord, is now aware of the problem and has stated that he will see that it gets resolved. As long as the problem of poor communication between residents and landlord remains, however, there is a possibility that a heating loss could recur and that the families would continue to have difficulty in notifying Mr. X.

The problem of poor communication has a low potential for change at this time, because neither the families nor the landlord appear motivated to work on improving their communication. The families are afraid that if they meet with Mr. X, he may think that they are complaining too much and raise their rent. Mr. X indicated that he is very busy, with no time to contact residents.

PROBLEM PRIORITIZATION: Because there was only one problem that the client system was presenting at this time, the social worker did not use the problem-prioritization tool. The need for heating was primary and urgent.

CONTRACTING: The social worker and the residents developed the contracted plan shown in Table 7.13 during their first meeting. The communication problem was added after the social worker had contacted the landlord.

V. Education Case

A. Agency: Keeney Elementary School

B. Client System

Jim G is an 8-year-old African American third-grader with regressive behavior in school and at home. (For additional background information, see Chapter 5, Ongoing Cases: Engagement Phase, V. Education Case.)

C. Summary of Preceding Phases

The problems, needs, goals, and tasks identified prior to a formal assessment are indicated in Chapter 6. Through play, Jim began to express his fear that his mother might leave him. Mrs. G shared feelings of anger and hurt regarding her husband and their relationship. She was finding it difficult to forgive him and to trust him. A meeting was arranged for the social worker to meet with Mr. and Mrs. G to discuss Jim's problems and how they were being affected by the problem between Mr. and Mrs. G.

D. Assessment

When the social worker met with Mr. and Mrs. G, they moved into the assessment phase of the General Method. Problems and goals were clarified, and a contracted plan was articulated by the social worker, Jim, and both of his parents.

ASSESSMENT STATEMENT: Jim has a problem being present at school physically, emotionally, and cognitively, owing to his upset feelings and his fears, which are caused by tension and quarreling at home between his parents. Jim has refused to fall asleep at night unless his mother is with him and a light is on in the room, because he is afraid that she will leave him, as he overheard her saying to his father. He was overly tired in school because he was trying to keep awake during the night. Jim did not want to go to school because he feared his mother would leave for good while he was gone. Mr. and Mrs. G have been quarreling because Mrs. G recently learned that her husband had gone out with another woman.

The change potential for Jim's school and home problems is assessed as high. The problems have had a short duration. Jim is reacting to external circumstances, and Mr. and Mrs. G are eager to improve the situation. Mrs. G is reassuring Jim that she will not leave him, and she and her husband are willing to go for professional help with their relationship.

PROBLEM PRIORITIZATION: The social worker used the problem-prioritization tool as shown in Table 7.14.

The change potential for the school tardiness and absenteeism problem was assessed as very high (9), because Jim did not have a history of missing school and the problem merely involved physical presence. The "person" change-potential score was assessed as medium (5). Even though Jim has the capacity to go to school, he did not appear to have the necessary motivation. The potential of the "environment" to change for problem resolution was assessed at a 9, very high, because Mr. and Mrs. G were being very cooperative and gave assurance that they would see that Jim came to school on time each day.

The change potential for the problem of declining academic performance was assessed as a 6 (medium—leaning toward high) because the nature of the problem was reactive (related directly to external circumstances) rather than internalized (present regardless of external circumstances) and because the problems had only become observable over the past month. It could become a serious problem if it persisted and Jim had to be removed from his classroom (asterisk in "severity" column).

The change-potential score for "person" as related to the school-performance problem was assessed as 5 (medium), because here, too, although Jim has the capacity to do the work, he is not motivated for school achievement at this time. The "environment" score was appraised as a 9 (high), because Jim was beginning to be helped by his parents and the school. His parents were committed to try to reduce the causes for Jim's decline in his school work.

The change potential for Jim's problem with falling asleep was given a 5 (medium), because of the somewhat serious nature of the problem, even though it had only recently developed. If Jim continued to get little sleep, he could become physically ill. The "person" potential was assessed as a 3 (somewhat low) because Jim was too upset to sleep and he

TABLE 7.14 ■ Problem Prioritization: Education Case

Problem List	Change-Potential Scores (0–10)			Total Change Potential	Problem Prioritization	Severity
	Problem	Personal Strengths	Environmental Resources			
School tardiness and absenteeism	9	5	9	23	1	
Declining academic performance	6	5	9	20	3	
Sleeping problem	5	3	5	13	4	*
Strain in marital relationship	6	8	9	23	2	

*Life-at-risk situation.

continued to want a night-light even after his mother assured him she would not leave. The "environment" score was a 5 for this problem, because Jim's parents were unable to make Jim fall asleep and they did not want to give him sleeping pills.

The change potential for the problem of a strained marital relationship was assessed as high (8) because Mr. and Mrs. G said that this was the first time they had had such a problem. Mr. G said that it was the first time he had gone out with someone else and that it would not happen again. The "person" potential was seen as high (8) because both Mr. and Mrs. G were motivated to work on their problem and to seek outside help. The "environment" potential was seen as very high (9) because several resources for marital counseling were available in the area.

Through problem prioritization, it became clear that the first two areas to be addressed were (1) Jim's school attendance and (2) Mr. and Mrs. G's marital relationship. With improvement in these two areas, it was hoped that Jim's school performance and sleeping at night would improve. Efforts for problem resolution and sleeping at night would improve. Efforts for problem resolution would be primarily directed, therefore, according to the following sequence: (1) Jim's school tardiness and absenteeism, (2) the strain in Mr. and Mrs. G's relationship, (3) Jim's declining school performance, and (4) Jim's sleeping problem.

CONTRACTING: When the social worker met with Mr. and Mrs. G, they reviewed the problems, goals, and tasks that were identified earlier, and they agreed on the contracted plan outlined in Table 7.15. As highlighted in the "contract" column, Mr. and Mrs. G planned to become actively involved in going for help with their marital relationship and in working with Jim and the school on Jim's school problems.

VI. Corrections Case

A. Agency: Juvenile Court

B. Client System

Seven male youths, age 14, are on probation and attending weekly group meetings led by co-workers at Juvenile Court. (For further background information, see Chapter 5, Ongoing Cases: Engagement Phase, VI. Corrections Case.)

C. Summary of Preceding Phases

The problems, needs, and goals identified by the group during engagement and data collection are outlined in Chapter 5. The youths in the group had low self-esteem and frequently referred to themselves as "stupid." All of the youths were in special classes at school for learning disabilities. The social workers also learned that all of the group participants were from single-parent homes and had trouble communicating with their parents. In visiting the homes and schools, the co-leaders learned that all seven youths were seen as "problems" by parents and teachers. The group members agreed to come to weekly group meetings in order to get off probation sooner (possibly a two-month reduction from a six-month probationary period).

D. Assessment

ASSESSMENT STATEMENT: The youths in the group are on probation because they committed the following crimes: three members—breaking, entering, and stealing from homes; two members—theft of automobiles; two members—shoplifting. The problem of

TABLE 7.15 ■ Contracted Plan: Education Case

Date Identified	Problem/Need	Goal	Task	Contract	Date Anticipated	Date Accomplished
11/1	1. Jim's school tardiness and absenteeism	1. Jim's regular school attendance (on time daily)	1. Get Jim to school on time each day.	1. Mr. and Mrs. G	11/5 and each school day thereafter	11/5-ongoing
11/21	2. Strain in Mr. and Mrs. G's marital relationship	2. Improved marital relationship (less quarreling, growing trust)	1. Explore counseling resources.	1. Social worker and Mr. and Mrs. G	11/27	11/27
			2. Select resource.	2. Mr. and Mrs. G	11/27	11/27
			3. Contact resource for appointment.	3. Mr. G	11/28	
			4. Attend counseling sessions.	4. Mr. and Mrs. G	Beginning week of 12/3	
11/1	3. Jim's declining school performance	3. Improved school performance (interest, participation, grades)	1. Talk with Jim about school problems in relation to home problem.	1. Mr. and Mrs. G, Jim, and social worker	11/27	11/27
			2. Check on Jim's performance.	2. Social worker with Jim's teacher	11/28 and weekly	
			3. Update Mr. and Mrs. G on Jim's school performance.	3. Social worker	12/4 and 12/11 telephone contacts	
			4. Continue to meet with Jim.	4. Social worker	11/29	
			5. Home meeting to evaluate progress.	5. Social worker, Mr. and Mrs. G, and Jim	12/17	
11/2	4. Jim's problem getting to sleep at night	4. Jim's going to sleep at night without mother in room	1. Continue to assure Jim that Mrs. G is not going to leave him.	1. Mrs. G	11/27 and each night thereafter	

law breaking is assessed as very serious for at least five of the youths (J, T, ML, B, and A). There is a history of law breaking in their families (by fathers or brothers), and little discipline or support is offered in their homes. All of these five express a desire to get off probation and to make sure they "don't get caught again." They do not have a strong motivation to keep within the law. Although C appears to be sincerely sorry that he got into trouble and upset his father, the problem could become serious if he continues with the street gang he has joined. MK's offense was shoplifting for the third time. His mother said she never has enough money to provide for the children, and she thinks MK was trying to bring home things for her and his sisters and brother. Although Mrs. K was finding it difficult to discipline MK, she said she had started attending a "parenting" class at church that was helping her to work better with him. She was trying to get her son to promise that he would not steal any more.

The youths in the group are having a problem generally with their development and their feelings because they are entering adolescence with low self-concepts and limited support systems at home and in school. Low self-esteem is reinforced by placement in special classes at school. All of the members have said that they don't like being told what to do, and that they get angry when someone puts pressure on them. They wish they could be independent, but they are afraid to try to make it on their own. They don't understand "the changes," physical and emotional, that they are going through, and they said there isn't someone they can talk to about them.

The lack of understanding about their "changes" has a high change potential because issues and topics related to the boys' development can be addressed and discussed in group meetings. Efforts can also be made through the group to help them with gaining temper control. The youths' motivation to work on both of these problem areas ("changes" and "temper") also contributes to an affirmative assessment of change potential.

PROBLEM PRIORITIZATION: In prioritizing problems, the social workers considered mainly those problems that the group members said they wanted to work on. Although parent-son conflicts and low self-worth were seen by the social workers as two problem areas, the group proceeded with identifying goals and tasks only for the following: (1) law breaking leading to probation, (2) bad tempers, and (3) lack of understanding of the changes they were experiencing.

All of the youths knew that probation requirements included abiding by the rules of society and school, attending school, and obeying at home. They were also expected to attend weekly group meetings and to actively participate in them. If the youths had not agreed to the group, they would have been required to have weekly contact individually with a probation officer.

In discussing the prioritization of problems and goals with the group, everyone said top priority was to be given to getting off probation in four months (shortest possible time period). They knew that to achieve this goal, they had to meet all of the requirements of probation. In order to get along and abide by the rules at school and at home, the youths knew that they needed to work on controlling their tempers. They listed this as the second most important problem to be addressed. Finally, they agreed that basically they really didn't understand themselves and what was happening to them. They wanted to talk about the changes they had to learn to deal with.

Without having to use the prioritization tool, therefore, the group prioritized and clarified their goals as follows: (1) to get off probation in four months, (2) to control their tempers at home and at school, and (3) to learn more about some of the changes they were facing (including becoming independent, understanding sex and family planning, and getting training and jobs).

There was a lengthy discussion over goal 1. Some wanted to add "and to stay off." What it would take "to stay off" was debated. Some said it meant they couldn't break the law any more. Others said they would just have to be more careful. The social workers said that, hopefully, as participants grew in understanding and respecting themselves and others, they wouldn't need to be involved in law breaking, and this would ensure their not getting caught again.

CONTRACTING: Using the prioritized problems and goals, a contracted plan was initiated with the group, as shown in Table 7.16. As indicated in the diagram, no goals or tasks were specifically planned at this time for problems 4 and 5, because the group didn't want to work on these problems. Since the group gave first priority to the goal of getting off probation, the planned contract centered on this problem. Later, additional tasks were added to the contract for accomplishment of goals 2 and 3 (described in Chapters 8 and 9).

E. Ongoing Evaluation

During the assessment period, as the plan was made to chart progress weekly in the areas required for probation, evaluation graphs (explained in detail in Chapter 10) were designed to show the following: (1) group attendance, (2) group participation, (3) behavior in school (i.e., compliance with rules and expectations), and (4) behavior at home (i.e., compliance with rules and expectations). (See Figures 7.1, 7.2, 7.3, and 7.4.) Assessments of group attendance and participation were first scored by the co-leaders, and eventually by the youths themselves. The home assessments were made by the parents and given weekly over the phone to the social workers. The school evaluation was made weekly by the youths' teachers and given to the school social worker, who had weekly contact with the court workers.

In addition to these weekly assessments, the social workers checked each week to see if any of the group members had been reported to or picked up by police. Any incident was recorded in the youth's record and discussed with the youth individually.

As indicated in Figure 7.1, group attendance was charted by a graph point that indicated the number of the meeting (1, 2, 3, etc.) and an attendance score of 0, 1, or 2. A score of 0 meant "no attendance." A score of 1 was used if a youth came late or left early. A score of 2 meant he was on time and stayed for the full meeting. The youths knew that to get a two-month reduction in probation, they needed to maintain a score of 2 every week unless they were excused by a social worker.

In Figure 7.2, group participation was assessed on a 0–4 vertical scale in terms of 0 = *none*, 1 = *little*, 2 = *some*, 3 = *much*, and 4 = *full*. The points were plotted to indicate (X) the number of the weekly meeting and (Y) the score for participation. An attempt was made to give more specific criteria for participation scores by the leaders. If a youth came and did not seem interested and never said anything at the meetings, he was given a 0. If he spoke at least once or twice at the meeting, he was given a 1. Speaking up about three or four times and being somewhat interested earned a 2. Sharing or responding five or six times and showing much effort at a meeting to participate was a 3, and being fully involved and fully sharing at a meeting was a 4. Group members were informed that they would need to average 3 points in group participation if they were to have a reduced probationary period.

TABLE 7.16 ■ Contracted Plan: Corrections Case

Date Identified	Problem/Need	Goal	Task	Contract	Date Anticipated	Date Accomplished
10/1	1. Law breaking leading to probation	1. To get off probation in four months	1. Attend and participate in weekly group meetings.	1. Seven members, two social workers	10/1 and each Monday at 4:00 P.M. for at least four months	10/1–8/15
			2. Participate in group meetings.	2. Seven members	10/1 and each Monday at 4:00 P.M. for at least four months	
			3. Obey rules of school, home, and community.	3. Seven members	10/1	
			4. Receive weekly reports on behavior from home and school.	4. Social workers, parents, school social workers	Week of 10/1 and once a week for four months	
			5. Chart progress at meetings.	5. Social workers and members	10/22 and at each meeting thereafter	
10/1	2. Bad tempers	2. To control tempers in school, home, and neighborhood	1. Discuss the problem of dealing with anger.	1. Social workers and members	10/22	
10/1	3. Need to understand "changes" of teenagers	3. To learn more about "changes" (including becoming independent, sex and family planning, and job training)	1. Select first topic.	1. Social workers and members	10/22	
10/1	4. Parent-son conflicts					
10/1	5. Low self-worth					

FIGURE 7.1 ■ Group Attendance

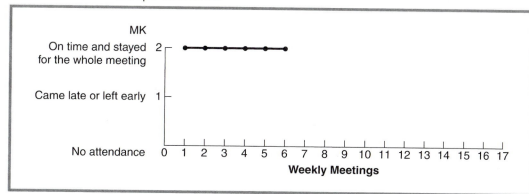

FIGURE 7.2 ■ Group Participation

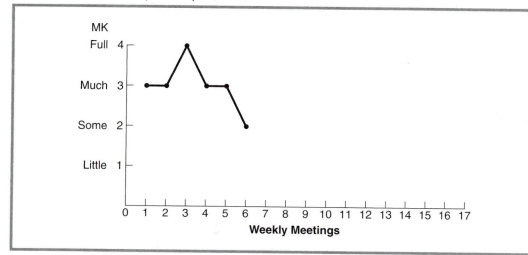

The graphs for charting home and school reports on behavior had scale points ranging from 0 to 4 (0 = *total noncompliance*, 1 = *poor*, 2 = *fair*, 3 = *good*, 4 = *excellent*). The social workers requested descriptions of behaviors and incidents if a youth was assessed by his parent or teacher as showing "poor" or "fair" behavior (Figures 7.3 and 7.4).

VII. Homelessness Case

A. Agency: West End Community Shelter

B. Client System

José Romano, a 37-year-old Hispanic male, is homeless and HIV positive. (For additional background information, see Chapter 5, Ongoing Cases: Engagement Phase, VII. Homelessness Case.)

FIGURE 7.3 ■ School Behavior (Compliance with Rules and Expectations at School)

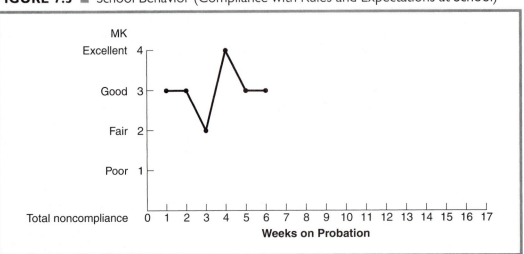

FIGURE 7.4 ■ Home Behavior (Compliance with Rules and Expectations at Home)

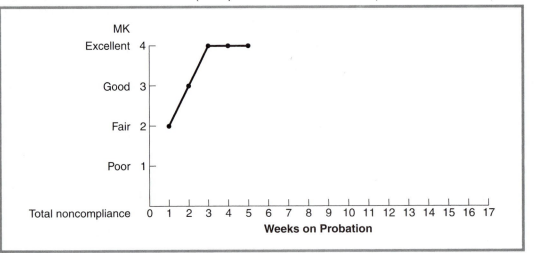

C. Summary of Preceding Phases

During engagement and data collection, the social worker learned that Mr. R completed a drug detoxification program over six years ago. Since that time, he had been living a productive, independent life until he learned that he was HIV positive. At the time of intake, Mr. R was homeless and without any medical care. He had strong feelings of depression and loneliness. In addition to a recognized need for food, shelter, and health care, Mr. R expressed a need for more information about his illness and a desire to return to his church (see Chapter 6). During data collection, the social worker and Mr. R had some success in locating possible resources. These included a local free health clinic, a support system of HIV/AIDS victims, a Catholic church with a large Hispanic Outreach Program, and two residences for individuals with AIDS. They were also exploring possible full- or part-time job opportunities.

D. Assessment

ASSESSMENT STATEMENT: Mr. R is not receiving any health care because he has no money or health insurance and because he is afraid of taking medications due to his past history of drug addiction. His physical condition (HIV positive) is expected to become increasingly worse because he has a progressive terminal illness (currently). Mr. R is homeless and without food because he does not have a job and his financial resources have been depleted. He does not have a job because he left his employment as chef in a nursing home when he learned he was HIV positive, and he has limited occupational skills (cooking and farming). Mr. R is recognizing a spiritual void in his life because he has been thinking about the terminal nature of his illness. He dropped away from church ("and God") as he became involved with drugs.

Although the change potential for Mr. R's illness is low because he has a progressive terminal illness, the social worker assessed a moderate to high change potential in other problem areas because of Mr. R's strong motivation and the number of available resources. Both the social worker and Mr. R recognized that progress in achieving goals was greatly dependent on the extent to which his illness progressed.

PROBLEM PRIORITIZATION: The problems identified in Chapter 6 were prioritized using the problem-prioritization tool as shown in Table 7.17.

TABLE 7.17 ■ Problem Prioritization: Homelessness Case

Problem List	Change-Potential Scores (0–10)			Total Change Potential	Problem Prioritization	Severity
	Problem	Personal Strengths	Environmental Resources			
HIV+	2	4	4	10	6	*
Lack of knowledge re: HIV	8	8	8	24	3	
Homeless/Hungry						
a. Emergency	9	9	9	27	1	
b. After 60 days	5	5	5	15	5	
Unemployment	6	6	6	18	4	
Spiritual Void	8	8	9	25	2	

*Life-at-risk situation.

TABLE 7.18 ■ Contracted Plan: Homelessness Case

Date Identified	Problem/Need	Goal	Task	Contract	Date Anticipated	Date Accomplished
5/7	1. Homeless a. Short term	1. To obtain emergency shelter	1. Enroll in shelter.	1. Mr. R and social worker	5/8	
5/8	2. Spiritual void	2. To reunite with church	1. Go to service.	1. Mr. R	5/10	
5/8	3. Lack of knowledge re: HIV	3. To gain information	1. Review information at shelter.	1. Social worker and Mr. R	5/9	
			2. Go to free clinic and ask for help.	2. Mr. R		
5/8	4. No income/ job	4. To get income	1. Search for job.	1. Mr. R. and social worker	5/9– 5/15	
			2. Apply for job.	2. Mr. R	5/20	
			3. Start job.	3. Mr. R		
			4. Seek SS/ public assistance.	4. Mr. R	Depends on illness	
5/7	5. No housing after 60 days	5. To locate residence	1. Look for apartment or home for AIDS victims.	1. Social worker and Mr. R	5/8	
			2. Get on waiting list of home for persons with AIDS.	2. Mr. R	5/11	
5/8	6. HIV positive	6. To receive medical care	1. Make appointment.	1. Social worker and Mr. R	5/8*	
			2. Go to free clinic.	2. Mr. R	5/9	
			3. Continue treatment.	3. Mr. R	Next appointments	

*Because of the asterisk at problem 6 (life-threatening problem), the worker continued to keep this problem in focus even though the problem has the lowest change potential.

The illness received a score of 2 on the problem prioritization scale. Although there currently is no cure for AIDS or HIV, research continues and medications are available to provide some relief from pain and some delay in disease growth. "Person" (Mr. R) received a 4 due to Mr. R's high motivation, and "environment" received a 4 because of the availability of the health clinic. The change potential for "lack of knowledge" received a high score (8) because of the increasing amount of information available about the disease, particularly at the free clinic. The shelter could provide immediate shelter and food (total of 27), but, after 60 days, Mr. R would need to go to one of the residences for AIDS patients or find another location (15). Finding a job for Mr. R was seen as possible, since he was highly motivated with a good work history, and currently his illness was not too severe to prevent at least part-time employment. It was also possible that if Mr. R's health did become worse, he could start to receive public assistance and social security (rated a total of 18). Having Mr. R return to church was highly rated, since he was very anxious to go to the church in town where he could be with people of his native culture (25).

CONTRACTING: After prioritizing the problems, Mr. R and the social worker developed a contracted plan of action (see Table 7.18).

E. Charted Progress

Mr. R's progress in the problem-solving process was summarized in ongoing summary recordings. The problem-prioritization tool and the contracted plan developed during assessment were placed in his record for additional information and ongoing indication of progress. A copy of the planned contract was given to Mr. R to remind him of the goals, tasks, and dates he and the worker decided on.

SUMMARY

In this chapter, the assessment and contract planning phase of the General Method was described as consisting of the three major dimensions of (1) assessment statement, (2) problem prioritization, and (3) contracted plan. Tools were presented to assist the general practitioner in this phase of the General Method.

A point emphasized in this chapter is the need for documented assessments and contract plans for each case before a social worker takes action. Even when working with a crisis, the social worker needs to demonstrate skill in planning where, when, and how to intervene. Through practice and supervised experience, the generalist practitioner learns to apply the tools in the process of assessment very quickly and accurately.

The Generalist Method and each of its phases is a dynamic process. As circumstances change, the social worker needs to be open to the possibility of having to reassess a situation or to reformulate a contract. There has been an indication that some social workers resist finding out new information that would necessitate a reformulation of goals and plans. A major challenge of general practice is to be able to stand on a diversified but solid foundation where one is expected to demonstrate flexibility and adaptation to emerging tensions, growth, and change.

Although the range of tasks and interventions by a generalist appears to be limitless, some parameters and guidelines need to be identified. An entry-level social worker does have limitations in knowledge and skills. A skillful assessment may lead to a plan for referral to a specialized service. In the next chapters, an effort will be made to clarify the interventions of a generalist practitioner during the fourth phase of the Generalist Method. In the intervention phase, the social worker collaborates with other resources and service systems in carrying out the plan that was contracted during assessment.

REFLECTION POINTS

Becoming a skilled social work practitioner requires knowledge and skills, including the ability to reflect on practice endeavors. The following reflection points are designed to strengthen critical thinking and mastery of knowledge of key points in this chapter.

1. Define the following key concepts in generalist social work:
   - Goal analysis
   - Contract review and reformulation
   - Evaluation questions
   - Ongoing evaluation
2. How might each of these concepts influence your professional behavior in practice with client, action, and target systems at micro, mezzo, and macro levels of practice?
3. Select two case examples presented in this chapter and develop alternative evaluations of client outcomes using the tenets of evidence-based practice (Chapter 3). Provide examples of the evidence-based questions used in evaluating the outcomes.
4. How might human diversity influence practice evaluation at different levels of practice?
5. Review Section 5.02, Evaluation and Research, of the *NASW Code of Ethics* (www.socialworkers.org). How might these standards influence professional behavior?
6. For further reading and research, use the concepts in Question 1 to locate social work references related to this chapter's content. (See Appendix A, Selected Internet Resources, and Appendix B, Selected Social Work Journals.) What underlying theoretical concepts are evident in the articles? How are they applied in the articles? How might they be applied in one of the seven ongoing cases in this chapter or in a case in your field internship?

Intervention in Micro and Mezzo Generalist Practice

The strengths-based problem-solving processes and strategies of direct intervention with micro and mezzo client systems form several practice models within the General Method. Each model is designed to address particular problems and needs, goals, and contracted plans with micro and mezzo client systems. This chapter focuses on five General Method intervention models that are primarily applicable at micro and mezzo practice levels: counseling with individuals and families, information and referral, crisis intervention, small group intervention, and case management and teamwork.

Overview

The goal of social work intervention with micro and mezzo client systems is to facilitate empowerment transactions between client systems and their environments. More specifically, the goal is to enable people to overcome those conditions that keep them from participating in the benefits of society and to find ways of meeting their needs so that they may develop and function within their environment to the best of their potential. Facilitating a client system's ability to engage in empowerment transactions with their environment involves:

▶ Strengthening the client system's attitudes and beliefs about their efficacy in taking action
▶ Developing the client system's ability to think critically about its world
▶ Facilitating acquisition of the knowledge and skills needed to take action
▶ Facilitating development and availability of support and mutual aid systems
▶ Developing the client system's ability to take action that leads to change in the face of impinging problems (Saleebey, 1997)

To achieve the goal of client system empowerment, the generalist social worker stands at the interface of client systems and their environments and carefully tries to collaborate with both in a planned change process that enhances their fit and interaction with each other. Thus, the role of the social worker during the intervention phase of the General Method evolves according to the principles of empowerment through the goals and tasks identified in the contracted plan described in the previous chapter.

■ CONCEPT 8.1

Empowerment is a generative process through which the disenfranchised and vulnerable are enabled to (1) mobilize personal, familial, organizational, and community resources; (2) exercise greater control over their environment; and (3) meet their needs and attain their aspirations (Cowger, 1997; Pinderhughes, 1995; see Chapter 1).

Because power is a critical component in any client system functioning, empowerment is a key process in planning interventive strategy (Maluccio, 1981). Social work intervention takes place in the transactions between individual client systems and their environments. The power differential between individual client systems and environmental systems is often so great that individual client systems sometimes cannot perceive themselves as competent to take action on their own behalf. This marginalized status may increase from being perceived and labeled by others as simply different to being perceived and labeled as deviant and devalued by society.

When planning an intervention, seven interrelated practice components must be present for the intervention to contribute to the empowerment of client systems (Parsons, Jorgensen, & Hernandez, 1994):

▶ Power-shared relationship
▶ Competency-based assessment
▶ Normalization
▶ Collectivity for mutual aid
▶ Critical thinking and problem solving
▶ Knowledge and skills for finding resources
▶ Skills for taking action

In a *power-shared relationship*, client systems are viewed as having equal and legitimate expertise in relation to their own problems and solutions. Being able to accept clients' definitions of their own problems is a critical part of empowerment practice (Gutierrez, 1990). Although the generalist social worker brings expertise about social problems, problem definitions, assessment, goal setting, planning, contract setting, and intervening to the collaborative process, client systems generally know what they need and, with heightened self-awareness and support, are able to choose a good alternative for action on their own behalf. They are competent to identify and understand their problems and to choose adequate solutions.

To understand client systems' strengths and coping skills rather than their weaknesses and deficits in coping, the social worker needs to uncover their motivation, capacity, and opportunities for change (Maluccio, 1981). To plan an intervention that will empower the client system, the social worker and the client system engage in a *competency-based assessment,* or power analysis, which examines the conditions of powerlessness affecting the presenting situation, the power resources, and the effects of the social-structural context (Gutierrez, 1990). Specifically, the generalist practitioner looks for the client system's desire, perceived hope, belief that change can come about, knowledge and skills for making change, and environmental impingements that may facilitate or hinder change.

The development in client systems from powerlessness to personal autonomy and from alienation to interdependent mutual aid and personal or political power requires a blending of action, reflection, and consideration of environment. The screen of *normalization* implies viewing the client systems' problems in terms of the environmental context, cultural conventions and values, and purposefulness of behavior. The idea of building *collectivity for mutual aid* is inherent in this helping process. Collectivity offers clients an opportunity to interact with other people who have similar problems and concerns and to receive validation from others in their situation. Through mutual collective aid, for example, parents gain the support to act on their own behalf as well as learn to solve parenting problems and develop new ways of coping with child-rearing issues.

Dialogue, interaction, and education with others in similar circumstances help client systems develop critical consciousness regarding their own subjective conditions and problems. Acquisition of knowledge and skills for common problem solving most often occurs through the group process (Gutierrez, 1990). Gaining specific information regarding the problem at hand as well as the *skills for taking action* are important parts of empowerment. For example, when working with client systems struggling with chronic illness, dialogue around the illness condition and health needs can provide an opportunity for individuals to tell their stories to people who understand their plight, listen to others, find out about resources, discuss ways of coping with the condition and general life stress, or share skills and understanding. Specifically and most importantly, chronically ill persons and their support systems receive a critical education by expanding their understanding of their own personal and collective problems from an inward context to a broader collective socio-environmental context and back to a focus on self and how to cope. Acquisition of critical thinking skills, knowledge regarding resources, and skills for taking action are necessary components of successful living.

When a social worker, in agreement with a micro or mezzo client system, intervenes directly with the client system, that social worker is engaging in *direct intervention*. The goal of direct intervention is to promote client system empowerment through the objectives of:

1. Educating the client system about resources, critical problem-solving, and skills for taking action
2. Providing support as the client system carries out contracted tasks
3. Creating opportunities for the client system to be successful in strengths-based problem-solving and become empowered
4. Assisting the client system to bring about planned change
5. Creating opportunities for the client system to gain mutual collective aid

■ CONCEPT 8.2

> *Counseling* is the professional application of generalist social work methods to client system problems in psychosocial functioning that arise out of a disequilibrium in transactions between person and environment.

Counseling with Individual and Family Client Systems

Counseling that directly involves an individual or family client system and a social work generalist may be brief or extended, depending on the identified need or problem and the strengths and coping capacities of the client system. In counseling, strengths-based problem-solving takes the form of dialogue, questions, actions, and transactions that guide client systems through the change process and facilitate:

▶ Resolution of problems or issues and mitigation of their effects
▶ Acquisition of internal personal resources and external environmental resources
▶ Development of affective coping and adaptation
▶ Enhancement of well-being

The extent of direction or leadership offered by the social worker in counseling is influenced also by the seriousness of the situation and by the strengths and coping capacities of the client system. The nature of the counseling interaction promotes growth and encourages the client system in self-direction as much as possible without creating harm to the well-being of the client system.

The generalist uses a broad range of relationship and strengths-based problem-solving processes and strategies in the course of intervening with members of a client system. The relationship itself is central to the entire process. Particularly in the intervention phase, a strong working relationship is necessary. During the course of the counseling, the social worker may use the processes, strategies, and skills of listening, responding, guiding, paraphrasing, clarifying feelings, sensing, and, possibly, confronting. In addition, the strengths-based problem-solving processes of problem and need identification, data collection, assessment, problem prioritization, goal setting, planning, contract setting, and evaluating may be repeated as problems are added or changed.

A client system may begin with identifying immediate material needs or problems with institutions. As a working relationship develops and the social worker is able to help with the presenting problems and needs, client systems frequently begin to discuss more interpersonal or personal problems. Information is gathered and assessments are made regarding each of these problems. The social worker and client system may agree to tasks in the contracted plan that entail direct, ongoing counseling contact between social worker and client system. This contact may be seen as a means for the client system to achieve greater understanding of self and others or to bring about a change in self. If the goal identified is to bring about a change in someone outside of the client system, the intervention will need to include the outsider directly (becoming a part of the client system) or indirectly (becoming a target system). For example, if Mrs. N wants her husband to overcome his drinking problem, there is little chance of accomplishing this goal by counseling only with Mrs. N.

In addition to the foundation skills identified in Chapter 1, contemporary strategies and techniques are used in counseling with particular client systems. For example, eco-maps (Hartman & Laird, 1983), sculpting (Bardill, 1997), and genograms (McGoldrick, Giordano, & Pearce, 1996) are valuable tools to use when working with a family. They provide a technical and vivid means for helping clients understand diverse perceptions of the family. These techniques may also be adapted for use in working with individuals, groups, and communities.

For working with groups, techniques and concepts have been identified to enable a social worker to handle disruptive behavior (Brown, 1992) and scapegoating (Worden, 1999). The use of force-field analysis (Brueggeman, 1996; Lewin, 1951) helps a social worker pinpoint the supportive and the constraining forces that have impact on the life and growth of a family, group, or organization. Techniques to handle disruptive behavior and prevent scapegoating may be adapted for use with individuals and families as well as organizations and communities.

For working with adolescents, an effective technique to promote greater self-awareness is the use of the adolescent grid (Anderson & Brown, 1980). By recalling major events within a visible framework, the adolescent can avoid the discomfort often felt in face-to-face interviewing. The grid identifies crisis points chronologically, according to place, family, school, health, activities, and other areas. Adults or children, individuals, groups, or families may also find that this structured instrument is a helpful device for overcoming their fears of interacting with a social worker.

As a social worker counsels any person, family, or group, it may become clear that giving support or understanding is insufficient to achieve certain goals. For a change to take place in a client system, the social worker may use some techniques from behavioral modification, as well as strengths-based problem-solving skills. In addition to helping a client system develop a rational, systematic way to solve problems, a social worker may use specific behavioral techniques for more immediate control of undesirable behaviors, thoughts, or feelings. Although behavior modification in its entirety is a specialized treatment approach, individual learning techniques such as behavior reinforcement, cognitive restructuring, relaxation exercises, and thought stopping can be selected for use in generalist practice (Doyle, 1998).

All of the contemporary techniques that have been cited are supplementary to the basic skills identified in the foundation of generalist practice (Chapter 1). Eco-maps, genograms, techniques for handling disruptive behavior and scapegoating, force-field analysis, the adolescent grid, behavior reinforcement, cognitive restructuring, relaxation exercises, and thought stopping are among the tools that enable a client system to grow in understanding. They facilitate change in a client system by helping to clarify, objectify, and promote greater control of self or a situation.

There are times when it becomes clear that a client system needs to change through gaining personal understanding. If General Method counseling is insufficient to bring about the change necessary for goal achievement, the social work generalist has to be able to realize that a client system may need more intensive help to overcome its problematic behavior. For the individual, family, or group, this could involve delving into buried feelings or past experiences over a prolonged period. In time, the client system can be helped to connect current behaviors with feelings that are triggered by certain situations that relate to past experiences. Barriers and dynamics that create conflict and broken relationships can be exposed. Through this intensive work, the client system may be freed to choose more acceptable behaviors in the future.

However, this intensive counseling work is not within the parameters of entry-level generalist social work practice. Occasionally, a client system may come with enough strengths or past experiences to be able to grow in such insight with support from the generalist practitioner. Usually, however, the generalist brings the client system with this type of need to the point of realizing that more specialized help is needed. They then enter into the process of referral. Whether the client system is an individual, family, or group, there are times when the generalist social worker is unable to help the client system bring about the change needed through counseling, and a referral is made.

■ CONCEPT 8.3

Information and referral is the professional application of generalist social work methods to client system problems that arise out of inadequate knowledge about or linkage with environmental resources.

Information and Referral

At times, it becomes apparent that a client system does not have the information needed for problem resolution. Often, client systems have received misinformation or they have misconceptions about environmental resources. They may contact a social worker to receive assistance that the social worker or agency may not be able to provide. In these cases, the social worker's intervention is primarily that of information and referral.

The process in which a social worker directs a system to another resource for help with an identified problem or need is called *referral*. In referring client systems, the social worker should be guided by the principles of least restrictive environment, normalization, empowerment, and self-determination. These principles suggest that the more informal network systems of help, including mutual-aid and self-help groups, be explored before seeking help from formal helping organizations. Referral and linkage of client systems with informal and formal helping systems is done under the assumption that client systems may seek out additional resources or help on their own. Often, social workers are surprised to learn that a resource has not picked up on a case as expected. Several factors can lead to an unsuccessful referral. There is, in fact, an art to knowing where, when, and how to make a referral. Time, planning, and processing are needed for an appropriate match between the client system in need and an available resource. The act of referral contains six tasks. If any one is overlooked, the referral may fail. The experience of an unsuccessful referral may build up in the client system feelings of negativism and fear, as well as resistance to reaching out and trying again with another resource. The referral tasks include:

1. Clarifying and explicitly stating the problem or need for which help is sought and the goals to be accomplished
2. Researching appropriate and available resources and informing the client system about them
3. Discussing options and selecting resources with the client system in need
4. Planning and contracting the means of contact with the selected resource (initial contact, sending information, providing transportation, client-resource meeting)
5. Meeting of the client system with the resource
6. Following up by the social worker to see if the goal is being or has been accomplished

The basic principle of having the client system do for itself is paramount throughout the referral process. Only when it is clear that the client system does not have the knowledge or ability to carry out a task in the process should the social worker intervene and take action.

In referral task 1, the generalist helps the client system clarify what the problem or need is that cannot be taken care of by the generalist practitioner. The feelings and goals that relate directly to the identified problem or need are also expressed. The feelings both client system and social worker may have about sending the client system to a different resource need to be expressed. Either one might see a referral as a personal failure and feel somewhat guilty. The limitations of the social worker and/or the agency in relation to the problem, need, and goal should be presented as factually as possible. The client system should be reassured that the referral is not a rejection by the social worker. The social worker conveys to the client system a sincere desire to see the client system achieve its goals and a strong belief in the ability of a resource to make this possible.

In referral task 2, the social worker and, if possible, the client system work on locating resources to meet the identified needs and goals. Both formal and informal resources are explored. If a need or problem can be resolved through utilizing informal resources (family, friends, community), this may be more desirable to the client system. Some may prefer not to have these local support networks know about their problem, and formal resources (agencies, programs, institutions) will need to be considered.

It is imperative to find resources that are appropriate, available, and acceptable. A resource is appropriate not only because it provides services that address the identified problem or need but also because it suits the persons and environment of the particular system in need. For example, a person who speaks only Spanish could best receive help from a social worker who understands and works with Hispanic people. Further, if the resource is not accessible to people from the neighborhood or environment of the client system, it is usually not an appropriate resource. If contact with the resource is expected to be brief and transportation can be assured, it is possible to use a resource that is not located near the environment of the client system. Sometimes, however, social workers incorrectly assume that client systems are able to find bus fare or transportation on their own.

Agency resources may not be available for certain clients, given the hours when services are provided. Although a resource may be appropriate, it may have a long waiting list because of an insufficient number of staff members available to deliver the services. Moreover, the cost for the service may be outside the price range of some clients and therefore the resource is not available to them.

In referral task 3, the social worker and the client system share their findings about possible resources, but the client system is the one to choose the resource to be contacted. The social worker helps the client system consider alternatives, with probable outcomes or consequences for each option. If there is some question or doubt about a resource, this should be explored. No false hope or reassurance should be given. Even when it appears that an appropriate and available resource has been located and selected, it may prove beneficial to help the client system identify a second choice in case the first does not work out.

In referral task 4, time is given for planning and contracting to decide who will:

▶ Make the initial contact with the resource (usually by phone)
▶ Give whatever information is necessary for the referral to be accepted
▶ Arrange for transportation or provide it
▶ Meet with the resource to initiate the services

A whole range of possible ways exist to achieve each of these four activities. The two extremes on a scale to indicate the range of options would be (1) the client system carrying out the activity and (2) the social worker carrying it out. In between are different social worker–client system combinations for which the activity may be subdivided. For example, in the first activity of initial contact, the social worker could (1) dial the number and have the client speak; (2) dial and speak first and then put the client on the phone; (3) have the client dial, but the social worker speaks; (4) have a three-way conference call in which social worker, client system, and resource person all speak together. The initial contact might also involve writing a letter or going to the agency to set up an appointment. These activities also could be done by the social worker, by the client system, or by some combination. The same range of options exists for deciding about giving information, arranging transportation, and having the first client system-resource meeting. The guiding principle of having the members of the client system do for themselves whenever possible should be used as the contract is formulated and tasks are planned.

In referral task 5, the new helping process begins as the client system meets directly with the resource. Here, too, the art of referral operates in the social worker's careful assessment of whether the client system can or should have the first session alone with the resource. The social worker considers not only the motivation and capacity of the client system to have this be a fruitful encounter but also the capacity of the resource itself to be of help to the system in need. In some individual situations, it may be better to have the social worker present in the first contact to offer support, information, or advocacy if needed. As soon as possible, however, the social worker should back out and let the client system become involved with the resource on its own.

Finally (referral task 6), every referral should have some type of follow-up by the social worker. When a person, family, or group comes to a professional person or agency for help, they share—sometimes painfully—their problems, needs, and aspirations. The professional person and human service agency show a sense of respect and commitment to people in need by working diligently at getting the necessary help for them. People asking for help are often vulnerable and dependent on the expertise and sensitivity of those sanctioned to give service. Social workers are expected to know what resources are available and how to help people utilize them. It is true that many times circumstances outside of the control of a social worker or agency prevent a service from being carried out. However, the social worker must find out if the person who asked for help did receive it. If the person did not receive help, the social worker needs to find out why help was not given and to consider whether anything else could have been done.

The social worker finds out if help was provided by checking directly with the resource, with the client system, or with both. It is important that both the resource and the client system know that the social worker will be calling back, and when to expect the follow-up. This should be clarified prior to the social worker's last contact with each. In planning, the social worker will skillfully discern what a follow-up contact with the client system might do to the beginning working relationship of the client system and the new resource. The social worker will also need to consider what effect it might have on the client system to hear that the social worker called the resource to see how things were going. Negative repercussions will be avoided as long as all three parties (social worker, client system, and resource system) know in advance that the social worker will be doing a follow-up and it is clear who will be contacted and when.

When it appears that the goals for the referral are being accomplished, the social worker is able to close the case. If there are other problems or needs that are not being addressed by the resource, and the client system continues to ask for the services of the social worker, a collaborative arrangement must be worked out between the resource and the social worker. Using a holistic perspective, the generalist knows that problems and needs of a client system are interdependent, and that when service provision is carried out by more than one resource, collaboration and teamwork among the resources are needed.

■ CONCEPT 8.4

> *Crisis intervention* is the brief professional application of social work generalist methods to acute client system problems in psychosocial functioning arising from stressful events perceived as threats to well-being.

Crisis Intervention

At times, persons may perceive and respond to a life event as an overwhelming and debilitating situation or crisis. Examples of such life crisis events include:

1. Environmental events
   - Natural disasters triggered by wind, fire, flood, and drought
   - Person-made disasters such as war, terrorism, forced migration, famine, and health epidemics
2. Situational events
   - Human loss experiences such as death of a family member or significant other, break-up of a family, loss of a job, moving from place to place
3. Developmental events
   - Interference with achieving developmental life tasks
   - Experiences representing life transitions such as graduations, marriage, birth of a child, birthdays, anniversaries, cultural celebrations

It is, however, important to underline that it is the personal meaning of a particular event that determines whether or not the event is perceived as a critical threat to well-being and triggers a crisis state. Meanings that transform life events into life crises include:

- ▶ Threats to life and limb
- ▶ Threats to the security of a known way of life
- ▶ Threatened loss of significant persons, places, or activities
- ▶ Threats and challenges inherent in new life stage developmental experiences

The initial personal response to a crisis event is likely to be disorganization, blocking or stopping thoughts about the impact of the event, and emotional numbing (James & Gilliland, 2004; Parad & Parad, 1990; Slakieu, 1990). Involuntary flooding of the client system with feelings, thoughts, and images about the trigger event follows the initial response. These *blocking* and *flooding responses* are apparent in affect, thoughts, and behaviors including:

▶ Tension, anxiety, confusion, helplessness, tiredness, and physical complaints
▶ Psychosocial dysfunction in work, family, social relationships, and activities

The next personal response involves *mobilizing strengths and resources* for coping and problem-solving. It includes taking stock of the situation, identifying resources and barriers, strengths-based problem-solving, and working through feelings, thoughts, and images related to the crisis event. This mobilization of strengths and resources takes into account that the person's customary methods of problem-solving and coping are unable to handle the temporary disorganization and flooding of the crisis event. It also involves acknowledging that this temporary inability creates both vulnerability in psychosocial functioning and opportunity for adaptive change and growth. It is important to note that this opportunity is mediated by the severity of the trigger event, personal strengths and problem-solving resources, and the availability of social supports and environmental resources (Parad & Parad, 1990; Slakieu, 1990). Possible outcomes include:

▶ Growth in adaptive psychosocial functioning and problem-solving
▶ Return to the previous level of psychosocial functioning and problem-solving
▶ Development of psychosocial dysfunction

Some persons do not have the strengths and resources to handle crisis events without professional help. In these instances, generalist social workers engage them as client systems and quickly assess problems, needs, current psychosocial functioning, personal strengths and resources, and social support resources. In view of the stressful and temporary nature of life crisis events, crisis intervention services are best delivered immediately for a brief period of time. There are four major service goals:

1. To alleviate the stressful impact of the crisis event
2. To mobilize client system strengths and resources
3. To enable the client system to develop strengths-based problem-solving skills
4. To enable the client system to achieve equilibrium in psychosocial functioning and begin to integrate the crisis experience

The multiple processes, strategies, and tasks involved in implementing these goals vary with the nature of the crisis event, client system strengths and resources, and the availability of environmental resources. For example, in the face of natural and person-made disasters, alleviating the stressful impact of the crisis event with client systems includes identifying and providing for immediate material needs and provision of concurrent emotional support. Since service delivery is often beyond the scope of one agency, advocacy, service mobilization, and interagency coordination and collaboration become important initial tasks for the generalist social worker. In addition, the social worker provides emotional support and explores with the client system: *Who is available to provide material and emotional support? What kind of support? For how long?* Such exploration focuses the client system on mobilizing available resources, identifies resource gaps, and identifies the possibility of referral to supplemental support services. The answers to these questions and assessment of the client system's current psychosocial functioning and assets will also suggest whether a facilitative or more directive approach may be needed for resource mobilization, emotional support, and reactivation of strengths-based problem-solving capabilities.

Client systems experiencing situational loss and developmental events typically require less immediate material assistance. Generally, they need initial emotional support and clarification to alleviate the stress and mobilize their strengths and resources. The generalist social worker provides emotional support by helping the client system feel acceptance, giving permission to reflect on the personal meaning of the event and the associated stress, and providing encouragement to express feelings and reactions.

Enabling client systems to develop strengths-based problem-solving skills first involves reactivating and assessing general problem-solving capabilities and prior efforts to cope with the current crisis event. Next, the social worker and the client system partialize problems and needs triggered by the crisis event and consider possible alternative solutions. To achieve the selected solution, they identify concrete actions to be taken by the client system. When possible, the social worker assumes a facilitative stance in this process. If the client system appears unable to act, the social worker becomes more directive and takes action along with the client system. When the client system begins to implement assigned tasks, the social worker returns to a more facilitative stance.

■ CONCEPT 8.5

Small group intervention is the professional application of generalist social work methods through group process designed to meet members' needs, resolve targeted problems in psychosocial functioning, and complete specified tasks.

Small Group Intervention

Small group intervention in the General Method includes task groups and psychosocial intervention groups. Depending on their purpose and goals, these groups may have brief or extended time frames and open or closed memberships.

Task Groups

Social work generalists often work with small collectivities of persons drawn together by mutual concerns and interested in accomplishing specific tasks. The goals, forms, and outcomes of these task groups include:

- ▶ *Individual goal:* Identify and plan ways to meet the needs of client systems. *Forms:* Case conferences, team meetings. *Outcome:* Coordinated client system case plans
- ▶ *Organizational goal:* Identify and plan ways to address organizational needs and issues. *Forms:* Staff meetings, committees, boards. *Outcome:* Reports documenting organizational needs, issues, and proposed solutions
- ▶ *Community goal:* Identify and plan ways to address the needs and social concerns of the community. *Forms:* Citizen coalitions, delegate councils, neighborhood advisory committees. *Outcomes:* Reports documenting community needs and social concerns and recommending service delivery policies and plans; political platform statements with proposals for influencing legislation

During the intervention process, task groups move through five developmental phases (Anderson, 1997; Brown, 1991; Garvin, Galinsky, & Gutierrez, 2004):

1. *Phase 1—Orientation:* As leader, the social worker orients members to the group's purpose and task, enables members to provide relevant information, and elicits group discussion and consensus about the designated task. The social worker enables the group to develop task-related goals, activities, a plan, and a time frame for task achievement.
2. *Phase 2—Accommodation of group members to each other:* As leader, the social worker facilitates communication, elicits comments and ideas, and enables the group to establish parameters, norms, tasks, and time frames for task achievement.
3. *Phase 3—Generation of ideas about needs and solutions:* As leader, the social worker facilitates open communication, supports sharing, and stimulates development of alternative ideas and solutions. As necessary to expedite group process, the social worker provides feedback about what is occurring in the group, helps the group clarify points of confusion, and enables the group to focus on the task.
4. *Phase 4—Integrative problem-solving:* As leader, the social worker builds the capacity of the group as a whole for pulling together the disparate ideas generated and engaging in integrative, strengths-based problem-solving and planning. The social worker mobilizes the group to clarify alternative ideas and solutions, overcome barriers to goal achievement, and address nonproductive behavior patterns.
5. *Phase 5—Task completion:* As leader, the social worker enables the group to sustain the task focus, contribute to task completion, and finish the product in timely fashion.

Psychosocial Intervention Groups

In psychosocial intervention groups, the focus is on enabling members to benefit from the group. The goals and forms of the groups include:

- ▶ *Goal:* Educate members about persons, issues, or topics. *Form:* Educational groups. *Outcome:* Increased knowledge and skill learning
- ▶ *Goal:* Enable members to acquire social skills, increase self-confidence, and invest energy in socially approved venues. *Forms:* Social skills groups, socialization groups. *Outcome:* Interaction and networking skills and confidence
- ▶ *Goal:* Enable members to provide each other with mutual support, encouragement, information, and shared problem-solving about common concerns, issues, and needs. *Forms:* Social support groups, self-help groups. *Outcome:* Successful coping with distressful experiences
- ▶ *Goal:* Enable members to build on their strengths, attain their potential, and achieve their personal goals. *Form:* Personal growth and well-being groups. *Outcome:* Personal growth and sense of personal competence
- ▶ *Goal:* Enable members to change troubling behavior, address issues of concern, meet needs, engage in strengths-based problem-solving, and develop more adaptive coping strategies. *Form:* Treatment groups. *Outcome:* Personal growth and behavioral change

In these groups, the leadership style is an enabling one that involves seeing that decisions are made by the group, not the social work practitioner, and seeing that the group knows what and how it is doing. Depending on the group's goal and form, the social work leader selects from the following practice principles to facilitate group dynamics and actualize group functioning (Anderson, 1997; Toseland & Rivas, 2005):

1. *Physical environment and emotional climate*
   - Sustain a comfortable physical environment as well as supportive emotional climate.
   - Interpret agency function and leadership in relation to the group's goal.
   - Build a cooperative group climate with shared group goals.
   - Model principles of inclusion and trust.
2. *Group communication patterns and culture*
   - Assess and interpret verbal and nonverbal communication patterns.
   - Enable the group to seek clarification so all points of view are understood.
   - Educate members about providing and receiving feedback.
   - Facilitate the group's clarification of verbal and nonverbal communications.
   - Attend to group power relationships and emotional bonds as needed.
   - Facilitate open, group-centered communication.
   - Facilitate the development of a group culture and functioning style.
   - Discourage overdependence of members on the group leader.

3. *Group interaction and cohesion*
   - Sustain group interaction and cohesion.
   - Acknowledge members' needs for affiliation and recognition.
   - Clarify expectations of positive and negative consequences of membership.
   - Promote sense of competence and confidence.
   - Promote the group's willingness to take responsibility for the maintenance, functioning, and goal attainment of the group.
   - Define conflict as belonging to the group and conflict resolution as the responsibility of the group.
   - Model mutual respect and acceptance of group differences and commonalities.
   - Mobilize strengths-based problem-solving efforts by the group.
4. *Social control*
   - Facilitate the development of appropriate norms and social control mechanisms to enable the group to function appropriately.
   - Enable the group to limit the participation of overly assertive members.
   - Limit behavior harmful to members and destructive to the environment.
   - Make expected ways of behaving explicit.
   - Encourage civility in discussion, sharing, agreements, and disagreements.
5. *Monitoring group process and progress*
   - Enhance the capacity of the group to observe and analyze processes and monitor progress in order to understand and share what is happening and why.

During the intervention process, psychosocial intervention groups move through five developmental phases (Toseland & Rivas, 2005):

1. *Phase 1—Orientation:* Members engage and make an initial commitment to the group and its goals. Patterns of functioning develop around orientation issues, belonging and dependency concerns, and the mutual needs of group members.
2. *Phase 2—Authority:* Members challenge the group's influence, power, and control. They compete and search for individual autonomy. Norms and values develop.
3. *Phase 3—Negotiation:* Members engage in conflict resolution. They design and adopt goals, roles, and tasks. Personal involvement and group cohesion intensify.
4. *Phase 4—Integration:* Members become part of a whole with reciprocal ways of functioning. Communication is more open. Diversity is more respected. Strengths-based problem-solving capacity develops.
5. *Phase 5—Disintegration:* The group bond lessens as does group influence on members. (See Chapter 11, Termination.)

■ **C O N C E P T 8 . 6**

Case management is the professional application of generalist social work methods to mobilize a comprehensive array of services that meet client system needs and facilitate client system psychosocial functioning. As an action system, *teamwork* involves mobilizing and collaborating with the various service providers needed.

Case Management and Teamwork

Problems and issues that client systems face often represent a combination of many forces impinging on the client system prior to the system seeking help. Thus, the solution to client system problems may necessitate that the problems be seen and addressed in the context of more than one level of intervention (micro, mezzo, and macro), outreach on behalf of the client system, and collaboration with other service provider resources. The generalist social worker has skills to form action systems with other resource persons in a cooperative effort to achieve their common purpose of providing human services.

Case management is a contemporary term that is used to refer to the actions taken by a social worker to mobilize and to bring together the various services and resources needed in a case for effective, efficient service delivery. A case manager:

► Aims to ensure a continuum of care to client systems with complex, multiple problems and disabilities
► Attempts to intervene clinically to ameliorate the emotional problems accompanying illness or loss of function
► Utilizes social work skills of collaborating, promoting teamwork, brokering, negotiating, mediating, and advocating as a boundary approach to service delivery (Vourlekis & Greene, 1992)

Specifically, a case manager aims to provide services in the context of the client system's least restrictive setting while promoting client system self-determination and normalization. In other words, case management focuses on linking client systems to the best services that will provide the most appropriate and most cost-effective help. Thus, the goals of case management include providing access and linkage to services, case coordination with client systems, and, at times, outreach on a client system's behalf. In achieving these goals, the social work case manager asks:

► *How do we best assess, monitor, and evaluate client system needs?*
► *What are the least restrictive and most empowering services possible?*
► *What is the least restrictive and most empowering path linking client systems with resources appropriate for meeting their needs?*
► *Which action systems possess the power for ensuring adequate service delivery?*
► *Which action system has the knowledge and resource capacity to oversee and assess whether utilized services have beneficial outcomes?*
► *What commitment of time and resources among community action systems is necessary to assure that client system's needs are likely to be met?*
► *What commitment and capacity by the social work case manager is necessary to ensure that selected services produce beneficial outcomes?*

Client systems receive case management services from a variety of sources. For example, state public social service sectors use case management to provide early intervention programs, foster care, child protective services, TANF, child care, housing, food distribution, employment, and job training. The criminal justice system uses case management in prisons, halfway houses, and program alternatives to incarceration. Mental health and health settings use case management to augment clinical social work, nursing, medical, and psychiatric services. Case management programs are used for the elderly and individuals who are developmentally disabled or chronically ill. Even agencies that do not identify their programs and services as including case management often assume that social workers will integrate case management knowledge and skills into their practice.

In order to function effectively as a case manager, the generalist social worker needs to possess knowledge of various service systems and the needs and functioning of client systems. In addition, the social work case manager must engage client systems in assessing their needs and environmental situation so that both can agree about what is to be done, by whom, when, and for which client goal. In addition, the social work case manager must have sufficient capacity, power, and authority to facilitate results and mitigate inefficiencies in service outcomes (Rubin, 1992). Therefore, case management functions include (Rose & Moore, 1995):

▶ Assessment of client system needs in relation to environmental challenges
▶ Assessment of the informal and formal social support available and accessible
▶ Identification of resources within the formal system of care
▶ Enabling and empowering client systems to use personal resources in meeting environmental challenges
▶ Enabling families and other primary groups to expand their caregiving capacity
▶ Facilitating effective negotiations for resources
▶ Facilitating effective interchanges between client systems and formal care systems
▶ Evaluating the extent to which client systems become integrated into naturally existing informal and formal systems of care

Although case management is viewed as a process of service coordination, accountability, and a method of ensuring a client system's right to service, its hallmark feature is to hold the social worker in the case management role responsible for overcoming fragmentation in the service delivery system. When identified as the case manager, the generalist social worker must use skill to work with the various resources for a case to develop an atmosphere of shared leadership and openness. When diverse resources work together in common planning, decision making, and consolidated action, the efforts of this organized group may be called *teamwork*. Unless the service providers who are working with one client system move to become a team, the generalist social worker may carry the heavy burden not only of managing the case but also of being seen as primarily responsible for its outcome. When resources truly become a team, there is a strong sense of sharing and commitment and of a group responsibility for final outcome.

Within case management, the aim of *multidisciplinary collaboration* is coordinated and integrated service delivery across education, health, and social services. Achieving this teamwork aim requires participating professionals from multiple disciplines to take an active role in blending not only the organizational purpose, policies, and procedures of their agencies but also their own diverse professional values, knowledge base, perspectives, and intervention approaches in the interest of promoting client service. The case management function of bridging organizational and professional boundaries and building well-functioning multidisciplinary teams is a complex effort that is well guided by the principles and practices of collaboration (Sabatino, 1999) and negotiation.

To understand case management collaboration, the social worker must first understand the multiple forms coordination assumes depending on the intended purpose (Mulroy, 1997). For example, from the perspective of organizational planning, collaboration is used as an intervention method for coordinating activities across administrative hierarchies. From the perspective of a generalist practitioner in a case management role, collaboration usually means a sense of cooperation among individuals working on a common task within a service system or across service systems (i.e., interprofessional collaboration and team building) (Sabatino, 1999).

In addition, one must understand the underlying assumptions in team collaboration. Multidisciplinary teams have more opportunity to deal with the whole picture in data collection, assessment, and contract planning. Thus, in developing and implementing a service delivery system for a client system, a multidisciplinary team addresses more of the nuances and complexities associated with specific problems and needs and this particular person-in-environment configuration. As team members become familiar with their teammates' understanding, their own knowledge base expands. As mutual understanding increases, team sharing in planning and delivering services builds interest, partnership, and consensus and thereby breaks through categorical approaches to health, education, and social services (Sabatino, 1999).

To begin to grow in the art of teamwork, it is important to realize that there is no *one* model of teamwork that should be used at all times. Some teams have a designated leader, and some have a rotating leadership. A leader needs to have an understanding of group process, as well as goal-directed abilities and skill in bringing forth contributions and leadership from other members of the group.

There are nine basic principles for effective teamwork. When a team is not achieving its goals, a review of the principles could reveal possible causes for difficulties incurred. The principles are summarized as follows:

1. *Obtain sanction:* Team members must be free to communicate openly in collaborative service planning and provision. The client system must sanction the team with the understanding that there will be open communication among members.
2. *Build supporting structure:* Each team member brings the professional knowledge, values, and skills of his or her own discipline and the concern (whether conscious or not) that blending interprofessional strategies will erase their discipline. In some instances, collaboration necessitates a shift in work culture and attitude about cooperation and acting together. In other instances, collaboration necessitates revisions in policy, job descriptions, and accountability requirements (Gallesich, 1982; Sabatino, 1999).

3. *Know yourself:* All members of the team must clearly know their own professional identities and the distinctive contribution they and their agencies can make to the team.

4. *Maximize resources:* Inclusion of professionals from multiple disciplines in joint planning and shared decision making creates the opportunity for maximizing resources by generating new paradigms for data collection, assessment, contract planning, intervention, and evaluation (Gallesich, 1982; Sabatino, 1999).

5. *Respect one another:* Members of the team must respect each discipline, recognizing similarities and differences without being threatened or "turf protective." They must understand the service orientation, recognize the competencies, trust the communications, and rely on the work of each team member (Sabatino, 1999).

6. *Meet regularly:* The team must meet on a regular basis for shared communication, planning, and evaluation.

7. *Define task assignments:* The team must define clearly each person's tasks and role in providing service. Roles and assignments must be explicit and agreed upon. Goals and methods must be clarified (Sabatino, 1999).

8. *Examine team process and achievement:* The team as a whole must systematically review its own process in working toward goal achievement. To ensure accountability in service delivery, the team must explore both its successful accomplishments and failures to understand what processes lead to effective teamwork (Gallesich, 1982; Sabatino, 1999).

9. *Share responsibility:* The team must assume collective responsibility for service outcome.

A team proceeds through stages that are similar to the phases of the General Method. Collectively, members of the team:

► Clarify the problem and purpose for organizing
► Share data
► Agree on goals and a plan for intervention
► Assign tasks
► Evaluate
► Terminate contact

The struggle for power or status, the emergence of conflict, and the development of group norms and expectations are important dimensions of a growing team, as they are for any human system.

At times, however, in order to achieve unified teamwork, or collaboration, the social worker has to negotiate, mediate, or even arbitrate between client systems and their impinging environments, between service systems on behalf of client systems, and between client groups. *Negotiation* involves direct communication between two parties. If conflicting parties cannot negotiate a solution, a third party is needed to mediate and promote communication and conciliation. If a third party is unable to promote negotiation between the parties, an arbitrator may be needed. The arbitrator does not attempt to promote communication and negotiation. Instead, like a judge, he or she hears both sides of the conflict situation and decides the resolution. Finally, if the arbitration is not successful, the social worker would refer the client systems for litigation, in which each party is represented by an attorney (Parsons, Jorgensen, & Hernandez, 1994).

Negotiation and mediation involve a process of facilitating communication between opposing positions around mutual interests. Mediating is appropriate only when there is perceived definable mutual interest; whereas when conflict of interest is perceived, advocating is more appropriate. In negotiating and mediating, the effort is to secure resolution of benefits through give-and-take on both sides. In advocacy, on the other hand, the effort is to win for the client or help the client win for himself or herself. In practice, both of these approaches tend to mesh and overlap.

Negotiating and mediating focus on behaviorally oriented change. The tactics or strategies do not focus on personality change, attitude change, or therapeutic process of the participants. Attitudinal change, however, may very well follow behavioral change. The goal is to create choices so that reconciliation, settlement, compromise, or understanding can take place between party systems. The process assumes that the involved parties are able to isolate issues, interests, positions, alternatives, and resources to find agreed-upon solutions. The desired outcome is a behavioral agreement mutually agreed on by the parties.

The framework for negotiating and mediating is based on integrative problem solving, which typically involves four steps (Fisher, Ury, & Patton, 1991):

1. Separate persons from problems.
2. Focus on interests instead of positions.
3. Create options for mutual gain.
4. Select criteria for choosing alternatives.

Although conflicts usually begin around some substantive issue, they often quickly progress into an emotional arena of the participants while the substantive issue itself is lost. The first step in negotiation and mediation is to ask each participant to describe the problem and state his or her feelings about the problem. The social worker's skills are to help clarify perceptions, reframe the problems presented in the interests of the participants present, and validate each participant by using reflective listening techniques. Each participant needs to be heard. The social worker often asks participants to repeat in their own words what they heard the other party saying and encourages each party to use "I" statements instead of "you" statements. By sharing with each other, the participants are able to begin to define the problem as separate from the person. Once the problems are out on the table, the social worker and the participants can begin to build an agenda for work.

As the problems are presented, the social worker enters the second stage by listening for the interests behind the positions, or the wants as opposed to needs of the participants. For example, a position of "My father does not want to go to a nursing home" may actually reflect an underlying interest of "I need to feel that my father is getting the best care available" or "I need to feel not guilty about the proposed plan of care for my elderly father." The key to interest-based problem-solving is to find the common interest of the participants or at least some compatible individual interests. When participants hear and see that their needs may not be so very different, they often are able to negotiate a solution out of those interests instead of remaining entrenched in their previous positions. Sometimes the social worker has to point out the areas of common interests because they are hidden behind emotions.

To pursue a client system's mutual interests, the social worker creates opportunities for generating options during the third step of integrative problem solving. The social worker encourages the participants to brainstorm and discuss various options that others may have used for solving the presenting situation. The social worker should refrain from premature feedback on potential solutions; rather, he or she should encourage the participants to critically explore and examine the path and consequences of presented options. Using humor and even exploring frivolous alternatives tends to help alleviate the emotional stress that parties sometimes feel in their pursuit of solutions.

Finally, when a number of alternatives have been generated, selection can take place. The social worker assists the participants in deciding how alternatives will be selected. As part of the final step in integrative strengths-based problem-solving, the social worker helps participants identify and select what objective criteria will be used for choosing a particular option. When participants can agree to select alternative solutions using an acceptable set of criteria, the resolution is practically complete. Criteria are often based on developmental, economic, and growth-promoting interests of the participants. For example, in elder care decision making, the objective criteria are likely to be based on economic feasibility, quality of care, and access to companionship. Once the criteria are chosen, alternatives are selected, spelled out procedurally, written down, and distributed to all relevant participants. Plans are then made to carry them out. This is also a time to decide about follow-ups or any check-in procedures. Fisher, Ury, and Patton (1991) note that a collaborative, integrative negotiation or mediation produces a wise agreement or an agreement that meets the main interests of all the participants.

Throughout the negotiation, the social worker is expected to assume neutrality subject to professional values and agency policies. Participants must be judged to be competent to negotiate. People who are chemically dependent or mentally incompetent are not considered appropriate participants, for they may not be able to follow through with a behavioral contract to resolve problems. Obviously, life-threatening situations are not amenable to negotiation. Instead, they must be handled in a more direct, expedient manner.

Common questions about this process include: *How does one get to the task or problems for resolution when emotions are running high? Don't people's feelings have to be considered before addressing their tasks?* Integrative strengths-based problem-solving does not discount emotions but they are not the focus of the process. Emotions must be heard, listened to, and reflected on. They must be dealt with to the extent that they get in the way of problem resolution. The goal is always to create workable solutions that promote mutual gain, decrease conflict, and empower the participants.

Although both the relationship of participants and the outcome of negotiation and mediation are important in the integrative strengths-based problem-solving process, the *outcome is the goal* and the *relationship is a by-product*. The emphasis may vary based on the anticipated future contact of the participants (Fisher, Ury, & Patton, 1991). That is, if participants are to maintain a close contact in the future, the relational component of negotiation becomes important and must be one of the options and selection criteria for alternatives sought. For example, if participants are family members, significant persons, or individuals who have to co-exist in close proximity, emotions must be addressed as part of the solutions sought. On the other hand, if participants are parties who will not be expected to maintain future close contact, as in the case of group members who come together for a specific task solution, the outcome or the mutual gain takes precedence over the relationship.

Although negotiation and teamwork may be emotionally draining and time-consuming components of case management, they avoid excessive demands on limited resources and prevent fragmentation and overlap of service delivery. Through a case management approach, client systems are not left with the burden of trying to integrate services on their own, and a sense of mutual aid, shared unity, and community is fostered.

Designs for Micro and Mezzo Interventions

The types of intervention by a generalist social worker may be depicted in designs composed of circle clusters. In Figure 8.1, the social worker (SW) is seen in interaction with a client system (C) through overlapping circles. This simple design is used to demonstrate *counseling*. A case example for Figure 8.1 is a generalist working with a family (father, mother, and son) as they grow in understanding the changing behaviors of their adolescent son (age 15).

In Figure 8.2, *information and referral* is pictured by a social worker (SW) interacting with a client system (C) as the client begins to interact with a resource (R). If contact with a particular resource system has not yet been actualized, but is the intent of the intervention, the resource system (R) may be depicted by a broken line. If both a social worker and a client system have direct contact with a resource, the SW circle would extend to the right and intersect the R circle also (Figure 8.3).

An example for Figures 8.2 and 8.3 would be a social worker whose client system is a depressed woman who is talking about suicide. As indicated in the designs, the social worker is trying to help the client face the seriousness of her problem and admit herself to the local mental health center. In Figure 8.2, only the client system has contact with the mental health center. In Figure 8.3, both the social worker and client system have contact with the mental health center.

In the design found in Figure 8.4, the social worker and other resources (A, B) join together in a team effort. Collectively, the social worker (SW) and other resources (A, B) interact with a client system (C). The overlapping circles reflect the *case management and teamwork* in human service provision. For example, in working

FIGURE 8.1 ■ Counseling

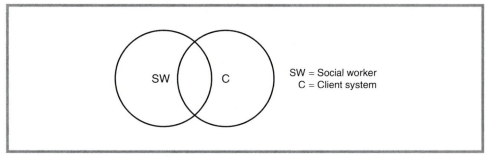

FIGURE 8.2 ■ Information and Referral

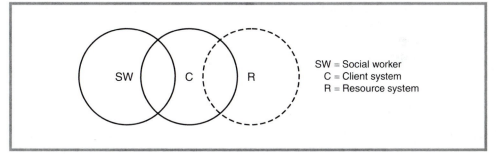

FIGURE 8.3 ■ Crisis Intervention

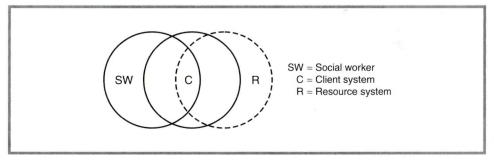

with a community that has experienced a number of unexplained fires lately, a generalist may be working with representatives from the fire department and the local police force to help community members express their concerns and to find ways to combat fires and to report suspected arsonists. In Figure 8.4, all three resources (social worker, fire department, and police) are shown as coming together to form a team for ongoing service to the community. In Figure 8.5, the social worker remains in the role of case manager because teamwork has not been established with all three resources to work together. The local police and the fire department are called on by the social worker to meet separately with the community on different occasions. The

FIGURE 8.4 ■ Case Management and Teamwork

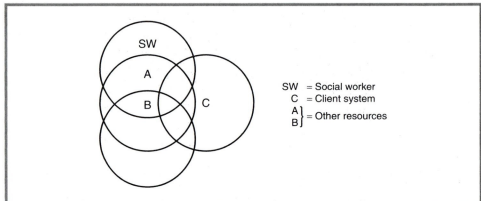

FIGURE 8.5 ■ Case Management

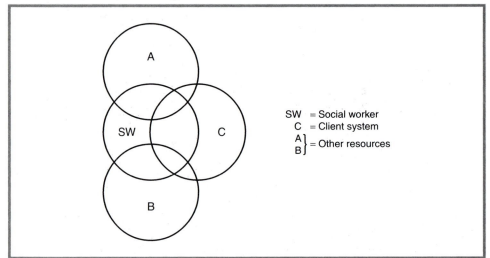

absence of an ongoing team effort is depicted in Figure 8.5 boundaries that do not overlap (A and B), except with the social worker (SW), who contacts and coordinates the services for the community.

Additional designs in intervention may be drawn up to reflect combined intervention types. Sometimes, as shown in Figure 8.6, a generalist (SW) may be involved with a number of community resources (A, B) in a team effort to influence a target system (T) for client service (C). For example, a generalist (SW) working on behalf of an elderly community (C) plagued by vandalism may join with town officials (A) and the local newspaper (B) to advocate better police protection (T) of the elderly community.

FIGURE 8.6 ■ Combined Interventions

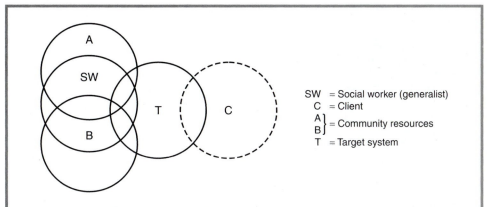

In the course of working with a system, a generalist may change the design of intervention as problems or needs emerge or are resolved. At any given time, a social worker should be able to identify the design (or designs) currently being used.

Monitoring Intervention

The intervention phase of the General Method evolves through ongoing dynamic interchanges between the client system and the social worker that are directed toward goal achievement. The results of these intervention processes may be monitored and documented as:

▶ Steps forward or progress toward goal achievement
▶ Standing still or no progress
▶ Steps backward or movement away from goal achievement

In the past, this documentation has often taken the form of narrative case record descriptions of process and progress, or the lack thereof, and qualitative assessment of the results achieved. Today, narrative documentation and qualitative assessment alone are no longer sufficient.

Shifting from narrative to evidentiary documentation of intervention process requires converting each case goal into a scale with ratings such as −1 *movement away from goal achievement* to 0 *no movement* to 1–2 *some progress, 3–4 progress,* and 5 *goal achieved.* In this way, client systems may be rated at various points in the intervention process on the degree of achievement of each individual goal as well as on the totality of all goals. Such ongoing monitoring is useful during the intervention phase in providing information about the rate and amount of progress being made (see Chapter 3). A more formal evaluation process (see Chapters 3 and 10) occurs prior to termination.

CAREL B. GERMAIN (1922–1998) developed and elaborated on the concept of *ecological perspective* in social work theory and practice. She authored seven books, including *The Life Model of Social Work Practice* (with A. Gitterman) and *Human Behavior and the Social Environment: An Ecological View*. She served on the social work faculties of the University of Maryland, Columbia University, and the University of Connecticut.

Working with Different Client Systems

As stated earlier, a generalist practitioner has skills and techniques for work with client, action, or target systems of any size. In addition to the relationship skills, problem-solving skills, and political skills, as categorized in the foundation framework (Chapter 1), there is a range of techniques that can be called on as needed with particular client, action, and target systems. Techniques may be appropriately identified as generalist practice techniques if they can be used with more than one type of system or problem. Specialized techniques are specifically designed for and used in a particular area of specialization, according to problem, population, institution, traditional or specialized method, or theoretical approach. Some techniques that originate in a specialized area may later be extended for use with a variety of social systems by the generalist social worker with additional knowledge, skills, and experience under supervision.

Using Social Work Foundation Knowledge in Intervention

Basic values, theories, and skills used by the generalist social worker during the intervention phase of the General Method are identified in the holistic conceptualization of the foundation for social work practice (Chapter 1). The practice principles that reflect the basic values of social work are very evident in the judgments and actions of the social worker as interventions are planned and implemented. Interventions by a social worker are dependent on the willingness of a system to accept and cooperate with the social worker. As much as possible, the system of contact is given the opportunity to determine for itself the types of involvement the social worker will provide. Each problem-person-environment situation is individualized as the social worker accepts or suggests certain roles or task responsibilities.

Knowledge used during intervention varies according to the task at hand. During counseling with micro and mezzo client systems, theories about the type of client system (individual, family, group) the social worker is interacting with are used. In referral, the social worker uses knowledge about resources. For teamwork to be successful, individual members must know about their own profession and other professions, as well as group dynamics and processes.

The heart of the General Method may be seen as intervention. The appropriate use of relationship and strengths-based problem-solving skills and techniques in this phase is crucial to the fulfillment of the process. As emphasized, the selection of skills and techniques is guided by a social worker's application of basic values and knowledge. The holistic conceptualization of the foundation for practice is a helpful reference for the generalist who must competently apply foundation knowledge, values, and skills when intervening in each unique situation.

Human Diversity in Intervention

The core human diversity issues related to social work intervention at the micro and mezzo level with client systems include institutional racism, cultural diversity, gender role expectations, sexual orientation, and socio-economic status. When a social worker is intervening directly with a client system of another culture, an interpreter may be needed to overcome language differences. In one sense, direct intervention becomes a type of teamwork when an interpreter is used. Although interpreters repeat what has been said verbatim as they translate, they also need the ability and sensitivity to convey the feelings and attitudes that are being communicated. Ideally, interpreters for social workers need to have some understanding of the basic principles and practices of the social worker. They need to realize the difference between relating to a friend and to a client, and to be able to convey the personal style of the social worker. Open communication with a strong sense of trust and mutual commitment should exist between the social worker and the interpreter. The social worker needs to make every effort to communicate directly and respectfully with a client system, even when an interpreter is being used. At no time should any member of the client system be made to feel like an object to supply information or to be talked about. Children should not be used as interpreters for their parents; such action puts them in a position that generally contradicts their role and place in their culture. It may also prevent a parent from dealing with content he or she does not wish to discuss in front of the children.

When an agency cannot supply the needed type of intervention, a referral must be made. The social worker looks for resources that appear to be sensitive to the culture, social stratification characteristics, and socio-demographic characteristics of the client system. This may become apparent by considering:

1. The cultural and social background and languages of those administering and providing the service
2. The location of the service

3. The involvement or input by the particular cultural and social group in the resource

4. The extent to which members of the cultural and social community have received satisfactory services from the resource in the past

Before contacting a formal resource, a social worker and client system should explore thoroughly the possibility of locating available informal resources. In meeting emotional, social, and personal needs, particularly for minority members, familial and community resources are often far more effective than formal agencies or programs. Also, informal resources usually provide greater stability through ongoing availability. It is in the black community, for example, that members of the African American culture receive their emotional support and positive identity (Chestang, 1982).

When a social worker intervenes through teamwork with other professionals, it is important to see that team members are sensitive to the diversity issues of the client system receiving service. Ideally, the service team should seek periodic consultation from someone with knowledge, experience, and demonstrated competence in working with people of the particular culture, social background, and socio-demographic characteristics.

Especially for those individuals who do not have a nurturing, accepting family or community networks, a group of people who share common values, problems, pressures, concerns, and lifestyle can be very supportive and strengthening. In working with vulnerable populations, a generalist practitioner will be promoting self-esteem and self-sufficiency by using the General Method because it is a collaborative, strengths-based problem-solving approach that encourages assertiveness and empowerment. As presented throughout this text, a guiding principle is to have members of a client system do whatever there is to be done for themselves whenever possible.

ONGOING CASES
Intervention Phase of Micro and Mezzo Generalist Practice

In the following section, the application of knowledge and skills during the *intervention phase* of the General Method will be demonstrated by entry-level generalist practitioners. The primary focus is micro and mezzo generalist practice.

In Exercise 8.1, questions are proposed for reflection and discussion about how practice in each of the seven ongoing case examples might change during the intervention phase if the client system represented a different

▶ *Culture:* Racial/ethnic group membership, national origin and social group identity, religion and spirituality

▶ *Social status:* Socio-economic status, environmental and rural/urban differences

▶ *Socio-demographic strata:* Age and developmental stage, gender roles, sexual orientation, challenges in mental and physical ability

EXERCISE 8.1
Impact of Human Diversity on Intervention Process

Consider the following questions in each of the seven client systems. In intervention, how might change in culture, social status, or socio-demographic strata:

1. Influence the client system's participation in intervention?
2. Influence the social worker's view of intervention?
3. Reveal values that influence timing, communications, content, and actions?
4. Affect the dynamics of the professional relationship in intervention?
5. Affect monitoring of the progress, timeliness, and completeness of intervention?

I. Child Welfare Case

A. Agency: State Department of Children's Services

B. Client System

K, a 15-year-old female, is moving from an emergency shelter into a group home. (For more background information, see Chapter 5, Ongoing Cases: Engagement Phase, I. Child Welfare Case.)

C. Summary of Preceding Phases

The problems, needs, goals, and contracted tasks identified during engagement, data collection, and assessment and contract planning are listed in Chapter 7. The three major problems were assessed in terms of change-potential scores and prioritized as follows: (1) permanent placement, 24; (2) school placement, 23; (3) personal problems— (a) depression, 21; (b) poor self-esteem, 20; (c) identity confusion, 20; and (d) sexuality, 19.

D. Intervention

The types of interventions by the social worker were (1) counseling, (2) referral, and (3) teamwork. In addition to working directly with K and making a referral to the group home, the child-welfare worker continued as K's state social worker (the state maintained custody) and formed an action system (teamwork) with the administrator and other members of the staff of the group home. The social worker also participated in school conferences on K, thus forming an alliance with the teacher and social worker of the school. Prior to K's placement in her present group home, the social worker had also worked collaboratively with the staff at the shelter. The design that primarily depicts the interventions of the child-welfare worker is found in Figure 8.7.

Counseling with K was primarily to give her support as she carried out the tasks identified in the contracted plan (Chapter 7) and to discuss her adjustment in the group home and in school. Contracts with personnel from the group home and school were mainly for the purpose of monitoring K's adjustment and personal growth and to see if any additional services were needed.

FIGURE 8.7 ■ Social Worker's Combined Interventions: Child Welfare Case

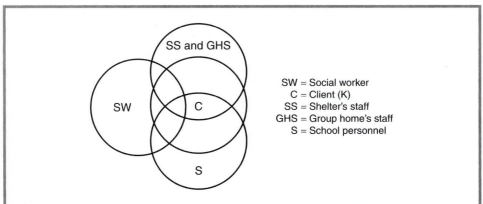

SW = Social worker
C = Client (K)
SS = Shelter's staff
GHS = Group home's staff
S = School personnel

A month after K's placement in the group home, K and the social worker reviewed the reasons for K's commitment to the state. K understood the need for the social worker to petition the court for a continuance of her commitment. This need and its related goals and tasks were added to the planned contract, as recorded in Table 8.1. After K was in the group home for three months, the social worker and K evaluated the progress that had been made.

II. Gerontology Case

A. Agency: Seaside Nursing Home

B. Client System

Mrs. J, an 80-year-old Portuguese woman, is in a skilled-nursing facility. (For additional background information, see Chapter 5, Ongoing Cases: Engagement Phase, II. Gerontology Case.)

TABLE 8.1 ■ Contracted Plan: Child Welfare Case

Date Identified	Problem/ Need	Goal	Task	Contract	Date Anticipated	Date Accomplished
2/24	4. Need to remain in custody of state (abusive parents)	4. To obtain continuance of custody	1. Discuss.	1. Social worker and K	2/24	
			2. Prepare case summary.	2. Social worker	2/24	
			3. Petition court for continuance.	3. Social worker	3/1	
			4. Attend court hearing.	4. Social worker and K	3/30	

C. Summary of Preceding Phases

The problems, needs, goals, and tasks identified during engagement, data collection, and assessment and contract planning are indicated in the contracted plan found in Chapter 7. During assessment and contract planning, problems were prioritized as follows: (1) unfamiliarity with staff and resources of the home, (2) fighting with nurses over bath, (3) reclusiveness (not leaving room), (4) calling residents names, and (5) cultural isolation.

D. Intervention

Interventions by the social worker in this case were (1) counseling with the client through twice a week sessions and (2) teamwork with the nursing-home staff (nurses, program planner, recreational staff, volunteer director, and a volunteer) as well as with the pastor of the church Mrs. J attended before hospitalization. The designs that demonstrate these primary interventions of the social worker are found in Figures 8.8 and 8.9.

Through working with the church pastor, members of his congregation who knew Mrs. J began to visit her and to take her out to special church celebrations (a concert and the

FIGURE 8.8 ■ Counseling: Gerontology Case

FIGURE 8.9 ■ Teamwork: Gerontology Case

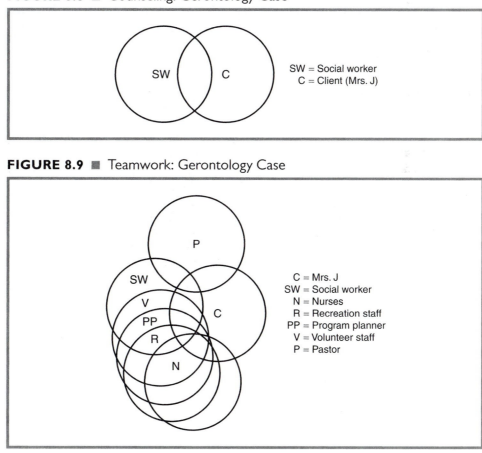

FIGURE 8.10 ■ Counseling: Gerontology Case

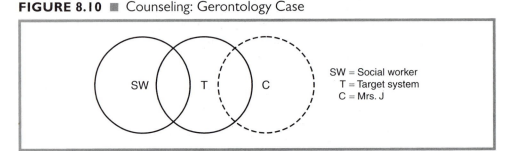

Christmas prayer service). Mrs. J was extremely happy to have them visit her and take her out to church activities. She also began to attend Bible services held in the nursing home. At first, she went with the social worker; later, she would go with other residents. Mrs. J began to carry on conversations with other residents at her dining-room table and on her corridor. She became friendly with her roommate, and they would go together to entertainments put on by the recreation department at the home.

Eventually, a Portuguese-speaking volunteer began to visit Mrs. J. This young woman came only three times before she dropped out of the volunteer program. The social worker continued to try to locate Mrs. J's family members but was unsuccessful. If family members had been reached, they would probably have been target systems, and the social worker's intervention would be depicted as shown in Figure 8.10. If Mrs. J's children had been responsive to the social worker's efforts and asked for the social worker's help, they would have become an extended part of the client system (Figure 8.8). If they joined with the social worker and the home in providing support for their mother, they would be seen as constituent members of the action system and perceived by the social worker and the staff as team members in collaborative effort for goal attainment (Figure 8.9).

E. Charted Progress

As the tasks of the contract were executed, the social worker recorded their completion by indicating the dates of accomplishment on the contracted plan. Visits by members of her former church were also recorded in the task column (see Table 8.2).

III. Public Social Welfare Case

A. Agency: State Social Services

B. Client System

Mr. and Mrs. P and their two children (2 and 4 years old) are in need of housing (emergency and long-term) and food (emergency and supply until TANF payment). (For additional background information, see Chapter 5, Ongoing Cases: Engagement Phase, III. Public Social Welfare Case.)

C. Summary of Preceding Phases

The problems, needs, goals, and tasks contracted as the social worker and Mr. and Mrs. P moved quickly (crisis situation) through the stages of engagement, data collection, and

TABLE 8.2 ■ Contracted Plan: Gerontology Case

Date Identified	Problem/Need	Goal	Task	Contract	Date Anticipated	Date Accomplished
9/27	1. Unfamiliarity with staff and resources of nursing home	1. To get to know the staff and resources of the nursing home	1. Meet twice a week with social worker.	1. Social worker and Mrs. J	10/4 and every Tuesday and Thursday	10/4, 10/9, 10/11, 10/16, 10/18, 10/23, 10/25, 10/30
			2. Meet with program planner.	2. Social worker, Mrs. J, and program planner	10/16	11/1, 11/6, 11/8, 11/13, 11/15, 11/20, 11/22, 11/27; 12/6, 12/11, 12/13
			3. Meet with a person from recreation staff.	3. Social worker, Mrs. J, and recreation-staff person	10/23	10/23
10/2	2. Fighting with nurses over bath	2. To work out bath schedule with nurses	1. Meet with head nurse to discuss bath schedule.	1. Mrs. J and head nurse	10/16	10/16
9/25	3. Reclusiveness: not leaving room alone	3a. To leave room alone (at least once a day)	1. Walk down to nursing station alone at least once a day.	1. Mrs. J	10/25 and each day thereafter	10/26, 11/6, 11/14, 11/20; 12/3 12/5, 12/12, 12/15
		b. To attend a house activity (at least once a week)	2. Go to a house activity, program, or meeting (at least once a week).	1. Social worker or staff member and Mrs. J first two times	Starting week of 10/22	10/24, 12/30
				2. Mrs. J with residents each week thereafter	Starting week of 11/5	11/5, 11/12, 11/21, 11/28; 12/3 12/7, 12/12, 12/17
10/2	4. Calling residents names	4. To stop calling residents names	1. Stop name calling. 2. Say "hello" to residents.	1. Mrs. J 2. Mrs. J	10/16 and thereafter 10/16 and thereafter	10/16 until 10/20 (argument 10/21) and thereafter
9/25	5. Cultural isolation	5. To share culture with others	1. Meet director of volunteers.	1. Mrs. J, social worker, and director of volunteers	10/25	10/25
			2. Visit with Portuguese volunteer.	2. Mrs. J and volunteer	?	11/13, 11/20, 11/30
			3. Visit with pastor of church.	3. Mrs. J and pastor	?	11/14, 11/20, 11/30
			4. Visit with member of church.	4. Mrs. J, pastor, and congregation	11/20	11/30
			5. Go off grounds to attend church activity.	5. Mrs. J and congregation (Mr. and Mrs. T)	12/4, 12/17	12/4, 12/17

assessment and contract planning are indicated in Chapter 7. The problems and needs of the family were prioritized as follows: (1) food—emergency food, (2) housing—temporary shelter, (3) food supply until TANF payment, and (4) long-term housing.

D. Intervention

The types of intervention by the social worker were (1) referral, (2) counseling, (3) crisis intervention, and (4) case management and teamwork. The social worker placed the family at Center City Motor Inn on the same day that they arrived at the agency. The family rejected the options of Salvation Army (mother and father would have been placed in separate facilities) and the City Hotel (disliked the location). Before going to the Motor Inn, the social worker took the family to the Good News Soup Kitchen for a meal and picked up a bag of groceries at the Center Churches Food Bank.

While at the motel, Mrs. P asked the social worker to try to get a medical card for her to take the children to the health center for a checkup. The social worker learned that the medical card was being processed at the central office and that it would take another eight days to arrive. The social worker offered case management services by writing a letter to the health center, verifying the status of the P family. The letter was cosigned by the family's income-maintenance technician. Medical transportation was requested and provided for Mr. and Mrs. P and the children to go to the health center.

Mr. and Mrs. P did not actively search for permanent living quarters. They said that they didn't think they liked the locations of the apartments listed in the paper. The social worker offered to drive them to look at places, but they only went to two places with him. By the end of 10 days, the social worker stressed that their time was running out, and the Ps requested an extension of time during this crisis situation. The application for an extension was denied, and the Ps asked for a fair hearing. They were again denied at the hearing and told that they would have to leave the motel by the following Monday. When Monday came, the Ps informed the social worker that they had located an apartment and requested help with moving their furniture from Mrs. P's father's house to the new apartment. After the family got the three required moving estimates, their moving expenses were covered through the Income Maintenance Department.

In their new apartment, the family requested help with obtaining fuel assistance. The social worker informed them that they needed to keep their fuel bills and showed them how to apply for assistance. Their TANF check was detained because of the address change, and the social worker hand-delivered the check and food stamps.

The family had a problem with the refrigerator and asked the social worker to help them obtain funding to have it repaired. The social worker suggested that they try the Salvation Army, which might pay for new parts. The social worker learned later that the Ps received a new refrigerator and that this was handled through the income-maintenance technician. Mr. P asked if the social worker thought he should reapply to social security for Supplemental Security Income benefits. The social worker inquired about the procedure for reapplication and encouraged Mr. P to begin the process.

Mrs. P asked if the social worker knew of any place where the family could go to receive a Thanksgiving basket. Mr. P also wondered if there was any place where he could get Christmas presents for the children. The social worker inquired and informed Mr. P that baskets were being given by several local churches and that the Salvation Army had children's gifts.

At one point earlier, when it seemed that the Ps were not going to find housing, the social worker had teamed up with the Protective Services Department. It appeared that placement of the children might be needed until housing for the family was located. Fortunately, this was not necessary.

In the case of the P family, a number of resources were mobilized by the B.S.W. worker. The social worker went with the Ps to obtain food and shelter. Initial contacts were made by the social worker for the Ps with the fuel-assistance program, social security office, medical transportation services, and Salvation Army (Figure 8.11).

In addition to information and referral, the social worker maintained ongoing counseling with the family for three months (Figure 8.12). Throughout this period, the social worker engaged in teamwork with the income-maintenance technician and with Mr. P's psychiatrist. Contact with the income-maintenance technician averaged once a week. The social worker spoke with the psychiatrist on five different occasions. These case management and team efforts (Figure 8.13) provided the family with coordinated services and offered the service providers an opportunity for shared service delivery.

E. Charted Progress

As various interventions were identified and enacted, the social worker recorded them, along with the dates of task accomplishment, on the contracted plan. After the Ps were placed in temporary shelter, the goal of locating a long-term residence took longer to accomplish than anticipated. The efforts to obtain a time extension for temporary placement were also recorded, as were additional problems and needs that surfaced. Goals and con-

FIGURE 8.11 ■ Referral: Public Social Welfare Case

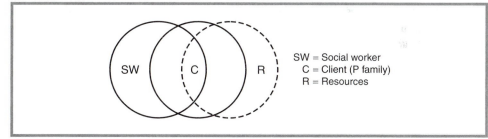

SW = Social worker
C = Client (P family)
R = Resources

FIGURE 8.12 ■ Counseling: Public Social Welfare Case

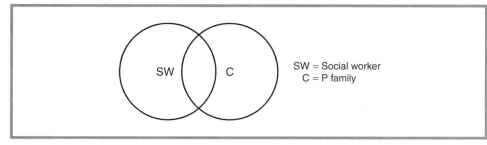

SW = Social worker
C = P family

FIGURE 8.13 ■ Teamwork: Public Social Welfare Case

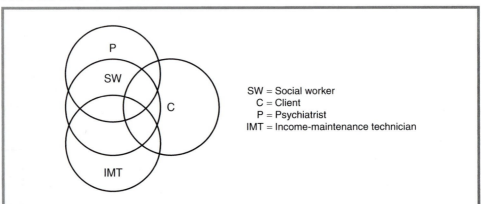

tracts for each new problem were developed with the Ps and charted on the contracted plan (see Table 8.3).

As indicated in the table, task 3 (move to new apartment) for problem 4 (housing—long-term) was not accomplished until 11/7, even though the anticipated date was "not later than 10/12." The additional needs of a medical exam for the children (including transportation), fuel assistance, TANF check delivery, refrigerator repair, Thanksgiving baskets, and Christmas presents for the children were also listed and contracted.

IV. Community Services Case

A. Agency: Clayton Neighborhood House

B. Client System

Four Hispanic families are without heat in their apartments on the second floor of 33 L Street. (For more background information, see Chapter 5, Ongoing Cases: Engagement Phase, IV. Community Services Case.)

C. Summary of Preceding Phases

The problem, need, goal, and contracted tasks developed by the social worker and the community of residents in earlier phases are outlined in Chapter 7. In addition to the need for heating in their apartments, the families recognized that they had a communication problem with their landlord. They were not, however, interested in trying to find ways to improve communication with him at this time.

D. Intervention

The interventions of the social worker included (1) crisis intervention, (2) task groups, and (3) advocacy. The social worker met with the residents directly to plan and monitor change. She also served as their advocate through work with Mr. X, the landlord. Designs depicting the social worker's intervention are found in Figures 8.14 and 8.15.

TABLE 8.3 ■ Contracted Plan: Public Social Welfare Case

Date Identified	Problem/Need	Goal	Task	Contract	Date Anticipated	Date Accomplished
9/28	4. Housing— long term	4. To move into an apartment for long-term residence	1. Explore resources.	1. Mr. and Mrs. P and social worker	9/29	9/30
			2. Contact resources.	2. Mr. and Mrs. P	9/29	9/30, 10/10
			3. Move.	3. The Ps	10/12	11/7
			4. Update.	4. Social worker, Mr. P's doctor, income-maintenance technician	9/29 and weekly	9/29; 10/6, 10/13, 10/20, 10/27; 11/3, 10/17
			5. Request extension for temporary placement.	5. Social worker	10/11	10/11
			6. Fair hearing.	6. Mr. and Mrs. P, social worker, and department board	10/31	10/31
			7. Request moving assistance.	7. Social worker	11/5	11/5
9/28	5. Poor money management					
10/1	6. Medical exam for children	6. To have children examined at health center	1. Find out about medical care.	1. Social worker	10/2	10/2
10/1			2. See if health center will accept letter of authorization.	2. Social worker	10/2	10/2
			3. Write letter.	3. Social worker and income-maintenance technician	10/5	10/5
			4. Make appointment.	4. Mrs. P	10/5	10/8
			5. Make arrangements for medical transport.	5. Social worker and income-maintenance technician	10/8	10/8
			6. Take children to health center.	6. Mr. and Mrs. P and medical transport service	10/12	10/12

(Continued)

TABLE 8.3 ■ Continued

Date Identified	Problem/Need	Goal	Task	Contract	Date Anticipated	Date Accomplished
11/14	7. Need for fuel assistance	7. To obtain fuel assistance	1. Explore resources.	1. Social worker	11/15	11/15
			2. Discuss.	2. Social worker and Ps	11/16	11/16
			3. Fill out application.	3. Ps with social worker's help	11/20	11/20
			4. Follow up if necessary.	4. Mr. P	11/26	
11/14	8. Check and food stamps	8. To receive TANF check and food stamps	1. To find out about delay in delivery.	1. Social worker	11/14	11/14
			2. Get check at central office.	2. Social worker	11/15	11/15
			3. Deliver check to Ps.	3. Social worker	11/16	11/16
11/20	9. Malfunctioning refrigerator	9. To fix refrigerator	1. Get estimates on repairs needed.	1. Mr. P	11/20	11/20
			2. Explore funding	2. Social worker resources.	11/20	
			3. Contact Salvation Army.	3. Mr. P	11/22	(Problem withdrawn 12/4—new refrigerator)
			4. Have refrigerator repaired.	4. Mr. P	11/23	
			5. Send bill to Salvation Army.	5. Mr. P	11/26	
11/20	10. Supplemental Security Income	10. To receive Supplemental Security Income	1. Contact social security office.	1. Social worker	11/21	11/21
			2. Discuss.	2. Social worker and Ps	11/22	11/22
			3. Complete application.	3. Mr. P	11/22	
			4. Follow-up call.	4. Mr. P	11/26	
			5. Go for interview.	5. Mr. P	11/27	
11/20	11. Thanksgiving food basket	11. To receive a food basket	1. Explore resources.	1. Social worker	11/21	11/21
			2. Contact churches.	2. Mr. P	11/22	
			3. Got food basket.	3. Mr. P	11/24	
11/27	12. Gifts for children	12. To obtain Christmas gifts for children	1. Explore resources.	1. Social worker	11/28	11/28
			2. Contact resources.	2. Mr. P	11/29	
			3. Pick up gifts.	3. Mr. P	12/5	

FIGURE 8.14 ■ Task Group: Community Services Case

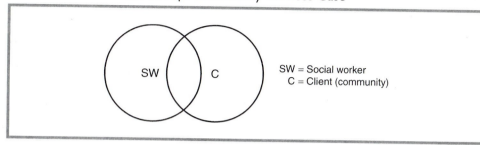

FIGURE 8.15 ■ Advocacy: Community Services Case

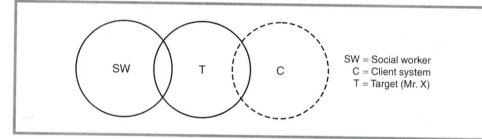

When the social worker returned to meet with the residents on the day after she contacted the landlord, she found that their apartments were heated. She had brought thermometers with her for each apartment. They registered 68°. The residents expressed gratitude and hoped that the heating would continue throughout the winter. The social worker told the group about her conversation with the landlord. They admitted that they didn't really know the man but continued to be afraid to have contact with him. They agreed to monitor the heating in their apartments by checking their thermometers each day. They would meet with the social worker in one week to report on their findings.

E. Charted Progress

As the social worker and the residents planned additional tasks, the social worker recorded the extended plan by adding items to the "task," "contract," and "date anticipated" columns of the contracted plan (see Table 8.4).

V. Education Case

A. Agency: Keeney Elementary School

B. Client System

Jim G is an 8-year-old third-grader with problems at school and at home directly related to his parents' problem with their marital relationship. (For further background information, see Chapter 5, Ongoing Cases: Engagement Phase, V. Education Case.)

TABLE 8.4 ■ Contracted Plan: Community Services Case

Date Identified	Problem/ Need	Goal	Task	Contract	Date Anticipated	Date Accomplished
			4. Monitor heat daily in each apartment.	4. One person from each family (Mr. T, Mrs. V, Mr. A, and CR)	12/5 to 12/12	
			5. Meet to review findings.	5. Social worker and residents	12/12	

C. Summary of Preceding Phases

The problems, needs, goals, and contracted tasks identified during preceding phases are outlined in Chapter 7. The two primary tasks prioritized and contracted with Mr. and Mrs. G were (1) getting Jim to school on time each day and (2) going together for marital counseling. Jim's poor school performance and his sleeping problem were seen as reactions to Mr. and Mrs. G's quarreling and, especially, to Mrs. G's threat that she was going to leave her husband and children. The social worker's primary contracted tasks included meeting with Jim, his teacher, and his parents regarding Jim's school performance and general progress.

D. Intervention

The interventions of the social worker may be identified as (1) counseling (Jim, Mr. and Mrs. G, Jim and his parents) (see Figure 8.16); (2) referral (marital counseling for Mr. and Mrs. G) (see Figure 8.17); and (3) teamwork (social worker and Jim's teacher, working with Mr. and Mrs. G to help Jim) (see Figure 8.18). The social worker also attended a student study task group on Jim with several members of the school faculty (principal, nurse, classroom teacher, learning-disabilities teacher, social service supervisor, social worker). Jim's parents had been invited to this conference but they said that they couldn't attend because they were working.

FIGURE 8.16 ■ Counseling: Education Case

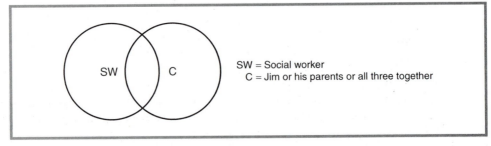

SW = Social worker
C = Jim or his parents or all three together

FIGURE 8.17 ■ Referral: Education Case

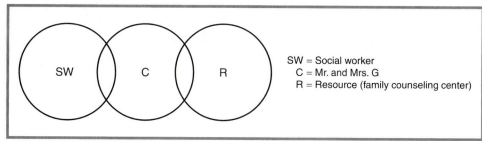

SW = Social worker
C = Mr. and Mrs. G
R = Resource (family counseling center)

FIGURE 8.18 ■ Teamwork: Education Case

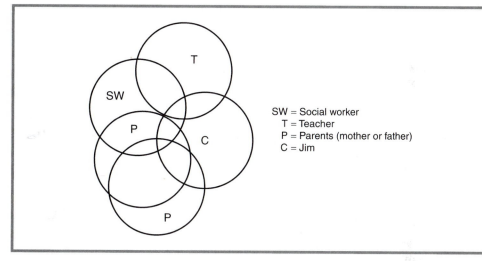

SW = Social worker
T = Teacher
P = Parents (mother or father)
C = Jim

During their meeting with the social worker at school, Mr. and Mrs. G invited Jim to join them before the end of the meeting. At this time, Mr. and Mrs. G informed Jim that they knew that he had been worried about them because he had heard them arguing. They admitted to Jim that they had been having some problems but assured him that they were going to get help themselves so they could learn to get along better with each other. They stressed that it was not Jim's problem and that he really didn't have to worry about them. They also assured Jim that neither one of them was thinking of giving up or leaving home. Jim was encouraged to try to do better in school. They said they knew it must have been hard for Jim. Mr. G said he knew it was hard enough for Jim to be "a little man in a big world," and that Jim didn't have to take onto his shoulders the problem of his mother and father. As he hugged his parents, Jim said he would try to work harder in school.

Before leaving this interview, it was agreed by all that the social worker would continue to see Jim twice a week and that the follow-up contacts between the social worker and Mr. and Mrs. G would be by telephone for two weeks. These would be followed by a home visit by the social worker, at which time they all would consider termination of planned contacts if progress was apparent.

In talking with Mrs. G on the telephone the following week, the social worker learned that Mr. G had made the appointment and that Mr. and Mrs. G had begun counseling sessions at the family counseling center. Mrs. G said Jim still wanted a light left on in his room at night but he didn't need to have his mother with him. He settled for a small night-light.

Jim's teacher reported that Jim was beginning to look happier and to show more interest in his schoolwork. The social worker continued to meet with Jim in her office twice a week, and Jim was interested in playing age-appropriate games. They drew up ongoing evaluation graphs to chart Jim's progress in school (to be presented in the next chapter).

E. Charted Progress

As tasks contracted in the plan developed by Mr. and Mrs. G, Jim, and the social worker (Chapter 7) were carried out, the social worker recorded the date they were completed in the "date accomplished" column of the contracted plan. At the last meeting of the social worker with Mr. and Mrs. G in their home, the social worker shared the updated plan with them as they reviewed and evaluated progress.

VI. Corrections Case

A. Agency: Juvenile Court

B. Client System

Seven male adolescents, age 14, are on probation for burglary, theft of automobiles, or minor larceny (shoplifting) and are attending weekly group sessions led by co-workers from Juvenile Court. (For further background information, see Chapter 5, Ongoing Cases: Engagement Phase, VI. Corrections Case.)

C. Summary of Preceding Phases

The problems, needs, goals, and contracted tasks identified in earlier phases are outlined in Chapter 7. The youths prioritized their problems as (1) law breaking leading to probation, (2) bad tempers, and (3) lack of understanding of the changes they were experiencing. Group members admitted that they didn't think much of themselves (low self-worth) and that they had problems with their parents (parent-son conflicts), but they didn't appear interested in working directly on these problems. In developing the contracted plan in the group, the need for ongoing evaluation instruments was recognized, and graphs were developed to monitor group attendance, group participation by members, and members' behavior at school and at home.

D. Intervention

The interventions of the B.S.W. worker were mainly small groups and teamwork. The social worker and her co-leader met with the seven youths in weekly group meetings, and the social workers engaged in ongoing communication with each other as team members. They met at least twice a week to discuss the process, problems, and progress of the group and any developments that were taking place with individual members. The social workers went together to visit every home of the group participants. They divided the task of visiting the schools (the B.S.W. went to four schools, the M.S.W. to three) and the tasks of receiving weekly reports from parents and school social workers. The approach used with teachers and parents also highlighted a team effort as they worked together to help the youths accomplish their goals.

The primary teamwork designs to depict the interventions of the B.S.W. worker are found in Figures 8.19 and 8.20.

After charting progress in group attendance, group participation, and school and home behavior, the group began to focus on their problem with their tempers. All saw a relationship between this problem and the problems they were having at home and at school. They agreed to take home an index card each week, and every time they lost their tempers, they would put a check on it. If they forgot during the day to check the card, they would try to remember the incidents and to mark the card each night before going to bed. They would bring the card back each week and report the total number of checks they had for the week

FIGURE 8.19 ■ Social Worker and Co-Worker Teamwork: Corrections Case

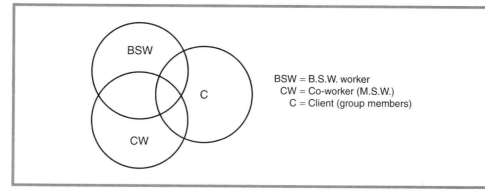

BSW = B.S.W. worker
CW = Co-worker (M.S.W.)
C = Client (group members)

FIGURE 8.20 ■ Extended Teamwork: Corrections Case

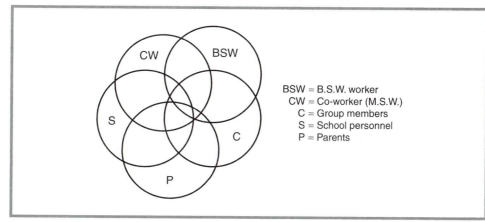

BSW = B.S.W. worker
CW = Co-worker (M.S.W.)
C = Group members
S = School personnel
P = Parents

FIGURE 8.21 ■ Temper Loss: Corrections Case

Weeks

Names	1	2	3	4	5	6	7	8	9	10	11	12	13	14	15	16
J																
MK																
T																
ML																
B																
A																
C																

FIGURE 8.22 ■ Temper Control: Corrections Case

Weeks

Names	1	2	3	4	5	6	7	8	9	10	11	12	13	14	15	16
J																
MK																
T																
ML																
B																
A																
C																

to the group. At the meeting, members entered their total number of checks for the week on a weekly chart. The group members said that they also wanted to check on the other side of the card every time they felt like losing their tempers but didn't (Figure 8.21). The cards were labeled on each side "temper loss" or "temper control." A matching weekly chart was designed to indicate temper control (Figure 8.22). During meetings, the group also discussed ways to let out anger that are acceptable and not seen as a loss of temper. For example, some said they find it helpful when they start to feel angry if they can get out and play ball. Others suggested turning on the radio and singing, going for walks, or finding a friend to talk with. One youth said he learned that taking deep breaths and thinking about something that makes him happy help. They joked about what he might be thinking.

After six group meetings, A was picked up by the police and charged with breaking into a store (fifth time). He was found guilty and sent to a correctional institution for six months. J and T often came late to the meetings and continued to say they came only because they had to.

As the group began to work on goal 3 (to learn about "changes"), a topic or issue of interest was selected each week by the members, and a plan was developed to study the issue the following week. Topics studied included living in prison, human sexuality and birth control, vocational training and jobs, managing money, and cooking. Films and guest speakers were used to provide information for discussion. The group also went on a trip to visit a vocational-training school.

E. Charted Progress

Each week, as additional tasks were planned by the group, the social worker would record them on the contracted plan. For example, the additional tasks that were developed for goal 2 (to control tempers) and for goal 3 (to learn about "changes") were added, as outlined in Table 8.5.

VII. Homelessness Case

A. Agency: West End Community Shelter

B. Client System

José Romano, a 37-year-old Hispanic male, is homeless and HIV positive. He has no family or close friends. He was referred to the shelter by the Department of Social Services. (For additional information, see Chapter 5, Ongoing Cases: Engagement Phase, VII. Homelessness Case.)

C. Summary of Preceding Phases

During engagement, Mr. R shared his history of past drug addiction and divorce. He worked out a plan with the worker that involved his going to the free health clinic located near the shelter. He also planned to attend a local church service. Data collection continued as the social worker and Mr. R began to implement the contracted plan. Mr. R's illness was diagnosed as slowly moving into the second stage of the virus. He was having night sweats and shortness of breath.

D. Intervention

Mr. R and the social worker carried out the "tasks" of the contracted plan. The social worker used counseling and information and referral throughout the process (see Figures 8.23 and 8.24). After the first week, both Mr. R and the social worker recognized his need for additional social supports. Mr. R did not have a car or any money for public transportation. The void in social supports was added to the list of "problems/needs" in the contracted plan (see Table 8.6). Mr. R agreed to contact Harmony, Inc., a service that offered a buddy system and transportation for persons with HIV or AIDS. Mr. R was assigned a buddy who would visit

TABLE 8.5 ■ Contracted Plan: Corrections Case

Date Identified	Problem/Need	Goal	Task	Contract	Date Anticipated	Date Accomplished
10/1	2. Bad tempers	2. To control tempers in school, home, and neighborhood	1. Discuss the problem of dealing with anger.	1. Social workers and group members	10/22	10/22
			2. Notice when angry.	2. Individual members	10/22 and each day	10/22–ongoing
			3. Find acceptable outlet.	3. Individual members	10/22 and each day	
			4. Keep track of successes and slip-ups on card.	4. Individual members	10/22 and each day	
			5. Report to group and chart number.	5. Individual members	10/29 and each Monday at group	
10/1	3. Need to understand "changes" of teenagers	3. To learn about some of the "changes" (including becoming independent, sex and birth control, and job training)	1. Select first topic—life in prison.	1. Group and members	10/22	10/22
			2. Plan program.	2. Group members	10/23	
			3. Call Prison Association for speaker.	3. Social worker	10/23	
			4. Have a talk and discussion.	4. Guest and group	10/29	

FIGURE 8.23 ■ Counseling: Homelessness Case

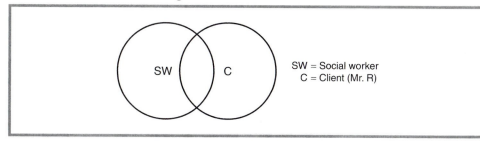

SW = Social worker
C = Client (Mr. R)

FIGURE 8.24 ■ Information and Referral: Homelessness Case

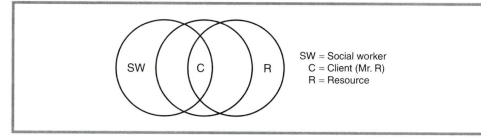

SW = Social worker
C = Client (Mr. R)
R = Resource

him at the shelter occasionally and take him to the Harmony social support group once a week. On the days when Mr. R wanted a ride to church because he didn't feel well enough to walk, he was able to call his buddy for transportation. While attending a church service, Mr. R met a man from his hometown in Puerto Rico. The man told Mr. R. that they were looking for additional help at the chicken farm where he worked. He agreed to pick up Mr. R and take him to see the farm supervisor. Mr. R was hired and worked for four weeks before he had to stop because of his illness. He then began working part time. On days when he felt able, he would call the supervisor to see if he could work. Mr. R applied for residence at Hope Home.

E. Charted Progress

As planned tasks were operationalized, the social worker would indicate on the contract the dates of accomplishment. She shared the process of charting progress with Mr. R to promote his sense of control over what was happening in his life.

TABLE 8.6 ■ Contracted Plan: Homelessness Case

Date Identified	Problem/Need	Goal	Task	Contract	Date Anticipated	Date Accomplished
5/7	1. Homeless—short term	1. To find emergency shelter	1. Enroll in shelter.	1. Mr. R & social worker	5/8	5/8
5/8	2. Spiritual void	2. To reunite with church	1. Go to service.	1. Mr. R	5/10	5/10
5/8	3. Lack of knowledge re: HIV	3. To gain information	1. Review information at shelter.	1. Social worker & Mr. R	5/9	5/9
			2. Go to free clinic, ask for help.	2. Mr. R		
5/8	4. No income/job	4. To earn income	1. Search for job.	1. Mr. R & social worker	5/9	5/17
			2. Apply for job.	2. Mr. R	5/15	5/19
			3. Start job.	3. Mr. R	5/20	5/21
			4. Seek SS/public assistance.	4. Mr. R	Depends on illness	
5/7	5. No housing after 60 days	5. To locate residence	1. Look for apartment or home for persons with AIDS.	1. Social worker & Mr. R	5/8	
			2. Get on waiting list for home for persons with AIDS.	2. Mr. R	5/11	6/24
5/8	6. HIV positive	6. To obtain medical care	1. Make appointment.	1. Social worker & Mr. R	5/8	5/8
			2. Go to free clinic.	2. Mr. R	5/9	5/9
			3. Continue treatment.	3. Mr. R	Next appointments	5/19
5/12	7. Social void	7. To obtain social support	1. Contact Harmony, Inc.	1. Mr. R	5/12	5/12
			2. Meet with staff person.	2. Mr. R	5/13	5/13
			3. Meet "buddy."	3. Mr. R	5/20	5/20

SUMMARY

This chapter focused on five General Method models of intervention with client systems that are primarily applicable at micro and mezzo practice levels—counseling, information and referral, crisis intervention, small group intervention, and case management and teamwork. Each of these models illustrated application of the strengths-based problem-solving processes and strategies discussed earlier as well as application of those processes and principles unique to the model. As the ongoing cases illustrate, the generalist social worker may apply more than one model in order to implement the contracted plan. When all of the tasks in the contracted plan have been accomplished, a formal phase of evaluation takes place. In the next chapter, the focus will be on models of intervention with client systems applicable at the macro practice level.

REFLECTION POINTS

Becoming a skilled social work practitioner requires knowledge and skills, including the ability to reflect upon practice endeavors. The following reflection points are designed to strengthen critical thinking and mastery of knowledge of key points in this chapter.

1. Define the following key models in generalist social work:
   - Counseling
   - Crisis intervention
   - Small group intervention
   - Information and referral
   - Case management and teamwork
2. How might human diversity influence intervention in micro and mezzo practice?
3. Drawing on human behavior and social environment theories, identify a change theory and consider it in relation to one of the seven ongoing cases. Discuss how to apply the theory to the intervention process in this case.
4. Provide examples of evidence-based questions (Chapter 3) about the intervention process for each of the models.
5. Review Section 1, Social Workers' Ethical Responsibility to Clients, of the *NASW Code of Ethics* (www.socialworkers.org) in relation to your professional behavior. How might these standards influence your professional behavior?
6. For further reading and research, use the models in Question 1 to locate social work references related to this chapter's content. (See Appendix A, Selected Internet Resources, and Appendix B, Selected Social Work Journals.) What underlying theoretical concepts are evident in the practice models described in the articles? How are they applied in the articles? How might they be applied in one of the seven ongoing cases in this chapter or in a case in your field internship?

CHAPTER 9

Intervention in Macro Generalist Practice

As with micro generalist practice, the strengths-based problem-solving and empowerment processes and strategies of macro-level intervention with large groups, organizations, and communities form several practice models within the General Method. Each of these macro-level intervention models is designed to address particular issues and client and action system needs, goals, and contracted plans in order to bring about planned change in client, action, and target systems. This chapter first presents an overview of macro generalist practice and macro practice knowledge and skills. Then, the chapter focuses on four macro-level intervention models of social and political advocacy, social planning and community development, locality development, and internal organizational change.

Overview

In macro generalist practice, as in micro- and mezzo-level generalist practice, the social worker stands at the interface of person-in-environment (client, action, and target systems and their environments) (see Figure 9.1) and targets large groups, organizations, and communities as the unit of attention in a planned change process designed:

1. To enhance the transactions and fit between the client system and the larger environment
2. To develop a sense of competence in the client system that is based on the actual exercise of power (Hardcastle, Powers, & Wenocur, 2004; Lee, 1997)

To enhance the transactions and fit between a community and its larger environmental surround (Goal 1), the generalist practitioner works with groups, organizations, and communities to modify conditions that impinge on the well-being of citizenry and that create barriers to the development of their potential. To develop a sense of competence in the macro client system that is based on the actual exercise of power (Goal 2), the generalist practitioner works within larger groups, organizations, and communities to enable citizens to set their own collaborative goals and modify conditions that create barriers to the well-being and developmental potential of its members.

Macro Practice Knowledge and Skills

Much of social work knowledge is applicable across the board in micro, mezzo, and macro social work practice using the General Method. Some specialized knowledge about empowerment as process and outcome, communities, organizations, funding sources, and group interaction skills, however, is particularly useful and applicable for macro practice.

Empowerment as Process and Outcome

In working with a macro client system to achieve strengths-based empowerment for the system as a whole, it is critical that both the generalist social worker and the client system pay close attention to factors that may affect building and maintaining their work together. Such factors may involve preconceived misbeliefs that:

▶ Service providers are the only or primary experts who possess the knowledge, skills, and resources and should therefore be the ones to assume full responsibility for the macro client system's goal achievement.
▶ Seeking help individually or collectively is a sign of weakness and a lack of expertise or power in selected roles.

FIGURE 9.1 ■ Person-in-Environment and Social Work Service Interface

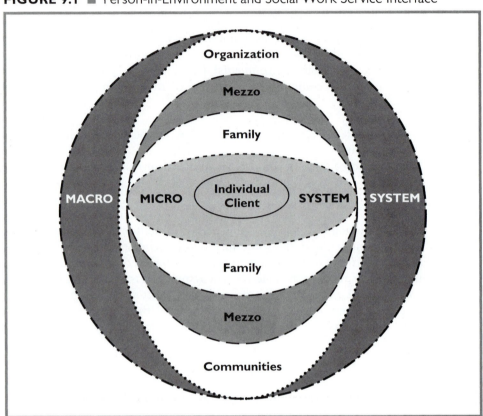

▶ Defining power in the collaborative decision-making process is unimportant.
▶ Appreciation, respect, and acceptance of each other's cultural diversity will implicitly happen and does not require explicit learning about role expectations in helping and being helped and in developing and maintaining a focus on goal accomplishment.
▶ Both the generalist social worker and the macro client system automatically share common interests in the political dimensions of the problems or issues that surround their contracted goals, working alliance, and goal accomplishment.

These faulty beliefs may translate into misplaced efforts to lodge responsibility and power for change solely with the generalist social worker and thereby avoid macro system responsibility for action and change.

    In reality, both the generalist social worker and the macro client system have power-related knowledge and expertise. At the outset of their engagement, it is essential that their respective power, expertise, strengths, capacities, and assets be recognized, identified, and explicitly acknowledged. The General Method acknowledges that the macro client system has the innate power and untapped assets and resources to effect change and achieve goals. Therefore, as with micro and mezzo client systems, it is the generalist social worker's responsibility to identify, strengthen, increase, and mobilize what the macro client system already possesses and harness it in the service of the issue or need identified by the macro client system. To accomplish this process, the generalist social worker facilitates the identification, development, and implementation of the macro client system's power and resources in collaborative ways that enable the macro client system to effect the desired changes.

As noted earlier, empowerment is a generative process through which vulnerable micro, mezzo, and macro client systems:

▶ Engage in dialogue that results in forming collaborative partnerships, articulating challenges, and defining directions.
▶ Learn about their strengths, capacities, and resources through the processes of discovery, analysis, and consideration of the pros and cons of possible solutions.
▶ Develop the means to activate resources, create alliances, expand opportunities, recognize successes, integrate gains, and monitor and evaluate outcomes.

Through this empowering process, all client systems are enabled to:

1. Increase their competence and problem-solving.
2. Apply their existing strengths.
3. Mobilize personal, familial, organizational, and community resources.
4. Exercise greater self-direction and control over their environment.
5. Meet their needs and attain their aspirations.

In promoting empowerment at the macro system level, a generalist social worker shifts between working with a client system to working with an action system to working with a target system, and often moves back and forth from working with one individual to working with many in large groups, organizations, or communities. In the beginning dialogue with the macro client system during the formation of an empowering alliance and working relationship, the generalist social worker draws on many skills designed to maximize macro client system power by encouraging cohesive development and distribution of leadership, information, and skill development. This process requires that the generalist social worker facilitate the development of power in as many members of the macro client system as possible and explicitly acknowledge or give voice to those macro system members who may initially perceive their contributions as insignificant.

Initially, the macro-level client system and the generalist practitioner join together to identify collective concerns, gather and evaluate evidence, and formulate an ongoing assessment of the internal and external components of the presenting social problem and its environmental context. Because the problems and needs of individual members are often symbolic of larger community needs and issues, the assessment process includes both individual and communal perceptions of need, thereby creating a path for collective decisions and actions. In other words, the assessment process is a dialectical one that takes into account sources of problems ranging from the individual's person-in-environment context to the community environment to the external environmental context surrounding the community (see Figure 9.2) and back and forth.

In macro client system assessment, the generalist social worker discovers and considers not only problems presented by the client and the target systems but also the naturally occurring strengths, assets, and resources of these systems and their interacting environmental systems that can be utilized in work toward goal achievement. During the discovery process in the data collection and assessment and contract planning phases (Chapters 6 and 7), the generalist practitioner and the macro client system engage in a consciousness-raising process to gain a better understanding of the issues and needs at hand, internal strengths and stresses, environmental strengths and stresses, and a clearer focus in determining the macro client system's preferred goals and objectives. They analyze and reflect on the meaning of the resource capabilities, explore the pros and cons of possible outcomes, and frame possible alternative solutions that incorporate the macro client system's preferred goals and objectives. This reflection and action pattern continues in cyclical fashion throughout the intervention process. As noted in Figure 9.2, the collaborative empowerment process follows the General Method phases of the strengths-based problem-solving process and includes multiple components. The generalist social worker joins with the macro client system to increase awareness, gather and assess information for collaborative decision-making, and formulate strategies for goals and objectives.

Specifically, social work generalists and their macro client systems collaboratively engage in the development of educational and developmental tasks, linkage and brokerage tasks, advocacy tasks, and social action tasks that target the interface of large groups, organizations, and communities and their surrounding environmental systems (Hardcastle, Powers, & Wenocur, 2004; Haynes & Mickelson, 2000; Rothman, Erlich, & Tropman, 1995; Schneider & Lester, 2001):

1. *Educational and developmental tasks designed to*
   - Enhance strengths-based problem-solving competencies and developmental capacities of macro client systems in their environmental contexts.
   - Educate macro client systems about resources and networks.
   - Enable macro client systems to use existing strengths and resources of both systems and their environments to increase macro system coping and resilience.
   - Promote the self-direction of macro client systems.
2. *Linkage tasks designed to*
   - Provide and broker connections and coordination between macro client systems and environmental resource systems that provide services and opportunities.
   - Collaborate with macro client systems to uncover and address unjust and unfair practices and policies in their environmental contexts.
   - Promote linkages and social networks that can legitimize the aspirations of macro client systems.
3. *Advocacy tasks designed to*
   - Enable the macro client system to promote fair and just operation of environmental resource and service systems.

FIGURE 9.2 ■ Macro Client Systems' Empowering Processes

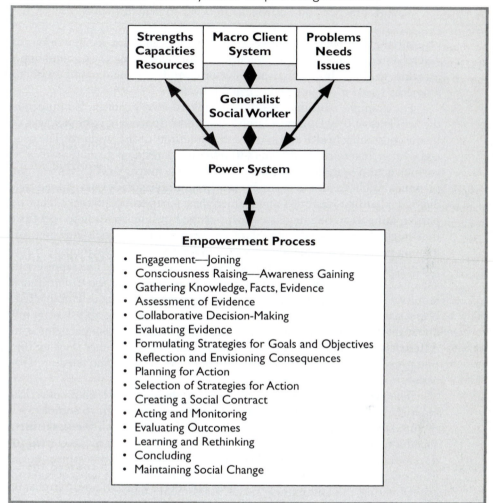

- Promote development of just and fair social policies.
- Enhance the macro client system's ability to apply evidence-based knowledge and skills to increase responsiveness of environmental service systems in meeting client system needs.
4. *Social action tasks designed to*
   - Join the macro client system and generalist social worker in promoting intra- and intersystem environmental change in order to increase macro system well-being.
   - Engage in social action to support the use of just and fair policies, services, and resources to promote the well-being of all human systems.
   - Use empirical evidence to support and evaluate the social action process and progress toward task completion and goal accomplishment.

- Use evidence-based knowledge and skills to advance macro system social work practice and knowledge in order to benefit society.

Overall, the empowerment process requires that generalist social workers assist their macro system clients in developing leadership, recognizing choices and opportunities, locating genuine but practical solutions, and enhancing and cultivating their strengths-based problem-solving capabilities.

For example, consider the following macro-level problem. Continued housing of the residents of City Courts, a large low-income apartment complex, was threatened by the continuing health and safety code violations of the landlord. The generalist social worker, macro client system (330 residents, 2 resident groups, and 5 leaders), and various action systems (city housing managers, mayor's office representatives, city planners, public health department workers, and legal advisors) joined together in a dialogue that first identified and formed their partnership alliances. They next began participating in an ongoing assessment of the housing situation to identify strategies that might help preserve or replace the targeted low-income housing. In this dialoguing process, the generalist social worker focused on facilitating the process of joining, coming together, and forming supportive alliances. The representatives from various community organizations and groups, including the disenfranchised community residents, began articulating the challenges and the disempowered residents began gaining voice. In the process, they began generating and sharing information about the situation. The client system and each action system participant focused on different aspects of the problem and needs but joined together in using the information to reformulate a collective assessment of the problem and needs and to create an action plan for goal achievement.

The generalist social worker assisted in the discovery, data collection, and assessment process by helping the various community members to complete a strengths-oriented, ecosystem community assessment. To accomplish this task, the generalist social worker met with targeted community representatives who elected to work on developing the items that would become part of this needs assessment questionnaire. This subgroup became the community advisory body that subsequently focused on implementing the community needs assessment survey with targeted community groups. They eventually presented the findings in several meetings with the macro client system. The needs assessment survey explored and considered several key dimensions of the housing problem by examining the City Courts community identity, profile, and audit of strengths and barriers:

▶ The knowledge and understanding of the history of the housing community
▶ The geographical boundaries of the resident community and other community systems existing in this identified area
▶ The existing services and their relationship to community residents and the landlord
▶ The interpretation of the presenting problem by various stakeholders
▶ The power structure in the community, their relationship to City Courts' residents, and their available resources
▶ The degree of governmental enforcement of its housing policies

▶ The degree of willingness for different community client systems to work together to help residents remain in their housing
▶ The community alliances in existence, how well they are working, and what connections are missing
▶ The solutions attempted in the past and present
▶ What else might change in the environment if community residents were able to resolve their landlord problems and stay in their housing
▶ What else might change in the community if the residents were forced to move or become displaced

Through the information gained in the needs assessment, the generalist social worker and the macro client system searched for naturally existing strengths in their community partnerships, explored their implicit and explicit expectations for goal accomplishments, and analyzed their resource capabilities, particularly their funding and the buy-in commitment to work on a just and fair resolution. They explored the consequences of taking different actions toward different solutions.

In promoting the empowerment of the City Courts community, the generalist social worker and resident leaders used the following macro strategies:

▶ Educating groups, organizations, and communities about resources, strengths-based problem-solving, and the benefits of collective action
▶ Providing training and creating opportunities for leadership development
▶ Building group, organization, and community capacity for participating in support networks, governance activities, and collective task achievement
▶ Engaging groups, organizations, and communities in social and political advocacy
▶ Creating opportunities for group, organization, and community success in strengths-based problem-solving, resource mobilization, and planned change
▶ Providing professional technical assistance

These strategies resulted in the development of a resident civic association but failed in negotiations with the landlord. The next steps included mobilization of wider community resources and more stakeholders for greater power and greater potential for successful action. The community advisory body and the resident civic association, along with the generalist social worker, created a plan that gained news media coverage, community meetings with the mayor and representative of the City Council, and, finally, governmental sanctions that enforced building code compliance. In turn, the landlord tried to eject all of the residents in order to rehabilitate the property, and legal action had to be solicited and taken to support residents' rights, according to city regulations, to remain in their apartments while rehabilitation work was being done.

In this example, the generalist social worker and the macro client system became part of the larger community group that came together to facilitate the process of social change. Consciousness-raising, self-awareness, resource identification and expansion, flexible leadership, harnessing power through ongoing dialogue, discovery and assessment, and development of resources became crucial in gaining an empowering solution for the City Courts community.

■ C O N C E P T   **9 . 1**

> *Communities* are comprised of groups of people connected with each other by the geographic locality in which they live and by their various interactions and transactions.

Communities

Geographic communities can be mobilized by generalist social workers to increase the collective participation and contribution of members, but it is important to note that different groups or people in the community have different preferences for the kinds of help they seek and use. For example, teen mothers in urban areas are more likely to respond positively to informal support from their families and friends compared to formal, institutional support from organizations (Bergman, 1989). Farm families, on the other hand, may prefer to seek assistance from clergy, family, and friends in that order (Martinez-Brawley & Blundell, 1989). The important point in these two studies is that no one community is exactly the same as another community even though they may share some similarities. The state of Maryland, for example, contains multiple geographic communities that differ markedly from each other: rural southeastern shore communities, central state river communities, District of Columbia suburban communities, Baltimore City communities, and rural northwestern Piedmont communities. As this example shows, many large communities are internally diverse by geography. They also may be diverse in ethnicity, social class, economy, education, and people's needs as reflected in the ways they earn a living, their income levels, their housing circumstances, and their preferred religious, cultural, social, and recreational institutions.

One way to understand and prepare for working with a given community is to take a road map and create an informational map overlay that conveys areas of diversity, available resources, and information about what it is like for people to live, work, attend school, seek services, attend religious institutions, play, and socialize within a given geographical area. As seen in Figure 9.3, this information can be organized along several topical dimensions prior to plotting it on an informational map.

Thus, in communities, generalist social workers need to pay attention to the values, economic circumstances, and political realities of each specific locality and to the diverse groups living within each portion of the community. Lack of understanding of culturally driven beliefs and practices often leads to inadequate service implementation. This, in turn, leads to poor client system utilization and poor client system and program outcomes. Indeed, studies show that when social services are not targeted appropriately to match the values held by community residents and their collective needs, the services are not likely to be effective in achieving communitywide change. For example, a study examining patterns of family intimacy in an urban community found a large variety of parenting practices associated with how children were bathed, sleeping arrangements among family members, and physical expressions of intimacy between parents and children. This study revealed that these patterns differed significantly between groups who identified themselves as Hispanic, Caucasian,

FIGURE 9.3 ■ Examples of Knowing a Community

Community Characteristics	Examples
1. What are the major characteristics of the people living in the community?	Percent of age range, citizens and foreign-born, ethnicities, religious denominations
2. What economic characteristics are represented in the community? Who and which organizations control jobs?	Types of employment, types of industries, sources of wealth and income, recent changes about job losses
3. What are the patterns of unemployment and what is the general income range? What services are available for the unemployed?	Percent of people unemployed, length of unemployment by ethnicity, and by reasons; percent of income distribution, and median income in the community
4. What is the housing pattern? Where do people live? What is their ethnic and income diversity?	Type of available housing and percent of people using different types of housing; percent of single homes, rentals, and public housing units
5. How many schools, location of schools, and other educational facilities are there in relation to where people live?	Types of educational and/or training facilities available for different age range of people
6. How many religious denomination facilities for worship are evident and where?	Types of churches, synagogues, mosques, and other spiritual/religious denomination meeting facilities; percent of people attending; types of services available
7. How is public information communicated across newspapers, radio, or electronic media?	Types of newspapers and other media; ownership; percent of use; and types of content being transmitted
8. What is the culture for socialization, music, art, athletics, and civics? What social support and charitable services do any of these organizations provide?	Types of organizations that provide services for art, music, athletics, civic and fraternal organizations; percent of people using and attending these services
9. What are the norms evident in seeking help by different members of the community and for what purpose?	Types of agencies that provide help with specific needs: health care, spiritual support care, end-of-life care, early childhood care
10. How does the local community government operate and how are people in the community involved?	Types of people attending public forums; types of public service available; percent of public services well maintained
11. What kind of community assistance can caregiving adults rely on for which kind of support?	Type of formal and informal networks and services available for parents with children of different ages and developmental needs; adult caregivers to other adults with health and disabilities difficulties; respite care availability; types of self-help groups or voluntary charitable associations

African American, Cambodian, Korean, and Vietnamese (Ahn & Gilbert, 1992). The study also found that child abuse prevention programs were likely to fail if the programs were not sensitive to personal and community values and customs.

Organizations

Working in macro settings requires generalist practitioners to become versed in the operations of the multiple organizations and agencies providing critical community services. For example, working with a community to address parental child abuse necessitates knowledge not only of the differing cultural patterns in parenting within the community but also knowledge about the availability, accessibility, and acceptability to the community of the organizations designed to help people who have difficulty parenting (public child welfare services and protective services, private nonprofit organizations such as Parents Anonymous, and religious organizations).

The following questions serve as guidelines for collecting organizational information that is relevant to community acceptance and utilization of services:

▶ How do the design and structure of an organization's mission and service delivery help the community groups it intends to help?
▶ Do the data provide evidence about how well the organization serves the community groups it intends to help?
▶ Does the community perceive the organization in a positive or a negative way? Why?
▶ Which governance auspice (public, private not-for-profit, private for-profit, religious) operates and funds the organizational service?

Generalist social workers also need to understand how organizations function. For example, they need to know:

▶ The resources and structures that sustain the organization's ability to accomplish its mission
▶ The barriers that impede or impair the organization's ability to accomplish its mission
▶ The processes and patterns of organizational change
▶ The motivational factors that sustain employees in their work toward accomplishing organizational goals
▶ The retention patterns of staff
▶ The sources of formal and informal power in decision making

Further, generalist practitioners need to understand organizational patterns of change that are associated with funding sources and patterns, personnel turnover, and the political realities of the communities in which service organizations compete for their survival (Frey, 1990). Organizational development along these lines is continuous and normal but not always apparent. Zastrow (2003) provides a useful reminder to social workers involved in organizational change when he notes "wars are won and lost by people who have a staying power in organizations and communities" (p. 236).

Funding Sources

All provision of services to individuals, families, groups, organizations, and communities depends on some kind of external funding. Each funding source has its own cycles or revolving time frames for allocating funds and conditions about substantiating its use with intended client systems. Specifically, funding sources may specify:

▶ How funds are to be used
▶ How the use of funds is to be documented
▶ How the appropriateness of this use with intended client systems is to be substantiated
▶ How outcomes are to be documented

Given these requirements, therefore, it is also useful to consider:

▶ Who controls the funds? Individuals or groups? Private or public?
▶ What is the funding calendar cycle in allocating and disbursing funds?
▶ What coalitions are the funds tied to? New services or repackaging and relabeling existing services? Matching funds?
▶ Are these conditions worth the funds received?

In addition, funding source requirements may influence not only the services delivered to client systems but also the employment, deployment, and professional role of personnel. That is, how the social work role is implemented in macro practice depends in part on what the macro project is intended to accomplish and whether the social worker is funded to work *inside* or *outside* the organizational entity. Outside work in neighborhood and community settings is essential for goal accomplishment in macro generalist social work practice.

Group Interaction Skills

A working knowledge of large groups, communities, and organizations translates into multiple techniques and decision-making skills for use in groups (Brueggeman, 1996; Rose, 1998; Sheafor & Horejsi, 2003; Ungar, Manuel, Mealy, & Campbell, 2004).

Brainstorming elicits multiple alternative ideas from group members for accomplishing goals and envisioning the consequences of proposed paths by which organizations and communities achieve solutions. This technique is helpful with groups whose members have achieved some level of acquaintance, trust, and comfort with each other. Brainstorming, however, can have an inhibiting effect in groups whose members do not know each other and are not committed to work toward a common goal and in groups whose leader or facilitator does not help the group commit to the idea of change.

Nominal group technique is designed to identify problems and solutions in organizations and communities and reflect the group problem-solving process. This technique is sometimes considered superior to brainstorming because it tends to avoid judging and evaluating the various options generated by the group. All ideas and options generated during discussion are posted for members to see and then rank ordered according to their preferences. Low-ranked items are dropped and the process is repeated in iterative fashion until the group choice is clear. At this point, facilitating group commitment to the top-ranked preference becomes a key task.

Negotiating is used to achieve mutually agreed on decisions acceptable to all involved. This process may take place when persons disagree, the identity of the person is merged with the problem, an adversarial situation is created, and little apparent progress is made in resolving the issue. Effective negotiation involves separating the person from the problem and creating alternative solutions. Directing attention to the mutual interests of all parties increases the probability of reaching an agreement that is satisfactory to those involved.

Needs assessment is used to identify assets and resources and to appraise the breadth and depth of organizational and community strengths, problems, and needs. Typically, needs assessments include questions such as:

- ► Who is asking for this needs assessment?
- ► Why is the needs assessment important?
- ► What information is being sought?
- ► How should questions be phrased to obtain the desired information?
- ► Who will benefit from knowing this information?
- ► What are the possible sources of information?
- ► What level of expertise is needed to develop, implement, collect, analyze, and present the needs assessment?

Needs assessments generally include a profile of community characteristics such as resident socio-demographic and socio-economic data; type, quality, and costs of community housing; employment and transportation; social, legal, economic, educational, and political issues; and health, education, and recreation facilities. The profile also identifies patterns of how people use community services, strengths and barriers in services utilization, means of communication, resource management, and political resource assessment. Needs assessment profiles may also be used in identifying organizational characteristics and patterns.

Public relations skills require generalist practitioners to become fluent in communicating ideas through public speaking, working with different types of media, and handling media exposure that ranges from written public service announcements to television interviews to testimony at public hearings.

Lobbying, or engaging in political activism, is designed to persuade elected and appointed officials and ultimately redress social conditions created by unjust or unfair practices. Lobbying requires advance preparation, skill, and developing working alliances with elected officials and power brokers. In lobbying, Zastrow (2003) recommends that generalist social workers follow three basic rules:

1. Get to know your legislative body or elected officials before you lobby them.
2. Create an environment in which elected officials get to know you before you lobby them.
3. Always be inclusive and respectful of other persons' opinions and positions.

■ **C O N C E P T 9 . 2**

Social and political advocacy involves professional application of generalist social work methods to help macro client, action, and target systems "acquire the personal, interpersonal, and political power they need to take control of their lives and bring about changes in the [laws,] policies, organizations, and public attitudes that are adversely impacting their lives" (Sheafor & Horejsi, 2003, p. 414).

Social and Political Advocacy

The generalist practitioner may find a potential resource that is resistant to the requests of a client system or the social worker. Such skills as providing evidence, publicizing, bargaining, organizing, demonstrating, taking legal action, and influencing policy development may have to be utilized. For example, a hospital social worker with refugee patients has been unsuccessful in obtaining services from a refugee program. The social worker knows that the program is being funded to offer the services requested. The generalist may need to present to her supervisor and to the administrator of the refugee program evidence that several requests were made without results. If this intervention is unsuccessful and efforts at bargaining are also unproductive, social and political advocacy may need to take place.

In this practice vignette, social and political advocacy begins with a micro-level practice situation and progresses to the macro level. Thus, the micro case becomes the impetus for macro-level change efforts.

The goals of social and political advocacy include improving the quality of life and meeting the needs of client systems through:

▶ Empowering client systems to act on their own behalf in meeting needs and achieving a better quality of life
▶ Empowering client systems to be active, responsible participants in governance processes
▶ Promoting service delivery policies and practices that respect client system rights and entitlements
▶ Educating the public about social issues and the rights of vulnerable populations
▶ Creating basic social changes in public policies about access to and distribution of public resources
▶ Creating basic social changes in organizational and institutional programs and service delivery practices that deny client system rights and entitlements

Depending on the problem, need, strengths, and goals in practice situations, social and political advocacy may involve efforts to achieve either incremental or fundamental change in the status quo of social inequities. Whenever it is feasible, the social work generalist employs a nonadversarial approach to the decision-makers who comprise the social and political power base of a community. Nonadversarial techniques include education, logical reasoning, bargaining, and mutual negotiation (Kirst-Ashman & Hull, 1997; Schneider & Lester, 2001). This approach is especially important in working incrementally to redress inequities for client systems in the application of policies and procedures about service or resource eligibility.

When more fundamental change is needed to reduce inequities in the distribution of public resources and the lack of power sharing in community decisions, the social work generalist may employ an adversarial approach in relation to the social and political power base of the community. This type of change includes ensuring fair access to existing entitlements, exercising existing rights, redistributing public resources, and developing new resources. Generally, such change requires public confrontation and community consciousness-raising strategies (Schneider & Lester, 2001).

One strategy often used in social and political advocacy efforts to change community inequities involves force-field analysis. Based on Lewin's (1951) field theory, this strategy has been developed as a tool in data collection, assessment, and intervention with large groups and organizations (Brueggeman, 1996). Whenever any macro system is not able to change the status quo, there are usually restraining forces operating that are stronger than the driving forces of change. The generalist social worker may try to offer the macro system support and increase its understanding of the situation through using and explaining the process of force-field analysis. Or, the social worker may use the analysis to build a plan for social and political advocacy. The strategy of force-field analysis has characteristics similar to those of the tool for problem prioritization (Chapter 7) and procedures used for evaluation through goal analysis (Chapter 10).

Basically, the force-field analytic strategy involves a framework to organize information as it relates to the accomplishment of a particular goal or task. The forces that influence those community persons responsible for enacting tasks necessary for goal accomplishment are organized and classified as either driving or restraining forces. The process begins with clarification of a specific goal. Then, the primary persons needed to achieve the designated goal or task are identified. Next, each of the driving and restraining forces is evaluated in terms of openness to and potential for change. The consistency and stability of each force during a time of change is also explored. For positive change to occur, the driving forces must be greater than the restraining forces. If the driving and restraining forces are equally balanced, it is likely that no change will occur. If the restraining forces are greater, change is likely to be in a negative direction. This assessment strategy can be used to help any group, community, or organization understand more clearly why certain tasks are not being performed and certain goals are not being accomplished. It also can identify planned intervention strategies to counteract restraining forces and build up driving, change-producing forces.

Other social and political advocacy strategies include (Brueggeman, 1996; Schneider & Lester, 2001; Sheafor & Horejsi, 2003):

▶ Employing consciousness-raising strategies to educate groups about resources to which they are entitled, the impact of laws on their lives, and service delivery barriers

► Building community coalitions to lobby for change in laws, policies, programs, and practices adversely affecting vulnerable populations
► Changing legislative policies to increase availability, adequacy, and acceptability of community services and resources
► Using knowledge about individual and collective rights to service, protections and entitlements based on laws and their interpretations, and avenues of appealing adverse decisions on behalf of client systems

In today's economic and political climate, social and political advocacy strategies and activities are used to address the overwhelming social problems and needs, the paucity of public funds and resources, and the competition among social welfare, health, mental health, and education programs for limited funds available. Indeed, advocacy activities of legislative analysis, lobbying, and testimony have become essential for the well-being of the individuals, families, groups, organizations, and communities served by generalist social workers.

Through their day-to-day practice, attention to the world around them, and ongoing professional development, social workers gain understanding of the causes of and possible solutions for a variety of social problems. They also collect information about the effects of existing and newly implemented public laws and policies on client systems and service delivery. Influencing existing and proposed legislation, however, involves more than narrative sharing of practice-derived information with key legislators and government officeholders. To exercise leverage and secure needed services and benefits for client systems at the policy level, the social work generalist obtains information about the following:

► Individual and collective rights, protections, guarantees, and entitlements based on existing laws and policies intended to alleviate the targeted social problem and need
► Implementation and programmatic application of laws and policies
► Avenues for appealing adverse decisions affecting client system functioning and well-being
► Resources available and accessible for informed social and political advocacy to change existing laws and policies and to promulgate new ones

With both existing and newly implemented laws and policies, the generalist social worker empirically monitors and documents their impact on the well-being of the targeted population, the numbers served, the degree of goal achievement, the long-term consequences, and the costs in both human and financial terms (see Figure 9.4).

With proposed legislation, the generalist social worker (Schneider & Lester, 2001; Sheafor & Horejsi, 2003):

► Analyzes the substance, purpose, and underlying values of the proposed changes to existing laws and policies
► Anticipates potential consequences and ramifications for the affected constituency
► Develops data that will support, modify, or defeat the proposed bill
► Acquires information about the committee structure and membership handling the proposed bill in order to identify central policymakers, learn about their

FIGURE 9.4 ■ Policy Analysis Framework

I. Facts about the target policy
  - Historical development and background
  - Problems addressed
  - Goals and objectives
  - Implementation, eligibility, and funding stipulations
  - Supporting database
II. Feasibility study of target policy
  - Explicit projected and implied outcomes
  - Underlying social values, beliefs, and assumptions
  - Social, economic, and political feasibility
  - Support for and opposition to the policy—who, what, why, how
  - Ramifications of policy for diverse population groups and human service delivery systems
III. Assessment of merit
  - Social, economic, and human costs and consequences
  - Differential impact on diverse population groups and client systems
  - Currency, accuracy, and adequacy of data purporting to support policy
  - Possible unanticipated outcomes
  - Overall merit or lack thereof

values and motives in relation to the proposed bill, and target them for lobbying efforts
▶ Acquires information about the fiscal requirements of the bill and sources of funding
▶ Acquires information about the political ramifications and sources of support and opposition to the bill
▶ Analyzes the evidence gathered
▶ Estimates the potential for mobilizing community support and political action to support, modify, or defeat the legislative initiative

After gathering and analyzing this evidence, the generalist social worker prepares a presentation for written or oral testimony (see Figure 9.5). The generalist also sets an action agenda for lobbying key policymakers that includes a factual definition of the problem and need from an action perspective; empirical evidence about needs, goals, and priorities for change; and plans for building advocacy coalitions. During this process, the social worker considers the values underlying the policy proposal on the table and the values underlying alternative options being considered. When presenting a proposed policy or information about an existing policy to power brokers and decision-makers, the generalist practitioner focuses on articulating facts about the target policy, analysis of its feasibility, and assessment of its merit and sets aside comments about competition among lawmakers and program directors to obtain limited resources for their preferred projects.

FIGURE 9.5 ■ Guide for Public Hearing Testimony on Pending Legislation

I. Create an informed knowledge base
   • Conduct a policy analysis (see Figure 9.4).
II. Prepare a position statement
   • Prepare a succinct, focused, evidence-driven statement of perceived problems (or assets) of the proposed legislation.
   • Present the position of the group, organization, or community represented.
   • Present recommendations of the entity represented.
   • Summarize these three major points in succinct outline form on 3 × 5 cards or PowerPoint presentations.
   • Prepare brief bio sketch outline on 3 × 5 cards or PowerPoint, including
     —social worker's name and relevant credentials, and
     —entity represented, its relevant goals and accomplishments.
III. Present testimony
   • Identify self.
   • Identify entity represented.
   • Present statement.
   • Answer questions briefly or reply, "I'm sorry I do not have the answer." If feasible, add "I will get back to you about that on _____."

A key component of social and political advocacy is building an action coalition of client systems, community citizens, professionals, members of civic and religious organizations, planning groups, and other interested stakeholders. The goal of this action coalition is to influence the thoughts and plans of lawmakers, government officials, and power brokers through participating in public hearings mandated by law, one-to-one or small group lobbying efforts, client system narrative testimony, and professional expert testimony by social workers and others.

Throughout the social and political advocacy process, the generalist social worker uses strengths-based problem-solving, empowerment processes, and evidentiary data to facilitate client and action system participation in obtaining needed resources. This partnership is designed to share knowledge, mobilize client and action system capabilities, and enable client and action systems to accept responsibility for identifying problems, selecting solutions, and bringing about change. As the systems become informed, exercise their capacities, and experience successes resulting from their work, they begin to comprehend that they have the power to control their lives (Ecklein & Lauffer, 1972). That is, the systems become empowered.

It is important to note that social work generalists are not limited to legislative analysis and advocacy related to policy proposed or developed by others. In developing policy, they may:

▶ Examine the social, economic, and political implications of a policy change that they support, and study its underlying values and reflected preferences.
▶ Analyze the human and financial costs and benefits.
▶ Identify key stakeholders.

▶ Collaborate with key stakeholders in bringing the proposed policy changes forward.

Such collaboration is essential because it is city council members, county council representatives, state legislators, congresspersons, and senators who hold the governing power and decision-making responsibility to accept or reject a local, state, or federal policy proposal.

Sometimes, social workers are asked: *Who gives you the right to advocate for this client system or social policy?* The authority to advocate for client, action, and target systems faced with social injustice and personal need derives from social workers' professional code of ethics, job descriptions, the permission of client systems, and the civil and legal rights of client, action, and target systems. In advocacy efforts, generalist practitioners first promote engagement and commitment of client and action systems and other key stakeholders. Later, if necessary, they may choose to employ strategies that are more confrontational and likely to polarize the client, action, and target systems involved. Polarizing strategies are not used without a great deal of contemplation, planning, and preparation for dealing with the possibility of community split.

■ C O N C E P T   **9 . 3**

> *Social planning and community development* involve professional application of generalist social work methods in building community capacity to use their strengths, resources, and political skills with identified power systems in order to bring about environmental change in political structures and organizations.

Social Planning and Community Development

A social worker who perceives needs on the broader societal level may wonder where to start and how to carry through with efforts to bring about social planning and community development. Time and energy limitations of the social worker should be realistically recognized, with activities carefully planned to avoid wasted effort. For social planning and community development, the General Method is somewhat modified, because the system of contact usually does not have the identified need, nor does that system see any reason to respond to the need, even though it has the power to do so. Although the method has been described repeatedly as a collaborative process between a social worker and a client system, in this type of work the social worker often executes the process alone. Sometimes the work involves advocacy for particular client systems. In these cases, every effort is made to involve and empower the client systems in each step of the process. At times, however, a social worker is advocating for a class of people or for a policy change that affects people in society at large. Although a social worker may try to join with others in coalitions, teams, or action systems to bring about the desired change, it is possible that the process will have to be initiated and perhaps completed by the social worker alone. Whether alone or with others, the procedure for work in the extended environment can be guided by the six phases of the General Method.

An outline of the General Method as designed in this text is repeated in Figure 9.6. Having first identified both a need in society and the systems primarily responsible for meeting the need, a social worker can follow the outline as a guide for action. The questions raised during each phase of the General Method may be modified or expanded for greater relevance. For example, the three main components of the first phase are shown as problems, feelings, and goals. When beginning to engage in the process, the generalist social worker studies the problem, need, or issue in the extended environment by asking the following questions:

1. *What is the problem or need as perceived by*
   a. *Me (social worker), my agency, my profession?*
   b. *The systems with the power to respond to the problem or need?*
   c. *Others*
      1. *The group of people feeling the problem or need?*
      2. *People in society at large?*

The social worker then proceeds to an inquiry about feelings and goals as the following questions are asked:

2. *What feelings surround the problem or need as felt by*
   a. *Me, my agency, my profession?*
   b. *The power systems?*
   c. *Others: those with the problem or need, society at large?*

FIGURE 9.6 ■ The General Method

I. Engagement
  • Problems
  • Feelings
  • Goals
II. Data Collection
  • Problems
  • Persons
  • Environment
III. Assessment and Contract Setting
  • Assessment statements
  • Problem prioritization
  • Contracting (plan)
	IV. Intervention
	  • Micro and mezzo levels
	  • Macro level
	V. Evaluation
	  • Goal analysis
	  • Contract review
	  • Contract reformulation
	VI. Termination
	  • Decision: transfer, refer,
	    terminate
	  • Plan: timing, follow-up
	  • Termination

3. *What goals related to the problem or need can be identified by*
   a. *Me, my agency, my profession?*
   b. *The power systems?*
   c. *Others: those with the problem or need, society at large?*

Moving into data collection (phase II), the social worker gathers information about problems, persons, and environment. In social planning and community development, the generalist practitioner uses both available and new data to consolidate information about community needs and service availability, adequacy, and acceptability. He or she also works with community leaders to identify what is needed in developing a plan for obtaining additional data that will facilitate problem definition and resolution. Designing, collecting, and analyzing this additional information so that it adds new information to and becomes part of the substantive database for social planning involves technical processes that the generalist social worker may not possess. In this instance, consultation with a macro social work specialist may be indicated.

In this task-oriented style of macro practice, it is important to identify and plan for the amelioration of need effectively, efficiently, and systematically (Rothman, Erlich, & Tropman, 1995). Thus, data collection typically requires empirical data and some computerized entry of the data. Social planning also may require computerized statistical data analysis to identify trends and clarify community development needs. When conducted in this manner, social planning becomes the means for assessing existing and newly collected data that, in turn, become translated into an assessment and eventually incorporated into goals, objectives, and an action plan. It is important that these goals reflect the change desired by a community if needs are to be met, resource gaps addressed, and the vulnerable empowered. Questions to be answered in this phase are as follows:

4. *What is the scope (number of people), the duration (length of time), and the severity (degree to which it is a life-or-death issue) of the problem or need?*
5. *Who are the persons suffering from the problem or unmet need? What is their motivation and capacity to work on the problem or need?*
6. *Who are the people in the power systems (titles, roles, personal characteristics)? What is their motivation and capacity to work on the problem or need?*
7. *What are the power systems—structure, channels, lines of authority, processes, rules of procedure? How are decisions made?*

Question 7 is extremely important if a generalist social worker is to intervene effectively in a power system. If, for example, a social worker enters the legislative arena with the intent to have a bill introduced or passed, it is imperative that he or she have knowledge of the legislative process, as well as of the legislators themselves. If the social development is occurring in a nondemocratic society, the social worker needs to understand the overt and covert governing and decision-making processes used by the society's formal and hidden power structures.

Supplementing information about the identified power systems, the generalist social worker needs to know the following:

8. *Are there any other systems with the potential for meeting the identified need or for resolving the problem?*
9. *Are there other systems that could influence or put pressure on the power systems?*
10. *Are there other resources to support, or to collaborate with, the social worker in his or her efforts?*

On the basis of the data collected, the generalist social worker is then in a position to make a clearer assessment of the problem or need and to plan interventions. The questions raised in the assessment (phase III) include:

11. *Who has what (problem or need) and why?*
12. *If more than one problem or need has been identified, how should they be prioritized?*
13. *What is the most effective plan to work on the problems or needs as prioritized?*

As a plan is developed, the social worker would recall and may plan to use political skills, strategies, and the testimony guide (see Figure 9.5). As tasks are listed sequentially on a contracted-plan sheet, a generalist social worker might include efforts to mobilize other individuals, groups, or organizations to work with him or her on mutual goals stated on the contract. If others become involved in the action, the tasks may be distributed and contracted among the participants. As pointed out, however, it is possible that all of the tasks will have to be carried out by the social worker alone.

In intervention (phase IV) during social planning and community development, a generalist social worker may have face-to-face contact with the power systems and use various political skills and tactics. The social worker may act as a team member in a coalition or may refer the issue to another resource for action. Throughout the intervention phase, the social worker (team) asks these questions:

14. *Am I (are we) completing the tasks as planned?*
15. *Am I (are we) ready to move on to the next planned task?*

As the generalist social worker moves into evaluation, the questions asked are the following:

16. *To what extent has (have) the goal(s) been accomplished?*
17. *If there has been goal accomplishment, was this the result of my (our) efforts? If there has not been goal accomplishment, why not?*

Here, too, the contracted plan for social planning and community development created during assessment is carefully reviewed if goals have not been accomplished. Timing anticipated, resources contracted, and tasks sequenced along with stated goals and problems on the plan are reconsidered.

The social worker (team) then asks the following question:

18. *Is there a need to reformulate goals or any other dimension of the plan? Are more overt political behaviors needed?*

In the final phase, the generalist social worker (team) makes the decision regarding termination of his or her involvement in the issue with the identified power systems. Questions raised in this phase include:

19. *Is it time for me (us) to refer, transfer, or terminate my (our) efforts to bring about change in the extended environment in relation to the identified problem or needs?*
20. *How do I (we) plan to terminate?*
    a. *When?*
    b. *Will there be a follow-up?*
    c. *In terminating, are there feelings or reactions that need to be expressed? by me? the power systems? others?*
21. *Using the life-cycle approach, what is the past, present, and future of my (our) involvement in working on these problems or needs in the extended environment?*

If the social worker is an entry-level generalist, the time may come in the process when a referral or transfer needs to be made to a social worker with advanced expertise in political strategies or policy formation. Systems with greater legal access and authority may need to step in and take over in social planning and community development. Social problems in society at large are seldom resolved fully. Even when legislation is passed and programs are initiated, ongoing monitoring of change is usually needed. Social workers may therefore build in a role of monitoring as part of their follow-up plan for the future.

Although entry-level generalists may not possess advanced, sophisticated political skills to work in complex political structures, they are the ones most likely to be aware of the pulse and the pain of the disadvantaged in society. Their firsthand experience and documentation, with a strong sense of commitment and perseverance, may be the most valuable forces to bring about change in the extended environment.

■ CONCEPT 9.4

Locality development involves professional application of general social work methods to enable rural and urban communities to:

▶ Identify and mobilize their assets and resources.
▶ Build social connectedness, cohesion, solidarity, and competence in dealing with common problems and needs.
▶ Increase their collaborative strengths-based problem-solving capacity.
▶ Assume responsibility for their quality of life.

Locality Development

In the ideal, local communities provide their residents with a delineated common living space, sense of identity and connectedness, social provisions, and friendship support networks. They form stable and cohesive primary groups that exert inter-

personal influence, provide mutual aid activities, and maintain linkages to local educational, religious, employment, and recreational networks and formal external supports and resources. In brief, such communities have assets and social capital clearly visible and available within their local environments and in their connections or linkages with their surrounding environments (Kretzmann & McKnight, 1993; Putnam, 2000; Scales & Streeter, 2004). By contrast, other communities have high resident mobility, a paucity of both informal and formal support networks and linkages, and multiple social problems and needs. Yet, these communities too have assets and social capital, albeit undeveloped and not readily apparent.

To develop the social capital of such communities, the generalist social work practitioner uses a communitywide intervention process to energize residents, obtain broad-based participation, and help residents act on their own behalf in (Hardcastle, Powers, & Wenocur, 2004; Kretzmann & McKnight, 1993):

▶ Identifying, making visible, and mobilizing community assets and resources
▶ Developing a common awareness of these assets and resources as the social capital to be used in addressing local problems
▶ Developing community solidarity and community control of assets and resources
▶ Becoming involved in improving the quality of community life through social networks, coalitions, and local initiatives
▶ Becoming empowered in dealing with social and political institutions
▶ Participating in a collaborative strengths-based problem-solving process in identifying community assets and resources to meet community needs

As these developmental goals suggest, the whole community is the context of intervention and change, the target of change, and the change mechanism for developing the social capital to redress issues of power imbalance in socio-political community structures and to address social problems and needs. Thus in locality development, the social worker's primary tasks include (Kretzmann & McKnight, 1993; Ungar, Manuel, Mealey, & Campbell, 2004):

▶ Identifying assets and resources
▶ Increasing asset and resource visibility, availability, and accessibility
▶ Mobilizing local indigenous leadership
▶ Eliciting commitment from power brokers
▶ Building social networks and coalitions to handle the work of the community and sustain communitywide progress

For such task-oriented efforts to be a success, the following conditions need to exist in the local community (Rothman, 2000):

▶ Leadership and organizational capacity within the community sufficient for the task at hand
▶ Identified tasks adequate for the targeted goals
▶ Small-scale project activities sufficient for accomplishing targeted goals
▶ Community as a whole and community representatives sufficiently committed to the project under consideration

> ► Sufficient knowledge and resources available to the community and community representatives to accomplish the identified tasks
> ► Community interest, community belief that the community will benefit from the project, and community investment in the project
> ► Projected benefits that outweigh overall costs

When local community conditions are adequate, addressing the identified goals and tasks requires process-oriented macro intervention (Kirst-Ashman & Hull, 1997; Scales & Streeter, 2004) that focuses on:

> ► Identifying, developing, and connecting community social capital
> ► Increasing the interpersonal relationships and social connectedness of community residents
> ► Building community capacity for problem-solving, achieving consensus, and engaging in collaborative mutual aid and self-help efforts
> ► Building community capacity for sustaining development

At the same time, however, the intervention must balance process with actions directed toward the goal of increasing the visibility and usability of community assets and resources in order to achieve real improvement in community life, sustain residents' interest, and create evidence of the whole community's progress and mastery. In turn, achieving the goal of increased usable assets reinforces the sense of community competence and empowerment as well as fosters further collaborative efforts (Kretzmann & McKnight, 1993).

In addition to the strength of the local economy, three asset clusters capture the resources and social capital of a community (Center for Visionary Leadership, 1998):

1. Capacities of individual residents, including personal skills, community involvement activities, and enterprise activities
2. Resident groups or associations that share common interests and activities (cultural, religious, recreational, political, self-help, volunteers)
3. Local community infrastructure of private, public, and nonprofit organizations and institutions (businesses, grocery stores, schools, daycare centers, libraries, parks, police and fire departments, hospitals and health clinics, pharmacies, social service agencies)

Once the generalist social worker recognizes and maps out the details of asset clusters on a community map, each becomes more visible and therefore more accessible and available for developmental purposes. Thus, locality development begins with the assets present in the community, not with community needs that represent what is missing or absent (Kretzmann & McKnight, 1993). Once the community is mobilized and invested in development, outside resources may be drawn in and used more effectively to meet need and further local community development.

Besides being asset based, locality development is internally focused on building the community's agenda for change and identifying the internal forces supporting change. These forces grow out of the strengths, investment, hope, creativity, and problem-solving capabilities of residents, resident groups and associations, and local institutions. Thus, locality development is also relationship driven and dependent on connecting the existing capacities of residents, resident groups and associations, and local organizations and institutions by building relationships within and among them.

Table 9.1 summarizes the similarities and differences found in locality development and the two previously discussed models of macro intervention: social planning and community development, and social and political advocacy. The table highlights characteristics such as goals and assumptions, strategies and techniques for change, social work practice roles and client system roles, organization of power structure, and perception of client systems.

■ C O N C E P T 9 . 5

Internal organizational change involves professional application of general social work methods in order to

▶ Change organizational conditions harmful to client systems served.
▶ Change organizational conditions harmful to staff service providers.
▶ Enhance the organizational effectiveness of service delivery.

Internal Organizational Change

Since the majority of generalist social workers are employed by social agencies and organizations, knowledge about how to effect agency-based organizational change while remaining employed can be a useful asset in the social worker's professional repertoire. Sometimes, the social worker notes that policies, programs, and practices are forming barriers to serving client systems and meeting their needs. Sometimes, the social worker notes that the presence of various "isms" is interfering with service delivery to diverse populations. Other times, the social worker may be concerned about the impact of management practices on staff morale, retention, and service delivery efforts.

To enhance organizational effectiveness in service delivery, the generalist social worker may decide to intervene in order to remove those organizational conditions harmful to the well-being and morale of staff providing service as well as to the client systems served (Frey, 1990; Resnick & Patti, 1980). First, the social worker must gain increased understanding of the agency organization as a social system influenced by internal forces from within and external forces in the community that impact its functioning in relation to its identified client systems. In conducting this initial organizational assessment, the social worker asks himself or herself:

▶ *What are the sources of the barriers to service delivery?*
Is it lack of knowledge? The method of service delivery? Lack of funds, staff, space, or other resources? Customary practices that are outdated? Other?

TABLE 9.1 ■ Comparison of Three Models for Macro-Level Practice

Characteristics	Locality Development	Social Planning and Community Development	Social and Political Advocacy
1. Goals	Enhance community living and well-being Use self-help or naturally existing local networks Focus on process goals	Resolve problems in community living Use various problem-solving strategies to create collaboration between individuals, groups, and communities Focus on accomplishment of task goals	Create institutional and community change to reduce oppression and promote human justice and fairness Use various power-based relationships and resources Focus on process and task goals
2. Assumptions	All local naturally existing network systems want the community living to improve and are willing to contribute to its improvement.	Problems in community living can be resolved by collaboration between planning experts and natural existing networks	The community has a stake in promoting the well-being of the oppressed group(s); social injustice is a problem for all, not just the oppressed; community has an identifiable power structure.
3. Strategy for Change	Broad cross-section of naturally existing networks of people who willingly come together to identify and solve their problems.	Experts engage in fact gathering and analysis of problems which are presented to identifiable community network representatives	Members of oppressed groups organize to advocate and create publicly visible dialogue with power structure or community hierarchy
4. Techniques for Change	Group discussion to create consensus	Group presentations and discussion to identify conflicts and achieve consensus	Group public confrontations, demonstrations, protests, speeches, announcements, direct action and negotiations, and policy change
5. Social Work Practice Roles	Facilitator, coordinator, broker, educator for problem-solving	Expert planner, evidence collector, analyst, program developer, implementer, and evaluator	Social advocate, social activist, group advocate, partisan broker, and negotiator
6. Organization of Power Structure	Power structure is primarily collaborative and facilitative among systems	Power structure is based on the concept of expertise or "employer" and "sponsor" among systems	Power structure is the target of removal or action by the oppressed system
7. Perception of Client systems	Clients are viewed as community citizens	Clients are viewed as consumers	Clients are viewed as the oppressed or victims
8. Client System Roles	Participants in the problem-solving process	Recipients or consumers of accomplished goals by invitation	Powerless constituents or employers that are induced to act

Source: Adapted from Zastrow (2003, p. 231); Hardcastle, Powers, & Wenocur (2004); Rothman, Erlich, & Tropman, 1995.

► *What are the organization's greatest assets and resources?*
Is it the mission? Prior accomplishments? Current reputation? Endowment? Other?
► *Who holds the power and makes the decisions in the areas within the organization that need to be changed?*
Board? Director? Line staff? Client systems? Community? Other?
► *How receptive are the decision-makers to change?*
Who or what influences this receptivity? Is the decision-making style hierarchical or egalitarian?
► *What are the forces and processes for change in these areas?*
Which support change? Oppose change?

In conducting an organizational assessment of service delivery issues, the social worker asks himself or her self:

► *What requires changing if client system needs are to be met more adequately?*
► *What is possible in the short term? The long term? Not possible?*

In conducting an assessment of the perceptions and reactions of staff members, the social worker asks himself or herself (Frey, 1990):

► *How do colleagues perceive the situation?*
► *What are colleagues' strengths and resources in relation to organizational change?*
► *What is the potential for colleague involvement in a change effort?*
► *What are the possible consequences of my change efforts for colleagues, client systems, and myself?*
► *What are the ethical implications and issues in the change effort?*
► *How committed am I to a change effort?*

If the change effort begins to seem feasible, the social worker continues to use the General Method framework in engaging colleagues and formulating a collective goal statement. Together, the participants review their collective understanding of agency functioning and invest energy in improving agency functioning. As an action system, the participants collectively gather additional information and analyze the forces supporting and opposing change. (See a discussion on force-field analysis presented earlier in this chapter.) They mobilize resources, consider alternative courses of action, and begin to formulate an action plan. Depending on the assessment, the proposed action plan may include a proposal to:

► Establish a task-oriented committee to study the problem and develop recommendations.
► Change a policy or procedure in view of the collected facts, assessment, professional ethics, and possible negative consequences for those served, the service providers, and the organization.

▶ Permit a revised or new service delivery approach to targeted client systems on a trial basis.

▶ Establish a staff-development program to increase effectiveness and morale.

The choice will also be influenced by the culture of the organization, the change being sought, the community context, and timing in relation to what else is occurring in the organization and in the community. During leadership change, for example, there is opportunity to influence selection of a new board member, director, or supervisor. There also may be an opportunity at this time to revisit and reinterpret policies and procedures and to revise intervention approaches (Resnick & Patti, 1980).

Organizational change typically causes uncertainty among personnel and upsets the previously established equilibrium of organizational functioning. Any change is likely to generate a certain amount of tension and resistance. Thus, it is important to mitigate tension and resistance by increasing staff involvement and investment in the proposed plan and its implementation (Frey, 1990).

Most internal organizational change efforts by staff are incremental and non-adversarial. Some, however, may become adversarial and include:

▶ Submission of petitions to board and director
▶ Confrontation in public meetings and board meetings
▶ Use of media for public confrontation and mobilizing targeted client systems
▶ Efforts to sanction the organization through professional associations, accrediting organizations, or licensing bodies

In this process, formal mediation efforts, arbitration, and litigation are often the final steps. When change efforts reach the point of litigation, there is an inherent risk for all involved.

Designs for Macro Intervention

As with the General Method micro and mezzo interventions in Chapter 8, the types of General Method macro interventions in this chapter may be depicted in designs composed of circle clusters. In social and political advocacy (Figure 9.7), the generalist social worker is seen in interaction with a macro client system. The two are interacting with a community action coalition. Through the community action coalition, the social worker and macro client system influence community power brokers. In turn, the community power brokers join the influence chain and influence the social policy decision-makers. In social planning and community development (Figure 9.8), the generalist social worker is seen interacting with a macro community client system to build community capacity to use its strengths, resources, and political skills in bringing about change in the community school board policy. In locality development (Figure 9.9), the social worker is working with the macro community

FIGURE 9.7 ■ Social and Political Advocacy

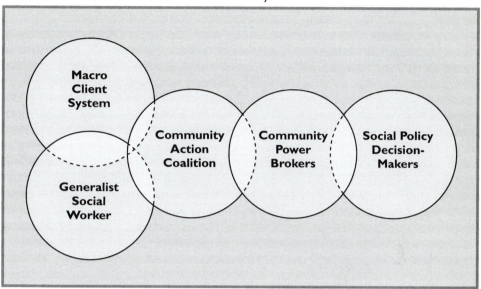

FIGURE 9.8 ■ Social Planning and Community Development

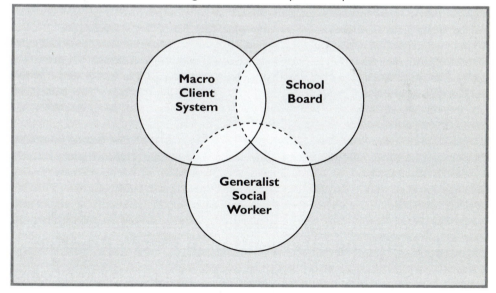

client system to facilitate community empowerment and resource development. In internal organizational change (Figure 9.10), the social worker is transacting with social work colleagues, and agency administrators in order to facilitate change in agency policies and practices by the board.

FIGURE 9.9   ■   Locality Development

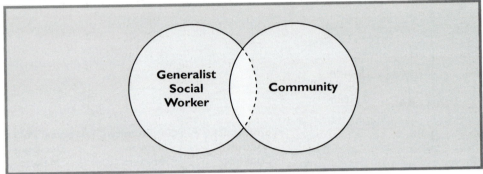

FIGURE 9.10   ■   Internal Organizational Change

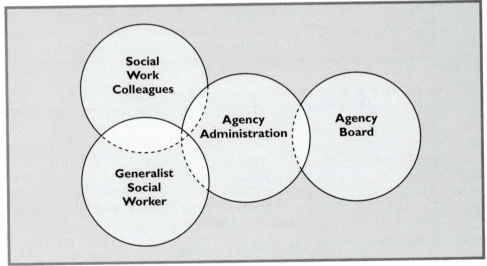

Monitoring Intervention in Macro Practice

To keep track of progress during the intervention phase in macro practice, the social worker rates the client or action system's progression in achieving its planned goals (see Chapter 7). In macro practice, such monitoring often requires development of community-specific measuring instruments that capture the planned activities and action steps in goal accomplishment. Monitoring and implementation may necessitate computerized techniques of data management and analysis. Systematic computerized collection and analysis of data enables generalist practitioners:

▶ To assess whether a program is accomplishing its planned goals and functioning effectively and efficiently

▶ To identify which intervention strategies are most effective with which populations under which circumstances

▶ To identify which programs and intervention strategies are underutilized and why

To assess whether and how change is occurring during intervention, it is important to establish baseline indicators to be used as markers of the macro change process as well as outcome indicators of goal achievement. As discussed in Chapter 3, other strategies may also be used to monitor intervention progress at the macro level. Chapter 10 addresses intervention outcomes.

Working with Different Client and Professional Systems

In a meeting of a group or community client system, a generalist social work practitioner strives to help member stakeholders envision the goals desired, the process of change in achieving these goals, and the possible consequences for all involved. Stakeholders may be asked to depict how they perceive the current climate of the system, the relationships among community subsystems, and the actions being taken. As special interests, fears, and feelings of insignificance are identified, they can be addressed and the communication patterns within the community enriched.

To interact effectively with members of different professions or with other social workers within their work environments, social work generalists are expected to understand both the professional system and the community environmental system. For example, social work practitioners working in a school system need to understand the educational language of the school systems and be able to translate their practice

WHITNEY M. YOUNG (1921–1971), a community organizer, campaigned for human rights and advocated for African Americans and the poor throughout his career. He served as dean of Atlanta University School of Social Work, executive director of the National Urban League, and president of the National Association of Social Workers. He also served as advisor to Presidents Kennedy and Johnson and received the Presidential Medal of Freedom in 1969.

process and outcomes into language meaningful to educators. Similarly, if social workers are to form alliances or adversary systems with lawyers, they need to have a working knowledge of the language, methods, and motivations of the legal system. Unfortunately, research shows that there is often a tense, untrusting relationship between the two professions (Swenson, 1993). The frustration that exists as these two interface may be due to issues of communication and lack of understanding since the use of language and the approach to problem-solving are different in each profession. One example is that use of the words *contract* and *fact* may cause confusion. A contract used in the strengths-based problem-solving approach of the General Method is not the same as a contract used in the legal process. Social workers collect data on problems and strengths, feelings and attitudes, and facts such as names, dates, and circumstances for assessment and contract planning. They are concerned not only with *what* happened to the client system but also with *why* it happened in order to arrive at a mutually determined contract plan for problem resolution. A lawyer is concerned with establishing evidence of *what* happened in order to determine if legal action can be taken. The *why* is considered relevant only in relation to what happened. Although a social worker may know that something is true for a client system, it is not useful information in court unless the facts can be substantiated and admitted into evidence. Whereas case law of the lawyer is technical and specific, the theory and method of the social worker are dynamic and evolving (Swenson, 1993).

Using Social Work Foundation Knowledge in Intervention

As in intervention with micro and mezzo client systems, basic values, theories, and skills used by generalist social workers during intervention with macro client systems are identified in the holistic conceptualization of the foundation for social work practice (Chapter 1). The knowledge used varies according to the intervention task at hand. For example, knowledge of policies, procedures, institutions, social change theory, exchange theory, and field theory are particularly relevant. Working on a scale greater than one-to-one or small group, however, requires that generalist social workers have strong communication skills and interpersonal skills, including empathy with, respect for, and belief in the collectivity. In macro-level practice, for example, acceptance by the community has as significant an effect on the generalist social worker's ability to gain cooperation, support, and approval for a targeted project as it does for improving micro and mezzo service delivery. Similarly, whether working with individuals, families, groups, organizations, or communities, it is important to be able to help client systems at the micro, mezzo, and macro practice levels:

▶ Problem-solve and clarify issues.
▶ Identify personal strengths and environmental assets and resources.
▶ Establish priorities.

▶ Set goals with attainable objectives.
▶ Decide on an appropriate course of action likely to yield a high success rate.
▶ Implement plans.
▶ Monitor progress by means of empirical evidence.
▶ Evaluate outcomes by means of empirical evidence.

One central skill in macro-level practice is using group dynamics, processes, and skills such as enabling, mobilizing, mediating, and brokering with large groups, organizations, and communities to facilitate progress toward goal achievement. Another is building social networks within the community, including connections with institutions, businesses, voluntary organizations, the media, and outside resources. For successful collaboration and teamwork, knowledge of the social work profession and other professions, political skills, and group dynamics and processes are central.

As noted, the selection and application of macro intervention skills and techniques are guided by a generalist social worker's use of professional values and basic foundation knowledge. Thus, the holistic conceptualization of the foundation for practice is a helpful reference for the generalist who must skillfully apply foundation knowledge, values, and methods in intervening in each unique macro-level situation (Chapter 1).

Human Diversity in Intervention

As in practice with micro and mezzo client systems, the core human diversity issues at the macro level include institutional racism, cultural diversity, gender role, sexual orientation, and socioeconomic status. When a social worker is intervening with a macro client system of another culture, a language interpreter or cultural facilitator may be needed to increase the accuracy of communication and to facilitate understanding and strengths-based problem-solving.

Additionally in intervention with macro client systems, a social worker may become actively involved in promoting legislation to ensure adequate income for all vulnerable children and families or in changing policies and structures of traditional agencies to ensure receipt of adequate services for members of vulnerable groups. Generalists may need to encourage agencies and organizations to join with representatives of diverse groups in order to develop more sensitive and relevant service provision. As brought out by Chestang and others (Chestang, 1982; Everett, Chipungu, & Leashore, 1991), the three essential criteria for programs serving minorities are proximity, relevance, and community participation. These three criteria are also important in developing communities.

When dealing with client, action, and target systems that are diverse in culture, social status, and socio-demographics, it is important that macro-level generalist practitioners enhance the capability of service delivery systems to promote client system dignity and to increase service accessibility and acceptability. In other words, the intent of macro-level generalist practice is to ensure dignity, fairness, justice, and excellence in service access and quality by attending to the service delivery issues and needs of client systems.

O N G O I N G   C A S E S

Intervention Phase of Macro Generalist Practice

In Exercise 9.1, questions are proposed for reflection and discussion about how practice in each of the seven ongoing case examples might change during the intervention phase if the macro client system represented a different

▶ *Culture:* Racial/ethnic group membership, national origin and social group identity, religion and spirituality
▶ *Social status:* Socio-economic status, environmental and rural/urban differences
▶ *Socio-demographic strata:* Age and developmental stage, gender roles, sexual orientation, challenges in mental and physical ability

E X E R C I S E   9 . 1
Impact of Human Diversity on Intervention Process

Consider the following questions in each of the seven client systems. In macro intervention, how might change in culture, social status, or socio-demographic strata:

1. Influence the client system's participation in intervention?
2. Influence the social worker's view of intervention?
3. Reveal values that influence timing, communications, content, and actions?
4. Affect the dynamics of the professional relationship in intervention?
5. Affect monitoring of the progress, timeliness, and completeness of intervention?

In previous chapters, the focus has been on engagement, data collection, and assessment and contract planning with client systems in the seven ongoing cases. For the majority, the primary intervention models used have been micro and mezzo (Chapter 8). In this chapter, however, the focus shifts to consideration of the knowledge and skills required for intervention with the client system at a macro level derived from the earlier micro and mezzo work. In each case, a question is proposed for reflection and discussion about how generalist practice in each of the ongoing case examples might be expanded if the broader community issues and needs were addressed by macro-level intervention.

I. Child Welfare Case

A. Agency: State Department of Children's Services

B. Client System

ONGOING MICRO-LEVEL PROBLEM: K, a 15-year-old female, is moving from an emergency shelter into a group home. (For background information see Chapter 5, Ongoing Cases: Engagement Phase, I. Child Welfare Case.)

CASE-DERIVED MACRO-LEVEL ISSUE AND NEED: What community supports do foster parents and foster adolescents need to sustain placements for adolescents in out-of-home care?

C. Intervention

The social worker selected the social planning and community development model of intervention as the action system for developing a communitywide needs assessment to identify foster parents' and foster adolescents' perceptions of needs and for stimulating interagency collaboration to establish a foster parent training program and a foster adolescent developmental program. The tentative planning goals included (1) building an empowering foster parent support network to strengthen their parenting and facilitate coping with adolescents; (2) establishing an educational program for foster parents to address the problems and needs of adolescents in out-of-home care and the parenting issues experienced by foster parents; and (3) developing a program for adolescents that would address their concerns and prepare them for moving out of foster care into independent living and for postsecondary school training and further education.

II. Gerontology Case

A. Agency: Seaside Nursing Home

B. Client System

ONGOING MICRO-LEVEL PROBLEM: Mrs. J, an 80-year-old Portuguese woman, is in a skilled-nursing facility. (For background information, see Chapter 5, Ongoing Cases: Engagement Phase, II. Gerontology Case.)

CASE-DERIVED MACRO-LEVEL ISSUE AND NEED: How can the community create a supportive resource system for isolated and vulnerable elderly who have few support networks and resources?

C. Intervention

The social worker selected the social and political advocacy model of intervention as the action system for identifying, publicizing, funding, and developing policies and programs designed to build support networks and resources for the community elderly. The Area Office on Aging was identified as the lead agency in mobilizing community advocates and developing a coordinated lobbying plan.

III. Public Social Welfare Case

A. Agency: State Social Services

B. Client System

ONGOING MICRO-LEVEL PROBLEM: Mr. and Mrs. P and their two children (2 and 4 years old) are in need of housing (emergency and long-term) and food (emergency and continuous supply until TANF payment). (For background information, see Chapter 5, Ongoing Cases: Engagement Phase, III. Public Social Welfare Case.)

CASE-DERIVED MACRO-LEVEL ISSUE AND NEED: How does the community take steps to assure safe and affordable housing and employment at a living wage for low-income families?

C. Intervention

The social worker selected the locality development model of intervention as the action system for developing a public/private partnership model that would bring together several stakeholders such as the Public Housing Authority, Chamber of Commerce, and Public Social Services to develop a program for meeting basic family needs of housing and employment, thereby protecting communities and families against homelessness, hunger, neglect, and abuse.

IV. Community Services Case

A. Agency: Clayton Neighborhood House

B. Client System

ONGOING MICRO- AND MEZZO-LEVEL PROBLEM: Four Hispanic families are without heat in their apartments on the second floor of 33 L Street. (For background information, see Chapter 5, Ongoing Cases: Engagement Phase, IV. Community Services Case.)

CASE-DERIVED MACRO-LEVEL ISSUE AND NEED: How are landlords in a community held accountable for providing safe and affordable housing?

C. Intervention

The social worker selected the social and political advocacy model of intervention as the action system for empowering families to address their housing needs in an organized, coherent fashion. The initial goals included (1) empowering families to address their needs and (2) involving representatives from the Advisory Neighborhood Commission, Zoning Commission, and Public Health Department to develop policies and inspection programs for sustaining safe and affordable housing.

V. Education Case

A. Agency: Keeney Elementary School

B. Client System

ONGOING MICRO-LEVEL PROBLEM: Jim G is an 8-year-old third-grader with problems at school and home directly related to his parents' problem with their marital relationship. (For background information, see Chapter 5, Ongoing Cases: Engagement Phase, V. Education Case.)

CASE-DERIVED MACRO-LEVEL ISSUE AND NEED: How can teachers in a school system be helped to understand the impact of health and mental health issues on children's school performance?

C. Intervention

The social worker selected the social planning and community development model of intervention as an action system for identifying and organizing community resources to provide staff with information and training about the impact of health and mental health on academic and socio-behavioral performance in schools. In addition, the action system's task was educating and mobilizing the Board of Education to obtain additional resources to mediate the impact of health and mental health issues on school performance.

VI. Corrections Case

A. Agency: Juvenile Court

B. Client System

ONGOING MEZZO-LEVEL PROBLEM: Seven male adolescents, age 14, are on probation for burglary, theft of automobiles, or minor larceny (shoplifting) and are attending weekly group sessions led by co-workers from Juvenile Court. (For background information, see Chapter 5, Ongoing Cases: Engagement Phase, VI. Juvenile Court Case.)

CASE-DERIVED MACRO-LEVEL ISSUE AND NEED: How can the community unite to engage their youth in constructive programs and activities to prevent juvenile delinquency?

C. Intervention

The social worker selected the social planning and community development model of intervention as the action system for conducting a needs assessment and involving representatives of Youth and Family Services, education, recreation, employment, and public health agencies. The initial goals included (1) conducting a needs assessment, (2) connecting representatives of stakeholder agencies, and (3) developing a Partnership for Youth organization to mobilize and sustain community development and delinquency prevention efforts for youth.

VII. Homelessness Case

A. Agency: West End Community Shelter

B. Client System

ONGOING MICRO-LEVEL PROBLEM: José Romano, a 37-year-old Hispanic male, is homeless and HIV positive. He has no family or close friends. He was referred to the shelter by the Department of Social Services. (For background information, see Chapter 5, Ongoing Cases: Engagement Phase, VII. Homelessness Case.)

CASE-DERIVED MACRO-LEVEL ISSUE AND NEED: How can faith-based community organizations be empowered to provide material, emotional, social, and spiritual support to persons with HIV and other chronic illnesses?

C. Intervention

The social worker selected the social planning and community development model of intervention as the action system for involving representatives from the shelter, religious institutions, employers, health, and housing to conduct needs assessments and build coalitions for developing programs to support in-home services and support networks for the chronically ill.

SUMMARY

In this chapter, multiple strengths-based problem-solving models of General Method intervention with macro client systems were presented. These models included social and political advocacy, social planning and community development, locality development, and internal organizational change. As the ongoing cases illustrate, the generalist social worker applies macro system intervention models to empower and strengthen the community and to implement the contracted plan. In the next chapter, the focus will be on the fifth phase of the General Method: evaluation.

REFLECTION POINTS

Becoming a skilled social work practitioner requires knowledge and skills, including the ability to reflect on practice endeavors. The following reflection points are designed to strengthen critical thinking and mastery of knowledge of key points in this chapter.

1. Define the following models in generalist social work:
   • Social and political advocacy
   • Social planning and community development
   • Locality development
   • Internal organizational change
2. How might human diversity influence intervention at macro levels of practice?
3. Drawing on human behavior and social environment theories, identify a change theory and consider it in relation to one of the seven ongoing cases. Discuss how to apply the theory to the intervention process in this case.
4. Provide examples of evidence-based questions (Chapter 3) about the intervention process for each of the models.
5. Review Section 1, Social Workers' Ethical Responsibility to Clients, of the *NASW Code of Ethics* (www.socialworkers.org) in relation to your professional behavior. How might these standards influence your professional behavior?
6. For further reading and research, use the models in Question 1 to locate social work references related to this chapter's content. (See Appendix A, Selected Internet Resources, and Appendix B, Selected Social Work Journals.) What underlying theoretical concepts are evident in the practice models described in the articles? How are they applied in the articles? How might they be applied in one of the seven ongoing cases in this chapter or in a case in your field internship?

CHAPTER 10

Evaluation

"Measure, evaluate, estimate, and appraise your results, in some form, in any terms that rest on something beyond faith, assertion, and 'illustrative case'" (Cabot, 1931, as cited in Bloom, Fischer, & Orme, 2003, p. xiii). As one of the basic prerequisites in helping people to help themselves, social workers are expected to justify the effectiveness and efficiency of their service efforts and intervention endeavors. *Effectiveness* is concerned with the accomplishment of client system goals, whereas *efficiency* seeks to assess the cost expenditures of services and interventions in money, time, and other resources. In general, the *evaluation phase* is a time of studying and measuring the results of the actions taken during intervention. It is expected to (1) determine that client goals are being met, (2) demonstrate accountability, (3) facilitate informed decisions about service quality, and (4) increase social workers' knowledge base (Gabor & Grinnell, 1994).

The earlier general discussion in Chapter 3 focused on building empirical evidence for practice. By contrast, this chapter focuses on evaluation as the fifth practice phase of the General Method. The conceptual framework and guiding principles of the evaluation phase are discussed and applied to generalist practice with client, action, and target systems at micro, mezzo, and macro levels of practice. The central conceptual elements and processes include:

▶ Goal analysis
▶ Contract review
▶ Contract reformulation
▶ Evaluation questions
▶ Ongoing evaluation

Goal Analysis

Developing a clear definition and description of the intervention goals is always the essential first step in all forms of evaluation. The social worker has helped the client system develop specific goals in the early phases of the change process (through goal refinement in engagement, data collection, assessment, and contract planning). Otherwise, the social worker will not be able to measure the desired outcome effects during the evaluation phase. Evaluation also always involves some type of measurement. The social worker has to select criteria by which to measure client system goal targets (e.g., client behaviors, group tasks, and community assets) that are expected to change during the intervention. The social worker has to possess a knowledge of research that organizes measurable entities into *dependent variables* or goals (outcomes or targets). When deciding what procedures to use to measure change in a client system, the social worker needs to bear in mind the following research tenets (Bloom, Fischer, & Orme, 2003; Kerlinger & Lee, 2000):

▶ The procedure or specific measuring device sought should be *valid*. It should measure what it is believed to measure and not something else. If a standardized instrument is used, care needs to be taken to examine the instrument's reported validity and whether the instrument was intended for use with a particular client system. If a measuring device developed by the social worker or agency is used, expert judges should assess whether the instrument actually measures what it purports to measure prior to its use with client systems.

▶ The chosen procedure should be *reliable* or yield similar results when the measurement is repeated under similar circumstances. If a standardized instrument is used, care needs to be taken to examine the instrument's reported reliability (typically presented as a correlation coefficient). An instrument that is judged reasonably reliable should have achieved a reliability correlation coefficient of at least 0.70. A reliability of less than 0.70 is considered suspect, as it may produce inconsistent responses to the same questions under similar conditions.

▶ The procedures should be *brief* (15 to 20 minutes maximum time), *easy to use* by the client system, and not require a specialist for administration or interpretation.

▶ The procedure should be able to detect *relatively small levels of change* as well as differences in the types of change achieved.

▶ The procedure should be *nonreactive* (i.e., able to detect differences without modifying or influencing the phenomena being measured).

▶ The design of measuring should lend itself to *tracking, monitoring, and evaluating change* using single subject designs. If the ongoing measuring is too complicated because it takes too long or requires special knowledge and/or training, *pre- and posttest measurements* may be more useful.

It needs to be emphasized here that practice evaluation measures only those things that are relevant and central to the provision of service to client systems and to understanding what happened as a result of that service.

To begin the fifth phase of the General Method, the social worker asks the following question: *Has the goal been accomplished?* For every task or set of tasks, a goal was stated on the contracted plan. That goal related directly to the problem listed in the column that preceded it. If the goal has been accomplished, the problem should now be resolved or modified, depending on how the goal was originally stated.

To answer the basic question cited, an intensive consideration is made of the change or progress that has taken place since the beginning of the social worker–client system interaction. First, the starting point is recalled; the social worker and system of contact ask: *What was the problem when we first met?* The description that follows the starting point (which may be referred to as the *baseline*) should be as precise and factual as possible. For example, if the presenting problem was Mr. and Mrs. S's constant quarreling, the social worker will try to be more specific by recalling that Mrs. S said every time she and her husband spoke to each other, they quarreled and that this was at least six times a week. On the contract that was agreed to by both Mr. and Mrs. S, the stated goal read, "To be able to talk and to listen to each other without quarreling." The social worker and client system would therefore ask: *Has the communication between Mr. and Mrs. S improved? Are they speaking together without quarreling? Can they lower the number of quarrels per week to less than the baseline number?*

Answers to such questions may be received from different sources. The primary respondents are the client system receiving service and the social worker. In addition, information for goal analysis may be requested from other knowledgeable resources, such as family members, teachers, employers, and others. If a social worker does not think that the perception of a client system together with the observations of the social worker is sufficient, reliable, or accurate, then outsiders may be brought into the evaluation process. As with data collection in the second phase of the General Method, the use of outside resources during evaluation with client systems should be discussed with and be sanctioned by the client system prior to contacting the resources.

If the answer to the basic question of goal accomplishment is not a clear 100 percent yes, a study is made to determine to what extent the goal has been accomplished. Beginning at the baseline starting point, the question is asked: *From where you started when we first had contact, how much closer to or further from the goal have you moved?* A scale may be used to help the social worker and the client system become more specific in answering this question (see Figure 10.1). It is a nine-point bipolar scale with an equal number of categories for progression and for regression. The midpoint on the scale (0) indicates the starting point. Descriptive criteria for this point should indicate the problem that led to the stated goal under study. The extreme right of the scale is numbered +4, and the anchoring description for this point is 100 percent "goal accomplished." More specifically, this score indicates that the problem or issue at the starting point has been eliminated or reduced, according to the way it is spelled out in the stated goal. Conversely, the opposite end of the scale is numbered −4, and the descriptive criterion is "goal given up," with no attainment. The intermediate points on either side of the 0 are balanced to reflect movement to a little, some, or a large extent better or worse than the starting point.

The number of scale points to be used depends on the individual goal in each situation. Sometimes the goal may be a single activity that cannot be broken down into a measurable sequence. For example, a goal may be to get food stamps for a family or tutoring for a child. It may be sufficient here to have a simple 3-point scale (−1 = goal given up, 0 = starting point, +1 = goal accomplished). If any movement, even slight, can be detected, it is important to have a scale that can show this. Too few scale points may prevent the recognition of some progress, which could increase hope and motivation. Even the identification of going backwards and a consideration of how the situation may end if regression continues may cause sufficient anxiety to promote greater effort and involvement.

With each individual situation, an attempt is made to use objective descriptors, including numbers or times and events. For example, in the situation presented earlier, the problem at the starting point was Mr. and Mrs. S's repeated quarreling whenever they tried to communicate (at least six times a week). The long-range goal was to have the couple speak and listen to each other without quarreling. During intervention, techniques were used to help them listen to each other and try to understand each other's viewpoints. A sensitivity to nonverbal communication was encouraged, and words were suggested to help them express their feelings. After the social worker and Mr. and Mrs. S worked together for the period of time indicated in the contracted plan, they began to evaluate goal accomplishment. The scale in Figure 10.2 was developed under the guidance of the social worker.

In finding regressive descriptors, the social worker and the client system discern what have been or could be ways in which the situation would grow worse than when

FIGURE 10.1 ■ Goal-Accomplishment Scale

−4	−3	−2	−1	0	+1	+2	+3	+4
Goal given up	Large extent worse	Some-what worse	Little worse than starting point	*Starting point*	Little better than starting point	Some-what better	Large extent better	Goal accomplished

FIGURE 10.2 ■ Communication Scale: Mr. and Mrs. S

−4	−3	−2	−1	0	+1	+2	+3	+4
Goal given up; injury and separation	Large extent worse; no communication without fighting	Somewhat worse; quarrels moving into physical fights half the time they talk	Little worse; quarrels moving into physical fights once or twice a week	<u>Start</u>: no communication without quarreling (at least six times a week)	Little better; communicating without quarreling once or twice a week	Somewhat better; communicating without quarreling half the time they talk	Large extent better; communicating without quarreling most of the time (may be one quarrel a week)	Goal accomplished; open communication without quarreling

the problem was first identified. In the case of Mr. and Mrs. S, they said that at one time they had started to physically fight, and they feared this might happen again. Therefore, the negative indicators reflect the typical pattern of regression for this client system. If they had feared an increasing withdrawal from any interaction with each other, then withdrawal would be indicated in the negative descriptors.

What needs to be emphasized is that during the evaluation phase of the General Method, there must be an opportunity to identify possible deterioration as well as growth in a situation. Even with general intervention, the communication between Mr. and Mrs. S, for example, could have become worse than when they first set the goal. The cause of this deterioration would need to be considered as the evaluation progresses. It could be that the intervention was inappropriate because the relationship was too dysfunctional or because Mr. and Mrs. S lacked sufficient motivation or capacity to work on it. The regression in the relationship could be caused by other factors, including those outside of the social worker's control, such as influences from individuals or systems unknown to the social worker. Before asking why the goal has or has not been attained, however, social worker and client system take time to judge what movement, forward or backward, has taken place on the goal-accomplishment scale. After this appraisal, they proceed to an analysis of why they have arrived at the particular point on the scale. Here again, the contracted plan is a helpful guide to social worker and system of contact as they analyze causation.

Contract Review

An evaluation does not stop at this point, even when the first question in the process is answered with a 100 percent yes. Although a goal has been attained, it is important to find out why this has happened. The question to be asked is: *Has the goal been accomplished through the planned interventions identified by social worker and client system in the contracted plan?* An honest appraisal of causality can build a stronger working relationship, and it can give direction for further interactions between social worker and client system. It is possible that a goal's accomplishment is due to negative circumstances that may have to be addressed with a reformulation of goals. For example, a goal of getting someone off welfare may have been accomplished because the person was imprisoned rather than because of the interventions of the social worker. More immediate goals may emerge, such as providing care for the children of the person incarcerated. If it appears that the goal has been accomplished as a result of the tasks identified in the contracted plan, then social worker and client system may move on to other problems and goals, or they may move into the process of termination (to be developed in the next chapter).

If a goal has not been accomplished by the date anticipated for the completion of tasks in a plan, the question must be asked: *Why not?* Again, the response may point to some unexpected circumstances; for example, a death or sudden tragedy may have caused the failure in goal accomplishment. If such circumstances are not readily identifiable, the social worker and the client system begin a systematic review of the planned contract, starting with the last column on the right, to find out why the goal has not been attained. *Why has the goal not been accomplished?* is the obvious question, but it is also important to ask: *Why has movement toward goal accomplishment reached the point identified on the goal attainment scale?*

The last column on a contracted plan indicates the dates when planned tasks have or have not been accomplished to date. For an example of a contracted plan, see Table 10.1. After recognizing which tasks have not been completed, focus should move over to the next column to find out when it was expected that these tasks would be accomplished. Questions to be asked at this point are: *Was there an error in date anticipation? Is more time needed? Why was our timing off?* If it appears that what is needed is an adjustment in the date anticipated, this can readily take place, and intervention will be continued. For example, a social worker may have worked out a contracted plan with a group of citizens in which it was anticipated that they would meet with a member of Congress by a certain date. It was found out later that the politician's schedule was fully booked until two weeks after the anticipated date on the plan. If the reason for a failure to accomplish a goal on the date expected is something other than insufficient time for task completion, evaluation continues by moving over to the "contract" column (the third column from the right) of the plan. (see Table 10.1).

In analyzing the "contract" column, a review is made of the people or system responsible for carrying out the identified tasks. Questions include: *Did the persons or system designated to carry out a task in the plan complete that task? If not, why not?* There are several possible reasons for a failure in task execution. Basically, a review of motivation, capacity, opportunity, and understanding of expectations should be made. The failure could be due to work overload, insufficient resources, or environmental pressures greater than anticipated. A change or redistribution in task responsibilities may be all that is needed to move forward toward goal accomplishment. Perhaps a social worker or resource will have to withdraw from carrying out tasks in order to have a client system become more directly involved in problem resolution. Perhaps the social worker or a new resource will have to become directly involved in collaborating with a client system to accomplish certain tasks. For example, a social worker and Mr. M may have planned that Mr. M would go to the Vocational Rehabilitation Office to complete a set of tests. He was then expected to call the social worker to let her know how he made out. What actually happened was that Mr. M changed his mind as the date for the testing drew closer because he was afraid to hear the results of his testing. When he called the social worker, he told her he didn't keep the appointment because he didn't feel well. The social worker asked Mr. M to come in to talk with her, and as they evaluated the plan they had made, Mr. M shared the fact that he couldn't face going for the tests and hearing the results by himself. The contract had to be changed so that the social worker would go with Mr. M to the Vocational Rehabilitation Office.

Through analysis of the "contract" column, it may become apparent that, even when everyone carries out the tasks as agreed to in the plan, goals may still not be accomplished (see Table 10.1). The next area to be considered, then, would be the "tasks" column, to see if there could be an error in identifying what tasks had to be performed to fulfill the stated goals. When the tasks outlined in the contracted plan are studied, the question to be asked should call for an evaluation not only of the iden-

TABLE 10.1 ■ Contracted Plan with Mr. M

Date Identified	Problem/Need	Goal	Task	Contract	Date Anticipated	Date Accomplished
2/6	1. Lack of self awareness of potential—Mr. M	1. To grow in awareness of potential (intelligence, skills)	1. Talk with Mr. M.	1. Social worker and Mr. M	2/13	2/13
			2. Talk with Mrs. M.	2. Social worker and Mrs. M	2/15	2/15
			3. Talk with Mr. and Mrs. M.	3. Social worker and Mr. and Mrs. M	2/22	2/22
			4. Call Vocational Rehabilitation.	4. Social worker	2/23	2/23
			5. Discuss Vocational Rehabilitation with Mr. M	5. Social worker and Mr. M	2/28	2/28
			6. Call Vocational Rehabilitation for appointment.	6. Mr. M	3/1	3/1
			7. Go to Vocational Rehabilitation.	7. Mr. M	3/14	
			8. Call social worker.	8. Mr. M	3/15	3/15
3/17 Evaluation	Evaluation of problem 1 (as cited above)	Goal 1 (as cited above)	1. Recall goal 1; evaluate why not accomplished; reformulate contract.	1. Social worker and Mr. M	3/17	3/17
3/17 Contract reformulation	Change in contract 7 and in task 8 and contract 8		7. Go to Vocational Rehabilitation.	7. Social worker and Mr. M	3/25	3/27
			8. Meet to review contract 7.	8. Social worker and Mr. M		

tified task but also of the sequencing of the tasks as listed in the plan. The social worker asks: *Were the tasks appropriately selected, clearly described, and properly sequenced in order to achieve the goal?* Perhaps some steps were omitted in the process. There may have been resources or influences in the environment that needed to be contacted but were overlooked in the planning. The nature of the task itself may have been inappropriate for a particular system. For example, Mrs. L did not follow through with a plan to take her mother to visit a nursing home. Although Mrs. L passively agreed with the social worker that a nursing home would be good for her mother, and Mrs. L said that she would take her mother on a certain date, she never completed the task. Placing an elderly parent in a nursing home might in some cases be a successful plan to achieve the goal of providing needed care for a parent or of getting relief for a family strained by caring for an elderly person. In this situation, however, sending an elderly parent to a nursing home was not an acceptable or possible option for the family because it was contrary to their basic cultural beliefs and customs.

Occasionally, tasks are identified, sequenced, and implemented and the stated goals are accomplished, but the problem may continue to be present. At this time, the social worker and the client system would have to review carefully the "goal" column to see whether the stated goal actually related to or reflected the opposite of the identified problem or need. The social worker asks: *Did the accomplishment of this goal resolve, reduce, or prevent further growth of the problem? If not, why not?* It could be that the goal indicated the outcome desired by the social worker but not by the client system. The needs of the client system may continue to be unmet until the social worker clearly understands and expresses the goal of the client system. For example, Mrs. F may have expressed strong dissatisfaction with her apartment, complaining about rats and cockroaches, and the social worker may have thought that Mrs. F was identifying the goal of extermination of rats and cockroaches from the apartment. When the problem of rats and cockroaches decreased after much activity involving the landlord and the Housing Code, Mrs. F was still dissatisfied with her apartment. Her true goal was to be relocated with the social worker's help.

If there is not an overall improvement in a situation even after a contracted plan has been fully implemented, another reason could be an inappropriate identification of the problem or need in the first place. In the case just cited, for example, the social worker thought that the client system was presenting the problem of infested housing when, in fact, she was trying to give reasons for the social worker to help her move. She felt isolated and did not get along with her neighbors. She hoped the social worker would be able to arrange for her to move to the south end of town, where some of her relatives lived. As the generalist practitioner reviewed the case during evaluation, the question would be asked: *What, in fact, was the problem?* With hindsight, the social worker would be able to see that the real problem with Mrs. F was a lack of social adjustment. The goal she really wanted to accomplish was relocation.

It is apparent, then, that a social worker may use the contracted plan for evaluation in the General Method. There are six areas or columns that can be analyzed to locate possible causes for failure in problem resolution. At any step in the evaluated process, an understanding may take place that highlights the error in planning and pinpoints where reformulation must take place in the contracted plan.

Planned Contract Reformulation

The General Method is a cyclical, ongoing process. It is more common than exceptional to have the helping process in social work move three steps forward and two steps backward all along the way. By the time the social worker and client or action system move into evaluation, however, they are often sensitive to the possibility that the next phase in their working together may be termination. If the evaluation leads to an awareness that little or no progress has been made and that the contracted plan has to be reformulated, there may be resistance or expressed frustration on the part of both social worker and client system. This is particularly true when it becomes apparent that there is regression in a situation after much time and energy has been invested by both social worker and client system. A social worker may need special support from his or her supervisor and a system of contact may need to receive special support from the social worker, if they are to find the energy necessary to persevere in the process of plan reformulation. A social worker needs to maintain a flexible, realistic attitude throughout the General Method, and this attitude must be conveyed to the client, action, and target systems with which he or she is working.

As problems, goals, tasks, planned contract, or dates are reformulated during the evaluation period, it is imperative that the client or action system play a major role in the revision. Learning to recognize and accept setbacks, to try again without giving up, to change expectations and plans when necessary, and, finally, to see results from planned and persistent action can be extremely valuable to the growth of any human being or client or action system.

When the evaluation has taken place that leads to a reformulation of some aspect of the contracted plan, the social worker records the dates of the evaluation and the planned revisions on the contracted plan. As shown in Table 10.1, in the "date identified" and "problem/need" columns, the social worker indicates the dates when the evaluation took place and the problems that were being evaluated. In the "problem/need" column, the social worker also states what reformulations are necessary. In the columns where reformulations are to be made, the social worker describes the changes or additions and then proceeds to fill in the other columns of the planned contract to reflect the revisions.

As shown in Table 10.1, the social worker had originally set the goal of having Mr. M grow in awareness of his intellectual potential and marketable skills. He was to complete a battery of tests and learn the results at the Vocational Rehabilitation Office. After he completed the tests and learned their results, he was to call the social worker. Mr. M failed to keep the appointment because he was afraid to hear the results. When Mr. M called to say he didn't go for the testing, the social worker arranged to meet with him. During this meeting, they evaluated how far they had come and identified where the plan was incomplete. The difficulty was in Mr. M's not being able to carry out task 7 on his own. After much discussion, the social worker offered to go with Mr. M to vocational rehabilitation. He agreed, and they also planned to meet again for a follow-up session. The evaluation, with reformulations of tasks and contract, is shown in Table 10.1.

Evaluation Questions

In essence, evaluation may be described as a process. In addition to those questions already identified that relate to the different areas of the contracted plan, the social worker raises questions about external and internal circumstances that may have affected goal accomplishment. As stated earlier, the social worker first considers the possibility that contract planning did not anticipate outside factors that may have caused failure or success in goal attainment. After considering outside factors and after reviewing the contracted plan, the social worker and client or action system should also ask if any internal factors or dynamics within their relationship have prevented progress. This would include an assessment of the level of trust, openness, and honesty within the relationship. If it is agreed that there has been some resistance or holding back in their interactions, this should be explored. A direct discussion about the social worker–client system relationship, its progress, and its setbacks can be a powerful source for movement during evaluation.

Basically, the essential questions to be asked during evaluation may be summarized as follows:

Has the goal been accomplished? (yes or no)
▶ *If yes, has the goal been accomplished as a result of circumstances outside of the contracted plan?* (external causes)
▶ *If no, the following questions should be asked:*
1. From when the problem was first identified, how much closer to or further from the goal has the client, action, or target system moved? (goal-accomplishment scale)
2. Has the goal not been accomplished as expected because of circumstances outside of the contracted plan? (external causes)
3. Was there an error in date anticipation? (timing)
4. Did a person or system of contact designated to complete a task fail to accomplish it? (contract)
5. Were the tasks inappropriately selected, sequenced, or described? (tasks)
6. If the goal has been accomplished, but the problem continues, was the goal inaccurately identified? (goal)
7. If the goal has been accomplished, but the problem continues, was the problem inaccurately identified? (problem)
8. Was there anything in the social worker–client system relationship that inhibited goal accomplishment? (internal causes)

As these questions are answered, the causes for failure in goal attainment become increasingly evident. The reason a goal has not been accomplished to the extent anticipated may be pinpointed to some area on the contracted plan or to external or internal circumstances. When there has been clarification of what prevented goal accomplishment, the social worker and the client system then begin to ask: *Why did this happen?* and *What can be done to remedy the situation and make goal accomplishment feasible?* A reformulation of the plan takes place.

Not all of the evaluation questions have to be asked if it becomes clear that a goal has not been attained for a reason suggested in earlier questions. Instead of proceeding with further questioning, the social worker and the client or action system move into an analysis of why the particular drawback existed and a consideration of what modifications or additions need to be made in the contracted plan. With a reformulation of identified problems, goals, tasks, contracted plan, or dates, the social worker and the client, action, or target system return to the intervention phase for further action. After the newly developed plan has been enacted, another evaluation takes place. If goals have been attained at this time, the social worker and the client or action system are then ready either to work on other problems and needs or to move into the final phase of the General Method, called *termination*.

Ongoing Evaluation

As stated, the formal phase of evaluation begins with this question: *Has the goal been accomplished?* This question is asked at the time when it was anticipated on the contracted plan that a particular goal would be attained. In addition to this formal evaluation phase, it is possible to integrate a systematic evaluation throughout the entire General Method. Increasingly, efforts and instruments for ongoing evaluation in social work practice are being described in the professional literature (Fischer & Corcoran, 1994; Kirk, 1999). The value of a concentrated ongoing evaluation is that it helps the social worker and the client system to be sensitive to movement and to the long-range goals throughout the process.

A tool may be used to assist a social worker and system of contact in an ongoing evaluation process. The tool is a two-dimensional graph, which may begin to be constructed during any phase of the method. The zero point on the graph represents the starting point when a problem is identified and a goal is first established. The vertical line of the graph intersects the zero point midway, and the line has an equal number of plus and minus points above and below the zero point. The vertical line is the goal line, which is used to chart movement toward or away from the goal as the problem gets better or worse. The highest point at the top of this line indicates goal accomplishment; the midpoint (0) identifies where the problem is when the goal is set; and the lowest point represents total failure in goal accomplishment. Each intermediate point should have some measurable descriptive criterion that indicates progression or regression. Whenever possible, all points should be described in behavioral terms that can be objectively measured.

The horizontal line of the graph is a time indicator. It may represent weeks, days, or months, depending on the nature of the problem. (For a crisis, the intervals may represent days or hours.) The line to the left of the midpoint indicates time intervals prior to the starting point, when there was no contact between social worker and client system (i.e., the baseline time frame). The right side of the line indicates time intervals during the course of service delivery.

Generally, the graph has four points from the midpoint on each line (see Figure 10.3). More intervals may be added as work progresses, if this appears to be appro-

FIGURE 10.3 ■ Ongoing Evaluation Graph: Mr. and Mrs. S

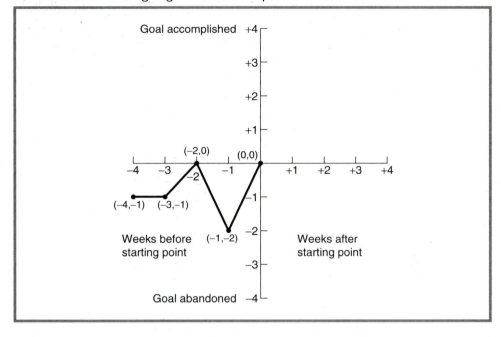

priate for a particular situation. During the data-collection phase of the General Method, information may be obtained for plotting dots on the left side of the graph. The social worker inquires about the severity of the problem prior to social worker–client system contact. Usually, this inquiry goes back to at least the previous four weeks. If it is a long-standing problem, a review may be made of the last four months or years. If it is a crisis that just recently began, the inquiry might cover the last four days or four hours. As the problem and goal become clear, the lines of the graph are drawn. As information is gathered about the history of the problem, person, and situation, dots are plotted on the left side of the graph. For example, if the intervals represent weeks, the social worker would ask what the situation was like one week, two weeks, three weeks, and four weeks before the system began to have contact with the generalist. As the situation for each time interval is described, an effort is made to locate a point on the goal line which matches the description. A dot is plotted where the time interval and goal indicator meet. In Figure 10.3, for example, one week before contact, the problem was assessed at the −2 point; two weeks before, it was at the 0 point (same as first contact with social worker); three weeks before, it was at the −1 level; and four weeks before, it was at the −1 level also. When the points are connected, it is apparent that the problem was at its worst one week before the system began to have contact with the social worker. In the case of Mr. and Mrs. S, this would mean that a week before they contacted the social worker, their quarrels were moving into physical fights half the time they talked.

If the tool in Figure 10.3 is used as an ongoing evaluation instrument, each time the social worker and the client or action system meet, they would plot a point on the graph to show what movement has taken place each week. During the assessment phase, the graph is refined with clear descriptors to measure movement toward or away from clarified goals within an expected time frame as indicated on the contracted plan. As points are plotted and connected, the social worker and the client system begin to envision the direction in which they expect to see the connecting line move, according to time intervals and dates anticipated on the contracted plan.

Plotting and charting movement could continue as the social worker and the client system go through the intervention, evaluation, and termination phases of the General Method. During the formal evaluation phase, a thorough analysis is made of the reasons why movement has been in the directions shown on the graph. The goal accomplishment scale and the contracted plan may still be used as described earlier to pinpoint the extent of goal accomplishment at the evaluation phase and to locate causal factors that resulted in arriving at the identified point. These tools may be complemented by the ongoing evaluation graph, which could provide a general perspective of movement throughout the process of service delivery.

Continuing to use the graph during termination helps the social worker detect any regression that may take place as the client, action, or target system begins to realize that contacts with the social worker will be terminated. As shown in Figure 10.4, for example, when Mr. and Mrs. S first began to express their problems to the social worker, tensions mounted between them. They accused each other of betraying confidences by talking with the social worker. The problem increased (point 1, −1). Through further contacts with the social worker, Mr. and Mrs. S began to grow in being able to listen to and understand each other. Progress toward the stated goal became evident. They were able to go for three weeks with open communication without quarreling. During the next two weeks of contact, some regression became apparent. The direction of the movement line went slightly downward. This regression was due to the fact that the social worker began to talk about termination with Mr. and Mrs. S. They began to talk about the anxiety they were feeling as they thought about having to work on their goals without the help of the social worker. A conscious awareness of the way they were responding to termination, with strong support from the social worker, helped them experience relief and find strength to move to goal accomplishment.

The intervals at the right side of the graph on the horizontal line are extended as long as may be needed to indicate length of time receiving service. Although the social worker may have gathered data only on the 4 weeks prior to the starting point (left side of line), the service may continue even beyond a year, and thus the horizontal line on the right would be extended. In Figure 10.4, for example, Mr. and Mrs. S were seen by the social worker for 12 weeks. Although there was some regression at the time of termination, they did not go back to where they were during the month before they contacted the social worker. The extended graph shows that their goal was attained by the time termination was finalized.

When the ongoing evaluation graph is used in working with a client system, it is very helpful to ask the client system to keep a daily log from the time the goal is first established. If a client is asked to recall what happened over a week or a month (depending on frequency of contacts), it is very likely that there will be some error in what is said. Often, a person's memory of what happened is influenced by how the

FIGURE 10.4 ■ Ongoing Evaluation Graph: Mr. and Mrs. S at Termination

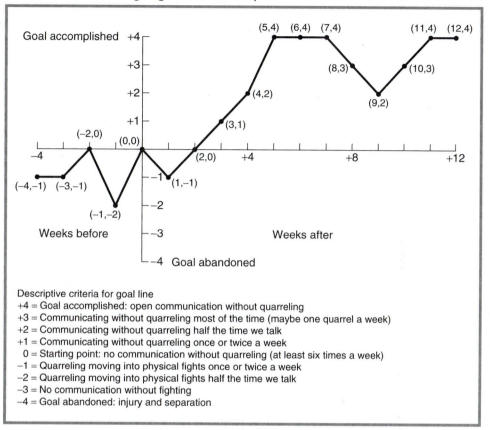

Descriptive criteria for goal line
+4 = Goal accomplished: open communication without quarreling
+3 = Communicating without quarreling most of the time (maybe one quarrel a week)
+2 = Communicating without quarreling half the time we talk
+1 = Communicating without quarreling once or twice a week
 0 = Starting point: no communication without quarreling (at least six times a week)
−1 = Quarreling moving into physical fights once or twice a week
−2 = Quarreling moving into physical fights half the time we talk
−3 = No communication without fighting
−4 = Goal abandoned: injury and separation

person is feeling at the time of recall. A daily log can be introduced when the graph is first formulated. The social worker asks the client system to indicate briefly in the log each day the extent to which the problem and the goal were present. More specifically, the system may be asked to record the number of times or the length of duration of a particular behavior or event. For example, Mr. and Mrs. S would have been asked to jot down at the end of the day in their log how many times they quarreled and also how often they communicated with each other without quarreling during each day. If they bring the log with them each time they meet with the social worker, a more accurate plotting of points on the graph can take place. The social worker and the client system need to articulate as exactly as possible the measurable behaviors that are to be recorded and used to indicate movement in goal accomplishment.

One of the main drawbacks in using the ongoing evaluation graph is the possibility that goals may change during the course of work with a client system. With a multiple-problem family, for example, a goal in one area may become abandoned or at least shifted in priority because of a crisis that arises in another area. Progress for the family is then recognized as movement toward a different goal. If more than one goal is being worked on at one time, a number of graphs may be used simultaneously.

For example, a child's health problem may be the working goal for a family, when suddenly they receive eviction papers. This new problem has to be addressed immediately. The new goal is to relocate the family within 30 days. A new graph indicating progression and regression in movement toward this goal would have to be developed.

The use of scales as depicted in Figures 10.3 and 10.4 is similar to that used in a single-subject research design. The research methodology includes measurement processes and statistical techniques for testing the significance of results. The short baselines and time frames of many interventions make the use of these techniques infrequent. The graphic visual presentation of results, however, is extremely beneficial in the course of charting progress.

The ongoing evaluation process used in single-subject design and in the related variation found in Figure 10.3 is applicable to work with a variety of problems, including those of a psychosocial nature. Examples include issues of adolescence, identity, alcoholism, loss or separation, and child abuse (Dean & Reinherz, 1986; Kirk, 1999; Salladin & Timberlake, 1995).

Working with Different Client Systems

No matter what type of system a social worker has been working with for goal accomplishment, time is needed to evaluate how far the client or action system has moved toward or away from the goal. A deliberate, objective study—which includes an analysis of change, identification of impediments to goal accomplishment, and planning or reformulating contracts—may help break through resistances and provide direction for future interactions between social worker and system of contact.

The tools and processes described in this chapter are general in nature; they may be used in evaluation with individuals, families, groups, organizations, or communities. The evaluation questions, the goal-accomplishment scale, the contracted plan, and the ongoing evaluation graph may be adapted for use with any system of contact. Even when working with action system teams or target systems, the generalist practitioner takes time to involve the client system in an evaluation, during which the tools and processes suggested may be utilized.

When working with an action system team, for example, evaluation questions are asked about the goals that the team identified collectively. The contract plan the team members developed is used to locate causal factors when goals are not accomplished. The timing, contract plan, tasks, problems, and goals found on the team contract are considered, along with external circumstances not anticipated by the team in planning. Internal circumstances are also considered as possible causal factors. A study would be made not only of the relationships of team members with the client, action, or target system but also of the relationships among the team members themselves (trust, openness) and how these relationships have affected the process of goal attainment. The goal-accomplishment scale may be used to show how much movement the team believes has taken place for each of the goals it stated. The ongoing evaluation graph may also be used to monitor direction over a period of time toward or away from the goals.

ANN SHYNE (1914–?), social work researcher and recipient of the first NASW Lifetime Achievement Award, narrowed the gap between research and practice by applying research methodology to practitioners' questions. Her 1948 question "Can planned short-term treatment be effective?" and later questions about placement prevention and family reunification yielded positive results supporting brief treatment and services to children in their own homes. During her career, Shyne directed research at the Community Service Society of New York and the Child Welfare League of America.

To cite an example of evaluation in teamwork, a vocational counselor from the State Department of Vocational Rehabilitation, a social worker from the East Side Women's Center, and a child welfare worker from the Department of Children's Services formed a team to coordinate service delivery for Mrs. Judy E and her 5-year-old daughter, Betty. Mrs. E had been reported three months previously for suspected child abuse. The child welfare worker was monitoring the home situation. She had helped Mrs. E reach the point where the client was asking for skill training to become employed. Mrs. E and the social worker developed a plan in which Mrs. E could be referred to the Women's Center and the Department of Vocational Rehabilitation. Mrs. E agreed also to have the social workers from the three resources form a team to provide ongoing, coordinated services for herself and her daughter.

Once the team was formed, goals were identified and tasks were distributed among the members of the team and Mrs. E. The main goals, tasks, and contracted plans that were collectively identified by the team are summarized as follows:

1. To help Mrs. E become employed by her going through a process of testing, training, job locating, and being hired (assigned to vocational counselor and Mrs. E)
2. To help Mrs. E grow in self-worth and self-confidence by her attendance at a weekly women's support group (assigned to social worker at the Women's Center and Mrs. E)
3. To help Mrs. E locate appropriate, available day care for Betty by searching for a resource and completing the application process (assigned to child welfare worker, Mrs. E, and Betty)
4. To have Mrs. E participate in the coordinated team effort by encouraging her to accept the invitation to join and become involved in all team meetings

The contracted plan also stated the anticipated dates for completing each of the identified tasks. As interventions were carried out, the team moved into the evaluation phase. If a goal and its planned tasks were apparently the direct responsibility of one social worker on the team (as in goals 1 through 3), this member was the one responsible for developing the ongoing evaluation graph and/or the goal-accomplishment scale for the particular goal. This team member was asked to lead the team as members took time to assess the extent to which that goal has been accomplished. Collectively, the team reviewed the evaluation questions and the contracted plan. This analysis was conducted with input from the client system.

The fourth goal in the team example is one of shared responsibility by all team members. Each member was expected to encourage Mrs. E to attend and to participate in team meetings. Together, the team designed a goal-accomplishment scale and an ongoing evaluation graph for this goal. Because the goal has the distinct dimensions of (1) attendance and (2) participation in team meetings, the team decided to draw up two graphs and two scales for clarity in assessment of goal 4. For example, in Figures 10.5 and 10.6 (goal-accomplishment scales) and Figures 10.7 and 10.8 (ongoing evaluation graphs), the team members—it is hoped including Mrs. E as a member—discussed and identified what they saw as criteria for identifying movement in goal accomplishment. The dual scales and graphs help highlight the multiple options that may exist when the two variables (attendance and participation) are considered necessary to achieve the one goal (Mrs. E's participating in the coordinated team effort). In Figure 10.5, Mrs. E is seen as attending the team meetings regularly (*4* is checked on Figure 10.5), but she is not yet participating fully at the meetings (*1* is checked on Figure 10.6). Both Figures 10.5 and 10.6 would have to reach a +4 if the goal is to be accomplished totally, according to the criteria developed by the team.

It should be noted that in the scales of Figures 10.5 and 10.6 and in the goal lines of the graphs of Figures 10.7 and 10.8, there are no minus numbers and line. This is because there is no degree to which the goal of attendance and participation at team meetings can be less than the starting point (0). The *0* on the scales means zero attendance and participation.

The ongoing evaluation graphs in Figures 10.7 and 10.8 show that there was 0 attendance and participation in team meetings prior to the starting point when Mrs. E was first invited to attend. The graphs also show the progress that took place as Mrs. E began to feel more in control of her life, more confidence in herself, and more comfortable with the other team members.

FIGURE 10.5 ■ Goal-Accomplishment Scale: Mrs. E's Level of Attendance at Team Meetings

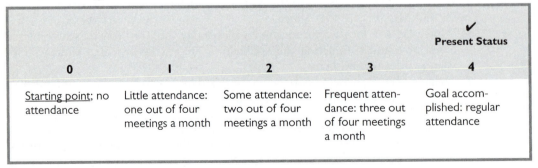

0	1	2	3	✔ Present Status 4
Starting point; no attendance	Little attendance: one out of four meetings a month	Some attendance: two out of four meetings a month	Frequent attendance: three out of four meetings a month	Goal accomplished: regular attendance

FIGURE 10.6 ■ Goal-Accomplishment Scale: Mrs. E's Level of Participation in Team Meetings

✔				
Present Status				
0	**1**	**2**	**3**	**4**
Starting point: no participation in meetings	Little participation: speaking up once or twice during a meeting or only when spoken to	Some participation: speaking up three or four times during a meeting	Frequent participation: speaking up and sharing five or six times	Goal accomplished: active—fully participating in flow of meetings

FIGURE 10.7 ■ Ongoing Evaluation Graph: Mrs, E's Attendance at Team Meetings

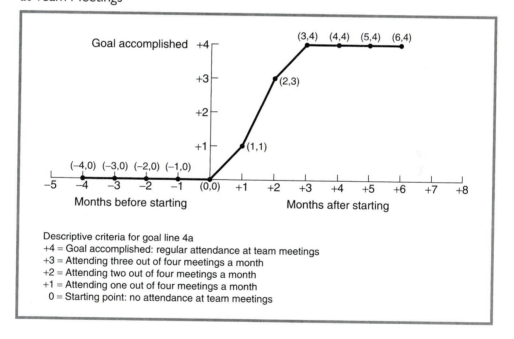

Descriptive criteria for goal line 4a
+4 = Goal accomplished: regular attendance at team meetings
+3 = Attending three out of four meetings a month
+2 = Attending two out of four meetings a month
+1 = Attending one out of four meetings a month
 0 = Starting point: no attendance at team meetings

In work with a target system rather than a team, client, or action system, the evaluation process may be somewhat different. Although a generalist may interact with a target system for goal accomplishment, the two may never arrive at a point where they develop a contracted plan together. A social worker alone, or with a client or action system or other resource, may initiate contact with a target system to request some assistance or change in service. The social worker and other members of

FIGURE 10.8 ■ Ongoing Evaluation Graph: Mrs. E's Participation in Team Meetings

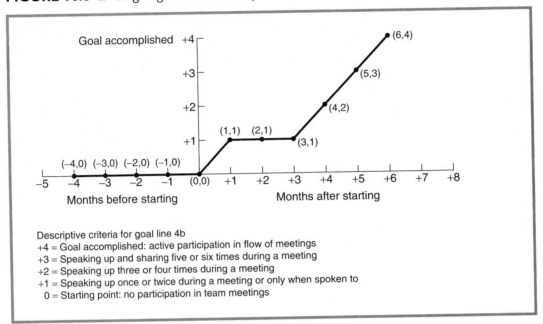

Descriptive criteria for goal line 4b
+4 = Goal accomplished: active participation in flow of meetings
+3 = Speaking up and sharing five or six times during a meeting
+2 = Speaking up three or four times during a meeting
+1 = Speaking up once or twice during a meeting or only when spoken to
 0 = Starting point: no participation in team meetings

FIGURE 10.9 ■ Evaluation Graph: Landlady Target System

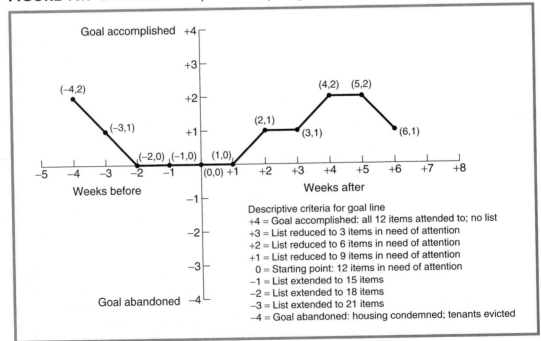

Descriptive criteria for goal line
+4 = Goal accomplished: all 12 items attended to; no list
+3 = List reduced to 3 items in need of attention
+2 = List reduced to 6 items in need of attention
+1 = List reduced to 9 items in need of attention
 0 = Starting point: 12 items in need of attention
−1 = List extended to 15 items
−2 = List extended to 18 items
−3 = List extended to 21 items
−4 = Goal abandoned: housing condemned; tenants evicted

the action system may state clearly at that time their purpose or goals in making the contact. The target system, however, may not respond favorably. If the social worker continues to try to change the target system through repeated contacts and pressures, there may be a time when the social worker evaluates with the target system what movement toward or away from the stated goal has taken place since their first contact. Here, a goal-accomplishment scale or an ongoing evaluation graph may be helpful as the social worker tries to make an objective presentation to confront the target system with the reality of the situation.

For example, on behalf of her tenants, a generalist practitioner may speak to the landlady of an apartment complex to try to get her to improve the conditions of the apartment. A list is presented indicating repairs, renovations, and improvements needed. To have all 12 items on the list taken care of is the ultimate goal. The generalist and the tenants involve a Housing Code Inspector and the Housing Court in efforts to pressure the landlady to make the improvements. Periodically, the generalist practitioner meets with the landlady to continue to bring to her attention the unattended needs of the tenants. As conditions improve or deteriorate, the social worker may choose to use an ongoing evaluation graph or a goal-accomplishment scale to demonstrate what has taken place since the problems and needs were first presented to the landlady (starting point). This evaluative approach may help create sufficient feelings for progress to be made.

As depicted on the graph in Figure 10.9, the conditions at the apartment complex had deteriorated during the weeks prior to the social worker's contact with the landlady. Through various pressures and continued contacts, some improvements were made. After the fifth week of contact, however, there was a tapering off of efforts to improve conditions, and problems increased. The social worker used the graph (Figure 10.9) to point out to the landlady what progress had been made, how conditions were starting to get worse, and how far they were from accomplishing the original goal (+4).

Using Social Work Foundation Knowledge in Evaluation

The holistic foundation for generalist practice (Chapter 1) identifies the fundamental values, knowledge, and skills used during evaluation. The social worker demonstrates care for a system and a commitment to quality service by taking time to analyze movement toward or away from goals. Even though the General Method requires ongoing evaluation and social work foundation knowledge, the principles of *individualization* and *self-determination* are emphasized. Any assessment of movement or change is strongly dependent on input from the system of contact. Any reformulation of a contract takes place only after a client system, an action system, or, if possible, a target system has spoken with the social worker and has given input and consent.

In practice, the social worker inquires about changes in feelings and attitudes as well as behaviors. He or she recognizes and encourages *purposeful expression of feel-*

ings during evaluation. If progress has not taken place, the social worker conveys a *nonjudgmental attitude* toward the client system, as focus is directed to exploring possible causal factors and a reformulation of the plan.

From scientific research, the generalist uses knowledge and skills for measuring, graphing, and scaling during evaluation. In addition to research skills, it may be necessary to use relationship, problem-solving, and political skills. Frequently, the social worker guides, clarifies, and confronts as goals are analyzed. Within the evaluation phase, such General Method skills as problem and need identification, data collection, assessment, and contract planning may be reviewed and repeated.

Foundation knowledge used during evaluation varies according to the problem or goal that is being evaluated. In order to identify indicators of improvement or regression in a problem, the nature and dynamics of the problem must be understood.

Through holistic knowledge, the generalist is enabled to conduct a comprehensive study of causal factors. As the evaluation questions are raised and internal and external circumstances are considered, the social worker is aided by the foundation knowledge base, which is integrated within the ecological-systems perspective of *person-in-environment*. The generalist is sensitive to the complex and multiple factors that interact and influence a client system.

Human Diversity in Evaluation

Core human diversity issues related to multiculturalism, social pluralism, and sociodemographics also need to be recognized and incorporated in evaluation. As noted earlier, examples of these issues include institutional racism, cultural diversity, gender-role expectations, sexual orientation, and socio-economic status among others.

As the social worker and client, action, and target system move into the evaluation phase of the General Method, they begin with the question: *Have the goals been accomplished?* The social worker must distinguish between long-range goals and short-range goals. Core human diversity issues may be readily identified as basically causing a client system to have unmet needs. Long-range goals may be the eradication of these two problems. Although the long-range goals may not be accomplished at the time of evaluation, the efforts made to work toward them should be evaluated. The identified immediate or short-range goals are usually articulated in more precise terms that can be measured for accomplishment. If they have not been fully accomplished, the contract review (described in Chapter 7) may help highlight the reason why plans are not carried out successfully. Again, the timing projected for goal accomplishment may not have been in line with the time orientation of the culture of the client system. The persons or resources expected to carry out the planned tasks, or the tasks themselves, may have been culturally inappropriate. It may be that the goals or the problems were not correctly understood or articulated.

As pointed out, a final question to raise during evaluation is: *Was there anything in the social worker–client system relationship that inhibited goal accomplishment?* To answer this question, a social worker needs to ask himself or herself: *How sensitive and accepting was I toward this person, family, group, organization, or com-*

munity? Self-awareness is necessary. If a social worker has come to understand and appreciate his or her own ethnicity, it is often easier to recognize and accept the ethnicity of others. As with the systems receiving service, a social worker also brings to any new relationship his or her ethnic history and personal experiences with certain cultural, social, and socio-demographic groups. Although, admittedly, it may be natural to transfer or stereotype, a working relationship can be very inhibited when those receiving help, or even those providing help, sense that they are not being treated as unique individuals. If goals are not being accomplished, the reason could be related to an absence of cultural sensitivity or of any shared cultural elements, with a resulting stereotyping by both the social worker and the client system receiving service. When stereotyping is present, studies have shown that participants begin to feel discomfort, and that they retreat into exaggerated behaviors that depict and confirm the ethnic-group stereotype.

In the evaluation phase, while making an appraisal of the extent of goal accomplishment and a comprehensive evaluation to locate possible reasons for any lack of accomplishment, a social worker who is knowledgeable about multiculturalism, social pluralism, and socio-demographic diversity can better recognize dynamics and factors that may affect or prevent the attainment of goals. In reviewing the contracted plan, it may become apparent that service providers or other persons who were expected to complete certain tasks may have taken longer than planned or may have changed their minds as the anticipated date arrived. The change on their part could be due to fears, threats, or insincere commitments that surfaced as the plan unfolded. Clients themselves may have changed their minds and plans as they began to experience pressures from family members, lawyers, judges, or others. An individual who seemed interested in joining a support group, for example, may have failed to show up for meetings because of increased fears of being identified with the group. And finally, here, too, it is possible that the social worker or the client system may be uncomfortable with the working relationship itself and that this discomfort has interfered with goal accomplishment. Perhaps the openness or support needed did not develop, owing to hidden biases or fears. Again, an honest evaluation of the social worker–client system relationship at this time may result in a breakthrough so that progress can begin.

When it is time to evaluate goals that relate to gender-role changes, progress in personal and environmental goals should be considered realistically. Both the social worker and those receiving service need to realize that only with continued efforts and much time and patience can there be any lasting change in prejudicial attitudes, practices, and policies. If a goal was to eliminate prejudice in a target system and this has not been accomplished, progress may have been made if at least some conscious awareness of its presence has begun to develop in the target system. On a personal level, to have an individual become aware of his or her self-image and bias may be a major accomplishment, even though the person may not change his or her behavior or life situation.

Here, too, a major factor to be reviewed when goals have not been accomplished is the expectations and attitudes of the social worker toward those receiving service. A social worker who is finding it difficult to support efforts to overcome bias and prejudice may be contributing to the failure in goal attainment.

ONGOING CASES
Evaluation Phase

In the following section, the application of knowledge and skills during the *evaluation phase* of the General Method is demonstrated by entry-level generalist social workers in cases from seven fields of practice: child welfare, gerontology, public social welfare, community services, education, corrections, and homelessness. In Exercise 10.1, questions are proposed for reflection and discussion about how practice in each of the case examples during the evaluation phase might change if the client system represented a different

▶ *Culture:* Racial/ethnic group membership, national origin and social group identity, religion and spirituality
▶ *Social status:* Socio-economic status, environmental and rural/urban differences
▶ *Socio-demographic strata:* Age and developmental stage, gender roles, sexual orientation, challenges in mental and physical ability

EXERCISE 10.1
Impact of Human Diversity on Evaluation Process

Consider the following questions with each of the following seven client systems. When evaluating the client system, how might change in culture, social status, or socio-demographic strata:

1. Influence the client system's attitudes and behavior about reviewing achievements?
2. Influence the norms, roles, and authority issues in evaluating each system?
3. Reveal values that influence timing, communications, and actions in evaluation?
4. Affect the dynamics of the professional relationship during evaluation?
5. Affect monitoring of the progress, timeliness, and effectiveness of service delivery?

I. Child Welfare Case

A. Agency: State Department of Children's Services

B. Client System

K, a 15-year-old female, was placed in a group home three months ago. (For more background information, see Chapter 5, Engagement Phase, I. Child Welfare Case.)

C. Summary of Preceding Phases

The problems, needs, goals, and tasks identified and implemented in earlier phases are found in Chapters 7 and 8. The social worker's interventions included counseling with K, the client;

a referral to the group home and a court petitioning for custody continuance; and teamwork with personnel from the shelter, the group home, and the school K is attending.

D. Evaluation

GOAL ANALYSIS: The primary goals of (1) obtaining and maintaining a permanent placement, (2) reentering school, and (3) personal growth were analyzed by K and the social worker. They agreed that a placement had been found and was being maintained (goal 1). K was also attending school regularly (goal 2). Her personal problems (3a–3d) were beginning to surface in casework and group sessions at the home, though she was still finding it difficult to believe that she was of any worth and to talk about her sexuality. Goal 4, to obtain continuance of custody, was achieved on 3/30.

Scales were developed to assess the extent to which the first two goals were accomplished. The two dimensions of goal 1 (obtaining placement and maintaining placement) were separated for greater clarity in evaluation (see Figures 10.10 and 10.11). The goal of school reentry was expanded at this time to include optimal school performance. Two scales were also used then to evaluate goal 2 (see Figures 10.12 and 10.13). The goal regarding personal growth (goal 3) had four subheadings (a–d). Because the child-welfare worker was not working directly on this goal with K, the four parts were reviewed in discussion and evaluated in general, on the basis of input from K, from the social worker who was seeing K individually, and from the group-home social worker who attended the peer-group meetings.

Goal 1a was evaluated by K and the social worker as accomplished (+2). K was placed in a group home where she could stay until adulthood.

According to K and the group-home staff, K was adjusting well to the placement. They thought, however, that she could try to participate more fully in group activities. She was completing her chores and getting along satisfactorily with the other residents. Because K had only been in the home for three months and said she was not completely comfortable there yet, the social worker and K evaluated the extent of accomplishment for goal 1b as +2 on the scale.

K was accepted into the local school; therefore, goal 2a was accomplished, as indicated with a +2 on the scale in Figure 10.12.

K and the social worker considered ways in which they could objectively assess her progress in school. They agreed that they would look at her grades and report card from school and that they would ask for verbal assessments from K's teachers through the school social worker. At the time of this evaluation, K's performance was described by her teachers as "satisfactory." They thought she could do better, especially in her writing and class participation. They expected that K would perform at a higher achievement level as she became more familiar with the school. K said that she liked school and her teachers and thought she was learning a great deal. She knew she could try harder and bring up her grades by the end of the semester. K did not believe that she needed a tutor or any additional help with her schoolwork at this time. The social worker and K assessed the extent of accomplishment for goal 2b as +2 on the scale (Figure 10.13).

K said she continued to find it hard to talk about herself and her personal problems (goal 3). She enjoyed the group meetings because the other residents were able to say things she couldn't. Deep down inside she knew she was feeling happier but was afraid it was "too good to be true." She said she would try harder to talk with her social worker about herself

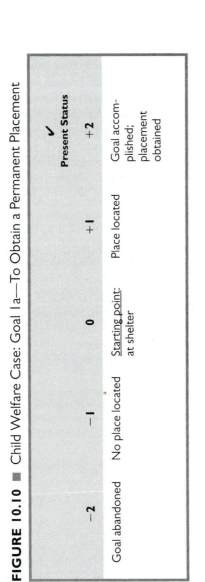

FIGURE 10.10 ■ Child Welfare Case: Goal Ia—To Obtain a Permanent Placement

−2	−1	0	+1	+2 Present Status
Goal abandoned	No place located	Starting point: at shelter	Place located	Goal accomplished; placement obtained

FIGURE 10.11 ■ Child Welfare Case: Goal Ib—To Maintain a Permanent Placement

−4	−3	−2	−1	0	+1	+2 Present Statu	+3	+4
Goal abandoned: removal from placement	Marked problems: high conflict level	Increased problems	Beginning problems in adjustment	Starting point; beginning placement at new group home	Beginning to adjust	Satisfactory adjustment, but room for improvement	Marked improvement, high comfort level	Goal accomplished; stabilized adjustment

FIGURE 10.12 ■ Child Welfare Case: Goal 2a—To Reenter School

–2	–1	0	+1	Present Status ✔ +2
Goal abandoned	No school located	Starting point; out of school	School located	Goal accomplished—returned to school

FIGURE 10.13 ■ Child Welfare Case: Goal 2b—To Achieve Optimal Level of Academic Performance

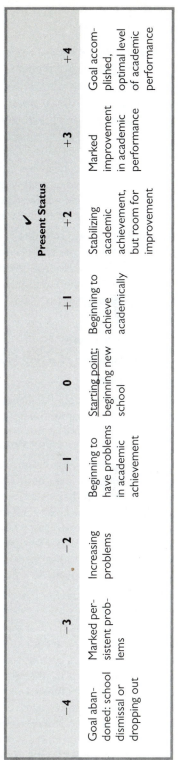

–4	–3	–2	–1	0	+1	Present Status ✔ +2	+3	+4
Goal abandoned: school dismissal or dropping out	Marked persistent problems	Increasing problems	Beginning to have problems in academic achievement	Starting point; beginning new school	Beginning to achieve academically	Stabilizing academic achievement, but room for improvement	Marked improvement in academic performance	Goal accomplished, optimal level of academic performance

and her feelings. K's social worker at the group home thought that K was beginning to relax more during individual sessions and that more time was needed before K would be able to talk freely about herself, her past, or her future.

CONTRACT REVIEW AND REFORMULATION: During planned contract review, the social worker and K recognized the need for more time before goals 1, 2, and 3 (especially goal 3) could be accomplished. In reviewing contracted tasks, the social worker and K agreed that the social worker did not have to continue to follow up with K every two weeks. K knew that she could always call the social worker if she needed her. They agreed that the social worker would begin to visit K once a month, unless there was some reason for additional contact. The social worker recorded the process of evaluation that occurred at this phase, indicating the reformulation of contract, as found in Table 10.2.

ONGOING EVALUATION: At this point, the social worker and K developed graphs to assess ongoing progress in (1) maintenance (adjustment) in the group home and (2) school performance. The graphs they designed are found in Figures 10.14 and 10.15. The social worker and K planned to use the graphs each month when they met for ongoing evaluation and charting of progress.

II. Gerontology Case

A. Agency: Seaside Nursing Home

B. Client System

Mrs. J, an 80-year-old Portuguese woman, is in a skilled-nursing facility. (For additional information, see Chapter 5, Engagement Phase, II. Gerontology Case.)

C. Summary of Preceding Phases

The contracted plan indicating the problems, needs, goals, and tasks identified in earlier phases is found in Chapter 7. The social worker's interventions were counseling with Mrs. J and teamwork with the staff of the nursing home and the pastor of the church Mrs. J used to attend. The prioritized goals for Mrs. J were the following: (1) to get to know the staff and the resources of the nursing home; (2) to work out a mutually satisfactory bath schedule with the nurses; (3) to leave her room alone (at least once a day) and to attend a house activity (at least once a week); (4) to stop name calling and yelling at residents; and (5) to share her culture with others.

E. Evaluation

GOAL ANALYSIS: After three months, the social worker and Mrs. J analyzed the extent of goal accomplishment for the five prioritized goals. Goals 2 and 4 had clearly been accomplished. Mrs. J's bath was scheduled earlier, and she no longer fought with the nurses. She also stopped calling the residents names and was beginning to feel more comfortable in the home as she got to know the staff and the resources available (goal 1). She met with the program planner, the director of volunteers, the head nurse and other nurses, the chaplain, and staff members from recreational therapy. Although there were occasional days when she did not leave her room, she was attending nursing-home activities with her roommate (goal 3) and appeared less fearful of having her possessions stolen. Regarding goal 5, Mrs. J's pas-

TABLE 10.2 ■ Child Welfare Case: Contracted Plan

Date Identified	Problem/Need	Goal	Task	Contract	Date Anticipated	Date Accomplished
4/25 Evaluation	Evaluation of problems 1,2,3,4	Goals 1,2,3,4	1. Recall each goal. 2. Assess extent of accomplishment. 3. Reformulate contract.	Social worker and K (with input from school and group-home personnel)	4/25	4/25
Contract reformulation	Change in 1. Date anticipated for task 4, goal 1; task 3, goal 3	Goal 1	Task 4—follow-up	Social worker, K, group home staff	5/25 and once a month thereafter	
		Goal 3	Task 3—follow-up	Social worker, K, social worker at group home	5/25 and once a month thereafter	
	2. Goal statement for problem 2; contract and date anticipated for task 2, goals 2a and 2b	2a. To reenter school 2b. To achieve an optimal level of academic performance	Task 2—follow-up	Social worker and school social worker	5/25 and once a month thereafter	

FIGURE 10.14 ■ Child Welfare Case Evaluation Graph: Goal 1b—To Maintain Permanent Placement

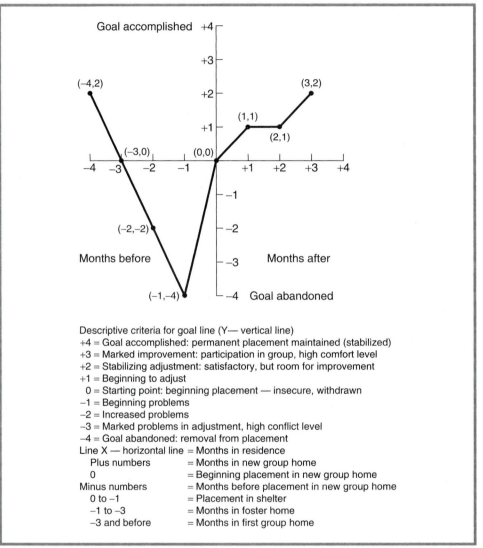

Descriptive criteria for goal line (Y— vertical line)
+4 = Goal accomplished: permanent placement maintained (stabilized)
+3 = Marked improvement: participation in group, high comfort level
+2 = Stabilizing adjustment: satisfactory, but room for improvement
+1 = Beginning to adjust
  0 = Starting point: beginning placement — insecure, withdrawn
−1 = Beginning problems
−2 = Increased problems
−3 = Marked problems in adjustment, high conflict level
−4 = Goal abandoned: removal from placement
Line X — horizontal line = Months in residence
　Plus numbers　　　　= Months in new group home
　0　　　　　　　　 = Beginning placement in new group home
Minus numbers　　　 = Months before placement in new group home
　0 to −1　　　　　 = Placement in shelter
　−1 to −3　　　　　= Months in foster home
　−3 and before　　 = Months in first group home

tor and two members of the congregation came to see her. They took her to their church for a Christmas prayer service and a concert. A volunteer who spoke Portuguese visited Mrs. J for three weeks in November but then dropped out of the program.

Scales to assess the extent of goal accomplishment for goals 3a and 3b were developed and drawn on a large sheet of paper (see Figures 10.16 and 10.17). The scale for goal 3a was expanded into an ongoing evaluation graph, which the social worker reviewed with Mrs. J each succeeding week (see Figure 10.18). The nurse at the head station agreed to help Mrs. J and the social worker keep track of the days when Mrs. J was able to leave her room on

FIGURE 10.15 ■ Child Welfare Case Evaluation Graph: Goal 2b—To Achieve an Optimal Level of Academic Performance

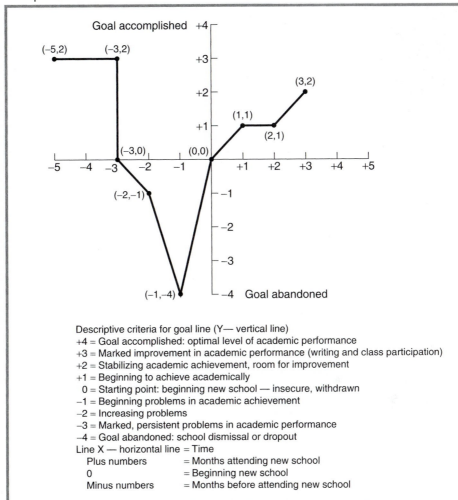

Descriptive criteria for goal line (Y— vertical line)
+4 = Goal accomplished: optimal level of academic performance
+3 = Marked improvement in academic performance (writing and class participation)
+2 = Stabilizing academic achievement, room for improvement
+1 = Beginning to achieve academically
  0 = Starting point: beginning new school — insecure, withdrawn
−1 = Beginning problems in academic achievement
−2 = Increasing problems
−3 = Marked, persistent problems in academic performance
−4 = Goal abandoned: school dismissal or dropout
Line X — horizontal line = Time
  Plus numbers   = Months attending new school
  0   = Beginning new school
  Minus numbers   = Months before attending new school

her own. A small calendar was kept at the head station, and the date was circled when Mrs. J came to the station to say "hello" to the nurse on duty.

The goal does not extend to Mrs. J's going outside the institution on her own. At this time, it is not seen as a possibility. The maximum goal accomplishment considered, therefore, was Mrs. J's being able to freely and frequently go out of her bedroom on her own. The graph in Figure 10.18 demonstrates that Mrs. J was able to live alone up to 3 weeks before she was hospitalized. She was in the hospital for 2 weeks prior to her placement in the nursing home. During her first 2 weeks at the home, she regressed. At the time of evaluation (12 weeks in residence), she progressed to occasionally leaving her room independently (averaging once a week), which is shown at point +1 on the goal line of Figure 10.18. With

FIGURE 10.16 ■ Gerontology Case: Goal 3a—To Leave Room Alone (At Least Once a Day)

			✔ Present Status			
−3	**−2**	**−1**	**0**	**+1**	**+2**	**+3**
Total refusal to go out of room—goal dropped	Increased refusal to leave room (once a day)	Occasional refusal to leave even when some-one offers to take her (about once a week)	<u>Starting point;</u> only leave when some-one takes her for meals	Occasional going out of room alone (about once a week)	Increased going out of room alone (once a day)	Going out of room alone freely; maximum goal accom-plished

FIGURE 10.17 ■ Gerontology Case: Goal 3b—To Attend House Activity (At Least Once a Week)

	✔ Present Status		
0	**1**	**2**	**3**
<u>Starting point;</u> attending no house activities (program or meeting)	Attending house activity with social worker or staff member (once a week)	Attending house activity with other residents once a week	Attending house activities with residents more than once a week; maximum goal accomplished

the added involvement of the nurses at the station on Mrs. J's floor, the goal reached the point +2 by one week after the evaluation, as shown in point 13,2 of Figure 10.18.

CONTRACT REFORMULATION: The evaluation conducted by Mrs. J and the social worker 12 weeks after she began residency in the nursing home was recorded on the con-tracted plan (Table 10.3). As indicated, the task for goal 3a was expanded to include Mrs. J's saying "hello" to the nurse at the station on her floor at least once a day after leaving her room on her own. The task of having the nurse chart on the calendar Mrs. J's visit to the sta-tion was also added to the contract. In addition, the head nurse and the social worker planned to meet once a week to review Mrs. J's progress, using the charted calendar. The social worker would use this information when she met with Mrs. J to chart progress in goal 3a on the evaluation graph each week. As shown in Table 10.3, the contract reformulation and the three-month evaluation were indicated on the contracted plan.

FIGURE 10.18 ■ Ongoing Evaluation Graph: Gerontology Case Goal 3a—To Leave Room by Herself

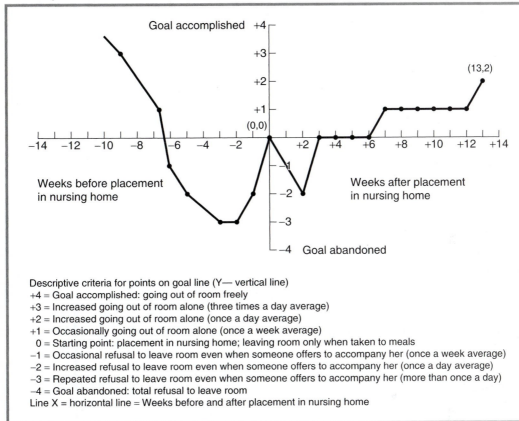

Descriptive criteria for points on goal line (Y— vertical line)
+4 = Goal accomplished: going out of room freely
+3 = Increased going out of room alone (three times a day average)
+2 = Increased going out of room alone (once a day average)
+1 = Occasionally going out of room alone (once a week average)
 0 = Starting point: placement in nursing home; leaving room only when taken to meals
−1 = Occasional refusal to leave room even when someone offers to accompany her (once a week average)
−2 = Increased refusal to leave room even when someone offers to accompany her (once a day average)
−3 = Repeated refusal to leave room even when someone offers to accompany her (more than once a day)
−4 = Goal abandoned: total refusal to leave room
Line X = horizontal line = Weeks before and after placement in nursing home

III. Public Social Welfare Case

A. Agency: State Social Services

B. Client System

Mr. and Mrs. P and their two children (ages 2 and 4) were placed in emergency shelter (Center City Motor Inn) for 44 days and are currently living in an apartment. (For additional background information, see Chapter 5, Engagement Phase, III. Public Social Welfare Case.)

C. Summary of Preceding Phases

The problems, needs, goals, and tasks identified and enacted in earlier phases are listed in Chapters 7 and 8. The interventions of the social worker were primarily (1) referral to several resources, (2) counseling with the P family, and (3) teamwork with the income-maintenance technician and Mr. P's psychiatrist.

TABLE 10.3 ■ Gerontology Case: Contracted Plan

Date Identified	Problem/Need	Goal	Task	Contract	Date Anticipated	Date Accomplished
12/8 Evaluation	Evaluation of problems 1–5	Goals 1–5	1. Review each goal. 2. Evaluate extent of accomplishment for each goal. 3. Reformulate contract.	Mrs. J and social worker	12/18 and 12/20	12/18 and 12/20
Contract reformulation	Change in tasks, contract, and dates anticipated for goal 3a	3a. To leave room alone (at least once a day)	(3a) 1. Leave room alone and walk down to nurse's station and say "hello" to nurse on duty. 2. Circle date of visit on calendar. 3. Meet to discuss Mrs. J's progress. 4. Evaluate progress toward goal 3a using graph.	1. Mrs. J 2. Nurse on duty 3. Head nurse and social worker 4. Social worker and Mrs. J	12/21 and each day thereafter 12/21 and each day thereafter 12/27 and each Thursday thereafter 12/27 and each Thursday thereafter	

D. Evaluation

GOAL ANALYSIS: After 10 weeks of service, the social worker and Mr. and Mrs. P evaluated the extent to which the goals of the contracted plan were accomplished. They agreed that goals for problems 1, 2, 3, 4, 6, 7, 8, and 9 were accomplished. These goals are the following: (1) to obtain an emergency food supply, (2) to move into emergency shelter, (3) to receive a food supply until TANF check and food stamps arrive, (4) to move into an apartment for long-term residence of family, (6) to have children examined at the health center, (7) to obtain fuel assistance, (8) to receive TANF check and food stamps, and (9) to have the refrigerator repaired.

Goals 10, 11, and 12 were not accomplished by the time of the evaluation. These goals are (10) to receive Supplemental Security Income, (11) to receive a Thanksgiving food basket, and (12) to receive Christmas gifts for the children.

No goal was ever stated on the contracted plan for problem 5 (poor money management) because Mr. and Mrs. P refused to recognize this problem. They continued to blame others and to deny that their evictions from past apartments were related to their poor management of money.

CONTRACT REVIEW: In reviewing the goals that were accomplished, the social worker asked if the attainment of goals was a result of the plan contracted. With the exception of goals 4 and 9, goal attainment directly followed the completion of planned tasks. The contract for goal 4 stated that the Ps and the social worker would collaborate on locating an apartment. For goal 9, the social worker and the Ps planned that Mr. P would contact the Salvation Army for financial assistance to pay for repairs. Instead, the Ps contacted their income-maintenance technician directly, and she arranged for them to receive a new refrigerator.

In analyzing goals that were not accomplished (goals 10, 11, and 12), the social worker noted that the barrier to goal accomplishment for each of these goals could be pinpointed to tasks contracted to Mr. P that he failed to complete. He did not follow up on his application for Supplemental Security Income, nor did he contact churches for a Thanksgiving food basket or the Salvation Army for Christmas presents for the children.

Even with goal 9 (refrigerator repair), instead of Mr. P's getting estimates on repair costs and contacting the Salvation Army, he and Mrs. P called the income-maintenance technician and requested a new refrigerator. (The social worker and the income-maintenance technician realized that they should have communicated with each other about this new request before either one enacted a plan thus avoiding teamwork breakdown.)

The social worker did not use scales to assess the extent of goal accomplishment during the evaluation phase because of the basic nature of the identified goals and the interventions utilized. Although the primary needs for housing and food were being met for the present, the social worker realized that there were two continuing problem areas: (1) poor money management and (2) excessive dependency on others to meet their needs. At the time of the evaluation, the Ps were not recognizing these problems and did not want to work on either of them. When the social worker pointed out that the tasks assigned to Mr. P had not been accomplished, he said he planned to do them when he felt up to it.

Since the Ps were not asking for help from the social worker with the two cited problems or with any additional problems or needs at the time of the evaluation, and because the social worker did not want to continue unnecessary dependency, he began to talk about terminating with the family. Both the Ps and the social worker agreed that they would begin the process of termination.

E. Charted Progress

The social worker recorded the evaluation process on the contracted plan as found in Table 10.4.

In the social worker's discussions with the Ps, their income-maintenance technician, and Mr. P's psychiatrist, the social worker shared his continued concern regarding the family's management of money and dependence on outside resources to meet their needs. The problem of the family's poor money management had been recorded on the problem list earlier. During evaluation, the family's problem of dependency became more obvious to the social worker, and it was added to the problem list when he recorded the evaluation (see Table 10.4). The social worker expected that the case of the P family would possibly need to be reopened at a later date, and he thought it would be helpful to have the basic problem of dependency highlighted in the summarized chart.

IV. Community Services Case

A. Agency: Clayton Neighborhood House

B. Client System

Four Hispanic families needed heat in their apartments on the second floor of 33 L Street. (For more background information, see Chapter 5, Engagement Phase, IV. Community Services Case.)

C. Summary of Preceding Phases

The problems, needs, goals, and tasks as identified and contracted in earlier phases are outlined in Chapter 7 and 8. The social worker's interventions were counseling and advocacy with residents and their landlord. By the third meeting of the social worker with the residents, they were ready to move into the evaluation phase of the General Method.

D. Evaluation

GOAL ANALYSIS: After the residents monitored the heat in their apartments for a week, they met to share their findings with the social worker. Each family reported that the heat was adequate, ranging from 65° to 70° each day. At night, the heat went down to 63° to 65°, and this was acceptable to the families. The residents expressed relief and gratitude to the social worker. They were hopeful that the heating would continue throughout the winter.

As the social worker and the residents began to recall their identified goal, she presented a scale (as found in Figure 10.19) for goal analysis.

The families agreed that at this time their heating during the day is checked as averaging 68° (see the ✔ in Figure 10.19). The goal of adequate heating was being accomplished. The continuation of heating throughout the winter remained in question. They wanted to continue monitoring the heat throughout the winter and asked how they could show it on the scale each week. The social worker introduced the ongoing evaluation graph found in

TABLE 10.4 ■ Public Social Welfare Case: Contracted Plan

Date Identified	Problem/Need	Goal	Task	Contract	Date Anticipated	Date Accomplished
12/4 Evaluation	Evaluation of problems 1–12	Goals 1–4 and 6–12 (no goal for problem 5)	1. Review goals.	1. Mr. and Mrs. P and social worker	12/4	12/4
			2. Assess extent of accomplishment.	2. Mr. and Mrs. P and social worker	12/4	12/4
			3. Analyze progress.	3. Mr. and Mrs. P and social worker	12/4	12/4
			4. Reformulate contract or begin termination.	4. Mr. and Mrs. P and social worker	12/4	12/4
Contract reformulation	Add problem 13: family's dependence on outside resources					

FIGURE 10.19 ■ Community Services Case: Goal 1—To Obtain Consistent, Adequate Heating

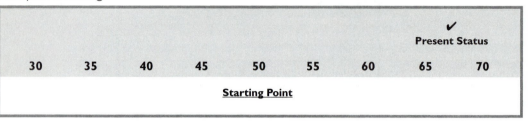

Figure 10.20. She explained that the horizontal line represented weeks and that the vertical line indicated temperature. She showed them when and how to plot their findings on the graph. They agreed to meet again the following week to plot their findings.

CONTRACT REVIEW AND REFORMULATION: In reviewing the contracted plan, the social worker reminded the residents that she had never met with the janitor (no entry in "date accomplished" for Task 1, Goal 1, in Chapter 7). They agreed that there was no need for anyone to say anything to him now that the upstairs was being heated adequately. The residents knew that they continued to have a problem communicating with the landlord, but they didn't want to do anything about it for the present.

FIGURE 10.20 ■ Community Services Case Ongoing Evaluation Graph: Monitoring Building Temperature

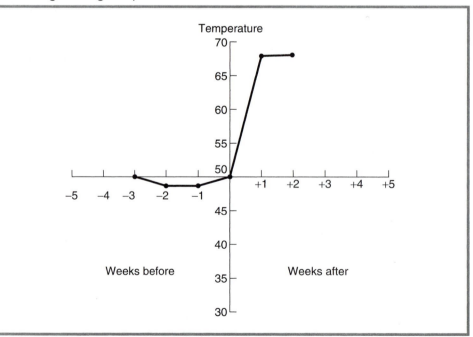

At this time, the social worker and the residents agreed to extend their contact for another week. If there was no further problem with the heating and if the residents had nothing else they wanted to work on with the social worker, she would terminate with them during the next meeting.

E. Charted Progress

The evaluation and contract reformulation by the social worker and the residents were recorded on the contracted plan as indicated in Table 10.5.

V. Education Case

A. Agency: Keeney Elementary School

B. Client System

Jim G, an 8-year-old third-grader, was showing regressive behavior in school and at home in reaction to his parents' strained relationship. (For additional background information, see Chapter 5, Engagement Phase, V. Education Case.)

C. Summary of Preceding Phases

The problems, needs, goals, and tasks that were identified in earlier phases are outlined in the contracted plan found in Chapter 7. After the joint session with Mr. and Mrs. G, Jim, and the social worker at school, Mr. and Mrs. G followed through with going for marital counseling at a local family counseling center, and Jim began to show improvement in his school work.

D. Evaluation

Progress in school performance was evaluated by Jim and the social worker as they met twice a week in her office. When the social worker called Mrs. G each week, they would evaluate what progress had been made. During the last home visit, the social worker, Jim, and his parents reviewed the contracted plan and analyzed the extent of goal accomplishment for all four problem areas.

GOAL ANALYSIS: As the social worker and Jim met together and focused on his school performance, they looked mainly at the extent to which Jim was (1) paying attention (showing interest in learning), (2) participating in class (raising hand to give answers or ask questions), and (3) bringing his grades up in math and spelling. These were specific areas in need of improvement identified by Jim's teacher. Each week, the social worker met briefly with Jim's teacher to receive a report on his progress in the classroom. The teacher showed the social worker Jim's weekly test scores in math and spelling. When Jim met with the social worker, the teacher's report was reviewed, and scales to evaluate goal accomplishment were used (see Figure 10.21).

By the end of the second week after the meeting with Jim and his parents, Jim's academic performance was assessed as +3 on the interest scale ("much interest") and as +3 on the scale for class participation ("much raising hand—five or six times a day"); his grades in math jumped from an average of 40 to 90, and his spelling grades went from 50 to 100 (see Figure 10.21). There was obvious progress in Jim's investment in school. His school attendance was no longer a problem. He arrived on time each day and was back to walking to school with the neighborhood children. Mrs. G also reported that he was sleeping better at night. When

TABLE 10.5 ■ Community Services Case: Contracted Plan

Date Identified	Problem/Need	Goal	Task	Contract	Date Anticipated	Date Accomplished
12/12 Evaluation	Evaluation of problems 1 (heating) and 2 (communication with landlord)	1. Adequate, consistent heating (no goal set for problem 2)	1. Review goal and problems.	Social worker and residents	12/2	12/12
			2. Evaluate extent of goal accomplishment.			
			3. Reformulate contract.			
Contract reformulation	Drop task 1, of goal 1, add tasks 6 and 7 for goal 1		6. Continue to monitor heat daily.	6. Mr. T, Mrs. V, Mr. A, and CR	12/12–12/19	
			7. Meet to review findings (and possible termination).	7. Social worker and residents	12/19	

418

FIGURE 10.21 ■ Education Case: Goal 3—To Improve School Performance

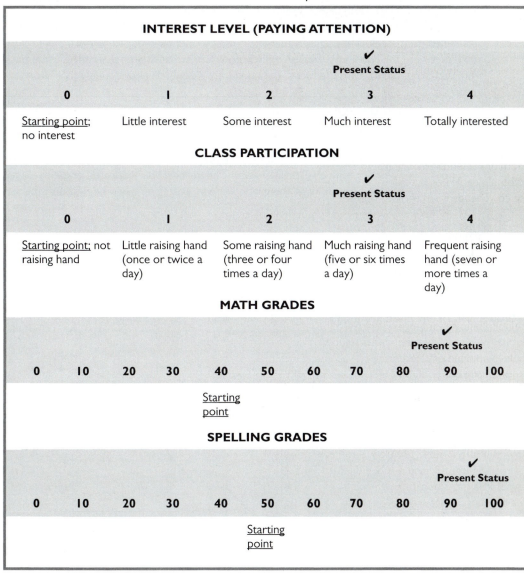

talking with Mrs. G on the phone, the social worker learned that Mr. and Mrs. G were not finding the counseling sessions easy, but Mrs. G did think that they were helpful.

CONTRACT REVIEW AND REFORMULATION: In the last planned visit with Mr. and Mrs. G and Jim, the social worker and the family recognized that all of their goals were being accomplished. More time was needed for Mr. and Mrs. G to work on their relationship, and they planned to continue in counseling for as long as was needed. Jim's problems had apparently subsided and he was back at his earlier functioning level (above average academically). Mr. and Mrs. G agreed that there was no reason for them to meet with the school social worker again unless additional problems developed with Jim.

Jim said he liked to meet with the social worker in her office and he didn't want to stop seeing her each week. They agreed that their visits would be reduced to once a week (instead of twice) for two more weeks (once before Christmas and once after he came back from vacation). During these sessions, they said they would talk about ending their work together.

ONGOING EVALUATION: Since the social worker and Jim would meet to review his progress, ongoing evaluation graphs were drawn and hung on the social worker's wall (see Figures 10.22 and 10.23). The graphs indicated Jim's progress in math and spelling from the time he began school in the fall. Each point on the horizontal line indicated weeks before or after he started working with the social worker. The vertical lines indicated grade averages each week, with the center point at the grade Jim was averaging when he first met the social worker.

E. Charted Progress

The evaluation of grades and the additional tasks planned at this time were recorded by the social worker on the contracted plan as shown in Table 10.6.

FIGURE 10.22 ■ Education Case Ongoing Evaluation Graph: Spelling

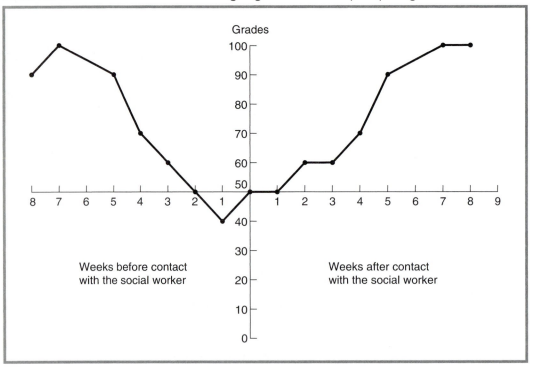

FIGURE 10.23 ■ Education Case Ongoing Evaluation Graph: Math

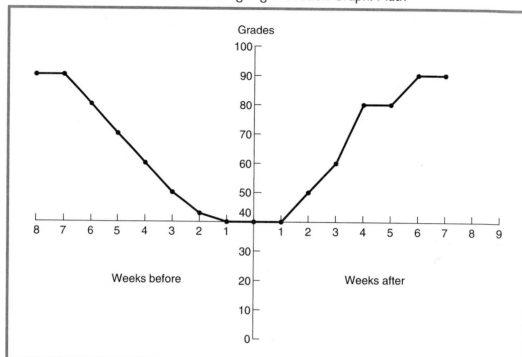

VI. Corrections Case

A. Agency: Juvenile Court

B. Client System

A group of six male youths, all age 14, are on probation and attending weekly group meetings led by co-workers at Juvenile Court. (For further background information, see Chapter 5, Engagement Phase, VI. Corrections Case.)

C. Summary of Preceding Stages

The problems, needs, goals, and tasks contracted in earlier phases are outlined in Chapters 7 and 8. Attendance and participation in group meetings and weekly behavior reports from home and school were charted on graphs from every member of the group at the end of each meeting. Issues of interest or "changes" for the members were selected and discussed each week. After three and one-half months (14 weeks), the social workers began to go through a formal goal analysis with the youths. They also talked about the group process and progress. The ongoing evaluation graphs and weekly charts that were developed and used earlier Chapters 7 and 8 were helpful in the evaluation process.

TABLE 10.6 ■ Education Case: Contracted Plan

Date Identified	Problem/Need	Goal	Task	Contract	Date Anticipated	Date Accomplished
12/4, 12/6, 12/13 Evaluation	Evaluation of problems 1, 2, 3, 4	Goals 1, 2, 3, 4	1. Review and evaluate goal 3 (school performance).	1. Jim and social worker	11/27, 11/29 12/4, 12/6	11/27, 11/29 12/4, 12/6
			2. Review and evaluate goals 1, 3, 4 (Jim's school functioning and sleeping).	2. Mr. and Mrs. G, Jim, and social worker	12/17	12/17
			3. Review goal 2 (Mr. and Mrs. G's relationship).	3. Social worker, Mr. and Mrs. G	12/17	12/17
			4. Reformulate contract or terminate.	4. Social worker, Mr. and Mrs. G, and Jim	12/17	12/17
Contract reformulation		To change task and date anticipated for task 4, problem 3 (see contracted plan, Chapter 7)	4. Meet once a week.	4. Social worker and Jim	12/20 and 1/8	

D. Evaluation

GOAL ANALYSIS: Since the four-month probationary period would be over in two weeks, all of the youths were eager to know if they would be getting off probation and if the group would be ending at that time. In evaluating goal 1 ("to get off probation in four months"), the members were reminded by the social workers of the criteria that had been stated earlier for achieving this goal: (1) to maintain a score of 2 for group attendance—present each week unless excused, (2) to maintain an average score of 3 ("much") or higher for group participation, (3) to maintain an average score of 3 ("good") or higher for behavior at home, (4) to maintain an average score of 3 ("good") or higher for behavior at school, and (5) to obey the rules of society (no further law breaking).

Each of the group members was asked to look over his graphs and to assess the extent to which he met the criteria for accomplishing goal 1. It was obvious that four of the youths (MK, ML, B, C) could be recommended for a reduction in probation from six to four months. One member (A) had already left the group and had been sent to a correctional center. The other two (J and T) had failed to attend and to participate in meetings regularly. J's home reports averaged "poor" to "fair," and T had "poor" school reports because he continued to get into fights at school. J and T realized that they had not accomplished goal 1 and would therefore need to continue to meet with the social workers each Monday. They were told that if they brought their scores up in all areas during the next six weeks, they could have their probation reduced by one month. They also knew that if they continued to do poorly, their probation period would be extended.

In evaluating goal 2 ("to control tempers"), each of the youths reviewed his scores on the weekly chart (in Chapter 8). All agreed that they had grown in recognizing when they were beginning to feel angry and it was time to "cool it." They verbalized ways they had learned to handle their feelings instead of "blowing up." In looking at the progression of their weekly scores, improvement in temper control was apparent for all of the youths except T.

In analyzing the third goal (to learn more about "the changes" of teenagers), the youths reviewed the topics that had been covered during group meetings. They indicated which issues or speakers they thought were the most interesting. They described the film on human sexuality as "kind of stupid," but the talk by the ex-prisoner and the trip to the vocational training school were "great." They all agreed that they had grown in understanding some of the changes they were going through.

After the evaluation, it was clear that four of the group members would probably be leaving the group in two or three weeks. Although the co-workers would continue to meet with J and T, the plan was made to begin to discuss in the following meetings "what it is like when you're off probation and there's no more group."

E. Charted Progress and Contract Reformulation

The social worker recorded the group evaluation and contract reformulation as outlined in Table 10.7. The outline indicates that the anticipated dates for group meetings would be extended to at least six additional weeks for J and T. Also indicated in the record is the plan made by the group to begin to discuss group termination and being off probation at the next meeting.

TABLE 10.7 ■ Corrections Case: Contracted Plan

Date Identified	Problem/Need	Goal	Task	Contract	Date Anticipated	Date Accomplished
1/14 Evaluation	Evaluation of problems 1, 2, 3	Goals 1, 2, 3	1. Review goals. 2. Evaluate goal accomplishment. 3. Reformulate contract or introduce termination.	Members and co-workers	1/14	1/14
Contract reformulation	1. Add goal 1a, task 1, contract date antici- pated to reflect plan to extend group meetings for J and T for at least 6 more weeks	1a. To get off probation by March 1	1. Attend weekly group meetings.	J and T and co-workers	Up to 2/25	
	2. Add beginning termination plan, tasks 1 and 2		1. Introduce termination. 2. Discuss being "off probation."	1. Co-workers 2. Co-workers and group members	1/14 1/22	

VII. Homelessness Case

A. Agency: West End Community Shelter

B. Client System

Mr. Romano, a 37-year-old Hispanic male, is homeless and HIV positive. (For additional background information, see Chapter 5, Engagement Phase, VII. Homelessness Case.)

C. Summary of Preceding Phases

Mr. R came to the shelter on May 7 feeling afraid and abandoned. During engagement, he informed the social worker that he had completed a drug detoxification program over six years ago and had tried to get his life in order ever since. Mr. R wanted to go back to work and to get more information about his illness. During assessment and intervention, the social worker and he developed and carried out a plan that included Mr. R's going to the free health clinic, getting involved with the Harmony, Inc. program, seeking employment, and returning to church.

D. Evaluation

GOAL ANALYSIS: Two days after Mr. R applied for residence at Hope Home, the shelter received a call from the social worker at Hope Home, who stated that they were anticipating an opening for Mr. R around the first of the month. They were making arrangements to move a resident to hospice in Florida where he could be near relatives. Mr. R could come over for a preplacement visit. The social worker and Mr. R decided it was time to evaluate what progress had been made in achieving goals and to plan for the future. In using the goal-accomplishment scales, it was apparent that the goals of obtaining emergency shelter, reunion with the church, gaining information regarding HIV/AIDs, obtaining medical care, and getting social support had been accomplished. The goal of locating housing after staying 60 days at the shelter was progressing (+3), but there was some regression in the goal of getting income (1.5) (see Figures 10.24 and 10.25). The reason for the regression was due to Mr. R's having to drop to part-time employment and his not being able to obtain social security and social services until his condition became worse (see Figure 10.24). The social worker recalled that during data collection she learned that even when Mr. R's testing indicates that he has AIDS (250 white T-cell count), and he is accepted for social security, there will be a 120-day wait before the first check is received. Mr. R could apply for general assistance during the interim period. During evaluation, Mr. R returned to the health clinic and learned that his white T-cell count was at 250. The doctor discussed with Mr. R the medications that would be prescribed.

FIGURE 10.24 ■ Homelessness Case: Goal 4—To Earn Steady Income

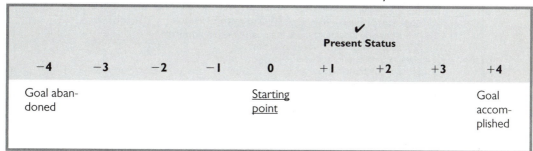

FIGURE 10.25 ■ Homelessness Case: Goal 5—To Locate Residence

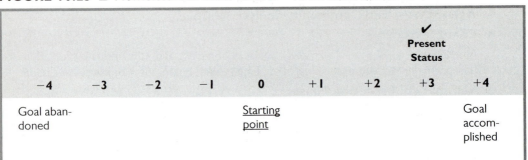

FIGURE 10.26 ■ Homelessness Case: Ongoing Evaluation Graph—Steady Income

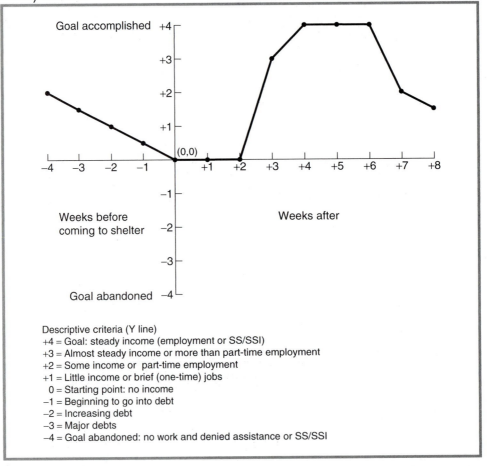

Descriptive criteria (Y line)
+4 = Goal: steady income (employment or SS/SSI)
+3 = Almost steady income or more than part-time employment
+2 = Some income or part-time employment
+1 = Little income or brief (one-time) jobs
 0 = Starting point: no income
−1 = Beginning to go into debt
−2 = Increasing debt
−3 = Major debts
−4 = Goal abandoned: no work and denied assistance or SS/SSI

ONGOING EVALUATION: While working with Mr. R, the social worker used the ongoing evaluation graphs for goals 4 and 5 (see Figures 10.26 and 10.27). These goals were selected because they appeared to be more complex and in need of more time than the other goals identified on the contracted plan.

CONTRACT REVIEW AND REFORMULATION: The only recognized contract reformulations that were needed at the time of the evaluation were additions to the tasks for goals 4 and 5. Mr. R needed to plan his move to Hope Home and apply for social security, SSI disability, and general public assistance. The contracted plan was augmented to reflect these anticipated developments for Mr. R (see Table 10.8).

E. Charted Progress

Progress in goal accomplishment was indicated on the contracted plan and the scales and graphs were placed in the record. The social worker entered information obtained from the Hope Home social worker and the doctor at the clinic in summary recordings.

FIGURE 10.27 ■ Homelessness Case: Ongoing Evaluation Graph— Permanent Residence after Shelter

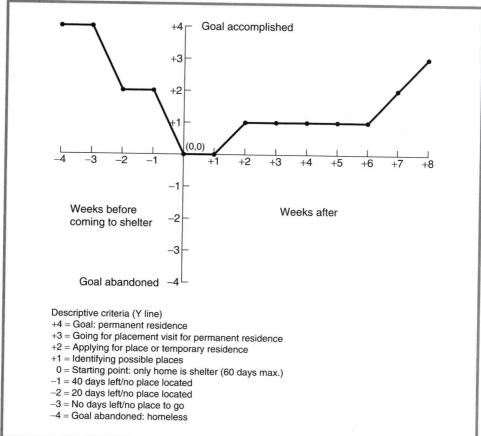

Descriptive criteria (Y line)
+4 = Goal: permanent residence
+3 = Going for placement visit for permanent residence
+2 = Applying for place or temporary residence
+1 = Identifying possible places
 0 = Starting point: only home is shelter (60 days max.)
−1 = 40 days left/no place located
−2 = 20 days left/no place located
−3 = No days left/no place to go
−4 = Goal abandoned: homeless

TABLE 10.8 ■ Homelessness Case: Contracted Plan

Date Identified	Problem/Need	Goal	Task	Contract	Date Anticipated	Date Accomplished
6/26	Evaluation of problems 1–7	Goals 1–7	1. Recall each goal. 2. Assess extent of accomplishment. 3. Reformulate contract.	1. Mr. R and social worker	6/26	6/26
Contract reformulation	1. Change task 4, date anticipated, and add tasks 5–8 for problem 4	Goal 4	4. Request doctor's report. 5. Get report. 6. Apply for SS and general assistance. 7. Get general assistance. 8. Get SS.	4. Mr. R 5. Mr. R 6. Mr. R 7. Mr. R 8. Mr. R	6/26 6/27 6/27 7/5 10/25 7/1	
	2. Add tasks 3 and 4 to problem 5	Goal 5	3. Go for preplacement visit. 4. Decide about placement.	3. Mr. R 4. Mr. R and Home social worker	7/2	

SUMMARY

In this chapter, the meaning and process of evaluation in the General Method were presented. Evaluation was recognized as a particular phase in and as an ongoing dimension of the General Method. The need and values of evaluation in social work practice were emphasized.

Tools and processes were introduced that may be used during evaluation with any type of system. Various examples were given to demonstrate their applicability. The art and the science of practice are very apparent as a social worker objectively and sensitively tries to assess progress and direction in each individualized situation.

As pointed out earlier, evaluation may lead to a reformulation of the contracted plan with additional interventions, or it may serve as a bridge to cross into the final phase of the General Method. Evaluation is a necessary prelude to termination.

REFLECTION POINTS

Becoming a skilled social work practitioner requires knowledge and skills, including the ability to reflect on practice endeavors. The following reflection points are designed to strengthen critical thinking and mastery of knowledge of key points in this chapter.

1. Define the following key concepts in generalist social work:
   - Goal analysis
   - Contract review and reformulation
   - Evaluation questions
   - Ongoing evaluation
2. How might each of these concepts influence your professional behavior in practice with client, action, and target systems at micro, mezzo, and macro levels of practice?
3. Select two case examples presented in this chapter and develop alternative evaluations of client outcomes using the tenets of evidence-based practice (Chapter 3). Provide examples of the evidence-based questions used in evaluating the outcomes.
4. How might human diversity influence practice evaluation at different levels of practice?
5. Review Section 5.02, Evaluation and Research, of the *NASW Code of Ethics* (www.socialworkers.org). How might these standards influence professional behavior?
6. For further reading and research, use the concepts in Question 1 to locate social work references related to this chapter's content. (See Appendix A, Selected Internet Resources, and Appendix B, Selected Social Work Journals.) What underlying theoretical concepts are evident in the articles? How are they applied in one of the seven ongoing cases in this chapter or in a case in your field internship?

Termination

Ending service with client and action systems takes place for a variety of reasons, including:

- ▶ When goals and objectives have been met
- ▶ When time limits are mandated by the agency or insurance company
- ▶ When progress suggests limited potential for change within existing services
- ▶ When needs are better served by a referral elsewhere for services
- ▶ When the client or action system withdraws from service
- ▶ When the social worker leaves the agency

Whatever the reason for ending, however, and whether the length of the service provided is long term or brief, the termination phase of the General Method contains the challenges of stabilizing progress and ceasing contact with the client or action system.

CONCEPT 11.1

> The *termination phase* consists of the time taken and the processes used in stabilizing progress, disengaging from the social worker–client system relationship, and formally ending services.

When the termination process is positive, the ending experience is more likely to stabilize progress and facilitate coping with future circumstances. Therefore, this chapter addresses the meaning of termination to client and action systems, identifies core tasks in the ending and transitioning process, and explores the variance in ceasing services with individuals, families, groups, organizations, and communities of diverse cultures, social status, and socio-demographic strata.

The Meaning of Termination

Ideally, the final phase of the General Method of social work practice involves a celebration of work well done and the beginning of a more autonomous existence in a newly enhanced environment. A successful outcome provides a sense of empowerment and accomplishment, a new view of the presenting problem or need, enhanced understanding of strengths and resources, and confidence in the ability to handle future situations. Thus, in a sense, termination—like graduation—is a rite of passage that involves these processes:

- ▶ Looking back to take stock of where one has been
- ▶ Integrating and consolidating goal achievements and mastery
- ▶ Mobilizing resourcefulness
- ▶ Dealing with reactions to ending
- ▶ Moving from the present toward a more autonomous future with enhanced strengths, assets, resources, and problem-solving ability

When the focus is on celebration and beginning anew, termination conveys the social worker's perception of the strengths and resourcefulness of the client or action system as well as the expectation of the system's ability to maintain the gains achieved. In other words, termination, like graduation, maximizes the empowering experience of celebration and renewed beginning and minimizes negative reactions to ending and loss.

Even when there has been minimal contact and sharing during the General Method process, the social worker and client or action system need ending time to:

▶ Integrate the earlier work and consolidate gains.
▶ Support personal and collective resourcefulness and strengths.
▶ Create a sense of accomplishment, mastery, and hope.
▶ Strengthen the ability to function in an enhanced environment.
▶ Build a bridge linking present and future.
▶ Complete the contractual relationship.

Thus, this final phase of the General Method serves as a culmination of all the work that has gone before and a transitional pathway into a better future.

Core Tasks in the Termination Process

The social worker and client or action system have several core tasks to complete in facilitating completion of the termination phase and enhancing the system's transition to a more autonomous existence:

▶ Deciding to terminate
▶ Reviewing progress
▶ Reinforcing strengths-based problem-solving skills
▶ Generalizing to the future
▶ Addressing reactions to ending
▶ Stabilizing change

For clarity, each of these tasks is presented separately and sequentially. In reality, however, these tasks are dynamic and form an overlapping cyclical process.

Deciding to Terminate

First, the social worker and client or action system must make decisions about when and under which conditions to terminate. The scales and graphs suggested in Chapter 10 will have empirically demonstrated the progress that has been made and highlighted whether the presenting problem or need was completely improved, substantially improved, slightly improved, or not improved. In addition to these empirical indicators of readiness to end, the social worker assesses the appropriateness of moving into termination by reviewing the work with his or her supervisor, observing and talking with the client or action system, and—with informed consent—talking with other knowledgeable sources about the system's readiness to terminate service. After this exploration, the social worker and the system may conclude that the purpose of their work together has been attained.

Sometimes, however, even before a social worker begins to discuss the issue, a client or action system indirectly conveys the message that it is time to terminate. Since systems often develop strengths-based problem-solving skills that are transferable, such messages are not surprising and often indicate decreased dependency and a desire to handle things more independently.

At other times, a social worker and client or action system terminate before the contracted goals have been accomplished. Such early termination may happen because the client or action system fails to engage in or continue services, has reached agency time limitations for service, or has depleted the means for payment for the service. Occasionally, loss of agency funding for service programs may result in ending early. Early termination may also happen when the social worker lacks the skill for resolving the client's or action system's needs or problems, becomes inappropriately emotionally involved in the change situation, or plans to leave the agency. It is always a good policy to document in writing issues related to early termination but to do so with sensitivity to the possibility that legal issues may arise in the future.

When termination is associated with client or action system failure to continue with service, the social worker has the responsibility to rethink the system's needs and strengths and the service barriers experienced, reflect on the nature of the social worker's relationship with the client system, and review the strengths-based problem-solving process of the General Method with his or her supervisor. In those instances when termination is being forced by insurance company or agency time limitations, the social worker has the responsibility of advocating for and linking the system to a network of continuous services whenever possible.

When the decision to terminate is based not on empirical evidence of the client or action system's goal accomplishment and readiness to end but on reasons related to the social worker's professional performance or life circumstances, the social worker and the agency have the responsibility to see that the system receives help from an appropriate resource. There also needs to be time to explain why termination is necessary and to give the system the opportunity to react to the unexpected closure. It is important for the client or action system that the termination discussion remain focused on the system's reaction and not the facts and feelings of the social worker's departure. The latter are best handled by entry-level social workers with their supervisor.

Reviewing Progress

In observing and talking with a client or action system about possible termination, the social worker and the client system review the extent of goal accomplishment and assess the current level of social functioning. Examples of the questions to be considered include:

- ▶ Have the goals been accomplished according to the contracted plan?
- ▶ Given the attained level of social functioning, can the client or action system continue to function, at least at this level, without further service?
- ▶ Given the attained level of social functioning, can the client or action system handle similar needs or problems in the future; or does the system know how to get help?
- ▶ If additional supportive resources are likely to be needed after the social worker and client or action system terminate, are they available?

If the preceding questions are answered affirmatively, then the client or action system and the social worker continue their work only for the length of time needed to stabilize change and complete the termination process. Part of the progress review includes the client system's own words about any changes and its perceptions of the reasons for them: *Tell me, in your own way, how are things now? What changes do you see? What do you think accounts for the change? Were the changes what you thought they would be? How well did these changes meet your expectations?*

Sometimes, the client or action system views the General Method as not successful in facilitating goal achievement. In this instance, it is the social worker's responsibility to understand the system's perspective and help the system reach out to a potentially more helpful service.

Reinforcing Strengths-Based Problem-Solving Skills

Human learning and problem-solving are aided by reinforcement of human competencies (Bandura, 1986; Thomas, 1967). Reinforcement of the client or action system's enhanced strengths-based problem-solving skills involves reminding the system of the positive impact of its earlier work in solving targeted problems. This process also involves having the social worker ask for specifics about what has helped in making expected and unexpected progress, assist the system in identifying the strengths evident in this progress, and raise awareness about the spread effect of the system's work to other circumstances. Praise and recognition for earlier large and small accomplishments serve as key strategies in strengthening problem-solving competencies.

Further reinforcement may be achieved by an explicit review of strengths-based problem-solving skills. Such a review enhances the client or action system's ability to:

▶ Identify the existence of the focal problem or need.
▶ Generate possible alternative solutions.
▶ View the circumstances from another's perspective.
▶ Develop a plan for achieving the chosen solution.

Generalizing to the Future

From the beginning, the General Method lays the groundwork for the client or action system to take the lead in planning for the future. As the review of strengths-based problem-solving progresses from focusing on the *past* to focusing on the *present*, it becomes clearer which goals have been addressed, which needs or problems necessitating help no longer exist, and whether it is time to consider what may lie ahead after termination. Sometimes independently and sometimes with prompting, the client or action system begins to inquire about the *future* and how to manage without the social worker. At this point, an explicit plan for ending and beginning anew may be formulated. In the process, the social worker and the system engage in a step-by-step review of the needs, issues, and problems that were identified in the *past* and the strengths, assets, and resources that became apparent in the *present* in order to envision and give hope for the *future*. Although the review of *past, present,* and *future* may not necessarily be addressed in exact sequence, this framework offers some direction and guidance for helping the client and action system move through the process of termination.

In this discussion, it is implied that the termination plan developed at this time will be individualized according to the needs and circumstances of the client or action system. The point being emphasized is that for an effective ending to take place, the termination plan has to be articulated, understood, agreed on, and implemented. Earlier in the General Method, specifically in the assessment and contracting phase, an initial time frame for goal accomplishment and termination was established. At this time, however, it is important that both the social worker and the system mutually agree on the actual termination date and on the number and spacing of the contacts prior to this date. For example, meetings may be gradually tapered off or may continue on the same basis until the closing date. If the review process has indicated that a system is ready to end but needs additional supports to function autonomously, referral, transfer, and mobilization of other environmental resources become essential components of the termination plan.

Addressing Reactions to Ending

Fortune, Pearlingi, and Rochelle (1992) found that the strongest client reactions to ending a variety of interventions were positive and included a sense of accomplishment. Reactions to ending the General Method process range from a sense of achievement and pride in work well done to mixed or negative feelings about the pending separation and loss of facilitative support. The intensity of these reactions during the termination phase may vary depending on a number of factors (see Table 11.1). Of these factors, the degree of client and action systems' investment in resolving needs and the social worker's skillfulness in facilitating General Method process from engagement to termination create the platform on which reactions are expressed. That is, when a system has been highly invested in addressing needs and issues, the reaction process is likely to be more intense. It is, however, important to note that a system's investment over the course of the intervention is subject to multiple influences such as prior experiences with help seeking, socio-demographic and cultural characteristics, and the match between identified needs and the services used for redressing these needs. Further, the intensity of the system's reaction to the unknowns inherent in transitioning to more autonomy may also be influenced by the availability of support networks and the particular structure and consistency of General Method service delivery. Lack of clarity in contracting about the problems and issues to be resolved and the needs/problems identified in contracting but remaining unresolved are likely to trigger intense negative reactions during the termination process.

Stabilizing Change

An important aspect of stabilizing or institutionalizing change is asking the client or action system what it will take to maintain the changes made, and then exploring the obstacles and barriers perceived by both the system and the social worker. For example, the social worker may ask questions: *How have you handled these obstacles and barriers earlier? What might you do if_____ happens? What do you think you need in order to continue the changes made?* Or, the social worker may make com-

TABLE 11.1 ■ Variance in Reactions to Ending

	More Intense	Less Intense
System investment	High	Low
Service delivery process	Inconsistent	Consistent
Structure of service		
• Length of contact	Open-ended	Time-limited
• Spacing of contact	Frequent	Infrequent
• Focus of contact	Personal issues	Environmental issues
• Emotional content	High	Low
Support networks	Absent	Present

ments: *It may be hard, but you have managed this in the past and now know what to look for and how to handle it. You also know how to get help.*

In stabilizing change, it is also important to identify the potential obstacles and barriers that may exist in the environment surrounding the client or action system. Explicit assignments that involve practicing strengths-based problem-solving about any remaining environmental issues can facilitate future handling of opposition and sustain the client system's changed ways of responding. Unless direct involvement by a social worker is absolutely necessary for the client system's well-being, the social worker tries negotiating a plan in which the system itself establishes linkages with the environmental supports and resources needed. Every effort is made to have client or action systems initiate and follow through on contacting and mobilizing resources on their own behalf. This approach is particularly important when resources are informal, such as family members, religious institutions, schools, or neighborhoods. Having client and action systems follow through in developing their own resources is empowering, fosters strengths, and provides the client system with an opportunity to see that it is possible to function more independently.

Monitoring the Termination Process

Careful monitoring of the central processes during the termination phase enables the social worker to assess phase-specific progress related to ending and moving on into the future. First, the social worker uses the formal outcome evaluation described in Chapter 10 to corroborate his or her professional judgment about the client or action system's present level of achievement and about the projected level of social functioning and competency after termination (see Figure 11.1). This professional judgment is made at the beginning of the termination phase, if possible, prior to discussing ending in order to highlight client and action system strengths and assets

FIGURE 11.1 ■ Rating Scale for Present Client and Action System Achievement and Projected Future Functioning

	No (0)	Somewhat (1)	Yes (2)	Excellent (3)
Present level of achievement				
• Met contracted goals				
• Achieved adequate level of current functioning				
Projected future functioning				
• Able to maintain current social functioning				
• Able to handle new challenges				
• Able to maintain social supports				
• Able to seek necessary help				

rather than any problems and needs that may be brought to the fore by temporary reactions to ending.

In Figure 11.1, the social work generalist reviews the present level of achievement by asking the following questions:

▶ *How well did the client or action system accomplish the contracted goals?*
▶ *Has the client system achieved an adequate level of social functioning?*

When considering the projected future functioning, the social worker asks:

▶ *How well is the system likely to maintain this level of social functioning?*

The rating system proposed in Figure 11.1 allows the generalist practitioner to quantify the present level of achievement and projected future functioning. For example, low item scores (0, 1) and low total summated scores (less than 12) suggest a minimal present level of achievement and projected future functioning. Such scores raise concerns about client or action system problems and needs in the future and suggest education about available supports and resources should the need arise. Item scores of 2 or 3 and total summated scale scores of 12 to 18 suggest adequate strengths and assets, client or action system well-being, and readiness to proceed with termination.

Figure 11.2 represents a rating scale for assessing completion of the termination phase. Here, the social work generalist focuses on and reviews six processes to determine whether the progress toward termination is as expected. This rating scale further allows the practitioner to track accomplishments with client and action systems and evaluate practice efforts. Low item scores (0, 1) and low total summated scale scores (less than 9) suggest minimal completion of this process and raise concerns about the adequacy of the termination process. Item scores of 2 and total summated scale scores of 9 to 12 suggest adequate completion of the termination phase.

FIGURE 11.2 ■ Rating Scale for Assessing Phase-Specific Termination Processes

	Not Addressed (0)	Addressing (1)	Adequately Addressed (2)
Integrating earlier work and consolidating gains			
Supporting personal and collective resourcefulness and strengths			
Creating a sense of accomplishment, mastery, and hope			
Strengthening the client system's ability to function within an enhanced environment			
Building a bridge linking the present with the future			
Completing the contract			

Working with Different Systems

Although the processes and tasks of the termination phase of the General Method are essentially the same for all client and action systems, there are some differences among and between them that are associated with variance not only in their contracted goals and service structure but also in their purpose, composition, and size.

Micro Client Systems

The broad goals of the General Method work with micro client systems, or individuals, involve meeting needs, resolving problems, increasing strengths-based problem-solving capacity, and strengthening social functioning. Whether the intervention has been long term or brief, termination with individuals follows the process and procedures previously discussed. First and foremost, individuals are proud of their accomplishments and look forward to being more autonomous. The impending losses of agency support and the social work relationship and the transition to more autonomy, however, may also trigger temporary ambivalence about ending and feelings of sadness, rejection and abandonment, and being unable to cope alone. A very strong negative reaction is usually associated with individuals whose life histories are replete with abandonment, rejection, and loss. These experiences may have increased vulnerability to endings and transitions, and can result in complex termination for such client systems. In these circumstances, coping styles and reactions during termination may be similar to stages of the grieving process (Kubler-Ross, 1969; Timberlake & Cutler, 2001). Although not necessarily in every case, nor in the exact order described here, the reactions to and the process of working through termination for vulnerable client systems may include:

▶ *Denial:* Some may ignore what the social worker is saying or try to avoid discussion of termination. This behavior may extend to missing appointments, coming late, or leaving early.

▶ *Anger:* There may be outbursts of verbal assaults directed toward the social worker, family members, or members of the support system. Anger may also be turned inward as the individual displays lack of concern for self. There may be a return to earlier troubling behavior in an attempt to delay ending.

▶ *Bargaining:* The individual may try to negotiate an extension of time or a modified cutback in meetings. Promises of *being good if* or gifts may be offered.

▶ *Depressive symptoms:* The individual may manifest listlessness, withdrawal, sadness, and helplessness.

▶ *Acceptance:* With the social worker's assistance and continuing focus on strengths-based problem-solving, the individual begins to accept termination. There is an increase in energy and ability to focus more on accomplishments and less on separation. He or she returns to the level of social functioning prior to the initial discussion of termination and moves away from self-centeredness.

Throughout the complicated grief process triggered by some terminations, the social worker stimulates the individual's memories and awareness that the growth and change are related to the strengths-based problem-solving of the General Method. After reinforcing the idea of strengths-based problem-solving skills, the social worker continues working with the client system to stabilize and extend the growth and change to everyday life and project them into the future.

Mezzo Client Systems

FAMILIES The broad goals of family work involve enhancing family relationships and structure, strengthening communication within the family and between the family and its environment, and increasing the family's strengths-based problem-solving capacity. Over the course of the General Method, family members have worked collaboratively on common tasks to strengthen their family unit. They have shared changes in internal family capability and in family functioning within their environment. When the contracted goals have been achieved and service ends, the renewed family continues and is usually in a better position to support its members and solve problems autonomously.

In reviewing and assessing progress during the termination phase, the social worker asks the family, as a unit, how family members see the changes that have occurred for the family as a whole and for individual members. As they review together the problems addressed during intervention and the changes made, the social worker reinforces the family's achievements and enables family members to reinforce each other's accomplishments.

In considering the family's future, key problem resolution strategies and skills that have been learned and employed are highlighted. The family explores how family resources have been strengthened to sustain the changes achieved and even to extend them. In addition, family members explore their thoughts, feelings, and concerns about ending service and separating from the social worker. Generally, they are pleased with their accomplishments but may simultaneously express relief, sadness, and anxiety about the social worker's departure from their lives. In some instances, family vulnerability to loss may trigger strong feelings about ending and complicate the termination phase in a manner similar to that of vulnerable individuals.

SMALL GROUPS   The wide-ranging goals of small General Method groups include, among others, modifying behavior, obtaining support and mutual aid, increasing social skills, collecting information, raising one's consciousness (about oppressed persons), and accomplishing tasks. The particular purpose of a group affects its interaction patterns and character, intensity and duration, development as a group, and termination. By the end of social work service, group members have worked collaboratively on common group activities, created a shared mutual aid experience with one another, and built a relationship with the social worker as part of the group entity. As closed membership groups anticipate the future, members must face the reality that the group will soon cease to be a resource in their lives, the membership will disband, and the social worker will no longer be present. Thus, each member of a closed group is ending multiple relationships—with the group, with each member, and with the social worker.

In reviewing the group's work, members help each other assess the changes that have occurred for the group as a whole and for individual members. Specifically, they recall their purpose in convening and explore how the group has functioned as an entity in achieving group and individual goals. The social worker enables the group to reinforce the strengths and achievements of members in taking responsibility for the group and helping each other accomplish group tasks and goals. The members are encouraged to look ahead and discuss how the benefits of the group can be incorporated into their social functioning outside of the group. They assist each other in developing future plans and in identifying and framing ways to overcome barriers to these plans. In the process, members review their collective and individual strengths-based problem-solving skills and assist each other to overcome common errors in solving problems.

In planning for the future, group members also explore their thoughts, feelings, and concerns about the group and their reactions to ending the group, losing contact with other members, and separating from the social worker. Usually, they acknowledge mixed feelings that include success in the group's and their own accomplishments, sadness over the ending, and some trepidation about the loss of mutual aid and support. The social worker points out that the lessons learned and memories of the group will remain with them for a long time. Sometimes at termination, there are graduation ceremonies and sometimes breaks in the middle of the last session for saying formal good-byes to individual members. In any event, some type of ending ritual is useful in facilitating members' ability to move on with their lives apart from the group (Rose, 1998; Tolson, Reid, & Garvin, 2003; Toseland & Rivas, 2005).

Task groups, by contrast, end when their assigned work is completed and a report is generated. Debriefing includes analysis of the strengths, cohesiveness, successes, and failures of the group in task completion. Usually, the report and debriefing include a consideration of what the future may bring. At this point, however, when the group's authority to operate ends, there is generally cause for celebration and relief.

Termination in groups with open-ended membership provides another variation on the theme. At the same time the social worker and group are ending with one member, they are beginning with another. As the group process incorporates these individual endings and beginnings, members experience commonality with the group as a whole in the ending or beginning of a member. Members also experience the divergence associated with the individualized group developmental levels and the diverse needs and strengths of ongoing members. The successes of departing members activate or reactivate the investment of new and ongoing members. Thus, these life space endings and beginnings in the course of the open-ended group are used to help members who will later experience their own termination.

Macro Client Systems

When members of large groups, organizations, and communities become client systems, their broadly stated goals may include:

▶ Building community empowerment and capacity to use their strengths, resources, and political skills in the service of community development
▶ Facilitating locality empowerment, capacity, and resource development for the benefit of the locality
▶ Facilitating organizational change in policies and practices for the benefit of staff and client systems
▶ Engaging a community in advocacy to achieve social and political changes of increased resources and social justice
▶ Developing political power in communities and localities to ensure a voice in decision-making

Once the decision to conclude services is reached, the macro client system and the social worker review the changes achieved in light of the established goal(s). The work products supporting these goals and changes may take various forms, including needs assessments, quality assurance assessments, planning reports, vision statements, grant applications, legislation, institutional rulings, or constitutions for community organizations.

During this review, the social worker makes the changes explicit and ascertains whether (Harrington, Fauri, & Netting, 1998; Netting, Kettner, & McMurtry, 1993):

▶ The instituted changes are the ones planned.
▶ There are any unintended consequences to be addressed prior to the conclusion of their work together.
▶ The changes are acceptable.
▶ The changes are sustainable with local resources.

If the review suggests that their strengths-based problem-solving work together is satisfactory and acceptable, the social worker and the macro system work together to consolidate and institutionalize the collective gains. This stabilization of change requires crystalizing the change situation, promoting strengths, and completing the transfer of power and authority to the macro client system (Lippett, Watson, & Westley, 1958). This process is a key aspect in generalizing to the future and preparing the macro client system for transition to autonomy and self-governance. The intent is to sustain empowered functioning of the macro system in the future.

At the final point of the termination process, the social worker concludes his or her role by separating from the change situation so that the macro client system may integrate the change and thereby fully own it (Harrington, Fauri, & Netting, 1998). If the social worker is an ongoing member of the large group, organization, or community in which the change occurred, his or her future participation must be circumscribed and limited to a clearly defined role and explicit responsibility apart from the completed change effort. The intent is that the accomplished changes become institutionalized within the macro client system and not continue in the person of the social worker (Mondtos & Wilson, 1994). That is, for the system to become fully autonomous, the social worker needs to remain mindful that it is his or her role and responsibility to provide the leadership, structure, and processes as set by the planned contract to ensure that change occurs. Once the change has been accomplished, the social worker terminates the generalist practitioner role established for this project, leaving the capacity for strengths-based problem-solving in place. In future projects with the same macro system, however, the social worker may once again negotiate a contract involving his or her role of generalist practitioner.

Action Systems

When social workers and client systems join existing action systems or come together to develop new ones, their purpose is working toward goals such as:

▶ Developing localities to benefit the client system and the community in which the client and action system live and work
▶ Engaging in community advocacy about unmet community needs
▶ Engaging in social planning for community betterment

Action systems, for the most part, are collaborative partnerships focused on task and goal completion. They end when the tasks are completed and the goals achieved.

Debriefing of the system as a whole during the termination process includes analysis of the strengths, cohesiveness, successes, barriers, and failures encountered during the social worker's and action system's General Method work together. Usually, the debriefing includes consideration of remaining community issues or needs and what the future may bring. At ending, there is usually cause for celebration and sometimes a decision to retain the action system membership for further work. Whether or not the social worker remains a member, the action system takes ownership of the changes that have occurred and the processes by which future change may be engendered and sustained.

Reactions of Social Workers

As human beings, social workers become attached to others. If there has not been the opportunity to anticipate both the loss and celebration, move through the reactions, and express the related feelings prior to final termination, a service provider may demonstrate withdrawal or burnout after several terminations of this nature.

For example, when a service provider is employed in an emotionally charged service, such as child protection or work with the terminally ill, the need for supportive outlets is especially apparent. In one case, in a residential setting for disturbed children, the child-care director became the main significant adult for a 5-year-old boy. The child progressed remarkably and was moved into a foster home. Following his placement, the director became obviously antagonistic toward the social worker and increasingly irritable toward the other children. It was not until the social worker and the director took time to look painfully at what was happening that the director began to recognize her feelings of distress due to the loss of the young boy. If the social worker or others at the facility had been more sensitive to the natural feelings of the director, more time could have been given to deal with termination prior to the child's discharge—a step that would have prevented some of the reactions that followed.

In a second example, a social worker who serves as a case manager for a team that is about to terminate with a client system shows sensitivity to the needs of the team members by building in a time to talk about the feelings they might have as they anticipate closing the case. Supervisors and administrators also have a major responsibility to help prevent burnout in their employees. If they understand the significance of termination in the provision of services, they can find various ways to assist their social workers. In a hospice facility where social work generalists and other service providers were repeatedly experiencing the deaths of their patients, an administrator not only set aside times for peer support meetings but also designated a room on the top floor as "the Tower," where staff could go whenever they felt the need "to yell, cry, or pray." Unless a service provider can reach a point of acceptance with a termination, he or she will not be able to have the anticipation, hope, and energy necessary to invest in new client system work assignments.

An example is given in Table 11.2 of a termination plan for a group of young adolescent girls called "the Angels." This group was one of many offered at a neighborhood center each year. All groups terminated at the end of June and began again in September. The social worker knew who was expected to take "the Angels" the following year; therefore, the new social worker was invited to meet with the group as part of the termination plan.

Developing Sensitivity and Skills

The ideas about termination that are presented in this chapter are often rejected as an overexaggeration. New social workers, in particular, find it difficult to believe that their leaving a client or action system can have an impact on the system or on themselves. A verbal presentation on the dynamics of termination may be only an intel-

TABLE 11.2 ■ Contracted Plan: The Angels

Date Identified	Problem/Need	Goal	Task	Contract	Date Anticipated	Date Accomplished
5/3	21. Funding for trip to beach	21. To raise $50 for trip	1. Explore ways to raise funds; begin to plan.	1. Group and social worker	5/3	8/3
			2. Finalize plans for bake sale.	2. Group and social worker	5/10	5/10
			3. Have bake sale.	3. Group and center	5/15	5/15
			4. Critique bake sale; set date and plan for beach trip; begin to discuss year-end evaluation.	4. Group and social worker	5/17	5/17
5/24 Evaluation	Year-end evaluation of problems/needs	1–21, as cited above	1. Recall goals.	1. Group and social worker	4/24 and 6/1	5/24 and 6/1
			2. Evaluate extent of goal accomplishment.			
6/1	Termination process	Satisfactory termination (progress stabilized)	1. Introduce termination.	1. Group and social worker	6/1	6/1
			2. Discuss feelings and reactions to ending the group; clarify final termination date.	2. Group and social worker	6/7	6/7
			3. Identify present strengths, discuss the future; plan termination.	3. Group and social worker	6/14	6/14
			4. Invite new social worker (who will have the group after summer vacation) to the next meeting.	4. Mary C (for the group)	6/15	6/15
			5. Meet with new social worker.	5. Former social worker, group, and new social worker	6/21	6/21
			6. Go on beach trip.	6. Former social worker, group, and new social worker	6/26	6/26
			7. Conduct closing session and have party.	7. Former social worker and group	6/28	6/28

lectual consideration unless some aspect of experiential learning can be included. Three basic exercises (Exercises 11.1, 11.2, and 11.3) may be used to help social workers grow in sensitivity and skill for working with termination.

EXERCISE 11.1
Using Imagery

All the individuals participating in this experience are asked to close their eyes and picture a significant person in their lives. They are then asked to imagine that this person is talking with them and saying that he or she is going away and does not plan to return. Participants are then asked to identify their immediate feelings. They are next asked to imagine that they express these feelings to the person, but that the person repeats his or her plan to leave. They then imagine the person getting up and walking out. They are asked to let themselves enter into what they would feel when the person has left, and to try to find words to express these feelings. Finally, the participants are asked: What would you do next? The individuals are then asked: What do you need at this time?

This exercise helps a person sense some of the feelings that often emerge as one perceives the loss of a meaningful other. Talking about the experience may also lead to a discussion about what actions a person may take in trying to cope with such a loss and what resources might help the person through the experience.

EXERCISE 11.2
Small Group Experience

Participants are divided into small groups to discuss a topic, such as "timing needed for termination" or "writing up a termination plan." The facilitator moves around to different groups and eventually asks a member of one group to leave and join another identified group. After a few minutes, the facilitator moves to the next group and again directs a member to leave and join a different group, with no explanation for the move. This procedure is continued until every group has lost one of its original members.

In the discussion that follows, participants are asked to describe any thoughts or feelings they had when one of their members was asked to leave. They usually say that they wondered why the person was removed from the group and that they felt some frustration over the departure. They are then asked how they felt about another person joining the group. Here, too, feelings of anger and frustration were often experienced over having to adjust to the entry of a new person. The leaving or entering may have slowed down or stopped the group process. In addition, participants may share feelings of anger toward the facilitator for interrupting the group. Those that were directed to leave a group may disclose that they felt disoriented, isolated, rejected, or perhaps withdrawn as they entered a new group.

EXERCISE 11.3
Role-Play

In this role-play between a social worker and a client system, there is a partial script that is given only to the actor who plays the role of the client system. The person in the role of the social worker is directed to begin the play by saying, "I will be leaving the agency in May." To what the social worker says, the person playing the client system is directed to feel free to respond as he or she feels like responding. Eventually, however, the "client system" is expected to make the statements (in whatever order seems appropriate) identified in the script.

Termination Script

SW: I will be leaving the agency in May.

CLIENT SYSTEM: Will I be seeing someone else?

SW: (?)

CLIENT SYSTEM: I had a fight with that neighbor again.

SW: (?)

CLIENT SYSTEM: Why did I bother coming here for anyway? You're not really helping me.

SW: (?)

CLIENT SYSTEM: I'll come to see you where you are going—maybe just for a few months.

SW: (?)

CLIENT SYSTEM: Nobody cares about what happens to me anyway.

SW: (?)

CLIENT SYSTEM: May I take your picture before you leave?

SW: (?)

CLIENT SYSTEM: Thanks for everything.

SW: (?)

This exercise may also be done as a "fishbowl" experience. Here, anyone watching the role-play who believes he or she may have a more appropriate way to respond to the client may come in back of the person playing the role of the social worker and tap him or her on the shoulder. The social worker then exchanges places with this person, and the new response is given.

In the discussion that follows the role-play, the facilitator asks the participants to consider what both actors were feeling as they made different statements. A basic question asked is: *Was the social worker responding to the content literally, or was he or she tuning into the feelings of the client system?* Participants are asked to consider other responses the social worker could have made to particular statements by the client system. The most important question is: *What does the client system need to hear at this time?*

HELEN HARRIS PERLMAN (1906–2004), social work practitioner and educator, authored over 80 articles and eight books in which she examined social work's mission, theory, principles, and practices. Her landmark publications included *Social Casework: A Problem-Solving Process* and *Persona: Social Role and Personality and Relationship.* A faculty member at the University of Chicago School of Social Service Administration, Perlman served on the editorial boards of several professional journals and on national committees of social work associations. She received the NASW President's Award for Excellence in Social Work Education.

By using these three exercises, social workers can become more aware of the following central ideas:

1. Terminations may cause a variety of feelings and reactions that lead to a need for help from others.
2. Departures may cause disorientations and frustration, leading to an arrest in progress or to withdrawal or anger toward the person who initiated the separation.
3. There are ways to respond to client or action systems who are facing terminations that can help let them know that you understand what they are going through.
4. Social workers themselves may have feelings and reactions that they need help with during terminations.

There are also other exercises and activities that can enhance a social worker's knowledge and skills in the process of terminating with a particular client system. For example, recording an individual interview on termination and then reviewing the recording by oneself or with one's supervisor or peers can help a social worker understand the dynamics taking place and locate where the client system and the social worker are in the termination process. During this last phase of the General Method, a social worker's feelings may at times be so intense that it is difficult to maintain an objective perspective. Using such exercises as recording, role-play, and imagery can help strengthen the social worker's comprehension and self-control.

Using Social Work Foundation Knowledge in Termination

As stated earlier, there is a competency in termination that calls on the values, knowledge, and skills of a social worker. The social work generalist demonstrates this competency as various elements from the holistic foundation for social work practice (Chapter 1) are selected, integrated, and applied throughout the termination process.

As a social worker and a client or action system begin to bring their relationship to an end, all of the value principles of individualization, acceptance, self-determination, nonjudgmental attitude, controlled emotional involvement, purposeful expression of feelings, and confidentiality are utilized. The timing, planning, and processing of termination have to be *individualized* according to each system's unique circumstances. If a client or action system is avoiding or denying the termination, the social worker patiently *accepts* the reaction pattern. Keeping in mind the principle of *controlled emotional involvement,* the social worker encourages the *purposeful expression of the system's related feelings.* If a system does not choose to identify new problem areas or to be referred for additional support, the social worker maintains a *nonjudgmental attitude* and respects the right to *self-determination.* When a referral or transfer is made or data are collected from an outside resource, all information about the client or action system is treated as *confidential* and released only with the informed consent of the system.

Knowledge of human development, group dynamics, organizations, and ecological systems are among the concepts and perspectives that give direction and understanding to a social worker in the termination phase. In human development theory, the social worker learns about the need all human systems have for attachments throughout the life cycle. Through theories of group dynamics and organizations, the social worker learns about the conflicts, tasks, and processes a group, community, or organization undergoes when a person who was seen as the leader (or someone with power and control) leaves the client, action, or target system.

Using an ecological-systems perspective, the social worker perceives the interdependence that develops between a client system and its service-providing environment. This perspective helps social workers understand that it may not be feasible to expect a client system to maintain its functioning level when a major nurturer and sustainer in its environment is removed. Therefore, the need for a careful assessment of a client system's available internal and external resources after termination with a social worker is highlighted.

Essentially, the four primary skills needed during termination may be described as

- ▶ *Sensing skills:* Recognizing feelings and reactions
- ▶ *Timing skills:* Knowing when to identify, wait, or stop
- ▶ *Processing skills:* Moving from past to present to future
- ▶ *Planning skills:* Knowing how to analyze and organize

The competence of termination rests in a social worker's demonstrated sensitivity to the time and movement needed for a client or action system to be ready to accept termination. All of the actions of a social worker, throughout the process, reflect an artful integration and application of values, knowledge, and skills.

Human Diversity in Termination

In addition to foundation knowledge, entry-level social workers need to understand and address the ways in which issues associated with cultural diversity, social status, and socio-demographic strata influence the termination process and inhibit or facilitate maintenance of the gains achieved by client and action systems at the micro, mezzo, and macro levels.

As brought out in this chapter, termination is a phase when skills in timing and sensing of feelings are especially needed. Again, knowledge of a culture's orientation toward the expression of feelings and the meaning of time is imperative. If a social worker has played a meaningful role in the life of a client or action system, the system will naturally have some feelings of pride and a sense of loss when the social worker terminates. The reactions will be culturally derived. A skilled social worker will understand and enable the system to find the time and the opportunity to express feelings and reactions and prepare for the termination. Feelings and reactions may vary according to cultural orientation toward separation and death. The process of moving from past to present to future may also be influenced by the time orientation of one's cultural background. As indicated earlier, members of Asian/Pacific American, Native American, and African American cultures tend to lean toward emphasizing the past, whereas Mexican Americans tend to be more concerned with the present and Anglo-Saxon Americans tend to be more future oriented. Recognizing such differences enables a social worker to have more realistic expectations of the pace needed to move to the point of acceptance in the process of termination.

After an evaluation, the social worker and the client or action system may decide to terminate, even though long-range goals for social change have not been achieved. With personal, interpersonal, or short-range goals attained, they may decide to continue to address the need to change target systems on their own or in other ways. The social worker may continue to advocate equal opportunities and services for vulnerable client systems through introducing or supporting related legislation, policies, programs, or practices. When the decision to terminate is reached by both social worker and client or action system, it is important for the system to feel welcome to return to the social worker or the agency for additional services after termination, if needed.

As with any working relationship, a deep attachment may develop between social worker and client system in the course of their working together. For client or action systems, it may be the first time they have met someone who has been able to listen to their questions and concerns and been able to accept and respect them as unique individuals. For social workers, it may be the first time they have had the opportunity to get to know and work with a particular cultural, social, or socio-demographic group. Terminating the relationship may evoke positive and negative feelings for both social worker and client system. It will be easier for both to accept termination if a sense of acceptance has existed throughout the time they have been together. If there has not been acceptance, either one may continue to feel a need to try to prove something to or to change something in the other.

Each phase of the General Method calls for a sensitive application of values, knowledge, and skills as a social worker interacts with systems of diverse cultures, social status, and socio-demographic strata. A knowledge of human diversity and an awareness of one's own human responses to various individuals, cultures, lifestyles, roles, and environments, thus, are essential for an effective application of the General Method.

ONGOING CASES
Termination Phase

As in the earlier chapters, the following section demonstrates the application of knowledge and skills during the *termination phase* of the General Method by entry-level generalist social workers in seven diverse fields of practice. In Exercise 11.4, questions are proposed for reflection and discussion about how practice in each of the case examples during the termination phase might change if the client system represented a different

- ► *Culture:* Racial/ethnic group membership, national origin and social group identity, religion and spirituality
- ► *Social status:* Socio-economic status, environmental and rural/urban differences
- ► *Socio-demographic strata:* Age and developmental stage, gender roles, sexual orientation, challenges in mental and physical ability

EXERCISE 11.4
Impact of Human Diversity on Termination Process

Consider the following questions with each of the seven client systems. In terminating with each, how might change in culture, social status, and socio-demographic diversity:

1. Influence the norms, roles, and authority issues in work with each client system?
2. Reveal values that influence timing, communications, and actions?
3. Influence professional view of the pressures, problems, needs, strengths, and resources that persist in the life of this client or action system?
4. Affect the dynamics of the professional relationship?
5. Affect monitoring of the progress, timeliness, and effectiveness of service delivery?

I. Child Welfare Case

A. Agency: State Department of Children's Services

B. Client System

K, a 15-year-old female, was placed in a group home six months ago. (For more background information, see Chapter 5, Ongoing Cases: Engagement Phase, I. Child Welfare Case.)

C. Summary of Preceding Phases

The problems, needs, goals, and tasks identified and implemented in earlier phases are found in Chapters 5 through 9. A summary of the evaluation of goals and contract reformulation may be found in Chapter 10. Basically, progress was identified during evaluation for all of the stated goals. The goal related to personal growth was the slowest in achievement, and more time was recognized as needed for progress in this area. The contract was reformulated to extend goal 2 to include optimal academic performance and to change the frequency of social worker contact to once a month rather than once every two weeks.

D. Termination

After K had been in her group home for six months, the social worker began to terminate because she was leaving the Department of Children's Services. K's first reaction to the termination was total indifference. She said she didn't "need the state any more," and hoped she would not have to get another state social worker. She was helped to express anger and fear of being abandoned. She admitted that she liked the social worker and would miss her very much. She was assured that the social worker would miss her also.

As the social worker and K began to review their work together, the ongoing evaluation tools described in Chapter 10 were used. Her academic performance and group home maintenance were assessed as +3. They recalled what the past was like for K and how far she had progressed, particularly in her present group home and in school. K knew that she continued to need help with her personal problems (goal 3).

In considering the future, K said she wished to remain in her present group home and school for at least another few years. Her long-range goals included returning to live with her real mother some day. K knew that this was not possible in the near future.

K's case was transferred back to a social worker (recently returned from sick leave) who had originally worked with her. K remembered her original social worker and said she was glad she didn't have to start all over with someone new. Two weeks before termination, K and the two state social workers had a meeting, at which time goals and progress were reviewed. For their last meeting, K and her social worker went for a walk. They took and exchanged pictures of each other. K asked if she could write the social worker after she left Children's Services, but this continued contact was discouraged.

E. Charted Progress

The termination plan that was developed and implemented by the social worker and K is found in Table 11.3. In recording, this plan was added to the contracted plan that was used during assessment and evaluation.

TABLE 11.3 ■ Contracted Plan: Child Welfare Case

Date Identified	Problem/ Need	Goal	Task	Contract	Date Antici- pated	Date Accom- plished
7/26	Termination process	Satisfactory termination	1. Introduce termination.	1. Social worker	7/26	7/26
			2. Discuss feelings and termination.	2. Social worker and K	7/26 and 8/5	8/5
			3. Do a work review.	3. Social worker and K	8/15	8/15
			4. Meet with transfer social worker.	4. K, social worker, and transfer social worker	8/22	8/22
			5. Conduct final session.	5. Social worker and K	8/30	8/30

II. Gerontology Case

A. Agency: Seaside Nursing Home

B. Client System

Mrs. J, an 80-year-old Portuguese woman, is in a skilled-nursing facility. (For additional information, see Chapter 5, Ongoing Cases: Engagement Phase, II. Gerontology Case.)

C. Summary of Preceding Phases

The problems, needs, goals, and tasks identified and contracted in earlier phases may be found in Chapters 5 through 9. The evaluation process and contract reformulation of the preceding phase are outlined in Chapter 10. At the time of evaluation, progress was noted for all of the stated goals. The least amount of progress was shown for goal 3a (to have Mrs. J go out of her room on her own at least once a day). Additional efforts to work on goal 3a were developed and contracted during the evaluation phase. These included the creation of an ongoing evaluation graph (in Chapter 10) and more involvement by nursing staff in helping to chart the frequency of Mrs. J's leaving her room by herself. Mrs. J and the social worker agreed to assess progress in goal 3a weekly.

D. Intervention

After working with Mrs. J for seven months, the social worker began the process of termination because she was leaving the agency. When the social worker informed Mrs. J that she would be working at the nursing home for only four more weeks, Mrs. J repeated, "No, you won't" or "You won't go" and refused to discuss it any further. Mrs. J would turn on her television whenever the social worker tried to talk about her leaving. One day, the social worker went to see Mrs. J at their regular meeting time and Mrs. J was not in her room. She was later located walking on the floor downstairs by herself. She said she didn't know why she was there.

The social worker told Mrs. J that she could see that she was upset and angry with her. Mrs. J said she could not understand why the social worker had to go. The social worker tried to review the progress Mrs. J had made, but Mrs. J said she didn't want to talk about it. She became very silent and refused to speak at all after the social worker said she would not be coming back, even to visit Mrs. J. Mrs. J was told that the social worker's supervisor would come to see her occasionally and would be available if Mrs. J needed to talk to a social worker. Mrs. J did not respond and remained withdrawn throughout the remainder of the time the social worker was at the home.

Realizing that Mrs. J was finding it difficult to accept the termination, the social worker's supervisor agreed to see Mrs. J at least once a week for a while after the social worker left. During the second-to-last meeting of the social worker and Mrs. J, the supervisor dropped in, but Mrs. J said very little to her.

E. Charted Progress

The termination plan was drawn up by the social worker, who kept trying to get Mrs. J involved in the process. The plan was recorded as found in Table 11.4.

As apparent in Table 11.4, tasks 2 and 3 (discuss feelings, review working relationship) of the termination plan were not accomplished. No dates are entered in the last column ("date accomplished") for tasks 2 and 3. The social worker was not able to engage Mrs. J either in a discussion of feelings about the termination or a review of their work. Thus, in the termination summary left in the record, the social worker emphasized the fact that the termination process had not been attained. The social worker's supervisor planned to focus on tasks 2 and 3 when she met with Mrs. J after the social worker's termination.

TABLE 11.4 ■ Contracted Plan: Gerontology Case

Date Identified	Problem/ Need	Goal	Task	Contract	Date Anticipated	Date Accomplished
4/29	Termination process	Satisfactory termination	1. Introduce termination.	1. Social worker	4/29	4/29
			2. Discuss termination and feelings.	2. Social worker and Mrs. J	5/1 and 5/6	
			3. Do a work review.	3. Social worker and Mrs. J	5/1 and 5/6	
			4. Meet with supervisor.	4. Social worker, Mrs. J, and supervisor	5/15	5/15
			5. Conduct final session.	5. Social worker and Mrs. J	5/22	5/22

III. Public Social Welfare Case

A. Agency: State Social Services

B. Client System

Mr. and Mrs. P and their two children (ages 2 and 4) were placed in emergency shelter (Center City Motor Inn) for 44 days and then relocated in an apartment. The family was receiving TANF because of Mr. P's mental incapacity. (Additional background information may be found in Chapter 5, Ongoing Cases: Engagement Phase, III. Public Social Welfare Case.)

C. Summary of Preceding Phases

The problems, needs, goals, and interventions of earlier phases are outlined in Chapters 5 through 9. A summary of the evaluation that was completed is charted in Chapter 10. The basic goals for food, housing, medical examination, fuel assistance, TANF payment, and a functioning refrigerator were accomplished mainly through extensive involvement by resources outside of the family. The goals of obtaining Supplemental Security Income, a Thanksgiving food basket, and Christmas gifts for the children were not accomplished (to date) because of Mr. P's failure to complete contracted tasks. The problems of poor money management and excessive dependence on outside resources were identified by the social worker but left unresolved because Mr. and Mrs. P refused to recognize them as problems in need of attention. The evaluation culminated with both the social worker and the family agreeing to begin the process of termination.

D. Termination

Although the Ps said they had no immediate need for continued social services, they appeared a little angry, as judged by their words and behavior, with the social worker when the idea of termination was first introduced. They were able to admit that they were disappointed when the social worker did not take care of fixing their refrigerator and also when the social worker didn't get them a food basket for Thanksgiving. They knew that they should try to do more for themselves and said it was easier for a social worker to deal with other programs and services. The social worker reminded them that when they really had to get something done, they were able to work it out (such as locating an apartment). At this point, they admitted that Mrs. P's father was actually the one who found the apartment for them. They asked if the social worker couldn't come by at least once every month to see how they were getting along. The social worker did not agree to this, because he felt it was better for the family to try to solve their problems as they arose and not to hold them until the social worker came each month. Again, the social worker cautioned them about their need for careful planning in money management and said that if they ever wanted help in developing their skill in this area, they could bring this to the attention of their income-maintenance technician or they could call the Social Services Department directly.

The social worker planned to meet three additional times with the family before their final termination. During these last visits, the family continued to complain about how hard it is to maintain a home and raise children these days. They repeated their desire for Christmas presents for the children, and the social worker reviewed the tasks identified in the contracted plan. Mr. P did call the Salvation Army (task 2, problem 12) on the day of the social worker's last visit.

E. Charted Progress

The termination plan carried out by the social worker and the Ps is recorded in Table 11.5. In the closing summary for the record, the social worker emphasized that although problems 5 (poor money management) and 13 (excessive dependency) were never recognized by the Ps, these were assessed as continuing and serious by the social worker.

IV. Community Services Case

A. Agency: Clayton Neighborhood House

B. Client System

Four Hispanic families needed heat in their apartments on the second floor of 33 L Street. (For more background information, see Chapter 5, Ongoing Cases: Engagement Phase, IV. Community Services Case.)

C. Summary of Preceding Phases

The problems, needs, goals, and tasks identified and enacted during early phases are described in the contracted plan found in Chapters 5 through 9. Although the families initially felt victimized and helpless, they expressed feelings of relief and gratitude during the evaluation phase. There was adequate heating in their apartments, and they were actively monitoring the temperature daily. They knew that they continued to have a problem in communicating with their landlord, but they did not want to try to improve their communications at this time.

D. Termination

When the social worker returned to meet with the families and review the heating situation, she learned that consistent heat had been provided throughout the week. This finding was charted on the ongoing evaluation graph given in Chapter 10. The social worker had mentioned to the families the previous week that if there didn't seem to be any remaining problems to work on when she came for this meeting, she would talk with them about terminating her contacts with them.

TABLE 11.5 ■ Contracted Plan: Public Social Welfare Case

Date Identified	Problem/ Need	Goal	Task	Contract	Date Anticipated	Date Accomplished
12/4	Termination process	Satisfactory termination	1. Introduce termination.	1. Social worker	12/4	12/4
			2. Discuss termination and feelings.	2. Social worker and Ps	12/11	12/11
			3. Do a work review.	3. Social worker and Ps	12/11	12/11
			4. Conduct final session.	4. Social worker and Ps	12/21	12/21

Residents first expressed a wish that the social worker would continue to visit with them at least once a week. Comments were made, such as "Don't you like us any more?" One tenant said that he had heard that the landlord was selling the apartment building and that maybe they all would be put out on the street. The social worker assured the residents that if they received notice that they had to leave the building, they could contact Clayton House for assistance with relocation.

In reviewing their work together, the social worker recalled their first meeting and the way in which they worked on the heating problem. The families were happy to know that they could drop into Clayton House if they ever wanted help with any problem. They were also informed of the regular community meetings and activities that went on at Clayton for children and adults.

The tenants decided that they wanted to continue their daily monitoring of the heat in their apartments throughout the winter. Mrs. T offered to keep track of their findings by marking temperature points on the graph in Chapter 10 once a week. If there was any marked regression, she would contact the social worker and call a meeting.

The social worker shared how much she had enjoyed working with them, even though their contact had been brief. She was invited to drop in any time she was in the neighborhood.

E. Charted Progress

The termination plan was carried out and recorded as outlined in Table 11.6.

V. Education Case

A. Agency: Keeney Elementary School

B. Client System

Jim G, an 8-year-old third-grader, was showing regressive behavior in school and at home in reaction to his parents' problems with their relationship and Mrs. G's threat to abandon the family. (For additional background information, see Chapter 5, Ongoing Cases: Engagement Phase, V. Education Case.)

TABLE 11.6 ■ Contracted Plan: Community Services Case

Date Identified	Problem/ Need	Goal	Task	Contract	Date Anticipated	Date Accomplished
12/19	Termination process	Satisfactory termination	1. Introduce termination.	1. Social worker	12/12	12/12
			2. Discuss termination and feelings.	2. Social worker and residents	12/19	12/19
			3. Do a work review.	3. Social worker and residents	12/19	12/19
			4. Conduct final session.	4. Social worker and residents	12/19	12/19

C. Summary of Preceding Phases

The contracted plan developed and implemented by Jim, his parents, and the social worker is found in Chapter 7. During evaluation, progress was noted for all four identified goals. The goal to improve Mr. and Mrs. G's marital relationship was recognized as needing more time before its accomplishment. Mr. and Mrs. G were motivated to remain in counseling at the family counseling center.

D. Termination

During one of the last interviews with Mr. and Mrs. G and Jim, termination was introduced and discussed. Although it was agreed that the social worker did not need to meet with Mr. and Mrs. G again, the contract with Jim was extended to include two additional sessions at school.

As the social worker and the Gs recognized the progress that had been made, Mr. and Mrs. G expressed gratitude to the social worker for her interest in Jim and in them. They said it was good to know that the social worker was at the school to help the children and their families. They admitted that they probably would not have gone for help for themselves if it hadn't been for the social worker. They were reminded by the social worker that it was Jim who was feeling their pain and reacting to the situation. It was Jim who led them to look closer at what was happening to them and to their family. Reviewing their work, the social worker moved from the past to the present and then to the future. In considering the future, the social worker strongly encouraged Mr. and Mrs. G to continue their work at the family counseling center, even if it got rough at times. They were assured also that they could contact the social worker at school if she could be of any further assistance.

When the social worker began to talk with Jim about termination during their last two meetings, he said he didn't want to stop coming. He liked to play with the toys in the office and he liked talking about his grades and keeping track of his improvement on the graphs.

During these sessions, Jim repeatedly asked if the social worker had started to see some other child in his place. He was assured that no one could take his place. Jim said he was happy about home, but he was sad that he couldn't continue to see the social worker. He told her that he might "surprise" her and drop in to see her on his own sometime. Before leaving, he took the graphs that were hanging on the wall with him. He brought the social worker a drawing he had made of himself and his family and hung it on her wall. He said that she could keep it—for a while.

E. Charted Progress

The plan for termination was recorded on the contracted plan as outlined in Table 11.7.

VI. Corrections Case

A. Agency: Juvenile Court

B. Client System

A group of six (originally seven) male youths, all age 14, are on probation and attending weekly group meetings led by co-workers at Juvenile Court. (For additional background information, see Chapter 5, Ongoing Cases: Engagement Phase, VI. Corrections Case.)

TABLE 11.7 ■ Contracted Plan: Education Case

Date Identified	Problem/ Need	Goal	Task	Contract	Date Anticipated	Date Accomplished
12/13	Termination process	Satisfactory termination	1. Introduce termination.	1. Social worker	12/17	12/17
			2. Discuss termination and feelings.	2. Social worker, Mr. and Mrs. G, and Jim	12/17	12/17
			3. Terminate with Mr. and Mrs. G.	3. Social worker	12/17	12/17
			4. Further discussion of termination and feelings.	4. Social worker and Jim	12/20 and 1/8	12/20 and 1/8
			5. Conduct final session.	5. Social worker and Jim	1/8	1/8

C. Summary of Preceding Phases

The group met weekly and focused on the three prioritized goals of (1) to get off probation in four months, (2) to control tempers at home and at school, and (3) to learn more about "the changes" they were facing as teenagers. After three and one-half months, the group evaluated their progress in goal accomplishment. Four of the members were achieving the stated goals as planned. They were being recommended for termination of probation. One youth was sent to a correctional center after he had attended six meetings, because he was found breaking into a store. The remaining two were not meeting the requirements for a reduction in probation. Group meetings were extended for at least six more weeks for these two members. After the evaluation, the group began to focus on termination.

D. Termination

As the group began to discuss what it would be like to be off probation, MK and B said that they were glad they were getting off probation but that they would miss seeing everyone in the group. They asked the group leaders to let them know about any upcoming trips in which they could join the group. J and T expressed anger over having to come back for group meetings. They began to blame the co-workers for not recommending that they get reduced time, but other group members reminded J and T that they themselves didn't keep up their scores.

As the group discussed their work together (i.e., past, present, and future), they began to recall what it was like when they first started attending. Most of the youths admitted that they didn't think that they could trust the social workers and doubted that they would give them time off. C reminded the group about A, saying he was sorry A didn't make it but that A should have listened to the probation officers. C also shared how excited he was because his mother and little sister and brother were coming from Puerto Rico to live with him and his father.

All of the youths said that they thought they were doing better than when they first were put on probation. They didn't know if they would be able to stay out of trouble once they were off probation. J and T said they probably would never get off probation. They knew that if they began to do better, they still could have a probation reduction of one month (rather than two). In looking toward the future, J and T were told by the social workers that if they continued to fail to meet the requirements, the group would stop at the end of its fifth month, but J and T would be expected to meet individually with a social worker each week for as long as they remained on probation.

In talking about the future for those who were leaving in two weeks (MK, B, ML, and C), the leaders encouraged each of them to try to get active with local churches or recreational centers. Specific places were identified for each of the youths. They were encouraged also to ask to see the school social worker if they started to have any problems in school.

At the end of the last meeting with all six members, the group had a pizza party. In the following weeks, J's behavior markedly improved at meetings, at home, and in school. He was recommended to be removed from probation one month early. T continued to come late to meetings. His fighting at school continued, and he was not obeying his grandmother. His probation period was extended beyond five months, and he was required to come to see the male social worker once a week.

E. Charted Progress

The termination plan was recorded as outlined in Table 11.8.

VII. Homelessness Case

A. Agency: West End Community Shelter

B. Client System

Mr. Romano is a resident at the homeless shelter and he has AIDS. (For further background information, see Chapter 5, Ongoing Cases: Engagement Phase, VII. Homelessness Case.)

C. Summary of Preceding Phases

When Mr. R came to the shelter in May, he was unemployed, homeless, and testing HIV positive. During his stay at the shelter, he found a job and worked full and part time on a chicken farm. He has become active with the Harmony Program and with Saint John's Church. He started and continues to be seen at the free clinic located near the shelter. Recently, the doctor informed Mr. R that test results indicate that he has AIDS. Mr. R is not able to continue working. He has applied for TANF and social security. He applied also for residence at Hope Home and was invited for a preplacement visit.

D. Termination

The decision was made by Mr. R and the staff at Hope Home that Mr. R would move to Hope Home on July 8. The shelter social worker and Mr. R took time to plan his termination from the shelter. Mr. R recalled how hopeless he felt that first night when he came to

TABLE 11.8 ■ Contracted Plan: Corrections Case

Date Identified	Problem/Need	Goal	Task	Contract	Date Anticipated	Date Accomplished
1/14	Termination process	Satisfactory termination	1. Introduce termination.	1. Social workers	1/14	1/14
			2. Discuss termination and feelings.	2. Members and social workers	1/21, 1/28	1/21, 1/28
			3. Do a work review.	3. Members and social workers	1/21, 1/28	1/21, 1/28
			4. Conduct final session for MK, ML, B, and C—pizza party.	4. Members and social workers	1/28	1/28
			5. Continue weekly meetings for a month.	5. J, T, and social workers	2/4, 2/11, 2/18, 2/25	2/4, 2/11, 2/18, 2/25
			6. Evaluate progress of J and T.	6. J, T, and social workers	2/11	2/11
			7. Conduct final session for J.	7. J, T, and social workers	2/25	2/25
			8. Continue to meet once a week.	8. T and social worker (M.S.W.)	3/4 and each week until off probation	

TABLE 11.9 ■ Contracted Plan: Homelessness Case

Date Identified	Problem/ Need	Goal	Task	Contract	Date Antici- pated	Date Accom- plished
7/2	Termination process	Satisfactory termination	1. Discuss termi- nation past/ present/future.	1. Social worker and Mr. R	7/3	
			2. Plan move.	2. Social worker, Mr. R, and "buddy"	7/3	
			3. Have last meeting.	3. Social worker and Mr. R		7/7
			4. Move to Hope Home.	4. Mr. R with help of buddy		7/8

the shelter and signed in for a bed. He expressed deep appreciation for the help he received from the social worker and said he would like to come back if he could to visit everyone sometimes. They recognized that Mr. R has been going through a lot of changes in his life and that the road ahead may not be easy. Mr. R said that the doctor helped him to under- stand the virus better and what he might expect. He said that he was very glad that he had "made peace with God" and his church. He still was afraid but not as much as when he first learned he was HIV positive. He said that he thought he would like the people at Hope Home. He was looking forward to sharing a room with only one person.

E. Charted Progress

A termination plan was added to Mr. R's contracted plan as found in Table 11.9.

SUMMARY

In reviewing the content of this chapter, it may be seen that the process of termina- tion includes all of the phases of the General Method (engagement, data collection, assessment and contract planning, intervention, evaluation, termination). During ter- mination, the social worker and the client system begin with an identification of the meaning of termination (engagement). They proceed to gathering information as they move from past to present (data collection). They move on to assessing and planning for the future (assessment and contract planning). The plan is then implemented (in- tervention) and evaluated (evaluation). Finally, there is closure (termination). The

General Method is a cyclical process with the process repeated and completed in the termination phase.

New social workers frequently say that the most difficult part of working with a client or action system is getting started. In time, social workers generally say the most difficult part is the ending. At the beginning, there may be some fears and emptiness because of little experience or knowledge of a system. Seasoned social workers know, however, the awesome reality that the emptiness after termination may be filled with memories of the experience and the achievements, particularly in the final phase, that live on.

REFLECTION POINTS

Becoming a skilled social work practitioner requires knowledge and skills, including the ability to reflect on practice endeavors. The following reflection points are designed to strengthen critical thinking and mastery of knowledge of key points in this chapter.

1. Define the following key concepts in generalist social work:
   - Termination process
   - Termination tasks
   - Reinforcing strengths-based problem-solving skills
   - Generalizing to the future
   - Reactions to ending
   - Stabilizing change
2. How might these concepts influence your professional behavior in practice with client, action, and target systems at micro, mezzo, and macro levels of practice?
3. How might human diversity influence client system behavior and your professional behavior in the termination process at micro, mezzo, and macro practice levels?
4. Review Section 1.16, Termination of Services, of the *NASW Code of Ethics* (www.socialworkers.org). How will these standards influence your professional behavior?
5. For further reading and research, use the key words in Question 1 to locate social work references related to this chapter's content. (See Appendix A, Selected Internet Resources, and Appendix B, Selected Social Work Journals.) What underlying theoretical concepts are evident in the articles? How are they applied in the articles? How might they be applied in one of the seven ongoing cases in this chapter or in a case in your field internship?

Appendix A
Selected Internet Resources

Professional Social Work Organizations

Association of Social Work Boards
www.aswb.org

Council on Social Work Education
www.cswe.org

International Federation of Social Workers
www.ifsw.org

National Association of Social Workers
www.socialworkers.org

Diversity in Population Data

U.S. Bureau of Census
www.census.gov

Rural Social Work Caucus
www.uncp.edu/sw/rural

Multicultural Diversity

Center for Cross-Cultural Behavioral Pediatric
Health www.unt.edu/pediatric

Center for Disease Control, minority health
issues www.cdc.gov/omh

International Association for Cross-Cultural
Psychology www.iacco.org

National Center for Minority Health and
Health Disparities
www.ncmhd.nih.gov

Office of Minority Health
www.omhrc.gov/omhrc

Transcultural Mental Health Care
www.tmhc.nsw.gov.au

Challenges to Mental and Physical Ability

Center for Mental Health Services
www.samhsa.gov

Agency for Health Care Research and Quality
www.ahrq.gov

National Library of Medicine
www.medlineplus.gov

Fields of Practice

Child Welfare: Abuse www.ispcan.org

Forensics, Violence www.nofsw.org
www.nm.nih.gov/medlineplus/
domesticviolence.html

Gerontology www.agesocialwork.org
www.nia.nih.gov
www.aoa.gov

Health www.nih.gov

HIV/AIDS www.aidsinfo.nih.gov

Homelessness www.nationalhomeless.org

Hospice www.nhpco.org/

Mental Health www.samhsa.gov

Multiple Fields
www.nyu.edu/socialwork/wwwrsw/ip

Oncology www.aosw.org/

Poverty www.nccp.org

School www.sswaa.org/

Substance Abuse www.casacolumbia.org
www.samhsa.gov

Social Work Research Development Centers

The Center of Poverty, Risk and Mental
Health of the School of Social Work, at
University of Michigan
www.ssw.umich.edu/nimhcenter/

The Children's Mental Health Services
Research Center of the College of Social
Work, University of Tennessee
http://utcmhsrc.csw.utk.edu/

The Center for the Study of Mental Health
Policy and Services of the Graduate School
of Social Work, Portland State University
www.rri.pdx.edu/index.php

The Social Work Prevention Research Center
of the School of Social Work, University of
Washington
http://depts.washington.edu/sswweb/ioe/

Centers on religion and poverty, children and families, HIV/AIDS, advocacy, schools and communities, aging, and women and girls at the Graduate School of Social Services, Fordham University
www.fordham.edu

Centers on mental health, comorbidity and addictions, American Indian studies, social development, and social policy studies at the George Warren Brown School of Social Work, Washington University
http://gwbweb.wustl.edu

Centers: Cartographic modeling lab, youth and social policy, children's policy, practice and research, and religion and social policy at the School of Social Work, University of Pennsylvania
www.sp2.upenn.edu

Empirical Evidence for Practice

Institute for Advancement of Social Work Research www.iaswresearch.org

Society for Prevention Research www.preventionresearch.org

Society for Social Work and Research www.sswr.org

Practice Research Network (PRN) www.socialworkers.org/

What Works Clearing House (education) www.w-w-c.org

The Campbell Collaboration www.campbellcollaboration.org

The Cochrane Collaboration www.cochrane.org

Appendix B
Selected Social Work Journals

Administration in Social Work

Affilia, Journal of Women and Social Work

Arete

Asia Pacific Journal of Social Work

Australian Social Work

British Journal of Social Work

Child and Adolescent Social Work Journal

Child and Family Social Work

Child and Youth Services

Child Welfare

Children and Schools

Children and Youth Services Review

Clinical Social Work Journal

The Clinical Supervisor

Families in Society: The Journal of Contemporary Human Services

The Gerontologist

Group Work

Health and Social Work

Indian Journal of Social Work

International Journal of Social Work

Jewish Social Work Forum

Journal of Analytic Social Work

Journal of Baccalaureate Social Work

Journal of Community Practice

Journal of Continuing Social Work Education

Journal of Ethnic and Cultural Diversity in Social Work

Journal of Family Social Work

Journal of Gay and Lesbian Social Services

Journal of Gerontological Social Work

Journal of Health and Social Policy

Journal of HIV/AIDS and Social Work

Journal of Human Behavior in the Social Environment

Journal of Immigrant and Refugee Services

Journal of Law and Social Work

Journal of Marriage and Family Therapy

Journal of Religion in the Social Services (Social Thought)

Journal of School Social Work

Journal of Social Service Research

Journal of Social Work Education

Journal of Social Work and Human Sexuality

Journal of Social Work Practice (England)

Journal of Social Work Practice in the Addictions

Journal of Social Work Research and Evaluation, An International Publication

Journal of Sociology and Social Welfare

Journal of Teaching in Social Work

Multicultural Social Work

The New Social Worker: The Magazine for Social Work Students and Recent Graduates

Professional Development in Social Work, The International Journal of Continuing Social Work Education

Psychoanalytic Social Work

Public Welfare

Research on Social Work Practice

Scandinavian Journal of Social Welfare

School Social Work Journal

Smith College Studies in Social Work

Social Policy Journal

Social Service Review

Social Work

Social Work Abstracts

Social Work and Christianity: An International Journal

Social Work in Health Care
Social Work Research
Social Work and Social Sciences Review
Social Work with Groups

The Social Worker / Le Travailleur Social
    (France)
Trabajo Social (Chile)

Bibliography

Addams, J. (1910). *Twenty years at Hull House.* New York: Macmillan.

Ahn, H., & Gilbert, N. (1992). Cultural diversity and sexual abuse prevention. *Social Service Review, 66,* 410–427.

Alter, C., & Egan, M. (1997). Logic modeling: A tool for teaching practice evaluation. *Journal of Social Work Education, 33,* 103–118.

Ammerman, R., Kolko, D., Kirisci, L., Blackson, T., & Dawes, M. (1999). Child abuse potential in parents with histories of substance abuse disorder. *Child Abuse and Neglect, 23,* 1225–1238.

Anderson, J. (1997). *Social work with groups.* New York: Longman.

Anderson, J., & Brown, R. (1980). Life history grid for adolescents. *Social Work, 25,* 321–323.

Anthony, W. (1993). Recovery from mental illness: The guiding vision of the mental health system in the 1990s. *Psychosocial Rehabilitation Journal, 14,* 11–23.

Appleby, G., & Anastas, J. (1998). *Not just a passing phase: Social work with gay, lesbian, and bi-sexual people.* New York: Columbia University Press.

Applegate, J., & Bonovitz, J. (1995). *The facilitating partnership.* Northvale, NJ: Jason Aronson.

Applewhite, S. (1995). Curanderismo: Demystifying the health beliefs and practices of elderly Mexican Americans. *Health and Social Work, 20,* 247–253.

Axinn, J., & Levin, H. (1997). *Social welfare: A history of the American response to need* (4th ed.). New York: Longman.

Bandura, A. (1986). *Social foundations of thought and action: A social cognitive theory.* Englewood Cliffs, NJ: Prentice-Hall.

Bardill, D. (1997). *The relational systems model for family therapy.* New York: Haworth.

Barker, R. (1999). *The social work dictionary* (4th ed.). Washington, DC: NASW Press.

Bartlett, H. (1958). Toward clarification and improvement of social work practice. *Social Work, 3,* 5–8.

Begman, A. (1989). Informal support systems for pregnant teenagers. *Social Casework, 70,* 526–533.

Belanger, K. (2001). Social justice in education for undocumented families. *Journal of Family Social Work, 6,* 61–73.

Berkowitz, E. (1987). *Disabled policy: America's programs for the handicapped.* London: Cambridge University Press.

Berl, F. (1979). Clinical practice in a Jewish context. *Journal of Jewish Communal Service, 55,* 366–368.

Berlin, S., & Marsh, J. (1993). *Informing practice decisions.* New York: Macmillan.

Bertalanffy, L. von. (1968). *General systems theory* (Rev. ed.). New York: Braziller.

Biestek, F. (1957). *The casework relationship.* Chicago: University of Chicago Press.

Bisman, C. (1994). *Social work practice: Cases and principles.* Pacific Grove, CA: Brooks/Cole.

Bloom, M., Fischer, J., & Orme, J. (2003). *Evaluating practice: Guidelines for the accountable professional* (4th ed.). Boston: Allyn and Bacon.

Blundo, R. (2001). Learning strengths-based practice: Challenging our personal and professional frames. *Families in Society, 82,* 296–304.

Boyer, D., & Fine, D. (1992). Sexual abuse as a factor in adolescent pregnancy and child maltreatment. *Family Planning Perspectives, 24,* 399–408.

Brice-Baker, J. (1996). Jamaican families. In M. McGoldrick, J. Pearce, & J. Giordano (Eds.), *Ethnicity and family therapy* (2nd ed., pp. 85–96). New York: Guilford.

Briggs, H., Leary, J., Cox, W., & Shibago, M. (2005). Group treatment of separated parents and child interaction. *Research on Social Work Practice, 15,* 440–451.

Bronfenbrenner, U. (1999). Environments in developmental perspective: Theoretical and operational models. In S. Friedman & T. Wachs (Eds.), *Measuring environment across the life span: Emerging methods and concepts* (pp. 3–30). Washington, DC: American Psychological Association.

Brown, L. (1991). *Groups for growth and change.* New York: Longman.

Brown, N. (1992). *Teaching group dynamics.* Hartford, CT: Praeger.

Browne, C., & Broderick, A. (1994). Asian and Pacific Island elders: Issues for social work practice and education. *Social Work, 39,* 252–259.

Brueggeman, W. (1996). *The practice of macro social work.* Chicago: Nelson-Hall.

Buechner, F. (1983). *Godric.* San Francisco: Harper-Collins.

Bullis, R. (1996). *Spirituality in social work practice.* Washington, DC: Taylor & Francis.

Canda, E. (1983). General implications of Shamanism for clinical social work. *International Social Work, 26,* 14–22.

Canda, E. (1998). *Spirituality and social work: New directions*. Binghamton, NY: Haworth Pastoral Press.

Canda, E., & Furman, L. (1999). *Spiritual diversity in social work practice: The heart of helping*. New York: Free Press.

Caplan, N., Choy, M., & Whitmore, J. (1992). Indochinese refugee families and academic achievement. *Scientific American,* February, 36–42.

Carkhuff, R., & Anthony, W. (1979). *The skills of helping: An introduction to counseling skills*. Amherst, MA: Human Resource Development Press.

Castex, G. (1994). Providing services to Hispanic/Latino populations: Profiles in diversity. *Social Work, 39,* 288–297.

Center for Visionary Leadership, in cooperation with Milton Eisenhower Foundation. (1998). *A guide to best practices: Practical information for developing and implementing programs to enhance the safety and security, personal empowerment, and economic self-sufficiency of public housing residents*. Washington, DC: U.S. Department of Housing and Urban Development, Office of Public and Indian Housing, Office of Public and Assisted Housing Delivery.

Chao, C. (1992). The inner heart: Therapy with southeast Asian families. In L. Vargus & J. Koss-Chioino (Eds.), *Working with culture: Psychotherapeutic interventions with ethnic minority children and adolescents* (pp. 157–181). San Francisco: Jossey-Bass.

Chestang, L. (1982). The delivery of child welfare services to minority group children and their families. In L. Chestang (Ed.), *Working with Black families and children*. Richmond, VA: Region III Child Welfare Training Center.

Chodorow, N. (1978). *The reproduction of mothering*. Berkeley, CA: University of California Press.

Chung, D. (1992). Asian cultural commonalities: A comparison with mainstream American culture. In S. Furuto, R. Biswas, D. Chung, K. Marase, & F. Ross-Sheriff (Eds.), *Social work practice with Asian Americans* (pp. 27–44). Newbury Park, CA: Sage.

Clarke, G., Hornbrook, M., Lynch, F., Polen, M., Gale, J., Beardslee, W., et al. (2001). A randomized trial of a group cognitive intervention for preventing depression in adolescent offspring of depressed parents. *Archives of General Psychiatry, 58,* 1127–1134.

Cnaan, R. (1999). *The newer deal: Social work and religion in partnership*. New York: Columbia University Press.

Cnaan, R., & Boddie, S. (2002). Charitable choice and faith-based welfare: A call for social work. *Social Work, 47,* 224–235.

Coggins, K. (1991). *Cultural considerations in social program planning among American Indians*. Unpublished manuscript. School of Social Work, University of Michigan, Ann Arbor.

Compton, B., & Galaway, B. (1994). *Social work processes* (5th ed.). Pacific Grove, CA: Brooks/Cole.

Compton, B., Galaway, B., & Cournoyer, B. (2005). *Social work processes* (7th ed.). Pacific Grove, CA: Brooks/Cole.

Conger, R., & Elder, G. (1994). *Families in troubled times: Adapting to change in rural America*. Hawthorne, NY: Aldine de Gruyter.

Cooper, M., & Lesser, J. (2005). *Clinical social work practice: An integrated approach* (2nd ed.). Boston: Pearson Education.

Cornett, C. (1982). Toward a more comprehensive personology: Integrating a spiritual perspective in social work practice. *Social Work, 17,* 1–10.

Cournoyer, B., & Powers, G. (2006). Evidence-based social work: The quiet revolution continues. In A. Roberts & G. Greene (Eds.), *Social workers' desk reference* (pp. 798–807). New York: Oxford University Press.

Coward, R., & Dwyer, J. (1993). The health and well-being of rural elderly. In L. Ginsberg (Ed.), *Social work in rural communities* (2nd ed., pp. 164–182). Alexandria, VA: Council on Social Work Education.

Cowger, C. (1997). Assessing client strengths: Assessment for client empowerment. In D. Saleebey (Ed.), *The strengths perspective in social work practice* (2nd ed., pp. 59–74). New York: Longman.

Cummins, J., Sevel, J., & Pedrick, L. (2006). *Social work skills demonstrated*. Boston: Pearson Education.

Danziger, S., & Haveman, R. (2001). *Understanding poverty*. New York: Russell Sage Foundation.

Davis, L., & Proctor, E. (1989). *Race, gender, and class: Guidelines for practice with individuals, families, and groups*. Englewood Cliffs, NJ: Prentice-Hall.

Dean, R., & Reinherz, H. (1986). Psychodynamic practice and single-system design: The odd couple. *Journal of Social Work Education, 22,* 71–81.

DeJong, G., Batavia, A., & McKnew, L. (1992). The independent living model of personal assistance in long-term-care policy. *Generations, 16,* 89–95.

DeJong, P., & Berg, I. (2002). *Interviewing for solutions* (2nd ed.). New York: Brooks/Cole.

DeJong, P., & Miller, S. (1995). How to interview for client strengths. *Social Work, 40,* 729–736.

Derezotes, D. (1995). Spirituality and religiosity: Neglected factors in social work practice. *Arete, 20,* 1–15.

Deselle, D., & Proctor, T. (2004). Advocating for the elderly hard-of-hearing population: The deaf people we ignore. *Social Work, 49,* 277–281.

De Shazer, S. (1988). *Clues: Investigating solutions in brief therapy*. New York: Norton.

Devore, W., & Schlessinger, E. (1999). *Ethnic-sensitive social work practice* (5th ed.). St. Louis, MO: Mosby.

Doe, S. (2004). Spirituality-based social work values for empowering human service organizations. *Journal of Religion & Spirituality in Social Work, 23*, 45–65.

Doyle, R. (1998). *Skill and strategies in the helping process* (2nd ed.). Pacific Grove, CA: Brooks/Cole.

Drower, S. (1996). Social work values, professional unity, and the South African context. *Social Work, 41*, 138–151.

DuBois, B., & Miley, K. (2005). *Social work: An empowering profession* (5th ed.). Boston: Pearson Education.

Dunlap, K. (1996). Functional theory and social work practice. In F. Turner (Ed.), *Social work treatment* (4th ed.). New York: Free Press.

Dunst, C., Trivette, C., & Deal, A. (1994). *Supporting and strengthening families: Methods, strategies, and practice* (Vol. 1). Cambridge, MA: Brookline.

Durant, R., Treiber, F., Getts, A., McCloud, K., Linder, C., & Woods, E. (1996). Comparison of two violence prevention curricula for middle school adolescents. *American Journal of Preventive Medicine, 12*, 91–100.

Duryea, M., & Gundison, J. (1993). *Conflict and culture: Research in five communities in Vancouver, British Columbia*. Victoria, BC: University of Victoria, Institute for Dispute Resolution.

Early, T., & GlenMaye, L. (2000). Valuing families: Social work practice with families from a strengths perspective. *Social Work, 45*, 118–130.

Ecklein, J., & Lauffer, A. (1972). *Community organizers and social planners*. New York: John Wiley & Sons and Council on Social Work Education.

Egan, G. (1998). *The skilled helper* (6th ed.). Pacific Grove, CA: Brooks/Cole.

Epstein, L. (1985). *Talking and listening: A guide to the helping interview*. St. Louis, MO: Times Mirror/Mosby.

Erikson, R., & Goldthorpe, J. (1993). *The constant flux: A study of class mobility in industrial societies*. Oxford: Clarendon Press.

Everett, J., Chipungu, S., & Leashore, B. (1991). *Child welfare: An Africentric perspective*. New Brunswick, NJ: Rutgers University Press.

Farley, J., (1994). *Sociology* (3rd ed.). Englewood Cliffs, NJ: Prentice-Hall.

Ferguson, K. (2004). Shaping street children organizations across the Americas: The influence of political, social, and cultural contexts on Covenant House and Casa Alianza. *Journal of Religion and Spirituality in Social Work, 23*, 85–102.

Finn, J., & Jacobson, M. (2003). Just practice: Steps toward a new social work paradigm. *Journal of Social Work Education, 39*, 57–78.

Finney, J., & Moos, R. (1992). Four types of theory that can guide intervention evaluations. In H. Chen & P. Rossi (Eds.), *Using theory that can guide treatment evaluations* (pp. 15–27). New York: Greenwood.

Fisher, J. (1973). Is casework effective?: A review. *Social Work, 18*, 5–21.

Fischer, J., & Corcoran, K. (1994). *Measures for clinical practice* (Vols. I, II). New York: Free Press.

Fisher, R., Ury, W., & Patton, B. (1991). *Getting to yes: Negotiating agreement without giving in*. New York: Penguin.

Flexner, A. (1915). Is social work a profession? *Proceedings of National Conference on Charities and Corrections*, 575–590.

Fortune, A., Pearlingi, B., & Rochelle, C. (1992). Reactions to termination of individual treatment. *Social Work, 37*, 171–178.

Fraser, M. (1997). The ecology of childhood: A multisystems perspective. In M Fraser (Ed.), *Risk and resilience in childhood: An ecological perspective* (pp. 1–10). Washington, DC: National Association of Social Workers Press.

Fraser, M., & Galinsky, M. (1997). Toward a resilience-based model of practice. In M. Fraser (Ed.), *Risk and resilience in childhood: An ecological perspective*. (pp. 265–275). Washington, DC: National Association of Social Workers.

Fraser, M., Nash, J., Galinsky, M., & Darwin, K. (2000). *Making choices: Social problem-solving for children*. Washington, DC: National Association of Social Workers Press.

Fraser, M., Nelson, K., & Rivard, J. (1997). Effectiveness of family preservation services. *Social Work Research, 21*, 138–153.

Freedman, J., & Combs, G. (1996). *Narrative therapy: The social construction of preferred realities*. New York: Norton.

Frey, G. (1990). A framework for promoting organizational change. *Families in Society: The Journal of Contemporary Human Services, 71*, 142–147.

Friedman, S., & Wachs, T. (1999). *Measuring environment across the life span: Emerging methods and concepts*. Washington, DC: American Psychological Association.

Gabor, P., & Grinnell, R. (1994). *Evaluation and quality improvement in the human services*. Boston: Allyn and Bacon.

Gallesich, J. (1982). *The profession and practice of consultation*. San Francisco: Jossey-Bass.

Gambrill, E. (1999). Evidence-based practice: An alternative to authority-based practice. *Families in Society, 80*, 341–350.

Gambrill, E. (2001). Social work: An authority-based profession. *Research on Social Work Practice, 11*, 166–175.

Gambrill, E. (2006). *Social work practice: A critical thinker's guide* (2nd ed.). New York: Oxford University Press.

Gans, H. (1979). Symbolic ethnicity: The future of

ethnic groups and cultures. *American Ethnic and Racial Studies*, 2, 1–20.

Garcia-Preto, N. (1996). Puerto Rican families. In M. McGoldrick, J. Giordano, & J. Pearce (Eds.), *Ethnicity and family therapy* (2nd ed., pp. 183–199). New York: Guilford.

Garland, D., & Conrad, A. (1990). The church as a context for professional practice. In D. Garland & D. Pancoast (Eds.), *The church's ministry with families*. Dallas, TX: Word Publishing.

Garrett, A. (1972). *Interviewing: Its principles and methods* (2nd ed.). New York: Family Service Association of America.

Garvin, C., Galinsky, M., & Gutierrez, L. (2004). *Handbook of social work with groups*. New York: Guilford.

Gaston, L. (1990). The concept of the alliance and its role in psychotherapy: Theoretical and empirical consideration. *Psychotherapy*, 27, 143–153.

Germain, C. (1973). An ecological perspective in casework practice. *Social Casework*, 54, 323–330.

Germain, C. (Ed.). (1979). *Social work practice: People and environments—An ecological perspective*. New York: Columbia University Press.

Germain, C., & Gitterman, A. (1979). The life model of social work practice. In F. Turner (Ed.), *Social work treatment: Interlocking theoretical approaches* (2nd ed., pp. 361–384). New York: Free Press.

Germain, C., & Gitterman, A. (1995). Ecological perspective. *Encyclopedia of social work* (19th ed., pp. 816–824). Washington, DC: National Association of Social Workers Press.

Germain, C., & Gitterman, A. (1996). *The life model of social work practice: Advances in theory and practice*. New York: Columbia University Press.

Gibbs, L. (2003). *Evidence-based practice for the helping professions: A practical guide with integrated multimedia*. Pacific Grove, CA: Thompson Learning.

Gibbs, L., & Gambrill, E. (1999). *Critical thinking for social workers: A workbook*. Thousand Oaks, CA: Pine Forge.

Gibbs, L., & Gambrill, E. (2002). Evidence-based practice: Counterarguments to objections. *Research on Social Work Practice*, 12, 452–476.

Gilgun, J. (2005). The four cornerstones of evidence-based practice in social work. *Research on Social Work Practice*, 15, 52–61.

Gill, D. (1998). *Confronting injustice and oppression: Concepts and strategies for social workers*. New York: Columbia University Press.

Gilligan, C. (1982). *In a different voice: Psychological theory and women's development*. Cambridge, MA: Harvard University Press.

Ginsberg, L. (1998). *Social work in rural communities* (3rd ed.). Alexandria, VA: Council on Social Work Education.

Glathorn, A., & Baron, J. (1991). The good thinker. In A. Costa (Ed.), *Developing minds: A resource book for teaching thinking* (Vol.1, p. 65). Alexandria, VA: Association for Supervision and Curriculum Development. www.ascd.org.

Goldberg, H. (1978). *The new male*. New York: New American Library.

Goldstein, H. (1990). The knowledge base of social work practice: Theory, wisdom, analogue, or art? *Families in Society: The Journal of Contemporary Human Services*, 71, 32–43.

Gordon, W. (1962). A critique of the working definition. *Social Work*, 7, 3–13.

Graham, M., Kaiser, T., & Garrett, K. (1998). Naming the spiritual: The hidden dimension of helping. *Social Thought*, 18, 49–61.

Granvold, G. (Ed.). (1994). *Cognitive and behavioral treatment*. Pacific Grove, CA: Brooks/Cole.

Green, J. (1999). *Cultural awareness in the human services: A multi-ethnic approach* (3rd ed.). Boston: Allyn and Bacon.

Guarnaccia, P. (1993). Ataques de nervios in Puerto Rico: Culture-bound syndrome or popular illness? *Medical Anthropology*, 15, 157–170.

Gutierrez, L. (1990). Working with women of color: An empowerment perspective. *Social Work*, 35, 149–153.

Gutierrez, L. (1994). Beyond coping: An empowerment perspective on stressful life events. *Journal of Sociology and Social Welfare*, 21, 201–219.

Gutierrez, L., Alvarez, A., Nemon, H., & Lewis, E. (1997). Multicultural community organizing: A strategy for change. In P. Ewalt, E. Freeman, S. Kirk, & D. Poole (Eds.), *Social policy: Reform, research, and practice*. Washington, DC: National Association of Social Workers Press.

Gutierrez, L., & Cox, E. (1998). *Empowerment in social work practice: A source book*. Pacific Grove, CA: Brooks/Cole.

Gutierrez, L., & Lewis, E. (1999). *Empowering women of color*. New York: Columbia University Press.

Gutierrez, L., Parsons, R., & Cox, E. (1998). *Empowerment in social work practice*. Pacific Grove, CA: Brooks/Cole.

Guyatt, G., & Rennie, D. (2002). *Users' guide to the medical literature*. Washington, DC: American Medical Association Press.

Hallowitz, D. (1979). Problem-solving theory. In F. Turner (Ed.), *Social work treatment: Interlocking theoretical approaches* (2nd ed., pp. 93–122). New York: Free Press.

Hardcastle, D., Powers, P., & Wenocur, S. (2004). *Community practice: Theories and skills for social workers*. New York: Oxford University Press.

Harrington, M., Fauri, D., & Netting, F. (1998). Termination: Extending the concept for macro social work practice. *Journal of Sociology and Social Welfare, 25,* 61–80.

Hartman, A., & Laird, J. (1983). *Family-centered social work practice.* New York: Free Press.

Haynes, K., & Mickelson, J. (2000). *Affecting change: Social workers in the political arena.* Boston: Allyn and Bacon.

Hearn, G. (1969). *The general systems approach: Contributions toward an holistic conception of social work.* New York: Council on Social Work Education.

Hearn, G. (1979). General systems theory and social work. In F. Turner (Ed.), *Social work treatment: Interlocking theoretical approaches* (2nd ed., pp. 333–360). New York: Free Press.

Hepworth, D., Rooney, R., & Larsen, J. (1997). *Direct social work practice: Theory and skills definition* (5th ed.). Belmont, CA: Brooks/Cole.

Hepworth, D., Rooney, R., Rooney, G., Strom-Gottfried, K., & Larsen, J. (2006). *Direct social work practice: Theory and skills* (7th ed.). Pacific Grove, CA: Brooks/Cole.

Herbst, A., Ulfelder, H., & Poskanzer, D. (1971). Adenocarcinoma of the vagina: Association of maternal stilbestrol therapy with tumor appearance in young women. *New England Journal of Medicine, 284,* 878–881.

Hollis, F. (1964). *Social casework: A psychosocial therapy.* New York: Random House.

Hollis, F. (1965). Casework and social class. *Social Casework, 46,* 466–469.

Horvath, A., & Symonds, B. (1991). Relations between working alliance and outcome in psychotherapy: A meta-analysis. *Journal of Clinical and Consulting Psychology, 38,* 139–141.

Horwitz, A., & Scheid, T. (1999). *A handbook for the study of mental health: Social contexts, theories, and systems.* New York: Cambridge University Press.

Huang, K. (1991). Chinese Americans. In N. Mokuau (Ed.), *Handbook of social services for Asian and Pacific Islanders.* New York: Greenwood.

Ivey, A., & Ivey, M. (2007). *Intentional interviewing and counseling: Facilitating client development in a multicultural society* (6th ed.). Belmont, CA: Brooks/Cole/Thomson Learning.

James, R., & Gilliland, B. (2004). *Crisis intervention.* Belmont, CA: Brooks/Cole/Thomson Learning.

Jayaratne, S., & Levy, R. (1979). *Empirical clinical practice.* New York: Columbia University Press.

Jenkins, L., & Cook, A. (1961). The rural hospice: Integrating formal and informal helping systems. *Social Work, 26,* 415–416.

Johnson, W. (1993). Rural crime, delinquency, substance abuse, and corrections. In L. Ginsberg (Ed.), *Social work in rural communities* (2nd ed., pp. 203–217). Alexandria, VA: Council on Social Work Education.

Jones, S., & Zlotnik, J. (1998). *Preparing helping professionals to meet community needs: Generalizing from the rural experience.* Alexandria, VA: Council on Social Work Education.

Jordan, J., Kaplan, A., Miller, J., Stiver, I., & Surrey, J. (1991). *Women's growth in connection.* New York: Guilford.

Joseph, V. (1975). The parish as a social service and social action center: An ecological systems approach. *Social Thought, 13,* 12–23.

Joseph, V. (1987). The religious and spiritual aspects of social work practice: A neglected dimension of social work. *Social Thought, 13,* 12–23.

Joseph, V. (1997). Toward the future: Call, covenant, mission. *Society for Spirituality and Social Work Newsletter, 4,* 1–5 & 11–12.

Kadushin, A., & Kadushin, G. (1996). *The social work interview: A guide for human service professionals.* New York: Columbia University Press.

Karger, H., & Stoesz, D. (1990). *American social welfare policy: A structural approach.* White Plains, NY: Longman.

Keith-Lucas, A. (1972). *Giving and taking help.* Chapel Hill: University of North Carolina Press.

Keith-Lucas, A. (1985). *So you want to be a social worker: A primer for Christian students.* St. Davids, PA: North American Association of Christians in Social Work.

Kelley, P. (1996). *Narrative theory and social work treatment.* In F. Turner (Ed.), *Social work intervention* (pp. 461–479). New York: Free Press.

Kerlinger, F., & Lee, H. (2000). *Foundations of behavioral research.* Fort Worth, TX: Harcourt College Publishers.

Kirby, L., & Fraser, M. (1997). Risk and resilience in childhood. In M. Fraser (Ed.), *Risk and resilience in childhood: An ecological perspective* (pp. 10–33). Washington, DC: National Association of Social Workers Press.

Kirk, S. (1999). *Social work research methods.* Washington, DC: National Association of Social Workers.

Kirst-Ashman, K., & Hull, G. (1997). *Generalist practice with organizations and communities.* Chicago: Nelson-Hall.

Kirst-Ashman, K., & Hull, G. (1999). *Understanding generalist practice* (2nd ed.). Chicago: Nelson-Hall.

Kochman, T. (1981). *Black and white conflicts.* Chicago: University of Chicago Press.

Kretzmann, J., & McKnight, J. (1993). *Building communities from the inside out.* Evanston, IL: Northwestern University, Center for Urban Affairs and Policy Research.

Kubler-Ross, E. (1969). *On death and dying.* New York: Macmillan.

Laborde, P., & Seligman, M. (1991). Counseling parents of children with disabilities. In M. Seligman (Ed.), *The family with a handicapped child* (2nd ed., pp. 337–369). Boston: Allyn and Bacon.

Laird, J. (Ed.). (1999). *Lesbians and lesbian families: Reflections on theory and practice.* New York: Columbia University Press.

Laird, J., & Green, R. (Eds.). (1996). *Lesbians and gays in couples and families: A handbook for therapists.* San Francisco, CA: Jossey-Bass.

Land, H., & Hudson, S. (1997). Methodological considerations in studying Latina AIDS caregivers: Issues in sampling and measurement. *Social Work Research, 21,* 233–246.

Larkin, H. (2004). Justice implications of a proposed Medicare prescription drug policy. *Social Work, 49,* 406–414.

Lee, J. (1996). The empowerment approach to social work practice. In F. Turner (Ed.), *Social work treatment* (pp. 191–218). New York: Free Press.

Lee, J. (1997). The empowerment group: The heart of the empowerment approach and an antidote to injustice. In J. Perry (Ed.), *From prevention to wellness through group work* (pp. 15–32). Binghamton, NY: Haworth.

LeResche, D. (1992). Comparison of the American mediation process with Korean American harmony restoration process. *Mediation Quarterly, 9,* 323–339.

Levy, C. (1973). The value base of social work. *Journal of Education for Social Work, 9,* 34–42.

Lewin, K. (1951). *Field theory in social science.* New York: Harper and Row.

Lewis, E. (1991). Social change and citizen action: A philosophical exploration for modern social group work. *Social Work with Groups, 14,* 23–34.

Lie, G. (1999). Empowerment: Asian-American women's perspectives. In L. Gutierrez & E. Lewis (Eds.), *Empowering women of color* (pp. 187–207). New York: Columbia University Press.

Lieberman, A., & Lester, C. (2004). *Social work practice with a difference.* New York: McGraw-Hill.

Lineberry, R. (1975). Suburbia and metropolitan turf. *The Annals of American Academy of Political and Social Science, 422,* 3–11.

Linzer, N. (1999). *Resolving ethical dilemmas.* Boston: Allyn and Bacon.

Lippett, R., Watson, J., & Westley, B. (1958). *The dynamics of planned change.* New York: Harcourt, Brace, & World.

Loewenberg, F. (1988). *Religion and social work practice in contemporary American society.* New York: Columbia University Press.

Lum, D. (1999). *Culturally competent practice.* Pacific Grove, CA: Brooks/Cole.

Lum, D., & Lu, E. (1999). Skill development. In D. Lum (Ed.), *Culturally competent practice* (pp. 113–144). Pacific Grove, CA: Brooks/Cole.

Mackelprang, R., & Salsgiver, R. (1996). People with disabilities and social work: Historical and contemporary issues. *Social Work, 41,* 7–14.

Mackelprang, R., & Santos, D. (1992). *Educational strategies for working with persons of disability.* Faculty Development Institute presented at the Annual Program Meeting of the Council on Social Work Education, Kansas City, MO.

Magura, S., & Moses, B. (1986). *Outcome measures for child welfare services: Theory and applications.* Washington, DC: Child Welfare League of America.

Mallon, G. (2004). *Gay men choosing parenthood.* New York: Columbia University Press.

Maluccio, A. (1981). *Promoting competence in clients.* New York: Free Press.

Mancoske, R., & Hunzeker, J. (1990). *Empowerment based general practice: Direct services with individuals.* New York: Cummings & Hathaway.

Marin, G. (1993). Defining culturally appropriate community interventions: Hispanics as a case study. *Journal of Community Psychology, 21,* 149–161.

Marin, G., & Marin, B. (1991). *Research with Hispanic populations.* Newbury Park, CA: Sage.

Marlatt, A., & Gordon, J. (1985). *Relapse prevention: Maintenance strategies in addictive behavior change.* New York: Guilford.

Marmor, J. (1980). *Homosexual behavior: A modern reappraisal.* New York: Basic Books.

Marsella, J. (1993). Counseling and psychotherapy with Japanese Americans: Cross-cultural considerations. *American Journal of Orthopsychiatry, 63,* 200–208.

Marsh, D. (1992). *Families and mental retardation.* New York: Praeger.

Marsh, J. (2004). Using evidence in social work practice. In H. Briggs & T. Rzepnicki (Eds.), *Using evidence in social work practice: Behavioral perspectives* (pp. 20–35). Chicago: Lyceum.

Marshak, L., & Seligman, M. (1993). *Counseling persons with disabilities: Theoretical and clinical perspectives.* Austin, TX: ProEd.

Martens, W., & Holmstrum, E. (1974). Problem-oriented recording. *Social Casework, 55,* 554–561.

Martinez-Brawley, E. (1990). *Perspectives on the small community.* Silver Spring, MD: National Association of Social Workers.

Martinez-Brawley, E., & Blundell, J. (1989). Farm families' preference toward the personal social services. *Social Work, 34,* 513–522.

Maslow, A. (1968). *Toward a psychology of being.* New York: Van Nostrand.

Maslow, A. (1970). *Motivation and personality* (2nd ed.). New York: Harper and Row.

Mattaini, M., Lowery, C., & Meyer, C. (Eds.). (1998). *The foundations of social work practice* (2nd ed.).

Washington, DC: National Association of Social Workers.

McGoldrick, M., Garcia-Preto, N., Hines, P., & Lee, E. (1989). Ethnicity and women. In M. McGoldrick, C. Anderson, & F. Walsh (Eds.), *Women in families: A framework for family therapy* (pp. 169–199). New York: Norton.

McGoldrick, M., Giordano, J., & Pearce, J. (Eds.). (1996). *Ethnicity and family therapy* (2nd ed.). New York: Guilford.

McMahon, M. (1996). *The general method of social work practice: A generalist perspective* (3rd ed.). Boston: Allyn and Bacon.

McMillen, J. (1999). Better for it: How people benefit from adversity. *Social Work, 44,* 455–467.

McMiller, W., & Weisz, J. (1996). Help-seeking preceding mental health clinic intake among African American, Latino, and Caucasian youths. *Journal of American Academy of Child and Adolescent Psychiatry, 35,* 1086–1094.

McNaught, B. (1981). *A disturbed peace.* Washington, DC: A Dignity Publication.

Mechanic, D. (1978). *Medical sociology* (2nd ed.). New York: Free Press.

Merton, R., & Nisbet, R. (1971). *Contemporary social problems.* New York: Harcourt.

Messinger, L. (2004). Comprehensive community initiatives: A rural perspective. *Social Work, 49,* 535–549.

Meyer, C. (1993). *Assessment in social work practice.* New York: Columbia University Press.

Miley, K., O'Melia, M., & DuBois, B. (2001). *Generalist social work practice: An empowerment approach.* Boston: Allyn and Bacon.

Miller, J. (1976). *Toward a new psychology of women.* Boston: Beacon Press.

Mizrahi, T., & Rosenthal, B. (1993). Managing dynamic tensions in social change coalitions. In T. Mizrahi & J. Morrison (Eds.), *Community organizations and social administration* (pp. 11–40). New York: Haworth.

Mondtos, J., & Wilson, S. (1994). *Organizing for poverty and empowerment.* New York: Columbia University Press.

Morales, R. (1976). *Asian and Pacific American curriculum in social work education.* Los Angeles: Asian American Community Mental Health Training Center.

Mullen, E., Dumpson, J., & Associates (Eds.). (1972). *Evaluation of social work intervention.* San Francisco: Jossey-Bass.

Mullen, E., & Streiner, D. (2006). The evidence for and against evidence-based practice. In A. Roberts & K. Yeager (Eds.), *Foundations of evidence-based social work practice* (pp. 3–20). New York: Oxford University Press.

Mulroy, E. (1997). Building a neighborhood network: Interorganizational collaboration to prevent child abuse and neglect. *Social Work, 42,* 255–264.

National Association of Social Workers. (1999). *Code of ethics.* Washington, DC: NASW Press.

Netting, E., Kettner, P., & McMurtry, S. (1993). *Social work macro practice* (2nd ed.). New York: Longman.

Newman, J. (1991). Handicapped persons and their families: Philosophical, historical, and legislative perspectives. In M. Seligman (Ed.), *The family with a handicapped child* (2nd ed., pp. 1–26). Boston: Allyn and Bacon.

Nichols, M., & Schwartz, R. (1995). *Family therapy: Concepts and methods.* Boston: Allyn and Bacon.

Nickerson, R. (1988–1989). On improving thinking through instruction. In E. Rothkopf (Ed.), *Review of research in education* (pp. 3–57). Washington, DC: American Educational Research Association.

Nugent, W., Sieppert, J., & Hudson, W. (2001). *Practice evaluation for the 21st century.* New York: Brooks/Cole/Thomson Learning.

Nussbaum, M. (2000). *Women and human development: The capabilities approach.* Cambridge: Cambridge University Press.

O'Hare, T. (2005). *Evidence-based practices for social workers: An interdisciplinary approach.* Chicago: Lyceum.

O'Neil, M., & Ball, J. (1987). *The general method of social work in rural environments.* Paper presented at Council on Social Work Education Annual Program Meeting, Saint Louis, MO.

Ordaz, M., & DeAnda, D. (1996). Cultural legacies: Operationalizing Chicano cultural values. *Journal of Multicultural Social Work, 4,* 57–68.

Parad, H., & Parad, L. (1990). *Crisis intervention: Book two.* Milwaukee, WI: Family Service America.

Parker, L. (2003). A social justice model for clinical social work practice. *Affilia: Journal of Women and Social Work, 18,* 272–288.

Parsons, R., Jorgensen, J., & Hernandez, S. (1994). *The integration of social work practice.* Pacific Grove, CA: Brooks/Cole.

Patterson, O. (1995). Affirmative action on the merit system. *New York Times,* August 9, p. 13.

Payne, M. (2005). *Modern social work theory* (3rd ed.). Chicago: Lyceum.

Pearl, W., Leo, P., & Tsang, W. (1995). Use of Chinese therapies among Chinese patients seeking emergency department care. *Annals of Emergency Medicine, 26,* 735–738.

Pedersen, P. (1997). *Culture-centered counseling interventions.* Thousand Oaks, CA: Sage.

Perkins, D. (1992). *Smart schools: From training memories to educating minds.* New York: Free Press.

Perlman, H. (1957). *Social casework: A problem-solving process.* Chicago: University of Chicago Press.

Petrosino, A., Turpin-Petrosino, C., & Finkenauer, J.

(2000). Well-meaning programs can have harmful effects! Lessons from experiments of programs such as Scared Straight. *Crime and Delinquency, 46,* 354–379.

Pincus, A., & Minahan, A. (1973). *Social work practice: Model and method.* Itasca, IL: Peacock.

Pinderhughes, E. (1995). Empowering diverse populations: Family practice in the 21st century. *Families in Society,* 76, 131–140.

Polack, R. (2004). Social justice and the global economy: New challenges for social work in the 21st century. *Social Work,* 49, 281–290.

Popper, K. (1992). *In search of a better world: Lectures and essays from thirty years.* New York: Routledge.

Popper, K. (1994). *The myth of the framework: In defense of science and rationality.* New York: Routledge.

Poulin, J. (2005). *Strengths-based generalist practice: A collaborative approach* (2nd ed.). Belmont, CA: Brooks/Cole.

Putnam, R. (2000). *Bowling alone: The collapse and revival of American community.* New York: Simon & Schuster.

Ragg, D. (2001). *Building effective helping skills: The foundation of generalist practice.* Boston: Allyn and Bacon.

Rapp, C. (1998). *The strengths model: Case management with people suffering from severe and persistent mental illness.* New York: Oxford University Press.

Reamer, F. (1993). *The foundations of social work knowledge.* New York: Columbia University Press.

Reese, S. (1991). *Achieving power.* Sydney, Australia: Allen & Unwin.

Reid, W., & Popple, P. (Eds.). (1992). *The moral purposes of social work: The character and intentions of a profession.* Chicago: Nelson-Hall.

Resnick, H., & Patti, R. (1980). *Change from within: Humanizing social welfare organizations.* Philadelphia, PA: Temple Press.

Reynolds, B. (1951). *Social work and social living.* New York: Citadel Press.

Richman, J., & Bowen, G. (1997). School failure: An ecological-interactional-developmental perspective. In M. Fraser (Ed.), *Toward a resilience-based model of practice* (pp. 265–276). Washington, DC: National Association of Social Workers Press.

Richmond, M. (1922). *What is social casework?* New York: Russell Sage.

Richmond, M. (1917). *Social diagnosis.* New York: Russell Sage.

Rivera, F., & Erlich, J. (1998). *Community organizing in a diverse society* (3rd ed.). Boston: Allyn and Bacon.

Roberts, A., & Greene, G. (Eds.). (2002). *Social workers' desk reference.* New York: Oxford University Press.

Roberts, A., Yeager, K., & Regehr, C. (2006). Bridging evidence-based health care and social work: How to search for, develop, and use evidence-based studies. In A. Roberts & K. Yeager (Eds.), *Foundations of evidence-based social work practice* (pp. 21–34). New York: Oxford University Press.

Robbins, S., Chatterjee, P., & Canda, E. (1998). *Contemporary human behavior theory: A critical perspective for social work.* Boston: Allyn and Bacon.

Rogers, C. (1957). The necessary and sufficient conditions of therapeutic personality change. *Journal of Consulting Psychology,* 22, 95–103.

Rose, S. (1998). *Group therapy with troubled youth.* Newbury Park, CA: Sage.

Rose, S., & Moore, J. (1995). Case management. In R. Edwards (Ed.), *Encyclopedia of social work* (19th ed., pp. 335–340). Washington, DC: National Association of Social Workers Press.

Rosen, A., & Proctor, E. (1978). Specifying the treatment process: The basis for effectiveness research. *Journal of Social Service Research,* 2, 25–43.

Rosen, A., & Proctor, E. (Eds.). (2003, 2006). *Developing practice guidelines for social work interventions: Issues, methods, and research agenda.* New York: Columbia University Press.

Rosen, A., Proctor, E., & Staudt, M. (1999). Social work research and the quest for effective practice. *Social Work Research,* 23, 4–14.

Ross, M. (1995). *Community organization: Theory and principles.* New York: Harper & Brothers.

Rossi, P., Freeman, H., & Lipsky, M. (1999). *Evaluation: A systematic approach.* Thousand Oaks, CA: Sage.

Rothenberg, P. (2001). *Race, class, and gender in the United States* (5th ed). New York: North Publishers.

Rothman, J. (2000). Collaborative self-help community development: When is the strategy warranted? *Journal of Community Practice,* 7, 98–105.

Rothman, J., Erlich, J., & Tropman, J. (1995). *Strategies of community intervention: Macro practice.* Itasca, IL: Peacock.

Rubin, A. (1992). Is case management effective for people with serious mental health illness? A research review. *Health and Social Work,* 17, 138–150.

Rubin, A., & Babbie, E. (2001). *Research methods for social work.* Belmont, CA: Wadsworth.

Rubin, H., & Rubin, I. (1992). *Community organizing and development* (2nd ed.). New York: Macmillan.

Sabatino, C. (1999). School social work consultation and collaboration. In R. Constable, S. McDonald, & J. Flynn (Eds.), *School social work: Practice, pol-*

icy, and research perspectives (4th ed., pp. 334–355). Chicago: Lyceum.

Sackett, D., Straus, S., Richardson, W., Rosenberg, W., & Haynes, R. (2000). *Evidence-based medicine: How to practice and teach EBM* (2nd ed.). New York: Churchill Livingstone.

Safran, J., Crocker, P., McMain, S., & Murray, P. (1990). Therapeutic alliance rupture as a therapy event for empirical investigation. *Psychotherapy, 27,* 154–165.

Saleebey, D. (1992). Introduction: Power in the people. In D. Saleebey (Ed.), *The strengths perspective in social work practice.* New York: Longman.

Saleebey, D. (1992). *The strengths perspective in social work practice.* New York: Longman.

Saleebey, D. (1997). *The strengths perspective in social work practice* (2nd ed.). New York: Longman.

Saleebey, D. (2006). *The strengths perspective in social work practice* (4th ed). New York: Longman.

Salladin, L., & Timberlake, E. (1995). Assessing clinical progress: A case study of Daryl. *Child and Adolescent Social Work Journal, 12,* 289–316.

Saulnier, C. (2002). Deciding who to see: Lesbians discuss their preferences in health and mental health care providers. *Social Work, 47,* 355–367.

Scales, T., & Streeter, C. (2004). *Rural social work: Building and sustaining community assets.* Belmont, CA: Brooks/Cole/Thomson Learning.

Schneider, R., & Lester, L. (2001). *Social work advocacy.* Belmont, CA: Wadsworth.

Schon, D. (1983). *The reflective practitioner: How professionals think in action.* New York: Basic Books.

Schwartz, I., & AuClaire, P. (Eds.). (1995). *Home-based services for troubled children.* Lincoln: University of Nebraska Press.

Seligman, M., & Darling, R. (1997). *Ordinary families, special children* (2nd ed.). New York: Guilford.

Sevel, J., Cummins, L., & Madrigal, C. (1999). *Student guide and workbook for social work skills demonstrated.* Boston: Allyn and Bacon.

Sheafor, B., & Horejsi, C. (2003). *Techniques and guidelines for social work practice.* Boston: Allyn and Bacon.

Sheafor, B., Horejsi, C., & Horejsi, G. (1997). *Techniques and guidelines for social work practice* (4th ed.). Boston: Allyn and Bacon.

Shulman, L. (1999). *The skills of helping individuals, families, groups, and communities* (4th ed.). Itasca, IL: Peacock.

Shyne, A. (1959). *Use of judgments as data in social work research.* New York: National Association of Social Workers Press.

Shyne, A. (1973). *Service to children in their own homes.* New York: Child Welfare League of America.

Simon, B. (1960). *Relationship between theory and practice in social work.* New York: National Association of Social Workers Press.

Simon, B. (1994). *The empowerment tradition in American social work.* New York: Columbia University Press.

Siporin, M. (1975). *Introduction to social work practice.* New York: Macmillan.

Siporin, M. (1993). The social worker's style. *Clinical Social Work Journal, 21,* 257–270.

Slaikeu, K. (1990). *Crisis intervention: A handbook for practice and research.* Boston: Allyn and Bacon.

Smalley, R. (1967). *Theory for social work practice.* New York: Columbia University Press.

Smith, E. (1995). Addressing the psychospiritual distress of death as reality: A transpersonal approach. *Social Work, 40,* 402–412.

Smith, B., & Marsh, J. (2002). Client-service matching in substance abuse treatment for women and children. *Journal of Substance Abuse Treatment, 22,* 161–168.

Spencer, S. (1956). Religion and social work. *Social Work, 1,* 19–26.

Substance Abuse and Mental Health Services Administration. (1995). *Cultural competence series: A guide for alcohol and other drug abuse prevention practitioners working with ethnic/racial communities.* Rockville, MD: U.S. Department of Health and Human Services, Office of Substance Abuse Programs.

Sue, D., & Sue, S. (1999). *Counseling the culturally different.* New York: Wiley.

Sullivan, P. (1994). Should spiritual principles guide social policy? No. In H. Karger & J. Midgely (Eds.), *Controversial issues in human behavior in the social environment* (pp. 69–74). Boston: Allyn and Bacon.

Swenson, L. (1993). *Psychology and law for the helping professions.* Pacific Grove, CA: Brooks/Cole.

Tallman, K., & Bohart, A. (1999). The client as a common factor: Clients as self-healers. In M. Hubble, B. Duncan, & S. Miller (Eds.), *The heart and soul of change: What works in therapy* (pp. 91–92). Washington, DC: American Psychological Association.

Tangenberg, K. (2004). Spirituality and faith-based social services: Exploring provider values, beliefs, and practices. *Journal of Religion & Spirituality in Social Work, 23,* 3–23.

Tangenberg, K. (2005). Faith-based human services initiatives: Considerations for social work practice and theory. *Social Work, 50,* 197–206.

Taylor, J. (1997). Niches and practice: Extending the ecological perspective. In D. Saleeby (Ed.), *The strengths perspective in social work practice* (2nd ed., pp. 217–227). New York: Longman.

Taylor, R., Ellison, C., Chatters, L., Levin, J., & Lincoln, K. (2000). Mental health services in faith communities: The role of clergy in Black churches. *Social Work, 45,* 73–87.

Thomas, E. (1967). *The socio-behavioral approach and applications to social work.* New York: Council on Social Work Education.

Thyer, B. (2001). What is the role of theory in research on social work practice? *Journal of Social Work Education, 37,* 9–25.

Timberlake, E., & Cutler, M. (2001). *Developmental play therapy in clinical social work.* Boston: Allyn and Bacon.

Timberlake, E., & Sabatino, C. (2006). Individuals with Disabilities Education Act: Translating and implementing. In C. Franklin, M. Harris, & P. Allen-Meares (Eds.), *The school services sourcebook: A guide for social workers, counselors, and mental health professionals.* New York: Oxford University Press.

Tolson, E., Reid, W., & Garvin, C. (2003). *Generalist practice: A task-centered approach* (2nd ed.). New York: Columbia University Press.

Toseland, R., & Rivas, R. (2005). *An introduction to group work practice* (5th ed.). Boston: Allyn and Bacon.

Towle, C. (1957). *Common human needs.* Washington, DC: National Association of Social Workers.

Tripodi, T. (2002). Single subject designs. In A. Roberts & G. Greene (Eds.), *Social workers' desk reference* (pp. 748–771). New York: Oxford University Press.

Tropman, J. (1999). *The Catholic ethic in American society: An exploration of values.* San Francisco: Jossey-Bass.

Tropman, J., Erlich, J., & Rothman, J. (1995). *Tactics and techniques of community intervention* (3rd ed.). Itasca, IL: Peacock.

Truax. C., & Carkhuff, R. (1967). *Toward effective counseling and psychotherapy: Training and practice.* Chicago: Aldine-Atherton.

Turnbull, H., & Turnbull, A. (1998). *Free appropriate public education: The law and children with disability.* Denver, CO: Love Publishing.

Ungar, M., Manuel, S., Mealey, G., & Campbell, C. (2004). A study of community guides: Lessons for professionals practicing with and in communities. *Social Work, 49,* 550–561.

U.S. Bureau of the Census. (2003). Population profile of the United States. *Current Population Reports,* Series P23-189. Washington, DC: U.S. Government Printing Office.

Valentine, C. (1971). Deficit, difference, and bicultural models of Afro-American behavior. *Howard Educational Review, 41,* 137–157.

Valleroy L., MacKellar D., Karon, J., et al. (2000). HIV prevalence and associated risks in young men who have sex with men. *JAMA, 284,* 198–204.

Van Hook, M., Hugen, B., & Aguilar, M. (Eds.).

(2001). *Spirituality within religious traditions in social work practice.* Pacific Grove, CA: Brooks/Cole.

Van Soest, D., & Garcia, B. (2003). *Diversity education for social justice.* Alexandria, VA: Council on Social Work Education.

Vourlekis, E., & Greene, R. (1992). *Social work case management.* New York: Aldine de Gruyter.

Wakefield, J. (1993). Is altruism part of human nature? Toward a theoretical foundation for the helping professions. *Social Service Review, 67,* 406–458.

Wall, S., Timberlake, E., Farber, M., Sabatino, C., Liebow, H., Smith, N., & Taylor, N. (2000). Needs and aspirations of the working poor: Early Head Start applicants. *Families in Society, 81,* 412–421.

Webster's desk dictionary of the English language. (1990). New York: Portland House.

Weed, L. (1971). *Medical records, medical education, and patient care.* Cleveland, OH: Case Western Reserve University Press.

Weick, A. (1992) Building a strengths perspective for social work. In D. Saleebey (Ed.), *The strengths perspective in social work practice.* New York: Longman.

Weick, A., Rapp, C., Sullivan, P., & Kisthardt, W. (1989). A strengths perspective for social work practice. *Social Work, 34,* 350–354.

Weil, A. (1995). *Spontaneous healing.* New York: Knopf.

Williams, E., & Ellison, F. (1996). Culturally informed social work practice with American Indian clients: Guidelines for non-Indian social workers. *Social Work, 41,* 147–151.

Williams, J. (1983). *The state of black America— 1983.* New York: National Urban League.

Wilson, S. (1978). *Confidentiality in social work: Issues and principles.* New York: Free Press.

Wrenn, L. (2002). Postmodernism and social work: Bridging clinical and social justice perspectives. *Praxis, 2,* 28–31.

Worden, M. (1999). *Family therapy basics* (2nd ed.). Pacific Grove, CA: Brooks/Cole.

Wright, E. (1985). *Classes.* London: Verso.

Yamashiro, G., & Matsuoka, J. (1997). Help-seeking among Asian and Pacific Americans: A multiperspective analysis. *Social Work, 42,* 176–186.

Yeager, K., & Roberts, A. (2006). A practical approach to formulating evidence-based questions in social work. In A. Roberts & K. Yeager (Eds.), *Foundations of evidence-based practice* (pp. 47–58). New York: Oxford University Press.

Yeaton, W., & Sechrest, L. (1981). Critical dimensions in the choice and maintenance of successful treatment: Trends, integrity, and effectiveness. *Journal of Consulting and Clinical Psychology, 49,* 156–167.

Zastrow, C. (1999). *The practice of social work* (6th ed.). Pacific Grove, CA: Brooks/Cole.

Zastrow, C. (2003). *The practice of social work* (7th ed.). Belmont, CA: Brooks/Cole/Thomson Learning.

Index

Photo Credits

CROSS-REFERENCE GUIDE TO CASES BY FIELDS, LEVELS, AND PHASES OF PRACTICE

PHASES OF PRACTICE

Fields of Practice	Case Name	Levels of Practice	Engagement	Data Collection	Assessment and Contract Planning	Intervention	Evaluation	Termination
Child Welfare	K	micro	187–189	228–229	266–269	319–320, 375	402–409	451–452
Gerontology	Mrs. J	micro	189–190	229–231	270–273	320–322, 375	406, 408–412	452–453
	Directors	macro			252–253			
Community Services	Mrs. T	micro	191–193	234–235	275–278	326–329, 376	414, 416–418	455–456
		mezzo						
		macro						
	Peter	micro			24–25			
		mezzo						
	N. C. City	macro			247			
	South End	macro			258–263			
	Family	micro			252			
	E Family	mezzo					394–399	
	Tenants	macro					398–399	
	The Angels	mezzo						443–444
	City Courts	macro				346–347		
Public Social Welfare	P family	mezzo	190–191	231–234	273–275	322–326, 376	411, 413–415	436–438
	Mr. L	micro			246–247			
	Mr. M	micro					385–386, 388	

PHASES OF PRACTICE

Fields of Practice	Case Name	Levels of Practice	Engagement	Data Collection	Assessment and Contract Planning	Intervention	Evaluation	Termination
Education	Jim G	micro mezzo macro	193–194	235–237	278–280	329–332, 376–377	417, 419–422	456–457
	Mrs. B	micro mezzo macro	159–171					
	Jerry	micro		217				
	Student	micro mezzo macro	143–144					
Corrections	Youth group	mezzo	194–196	238–239	280–285	332–335, 377	421, 423–424	457–459
Homelessness	Mr. R	micro	197–198	239–240	285–289	335–338, 377	425–428	459–461
Health	Mrs. Armez	micro mezzo	176–182	209–210				
	Mr. D	micro		215–216				
Mental Health	Group	mezzo		221–222				
	C Family	mezzo			254–256			
	Mr., Mrs. S	mezzo					381–384, 390–394	